More Murders of the Black Museum

The Criminal Museum at the Convict Office, Metropolitan Police Department, Scotland Yard (1883) *(Illustrated London News Picture Library)*

MORE MURDERS OF THE BLACK MUSEUM 1835–1985

GORDON HONEYCOMBE

By the same author

Neither the Sea Nor the Sand
Dragon under the Hill
Adam's Tale
Red Watch
Nagasaki 1945
The Edge of Heaven
Royal Wedding
The Year of the Princess
The Murders of the Black Museum
Selfridges
TV-am Celebration of the Royal Wedding
Siren Song

More Murders of the Black Museum 1835–1985

Gordon Honeycombe

Premier

This edition first published in 1993 by Premier Books (UK) Ltd
by arrangement with Hutchinson

Random House UK Limited
20 Vauxhall Bridge Road, London SW1V 2SA

Random House Australia (Pty) Ltd
20 Alfred Street, Milsons Point, Sydney, NSW 2061, Australia

Random House New Zealand Ltd
18 Poland Road, Glenfield, Auckland 10, New Zealand

Random House South Africa (Pty) Ltd
PO Box 337, Bergvlei, 2012, South Africa

A CIP catalogue record for this book is
available from the British Library

ISBN 0 09 182093 6

Typeset in Sabon by
SX Composing Ltd, Rayleigh, Essex
Printed and bound in Great Britain by
Clays Ltd, St Ives PLC

Contents

★

The years given above refer to the year in which the named victim was killed, not to the year of the ensuing trial.

In cases of multiple murder, the victim named is the one for whose death the accused was charged and tried.

Foreword

The Black Museum came into being in 1875, when exhibits that had been acquired as evidence and produced in court in connection with various crimes (not just murder) were collected and displayed in a cellar at 1 Palace Place, Old Scotland Yard, Whitehall. Ten years later the augmented collection was moved to a small back room on the second floor of the offices of the Convict Supervision Department. By then, the objects on display, consisting mainly of weapons, and all carefully labelled, numbered about 150.

In 1890, when the Metropolitan Police began moving into their new headquarters at New Scotland Yard, between Whitehall and the Victoria Embankment, the museum went too. Now called the Police Museum, its primary object was to provide some lessons in criminology for young policemen, and secondly to act as a repository for artefacts associated with celebrated crimes and notorious criminals. Privileged visitors, criminologists, lawyers and people working with the police were shown round the museum by a curator, who for the last 100 years has always been a former policeman, with a special responsibility for the cataloguing, maintenance, collection and display of the exhibits, and for dealing with correspondence from criminologists and policemen all over the world.

In 1968, the Metropolitan Police moved into their present modern high-rise premises at 10 The Broadway, London SW1. The museum, now officially designated the Crime Museum, was housed in a large room on the second floor. Eleven years later, on the 150th anniversary of the founding of the Metropolitan Police force, the museum was reorganised, redesigned and resited on the first floor of the Yard. Its original title was restored, and on 12 October 1981 the Black Museum was officially reopened by the Commissioner, Sir David McNee. It is not, however, open to the public.

The Black Museum's collection of articles, documents, photos and exhibits is unique. It covers more than murder. Other sections deal with Forgeries, Espionage, Drugs, Abortions, Offensive Weapons, House-breaking, Gaming, Bombs and Sieges, and Crime pre-1900. The museum also contains displays concentrating on particular crimes, such as the Great Train Robbery and the attempted kidnapping of Princess Anne, and possesses such peculiar exhibits as Mata Hari's visiting-card, a fake Cullinan diamond, a loving-cup made from a skull, two death masks of Heinrich Himmler, and 32 plaster casts of the heads of hanged men and women, executed in the first

70 years of the nineteenth centry at Newgate Prison, and at Derby and at York. Some of these shaven heads are said to have been made to record the features of those who were hanged. Many criminals then used aliases, and the only way of identifying them, if necessary, after death (before the use of photographs and fingerprints) was to make a plaster likeness. Most of these heads were probably made for doctors or phrenologists intent on proving theories about the physiognomy of criminal types by examining the shape and every aspect of a criminal's head after its owner was dead and gone.

Some items are not on show. There is a mass of other material (newspaper cuttings, photographs, documents, letters and miscellaneous artefacts) relating to the exhibits and to other crimes, which is kept in cupboards under lock and key, mainly because space is restricted, but also because some of the items, such as police photographs of mutilated murder victims, are too horrible to be shown.

Those on display are gruesome enough: a glass tank of formaldehyde containing a murderer's severed arms; a skeletal hand; a pickled brain; and a grim assortment of instruments of death. Even an innocuous household object like a tin-opener becomes very sinister when you know how and on whom it was put to use. The total effect of the museum's exhibits and showcases is cumulatively shocking. They present a dreadful picture of ruthlessness, cruelty, greed, envy, lust and hate, of man's inhumanity to man – and especially to women. There is nothing of kindness or consideration. There is no nobility, save that of the policemen murdered on duty. There is no pity or mercy; there is pain and fear. But the museum makes you realise what a policeman must endure in the course of his duty: what sights he sees, what dangers he faces, what depraved and evil people he has to face so that others may live secure.

This book covers a period of 150 years and contains murders investigated by the Metropolitan Police which were not included in my previous book, *The Murders of the Black Museum*. Charles Peace and the murder of Arthur Dyson appeared in that book; but after it was published, a manuscript written by the investigating inspector was sent to me by one of his descendants and passed on to the museum. This added so much new detail that Peace's story was rewritten and reappears here. Indeed, if any reader has any objects, documents, photographs relating to any of the murders described herein, the museum would be glad to receive and preserve them.

The accounts of these murders have been dealt with as case histories, with an emphasis on factual, social and historical detail, and on the characters and background, so far as it is known, of both victim and murderer. Principal sources are listed at the back of the book. But in the main, statements to the police and to reporters, as well as court proceedings, have formed the basis for each account. No dialogue has been invented: it has been reproduced from statements and what was said in court – by the accused, by witnesses, and by the judiciary and the police. The whole truth is of course never told in court, or revealed. In some respects a court of law is a theatre of deception, where the witnesses, defendants and barristers seek to deceive the jury and each other. All the relevant facts are seldom disclosed. Even the judge, the arbiter of truth, can mislead and be misled. That is why there is always some doubt, when motives and some matters are not fully explained or known, about even the most clear-cut evidence. This is the fascination of murder – the wanting to know not just about what happened, about who and how, and where and when – but *why*.

Another reason for this fascination is the exceptional nature of murder, and of those who commit murder. They are not like us – they may seem to be, but they are not. There is something missing in their genetic make-up, something like an extra Y chromosome, that turns people into psychopaths and possibly killers. There is undoubtedly a rage in the blood and in the mind of those who murder, who see no solution to a personal dilemma except to kill. What the murderers in this book all have in common, apart from their use of pseudonyms and a nonentity's yearning for notoriety, is that to some degree they are all amoral, vain, crafty, cruel, avaricious, selfish, stupid and downright bad. And without exception they are all, and behave like, fools.

Murder is also a very rare event – considering the pressures and overcrowding of life in Britain and the size of the population. Many more people are killed on the roads, which were none the less the safest in Europe in 1991. Between June 1990 and June 1991, when 24.7 million cars were on the roads in Britain, there were 4,655 deaths. Compare this with the death toll for 1948, when a mere 2.5 million cars were on the road: it was then comparatively very high – 4,513. Those who were injured in 1950 numbered 196,000. But in 1990 that figure had soared to 336,000.

The number of homicides recorded in England and Wales in 1990 – which includes murder, manslaughter and infanticide – was 669. In 1980 the figure was 564 and in 1970 it was 339. These figures, seen as a percentage per million of the population in England and Wales, show a slight increase, from 7 in 1970, to 11.5 in 1980 and 13.6 in 1990.

On the other hand, homicides recorded in London by the Metropolitan Police over the decade 1980–1990 show a decrease:

1980	*1987*	*1988*	*1989*	*1990*
204	194	148	176	185

Of the 185 homicides recorded in London in 1990, 150 were resolved – a clear-up rate of 79 per cent. There were a further 109 cases of *attempted* murder in 1990, of which 89 were resolved.

The incidence of murder in this country is, however, very small compared with that in America, where more than 24,000 people were murdered in 1991 – the highest-ever figure. The previous year the figure was 23,438. More than 10 per cent of the murders took place in Los Angeles, and the increase has been blamed on the rise in hard-core drug addiction, the availability of weapons, and the number of youths joining gangs and indulging in violent and criminal activities. The incidence of murder is also high in New York: in the first week of September 1990 (an average week) 35 people were shot, stabbed, strangled or burnt to death.

In view of the fact that in Britain persons found guilty of murder are now sentenced to life imprisonment, it is worth noting that at the end of 1990,

175 prisoners had spent more than 15 years in prison and 54 more than 20 years. Of the latter, 40 had served up to 25 years in jail; 9, between 25 and 30 years; and 5, more than 30 years.

Finally, what's in a name – like Tonbridge? It was in Tonbridge that Daniel Good was arrested, Ernest Walker confessed, Florence Ransom first appeared in court, and Ruth Ellis was married. And how odd that three of the murderers in this book should be called Ruth Neilson, Donald Neilson, and Dennis Nilsen. In fact, in none of the cases was the surname really theirs. It was assumed. Their original family names were Hornby, Nappey and Moksheim. What's in a name?

Prologue

For 400 years the most popular and most frequently used place of execution other than the Tower of London was the gallows at Tyburn, situated at a crossroads two miles north-west of Westminster and in the county of Middlesex. It took its name from the Tyburn stream that ran near by. The earliest record of an execution there is dated 1388. The last, that of a man called Ryland, who was hanged for forgery, took place at Tyburn in 1783.

The gallows, at the western end of what became Oxford Street, was so often used that it became a standing fixture. A triangular structure, it enabled three felons to be hanged at the same time, hauled aloft or displaced from a ladder, a cart, or the back of a horse. In 1783, when executions were transferred to Newgate Prison, the gallows was purchased by a carpenter, cut up and shaped into supports for beer casks in the cellars of the Carpenter's Arms in Adam Street (now Seymour Place).

The site of the gallows is marked by a plaque on a traffic island opposite the Odeon cinema at Marble Arch, at the bottom of Edgware Road.

Newgate Prison was originally part of the New Gate, one of several fortified gates in the walls enclosing the old City of London. Built in the reign of Henry I, the use of some of its rooms as prison accommodation is first recorded in 1207. In 1241 the New Gate was repaired and restored, and it was entirely rebuilt as a prison in 1422, from funds provided in the will of the former Lord Mayor, Sir Richard Whittington. Destroyed in the Fire of London in 1666, Newgate Jail was again rebuilt about 1770. Ten years later it was almost burnt down again, and wrecked, in the No Popery riots, during which 300 prisoners were released. Repaired and enlarged, the prison became the focus of executions in London in 1783, the scaffold being erected outside its walls. Fifteen people were executed on one day at Newgate, on 23 June 1784. Ninety-six were hanged the following year.

In 1808, the Quaker, Mrs Fry, began her attempts to improve the prisoners' living conditions. They were crammed into large rooms, up to 30 in each. Only those condemned to death had individual cells. There were five of these on each of the prison's three floors. Vaulted, they were nine feet high, and as long, and six feet wide, with a small, double-grated window high up at one end. The walls were lined with planks embossed with broad-headed nails, and the doors were four inches thick. The only furniture was an iron bedstead.

In 1815 the prison ceased to be used as a prison for debtors, of whom there might be as many as 300 in residence at one time.

In 1829, the Home Secretary, Sir Robert Peel, introduced a Bill in the House of Commons which became law on 19 June as an 'Act for Improving the Police'. In the Act, the Metropolitan Police District and its duties were defined, and on 29 September 1829 a Police Office opened for business in Westminster, at 4 Whitehall Place. At police houses around the capital 1,000 paid and uniformed police constables went to work. Their predecessors, the Bow Street Runners, were disbanded in 1839, in the same year as the creation of the City of London police force, a separate entity from the Met.

Control of the 'New Police' was in the hands of two so-called Justices, soon renamed Joint Commissioners. They were both Irishmen: Charles Rowan, aged 46, a retired colonel; and a lawyer, Richard Mayne, aged 33.

Early in 1840, Captain William Hay was appointed as the Inspecting Superintendent of the Metropolitan Police at a salary of £600 a year. He became, in effect, the Assistant Commissioner. Two years later, Rowan and Mayne proposed the setting-up of a plain-clothes Detective Force, which came into being in June 1842. It consisted of two inspectors, the senior being Nicholas Pearce, and six sergeants. Two more sergeants were added later. There was no further increase in detectives until 1864. When Sir Richard Mayne died in 1868, they only numbered 15 out of a Metropolitan Police force of nearly 8,000 men, whose task it was to maintain law and order in a city of over three million potential miscreants – including some murderers.

More Murders of the Black Museum

1835–1985

CHAPTER 1

James Greenacre and Sarah Gale

The Murder of Hannah Brown, 1836

The New Police, in their top hats and blue-belted coats, were but seven years old when they were faced with the kind of murderer whom their successors would often encounter over the next 150 years: a plausible and persuasive man, charming, amoral, avaricious, egocentric, self-deceiving, stupid and vain, with an urge to talk and write, to make his cleverness known, but not to acknowledge his evil and guilt – and to give himself away. For having killed and dismembered his victim, who but such a murderer would scatter the separate parts around London for anyone to find? The police involved efficiently pieced together the body, and the case. But, as would be the case in years to come, it was solved for them by the killer's crazy carelessness, by helpful witnesses and citizens, and also by sheer chance.

The Whigs, led by Lord Melbourne, were in power in 1836. William IV, aged 71, the third son of George III, was king. An old sea-captain and now Lord High Admiral, he was married to the much younger Queen Adelaide. Their children had all died in infancy, and the teenage Princess Victoria, only daughter of William's brother, the late Duke of Kent, was now heiress presumptive. William's seven-year reign was approaching its end. It had begun in 1830, when the Duke of Wellington attended the opening of the Manchester and Liverpool railway – an event of as much significance as his victory at the Battle of Waterloo, 15 years before. Times were changing: machines driven by steam were being dreamt of and made; trade unions were being formed; the Tolpuddle Martyrs, sentenced to transportation in 1834, had been pardoned; and in 1835 the word 'socialism' was coined. Winters were worse in those days: it was colder, and there was more snow.

It had been snowing in London since Christmas. On the afternoon of Wednesday, 28 December 1836, a labourer, Robert Bond, was trudging down the western side of Edgware Road near a toll-gate called Pineapple Gate, when he noticed a large bundle stowed behind an up-ended flagstone propped against a wall. The road was being widened thereabouts and new buildings built, so the snowy footpath was obstructed with piles of bricks and builders' supplies. No doubt on the look-out for something to filch, Bond examined the bundle, whose bulky contents were wrapped in a sack partly covered in snow and tightly parcelled with cord.

'I pulled the stone aside,' he said later. 'At first I thought it was meat, but on feeling it and pulling it about, I felt a hand.'

Alarmed, he summoned another labourer, James White, who was employed in the construction of Canterbury Villas near by. He cut the cords around the bundle and the twine at its neck. After removing various bloody bits of cloth and rag that enveloped what was hidden within, the two men exposed a headless torso with its folded arms tied across its breast.

Bond ran off to find a policeman and hailed PC Sam Pegler, who was on the other side of the road. On inspecting the workmen's grisly discovery, he sent Bond to fetch a wheelbarrow from the Paddington poorhouse, whither the remains, the rags and cords were conveyed about half-past two. It was not until then, when the torso was removed from the coarse, dirty sack and the arms untied, that the naked trunk, without legs, was seen to be that of a mature woman. The ragged bandages proved to be torn parts of a child's frock, a towel, and a shawl, some of which had been secured by small safety-pins, of a sort used on children's clothes.

PC Pegler, carefully examining these items, noticed that the sack smelled of mahogany dust, and that some mahogany shavings were lodged within – 'similar', he said later, 'to what a cabinet-maker would scrape off a mahogany table with a steel instrument'. He had also astutely observed, while in Edgware Road, that there had been no snow under the sack. It had evidently been dumped behind the flagstone on or before Christmas Day.

A post-mortem examination was carried out later that afternoon in the 'deadhouse', or mortuary, attached to the poorhouse, by a local surgeon, Gilbert Girdwood. He reported: 'The hand is a full woman's size, and dirty; there is no mark of needlework on the left forefinger; the mark of a ring exists on the left ring-finger . . . There are no marks of violence on the body . . . The thigh-bone on both sides . . . is sawn through . . . and then broken off.' The organs and the body were healthy, he said, and entirely drained of blood, which led him to suppose that the woman had been dismembered after death – after her throat was cut. She had eaten a meal and drunk some spirit shortly before her death, which must have been sudden. She was aged about 40, had been about 5′ 6″, and had never produced a baby. This latter fact was substantiated by what Girdwood called a 'remarkable peculiarity' – the dead woman had no uterus.

An inquest was held in a large room in the White Lion tavern in Edgware Road on the Saturday morning before a 'venerable' coroner, Mr Stirling, who was attended by his barrister son. Evidence was heard, and the proceedings observed by Inspector George Feltham, who had been put in charge of the case. He made copious notes. After retiring to the far end of the room for a discussion, the 12-man jury returned a verdict of 'wilful murder against some person or persons unknown'. *The Times* reporter noted 'a most singular coincidence'. Behind the coroner's chair was a full-length painting of an execution at Valencia in Spain, in which the executioner held up the decapitated head before the assembled multitude, who exhibited 'the greatest horror at the sight'.

A week after the inquest, the woman's head was found.

Matthias Rolfe, a lock-keeper on the Regent's Canal, was shutting the gates of the Ben Jonson lock at Stepney at 8.30 am after the passage of a coal barge, when the falls, or sluices, failed to close. Investigating the cause, he was horror-struck to see a human head, to which he assumed a body was attached. Summoning assistance and climbing down a ladder into the lock, his groping hand in the water informed him no body was attached. The head was a hideous sight, bloated and disfigured, with long dark slimy hair. It also lacked one eye.

Taken to the bonehouse in Stepney churchyard, it was examined by a surgeon, who deduced it was that of a woman aged between 40 and 45, and had been in the water for about five days. In fact, it had been in the freezing water of the lock for about two weeks. The jaw had been crushed and twisted by the gates. The right eye had evidently not been dislodged by them, but by a heavy blow that had caused severe bruising and swelling to the brow and cheek.

The canal superintendent, thinking that the head had been severed from the body of someone who had fallen into the water, had the locks emptied and the canal dragged – without result. Meanwhile, Inspector Feltham, hearing of the discovery while at the station-house in Hermitage St, Paddington, sought official permission to obtain the head from Stepney. Although he went to fetch it himself, accompanied by PC Pegler, it was not handed over until 10.00 pm on Sunday night. It seems the local police and parish authorities were reluctant to let it leave Stepney town hall, where the head now reposed and where a large crowd clamoured outside, wanting to view the find. It was wrapped up and taken to Paddington in a basket, as the torso, which had been buried on Thursday, was being exhumed.

On Monday morning Mr Girdwood, surrounded by medical men and parish officials in a poorhouse room, successfully joined the torso to the head. Both were closely examined for over two hours and Girdwood issued another report. He said:

> The head is that of a female, and of middle size; the skin is fair, and the hair is of a dirty brown colour, with a trace of grey here and there in it. The longest tresses are two feet long. The eyebrows are well marked, and, with the eyelashes, which are not very long, are of a dark brown colour. The eye is gray, with a shade of hazel in it. The frontal sinuses are strongly marked . . . The mouth is middle-sized, the lips large, more especially the upper, and prominent. The front teeth are good . . . Both ears are pierced for the ring. The left ear for that purpose has been pierced a second time, the original hole having apparently given way . . . The profile struck all of us as being very much that of the lower order of Irish.

A couple called Spencer, from the village of Willesden, were brought by PC Pegler to view the head. They thought it might be that of Sarah Ricketts, who had left the village to collect a legacy and never returned. But having seen the head they declared its features were not those of Mrs Ricketts and they went away.

Reports of missing women had proliferated since the finding of the trunk and arms. Now the one-eyed head excited even more interest and morbid curiosity. It was preserved in a jar of spirits in the Paddington poorhouse and shown to those whom the churchwardens deemed to have reasonable grounds for supposing it might belong to their mother, sister, daughter or wife. The trunk was reinterred, but not before the severed thigh-bones had been removed from their pelvic sockets, in case a match was required for the missing pair of legs. In the meantime, the Regent's Canal, which skirted northern London from the lower to the upper Thames, was dragged where it passed under Edgware Road. For it was surmised that the head and missing legs might have been dumped in the canal, not far from the trunk, and that the head's hair, becoming entangled in a barge's steering gear, might have been dragged all the way to Stepney lock. But although reports and rumours abounded over the rest of January, nothing relevant occurred until 2 February 1837.

A labourer, working in a bed of osiers (willows) in a marshy meadow beside Coldharbour Lane (between Brixton and Camberwell), discovered and opened a large sack. It contained a pair of bloodless legs, severed below the thighs. Each was bent backwards and tightly tied, like the trunk and arms, to make a compact bundle.

They and the sack were removed to a police station and examined the following day by the Paddington surgeon, Mr Girdwood, and by Inspector Feltham. The broken thigh-bones made a perfect fit, and Girdwood was now able to say that the dead woman had been 5′ 6″, that her legs, though large, had been well proportioned, with very small ankles, and that her feet, which were 'large and broad', had the appearance 'of having belonged to a person accustomed to walk barefoot'.

The piece of torn sack containing the legs was marked with capital letters: LEY and ERWELL. It was soon identified as being the property of a coal and corn merchant from Camberwell, Mr Moseley. He had many such sacks, but had no idea who might have so misused one, or when or how. However, the cords employed were the same as those used to tie up the Edgware sack, though that one was quite different from Mr Moseley's. All the evidence was taken to Paddington, and the legs interred in the churchyard with the trunk. The head remained on show.

Seven weeks passed without any further developments. It seemed as if the murdered woman's identity would never be known, nor the murderer found. Then, nearly three months after the torso was discovered in Edgware Road – on Monday, 20 March – an anxious man called William Gay expressed a wish to see the head. Reluctantly, the churchwarden concerned complied. Mr Gay stared at the terrible object with emotions that can scarcely now be imagined. But he said he was certain the head was that of his sister, Mrs Hannah Brown, aged 46, who had disappeared on Christmas Eve.

It was not, however, until the Thursday that Inspector Feltham heard Mr Gay's story and that of his sister's few friends. Within a few days he was able to make an arrest.

Hannah Gay was born in Norfolk in 1790, on a farm two miles from Norwich. Her father was a yeoman farmer. Apart from her brother William, she had two sisters, Mary and Rebecca; there were probably more. Aged 16 (and about a year after the Battle of Trafalgar), she went into service at Crimley Hall, the home of Lord Wodehouse. She was there for four years, after which she came to London and married a shoemaker, Thomas Brown. It was not a happy marriage. But after two years her husband sailed for the West Indies, in the expectation of claiming some property there as an inheritance. However, during the voyage he fell overboard, and was drowned. This would have been in about 1812, three years before Waterloo.

Over the next 20 years Mrs Brown worked for various respectable families as a cook, ending with a hatter, Mr Perring, in the Strand. During these years of hard kitchen work, being of frugal and temperate habits, she saved a good deal of money, some of which she then used to set herself up in business, buying a mangle and renting a kitchen basement at 45 Union Street (now Riding House Street), where she took in washing. The house, behind the Middlesex Hospital, belonged to a shoemaker, Mr Corney, and his wife who, like most shop-owners in London, took in lodgers paying a weekly rent. Here Mrs Brown lived quite comfortably, with a caged bird for company. Her savings consisted of a bag of sovereigns. But she also possessed some valuable pieces of jewellery: brooches, ear-rings and rings.

In appearance she was a tall, big woman – 5′ 6″ was tall for a woman in those days. She was 'very high chested', with strong large hands, long fingers, a high forehead and 'short, thickish teeth'. Her long brown hair was streaked with grey. She was very reserved, even secretive, and sometimes never spoke to anyone for several days.

About two years before her death her brother, William Gay, came to London, and Mrs Brown was instrumental in getting him a job as an assistant to a broker (a dealer in second-hand furniture etc), called Mrs Blanchard, whose business was at 10 Goodge Street, off Tottenham Court Road, a few hundred yards from his sister's lodging. He and his wife also lodged there. Brother and sister were very friendly at first, but after some disagreement Mrs Brown cold-shouldered her brother, even ignoring him when she visited Mrs Blanchard's shop.

The last time he saw her was on Thursday, 22 December, when she called on Mrs Blanchard to tell her that she was going to marry a Mr James Greenacre in Camberwell on Christmas Day. The banns had already been read at St Giles's Church. Greenacre waited for Mrs Brown outside the shop, and when she rejoined him, her brother William watched them walk away.

Her women friends would later say that she could not have known Greenacre for more than three months. Mrs Corney knew of the proposed marriage, and also that Mrs Brown had sold or disposed of her mangle and furniture prior to the marriage, saying that Mr Greenacre had told her to keep what she got for them as pocket money. The rest of her belongings she packed into some boxes before her departure.

None of her friends, or family, had met Greenacre before 22 December, apart from Evan Davis and his wife. They had known Hannah Brown for five years. He was a cabinet-maker, and they lived in Bartholomew Close, near Smithfield Market. About nine days before Christmas, Mrs Brown brought Greenacre to their house and introduced him as her beau. The two men went out to a pub, the Hand and Shears, for a drink, and Davis learned that Greenacre had an estate of about 1,000 acres at Hudson's Bay in Canada, from where he had returned about five weeks ago and whither he would return with his bride. The Davises then entertained the couple to supper in their home. Mr Davis would later say of Hannah Brown that she was 'remarkably sober, and a more social, agreeable woman did not exist'.

On 22 December, about 6.30 pm (after seeing Mrs Blanchard), Mrs Brown and her beau again visited the Davises' home. According to Mrs Davis, they 'appeared to be cordial, and like people who were about to be married'. She approved of the match, but advised Mrs Brown, when they were on their own, to be cautious about going abroad. The two men again went out to the pub for a drink, where Greenacre once more talked about Canada and America. After supper, while he and Mrs Brown sat on the sofa, he said:

> Well, we may as well tell you our intentions, as we aren't children. We intend to get married on Christmas Day, Sunday morning, at ten o'clock, at St Giles's Church. And as you've kindly offered us a dinner on that occasion, we accept of it. You, Mr Davis, will act as the father and give her away, and your daughter shall be bridesmaid. Meet us at Ramsay's public house near the church, and then we'll all go in together.

Mrs Brown also invited the Davises to visit her temporary new house in Camberwell, and Greenacre said they would have to excuse its appearance, as on account of their impending departure, it was in something of a mess.

Not long after this the happy couple left Bartholomew Close, with Mr Davis accompanying them a short distance down the road. Neither he, nor his wife and daughter, who were both called Hannah, ever saw Hannah Brown, alive, again.

She was seen by a friend, a plasterer's wife, Mrs Glass, at noon on Saturday, 24 December, when Mrs Brown called at the Glasses' house in Windmill Street to confirm that she would stay there that night, the night before her marriage. That afternoon, in Union Street, assisted by Greenacre, Mrs Brown put her trunk and boxes into a hackney-coach and told Mrs Corney she would return on the Monday, to pay the final instalment of her rent and remove the rest of her things. Mrs Corney said later: 'I received the key of Mrs Brown's room from one of my lodgers on the Tuesday . . . A week's rent was due on the Tuesday, and on the following day my husband and I went into the room and found nothing there but a bird cage.'

That night, about 11.00 pm, Mrs Davis was very surprised to be visited by Greenacre, without his future wife. She was even more taken aback when he asked her if Mrs Brown was there. Mrs Davis said later: 'I said No, and that I did not expect her. He then told me that he had broken off the match, having found out that Mrs Brown had no property, and it would not do to plunge themselves into poverty. I asked him to walk in, but he declined, and seemed agitated.'

Three days later, about 7.00 pm on Tuesday, 27 December, it was Mrs Blanchard's turn to receive a visit from Greenacre.

Unknown to him, William Gay, who was in the broker's shop at the time, listened to their conversation. He said later:

> I heard him tell my mistress that the wedding was broken off, and that he did not approve of [my sister's] character. He had heard that she had no property, and said he should take a shop in London instead of going to America . . . He said he went to the people, where they were to have dined on the Sunday, at 11 o'clock on the Saturday night to decline the invitation, because [Mrs Brown] and he had had a few words that night, and she had refused to go herself.

He could not, Greenacre said, in all justice, allow the Davises to be put to unnecessary trouble and expense. He said Mrs Brown had run him into debt in the Strand, and if she did that before the marriage she could do it after. He told Mrs Blanchard that the representations made by Mrs Brown and her friends concerning her property were incorrect, and that he had been deceived by her and them. Asked by Mrs Blanchard where Mrs Brown was now, he replied that she had, he believed, taken some lodgings in Camberwell, as it was too far to bring her boxes back to Union Street.

Mrs Blanchard, noticing that Gay was near by, then pointed at him and said: 'This is Mrs Brown's brother. You had better walk in.' Greenacre's expression altered. 'No, thank you. I'm in a hurry,' he said. 'I have an appointment to keep at ten o'clock.' He muttered something, bowed to Gay, and a few minutes later he left the shop.

When William Gay got home, he told his wife, Sarah, about this strange turn of events. Mrs Blanchard, in the meantime, expected that Mrs Brown would soon return to Union Street, to give her own account of what had happened. But when she failed to appear after a fortnight, Mrs Blanchard called on Mrs Corney, who had also seen or heard nothing of Mrs Brown since Christmas Eve. The room key had, however, been returned – given to a lodger by a boy, who had been given it by a man.

The two women concluded that the disagreement between Mrs Brown and her beau had been resolved, that they had married privately, and gone to America. Neither expected to see Mrs Brown again.

William Gay, however, was a worried man. The lurid newspaper reports of the finding of the torso, head and legs of a female in various suburbs had filled him with unease, especially the detailed description of the head. When he read that the legs had been found in Camberwell, where his sister's intended husband was believed to have dwelt, he decided, without telling his wife, to make casual enquiries as to her whereabouts.

To this end he visited her few known acquaintances and friends. It was a slow process as, like every shopman, he worked 12 hours every day: he was only free on Sundays. He walked, rather than travel by horse-drawn omnibus or hackney-cab. It transpired, however, that no one had had any news of his sister for more than two months, since Christmas. When the Davises provided him with Greenacre's alleged address in Camberwell, he decided to pursue his enquiries there.

He did so on Sunday, 12 March. There were people residing in 6 Carpenter's Place, but Greenacre was not among them; nor did they know where he lived. He made various enquiries locally, and hearing about a certain Mrs Gale and her child and other matters prejudicial to James Greenacre, Gay concluded at last that his sister had been murdered.

But before going to the police he was, it seems, determined to discover where Greenacre lived. For on Sunday, 19 March he returned to Camberwell, to talk further with the occupants of 6 Carpenter's Place (now Mission Place, off Peckham High Street).

Mrs Susan Dillon, who rented the house, told Gay that Greenacre had called there the previous Monday to collect his rent – he owned the house. He would not call tomorrow (the 20th), she said, but would send a representative. Gay suggested to Mrs Dillon that she should refuse to pay the rent to anyone other than Greenacre, thereby hoping that he would be forced to call and that his whereabouts, as well as himself, would be revealed. As it happened, Mrs Gale appeared on the Monday, and when no rent was forthcoming she agreed that Greenacre would call the following week.

But Gay had done enough. When he went home to Goodge Street, on the night of Sunday the 19th, he decided not only to tell his wife about his mysterious outings, but to go and look at the dead woman's head. 'Oh, heavens!' he said to Mrs Gay. 'I'm sure my poor sister has been murdered, and if the Lord spares my life until tomorrow I'll go and see her features!'

Why did he not do so sooner? Possibly it was a truth he was reluctant to face. But on the morning of Monday, 20 March he made his way to the Paddington poorhouse, and having explained his reasons for wanting to see the head to its guardian, a churchwarden, Mr Thornton, he was allowed a viewing. Battered and one-eyed, its long tresses floating in spirit, it must have presented a horrid sight. But William Gay was able at last to aver that the profile was that of his sister, whose left ear had been pierced a second time, after a fellow-servant had torn off an ear-ring.

Corroboration was needed, however, before the churchwarden was convinced – many people had wanted to see the head over the past two months – and Gay returned on the Wednesday night with two others (possibly the Davises) to confirm his conviction that the head was that of Hannah Brown. Even then the churchwarden had to be persuaded to pass on the outcome of all Mr Gay's patient enquiries to the police.

On Easter Sunday, 26 March, Inspector Feltham, accompanied by PC Pegler, went to Lambeth to arrest James Greenacre and Mrs Gale, arriving at 1 St Alban's Place about 10.45 pm. It is not known how he discovered the whereabouts of Greenacre's new abode, but *The Times* believed the information came from 'a gentleman connected with the family of one of his former wives'. Feltham later told the court:

> The landlord told me that [Greenacre] was in bed in the front parlour. I

> knocked at the door, when a voice from within said: 'What do you want?' I said: 'Open the door,' and the prisoner said: 'Wait until I strike a light.' I heard him in the room, and having raised the latch I entered and saw him standing beside the bed. I told him I had a warrant against him for the wilful murder of Hannah Brown. I then asked him if he knew such a person, and he answered that he did not. I then said to him: 'Were you not both asked in church?' He replied: 'Yes, we were.' He was then putting on his stockings, and I again asked him if he knew where Hannah Brown was. He answered: 'No, I do not, and you have no right to ask me such questions.' I then said: 'I do not intend to question you any more, but mind, whatever else you may say I shall be bound to repeat elsewhere.' I was then in the act of searching the trousers of Greenacre when I saw the woman Gale in bed for the first time. I said: 'Hallo! What woman is that?' Greenacre said: 'She is a woman that sleeps with me.' Hearing something rattle in the bed, and observing the woman endeavouring to hide something, I said: 'What have you got there?' Gale handed me the watch now produced. I then said I must take her into custody also, and as she was dressing herself I searched her pockets, and took from them several pawnbrokers' duplicates, a pair of cornelian ear-rings and other articles . . . After Greenacre had put on his clothes, he observed that it was a cold night, and requested that he might be allowed to put on a greatcoat, which was in a box, corded up. I objected at first, but subsequently opened the box, and gave him the coat. As soon as Gale had dressed herself I desired a constable, who was with me, to go for a hackney coach, when Gale said: 'My little boy is sleeping in the next room, and he must go too' . . . Greenacre said it was lucky I had come so soon, as he should have sailed for America on the following day.

A later search of the room produced a quantity of female attire which was identified as having belonged to Mrs Brown. Other articles had been pawned near Walworth Road by Mrs Gale on 17 January. These included a pair of shoes, two veils and a handkerchief, all of which were wrapped in an old silk handkerchief stained with blood. Mrs Gale would later insist the cornelian ear-rings were hers.

She and Greenacre were taken to Hermitage Street police station, Paddington, and at 11.30 am were locked in separate cells. It seems that her little boy, George, aged 4, accompanied his mother. Soon after this, at 12.25, the police sergeant on duty happened to visit Greenacre and found him unconscious, 'black in the face' and lying on his back. He had tried to strangle himself, using a handkerchief as a noose. When he was revived he said: 'I don't thank you for this. You might as well have let me die. I wished to die . . . Damn the man that's afraid to die! I am not!' As a result of this suicide attempt he was put in a strait-jacket and closely guarded day and night.

Later on that day, Easter Monday, Feltham and Pegler were searching Greenacre's rooms in St Alban's Place when a man knocked at the door. He enquired whether Mr Greenacre was at home and was greatly surprised to learn that he was in custody, charged with murder. The man turned out to be Captain Henry Tanner, with whom Greenacre had planned to sail to America on the Tuesday. Tanner was taking his wife, but Mrs Gale was apparently not included. Greenacre said later: 'Three of us were to have gone to America together, Captain Tanner and his wife, who were entered in the ship's books as Mr and Mrs Henry Thomas, and I. I signed my name as James Thomas, and we paid £24 for our passage. This Tanner took out a cargo some time ago, and sold it, and came back after selling it.'

The Tanners had in fact paid £18 for the voyage and Greenacre £6 – which meant he would have travelled as a single man in the steerage, and not in a cabin. The departure for Quebec of the sailing-ship, the *Mediator*, was delayed, and four large chests were found in the hold in Greenacre's assumed name. Three were full of 'very valuable tools and implements of various descriptions'. The fourth belonged to Mrs Brown and contained household items and other belongings which she had packed away before her 'marriage'.

The *Mediator* sailed on 3 April, two days after Greenacre and Mrs Gale appeared in Marylebone magistrates' court. From there they were separately taken for their own safety to the New Prison and the House of Correction in Clerkenwell – so violent were the demonstrations against them in Marylebone High Street.

It was at the magistrates' court on 1 April, in a police court cell, that Greenacre began to confess, while talking to the constable, PC Brown, who was with him. Brown commented on all the people who had come to look at Greenacre. He agreed that the affair had caused much excitement, more than any that had occurred in London for some time. Many people, he added, seemed to think that 'it' had been carried to Edgware Road in a cart. 'What do you mean?' enquired PC Brown. 'The body?' 'Yes,' said Greenacre. 'It wasn't moved in a cart, but in a cab.' After cautioning him, Brown asked: 'Was it on the same night that it happened?' 'No,' the prisoner replied, and continued: 'I believe it was between 2 and 3 o'clock . . . There has been a great deal of mystery about the head, and people appear to run away with the idea it was thrown into the tunnel at Maida Hill . . . There is, in fact, no proof to the contrary.' PC Brown warned the prisoner again. He retorted: 'Oh, never mind that! All I've said to you would go for nothing.'

From then on Greenacre became loquacious, and when not talking was writing. His hands, it seems, were not confined by the strait-jacket all the time.

After hearing the evidence against him for the first time in the magistrates' court, he made a long and voluntary statement, which he signed. He said:

> On the Saturday night before Christmas Day, Mrs Brown came down to my house, rather fresh from drinking, having in the course of the morning treated the coachman, and insisted upon having some more rum, a quantity of which she had had with her tea. I then thought it a favourable opportunity to press upon her for the state of her circumstances. She was very reluctant to give me any answer, and I told her she had

> often dropped insinuations [that] she could command at any time £300 or £400. I told her I had made some inquiry about her character, and had ascertained that she had been to Smith's tally-shop in Long Acre, and tried to procure silk gowns in my name. She put on a feigned laugh, and retaliated by saying she thought I had been deceiving her with respect to my property . . . During this conversation she was reeling backwards and forwards in her chair . . . I put my foot to the chair, and she fell back with great violence against a chump of wood that I had been using. This alarmed me very much, and I went round the table and took her by the hand . . . But she appeared entirely to be gone. It is impossible to give a description of my feelings at the time; and in the state of excitement I was in I unfortunately determined on putting her away . . . I thought it might be more safe that way than I gave an alarm of what had occurred.

He insisted that Mrs Gale, who was not in the house, had no knowledge of the accident or what he did thereafter. He had sent her to another lodging before Mrs Brown's arrival and did not see her, he said, for several days. When Mrs Gale returned to Carpenter's Place, he told her that as Mrs Brown had left all her boxes and other things behind, they would pledge all they could. 'The whole of the articles pawned,' he said, 'fetched only £3.' He added that Mrs Brown had eleven sovereigns on her and a few shillings in silver.

Mrs Gale stated that she was not at Camberwell at the time of Mrs Brown's demise. It was later proved in court that she had lodged, without giving her name, with a Mr and Mrs Wignell in Portland Street, off Walworth Road, on 22 December. She brought her little boy with her. Greenacre visited her on the morning of the 23rd, as he did on the 24th, and that night she went out between 9.00 and 10.00. She and Greenacre dined on 'a scrag of mutton and turnips' on Christmas Day, when he was with her between 2.00 and 9.00 pm. The following night she was away all night, leaving her child locked up in her room. He was heard calling 'Mother! Mother!' On Thursday, 29 December, the day after the torso was discovered in Edgware Road, Mrs Gale paid her rent and went away, taking the child. She returned the following day. On Sunday, 1 January, while she and Greenacre were in her room, Mr Wignell read aloud to his wife a newspaper account about the finding of the torso. On the Monday morning, Greenacre, who had spent the night with Mrs Gale, left the house with her, helping her with her things.

Neighbours noticed that the windows of 6 Carpenter's Place were shuttered on Christmas Day and remained so for three days. They saw Mrs Gale (whom they knew as Mrs Greenacre) leave the house at 7.00 pm on Boxing Day (Monday) with 'her bonnet carelessly on'. Her child was crying, and she picked him up, saying: 'You naughty cross thing!' Earlier that evening, Frances Andrews, who lived at No. 11, called on Mrs Gale to give little George a piece of plum pudding. She called again on the evening of the 28th, when Greenacre offered her a glass of whisky. Before Christmas, Mrs Gale had told Mrs Andrews that a lady, a friend of Greenacre, was coming to stay for a few days. No one seems to have seen Mrs Brown, and her boxes, arrive. And none was aware that Mrs Gale had temporarily moved out of the shuttered house.

A week or so after Christmas, an out-of-work shoemaker called Chisholm was walking along a lane in Camberwell when he was tapped on the shoulder by Greenacre and asked if he wanted a job – which was to assist in moving some goods. A boy was co-opted as well. All three went to Carpenter's Place. Chisholm said later: 'A number of boxes were placed all ready, tied up. Greenacre placed the boxes on a truck, together with some articles of furniture, and having secured them all together with ropes, he appeared very much agitated, and said: "Now all's right, I'm going to leave the country." A woman with a plaid cloak on [Mrs Gale] was standing by, and said to Greenacre: "Now you have done for yourself."'

Chisholm and the boy, who were paid 6d and 3d, pulled the truck to the Elephant and Castle, to a pawnbroker's shop. Greenacre and Gale accompanied them. Soon after this, the house at 6 Carpenter's Place was advertised as being *To Let*. Callers noticed that it had been fumigated with brimstone and that the fireplace had been boarded up. Mrs Dillon moved in.

It seems evident from all this that Mrs Gale was not as innocent as she claimed. She may not have been in the house when Hannah Brown was killed and dismembered. But she clearly helped Greenacre dispose of Mrs Brown's possessions and probably cleaned the house before it was let.

In ascertaining these matters the police, and *The Times*, also pieced together, partly from Greenacre himself, an account of his life, previous marriages, and career. He also wrote his own high-flown account, which was published by a paper on 9 April.

James Greenacre, at the time of his trial, was 51. He was born in 1785 – in Norfolk, like Hannah Brown; and his father, like hers, was a farmer. His birthplace was a hamlet called West Winch, two miles south of King's Lynn, and he was one of seven children. When his father died, about 1807, his mother remarried a local farmer called Old Towler, who had two young children of his own. It was about then, when Greenacre was 23, that he was sent on spec to a grocer in King's Lynn. But after four months he felt he had learned all he could and asked his parents to send him to London, where he expected to learn more, and more quickly, and be a success. They gave him 20 guineas, part of which was for the purchase of an apprenticeship. By somehow contriving to see the manuscript of *Times*' job vacancies before they were printed, he obtained work with a grocer at Tower Hill. There he remained for three years, during which he saved £45, and thence moved to a shop in Oxford Street. When Greenacre was 19, Old Towler helped to set his stepson up in business by buying a grocer's shop and putting him in charge. He also sent his daughter Betsy Towler, aged 16, to London to act as Greenacre's housekeeper. This was a mistake, as Greenacre tried by various means to seduce her and then to rape her. Betsy succeeded in fighting him off and fled back home. Her father turfed Greenacre out of the shop, although the young man tried to prevent this by barricading himself inside.

Soon after this Greenacre married the 18-year-old daughter of a publican,

Charles Ware, in Woolwich, where he opened his own grocer's shop. She had two children, and then died 'of a putrid, sore throat'. His second wife was an Essex farmer's daughter, and she also died, 'of brain fever', after bearing two children. Despite these domestic tragedies, his business thrived. For in 1814, aged 29, he took over a more prestigious establishment in the Borough (Southwark) and married Jane Simmonds of Bermondsey. She bore him seven children, of whom two survived – as did three from his first two marriages. For nearly 20 years he lived and prospered in the Borough, becoming a very well-known local tradesman. He wrote of himself: 'I have always abhorred a public-house and the babble of drunken men: the society of my books, my wife and children, have always been to me the greatest source of delight that my mind could possibly enjoy . . . My apprentices and servants have always manifested much pleasure in their situations . . . As a friend I can give the most incontrovertible testimony.' So what went wrong?

In 1833, after committing some offence against the excise laws, he absconded to America, taking his eldest son, James, aged 14, with him, and leaving his third wife and other children in London to await his summons to join him. Three weeks after his departure, however, she died of cholera. He stayed in New York for two years. Later he complained that in this period he was swindled and cheated out of nearly all the property he took with him by pretended friends. He also said he was imprisoned in New York for libel. On his release, he went with his son to Boston and married for a fourth time. But before long he was arrested again for a similar offence and jailed once again in New York. Clearly, he was incautious about expressing his grievances in letters to individuals, to officials and to the press. According to him, this arrest was so sudden – it occurred in the street – that he saw neither his wife nor his son again before he returned to London. This may have been of his own choosing. Or he may have been deported.

Back in London (in 1835), he waged an epistolary war against his creditors, who had declared him bankrupt, and against his third wife's relatives, who had disposed of the property left to him when she died. He succeeded in obtaining possession of 6 Carpenter's Place, and the house next door, and embarked on the manufacture of what he called 'amalgamated candy', made of cinnamon, peppermint, lemon and cloves. The secret ingredient was a herb which he had discovered while in America. Medicinal, the candy was advertised as a cure for coughs, colds, sore throats, hoarseness, asthma, and shortness of breath. He also invented and patented a washing-machine. At some point he met Sarah Gale, and she and her child moved in with him in October 1835. Her maiden name was Sarah Farr.

It seems she had 'married' more than once, and was living with a man called Thomas Gale, near the Elephant and Castle, when on 30 January 1833 she gave birth to a boy, who was named George. While living with Greenacre she bore another baby boy, at about 5.00 am on 17 February 1836. But the doctor who attended her never saw the infant after that day. Three days after the birth she was up and well – but the baby had disappeared. A day later, a male baby was found buried under a clod of grass by a ditch near Bermondsey. It was said by a doctor to have been dead for about 24 hours and to have been three days old when it died. Accused by a neighbour of murdering the child, Mrs Gale retorted that it was alive and well and being cared for by a friend in the Old Kent Road. Greenacre, when questioned, told one person that the baby was with a friend in Edgware Road. He told another the infant was dead.

It is not known how or when he met Mrs Brown. But the introduction, perhaps in September 1836, was made by a carpenter called Ward, who lived in Chenies Mews, off Tottenham Court Road. Ward is also described in *The Times* as a cabinet-maker and mangle-maker. By the time the police began their investigation, he had disappeared. Perhaps Mrs Brown was having her mangle repaired or buying a new one when Greenacre met her at the carpenter's shop, where he, perhaps, was having a discussion about his washing-machine with Ward – who may have constructed it. Somehow he learned that she had money, as well as jewellery, and determined, by offering her marriage, to rob her of all her possessions, and her life.

Why? He probably needed extra finance for his business ventures, and to restore a life-style he had lost. He would also have required money for the voyage to America and to set himself up in business once again, selling candy and washing-machines. Mrs Brown's death was clearly calculated, and not an accident, as he claimed.

He and Sarah Gale appeared for the third time before the magistrates on Wednesday, 5 April 1837, in the unusual setting of a large room in the Governor's residence in the New Prison, Clerkenwell. Gale was brought there by coach. Very pale, she trembled from head to foot when she alighted, followed by her child, who held her hand and smiled as he tripped along.

She and Greenacre sat on a bench before the magistrates, with a sturdy policeman between them. Evidence given by witnesses at the previous hearings was read, as were the statements of the accused. Greenacre proposed a minor correction and cheerfully rose to sign his statement. Gale was fearful of signing hers. 'Sign! Sign!' Greenacre urged her. 'Don't frighten yourself at what people say about your going to be hanged, and all that sort of stuff!'

The question of whether the trial should be postponed until the next session was debated. But Mr Price, Greenacre's counsel, urged on the prisoner's behalf that it should take place without delay. After being committed for trial the following week, both the accused were removed in a prison van to Newgate Prison, which was situated at the western end of Newgate Street, not far from St Paul's and near the street known as Old Bailey. In existence since the reign of Henry I (1100–35), the prison was rebuilt several times, having been destroyed in the Great Fire of London in 1666 and again in the No Popery riots of 1780. The Central Criminal Court, established in 1834, was next door.

Here the trial of James Greenacre and Sarah Gale began on Monday, 10 April 1837 at 10.00 am. The streets outside, like the court, were packed. Greenacre, dressed in a blue coat, fancy waistcoat and black stock, was remarkably self-possessed throughout the proceedings; Gale sat with lowered head and eyes. Lord Chief Justice Tindal headed the trio of judges, the other two being Mr Justice Coleridge and Mr Justice Coltman. The Recorder of

London sat with them. Mr Adolphus appeared for the prosecution, assisted by Mr Clarkson and Mr William Henry Bodkin. The prisoners, who were allowed to sit, were defended by Mr Price and Mr Payne.

The indictment against Greenacre contained three lengthy counts, in which he was accused of killing Mrs Brown by various means and dismembering her. This was called 'mutilation' by the court. Mrs Gale was charged with feloniously 'aiding, assisting and counselling' him in the murder. They both pleaded 'Not guilty'.

After outlining the prosecution's case, Mr Adolphus remarked: 'Happily but few instances have occurred in this country of similar atrocity [involving dismemberment].' These few he then listed – the case 'of Catherine Hayes about 100 years ago' who murdered her husband; of a Frenchman named Bardell, who murdered his landlady 70 years ago; of the murder of Mr Paas, of Holborn, by a man named Cook. The Bardell case was remarkably similar, said Mr Adolphus, in that the Frenchman had also made a statement saying that after a row, he had pushed his landlady's chair and caused her to fall backwards and fracture her skull. Mr Adolphus commented that Greenacre and Gale 'would have one advantage which persons in their situation were, until lately, deprived of – the advantage of having a speech from counsel in their favour'. This would, however, he felt sure, be largely unsupported by evidence. Twenty-seven witnesses were called by the prosecution and proceedings ended at 8.00 pm. The jury were lodged overnight in a nearby coffee-house.

On the second day of the trial the statements made by Greenacre and Gale before the magistrates were read in full. They were both found guilty. But such was the riotous behaviour of the mob outside the court that sentence was not passed, as was then the custom, on the last day of the sessions, but in secret on the following afternoon by the red-robed Recorder. It was prefaced by a legal dispute about the wording of the indictment, engineered by Mr Payne, and by Greenacre's attempt to make a speech in his defence. In it he complained about press prejudice and false evidence – 'such as might be collected in any pothouse or ginshop' – and said: 'It is contrary to reason and common sense to suppose that I should have meditated the death of the woman . . . because of the property she had. If that had been my object, I could have had it all on the next morning, when our marriage was to have taken place, and then it would have been mine. Where, then, was my motive for the murdering of her? It is –'

The Recorder interrupted, saying that this should have been urged by Greenacre's counsel during the trial and should be directed now to the Secretary of State. Greenacre then reaffirmed Mrs Gale's innocence, concluding: 'I deem it a religious duty to exculpate her from having any concern in this unfortunate affair. I have no more to say.'

He stood as sentence of death was passed, and while Mrs Gale sat on a chair at the rear of the dock. He stood for some time, as the Recorder had much to say and was much moved by his own strongly worded sentiments and observations. He said: 'The appalling details of your dreadful case . . . will long live in the memory and . . . in the execration of mankind, and generations yet to come will shudder at your guilt. You have, indeed, required for yourself a revolting celebrity, an odious notoriety in the annals of cruelty and crime.' The Recorder went on to refer to 'the amputated limbs and the dissevered body', to 'the mutilated trunk and mangled remains'. He said: 'The still warm corpse was barbarously mutilated and mangled by you, in the hope that the eye of man would not detect your guilt. But the eye of God was upon you!' He conceded that he was addressing 'an individual not devoid of education, of reasoning faculties, and strength of mind', and attempted to revive 'the last remaining sparks of virtue and religion' in Greenacre's heart by reading a long passage about repentance from 'an excellent work' – *The Analogy of Religion, Natural and Revealed*.

Greenacre listened without moving, and unmoved, even when the death sentence was eventually passed. He was led to the back of the dock as Mrs Gale was brought forward to be sentenced, in fewer words. 'Perhaps you considered that what had been done could not be undone,' said the Recorder, concluding: 'This Court do adjudge that you be transported beyond the sea to such place as His Majesty, with the advice of the Privy Council, shall direct and appoint, for the term of your natural life.'

That night Greenacre, back in the prison ward at Newgate, and confined in a 'strait-waistcoat' every night when he went to bed in case he tried again to kill himself, saw, at his request, an alderman he had known when he lived in social affluence in Southwark. He now gave a different version of the manner of Mrs Brown's death, in order, it seems, to remove any aspect of premeditation and hopefully have his sentence reduced to transportation for life. He told the alderman that while Mrs Brown was washing up the tea-things she admitted she had deceived him about the property she possessed, and laughed. Whereupon he had lost his temper, and struck her with a piece of wood used as a rolling-pin, which was originally a roller for silk – 'a sort of swinging side blow on the right eye'. She fell insensible to the floor and he fled from the house for an hour. On his return he deemed her to be dead, and decided then and there to dismember her and dispose of the parts. He attributed the fact that the neighbours had heard no sounds of altercation to their absence at market, it being Christmas Eve, and accounted for the absence of blood-stains on the floor when he cut up the body by saying that he had soaked up the blood with a flannel and thrown it in the privy.

Advised to make a detailed statement to this effect, for forwarding to the Home Secretary, Lord John Russell, Greenacre spent the whole of Thursday in writing, and in reading what he had written to the two turnkeys (warders) who closely observed him day and night. Frequently dissatisfied with his composition, he would tear it up and thrust it into a fire in the room, exclaiming: 'No, that won't do!' In so doing he used up a quire of foolscap.

Cheerful and loquacious, he continued to say that Mrs Gale knew nothing of Mrs Brown's death and dismemberment – and so did she. When she returned to his house, she said, and asked about all the boxes, he told her that Mrs Brown had left them there and wondered when she would retrieve them.

Greenacre completed his statement on Thursday morning and handed it to his counsel, Mr Price. He was also visited by the Sheriff and Under-Sheriff, but (said *The Times*) he refused to see 'a well-meaning and pious gentleman, who has been for some years in the habit of visiting capital convicts in the prison for the purpose of affording them religious consolation'. Greenacre said he had always despised 'religious cant'. However, he did not object to the prison chaplain's visits, although he remarked: 'The reverend gentleman might spare himself the trouble of advice and admonition, as I want no priest to tell me how to die.' *The Times* commented: 'How long this feeling will sustain him remains to be seen; but it would appear from his occasional abstracted and meditating moods, and the seeming attention which he bestows upon the Bible with which he is provided . . . that the light of religion may yet break in upon his mind.'

In his latest statement, Greenacre now claimed that after striking Mrs Brown with the roller on Christmas Eve he did not leave the house but paced up and down the room, 'not knowing how to act'. On realising she was dead, he considered how to dispose of the body and decided eventually to cut her up. This he did, he now said, with a dinner knife. He did not, however, as stated in a morning paper, hold the severed neck over a pail 'until the blood had ceased to flow'. He wrapped the head in a silk handkerchief and then put it in a canvas bag. Uncertain about what to do with it at first, he resolved at last 'to hide it in some distant place'. So he left the house, locked the door, and walked to the Elephant and Castle, with the head under his arm. From there he travelled by omnibus to Mile End, with the head in his lap, and then walked down to the Ben Jonson lock where, unwrapping the head, he 'shot it into the Stepney lock'. On his way back to Camberwell, he called on the Davises in Bartholomew Close. He spent the night in his own home – with the headless corpse. On the morning of Christmas Day, a Sunday, he cut off the legs, and carried them on his back to Coldharbour Lane, where he dumped them in the osier bed. After returning to Carpenter's Place, he put the torso and arms in a sack and tied it up, and on leaving the house with the sack on his back he hitched a lift with a carter as far as the Elephant and Castle, from where he and his bulky parcel were taken by cab to Edgware Road. Unobserved, he shoved the sack behind the flagstone near the Pineapple Gate.

He said later he chose to get rid of the dismembered body by day because he was less likely to be noticed by the police: carrying a large sack at night would look much more suspicious. Why he ventured as far as Stepney and Edgware Road – both were about seven miles from Camberwell – and why he chose these particular locations, remains as much a mystery as his carelessness about concealment. He could have buried his parcels, or, like the head, thrown them, weighted, into a pond or in the river. Asked what he had done with the roller and the silk handkerchief, he said he had burnt them with those of his clothes that were stained with blood; and that after washing out any stains on the floor, he went out to dine that afternoon with Mrs Gale in Walworth.

Further evidence of Greenacre's iniquity was published by *The Times* on 17 April, when it was revealed that a month after the death and dismemberment of Hannah Brown, Greenacre had advertised on 23 January on the front page of *The Times* as follows: 'Wanted, a partner, who can command £300, to join the advertiser in a patent to bring forward a new-invented machine, of great public benefit, that is certain of realizing an ample reward. Applications, by letter only, post-paid, for JG, at Mr Bishop's, No. 1 Tudor Place, Tottenham Court Rd.'

Perhaps it was through some similar device that he met Mrs Brown. For among the replies he received to this ad was one, *The Times* said, from 'a female of great respectability', who 'indiscreetly wrote to him on the subject, and afterwards had two or three interviews with him'.

He responded to this woman's initial letter with an unabashed offer of marriage. Writing on 4 February (the day of the inquest on the reunited pieces of Hannah Brown), he said:

> It is my wish to meet with a female companion, with a small capital, one with whom a mutual and a tender attachment might be formed, who would share with me in those advantageous pecuniary prospects which are now before me . . . No man can have a greater aversion than myself to advertising for a wife; nevertheless, this advertisement was intended to give an opportunity, by which I might make propositions of an honourable nature to one whom I might prefer as a companion for life . . . I am a widower 38 years of age, without any encumbrance, and am in the possession of a small income arising from the rent of some houses . . . Excuse the dissimulation by which I have obtained an introduction to you, and believe that my present proposal is dictated by every honourable and affectionate feeling towards you. I am, dear Madam, yours most sincerely, James Greenacre.

Perhaps the temporary success of this or other ventures caused him to defer his departure for America to the end of March. But *The Times* was censorious, exclaiming that 'at the very moment he wrote that letter, not only was he cohabiting with his fellow-convict, Sarah Gale, but was then, and is now, a married man, having left his fourth wife, a young woman of considerable personal attractions, behind him in America'. The newspaper had also learned that she, and his son by his first wife, were 'in a state of distress' in New York, where Greenacre had abandoned them.

The Times also reported two conversations which Greenacre had had in Newgate Prison with Alderman Humphrey, in which he denied having a wife in America. He said: 'A wife! No such thing! I never was married there. It is true I knew a woman called Martin there, and was as intimate with her as if I was her husband, and I intended to marry her, but I never did . . . There were two sisters of the house, and I was to have married one of them. But nobody knew anything about it.' Asked whether, as was rumoured, he was one of the Cato Street conspirators, who in 1820 had plotted to murder most of the Government at a banquet and then set fire to London, Greenacre replied: 'I never had anything to do with it. But I must be great food for the newspapers. Their business is to find out everything against me, and then to invent. I hope that report will be contradicted. It is quite absurd.'

He denied that Mrs Gale's baby had been murdered, and said that the silk roller, with which he struck Mrs Brown, belonged to her: 'It was in her trunk. It did not belong to me.' He also denied that she was killed upstairs, where some suspicious stains had been found. He said: 'It is true she went upstairs to make the bed in the back room, while I was lighting the fire, but she soon came down again.' Asked how no blood splashed over the walls and floor, he replied: 'I took care to let all the blood out of the throat before I cut off the head.' 'Into what did you let it flow?' Humphrey enquired. Greenacre answered: 'Into a brown pan, and I wiped up what was spilled with two flannel cloths, which I threw, blood and all, into the privy . . . There are two cesspools, and it is impossible they could be found.' He added: 'If I'm going to be hanged, I wish they'd hang me at once. I wish they'd hang me tomorrow.'

Hoping somehow, perhaps, to realise his wish and forestall the hangman, he wrote to Lord John Russell, ten days after he was sentenced to death, saying:

> Could I, my Lord, be relieved from the torture of the strait-jacket, and be permitted to recline upon my mattress occasionally, by day, instead of being compelled to sit in close company with two talkative keepers, I could derive that consolation of self-communion and secret prayer which the Bible so often enjoins us to strive for, by pouring out our sorrows before God in prayer, and by watering our pillows and our couches with our tears . . . I have, my Lord, another complaint to make of cruel, hard, and unfair usage . . . I mean, my Lord, the cruel falsehoods, the fabricated reports, and the perverted statements of newspaper advertisements. It is these falsehoods that make my death terrible indeed . . . PS. Should you feel disposed to permit me more liberty to pursue my devotions, there is, indeed, my Lord, no danger in me abusing that liberty.

Nothing, it seems, was done about Greenacre's request. The sheriffs reported to the Home Office that 'the strait-waistcoat which is placed upon Greenacre does not confine him to any uneasy position, it being so loose as to enable him partially to move his hands and arms'.

The order for his execution was communicated by the prison chaplain, Dr Cotton, and the Governor, Mr Cope, on 26 April. Greenacre was writing at a table in his room. On seeing the chaplain with a paper in his hand, to which a black seal was attached, he rose to his feet – strait-jacketed still, it would seem. As reported in *The Times*, the chaplain formally announced: 'The Recorder has made his report to the King, and I am sorry to inform you that it is unfavourable to you.' 'It cannot be helped,' Greenacre said. 'I am sacrificed through prejudice and falsehood.' Dr Cotton expressed the hope that the condemned man would occupy the time that was left to him 'in earnest and hearty prayer'. Greenacre replied: 'I have a confidence in the mercy of God, and will trust to that. I care not a pin for death. But I abhor the thought of going out of the world branded as a wilful murderer. I committed no murder.' On being handed a book of prayer, he said: 'I can't attend to those long prayers. I must look to inward prayer for relief. All prayers from the heart are short.' Said Dr Cotton: 'The blood of the unfortunate woman is upon your hands. For it was by your means she came by her death.' 'Yes,' said Greenacre. 'But it might as well be said that I murdered her, if a cart-wheel passed over her and I afterwards committed the mutilation. I have fallen a sacrifice to prejudice and the press.'

Dr Cotton aroused Greenacre's displeasure after the service in the prison chapel on Sunday, 30 April. Greenacre was now lodged in the condemned cell. He said: 'Sir – I do not know whether it was your duty to make the allusions you did in your sermon today. But whether your duty or not, you treated me as though I was a murderer.' Dr Cotton replied: 'My dear sir, you stand a convicted murderer by the verdict of a jury of your country, and as such I must speak of you.' 'But you said a good deal of the necessity of a confession,' Greenacre protested. 'Why need you have done that? You know I have already confessed. What can I say more?' To which the chaplain said: 'I am aware you have made statements more than once. All that is required is that there should be no mental reservation.' 'But sir,' retorted Greenacre, 'you spoke of me as a murderer! I have never acknowledged myself as such. Why should I – when I know to the contrary? . . . I consider that you made observations which might have been spared.' He was also upset when the authorities refused to allow him to see Mrs Gale before he died.

James Greenacre was hanged outside Newgate Prison at 8.00 am on Tuesday, 2 May, by which time some 20,000 persons had crammed the Old Bailey and every adjacent street, from Ludgate Hill to Smithfield Market.

They began gathering outside the prison well before midnight, where a sort of fair was held: piemen sold penny sandwiches and Greenacre tarts; ballad-mongers touted their wares; some hawkers sold pictures and life stories about Greenacre and Sarah Gale, as well as fake confessions. Others distributed religious tracts; and pickpockets plied their trade. Coffee-shops and pubs were open; first-floor rooms opposite the scaffold could be hired for as much as £12; windows were thronged. Every new activity or event was greeted with excited cheers and whistles, hisses and boos, even when women fainted or boys were trampled underfoot. Despite barriers and policemen, the crush and riotous incidents increased. At 4.00 am workmen emerged from the Debtors' Gate of the prison to erect the scaffold, a process that was hailed at every step by a cacophonous crescendo of sound, culminating in the executioner's appearance to fix the noose to the overhead beam. At 7.45 the bell of St Sepulchre's Church began to toll. Said *The Times*: 'From the moment that signal of the approaching execution was heard, the screams and groans occasioned by the pressure from the two extremities of the crowd upon the centre was perfectly appalling.' A few minutes before Greenacre appeared there was a general cry of 'Hats off!' and every man uncovered his head.

Within Newgate the condemned man had slept little, getting up and dressing himself at 3.45 am, after which he wrote several letters and conversed with the turnkeys. The previous night he had refused to take the sacrament with Dr Cotton, and when the chaplain entered his cell and offered consoling words and advice, Greenacre said he had no doubt Christ was a very good man, but he did not believe him to be the Son of God. About 7.00, while he drank a cup of tea and ate some bread and butter, he wept. It was the first time he had shed tears since being jailed. He remarked that he was very differently situated now to what he was some years ago: he had been highly respected then, and had been returned as one of the overseers of St George's parish with one of the largest majorities ever known. As 8 o'clock approached he became very agitated, but said nothing. The sheriffs and other officials assembled at 7.45 and Greenacre's arms were pinioned by Calcraft, the chief executioner, who had performed this office since 1828. The procession formed up, and set off through the prison to the Debtors' Gate. Greenacre's last request, after giving a small parcel to a sheriff for Mrs Gale (said to be his spectacles), was that he would not be exposed to the multitude for too long and his execution be swiftly done. *The Times* said:

> No sooner did those officers, who usually precede the criminal to the place of execution, become visible, than [the concourse] burst forth in a loud, deep and sullen shout of execration against Greenacre . . . As soon as he had mounted the scaffold, which he did with a firm and steady step, the populace again exhibited their detestation . . . by setting up a wild hurrah in approval of the retaliation which he was about to endure under the hands of justice . . . It appeared as if he was either perfectly unmoved by it, or regarded it as no additional bitterness to the agony of the hour . . . The bolt was withdrawn, Greenacre fell, and the vengeance of the law was accomplished. In two minutes from his first appearance on the platform he ceased to be a living man. He died, we think, instantly. One convulsive grasp of the hands was observed – nothing more.

He hung there for an hour. Then his body was cut down to 'a yell of triumph' from the crowd. A plaster cast was taken of his shaven head, and he was buried within the jail at 9 o'clock that night, near the graves of five of the Cato Street conspirators.

Before his death he had penned long and moralising letters of farewell to his family; to Mr Price; to Mr Hobler, his solicitor (to whom he left his silver hunting-watch, with its gold chain, and a key); and to his five surviving children, most of whom, it seems, were boys. He proclaimed his innocence to all. He also left a manuscript, written in Newgate and entitled *An Essay on the Human Mind*. This was seized by the sheriffs, denounced as 'a crude and wild farrago of visionary speculations founded upon the excellence of a moral religion', and destroyed.

To his sons he said:

> No precaution can be of any avail, for that which has happened to me may prove the Fate of any man . . . To avoid such a Fate I might admonish you never to throw at any person, nor to yield to passion . . . I would have you blend in your Hearts' Study your Worldly as well as your Spiritual welfare. For be you assured that upon your Temporal circumstances depends your Happiness or your Wretchedness in this life . . .

> There is no enemy to man equal to that of poverty. It is poverty fills the country with sin and crime.

To his brothers and sisters he said:

> Most sorry am I that the name of our family should be disgraced by any act of mine . . . that name which has not been stained by any crime cognizable to the laws of our country for centuries past . . . I feel this the more since I know that none amongst you, nor any person in London, has been more careful to maintain a good character than myself . . . Sobriety, industry, integrity, humanity and a quiet demeanour have always been the careful study of my life . . . My untimely end is an awful proof of the vicissitudes of life, and that no care or prudence can protect us from the decrees of fate.

He was an extraordinary murderer, and a more than ordinary man.

Three weeks after James Greenacre was hanged, Princess Victoria celebrated her 18th birthday on 24 May. Four weeks later, in the early hours of 20 June, her uncle, King William IV, died at Windsor Castle. The Archbishop of Canterbury and the Lord Chamberlain were driven from there to London, to Kensington Palace, and at 6.00 am Victoria, aroused from bed by her mother, the Duchess of Kent, put on a dressing-gown and went to meet the two gentlemen, alone, in an outer room. They told the short, slim, fair-haired girl that she was Queen.

CHAPTER 2

Daniel Good

The Murder of Jane Jones, 1842

Times were increasingly hard in 1842 for the teeming urban and industrialised mass of the population. Children aged six were working in mills and mines for 12–14 hours a day; the boys earned at most 3s 6d a week, the girls much less. An Act of 1840 had prohibited the employment of anyone under the age of 21 in sweeping chimneys by climbing them, but the Act was ignored for many years. Chartism, a nationwide movement for social, industrial and political reform, particulary where it affected the artisan and labouring classes, was rampant, resulting in torchlit meetings, processions, petitions and strikes. Transportation, although it had ceased to New South Wales in Australia, still continued. But gas-lighting, level wooden-blocked streets, umbrellas and waterproofing had provided some general benefits, as had the railways. Ninety-three Railway Acts had been passed since 1825, and 1,500 miles of track had been laid: London was now linked to Birmingham, to Southampton, Dover and York. The middle classes prospered, as did those values of family morality epitomised by the young Queen, now 23, and her young German husband, Prince Albert. Married in February 1840, they had already produced two children, the future Princess Royal and the Prince of Wales, and would have nine in all.

The Tory Prime Minister was Sir Robert Peel. The New Police that he had fathered were still getting a bad press. Punch, *launched the previous year and with W. M. Thackeray now on its staff, treated policemen with derision, even contempt. The police themselves still suffered from problems of credibility and poor communications, and were over-eager to be open about their activities with the press. As Charles Dickens said, they were forever 'jobbing and trading in mystery and making the most of themselves'. Their mishandling of the Jane Jones murder – a case of much bad luck for all concerned, including Good – caused considerable public criticism and internal ructions. But it led to the creation of a detective branch, which later became the CID.*

It was unfortunate for Daniel Good, and for PC William Gardiner, that both of them happened to be in Wandsworth High Street at about 8.45 pm on Wednesday, 6 April 1842, and that the casual theft of a pair of trousers would lead to the revelation of what *The Times* would describe as 'a murder of a most frightful and appalling nature'.

PC Gardiner was on patrol in the High Street when a shopboy ran up to him to report a theft. Led by the boy, he proceeded to a pawnbroker's owned by a Mr Collingbourne, who complained that an Irish coachman had filched a pair of black trousers, after haggling over, and buying, a pair of black knee-breeches. The shopboy, Sam Dagnell, had noticed the swarthy coachman conceal the trousers under his greatcoat, before stuffing them under the cushions of a four-wheeled pony chaise. He told Mr Collingbourne, who darted outside and asked the coachman if he had made some mistake. The coachman was at first dismissive, and then became abusive when accused of theft and drove the chaise away.

All this had been observed by a youth called Robert Speed standing outside an adjacent grocer's shop, where he lived and worked as Mr Cooper's assistant. He had recognised the Irish coachman – as did Mr Collingbourne, who also knew for whom the coachman worked, and where in Putney Park Lane. Armed with this information and determined to bring the felon to justice, PC Gardiner set off at once, with Speed and the shopboy, Sam, both of whom he evidently enlisted to identify the thief. Perhaps they also went along for a bit of excitement. If so, they would not be disappointed. It would be a night they would remember all their lives.

Putney Park Lane, a long avenue lined by trees running north and south between Upper Richmond Road and Putney Heath, was nearly two miles away, with the little village of Roehampton near its foot. No doubt, being early April, the night was cold as well as dark. But Gardiner had a lantern to guide him and the boys along the rough and unlit roads.

The district was then a pleasant one of parks and fields dotted with large country-houses, in one of which, called Granard Lodge, lived an aged, retired East India merchant, Mr Queeley Shiell. According to the 1841 census, he and his wife were in their early eighties. With them lived their son John, a barrister in his fifties, his much younger wife and four children, all girls, the youngest of whom was two. They employed about a dozen servants, most of whom were female.

On entering the gates of Granard Lodge, Gardiner and the boys approached the front door, where he rang the bell. The door was opened by a footman, who, when asked where the coachman might be, directed the PC to a farming complex of stables and kitchen gardens a few hundred yards up the road. There were two blocks of stables, with different sections for horses, conveyances, feed and equipment. Above one block were four rooms, which were used as sleeping quarters by some of the staff, including the Irish coachman and the son of Mr Shiell's chief gardener and bailiff, Thomas Houghton. That night the son, John Houghton, the estate's second gardener, was in his father's dwelling beside this stable block.

The stable-yard had a bell by a gate, which was rung, on PC Gardiner's instruction, by Speed, and a thin, dark man in his forties appeared, attended by a smaller boy.

'Has the coachman come home?' Speed enquired. 'I am the coachman,' replied the other man. 'Daniel Good.' Whereupon Gardiner stepped forward and, as he attested later, said: 'I have come to take you into custody on a charge of stealing a pair of black trousers from the shop of Mr Collingbourne, the pawnbroker, of Wandsworth.' Good replied: 'Why, yes. I bought a pair of breeches from Mr Collingbourne. But I haven't paid for them yet.' He took a purse out of a pocket and added: 'I'll give you what we agreed on, and you can take the money to him.'

Gardiner reported later: 'I told him I could not take the money as it had nothing to do with the charge I came upon. He then said: "Very well, I'll go with you to Wandsworth, and settle with Mr Collingbourne." I asked him if he would allow me to look into the chaise, and over the stables, to which he said: "Yes." And I went in, accompanied by the lads.'

First Gardiner searched the chaise-house and the stable on the north side of the yard. Then he moved towards the stable on the south side. Suddenly Good put his back to the door and refused to let the others enter. There was an altercation, heard by Houghton, the chief gardener, aged about 57. He emerged from his dwelling, and when he understood what the matter was about, told Good to stand aside and let the search proceed. All six entered: Gardiner, holding his lantern, Houghton, Good, Speed, Sam, and the small boy who had been with Good.

PC Gardiner told Speed and Sam to keep an eye on Good while he inspected the first two stalls, which were empty, and the hay-racks. Good seemed very uneasy, and shifted about, like the two ponies in the third stall. As Gardiner inspected the interior of a corn-bin, Good exclaimed that he would willingly go back to Wandsworth to pay what he owed. Gardiner refused to listen and said: 'No. I'll not go until I've searched the stable and made a diligent search.' He said later:

> I then desired the lad Speed, in the presence of Good, to stand by him while I finished the search; and Good having walked to the bottom stall while I was searching the bin, I followed him. I saw him move the hay from one side of the stall to the other – which I forbid – and told him to go and stand outside [the stall] with the lad. I then moved two trusses of hay . . . and on disturbing some loose hay I discovered something under it. I said: 'What is this here? A goose?'

Suddenly, Daniel Good ran for the door. Surprised, the others were too late to prevent him closing the door behind him and locking them in. 'Now we are done!' cried Gardiner, and added, according to Speed: 'Oh, my God! We have lost the prisoner!' For some seconds Gardiner, aided by Speed, attacked the door with a pitchfork, before resigning himself to official displeasure, even dismissal, over the departed thief, and he went back to examine his peculiar find, the plucked goose. On closer inspection it proved to be too large for a goose. Was it the carcass of a sheep, or, as the little boy thought, a pig? None of the five had seen anything like it before. 'Oh, my God!' cried Sam, who was now holding the lantern. 'It's a human being!' Speed turned the body over and they saw it had breasts. They now realised, aghast, they had found a naked female torso, without head, legs or arms, and with the lower stomach ripped open and the entrails removed.

PC Gardiner must now have felt even more sick: he had let a murderer, not a thief, escape. But it was 15 minutes before he was able to break open the stable-door and send Sam to raise the alarm.

After 20 minutes or so, PC Hayter and then PC Tye arrived. The latter galloped off on one of Mr Shiell's ponies to Wandsworth station-house, while Hayter made a brief search of the neighbourhood. He found a broken paling in a fence and footprints heading for Putney in the soft earth of a field.

When Sergeant Palmer arrived at about 11.00 pm he took charge. A further search was made of the stables. A dried-up pool of blood was found near the torso, and in another stall, hidden under hay, a mattress stained with blood and urine was found, rolled up with two blankets and tied. In the separate but adjacent harness room, whose locked door had to be forced, 'a very fulsome smell' was noticed by PC Tye. 'It resembled the odour of the rind of pork when burnt,' he said later. 'It nearly threw me on my back,' said Palmer. They investigated – Houghton senior was with them. He later told the court: 'The grate is what is called Cobbett's register-grate, much larger than an ordinary one, and the fire was laid when I entered with the officer. It was composed of wood and coals, of an unusual quantity. I should think about two wheelbarrows full . . . The day before the search was made I observed a quantity of smoke issuing from the harness room, from which I found a smell similar to that from the singeing of horse-hair.'

So he must also have told Sgt Palmer. Houghton's son, John, aged about 22, would later add to this, saying:

> On Tuesday morning, about half-past six o'clock, I came down from my room and perceived a very uncommon smell. [Good] was in the stable and I asked him if he been singeing the horses. He replied that he had been in liquor overnight, and had been roasting some cheese to refresh him. I did not see the fire in the harness room at the time, but I heard the cracking of wood . . . Good said he was drying the harness.

In the ashes of the grate the policeman discovered some calcined bones, including two pieces of a skull. A further search revealed two strips of flannel petticoat on the saddle-rack, some torn female linen, a bloody knife in a table drawer, a saw, and by the fireplace a blood-stained axe. An assistant surgeon, Alfred Allen, a local man, inspected the torso and pronounced that the dismemberment had been done after death about three days earlier. Apart from a portion of the bladder, the abdominal and pelvic viscera had been entirely removed.

It seems that some of the Shiell family were not at home at this time. Granard Lodge had been sold and the Shiells were about to move to a grand house in Clarges Street, off Piccadilly. None of the Shiells gave evidence later on, and of their servants, only the two male Houghtons, as well as the footman and cook, appeared in court. The Shiells may have been making the most of Easter – the previous Monday had been Easter Monday (4 April) – and they may have been staying with relations or friends. This might explain why Good had had so much free time, and was able to borrow the chaise on Wednesday, 6 April for about eight hours.

The Houghtons, and in particular the son, John, whose room in the stables was next to Good's, had much to tell the police. John said of the coachman: 'He never had a good character. No one would trust him much . . . He was a kind of swindler.' None the less the young gardener, who, having seen the remains – 'What a wretch he must be!' – and having sworn never to sleep in the stables again, had to admit that he had heard nothing unusual on the Sunday, Monday and Tuesday nights. This was not because he was inebriated – he went to bed sober – but because he was a heavy sleeper, he said.

Both Houghtons, father and son, added further details to their accounts of the stench and smoke emanating early on Tuesday morning from the harness room and its chimney.

Good, who had been with the Shiells for two and a half years, had been visited at the stables by two women, with whom he had had tea in the harness room. One of them, the younger one, who had worked at the Rose and Crown in Wimbledon, had been to the stables four or five times over the past year. On her last visit, a fortnight ago, she had stayed the night – thus the mattress in the stall. The other woman, Good had said, was his sister. She had been seen at the stables three times, the last time at the end of March. The police also learned that this sister had looked after the coachman's 10-year-old son, also named Daniel Good.

Where was the boy? He was in Thomas Houghton's cottage, whither he had fled in tears at 9.30 that night, after escaping from the stables. He had been locked in with the others, and seen the torso. He had also been out most of that day with his father in the chaise. Now he sobbed because his father had run away – and where was his aunt?

What little Daniel told the police, and when, we do not know. But this is what he told the magistrates' court.

He had lived with his aunt, whom he called 'Mother' to please her, in the front kitchen of 18 South Street, Marylebone for just over two years. His father used to come and visit them there. He last saw his mother in South Street on Easter Sunday, when he went to a C. of E. Chapel in Baker Street. On his return, she had gone. But this was not unexpected, as she had arranged for him in her absence to spend the night with a widow, Mrs Young, at 99 East Street, which he did, going to school as usual on Monday morning in Dorset Street. Later that day his father fetched him from the school and told him that his mother had gone into service and that he would not see her again for six months. On leaving South Street they went to Blandford Street and then to George Street. A man put him on an omnibus, which took him to Roehampton. A publican there, Mr Ricks, then escorted him to Mr Shiell's house, where he arrived about 9.00 pm. He slept there that night (presumably with his father in a room above the stables) and at 5.00 pm the following day, Tuesday, was taken by his father to sleep at Mrs Hester's house in Pear Place, Roehampton. She was out, but returned at half-past eight. On Wednesday, 6 April, he returned to the stables, and that afternoon he and his father set off in the chaise for Woolwich, for 13 Charlotte Place, arriving there about 1.00 pm. His father had a small band-box with him, in which was a blue bonnet that had been worn by his mother for about a year. At Woolwich his father took him to see Susan Butcher, saying that she was a cousin, and gave her some apples and pears and other items in the kitchen, where they had tea with Susan's little sister. Her father was a shipwright. Afterwards, Susan came with them in the chaise as far as New Cross Station, where she and his father went into a public house. On the way he was allowed to drive, after he had agreed to call Susan Butcher 'Mother'. Later, on their way back to Putney Park Lane, his father had pulled the chaise up in Wandsworth High Street to buy a pair of black trousers, which he put under the cushions on which little Daniel sat. Back at the stables, a policeman arrived looking for his father, who before long locked them all in the stables and ran away.

No one knows what little Daniel thought, and suffered, that night. But the police now knew that Susan Butcher could not have been the woman murdered in the stables. The victim must have been the little boy's 'mother' and his father's 'sister', last seen on Easter Monday. She called herself Jane Good. Before that she had been Jane Jones.

The police had much to do and a murderer to find. There was never any doubt in their minds, and in the papers, that Good *was* the murderer. But having caught him by chance, they had let him escape. Thereafter, because of their parochialism, poor communications, inter-divisional rivalries, and a shortage of men, he would evade arrest for more than a week. Even then he was caught by sheer chance. Daniel Good had some very bad luck.

The police would later claim, in an official document headed 'Outline of Steps taken by the Police', that 'about half-past nine o'clock on Wednesday night, the 6th of April . . . information of the charge and the escape, with a description of Good, was circulated immediately to all the Divisions of the Police . . . and known at every Police Station of the Metropolitan Police District [being a circumference of about sixty miles] before four o'clock'. This may have been the intention, but it could never have happened, for Gardiner and the others did not break out of the stables until half-past nine, when the coachman's little boy went crying to the gardener's home. The next policemen to appear, PCs Hayter and Tye, arrived some 20 minutes later. Gardiner himself declared: 'I sent the younger lad to give information of the circumstances to all the police he could meet with, while I remained with the body. In about half an hour Constable Hayter, who said he knew the prisoner well, arrived, and he, accompanied with another constable, went to give information to Superintendent Bicknell, who on his arrival proceeded with me and others to make a further search.'

The information could not have been given to Bicknell before about half-past ten, and it is unlikely that he passed it on straightaway. But even if the murder report had reached the police stations in central London by 4.00 am, the policemen on the beat would probably not have known about it until they paraded at 6.00 am – by which time Good had entered and slept in Jane

Jones's room, before absconding by cab with a large box, a large bundle and a bed. This he did at 5.15 am.

An internal inquiry would later be held into the police failures that night and various officers were censured for a less than urgent and efficient application to their duties. Some were suspended. PC Gardiner was discharged.

The next policeman to displease his superiors was Police Sergeant Stephen Perdrian, who had happened to observe Good order a cab in South Street at about 5.00 am and had noted its number, 726. He said later: 'While I was talking to the cabman, [Good] came out and called the cabman. I then crossed to the other side, and saw Good pass a large trunk to the cabman.'

But it was not until 4.30 on the afternoon of Thursday, 7 April that Sgt Perdrian was sent for by an inspector and told to find out where the cab had gone. No doubt Perdrian was already being blamed for not having had the foresight to question Good when he left South Street so conspicuously that morning, or to arrest him on suspicion.

By this time the police had decided that Jane Jones, missing from South Street since Easter Sunday, was most probably the murdered woman. Said to have been about 40, she had lodged at No. 18, where John and Jane Brown had a greengrocer's shop, for three years, and for most of this time had lived in the front kitchen, where she took in washing. A painted sign outside the house said: *Mangling done here by J Good*. She had begun calling herself Mrs Good about the time she moved into the kitchen, which was rented and paid for by Daniel Good. His small son, Daniel, had been living with her for about two years. He called her 'Mother'. Good told Mrs Brown that the boy's real mother had died a year and a half previously. Mrs Brown said later:

> He used to come daily to see Jane Jones, but not so frequently after he went to live at Putney. He never stayed long . . . She was a neat-looking woman, not stout, about five feet two inches high, and a person of close habits. I had no means of knowing whether she was in the family way or not . . . I last saw her alive on Sunday, 3 April. She had on a blue bonnet, a black shawl with flowers on it and a cotton dress. She went out between two and three o'clock in the afternoon.

Before she departed, Jane Jones told Mrs Brown she was going to visit her husband's place of work and that if she took the little boy, who called her 'Mother', he would 'massacre' her. Jane hoped it would pour with rain to prevent her having to go, as she was worried about what her husband wanted. She didn't know why he had sent for her or what he was up to.

Earlier, she chatted to Elizabeth Christie, who occupied the first floor of No. 18. She said she had been sent for by Good, and was distressed about where the boy would sleep that night, having been instructed not to bring him with her. Christie later said:

> She came to my door at twelve o'clock and said 'Do you think it will rain? I hope it will pour with rain all the afternoon.' I have known her to go to Putney, but never to stay out all night. Good used to visit her as early as five o'clock. I often heard him say on going away: 'Goodbye, my dear. Take care of yourself' . . . She told me, about three months back, that she thought she was pregnant, but subsequently that she was not.

South Street (now an extension of Blandford Street) was a few hundred yards north of Manchester Square, and it must have been the starting-point of Sgt Perdrian's investigation, which he pursued with great single-mindedness, evidently hoping to find Good and arrest him on his own. Promotion and praise were on his mind, not the public censure that ensued. It took him nearly 12 hours to trace the cab and its driver, John Littlebody, during which time he must have visited nearly every cabstand in central London. But at 3.45 am on Friday, 8 April, he was back at Marylebone police station, reporting that Good and his luggage had been dropped at Mr Shepherd's livery stables in Dorset Place, Pall Mall East at 5.45 am the previous day. It seems he was told, or decided himself, to make further enquiries, and succeeded in finding out that a second cab had taken Good on to the Spotted Dog in the Strand, where the luggage was booked in under the name of Stanley. At the Spotted Dog, Sgt Perdrian must have learned – as was later declared in court by a barmaid – that Good and a woman had collected the luggage at 11.30 am and driven away. A waiter also revealed that when the couple were in the tap-room, Good said he was very tired, as he had been 'travelling all night by the railway'. When asked which railway, he said he didn't know. Good was very restless, frequently going out into the street. As the waiter cooked Good some steak, he overheard him tell the woman: 'That bugger won't trouble you no more.'

All this must have much encouraged Sgt Perdrian. Fired with new enthusiasm, he now set out to find the *third* cab and its driver, assisted by a crossing-sweeper, who had seen Good and the woman leave the Spotted Dog, and knew the cabman who drove them away. He was found in Drury Lane. He said he had taken the couple, the bed and other articles to an address in Spitalfields. To save time, Perdrian hired the cab to take him on to Flower and Dean Street, to No. 4, where all the items had been unloaded and taken upstairs, to a room occupied by a Mrs Molly or Mary Good, aged 59, a fruit-seller in Bishopsgate.

What happened next that Friday morning was described by Perdrian himself, calling himself PS 16, in a report he later submitted to the Joint Commissioners of the Metropolitan Police.

> On PS 16 entering the House he ascertained the woman who lived upstairs was named Good but that she was out. PS 16 also found that Good had been there on Thursday morning and taken Mrs Good, his

wife, out with him and returned in the middle of the day, bringing with them a bed and a Trunk which they took away with them again in the afternoon when they went out together. While PS 16 was hearing this from the lodgers downstairs, Mrs Good came in and went upstairs. PS 16 then went upstairs to her and said to her good morning, I think I saw you at the Spoted Dog in the Strand yesterday. She said she went there with her Husband who she had not seen for the last 7 year until Thursday morning when he came home and said he was in trouble and had left his place. She then called him a vilain and said he had left her to live with another woman. I said to Her whose things were those he had with him. She said she did not know, she also stated that Good took her out in the afternoon with the intention to go and see some relation he had living in the Strand, but subsequently left her in a coffee shop at 5 pm on Thursday, since which she as not seen anything of him. PS 16 considered that the only motive Good had for going to see his wife was to get her to assist him in disposing of the things which PS 16 found to have been pledged by Good and his Wife at F Somes No 200 Spitalfields – and identified the things as being those removed from 18 South St . . . PS 16 thought it better to be explicit with her being convinced that she would soon hear of it, then told her of the Murder. She said I hope he may be taken, for he as been a raskal to me. PS 16 remained with Mrs Good up to 6 pm on Friday and finding there was no chance of gaining any further clue in tracing Good left to give the above information to the H Division. PS 16 also has to state that he found a bundle and two small work boxes at Mrs Good which she said Good had brought there.

Mr Soames's pawnbroking assistant must have told Perdrian (as he later told the court) that Good first offered to pawn a bed. But as he was a stranger, Soames refused to take it in. Good went away and returned with Mary Good. She said he was her husband, who had just come ashore from a voyage, and that it was all right. Good added that he had come to London by train and that the articles he wanted to pawn had belonged to a person who had died on the voyage home from China. Later, he brought in some female apparel to pawn.

Alas for Perdrian. When at length he reported all his discoveries, his enterprise and initiative were met with disapproval and blame. The 'Outline', previously quoted, declared: 'The Sergeant of Police belonging to the Marylebone Division, who had traced Good to this place, not being acquainted with the neighbourhood, from perhaps an excess of zeal more than discreet, made inquiries in the neighbourhood without communicating – as he ought to have done – with the Superintendent of Police of the Division, and any certain trace of Good has been lost since that time.' Inspector Nicholas Pearce, who had been put in charge of the investigation, also complained about Perdrian's 'incautious conduct'.

Pearce was also vexed by the carping clamour of the press, typified by a paragraph in *The Times* on Saturday, 9 April: 'The conduct of the Metropolitan Police . . . is marked with a degree of looseness and want of decision which proves that unless a decided change is made in the present system, it is idle to expect that it can be an efficient detective police, and that the most desperate offender may escape with impunity.'

But the police were doing all they could. Instructions were sent to all Divisions to check on 'all persons going away by any Coach, Railroad, or by the River, or any of the roads out of Town'. A description of Good was also sent 'to all the sea ports and principal Towns' and posters, proclaiming MURDER! and printed on 7 April, were distributed far and wide. These contained the following description of Daniel Good: 'He is an Irishman, aged about 46 years, 5 ft 6 ins high, very dark complexion, black hair, long features, and bald at the top of the head; walks upright; was dressed in a dark Great Coat, Drab Breeches and Gaiters, and Black Hat.'

As a result, swarthy sinister Irishmen were sighted all over the place, although most sightings were reported hours, even days, after the event. The police themselves kept a watch on Mary Good, whom the papers invariably described as 'Old Molly'. Of this surveillance the 'Outline' said:

> It has been ascertained, that an Irishman who comes from the same place as Good has been in frequent communication with Mrs Good – apparently the Bearer of some messages to and from her. When he goes to her room the utmost caution is used to prevent observation, and a Cloth is hung up within the door to prevent anyone looking through the Keyhole or any opening. Upon his leaving her he has been followed to a Court near Tooley Street in the Boro', where great numbers of the low Irish people lodge, and from thence has been traced again to Mrs Good's . . . Observation is still kept upon the girl Lydia Susannah Butcher, with whom Good is known to have been intimate latterly, and at her father's house at Woolwich.

The watch on Molly Good produced another suspect, and another unhappy result, which was described in some detail by the *Morning Advertiser*. Soon after midnight on Saturday the 9th, a young man 'of rather diminutive stature, with a large bundle of papers under his arm' knocked loudly on the street door of 4 Flower and Dean Street. Old Molly descended but refused to open the door. Whereupon the youth wrote something on a slip of paper and passed it to her. Apprehended by a constable, he was taken to the police station at Spital Square, where he 'strutted about with great apparent indifference'. He told the duty sergeant that he had called on Mrs Good to offer the professional assistance of his master, a solicitor. Sgt Coleman rebuked the youth before releasing him, saying his action at such a late hour might show some industry and perseverance, but not much professional respectability. The young man responded that the Sergeant was mistaken. More than once, he said, he had obtained a client by this means. Besides, the trial would be notorious, and benefit his master if he were involved. And there were 'many very nice and critical points of law' concerning the identification of the remains.

This particular matter was in part resolved by a mole on the right side of the torso's neck – Jane Jones had had such a mole, so two of her female neighbours said. The torso itself was buried on 15 April in Putney churchyard by the parish constable, watched by over 200 people. He had retrieved it after what was left of Jane Jones was put on display in a pub the previous Sunday. 'It is even asserted', said the *Advertiser*, 'that money was received, on that sacred day, for admission to the heartrending and sickening spectacle.'

The horror and emotion aroused by the murder was compounded by the popular conviction that Jane Jones had been about four months' pregnant. So a Putney doctor, who examined the remains, would later aver in court. But Mr Allen, the only other doctor to comment on this, would not commit himself, as the evidence had been removed. A broadsheet published at that time reflected the general revulsion. It began:

> Great God of all, who rules on high, Our secret thoughts to Thee are known. The darkest deeds before Thine eye Are all exposed before thy throne . . . Worse than Greenacre we allow, Like him all feeling thou didst spurn; He cut his victim up, but thou The body afterwards did burn . . . A double murder thou hast done, Unequalled yet by savage wild. For when the mother's blood did run, Thou didst destroy her unborn child . . .

It was later deduced from the stinking state of the travelling-box on the chaise – 'I nearly fell back in a faint,' said PC Tye – that Jane Jones's entrails had been transported to the Lower Richmond Road near Putney Bridge and cast into the Thames. A piece of flesh was found on the tow-path.

Good neglected, however, to destroy her clothes, and behaving with the unbelievable thoughtlessness that characterises most murderers (those that are known) pawned Jane Jones's belongings, including her bed, and gave items of her clothing to Susan Butcher and Molly Good. He also stole three shawls and a fur tippet from a shop in Welbeck Street on 5 April, the day before he stole the fatal trousers from the pawnbroker's in Wandsworth. All of which was done with a characteristic indifference – or subconscious invitation – to being found out.

By this time the inquest, first held in the Angel Inn, Roehampton on 8 April and adjourned until Tuesday the 12th, had been adjourned again, and a reward of £50 was offered by the parochial authorities of Putney.

On the Monday, *The Times* had published an account of Molly Good's early life and her version of what had happened the previous Thursday. She claimed to have married Daniel Good when she was 26 or 27 and while she was a housemaid in a gentleman's house in Kinsale, near Cork. Good, she said, was then a footman in another such house, that of a captain. They married and came to London where, after three years, he deserted her. She saw him eight years later, when he said he now had a son. Then he vanished again, to reappear on Thursday, 7 April.

If this was true, he must have been about 13 when they met. More likely, she was about 31 and he 18 or so. Interestingly, *The Times* had revealed the previous week that Good had been an officer's servant throughout most of the Peninsular War (1808–14), since when he had received a pension of five shillings a week. His master (the Captain?) had been killed near the end of the war, after which Good may have returned to Kinsale, when, in 1814, he would have been about 18. Perhaps he married Molly then. His real name is said elsewhere to have been Sullivan, or Dinovan, not Good.

According to Molly Good, when Daniel turned up in Flower and Dean Street on the Thursday at breakfast-time, he told her he had been away at sea. She upbraided him, and he replied: 'What ails you, my heart? I know I've been a very bad man. But God Almighty has at last turned me to you, and we'll be happy and comfortable yet.' Whereupon he embraced her and burst into tears. He then gave her sixpence to buy some rum, which they downed with their breakfast. He also gave her some women's clothing, and left the oilskin cover for his hat in her room. At the pawnbroker's shop managed by Mr Soames (whom they must have visited about noon, after leaving the Spotted Dog in the Strand), Good, saying he was William Stanley, pawned a bed, a rug, a counterpane, four pillows, four blankets and five sheets, as well as two waistcoats, two pairs of boy's trousers and a tablecloth, several scarves and shawls, a tea-caddy, several cups and saucers and other pieces of china, plus two dozen knives and forks. He sold all he could of Jane Jones's possessions – he told Susan Butcher to take her mangle.

After this, according to Molly Good, they walked westwards to Cheapside, where they paused to have a coffee. Hungry, she asked him to get her an egg. He walked out, and never returned.

That's what she said. The following morning Sgt Perdrian called. From then on a watch was kept on the house in which she lived, and on Tuesday, 12 April Inspector Pearce replaced previous police observers with an experienced and soldierly sergeant, Stephen Thornton, who noted the almost daily visits paid to Molly Good by an Irishman, Richard Gamble, and endeavoured to trail him wherever he went. But there was still no sign of Good, although agitated Irishmen looking like him were spotted in Essex, in Greenwich, in assorted pubs and streets and eating-houses and barber's shops – apparitions who paled and fled when anyone mentioned murder. More interesting was a Mr Dixon's piece of information. He said that an Irishman called Daniel Good had been in his father's service about nine years previously as a coachman. This man committed a felony in Brixton and was sentenced to seven years' transportation, a sentence then commuted to one or two years which were spent in the Millbank Penitentiary.

The *Morning Advertiser* reported on Friday, 15 April: 'Yesterday the office of the Commissioner of Police in Scotland Yard was besieged with anxious inquiries as to whether the murderer Good had been taken into custody, and the police on duty were compelled to return the mortifying answer that he had not.' During the day, continued the *Advertiser*, several people had purported to have important information. But 'their intelligence was in most instances vague and shallow, and in some instances truly absurd'. A middle-aged gentleman had gravely informed the police that he had seen Good, dressed in female attire, selling apples in Finch Lane, Cornhill.

The police themselves were better informed about Good's appearance on 16 April, when a very detailed and useful description of him was circulated within the divisions. It originated in a report from an Inspector Macgill in Sidcup. He had visited Elmstead Farm, where Good had once worked as a coachman for a Mr Fitzgerald. His enquiries led him to a Mrs Head, who had 'lived as fellow servant' with Good in Mr Fitzgerald's service. She told Macgill:

> He speaks very fast, is quick in all his movements, eats fast, and his cheeks are thin and hollow from the loss of his back teeth; his eyes are small and very dark, his brow much wrinkled, and knits his brow and shakes his head when speaking; has a scowl upon his face and looks very morose, and when he smiles he seems altogether as well pleased; his nose is rather conspicuous, for near the point, it seems as if a small piece had been chopped off; this however is natural.

Macgill added: 'While in the service of Mr Fitzgerald Good was assaulted by his master, and Mrs Head bathed the wound whilst he lay on a dresser in the kitchen; this wound was on the left side of the upper lip near to the nose. Mrs Head states that Good speaks 4 languages, French, Italian, Irish and English.'

But he was unable to read or write. If he had been able to do so, he may, like Greenacre, have deluged others with his prose. As it is, he managed to send two letters to Mr Shiell, one of which was dictated to an Irish paviour, John McEvoy, taken by Good from his employment in the Poultry (a road in the City) to the Three Tuns in Coleman Street, where he was provided with some paper and a quart of gin to assist his literary output. This was at about 6.15 am on Thursday, 7 April. The letter that resulted was so badly written and spelt that McEvoy himself took an hour to read it aloud in court. It expressed the hope that Mr Shiell would take care of Good's 'destitute boy' and that £7 10s allegedly owed to Good would be used to look after his son. Among disjointed sentences it said: 'I am a single man since I buried my dear wife five years the 14th of January last . . . You will find two blankets and a mattress in the stable which Susan Butcher and me slept on. I was a RC until I became acquainted with Susan Butcher, and she was the cause of all my trouble and misfortune . . .'

Another poorly written epistle, but much shorter, was also sent to Mr Shiell. Now in the Public Record Office archives in Kew, it was also probably penned by an Irishman – or woman – and is hard to decipher. It says: 'Sur – i wright thys to inform u to pa the 7 pounds 10 due to mee to mi desolate boy. I shall thro miself into the thames just bi waterloo brydge tonight where mi body wil be found. Good by god bless yu all – tak kare of mi poor boy and I shall dy in piece. Dan Good.'

Although a man's body found in the Thames at Richmond was thought for a while to be that of Good, this proved wrong. On 15 April the *Advertiser* complained: 'The retreat of the murderer has not yet been discovered, and that unhealthy excitement which pervades all minds suffers no abatement, but on the contrary, it increases as the chances lessen of the police being able to capture a man of such atrocious and fiendish character.' He had been missing now for nearly ten days. Where *was* he?

On 16 April, through another piece of bad luck, Daniel Good was found.

It seems that he did not leave London until Sunday, 10 April. For on that day he entered a barber's shop in Bromley in Kent to have himself shaved. Dressed as a bricklayer – in a fustian jacket and trousers, dirty blue-striped shirt, black waistcoat, black neckerchief, low shoes and a dark cloth cap without a peak – he carried a large bundle and a new bricklayer's hod. The barber, Anthony Foyle, became suspicious when his customer insisted on moving his chair to a dark part of the shop. Foyle deliberately began to discuss the murder with another customer, a young market gardener, Bill Addis. 'What a dreadful thing that murder was at Putney,' Foyle remarked, razor in hand. 'I should like to have the punishing of the villain.' This upset his customer so much that the shaving was abandoned. But he paid his penny for the shave and was not averse to exchanging some words before he left. He said he'd been knocking about for several days and was on his way to the country to get a job. 'On a Sunday?' queried Foyle. 'I would venture to swear you haven't been a bricklayer's labourer for the past three months.' 'To tell the truth,' the stranger replied, 'I've not been so long. For I was in a capacity where I was obliged to shave every day, and I don't feel comfortable without it.'

He left, and proceeded on his way – on foot, although he may have got a lift in a cart – to Sevenoaks. From there he journeyed to Tonbridge where, it is said, he arrived at about 11.00 pm and lodged overnight at the Bull. At about 5.30 am on Monday, 11 April he entered the Angel public house (which was then on the southern edge of Tonbridge) and asked the landlord, Mr Adams, if there was any work to be had. Mr Adams said there was a good deal of building going on in the neighbourhood and that a job should be easy to get. After consuming a penny loaf and supping a half-pint of beer, Good succeeded in obtaining a job with a builder and began work on some cottages near the new South-Eastern railway station. He appeared to know his business, but spoke to no one. That night, he acquired a lodging at Mrs Hargreave's house, telling her he used to be a hawker and dealer in hare and rabbit skins. She said later he was very restless and could be heard sighing and moaning at night. Whenever anyone came to the door he became anxious, and wanted to know who it was.

For five days and nights he lived and worked in Tonbridge undisturbed. But on the morning of Saturday, 16 April, he was approached by another bricklayer, Thomas Rose, who was labouring on the new station near by, and thought there was something familiar about the other man. Rose happened to be not only a former police constable, but also one whose beat in Wandsworth less than two years ago had included Putney Park Lane.

'Why – you are the man Good!' he said. 'Your name is Daniel Good.' 'No, it's not!' retorted the Irishman. 'My name is James Connor.' Rose persisted: 'Why, you are he I've seen in Putney Park Lane. You was coachman to a gentleman there.' The Irishman insisted that Rose was mistaken – he had never been a coachman. Rose exclaimed: 'Oh, I've seen you frequently at the stables opposite to Mr Hulton's. And you know young Houghton.'

He went away to find a policeman, asking someone in his absence to keep an eye on Good. Rose told PC Humphrey, who duly had a careful look at the suspect, acquired two other constables, Ludlow and Peckham, as reinforcements and invited Good to join him in the Angel for a glass of ale. There Good was handcuffed and guarded while Humphrey hastened to Good's lodging to search his room. In a bundle were garments usually worn by a coachman, which had in fact been worn by Good on the night he fled from Putney Park Lane. Back at the Angel, a search of the suspect produced a silver watch, a purse containing £3 17s 6d, and an apron made from a black muslin petticoat and stained with blood.

News of the capture soon spread, and 'an immense crowd' attended Good's removal at 1.00 pm to the magistrates' office, where he was formally charged and remanded. Good, who gave his name as Richard Hall, said: 'I'm an innocent man, and evidence can be produced before the twelve judges to prove it.' He was then conveyed in a cart, accompanied by Ludlow and Peckham, to Maidstone Jail. Three times, as they passed through the villages of Hadlow, Mereworth and Teston, Good asked for permission to get himself shaved. The constables refused, in case he would attempt to cut his throat or escape. However, they stopped at the King's Head in Mereworth, so that the prisoner could partake of some bread and cheese and beer.

They reached Maidstone at 7.00 pm. The prison governor, after studying the descriptions of Good and narrowly viewing the suspect, pronounced him to be the murderer. This conclusion was happily reinforced when Good took a comb from a pocket and rearranged his hair to cover a bald patch.

On Sunday he was brought to London. The hackney-coach in which he was conveyed as far as Greenwich was assailed by so many people along the way, by booing, hisses, shouts and missiles – the windows were broken – that he was transferred to a prison van. Escorted thence by policemen on horseback, he reached Bow Street police station about 8.00 pm. Good now began talking freely, admitting his real identity and that Jane Jones had been with him on Sunday, 3 April. But how she died, he did not know. He conceded that appearances were 'rather black' against him, but joked about his escape and the locking-up of PC Gardiner and the others in the stables. He chatted with two constables detailed to sit with him, and after enjoying a pint of coffee and some bread and butter, fell asleep at 3.00 am.

The previous night (Saturday), Inspector Pearce and his observer, Sgt Thornton, had pounced on Molly Good and her visitor, Richard Gamble. Both were arrested and charged with receiving stolen goods, namely three old dresses.

The *Morning Advertiser* took the opportunity once again to disparage the police. It said:

> The old woman made no secret whatever of having these things; on the contrary, she exhibited them to various members of the police, and even asked many of them to take them away . . . For some reason best known to the police themselves, they were allowed to remain there for a whole week . . . The numerous respectable persons who have known the old woman for upwards of 20 years, believe her to be wholly incapable of the slightest participation in the frightful crime . . . and her apprehension, under the circumstances, is considered by them . . . as somewhat extraordinary. The secret of the matter appeared to be, that the police, feeling annoyed at the slovenly manner in which the case had been managed, as well as their own almost culpable negligence in permitting the murderer to escape, were determined to apprehend some person as a sort of *flash in the pan.*

Mrs Good herself objected strongly to being arrested, saying it was for 'Nothing at all, at all.' On being told of Good's arrest she said: 'Then bad luck to him! Serve him right – if he has done the deed!'

She became fractious again on the Monday, when she and Gamble were taken to Bow Street court, where the charge against them was changed to murder. Before being removed from Spital Square police station she was brought some breakfast by friends, who had also provided her with food and refreshment the day before. Constable Evans took the breakfast to her cell. But she insisted that her friends be allowed to bring it in person. On being told this could not be allowed, she became violent and abusive, claiming that the police had brought her there to murder her and were poisoning her food. She refused to leave the cell when a hackney-cabriolet arrived to take her to Bow Street and, still raving, was forcibly plucked from her cell by Sgt Coleman and dumped in the cab.

On that same Monday (18 April), at 10.30 am, Daniel Good appeared in Bow Street court, before Molly Good and Gamble were charged. *The Times* reporter remarked: 'His countenance was rather unpleasant, his eyes sunken, and his hair, nearly black, rather long and combed from the right side of the head to the left.' Dressed once again in his coachman's gear, he stood for most of the time with his chin on his left hand and his left elbow resting on the edge of the dock. Nine witnesses were called, including PC Gardiner, and Robert Speed. Lydia Susannah Butcher also gave evidence and wept throughout. Good was also moved to tears.

In reporting the proceedings in detail the following day, the *Advertiser* now thought it fit to commend the police, and declared:

> It is said to be rare that a man so accomplished in the art of crime has for so short a period evaded justice. From this it will be seen that the police, to whom so much blame has been attached, are, after all, anything but culpable, and that in the present instance the attribution of the want of energy and ability are, at least, unjust and unwarranted . . . The officers

employed, instead of exhibiting any negligence, seem to have been most vigilant and active.

When Good reappeared in Bow Street court on Thursday, 21 April, he was attired in blue prison clothes and attended by a jailer, Tyrrell, from Coldbath Fields Prison. The court was packed; tickets of admission, and seats, were the privilege of a favoured few, who included several noblemen, distinguished persons and MPs. This time the witnesses, 33 altogether, were questioned by a Treasury solicitor, Mr Maule, as well as by the magistrate, Mr Hall. The accused was also allowed to question the witnesses, although he seldom did so.

During PC Gardiner's evidence, Good fainted and was revived by the jailer. He also became emotional when Susan Butcher appeared, as did she; and when his ten-year-old son, Daniel, was brought in to the court to give evidence, which he did in a most clear and sensible manner, Good burst into tears and collapsed on a seat in the dock. At the conclusion of the boy's examination, during which Good sporadically wept, he said: 'Your worship – will you allow me to shake hands with the boy before he goes away?' Mr Hall acquiesced to this, and at the end of the hearing Good, again in tears, was allowed to embrace his son in front of the court before being removed to Newgate Prison.

The trial of Daniel Good, which lasted 11 hours, took place at the Central Criminal Court on Friday, 13 May. It began at 10.00 am, and was attended, among other notable persons, by the Queen's 69-year-old uncle, the Duke of Sussex. The prosecution was headed by the Attorney-General, Mr Waddington; the defence, by Mr Doane. The judges were Lord Chief Justice Denman, Baron Alderson and Mr Justice Coltman. On this occasion Daniel Good and Molly Good were arraigned side by side, he being indicted on 32 counts, which covered every possible way and means by which he might have killed Jane Jones. He pleaded 'Not guilty'. Mary Good was now charged with unlawfully harbouring, concealing and comforting him, knowing he had committed felony and murder. Mr Doane then applied for the prisoners to be tried separately. This was granted and Mary Good was removed from the court. The charges against her and Gamble were later dropped.

During the examination of Alfred Allen, the young surgeon, he stated that the torso of Jane Jones was 'in a most healthy state' and was empty of blood. He said: 'I should be inclined to think the deceased was pregnant, but I cannot speak decidedly . . . She was a plump, fine woman . . . The bosom was plump and full, and I do not think from their appearance that she had ever suckled a child.' The other doctor, Mr Ridge, who thought Jane Jones had been pregnant, said she died 'while in perfect health'.

Her movements on the Easter Sunday were pieced together in the evidence of five witnesses, who had seen her that day with Good. A confectioner, Lavender Layton, saw the couple at 3.45 pm walking arm in arm on the Barnes road, between the Red Lion and the Hammersmith suspension bridge. Good introduced Jones as his sister. 'We met by accident,' emphasised Mr Layton. 'I avoided conversing with them. My son, seven years old, was with me.' At 4.05, the landlord of the Coach and Horses in Barnes said the couple had some gin and water in his parlour. The woman was again introduced as Good's sister and said by him to be Welsh. He also said she had been good enough to bring him a present of some cream, sugar and tea. At 4.30 they called on Mrs Fanny Hester, the wife of an ornamental painter, whose husband was away in North America. The blue-bonneted woman was introduced this time as Good's sister-in-law. Mrs Hester offered them tea and they stayed for an hour. At one point Mrs Hester confided that the old gardener, Houghton, had been saying 'something disrespectful about Susan Butcher sleeping in the harness room'. This much upset Jane Jones, who told Mrs Hester that she knew nothing of this Susan Butcher, and demanded to know of Good who she was. He replied she was a friend of his and that it was time they left. Jones said she could plainly see that he wished to drop the subject. She clearly didn't, for at 6.15 they were seen by a policeman in the Upper Richmond Road, not far from Putney Park Lane, conversing 'in a loud angry tone'. The woman appeared, he said, to be 'finding fault with the man, and not him with her'.

At 7.00 pm they were in the King's Head in Roehampton, having bypassed Granard Lodge. They were again drinking gin and water. The landlord noticed that Good seemed to be urging the woman to drink, and that she did so with reluctance, pushing away the glass he offered her several times.

Good and Jane Jones finally reached the stables of Granard Lodge at about 7.30 pm. It was about then that Shiell's footman saw Good and told him his master wanted him to take some letters to the post office. Good collected them from the Lodge and told the footman he was going to the Green Man, a pub on Putney Heath, to see a person about taking his son to Ireland. Did Jane Jones go with him? Did he urge her to drink more gin? Did he kill her, as seems likely, later that night?

A motive for the murder seems to have been the fact that Susan Butcher, after spending a night at the stables a fortnight earlier, had agreed to marry Daniel Good. At his trial, between tears, she said he used to visit her when she was in service in Wimbledon. She was now out of work. He had been very kind to her, she said, and used to give her presents. He became her suitor, and told her his wife had been dead for five years. Although he asked her to marry him several times, she refused him at first, saying she wouldn't like to marry a Catholic. 'Nor I neither,' he said. On the night she slept in the stables, she slept alone, she said, on a mattress in the harness room. Good locked her in. The following morning she returned to Woolwich and to her father's home via the steam-boat from Putney. The last time she saw him was on 6 April, when he gave her several items which he said had belonged to his wife, including a blue bonnet, a shawl, a fur tippet and a pair of boots. He asked her to wear the bonnet, but she refused. With him on this occasion was his little boy, whom she had never met before. Good told the child, as they drove to New Cross, to call her 'Mother'.

Mr Doane, speaking on behalf of the prisoner, told the jury that there was nothing to show that Jane Jones met her death at the hands of another person, and that, on suddenly learning that the accused had been unfaithful to her, she took her own life. He begged the jury to bear in mind that 'the disgusting and horrible circumstances of the mutilation of the body' formed no part of any charge against the prisoner. And even if he did such a thing, to conceal her death, this did not mean that he had caused it. Why would he wish to kill her? She had no claims on him, and he could have ended the association when he pleased.

The Attorney-General, so sure was he of the prosecution's case, waived his right to reply.

In his summing-up, Lord Denman remarked that although the jury could not tell what motive might operate on the prisoner's mind, it was quite clear that no adequate motive could be assigned for the revolting and brutal act of dismembering the body after death and consuming the limbs by fire. If she destroyed herself, could a man with whom she had been living on friendly and intimate terms for a considerable time, be so lost of all proper feeling as to proceed to dismember her body without giving the least alarm or endeavouring to obtain any assistance?

The jury retired at 7.30 pm and returned at 8.05. The foreman declared the prisoner to be guilty. In sentencing Daniel Good to death, the Lord Chief Justice delivered a powerful speech condemning the 'most foul and wicked murder'. He said:

> There is no doubt that it is owing to the indulgence of your inclinations for one woman after another, that being tired of the unhappy deceased, and feeling that you could not enjoy to its full extent, in your view, the fresh attachment you had formed, that you resolved upon destroying the unhappy woman who was the former object of your affection . . . You coldly calculated, long before the act was committed, upon depriving the unfortunate woman of her little property . . . There is no doubt that on that Sunday night you lured the unhappy deceased to your stable intending to take her life, and to hide her afterwards from the eyes of men. That place was entirely under your control . . . But although you were watched by no human eye, your proceedings were brought to light in such a manner as to afford a powerful warning to all other criminals . . . It is absolutely necessary that your life should be forfeited to the laws of God and man.

In reply Good made a passionate attack on Susan Butcher, who was 'always getting intoxicated' and was the cause of Jane Jones's death. This he now explained in a spirited defence that took the court, and his counsel, by surprise. He said:

> When we left Mrs Hester's, Jane declared that she would destroy herself . . . I told her I could not let her sleep in the harness room, for that the old gardener told everything that occurred to my master. She was very

angry with me about Butcher, and declared she would drown herself. I told her she should not fly in the face of God by doing such a thing, and I prevented her going out of the stable. I shook down some hay in the stall where the trunk was found, and told her to stay there till I came back, and when I returned I found her lying dead in the same stall with her throat cut, and a razor and sharp penknife, with which she had done it, lying by her side. She was lying dead before me when I went into the stable, and I did not know what to do . . . I threw the knife over Hammersmith Bridge. I went out of the stable and locked the door, and did not know what to do. But I afterwards went back and covered her over with hay. On the Monday morning a man, of whom I had occasionally bought matches, rang at the bell, and I told him what had happened, and showed him the body, and asked him what I had better do, and he said: 'I'll tell you – we'll conceal the body.' I offered him a sovereign if he would conceal it for me, and he consented. And he came on the Tuesday morning and I gave him the axe and the knife, and left him in the harness room, and locked him in and told him not to make a noise . . . And he made a fire, and burnt the head and the limbs. I declare to God I had nothing to with it . . . He was to have come the next day and fetched the trunk and have thrown it into the river. But he did not come. I took her ear-rings out of her ears, and the ring from her finger. It was my wife's wedding-ring. *She* was not my wife . . . The next day I went to Susan Butcher and gave her the ring and the bonnet, and the shawl, and told her what had happened. And she said she was glad of it – that *she* was out of the way. She kept the cap, the shawl, and the ring, and did not give them up to the police . . . Ladies and gentlemen, I wish you all a very good night. I have a great deal more to say, but I am so bad I cannot say it.

By 'bad' he meant 'upset' or 'fatigued'. But more than bad did Good seem now. His blatant lies, the last-minute invention of the match-seller, the cruel incrimination of the servant-girl he had meant to marry, and the removal of Jane Jones's ear-rings and ring in addition to the disposal of her property and clothes, all made him seem like evil incarnate. He was removed from the dock as the great crowd that had gathered outside heard of his fate. 'They uttered a tremendous volley of cheers,' said the *Advertiser*. 'And the unhappy wretch was taken to his cell with the cheers of the multitude ringing in his ears.'

It seems likely that Jane Jones was killed – hit on the head with the axe – as she lay in the furthest stall on the mattress, wearing little except her petticoat. For the mattress was found to be stained with blood and urine; and no marks of blood were apparently found on her outer garments, which Good later gave away.

Daniel Good was hanged outside Newgate Prison on Monday, 23 May 1842. The crowd that assembled to witness his execution was said by prison warders to have been the largest they had ever seen. People began gathering outside the prison 12 hours before the execution. At 3.00 am, prison carpenters began erecting the scaffold, completing their task before 6.00 am.

Inside the prison Good, who had slept for less than three hours, got up at 5.00 am, remarking cheerfully to one of the warders that it was 'a very fine morning'. When the Governor, Mr Cope, appeared, Good assured him: 'Mind, I am no murderer – I am no murderer.' Meanwhile, the prison chaplain, the Revd Carver, had been exhorting the condemned man to confess – to no avail, as Good continued to deny any guilt. At 7.00 am he hungrily consumed the breakfast that was was brought to him.

But by 7.45, when the sheriffs, under-sheriffs, reporters and others arrived to witness his final minutes, Good broke down. Sitting on a bench beside the Revd Carver, he wept, clasping his hands and rocking from side to side. 'The Lord be with you all!' he cried. 'The Lord have mercy upon me!' He clung on to anyone who came near him, repeatedly shaking any hands that he could reach, thanking all and sundry for their kindnesses and attentions between saying again and again: 'I never took the life of that woman! I never took a life! I never took a life from anything!' To the Revd Carver he said: 'Oh, sir! You have done everything that a man could do. I love the very ground you walk upon.' Carver responded: 'Think now of what you are saying, and remember that you now have but a few minutes to live. And think of that text which I have so often endeavoured to impress upon you – "If we confess our sins, God is faithful and just to forgive our sins, and to cleanse us from all unrighteousness. But there is no forgiveness of sin without sincere repentance, and a forsaking of sin in the heart."' Good, placing his hand on his heart, replied: 'Oh, sir! I know it! I know it! I would confess everything to you. But I never took a life – I never took a life!' He said this so many times that one of the sheriffs rebuked him, saying: 'You had better remain quiet, as you are only making your case worse!' But Good would not be silent, and continued to declare his innocence and lament his fate.

Minutes before the procession to the scaffold formed up, the Governor gave Good a tumbler of port wine to drink, which he did. The executioner then tied his wrists together, pinioned his arms and removed the coachman's white cravat from his neck. He was wearing a long dark frock-coat, black trousers and a waistcoat, and looked thinner and less healthy than at his first appearance in court. By 7.55, when the grim procession set off through the jail and out to the scaffold, Good was temporarily more composed, though he still tried to shake people's hands.

The *Morning Advertiser*'s reporter wrote: 'The tolling of the chapel bell, the reading of selected portions of the funeral service, and the indistinctly heard shoutings of the mob without, altogether combined to produce a most solemn and impressive effect.'

Outside, Good was overcome with dread. He seemed terrified by the sight and sound of the crowd, and of the scaffold itself. He ascended it slowly, and looking 'more dead than alive' his lower jaw dropped as the rope was adjusted and the cap drawn over his face. It is said he cried: 'Stop! Stop!' and tried to address the crowd. But Calcraft, the executioner, told him not to waste his breath, and to pray. Seconds later, the lever was pulled, and the floor fell from under his feet. The *Advertiser* reported: 'He struggled very little, and appeared to die almost immediately. The only motion observed was about the hands, which, the instant he fell, he raised up in the attitude of prayer, as far as the pinioning rope would allow them to go.'

Before he died, Good dictated three letters, the longest being a general letter of thanks to several people, including the Lord Mayor and his wife (who had paid him a visit), the sheriffs, the Governor, the clergymen, and three of his former masters, Mr Dando, Mr Nottidge and Mr Shiell. In this letter he said: 'I put my trust in James Spencer and his wife, Mrs Spencer, that they will have an eye after my boy.' He also said:

> I do acknowledge, as I am parting this world, that Susan Butcher was the cause of that poor woman, Jane Jones, through jealousy, making away with herself; and Jane Jones told me that she would make away with herself through hearing about Susan Butcher . . . I wish to say I never cut her up. The matchman said he could not make away with the body without taking the limbs off. I locked him up in the stables, and I was cleaning my harness. He promised to come on the 6th of April and take the remaining part away, but he never came. He told me he lived in the neighbourhood of Brentford. I knew this man as coming with matches about fourteen or fifteen months.

A short letter was addressed to the Spencers, and a third to Molly Good. In this he said: 'My dear Molly – I write these few lines to bid you farewell, and I'm glad you got acquitted. I hope the things I put in pledge you will be able to redeem, and keep them for yourself. My best respects to you, with tears, and also your friends; and the Lord be with you all, and may the Lord have mercy upon my poor soul. From your unfortunate – Daniel Good.'

The one redeeming feature of Daniel Good's last months is his evident concern for his son, although he pawned the little boy's spare trousers. One wonders what happened thereafter to the boy and whether his father's last wishes were carried out. Was young Daniel rescued from the Lambeth Workhouse, where he had been dumped, and given a home by the Spencers – or by the Shiells? Or did he end up with Molly Good? Did he ever recover from the horrors of that April and May, from the dreadful deaths of his 'mother' and father? Unfortunately, murder trials and tales have little to say about those other victims, the family's survivors – and less if anything at all about the children of the hanged.

In June 1842 – as the result of the Jane Jones murder and that of a policeman on duty – the Joint Commissioners of the Metropolitan Police, Colonel Rowan and Richard Mayne, sent a memorandum to the Home Secretary, Sir James Graham, advocating the setting-up of a plain-clothes 'Detective Force' to co-ordinate and carry out investigations into certain crimes. This force, created that month, consisted of two inspectors and six sergeants.

Two more sergeants were soon added to the team, and from 1846 two constables from each Division were regularly trained in detective work to assist in operations. But there would be no increase in the basic complement until 1864. Even four years later the detectives numbered a mere 15, out of a police force of nearly 8,000 men.

Of the original eight who formed the Detective Force, forerunner of the CID, one was Sgt Stephen Thornton. Another, the senior detective inspector in charge of the force, was Inspector Nicholas Pearce.

CHAPTER 3

William Palmer

The Murder of John Cook, 1855

If speculation and other writers are to be believed, the murder of John Cook was the last in a series of murders that Palmer committed over a period of ten years, during which as many as 15 men, women and children were poisoned by him. His trial, the first for poisoning by strychnine – although none was found in the body of the deceased – was one of the longest and most sensational of the century. It was remarkable also for the length of the defence and prosecution speeches, the overt partiality of the judge, and the profusion and confusion of the medical experts. In its way, the trial was as much a damning contemporary comment on the medical profession, its ignorance and ineffectuality, as the recent deaths of thousands of soldiers in the Crimean War mainly through disease and despite Florence Nightingale's endeavours. The war came to an end in 1855 with the Russian surrender of Sebastopol – two months before the death in a Staffordshire inn of a young racehorse-owner, John Parsons Cook.

He was a slight and pale young man, aged 29, who played village cricket and regularly rode with a hunt. But he had a weak constitution and was liable to headaches and bilious attacks. He also had bad teeth, spots and ulcerations, some of the latter being minor syphilitic symptoms. Some two weeks before his death, he visited his doctor, Henry Savage, who noted that one of Cook's tonsils was red and enlarged and that there were some superficial ulcers on his lips. He assured Cook that he did not have syphilis and that his general health was good. Dr Savage said later: 'He was a weak man, and apt to take the advice of any person he might be in company with . . . I recommended him to go abroad for two years, as I wished to get him away from his turf associations.' One of them was William Palmer.

Cook had been a solicitor. But when he inherited some £12,000 he abandoned that profession, became a racehorse-owner and frequenter of race-tracks. He met Palmer about a year before his death. They soon became friends, and for a while they were joint owners of a mare, Pyrrhine, until, in settlement of a debt or loan, she became Palmer's property. Although both men owned several horses, they were virtually broke when on Monday, 12 November 1855 they went to the Shrewsbury Races, taking two bedrooms and a sitting-room at the Raven Hotel. Cook had some cash, which he had won at Worcester Races the previous week. But Palmer was deep in debt, owing one money-lender £11,500, and another, £2,000. Both, however, had horses running in the races, and it would literally be a matter of life and death, as to which horse, if either, won. In the event, Cook's won and Palmer's lost and Cook was doomed.

William Palmer was 31, boyish, blue-eyed, short and chubby, with thinning hair. Baptised at Rugeley in Staffordshire on 21 October 1824, he was the second son in a family of five boys and two girls, whose father, Joseph, a sawyer, had so improved his lot that when he died in 1836 he owned a sawmill and left his family £70,000 – of which William received about £9,000 when he was 21. Apprenticed to a firm of wholesale druggists in Liverpool, he stole from them and was redeemed by his mother, Mrs Sarah Palmer, who continued to rescue him from financial troubles (not always knowingly) for the rest of his life. She herself was already a source of local scandal – as were a drunken uncle and brother of William (both of whom he later killed) – because of various unseemly love affairs that followed her husband's death.

Apprenticed next to a surgeon near Rugeley, from whom he also stole and in due course absconded, William then moved to Stafford Infirmary to continue his medical studies. There he remained for four years, finally obtaining his diplomas as a surgeon at St Bartholomew's Hospital in London in August 1846. He then returned to Rugeley, setting up an alternative doctor's practice in the High Street to that of 74-year-old Dr Bamford. Palmer was 22.

The chief pleasures of his youth were women, horses, money and drink. Quite without scruples of any kind, he cheated, lied and stole to achieve his ends, while maintaining a good appearance of social respectability and concern: he was a regular church-goer and generous to his horsy friends. He also possessed an abundance of energy and boyish charm. It is said that, before he married, he fathered 14 illegitimate children of as many girls.

His first victim is said to have been a man called Abley. Palmer was having an affair with Mrs Abley, and her husband died after a drinking session with Palmer, who supposedly put strychnine in his brandy – partly to see how it worked. Then one of his illegitimate children, born to a local girl, Jane Mumford, died after visiting him. But it was not until the young Rugeley doctor married, in 1847, that poison became his panacea for any inconvenient problem.

His wife, Annie, was the illegitimate daughter of a Colonel Brookes, who had served in India and settled in Stafford; the housekeeper, Mary Thornton, was Annie's mother. When the Colonel died, his estate, amounting to about £20,000, was divided between the two women, although Annie's share was tied up in Chancery. No doubt it was her inheritance that made Annie so precious to Palmer – he wooed her for over a year, until she was 21 and free to choose whom she married. But she was obviously not unattractive. She produced five children in the seven years before she died. Four of those children also died in infancy, the first in January 1851; the eldest, Willie, was the only one to survive.

A letter that William Palmer wrote to his wife has also survived. Undated, it gives some indication of the literary style and measure of the man.

> My ever adored Annie. I feel certain you will forgive me for not writing to you last night when I tell you that since I last saw you I have not had two hours sleep. I do assure you I never felt so tired in my life. I am almost sick of my Profession. Sorry I am to say my Mother has had another attack & one of my Sister's children I think will be dead before morning . . . My dearest Annie, I purpose all being well being with you tomorrow about three & depend upon it nothing but ill health will ever keep me away from you. Forgive me my duck for not sending you the papers last night. I really could not help it – I will explain fully tomorrow . . . My sweetest and loveliest Annie, I never was more pleased with you in my life than I was on Friday afternoon last. It was a combination of things. God bless you. I hope we may live together & love each other for 100 years to come. Excuse now for I must go. Till tomorrow accept my everlasting love.

Annie's mother, Mrs Thornton, was the next to die. Said to have been an intemperate, domineering woman, she was not fond of her son-in-law, and suspicious. Invited in January 1849 to stay in Rugeley, she grimly remarked to a neighbour that she did not expect to survive more than a fortnight. She was wrong: she died sooner than that, screaming: 'Take that awful devil away!' when her attentive son-in-law appeared by her bed. According to the local physician, Dr Bamford, who, it seems, was not just aged but unqualified and accepted all his confident younger colleague's diagnoses and assertions, Mrs Thornton died of apoplexy. Her possessions and property were duly inherited by her daughter and absorbed by Palmer, and converted to cash, and spent.

The following year, after a visit to a race-meeting at Chester, Palmer found himself owing £600 to a companion and brewer called Bladon, a debt he was unable or reluctant to pay. Invited to stay with the Palmers at Rugeley, Bladon expired within a week. Mrs Bladon arrived just before her husband's very sudden demise, and although friends encouraged her to seek a post-mortem or involve the police, she neglected to do so, succumbing instead to the seductive charms of her host.

A similar calamity visited another racing companion, called Bly, whom Palmer owed £800. As with Bladon, Dr Bamford signed a blameless death certificate, and Bly's widow was told that it was her husband who owed Palmer £800, not the other way around, and that she should honour this debt.

But this was small beer, resulting in the cancellation of Palmer's debts without augmenting his income, and in 1852, when he abandoned his moribund and unprofitable medical practice to pursue a full-time career as a racehorse-owner and gentleman of the turf, he looked to his own family to finance his investments, which involved a string of horses and his own stud and stables at Hednesford.

Expecting to inherit a modest legacy at least from an uncle, Joseph Bentley, Palmer invited his debauched and drunken relation to take part in a brandy-drinking contest, which the uncle won, dying not unexpectedly a few days later, mourned by his less indigent nephew. A wealthy aunt was the next object of Palmer's familial attention. Taken ill while on a visit to the Palmers' house in Rugeley, she was given some special pills by her solicitous nephew, which he advised her to take before she slept. Feeling better, she dispensed with his remedy by disposing of the pills by throwing them out of a window. The following morning several occupants of an adjacent chicken-run were discovered to have died. Whereupon the blessed and not suddenly sainted aunt discovered she was well enough to travel and had urgent business elsewhere.

In 1852, in addition to Uncle Joseph, two of Palmer's infant children also died, in January and December that year. It is said that he let them suck at a finger while they were cradled in his arms, having dipped the finger in a fatal sauce of honey and some poison. 'What will people say?' wondered sad Annie, speaking to a sister-in-law. 'My mother died here, then Mr Bladon, and now all these children!'

Local gossip was presumably saying in whispers quite a lot. But infant mortality was far from unknown, and hard-drinking, over-eating and unhygienic adults might succumb suddenly and mysteriously to one of many virulent mid-Victorian diseases. And who among the racing fraternity and tradesmen of Rugeley really thought that carousing, church-going, cheerful William Palmer could be a killer in their midst? Nor could Annie Palmer ever believe that the loving man who had fathered her five children and called her his duck, was now plotting to kill her – but not before he had insured her life for £13,000.

In 1853, Palmer's financial situation, despite the benefits accruing from the deaths of family and friends, was worse than ever. With reckless abandon, he had placed bets amounting to £10,000 on his mare, Nettle, winning the Oaks. She lost, and he lost the lot. Other bets and gambles failed; he defaulted on some and was blacklisted by Tattersall's. To pay his debts he borrowed from money-lenders at high interest rates, and as security drew up documents in his mother's name and faked her signature. Eventually his debts, with interest and other charges added, amounted to some £20,000.

With the help of a round-faced Rugeley solicitor, Jeremiah (Jerry) Smith, who had been one of his mother's lovers, Palmer sought to insure his wife's life for £25,000. This failed, but he succeeded in January 1854 (soon after his fourth infant died) in effecting a policy for £13,000 at an annual premium, which was paid, of £760. It was not until September, however, that Annie Palmer fell ill and died, poisoned over a period of nine days by stiff doses of antimony. Palmer wrote in his diary for September 29, Friday: 'My poor, dear Annie expired at 10 past 1.' And Dr Bamford, now an octogenarian, wrote 'English cholera' in the section of her death certificate describing the cause of death. After some delay and with some reluctance, the insurance company paid.

Nine days after Annie's death, the sorrowing widower took his only surviving offspring, Willie, to church to receive the condolences of the community. Nine months later, his housemaid, Eliza Tharm, gave birth to their illegitimate child. It is said that he was in bed with her the night that Annie died.

Such was the success of this venture, although the money was soon swallowed up by Palmer's creditors, that he tried to duplicate it by insuring the life of his drunken younger brother, Walter, for £82,000. Three companies were approached, with Jerry Smith acting on Palmer's behalf. Eventually, as with his wife, he managed to take out a policy with the Prince of Wales Company for £13,000. This policy was lodged with a London money-lender, Thomas Pratt, as security to cover a number of debts, which then began to be slowly repaid. Palmer also forged his mother's name as a guarantor on various loans. To forestall the £13,000 going to brother Walter's widow after his death, William agreed to lend Walter £400 in return for all the policy's rights and to pay the premium. Again, the deed was witnessed by Jerry Smith for a £5 fee.

Two other brothers of William in Rugeley were respectable men, being an honest solicitor and a vicar. But Walter Palmer was a dissolute sot, allegedly downing three bottles of gin every day. It was not difficult to add some prussic acid to his intake, and on 16 August 1855, Walter Palmer died.

But this time the insurance company concerned were more than suspicious and sent agents to check on the circumstances of Walter's death. His doctor had warned the company that William had 'insured his late wife's life for many thousands, and after first payment, she died. Be cautious'. And the postboy at the Talbot Arms, where Walter died, James Myatt, attested that he had seen William put something in Walter's glass. Soon after this, Myatt was persuaded to have a drink with Palmer and was laid low with agonising pains in his stomach. He recovered after a couple of days. In the meantime, Walter's widow laid claim to the policy on her husband's death, on the grounds that the £400 loan had never been paid.

Palmer was now becoming desperate. Pratt was pressing him for part payment of some of his debts, as was another money-lender, Padwick. So, having suffered a setback with Walter, he looked elsewhere for another life to insure, and fastened on the overseer of his stud and stables, George Bates, a former farmer who was paid, though not regularly, a sovereign a week for his labours. Said Bates: 'I looked after his stud and saw that the boys who had the care of the horses did their duty. I had no fixed salary.' Bates, a single man, had lodgings in Rugeley, for which he paid 6s 6d a week. It was in September, after a dinner in Palmer's home (when the other guest was John Parsons Cook) that the subject of insuring Bates's life was broached.

In October the necessary application was formulated by Palmer and Jerry Smith (it seems that Bates was virtually illiterate, though he could sign his name) and his life was insured for £10,000. Smith, acting as the company's local agent, for which he received a percentage of the premium, described Bates as 'a Gentleman of good Property and possessing a Capital Cellar of Wine'. No doubt he was also paid well by Palmer. Unfortunately, the insurance company reneged on the policy after making some checks, and the agents investigating Walter Palmer's death threatened to call in the police. So Palmer had to consider other means and other persons to solve his ever-present pecuniary problems. He now owed the money-lender, Thomas Pratt, £11,500.

On 6 November, Pratt issued two writs for £4,000 against Palmer and his mother. The following Saturday (10 November), Palmer visited Pratt in London and paid him £300. He prevaricated about paying off two large loans made on the expected payment on Walter's policy, and Pratt apparently threatened him with the writs, which had not been served. If and when the writs *were* served, Palmer would be revealed as a forger of his mother's name, and possibly others – he had forged Cook's signature endorsing a cheque for £375. On 13 November, when Palmer and Cook were both at Shrewsbury, Pratt wrote that steps must be taken to enforce the policy on Walter Palmer's life. 'I count most positively on seeing you on Saturday,' said Pratt. At the same time Palmer was being blackmailed by Jane Burgess, a Stafford girl, whom he had paid to have an abortion. Letters concerning this and other matters were in her possession, and she asked him for £50 for their return. On 13 November he wrote to her: 'I cannot do what you ask. I should not mind giving £30 for the whole of them, though I am hard up at present.'

It was at Shrewsbury on Tuesday, 13 November 1855, that a temporary solution to Palmer's many money problems presented itself. Cook's horse, Polestar, unexpectedly won the Shrewsbury Handicap at 7–1. His winnings amounted, with the stakes, to £2,050. He was as good as dead.

According to another doctor friend of Cook, William Jones, who spent the day with him and whose home at Lutterworth in Leicestershire was where Cook lived when not chasing to race-meetings around England:

> After the race was run he was so excited that for two or three minutes he could not speak to me. He was elated and happy the rest of the day, but he was not at all intoxicated. He was a very temperate man . . . We dined together in the evening at the Raven Hotel. He accompanied me when I left the hotel at 10 o'clock for the station. On our way there we called at the house of Mr Fraill, the clerk of the course. I was present during a conversation they had along with Whitehouse, the jockey. Cook produced his betting book and calculated his winnings.

Palmer, it seems, was elsewhere that night, apparently in Rugeley, whither he had dashed to procure some antimony, or tartar emetic, with which to commence his poisoning of Polestar's owner.

On Wednesday, 14 November, Cook collected some of his winnings and, with what he had won at Worcester, now had some £750 on him in banknotes. He attended the races that afternoon with Palmer, and the two of them were seen in the Unicorn Hotel at about 9.00 pm before they returned to their rooms in the Raven, where several racing companions assembled about 11.00 pm to drink some grog (brandy and water). Among them were Cook's agent, a wine merchant, Ishmael Fisher; another wine merchant, George Reid; a law stationer, Thomas Jones; and a Rugeley saddler, George Myatt, who had arrived, at Palmer's invitation, in Shrewsbury that night. He later slept in Palmer's bedroom. They sat around a table, drinking from a decanter of brandy, and smoking. Myatt would say later that Cook 'seemed the worse of liquor', though Fisher said he 'certainly was not drunk'.

Earlier that evening, Mrs Anne Brooks of Manchester, an occasional attendant at races without her husband's knowledge, had met Palmer in the street at about 8.00 pm. They conversed about racing prospects and odds for the following day, when Palmer's horse, Chicken, would run. He asked her to procure some information about Lord Derby's horse, and at 10.30 pm she went to the Raven, leaving her friends to wait for her below. She went upstairs and found Palmer standing by a small table in a corridor, with a glass in his hand. 'I'll be with you presently,' he said, holding the glass up to a gas-light and shaking a small quantity of colourless liquid within the glass. He made some casual remark about the weather, to which Mrs Brooks replied, then entered an empty adjacent sitting-room (not his own), whose door was partially open. In a minute or so he reappeared, still carrying the glass, and went into his own room, shutting the door behind him. Before long he emerged from his sitting-room bearing a glass of brandy and water for Mrs Brooks. As she sipped it, they discussed the next day's racing.

She suffered no ill effects from her drink. But curiously, and probably coincidentally, several racing persons were taken ill that day. Mrs Brooks said later: 'There was a wonder as to what had caused their illness, and something was said about the water being poisoned. They were affected by sickness and purging.' We do not know *when* on Wednesday people were smitten; and as Palmer was apparently in Rugeley on Tuesday night and on Wednesday morning, he was probably not to blame. But what happened to John Cook on Wednesday night was certainly of Palmer's doing.

Some time before midnight the party in the Cook/Palmer sitting-room was coming to a jovial end. Thomas Jones had left, and George Reid had just arrived, when Cook complained about the taste of his glass of grog, and asked Palmer to get him another. Palmer said he would do so if Cook emptied his glass – which he did, protesting: 'It burns my throat dreadfully.' He also said: 'There was something in it.' 'There's nothing in it,' retorted Palmer, seeming to take a sip of what was left, after which he handed the glass to Reid, who said: 'What's the use of giving me an empty glass?' Myatt said nothing, while Fisher sniffed the glass and commented that it smelled of brandy, and strongly so. A few minutes later the party broke up. Reid departed, while Palmer and Myatt retired to their shared bedroom (the bedrooms seem to have been on an upper floor), remaining there undisturbed and probably in a drunken torpor until dawn.

Cook was left with Fisher, and in ten minutes or so Cook rushed out of the room to be sick. Returning, he took Fisher outside and into Fisher's sitting-room, where he said he thought Palmer had been playing a trick on him and had put something disagreeable in his drink. Some similar jest had happened to him before. He gave Fisher his £750 for safe-keeping and then was violently sick again. After a third such seizure, this time up in Cook's bedroom, Fisher sent for a doctor, Mr Gibson, who arrived about 12.30. Cook complained of pains in his stomach and a burning throat, and said he thought he had been poisoned. Gibson advised him to take an emetic, which he did and was sick yet again. After this Gibson dosed the young man with rhubarb pills containing calomel and a draught of mistura sennacum. Fisher sat up with Cook until 2.00 am, when he exhaustedly fell asleep.

The following morning, Thursday, Palmer sent Myatt to check on Cook, who was still unwell and in bed. He told Myatt about his sickness and the doctor's visit and demanded to know what had been put in his grog. Myatt expressed total ignorance and fetched Palmer, who proclaimed his amazed innocence and hurt. 'I never play such tricks with people!' he told Fisher later. 'But I can tell you what he was – he was very drunk.' It seems that Cook believed Palmer. At any rate, he recovered sufficiently to have some breakfast later in the sitting-room and, though looking pale and ill, accompanied the others that afternoon to the racecourse. The weather was poor: it was cold and damp. Palmer's horse, Chicken, ran, and lost, and in losing deprived its owner of £5,000 of potential winnings, not to mention some £500 in bets. If it had won, Cook might have lived.

But Palmer had more to make of Cook, and his signature, which he intended to forge on money transactions, as he had done before. That evening, after an early meal in the Raven, Palmer and Myatt returned to Rugeley, about 6.00 pm, taking John Cook with them. They travelled by train from Shrewsbury to Stafford (Palmer paid) and then drove for nine miles in a fly (a one-horse hackney-cab) to Rugeley, during which journey *Palmer* was sick, and vomited out of the window. On arriving, Cook found accommodation in the Talbot Arms in the High Street, which was opposite Palmer's house. Still feeling poorly, he went to bed about 10.00 pm.

On Friday morning he was visited at 10.00 am by Palmer's solicitor, Jerry Smith, a small-eyed, fat-bodied man, who later told the court:

> He was having breakfast in bed – a cup of tea with a wineglassful of brandy in it. I dined with him and Mr Palmer about two o'clock. We had a beef steak and some champagne. After dinner we had three bottles of port wine, of which Cook drank his share. We rose from the table between five and six, and Cook and I went to my house, and then to the Albion Hotel, which is next door, and had a brandy and water each.

Smith asked Cook for £50, which he was owed. Cook gave him £5, saying he would pay the balance when he returned from claiming the rest of his winnings at Tattersall's in London on Monday. He said he had already loaned Palmer some money to settle a debt. And indeed that day he had written to Ishmael Fisher in London, and told him to pay £200 to Mr Pratt of Queen Street, Mayfair, in part settlement of a £500 debt. 'It is of great importance to both Mr Palmer and myself,' wrote Cook, adding, 'I will settle it on Monday at Tattersall's. I am much better.' This was engineered by Palmer as a sop to forestall any action being taken on Saturday, as threatened by Pratt, who received a letter from Palmer, saying: 'A friend of mine will call and leave you £200 tomorrow.' This Fisher did.

On Friday night Cook again went early to bed. On Saturday morning the process of poisoning him began again and continued on Sunday. Antimony was apparently the poison used.

First, Cook was sick after drinking some coffee while Palmer was in his bedroom. Then Palmer's charwoman was sent to fetch some broth from the Albion, and after he had warmed it up (and doctored it) in his kitchen, she took it over to the Talbot Arms, having been instructed to say it came from Jerry Smith. Cook refused to sample it, but on Palmer's insistence, did so later and was sick again. Some barley water and arrowroot was next taken up to his room by the chambermaid, apparently without ill effects. They were probably ordered by aged Dr Bamford, whom Palmer, after lunching with Smith and another crony, the postmaster, Samuel Cheshire, prevailed upon to visit Cook about 3.00 pm. He also arranged, at the suggestion of the housekeeper at the Talbot Arms, for Jerry Smith to sleep in Cook's room that night (it had two beds) when Cook was sick after eating some toast and water. Cook was also constrained to use what Smith referred to as 'the night-chair'. Evidently he was also suffering from diarrhoea. The inn was noisy that night, but Smith seems to have slept like a log.

He was woken by the arrival in the morning of Palmer and Bamford. Cook said: 'I'm rather better this morning. I slept from about two or three o'clock, after the confounded concert was gone.' 'I'll send you some more medicine,' Bamford said. Later, Palmer sent the patient another large cup of broth, this time via his gardener. The chambermaid, Elizabeth Mills, took it upstairs, but not before sampling it in the kitchen. Half an hour later she was very sick. So was Cook. She retired to her bed about 1.00 pm, but recovered by 5.00. Cook also recovered, and when Mills saw him again about 10.00 pm he was in good spirits. So much so that Palmer, who was in constant attendance on his friend, assured the housekeeper, Miss Sarah Bond, that no one need sleep in the room that night, not even Daniel, the boots. Palmer knew that Cook would have an undisturbed night, and day, as he (Palmer) had to go to London. It would never do if Cook expired in his absence and when he was not in charge, and he had probably decided to use another, and more deadly poison.

He had also already written to Cook's friend in Lutterworth, William Jones, saying: 'Mr Cook was taken ill at Shrewsbury . . . Since then he has been confined to his bed here with a severe bilious attack, combined with diarrhoea, and I think it is advisable for you to come and see him.' Jones was ill on Monday and could not comply at once. Palmer probably needed him as an innocent witness to Cook's demise.

So, when Palmer saw Cook about 7.15 on Monday morning, the coffee Cook drank had no effect on him, and by one o'clock he was well enough to wash, shave and get dressed. Elizabeth Mills brought him some arrowroot, and he was visited later by, amongst others, his trainer, Mr Saunders, and Dr Bamford, and drank some brandy and water. About 4.30 pm, Cook had another cup of coffee, and at 8.00 Mills took a pillbox, sent by Dr Bamford, to Cook's room and placed it on the dressing-table. By this time Palmer was well on his way back from London, having caught the 5.00 pm express for Stafford at Euston Station. A slow, smoky and noisy train, it arrived three minutes late, at 8.45. Palmer was back in Rugeley by half-past nine.

In London he had seen an agent, George Herring, with the assumed purpose of settling Cook's debts on his behalf, using his Polestar winnings, which added up to £984. Herring was instructed to pay Padwick £550 out of the winnings and Pratt £450. After collecting all but £110 of the money at Tattersall's (a Mr Morris had only paid £90 of the £200 he owed), Herring sent a cheque for £450 to Pratt and wrote to Cook, care of 'Palmer, Rugeley', saying what he had done. This letter was intercepted by the postmaster, Cheshire, and given to Palmer. The two of them had been at school together and Cheshire had already been persuaded, with gifts and/or money, to intercept any official-looking letters addressed to Mrs Palmer.

After deluding Herring, Palmer then went to see Pratt, to whom he gave £50 and told him that £450 was on its way. This meant that with £200 already sent by Cook, the £2,000 once owed to Pratt had been reduced to £1,300. No doubt well pleased with himself, Palmer returned to Rugeley for the final kill.

On arriving he called at Dr Salt's pharmacy and persuaded the young assistant there, Charles Newton, to give him three grains of strychnine. Newton did so without charging Palmer or making any note in a poison register. He later told the court: 'Mr Salt was not on speaking terms with Mr Palmer, and I thought Mr Salt would be angry at my letting him have it.' Palmer then called on John Cook in his room at the Talbot Arms.

Some minutes before midnight, the inn's waitress, Lavinia Barnes, was in the kitchen when the bell for Cook's room rang madly on the wall. 'I went up to his room,' she said, 'and found he was very ill. He was screaming "Murder!" and was in violent pain. He said he was suffocating. He asked me to send for Mr Palmer. His eyes looked very wild, and were standing a great way out of his head. He was beating the bed with his hands. I sent the boots for Palmer, and went and called Elizabeth Mills.' Her bedroom was on the floor above Cook's room. Mills said:

> I heard a noise of violent screaming whilst I was dressing . . . I heard the screams twice. As soon as I entered the room I found him sitting up in bed. He desired me to fetch Mr Palmer directly. I walked to his bedside, and I found the pillow upon the floor. There was one mould candle burning. I picked up the pillow and asked him if he would lay down his head. At that time he was sitting up and was beating the bedclothes with both his arms and hands stretched out. He said: 'I can't lie down – I shall suffocate if I do! Oh, fetch Mr Palmer!' His body, his hands and neck were moving then. A sort of jumping or jerking . . . Sometimes he would throw back his head upon the pillow, and then he would raise himself up again. This jumping and jerking was all over his body . . . Both the eyes were much projected. It was difficult for him to speak, he was so short of breath. He screamed three or four times while I was in the room. He called aloud: 'Murder!' twice. He asked me to rub one hand. I found the left hand stiff. The fingers were something like paralysed.

Cook was conscious throughout. When Palmer appeared, he gasped: 'Oh,

Palmer, I shall die!' 'Oh no, you won't, my lad,' said Palmer. He went away, returning a few minutes later with some pills. Cook said he could not swallow them, so Mills gave him, at Palmer's instruction, a teaspoonful of toast and water. Cook's body was still contorted with spasms. She said later:

> He snapped at the spoon like *that* – with his head and neck, and the spoon was fast between his teeth. It was difficult to get it away . . . Mr Palmer then handed him a draught from a wineglass – three parts full, with a liquid of a dark, heavy-looking nature. Cook drank it. He snapped at the glass just the same as he did at the spoon. He swallowed the liquid, which was vomited up immediately. I supported his forehead . . . The stuff he vomited smelt, I should think, like opium. Palmer said he hoped the pills were not returned, and he searched for the pills with a quill. He said: 'I can't find the pills.' After this Cook seemed to be more easy.

Cook told Palmer he thought he was dying and he must not leave him. He asked Palmer to feel his heart. Palmer said it was all right, still going – perhaps with an edge of ironic surprise.

The waitress, Lavinia Barnes, was also present during most of this, but left the room before 1.00 am. Mills stayed until about three. When she left, Cook was dozing, and Palmer was asleep in a chair. She returned about 6.00 am, to find Cook alone – Palmer had left at quarter to five. When asked how he felt, Cook replied that he was no worse. He asked the chambermaid if she had ever seen anyone suffer such agony. She said: 'No, I never have,' and continued: 'What do you think was the cause of all that, Mr Cook?' And he said it was the pills that Palmer gave him at half-past ten. But this was apparently said without suspicion or any blame.

That Tuesday morning, 20 November, Palmer was still busy trying to make the most of Cook's Polestar winnings and concocting a conclusively fatal dose. The postmaster, Cheshire, was summoned to Palmer's house to write out a cheque, in Palmer's favour and at his dictation, for £350, which was what Cook allegedly owed him, but was in fact the total amount of the Shrewsbury Handicap stakes. Cook, said Palmer, was too ill to write the cheque himself. All Palmer had to do then was to forge Cook's signature and send the cheque to the Secretary of the Jockey Club.

Later that morning Palmer called at Mr Hawkins's chemist's shop, where he was served by an apprentice, Charles Roberts. He asked for some prussic acid, some opium and six grains of strychnine. Roberts was making up the order when Newton, Dr Salt's assistant, came in. Palmer, not wishing Newton to know what he was buying, turned him about and took him outside, where he indulged in idle chat. When another man happened to arrive and begin conversing with Newton, Palmer went back into the shop to pick up his purchases and then walked off towards his house. Newton, once he was free of the other man, re-entered the shop, and enquired what Palmer wanted – it was two years since he had bought anything there. Roberts is said to have replied that Palmer had bought enough poison to finish off the whole parish.

That afternoon, Cook's friend from Lutterworth, Dr William Jones, arrived in Rugeley by train and reached the Talbot Arms by half-past three. He examined Cook in Palmer's presence and found that the patient's pulse was normal and that his tongue was clean. 'You should have seen it before,' said Palmer. Jones also saw no symptoms of the bilious attack described in Palmer's letter.

Both men were in and out of the bedroom all afternoon, attending to Cook, who seemed to improve, although he vomited some coffee and toast and water, brought upstairs by Elizabeth Mills and handed to Palmer. Dr Bamford appeared at 7.00 pm, and the two doctors and Palmer had a consultation on the landing about the case, concluding that Bamford should make up some morphine pills and send them over later. Cook was now strong enough to get up and sit in a chair. 'He was very jocose,' Jones said later, 'speaking of what he should do during the winter, and of his future plans and prospects.' 'He was in very good spirits,' said Elizabeth Mills, 'and talked about getting up the next morning.' She brought him some arrowroot at about half-past ten. Palmer asked Cook if she could do anything more for him, and he said he would want nothing more. So she said goodnight and went downstairs to the kitchen, where she and Lavinia Barnes remained for some time, in case they were needed again. 'I was anxious,' said Elizabeth Mills.

At about 11.00 pm, Palmer entered Cook's room with a box of pills, which he said had been sent by Dr Bamford. He had in fact collected such a box from Bamford an hour earlier. Drawing Jones's attention to the directions on the box, Palmer remarked: 'What an excellent hand for a man upwards of 80 to write.' Jones agreed. Cook was reluctant to take two of the pills, protesting that they had made him ill the previous night. Reassured, however, by the other two men, he swallowed them with toast and water, and once again was sick. Palmer suggested that the utensil in which Cook had vomited be searched for the pills. But they had been retained. Satisfied, Palmer left the room and the inn, returning to his house.

With Cook seeming comfortable, Jones went downstairs for some supper, returning to Cook's room in half an hour, when he undressed while talking idly to Cook, who was sleepy and seemed quite well. Jones climbed into the other bed, leaving a single candle burning darkly in the room.

He was still awake when, ten minutes later, Cook sat up in his bed, crying: 'Doctor, get up! I'm going to be ill! Ring the bell for Mr Palmer!' Below, in the kitchen, the bell for Cook's room rang violently just before twelve. With what apprehension and alarm did the two servant-girls gaze at each other before running upstairs? Lavinia Barnes remained outside Cook's room, while Elizabeth Mills went in, to be told by the agonised man being supported by Jones, who was rubbing the back of his neck: 'Fetch Mr Palmer!' She ran out of the inn and across the street to Palmer's house. She said later: 'I rang the surgery bell at the surgery door. I expected him to come to the window, and as soon as I stepped into the road he was at the bedroom window. He did not put up the sash . . . I asked him to come over to Mr Cook directly, as he was much the same as he was the night before. I then went back to the hotel.'

She was in Cook's bedroom helping William Jones when Palmer entered a few minutes later, remarking: 'I was never so quickly dressed in my life.' He told her to wait outside, and produced what he said were two ammonia pills for Cook to swallow. Cook did so and began to scream, throwing himself back on the bed. He cried to Jones: 'Raise me up – or I shall be suffocated!' Then his whole body was seized by violent convulsions, so extreme that his head and heels bent back as if they would meet. Jones, with Palmer's assistance, tried to lift or control the contorting body but failed, because of the spasms and the rigidity of Cook's limbs. The convulsions lasted for about ten minutes, after which Cook's agony diminished and his heartbeat faded. He was dying. Jones sent Palmer out to fetch some spirits of ammonia, and on the landing he answered Mills's enquiry about the patient by saying he was not so bad as last night – 'not by a fiftieth part'. On Palmer's return, Jones turned Cook, at his request, on to his right side and listened to his heart, holding Cook's clenched left hand in his. He was not able to take the ammonia,' said Jones. 'His heart was gradually sinking, and life was almost extinct. He died so very quietly that I could hardly tell when he did die.'

Palmer sent Mills to fetch Dr Bamford. She did so, and when Bamford left the bedroom later he said: 'He's dead. He was dead when I arrived.' She sat on the stairs for a while until she was summoned into the room by Jones. 'Palmer wants you,' he said. She said to him: 'It's not possible that Mr Cook is dead?' 'Oh, yes. He's dead,' Palmer replied. They discussed who should lay out the body, and when Jones went downstairs to see Miss Bond, both Mills and Barnes, engaged in tidying the room, noticed Palmer rummaging through the pockets of Cook's clothes as well as under the pillow and bolster. They both left as Jones returned to find Palmer with Cook's coat in his hands. With smooth self-possession Palmer remarked that Jones, being Cook's closest friend, should take charge of his effects; and he handed over Cook's watch and purse, containing five sovereigns and five shillings. His betting-book, papers and the balance of his Polestar winnings had already been purloined by Palmer. As he left the inn, Palmer confided in Jones that Cook owed him about £4,000 and expressed the hope that his friends would honour these debts. 'If they don't assist me,' he said, 'all my horses will be seized.'

Palmer's blinkered and obsessive goal of gaining all he could and more from Cook's demise led him to further ill-considered and astounding acts of indifference to the opinions, suspicions and feelings of others. Having killed so often without being caught, he seems to have become convinced of his own immunity from discovery and retribution, presuming that people were more stupid than he, and that he who dares, wins.

On Wednesday, 21 November, Palmer noted in his diary: 'Cook died at 1 o'clock this morning.' Although busy later, making arrangements for Cook to be buried and lunching with Cook's trainer, he found time to write to Thomas Pratt in London:

> Ever since I saw you I have been fully engaged with Cook and not able to leave home. I am sorry to say, after all, he died this day. So you had

> better write to Saunders [Cook's trainer]. But mind you, I must have Polestar, if it can be so arranged, and should anyone call upon you to know what money or moneys Cook ever had from you, don't answer the question till I have seen you . . . I sat up two full nights with Cook, and am very much tired out . . .

To which Pratt replied: 'I have your note, and am greatly disappointed at the non-receipt of the money as promised, and at the vague assurances as to any money . . . If anything unpleasant occurs you must thank yourself.'

The following day Palmer made a more thorough search of Cook's room, ostensibly for a paper-knife. He also summoned Cheshire and produced a document, apparently signed by Cook, which acknowledged, in effect, that Cook owed Palmer £4,000. 'I want you to witness it,' Palmer said. To which Cheshire replied: 'Good God – the man is dead!' He refused to append his signature, as he was not present when the document was drawn up and signed (by Cook). Palmer seemed unconcerned: he would get someone else to witness the deed.

Meanwhile, William Jones had gone to London to inform Cook's step-father, William Stevens, of his stepson's death. Mr Stevens, a retired merchant, who had married Cook's mother 18 years previously, had last seen his stepson at Euston Station on 5 November, when he said: 'My boy, you look very well. You don't look anything like an invalid now.' Whereupon John Cook had manfully struck his chest and said he was quite well. Shocked by Jones's revelations about the manner of Cook's sudden and dreadful death, he travelled with Jones to Lutterworth to collect some personal effects, documents and Cook's will. The two men arrived in Rugeley on Friday, 23 November, and proceeded to the Talbot Arms. Stevens and Palmer had only met once before. Stevens said later:

> Mr Jones introduced us in the inn, and we then went up and viewed the body. I was greatly struck by . . . the tightness of the muscles across the face. We all then went down to one of the sitting-rooms, and I said to [Palmer] that I understood from Mr Jones that he knew something of my stepson's affairs. He replied: 'Yes. There are £4,000 worth of bills out of his, and I'm sorry to say my name is to them. But I've got a paper drawn up by a lawyer and signed by Mr Cook to show I've never had any benefit from them.' I told him I feared there would be no money to pay them, and asked if he [Cook] had no horses or property. He replied that he had horses, but they were mortgaged . . . I then said that whether Cook had left anything or not, he must be buried. Palmer immediately said: 'Oh, I'll bury him myself, if that's all.' I replied I could not hear of it . . . I said it was my business, as executor, to bury him, and that I intended to bury him in London in his mother's grave . . . Some short time afterwards I asked Palmer for the name of some respectable undertaker in Rugeley, so that I might order a coffin at once. He replied: 'I've been and done that. I've ordered a shell and a strong oak coffin.' I expressed my surprise, and said he had no authority to do so.

The three men had lunch together and Stevens left Rugeley by train at 4.15 pm. Before his departure he asked Jones to collect any correspondence, as well as the betting-book from Cook's room. Palmer went along with Jones, who returned empty-handed before long. 'No betting-book, Mr Jones?' exclaimed Stevens, then demanding of Palmer: 'How is this?' 'Oh, it's no manner of use if you find it,' said Palmer. 'No use, sir!' Stevens retorted. 'I'm the best judge of that.' 'It's no manner of use,' Palmer repeated. 'I'm told it *is* of use,' said Stevens. 'I understand my son won a great deal of money at Shrewsbury. And I ought to know something about it.' Palmer said: 'It's no use, I assure you. When a man dies, his bets are done with.' To which Stevens responded: 'Very well, the book ought to be found, and must be found.' 'Oh, it will be found,' said Palmer. 'No doubt of that.'

The next day, Saturday, Palmer entrained for London, where he gave Pratt £100 in part payment of his debts. Returning to Rugeley on the 2.00 pm from Euston he encountered Mr Stevens, who had been taking legal advice and now intended to employ a local solicitor to investigate his stepson's affairs and to arrange a post-mortem. This he told Palmer, who offered to introduce him to a solicitor (Smith). Over the weekend he kept checking on Stevens's intentions and offering advice, to no effect. By now Stevens had learned that enquiries were being made into Walter Palmer's death.

On Sunday, maintaining appearances and social conventions, William Palmer went to church. At some point he called on Dr Bamford about Cook's death certificate, and Bamford, at Palmer's suggestion (for he had been in regular attendance) attributed Cook's death to 'apoplexy'. Meanwhile a post-mortem was organised for the following day. That night Palmer summoned Mr Salt's young assistant, Newton, to his house. Said Newton later: 'There was no one else there. He asked me what dose of strychnine would kill a dog, and whether it would be found in the stomach. I told him a grain, and that there would be no inflammation, and I did not think it would be found. I think he said: "That's all right then", as if speaking to himself, and snapped his fingers.'

The post-mortem, held in a room in the Talbot Arms at about 11.00 am on Monday, 26 November, was one of the most imperfect and farcical ever held. Supervised by a physician from Stafford, Dr Harland, it was carried out by a medical student, Charles Devonshire, assisted by Newton, and attended by Drs Bamford and Jones, by local chemists, surgeons and tradesmen, by Smith and Cheshire, by the publican, Masters, and by William Palmer, who was now under suspicion of causing Cook's death six days previously. The corpse lay naked and pale on a table, the hands still clenched, before the curious and morbid eyes of up to 20 men.

Earlier, Palmer had met Dr Harland when he arrived in Rugeley. They had met several times before. 'I'm glad you've come to do the post-mortem,' said Palmer. 'Someone might have been sent whom I didn't know. I know you.' 'What is this case?' asked Harland. 'I hear there's a suspicion of poisoning.' 'Oh, no!' said Palmer. 'Not at all! He had an epileptic fit on Monday and Tuesday night, and you'll find an old disease in the heart and in the head.' Soon after this he told the nervous Newton, whom he invited to his house for a pre-post-mortem brandy: 'You'll find this fellow's been suffering from a diseased throat. He's had syphilis.'

The stomach and intestines were the first items to be removed and examined. As Devonshire was opening the stomach with a pair of scissors, Palmer gave Newton a shove, which made him bump into Devonshire – with the result that some of the stomach's contents were spilled. 'Don't do that!' said Dr Harland, thinking the persons concerned were just fooling about. What was left in the stomach, about three ounces of brownish liquid, was then inspected by the experts. Nothing unusual was noted there and so announced by Harland. Whereupon Palmer remarked to Bamford: 'They won't hang us yet!' The stomach was then placed in a jar, as was a portion of the intestines. The jar was then wrapped in a double layer of bladders, or parchment, tied up and sealed and placed on a table. It seems not to have had a lid.

The dissection continued: the liver, lungs and heart were examined, and the brain and throat removed. Harland suddenly noticed that Palmer, who had been restlessly moving about, was missing, as was the jar. 'Where's the jar?' demanded Harland. 'It's here,' replied Palmer, from the other end of the room. 'I thought it more convenient for you to take it away.' Harland reclaimed the jar, and discovered that a small cut or slit had been made in the parchment covering the jar. 'Who did this?' he demanded. But Palmer, Newton and Devonshire denied any responsibility. Harland rearranged and retied the wrapping, and the post-mortem eventually established that Cook had been moderately healthy, and had suffered from no disease or defects that might have caused his death. There were papillae or follicles at the back of his tongue which would have caused some discomfort in eating and swallowing. But there were no indications of syphilis, apart from a venereal scar.

It is not clear what Palmer was doing or hoped to do with the jar. Discovered at the end of a long room, near a door which was not the main entrance but a door that led to another room and then a passage, he may have been about to walk away with the jar. More likely, unobserved by the others, he hoped either to empty the stomach's contents through the slit or to inject some chemical that would neutralise the poison within.

It seems he may have succeeded. For when the contents of the jar were later examined by Professor Taylor, an expert in poisons at Guy's Hospital, there was nothing left in the cut-open stomach – which had been squashed by the intestines and much shaken about on the journey south. He tested the jar's contents for several poisons, for strychnine, prussic acid, oxalic acid, arsenic, mercury, antimony, hemlock and hellebore, among others. He also sent for Cook's kidneys, liver and spleen. All Taylor discovered were some traces of antimony – which might have caused Cook's death, although less than a quarter of a grain was found.

The jar had been taken to London by the wary Mr Stevens and a solicitor's clerk, two days after the post-mortem. Before the jar left Rugeley, Palmer made another crazily blatant attempt to destroy the evidence therein. He offered the postboy at the Talbot Arms (who was also a cab-driver) £10 to overturn the fly in which Stevens and the jar were about to be conveyed to Stafford. The postboy refused to comply.

But that was not the end of Palmer's machinations. On 1 December, when in London, he told the porter at a boarding-house to make up a hamper containing a brace of pheasants, a codfish, a turkey and a barrel of oysters, and send it anonymously to W. W. Ward, Esq, of Stoke-on-Trent. Mr Ward was the coroner who conducted the inquest on the death of John Cook. The inquest, held at the Talbot Arms and twice adjourned was much mismanaged by Ward. The jury asked more questions than he. It came to an end on Saturday, 15 December.

The previous day Palmer had written to Ward, most foolishly quoting from a letter written by Professor Taylor on 14 December to Mr Stevens's solicitor in Rugeley – which Cheshire intercepted and opened at Palmer's behest and whose contents were shown to him. On 14 December Taylor's conclusion appeared in Palmer's letter to Ward, in which a £10 note was also enclosed. Palmer wrote:

> My dear Sir – I am sorry to tell you that I am still confined to my bed. I do not think it was mentioned at the inquest yesterday that Cook was taken ill on Sunday and Monday night in the same way as he was on the Tuesday night when he died . . . I also believe that a man by the name of Fisher is coming down to prove he received some money at Shrewsbury . . . Had you better not call Smith to prove this? And again, whatever Professor Taylor may say tomorrow, he wrote from London last Tuesday night to Gardner to say 'We have this day finished our analysis, and find no traces of either strychnine, prussic acid, or opium.' What can beat this from a man like Taylor? . . . I know, and saw it in black and white, what Taylor said to Gardner. This is strictly private and confidential, but it is true. As regards his betting-book, I know nothing of it, and it is of no good to anyone. I hope the verdict tomorrow will be that he died of natural causes, and thus end it – Ever yours.

But that was not the verdict, nor was it the end; and William Palmer, apprehended earlier on a writ served by the money-lender, Mr Padwick, was arrested on a charge of wilful murder and taken to Stafford Jail.

Although the bodies of Annie and Walter Palmer were exhumed the following week and their murders ratified by a Grand Jury in Stafford in March 1856, Cook's murder was the only one with which William Palmer was indicted at the opening, on 14 May, of his trial at London's Central Criminal Court. Normally he would have been tried by an assize court in Staffordshire. But local feeling was so biased against him that it was felt he would not have a fair trial. An Act was accordingly passed in Parliament to allow for such a situation and for the trial to take place in London. It is still known as Palmer's Act.

The trial lasted two weeks, and was considered for many years to be one of the greatest trials in the history of English law. Most unusually, three judges presided, led by the Lord Chief Justice, Baron Campbell, then aged 77 and soon to become Lord Chancellor. The other judges were Mr Justice Cresswell and Mr Baron Alderson, aged, respectively, 62 and 68. The prosecution was led by the Attorney-General, Sir Alexander Cockburn, regarded as 'the most accomplished orator of his generation'. A QC since 1841, and a bachelor, he, like Campbell, came from an ancient Scottish family. Assisting him were Mr Edward James, QC, aged 44, who five years later would have debts amounting to £100,000, would be disbarred and become an actor in the USA; Mr W. H. Bodkin, aged 65, who was later knighted and became a judge; Mr William Welsby, aged 61, who had written numerous books about the law; and Mr John Huddleston, aged 41, a brilliant conversationalist and a devotee of both the theatre and the turf, who became a QC after the trial and then an MP, marrying when he was 57. The defence was led by Mr Serjeant Shee, a grey-haired Irishman, aged 51, who had never before defended in a murder trial and replaced another serjeant (ranked higher than a QC) who had been taken ill. Appointed a judge in 1863, Shee became the first Roman Catholic judge since the Reformation. He was assisted by Mr William Grove, QC, aged 45; Mr Edward Kenealey, another Irishman, aged 37; and a Scot, John Gray.

The court was packed. Many noble lords, aldermen and MPs attended the trial, including the Earl of Derby, and admission was by ticket. The *Illustrated London News* said: 'It was generally remarked that [Palmer] looked little like a man who had committed murder, and that he had grown exceedingly stout since his committal to prison. He is a good-humoured, ordinary-looking man and appears much older than he really is.'

Evidence for the prosecution, in which 40 witnesses were called, lasted six full days. Serjeant Shee's eight-hour speech for the defence took up the whole of the seventh day, and he called 21 witnesses, of whom 15 were medical experts. They dilated at length on the effects of strychnine on humans and assorted animals, drawing various conclusions as to the cause of Cook's death, and attributing it to traumatic or idiopathic tetanus, unknown causes, convulsions, arachnitis and even angina pectoris. This was the nub of the defence – that Cook's symptoms indicated he died from some *disease*, not strychnine, of which none was found in his corpse. Most of these experts were extensively cross-examined by the prosecution and the trial was largely a forensic contest full of hypothesis and disagreement. Ten medical witnesses had also been called by the prosecution, whose chief witness, Elizabeth Mills, spent several hours in the witness box.

Serjeant Shee's one-day speech endeavoured to make a detailed and innocent interpretation of some of Palmer's actions and words. Early on, Shee stated: 'I commence his defence – I say it in all sincerity – with an entire conviction of his innocence. I believe there never was a truer word pronounced than the words he pronounced when he said "Not guilty" to this charge.' This earned him the reproof of the Attorney-General and the Lord Chief Justice. Shee also erred when he spoke of Palmer's love for his wife, saying: 'He loved her as ardently as he now loves her first-born, his only surviving child, a boy of seven years old, who waits with trembling anxiety the verdict that will restore him to the arms of his father, or drive that father to an ignominious death upon the scaffold.' At this point the accused covered his face with his hands and wept. Shee went on to read a love-letter from Palmer (which ended: 'with best, best love, believe me, dearest Annie – your own William'); to speak of Palmer's 'dear sister' and 'a gallant and devoted brother', and his aged, grieving and agonised mother; and to urge the jury 'to stem the torrent of prejudice'. Shee was criticised for all these sentiments by a leading legal journal, which said:

> The defence of Mr Serjeant Shee was clever, ingenious and eloquent, but wanting in judgment and taste . . . The allusion to the family of the prisoner, and to his supposed affection for his wife, grated sorely, and almost ludicrously, on the sense of propriety in the face of the undisguised fact, known to all his audience, that he was accused of murdering his wife, that he slept with his maid-servant on the very night she died, and that he had confessed himself guilty of forgery upon his mother. Equally injudicious was the philippic against the insurances offices. In worse taste still was his solemn assertion to the jury that he was convinced by the evidence of the prisoner's innocence.

The Attorney-General's address to the jury, said to have been delivered without any notes, was a masterful exposition of the facts and an incisive refutation of the defence's claims. It was given on Saturday, 24 May.

The Lord Chief Justice, having spent 14 hours on the Sunday preparing his summing-up, began his charge to the jury at 10.00 am on the Monday. He spoke for ten hours, during which he dealt with the proofs for the prosecution. The case for the defence was less carefully treated on the Tuesday, much of it merely consisting of the reading of what witnesses had said.

A powerful and wealthy coterie of racing men later organised a concerted and abusive attack on the judge, by letter and in print, likening him to Judge Jeffreys and accusing him of bias and infamous conduct. They hoped to obtain a pardon or reprieve on the grounds that Palmer had not had a fair trial. They said:

> You weakened, by all the means within your power, the effect of the evidence when it told for the prisoner . . . Did you not step out of the way to comment (like an advocate) on the evidence? To get up this witness and to knock down that one, to praise those who supported Dr Taylor's theory, and to censure those who were independent of such nonsense? Did not your lordship convey, as clearly to the jury, by meaning looks, by thumping the desk with peculiar energy, by laying emphasis on certain parts of the evidence and then pausing and gazing intently upon the jurymen; by shaking your head, as if your thoughts of [Palmer's] guilt were too dreadful for utterance; by repeating over and over again those parts which told heaviest against him; by running on the evidence for the prisoner so that it was impossible for the jury to understand it?

Mr Baron Alderson was also lambasted as 'that learned functionary, who inaugurated the first day's proceedings by falling asleep and nearly tumbling over his desk during the Attorney-General's opening speech'. He was said to have

> amused himself during the progress of the trial by suggesting questions to Mr James, the counsel for the prosecution, by lifting up his hands in apparent astonishment when anything favourable to the prisoner was elicited, by looking at the jury with every mark of incredulity and contempt when Serjeant Shee suggested any matter beneficial to the prisoner, and by joining your lordship in overruling every legal objection which was raised by the counsel for the defence.

The jury retired for an hour and 18 minutes, returning with a verdict of 'Guilty'. Palmer was silent when asked if he had anything to say before being sentenced to death. It is said that after the Attorney-General's speech, he passed a note to his defence which said: 'It was the riding that did it.'

While in prison he was buoyant and cheerful, cracking grim little jokes.

He was hanged outside Stafford Jail at 8.00 am on Saturday, 14 June 1856, reiterating: 'I am innocent of poisoning Cook by strychnia.' And indeed this may have been, strictly speaking, correct, some other allied poison having been used in addition to antimony. The hangman was George Smith of Dudley, who wore a top hat and a long white coat.

Before a crowd of 30,000, some of whom were seated in grandstands, having paid a guinea for a place, Palmer composedly climbed the ladder to the scaffold and positioned himself directly below the noose. His body was buried in the precincts of Stafford Jail.

Some residents of Rugeley, embarrassed by the town's image as a sink of immorality, drunkenness, corruption and vice, and as a centre of mass murder, sought to change its name. They failed, and Rugeley is still on the map. The Talbot Arms, after its name was changed to the Shrewsbury Arms, is now called the Shrew Kafé-Bar. Palmer's house is now occupied by a video shop and a shop selling women's wear, and although the tombstone over the Palmers' family vault in the graveyard has been broken and battered by vandals, it still records the deaths of William's father in 1836, of his mother, Sarah, in 1861, and of his brother George and his wife in 1866 and 1870. William's brother, Walter, his wife Annie, and their four infants, are also buried there – but their deaths are not recorded. At a distance stands the unravaged gravestone of John Cook, singing his praises and saying: 'Whose life was taken away at Rugeley on the night of 22 November 1855 in the 29th year of his age.'

Robert Graves wrote a book, published in 1962, asserting Palmer's innocence and entitled *They Hanged My Saintly Billy*. In it a footnote records that Palmer's surviving son, Willie, committed suicide, aged 72, in 1925.

What a contemporary and a judge, Sir James Stephen, who had made a study of murderers, said of Palmer is worth quoting here, as it could apply to most murderers – few if any of whom are the 'monsters' created by the popular press.

> *His career supplied one of the proofs of the fact . . . that such a thing as atrocious wickedness is consistent with good education, perfect sanity,*

and everything, in a word, which deprives men of all excuse for crime. Palmer was respectably brought up; apart from his extravagance and vice, he might have lived comfortably enough. He was a model of physical health and strength, and was courageous, determined, and energetic. No one ever suggested that there was ever a disposition towards madness in him. Yet he was as cruel, as treacherous, as greedy of money and pleasure, as brutally hard-hearted and as sensual a wretch as it is possible ever to imagine. If he had been the lowest and most ignorant ruffian that ever sprang from a long line of criminal ancestors, he could not have been worse than he was.

CHAPTER 4

James Mullins

The Murder of Mary Emsley, 1860

Murder is mostly committed out of a compulsion to possess, or to dispossess – to get, or to get rid of, someone or something. When not motivated by rage, self-loathing, lust or frustration, most murderers kill in the course of a robbery, in taking what is not theirs. They could take without killing. But some basic denial of the owner, and his or her rights, seems to be an associated necessity. In order for the taker to feel fully secure and to take full possession, the owner, especially if weak or elderly, must lose not just property, but life as well.

On 17 August 1860, Inspector Hayes of K Division, which covered Stepney, sent a Murder Report to the Detective Department of the Metropolitan Police. He wrote:

> I beg to report that at 12 noon this day, Mr Rose, Solicitor, of No. 19 Change Alley, Cornhill, informed Sergeant Dillon, K19, that he had called at the house of Mrs Hemsley, Widow, No. 9 Grove Road, Mile End Road, Stepney, for the purpose of seeing her, but could not make anyone hear, & that he thought something was wrong. The Sgt went through the next house & over the garden wall, when he found the back door & window shutters of No. 9 unfastened; he proceeded upstairs & in the front room (2nd floor) he found Mrs Hemsley, dead, lying on her left side with her head against the doorpost. Dr Gill, of Bow, who was passing at the time examined deceased & stated that death had been caused by the fracture of the back part of the skull . . . There is a great quantity of congealed blood on the floor & it is supposed that deceased had been lying where found for – at least – 2 or 3 days. The deceased was last seen alive on Monday afternoon last. She was a very eccentric person, of independent means, & lived alone. I respectfully beg that one of the Detective Force may assist in the inquiry.

Inspector Stephen Thornton was put in charge of the case, and on 18 August he dispatched Sgt Dick Tanner, aged 28, and Sgt Bill Thomas, an ex-grocer from Bagshot, to investigate the circumstances surrounding the elderly woman's death.

Three days later Inspector Thornton penned his own report to the Assistant Commissioner. He wrote:

The deceased was about 70 years of age, resided quite alone in her house and was possessed of considerable house property situated in very low neighbourhoods of Bethnal Green, Ratcliff, Stratford, Barking, Dagenham, etc, and she was in the habit of personally collecting the greater portion of her rents on a Monday, and in consequence of her frequent litigation with the tenants, her very plain way of dressing and living, she became well known at the East End of London. On the 2nd August last the deceased purchased a large quantity of paper hangings at an auction (part of a bankrupt stock), the major portion of which was put into the room where the deceased's body was found, and I am of opinion that some person or persons called on the deceased on Monday evening last (13 August) under pretence of buying some of the said paper hangings, and she went upstairs to the top room to show it when she was murdered and robbed of 3 or 4 rings from her fingers and whatever rents she collected on that day estimated at present at about £40, which is all the property that at present can be ascertained to be stolen. I directed a thorough search of the Coal Cellar, privy, etc of the house in order if possible to find the weapon with which the deceased was murdered but it cannot be found, but a tin box containing £32 in gold, and £16-2-0 in silver has been found among the Coal in the cellar, and now is in the hands of the police. There is no doubt the deceased was murdered on Monday evening as she was not seen alive after that time and it was not discovered until about 12 noon the following Friday [17 August]. At present there is no clue to the perpetrator of the crime . . . There is nothing stolen which can be traced beyond a Ten pound cheque which has been stopped, but I am of opinion the murderer will not make use of that . . . The deceased employed a number of persons to assist to collect her rents, and many others to do her jobbing work at her houses; her custom of living alone, collecting and taking home rents on a Monday was also well known among her tenants numbering some hundreds, some of whom are of the most depraved and lowest class, and who have frequently threatened her. Her solicitor, Mr Rose, a very highly respectable man, informs me that he has frequently told the deceased that he thought she would be murdered, going about as she did alone among such bad and dangerous characters. The deceased has also a number of very poor relations who have also a great interest in her death, and she had made up her mind to make a will to build Almshouses with the whole of the money and not leave anything to her relatives which fact the deceased had talked publicly about and all the relatives knew it . . . Myself and Sergeants Tanner and Thomas are still pursuing the inquiry.

Among the many suspects was a soldier based in Portsmouth, Edward Jackson, said to be a nephew of Mrs Emsley and 'a very bad character'. Thornton, in another report, seeking instructions and also dated 21 August, wrote: '[Jackson] has often inquired by letter to his sister to know if his Aunt was dead, and has appeared anxious for her death, as he believes he will have considerable property at her death.' Thornton asked whether he should send

Tanner to Portsmouth to make enquiries, or telegraph the local police. The Assistant Commissioner replied, writing at the foot of Thornton's report: 'Telegraph inquiry to the Police – and if the soldier has been absent PS Tanner may be sent at once.' Promptly Thornton sent a message and on the same day received the following reply from the Portsmouth Superintendent: 'Edward Jackson was not absent but obtained leave today to go to London about the murder of a Relative.'

We do not know whether the soldier or any of those who claimed to be related to Mrs Emsley eventually inherited part of her fortune. It was a considerable one: she is said to have owned literally hundreds of houses and to have had an annual income of £5,000. Most people then earned £50 a year, or less. Her husband, another eccentric, and a building contractor and brickmaker, had died about four years earlier. They had been married for 17 years. Both, it seems, had had previous partners. So Mrs Emsley had been a very wealthy widow indeed. She was also very miserly and mean: she only bought the cheapest food at markets – stale vegetables and meat – and her house, without the attentions of a single live-in servant, exhibited every sign of dust, dirt and general neglect. Anything of value, like jewellery and silver plate, had been safely stored elsewhere or was hidden, like the tin box in the cellar containing coins of gold and silver. But every Monday, when she went out to collect her rents, she had the equivalent of a poor man's annual wage on her person. This money she brought home, no doubt to count and tabulate, before taking it that same evening to be locked away in a safe in the New Globe Tavern in Mile End Road.

On Monday, 13 August – as Thornton and his team soon established – Mrs Emsley was visited by a niece, Mrs Gotz, who apparently 'dined' with her. That afternoon she was out rent-collecting in Barnsley Street near Bethnal Green Station, one of her more insalubrious possessions. That evening she was seen by a neighbour sitting at a first-floor window of her house, between 7.00 and 8.00 pm. She was probably killed soon after this, before it got dark, as no shutters were closed and no candles were found to have been lit or taken to the second-floor lumber room where she died. The police thought she must have known and trusted her killer, as she was wary of letting anyone in, and there was no sign of a forced entry. Thornton's theory was that someone had called on her to collect or buy some of the paper hangings stored in the lumber room. Why else was she killed up there?

On the Tuesday, a youth called Edwin Emm went to the house to pick up two brass taps for his father, Walter Emm, a shoemaker, who did odd jobs for Mrs Emsley and sometimes acted as her rent-collector. No one answered his knocking at the front door. Nor was there any reply or reaction to the follow-up visits made on Wednesday, Thursday and Friday by Walter Emm. He reported the matter to Mrs Emsley's solicitor, Mr Rose, who went to see for himself; and when he also failed to gain entry, he sent for the police and notified a Mr Faith and a Mr Whitaker, who had each married a step-daughter of Mrs Emsley. The two sons-in-law, with Emm and Rose, waited in the street while Sgt Dillon entered the house at noon, via the garden wall and the unlocked back door. He let the others in and Mrs Emsley's body was found on the second floor, her head so badly battered by a blunt instrument that pieces of bone had been driven into the brain.

A search revealed that Monday's rental payments had been stolen, as well as some rings, a £10 cheque (received on the Monday), and a few knick-knacks, like spoons and a silver pencil-case. The lower rooms were in a state of considerable confusion: they had evidently been ransacked, and were littered with hundreds of documents, agreements and deeds. One of them, a receipt, had been signed in the house on the day of the murder by a paperer and plasterer, who like Emm did odd jobs for Mrs Emsley. His name was James Mullins.

A middle-aged man with a slight Irish accent, he had once been a police sergeant in K Division, until some misdemeanour caused him to be dismissed. About ten years ago he had been sentenced to six years' penal servitude for larceny, part of which was spent in the county jail at Leicester. An official said later: 'His conduct here was very bad and required constant watching by the officers.' He was removed as 'incurable' to Dartmoor Prison in November 1854, but despite that label and an attack on a police officer he was eventually released.

According to a charlady, it was Mullins who had carried Mrs Emsley's bargain buy of hundreds of paper-rolls up to the second-floor room on Saturday, 4 August – for which she paid him six shillings. It was because of his association with the scene of the murder, and his criminal record, and the receipt, that Inspector Thornton had Mullins briefly tailed and watched. Walter Emm was also under suspicion, as being another odd-job man who was known to enter the house. However, both men had alibis for the evening of 13 August, and much of the initial police inquiry was taken up in investigating a host of other suspects: German Jews, disaffected tenants and penurious relations headed the list. It was not in fact until 28 August that Mullins was interviewed by Sgt Tanner.

By this time there had been another, accidental death at 9 Grove Road. PC Watson, acting as a security guard, had been living in the house since Mrs Emsley's body was found. His family were with him. On the morning of Friday, 24 August, his four-year-old son fell out of a window at the back and was killed.

By this time also, a large reward amounting to £300 (£200 of which was contributed by Mrs Emsley's sons-in-law) had been offered for any information that might lead to an arrest. But no arrest was made, or seemed likely to be made, and *The Times*, on 8 September, three weeks after the body was found, reported that the police were 'ready to abandon the investigation as hopeless'. Then, on that very day, the killer, in trying to incriminate someone else and claim the reward, gave himself away.

The ex-policeman, James Mullins, visited Sgt Tanner at his home in Stepney, professing to have some information about the murderer, whom he suggested was Walter Emm. Mullins had earlier called on Inspector Thornton, but (it was a Saturday) he was out. Mullins said that ever since 28 August, when he had been interviewed by Tanner, he had been giving the case a good deal of thought, capitalising on what he had learned as a policeman, and had concluded that the most likely suspect was Emm. That morning, he said, he had secretly observed Emm's home at about 5.00 am, while pretending to be picking herbs, and had seen him leave his cottage and make his way to a ruined outhouse in a brickyard, 40 yards away, known as Emsley's Fields. He came out of the outhouse carrying a parcel, which he took into his cottage. Ten minutes later he reappeared bearing a much smaller parcel, which he concealed in an adjacent shed. Mullins felt certain that whatever was in the parcel had something to do with the case.

Tanner was properly cautious, and perhaps already suspicious of Mullins's manner as well as his words. He said he could not take any action before he had consulted Thornton, but agreed to meet Mullins the following day. As Mullins left he made a stupid and self-incriminating remark: 'If this goes off all right, I'll take care of you' – meaning that he would give Tanner part of the £300 reward.

On the Sunday morning, Sgt Thomas called at 11 Oakham Street, Chelsea, where Mullins was now lodging with his wife. They discussed the case. 'You know I am clever in these matters,' said Mullins. 'I've been working day and night to discover the murderer of Mrs Emsley, and I have found him out.' They teamed up with Thornton and Tanner, and all four travelled in a hackney-cab to the brickyard, where, telling Mullins to stay out of sight, they made (it seems intentionally) an inconclusive search of Emm's cottage, the shed and the ruined outhouse. No parcel, or anything untoward, was found. On being told this, Mullins was prompted to exclaim: 'You haven't half searched the place! Come – I'll show you!' Entering the shed, he said: 'Look there now! Pull down that bloody slab.' Sgt Thomas did, and discovered a small parcel, tied with tape and containing one large spoon, three small spoons marked WP, and a £10 cheque. Mullins seemed very pleased with himself.

Walter Thomas Emm was arrested and taken to Arbour Square police station and charged. Mullins went with the police, ostensibly as the happy recipient of the £300 reward. Then he was charged as well – on suspicion of also being involved in the murder. He exclaimed: 'Is this the way I'm to be served after giving you the information?'

Later, at the magistrates' court, Emm was discharged, for his alibi was unshakeable, and James Mullins was committed for trial.

Thornton and his sergeants now set about finding witnesses and other evidence to convince a jury of Mullins's guilt. His alibi for the night of the murder now seemed suspect – it had been provided by two of his sons. Emm's alibi was that on the Monday night, at about 9.00 pm, he had travelled to Bromley-by-Bow and Stratford in a pony-cart with his wife and two friends, returning at about 11.30 that night. And he had a toll-ticket to prove it. He was even able to prove, when he was supposedly concealing the parcel in the ruin on the morning of the 8th, that he was somewhere else and not even at home.

Sgt Thomas, in searching Mullins's lodgings at 33 Barnsley Street (where Mrs Emsley had been collecting rents on the afternoon before her murder), found some tape similar to that used to tie the parcel. He also found a plasterer's hammer which might well have been the murder weapon. At the lodgings in Orford Street, Chelsea where Mullins had lived at the time of the murder with his wife, Thomas noticed that Mrs Mullins had a spoon marked WP – later identified, by Mrs Gotz, as having belonged to Mrs Emsley. He also found a boot in a dust-hole (rubbish dump) which the landlady claimed to have seen being thrown out of the Mullinses' window. The marking on the boot's sole corresponded with a bloody boot-mark on the wooden stairs of 9 Grove Road. Thornton later produced the relevant piece of the stair in court, so that the jury could compare the boot with the mark. A silver pencil-case was also produced in court. It was said to have been sold by Mrs Mullins to a potboy in a pub.

The trial of James Mullins at the Central Criminal Court began on Thursday, 25 October 1869, and lasted two days. It was held before the Lord Chief Baron Sir Frederick Pollock, aged 77, and his son-in-law, Mr Baron Martin, aged 59. Sir Frederick Pollock, the son of a saddler of Scottish origins patronised by George III, had been the Lord Chief Baron for 16 years. He had previously held the post of Attorney-General and was also the Tory MP for Huntingdon. He married twice: his first wife had eleven children, and his second seven. He retired in 1866 and died four years later. His eldest daughter Fanny married Samuel Martin in 1838. He became a Baron of the Exchequer in 1850, was knighted, and died in 1883.

Serjeant Parry led for the prosecution, and Mr J. Best and Mr J. E. Palmer appeared for the defence. John Humffreys Parry was 44 and had been a Serjeant-at-law for four years. Born in London, the son of a Welsh antiquary and, like Pollock, twice married, he was noted for his 'admirable appearance and voice' and for the clarity of his thinking and of what he said.

The prisoner, according to *The Times*, looked 'hardly so old' as his alleged age, 58 – 'though he wears spectacles' – and had an 'intelligent and rather prepossessing appearance'. Witnesses were produced to say they had seen Mullins near Grove Road (now Globe Road) before and after the murder. One, a tailor, said that while waiting to enter a urinal at the end of Grove Road at 7.50 pm on Monday, 13 August, Mullins, in the working clothes of a plasterer, had emerged and walked off towards No. 9.

Thomas Mullins, aged 16, and his older brother, John, an unemployed dock-labourer, were called by Mr Best to substantiate their father's alibi, which was that the three of them were in 33 Barnsley Street from about 6.45 pm on 13 August until the following morning. After supper they had gone to bed about 9.00, although they then lay awake, talking, for another three hours. Mullins had slept on a trestle and some sacking, and his two sons on some rushes on the floor. They claimed that a Mrs Musick, who used to sleep in the back kitchen of the house, saw Mullins on the Tuesday morning; but she had since disappeared.

Serjeant Parry produced a laundress, Caroline Brinson, who swore that Mrs Musick, who had looked after her aunt at 33 Barnsley Street, was not there on the Tuesday morning (and by implication had left the previous night); for the laundress went there on Tuesday at 10.00 am to take Mrs Musick's place. She said she only saw Thomas Mullins there, and not his older brother or father. She added that the ceiling of a corridor in the house had not been waterwashed on the Tuesday by Mr Mullins, as his sons alleged, but on the Thursday.

In cross-examination, both the Mullins brothers gave confused and unconvincing replies about where they were and what they were doing on the days and nights before and after the murder. They were only certain about the events of the Monday night. 'I don't know why we didn't go to sleep at once,' said Thomas. 'Because we couldn't, I suppose.' 'You go along too fast for me,' John complained to Serjeant Parry – and there was laughter in court.

The Lord Chief Baron, in his summing-up, which lasted over three hours, was dubious about aspects of the prosecution's case. He was uncertain about the reliability of the identifications of Mullins around the night of the murder; and the two pieces of tape, of a very commonplace sort, did not correspond *exactly* – nor did the print on the stair with the sole of the boot. The hammer, he thought, had not been positively proved to be the murder weapon, or to belong to the accused. Moreover, a smear of blood on the pencil-case was not necessarily Mrs Emsley's. Nor were three hairs found on the hammer indisputably hers: plasterers used human hair in their mortar. The case against Mullins depended on whether or not the jury thought Mullins, and his sons, were lying about his whereabouts on the night of the murder, and whether he had deliberately lied about Walter Emm.

The judge's caution was probably caused by his injudicious acceptance of medical evidence in the trial of Dr Smethurst in August 1859 and his consequent summing-up against the accused. This evidence was reconsidered by the Home Office, found to be flawed, and Smethurst was released.

The jury at Mullins's trial had fewer doubts than the Lord Chief Baron. They retired at 6.15 pm on the Friday, and after an hour returned with a verdict of 'Guilty'.

Before sentence of death was passed, Mullins stated: 'I am not guilty. I know that I have not many days to live, and I am now speaking the truth. I am most happy to have had such a trial – an attentive jury and also such able counsel.' He said the hammer was not his, nor was the boot. In conclusion, he said, striking his breast: 'My heart is light at being able to tell all my friends about me that what I say to you now is the real truth. I am extremely obliged to the jury, and I am happy to have had such a patient jury. I am obliged to your lordship also, and to the gentlemen, both against and for me.' He also thanked Mr Best and his solicitor, Mr Ward, ' who has taken more trouble than I would expect a gentleman in his class to take. He has done all he could to find witnesses for me, and as yet I am sorry to say that I have not paid him'.

In passing sentence, the Lord Chief Baron managed yet again to indicate his dissatisfaction with the prosecution's case and with the evidence provided by the police. He said: 'I am still of the opinion that some of the circumstances urged against you [Mullins], instead of increasing the weight of evidence for the prosecution, only tended to embarrass the jury in coming to a conclusion. But with that conclusion I am bound to state I am perfectly satisfied.'

On 27 October, Inspector Thornton was able to report to his superiors, with some satisfaction, that 'James Mullins was yesterday found guilty at the Central Criminal Court of the Wilful Murder of Mrs Emsley on the 13th August last, and he was sentenced by the Lord Chief Baron Pollock to be executed'.

Before the execution, at Newgate Prison, Mullins was visited three times a day by his wife and children, and continued to proclaim his innocence. An appeal was denied by Sir George Lewis, the Home Secretary, on 16 November, and Mullins was hanged by Calcraft outside Newgate before a crowd of some 20,000 persons on Monday, 19 November. As he was a Roman Catholic, no words from the Anglican funeral service were read.

Minutes before his execution, he handed a lengthy written statement to the prison officials, in which he repeated he was innocent and reiterated the details of his alibi. 'My children proved the truth,' he said. 'But the truth was not believed.' He also asked for donations for his 'poor family' who were 'in the greatest destitution'.

Buried in this statement was a single sentence that seemed to acknowledge he had lied over one matter. He wrote: 'I believe Emm to be innocent of the murder of Mrs Emsley.' He had at least, and at the last, exculpated Walter Emm.

The hangman, William Calcraft, then aged 60, is said by the Dictionary of National Biography *to have been 'very fond of his children and grandchildren' and to have taken 'a great interest in his pigeons and other pet animals'. A kindly, mild-mannered, grey-whiskered man, he hanged about 1,000 people in his 45-year career. Born at Baddow, near Chelmsford, in 1800, he was a shoemaker, watchman, gentlemen's butler and hawker, before officially becoming the chief executioner in April 1829. He succeeded John Foxton, who died that year and had himself been executioner for 40 years. A chance meeting with Foxton had led to Calcraft being employed to flog boys at Newgate for ten shillings a week. Standing in for Foxton, he performed his first execution, a double hanging in Lincoln, in 1828. As the chief hangman, Calcraft was paid a guinea a week, and a guinea for every execution. He also received half a crown for every man he flogged, and was given an allowance to provide 'cats' and birch rods. For an execution out of town he might receive as much as £10. His last hanging was of James Godwin on 25 May 1874. He retired on a good pension of 25 shillings a week and died at Hoxton in London five years later, on 13 December 1879.*

CHAPTER 5

Franz Müller

The Murder of Thomas Briggs, 1864

Committed on a train, it was the first railway murder, and caused an outcry in the press. Although horse-drawn wagons conveying goods or coal had trundled along on rails in certain districts since 1800, the first conveyances carrying passengers and drawn by a George Stephenson locomotive would not rattle along the Stockton and Darlington line until 1825. Five years later, at the grand opening of the Liverpool–Manchester railway, the first passenger fatality occurred: Mr Huskisson, a VIP, was killed by a passing locomotive as he stood on the track. By 1848, some 5,000 miles of track had been laid in Britain and hundreds of bridges, cuttings and embankments had been built. The amalgamation of small regional companies had also led to the rise of the big national companies, like the LNER, LMS and GWR, and in 1863 people could travel from London King's Cross to Edinburgh without changing trains. They could also travel from Paddington to Hammersmith on the new Metropolitan Railway, the first underground railway in the world.

There were three classes of railway carriage, first, second and third, with separate compartments in each, and the top speed was 40–45 mph. Trains were symbols of progress in more ways than one. Noisy, bumpy, smoky and dark though they were, their standards of regularity, comfort, punctuality – and safety – were very high.

Mr Thomas Briggs was 69, and chief clerk in a City of London banking-house in Lombard Street, called Robarts, Lubbock & Co. After leaving his place of work at about 4.30 pm on Saturday, 9 July 1864, he journeyed south across the Thames to have an early dinner with his married niece and her husband, David Buchan, a woollen warehouseman, at 23 Nelson Square, Peckham. Formally dressed for work, he wore a high silk hat, and a heavy gold chain across his waistcoat attached to a heavy gold watch. In one hand he carried a black leather bag, whose contents he gave to the Buchans, and in the other a sturdy walking-stick with a solid handle. He was 5' 9" tall and the picture of Victorian respectability, portly, affable and silver-haired, with a full white beard.

Conversation at the dinner-table, apart from a mix of family and business matters, no doubt touched on recent battles and events in the American Civil War, on President Lincoln and Generals Grant and Sherman, on the aims and activities of the governing Liberal Party led by Viscount Palmerston, and on the unhappy situation of 45-year-old Queen Victoria, widowed since December 1861. Perhaps the merits of Dickens's latest novel, *Our Mutual Friend*, currently being published in monthly parts, was discussed.

Soon after the clocks in the house chimed the half-hour after eight, Mr Briggs departed, collecting his hat, stick and now empty bag and kissing his niece at the door. David Buchan walked with Mr Briggs to the Old Kent Road – the latter twice checked the time on his watch – and saw the elderly gentleman safely on to a horse-drawn omnibus. 'He was perfectly sober,' said Buchan later. 'Indeed, he was a man of very temperate habits.' The omnibus conveyed Mr Briggs back across the Thames to King William Street, where he descended, not far from his Lombard Street bank, and walking past the Monument, proceeded along Fenchurch Street to the railway station there. After showing his return ticket, he entered a first-class carriage and settled in a corner of a two-door compartment, his back to the engine. The train left the terminus at 9.50 pm, five minutes late, and proceeded via the North London railway line on its round of smoky northern London suburbs, via Shadwell, Stepney and Bow, to Hackney, Islington and Chalk Farm. Mr Briggs's destination was Hackney Central; his home was in nearby Clapton Square.

A dim ceiling-light glowed overhead. The night was warm. Perhaps Mr Briggs, having dined well and worked all day, gently dozed.

At Bow station, a property-owner and gentleman called Thomas Lee, who was waiting on the platform for the train (he was also going to Hackney Central), exchanged a few words with Mr Briggs through the open door or window before moving up the train to a second-class carriage. The two men were casually acquainted. 'Goodnight, Tom,' said Mr Briggs. Lee answered: 'Goodnight, Tom.' He was surprised to see the older man out so late and noticed there were two other men in the compartment: one was a thin, dark man, and the other, opposite Mr Briggs, was 'a stoutish thick-set man with light whiskers'.

At 10.01 the train left Bow. It was due at Hackney Wick four minutes later, at 10.05.

In a first-class compartment next to that in which Mr Briggs was seated sat a draper and a lady, unnamed. The draper, yet another Tom (Thomas Withall), would later say: 'When the train was near Hackney Wick I heard a horrid howling. I believe it was a dog. A lady, a stranger to me, who was riding in the same carriage as myself, remarked on it being a dog.' Another lady in an adjacent compartment would say that her dress was spattered with drops of blood flying in through an open window. She, however, said she heard nothing untoward, no sounds of violence or cries for help.

When the train pulled into Hackney Wick, two young clerks, Henry Verney and Sydney Jones, who both coincidentally worked at Mr Briggs's bank and were going to Highbury, stepped into the gloomy and now empty compartment where Mr Briggs had sat. After seating themselves Jones found there was blood on one of his hands. They then noticed there was blood on the seat cushions, on a window, on a black leather bag and a walking-stick.

Under a seat lay a black beaver hat, crushed, as if someone had stood on it. Much alarmed, they reported their discoveries to the guard, Benjamin Ames. He searched the compartment in the light of his hand-lamp, locked it, and as the train steamed on to Hackney Central, Ames telegraphed to the station-master at Chalk Farm, where the carriage was disconnected and shunted on to a siding to await the arrival of the police.

At about 10.20 the guard on a southbound train of empty carriages happened to see a dark object lying on the six-foot way between the railway lines. The train, which had just crossed a bridge over Sir George Duckett's Canal and was about 800 yards out of Hackney Wick station, was brought to a halt. The guard, William Timms, investigated, as did the engine-driver and the fireman. They found the body of Mr Briggs, lying on his back with his feet towards the City. Though badly injured and bloody about the head, he was still alive, albeit unconscious. With difficulty they carried him down the track to Wick Lane, where he was deposited on a table in the Mitford Castle tavern. A policeman, who chanced to be in Wick Lane, came to their assistance and a doctor was summoned. He arrived at about 11.00 pm. An examination revealed that wounds on the left side of Mr Briggs's head had probably been caused when he fell from his train. Two severe blows had also fractured his skull.

Mr Briggs's home was notified, and he was formally identified by one of his servants before his second son, Thomas James Briggs, a waterproofer, arrived with the family doctor at 6.00 am on the Sunday morning to take the injured and still-insensible man to his house in Clapton Square. He died there late on Sunday night.

'MURDER ON THE IRON WAY' proclaimed one newspaper. Another protested: 'It is monstrous that a thousand persons should be encased in a series of boxes and hurled along a line at the rate of forty miles an hour, and that they should be debarred from means of communicating with the only person who has control of the rushing mass.' 'Who is safe?' cried the *Daily Telegraph* on 13 July. 'It would be impossible to imagine circumstances of greater apparent security than those which seemed to surround Mr Briggs. Well known – expected at home – travelling First Class for a mere step of a journey, on a line where stations occur every mile or so, and fringed with houses – if we can be murdered thus we may be slain in our pew at church, or assassinated at our dinner table.' Train carriages were suddenly precincts of fear: women became very apprehensive about travelling at night, and alone; respectable men eyed rough-looking strangers with silent suspicion, concealing their watches and clutching their sticks or a hidden, protective life-preserver (a cosh).

Inspector Dick Tanner, assisted by Sgt George Clarke, was put in charge of the investigation, which soon established that the motive for the attack was robbery – although a diamond ring on the victim's little finger, a silver snuffbox, four sovereigns and some silver had not been taken. Missing were Mr Briggs's gold watch, valued at about £12, and its chain – as well as his high silk hat. The crushed black beaver hat was evidently the assailant's. Had he picked up the wrong hat in his flight, or deliberately purloined the more expensive item? It transpired that Mr Briggs's hat, which had a bell crown, had been specially made for him by a well-established hatter's managed by Daniel Digance and situated in Cornhill, near Lombard Street. It bore Briggs's name on an inner band. The beaver hat bore the name of its maker: Mr Thomas Walker of 42 Crawford Street, Marylebone. It had an unusual broad-striped lining and a merino rim.

Descriptions of the missing hat, as well as of the watch and chain, were published in the papers. They soon elicited a response from a Mr Death.

Robert Death, who apparently pronounced his name Deeth, was an assistant to his brother in a jeweller's shop at 55 Cheapside, a quarter of a mile west of Mr Briggs's place of work in Lombard Street. He told the police that on the morning of Monday, 11 July, a young man with a foreign accent had visited the jeweller's and offered to exchange a gold watch-chain in his possession for another of equal value. Death's brother, John, assessed the chain to be worth £3 10s, and in exchange the customer was given another gold chain (worth £3 5s) and a ring (5s) which were wrapped up in a small cardboard box.

There was no major development in the police investigation for a long frustrating week. It seemed the murderer would never be found.

Then, on Monday, 18 July, a 35-year-old cabman, Jonathan Matthews, began reading a poster outside the Great Western Hotel at Paddington Station, while his horse slaked its thirst at a trough. He had been prompted to do so after hearing the murder discussed on the cab rank. The poster – and hundreds had by then been splashed across London – announced that a reward totalling £300 (offered by the Government, Mr Briggs's bank and by the North London Railway) would be given for information leading to the capture of the murderer. Reading slowly through the details and noting the beaver hat, Matthews's eye was transfixed by the sight of 'Death'. Such a name, he recalled, had been inside a small cardboard box given to his daughter the previous Monday by a German acquaintance, a young tailor who wore a beaver hat – Franz Müller.

Matthews drove off at once to his home off Lisson Grove, found the box in a drawer and took it that evening to the Hermitage Street police station. He provided the police with a description of Müller, as well as his address and a photograph, and said that he had recently bought *two* beaver hats, one for Müller (for 8s 6d) and one for himself. He also revealed that the young German was no longer in London. He had emigrated to America four days ago, and was on his way to New York.

With commendable speed and enterprise, Inspector Tanner and his team soon discovered that Müller had pawned Mr Death's chain and some other items to raise the necessary cash to pay for his transatlantic voyage, as a steerage passenger, on the sailing-ship *Victoria*. The ship had left London a day late, at dawn on the previous Friday. On the Saturday, while the ship was still within view of the coast, Müller had written a farewell letter to the Blyths, in whose house he had recently lodged. The letter was posted at Worthing. It said: 'On the sea, 16 July, in the morning. Dear Friends, I am glad to confess that I cannot have a better time as I have, for the sun shines and the wind blows fair, as it is at present moment everything will go well.'

The Blyths, Ellen and George (he was a messenger), lived at 16 Park Terrace, Old Ford, Bow, not far from Wick Lane. Mrs Blyth told Inspector Tanner that Müller had lodged with them for about seven weeks, and that on the night of Saturday, 9 July, she had waited up for him until 11.00 pm.

As he had not returned by then, she and her husband went to bed. Müller had a latch-key. She said later: 'I saw him the next morning, Sunday, when he came down to breakfast with us, as usual. I did not notice anything unusual in his manner. He appeared to be a little lame from a sprain of the ankle, which he had spoken of on the Friday. He said he had got his foot between a bus and a kerbstone in crossing the road near London Bridge.' On Saturday he had, in fact, been wearing a slipper on the injured foot. On the Sunday, she said, Müller was in the best of spirits, laughing, chatting and enjoying his meals. He remained at home all Sunday, and went out with the Blyths in the evening. On Monday evening he showed the Blyths a gold chain which, he said, he had bought from a man at the docks. Müller, said Mrs Blyth, was 'a quiet, well-behaved, inoffensive young man, of a humane and affectionate disposition'.

Tanner followed up other leads provided by Mrs Blyth and the cabman, Jonathan Matthews, who had bought the beaver hat for Müller the previous December, in exchange for a waistcoat Müller made for him. Matthews identified the crushed beaver hat found on the train as Müller's. So did Mrs Matthews, who remarked that Müller, not liking a flat brim, had 'turned up the sides in the fashion worn by foreigners'. They had known him for nearly a year, having become acquainted through mutual friends, a couple called Repsch.

Godfrey Repsch was a tailor, living at 12½ Jewry Street, Aldgate. He and his wife had known Franz Müller for about two years, since he arrived in London from Germany, via Cologne. It was Mr Repsch who had helped Müller find a job with a tailor's, Mr Hodgkinson's, in Threadneedle Street (not far from Lombard Street), where he was paid 25 shillings a week. Müller left the business on 2 July, saying he was going to emigrate to America.

> The last time I saw him [said Mrs Repsch] was on the morning of Thursday, 14 July, the day he sailed. He told us he was going in the ship *Victoria* from the London Docks to New York. On the previous Saturday, the 9th, I had seen him at my house, where I left him at about half-past seven o'clock at night, talking to his friend, John Hoffa. He had not told me he was going anywhere. When I came back at about half-past eight, Hoffa was still there, at work, but Müller was gone. I did not see Müller at all on the Sunday. But he called on Monday between ten and eleven o'clock, and seated himself on the shop-board beside my husband. He then took out of his pocket the gold Albert [chain] and said he had paid £3 15s for it, and he showed us a ring upon his finger with a white stone and a peculiarly shaped head upon it, and he told us he had bought it for 7s 6d . . . He told us that he bought the chain and the ring of a man at the docks, whom he met when he was

> going down to take his passage ticket, and he thought it was a good bargain. I joked him about it and said it was not worth the money, upon which he took up the shears and scraped the chain, to show me the way of testing it. He said: 'You see it is pure gold.' I observed that the hat he was wearing was quite new, and I said to him: 'How extravagant you are with your hats!' He said he had smashed his old one and thrown it into the dust-hole. I had particularly noticed his old hat, because it had a striped lining . . . He used to put his letters in the lining.

When Müller said he had paid 14s 6d for his new hat, Mr Repsch remarked that it looked more like a guinea hat.

On Thursday morning, the day on which the *Victoria* was scheduled to sail, Mr Repsch had accompanied the young tailor to London Docks and saw him on to the ship. He was probably wearing his smart new hat. Why did he keep it? Perhaps, being a tailor, he appreciated its worth and appearance more than most, and had not the heart to throw it away.

John Hoffa was another young tailor and a friend of Franz Müller, having met him at Hodgkinson's, where he also worked. On the Saturday night referred to by Mrs Repsch, Müller told Hoffa when he left the house that he 'was going to see his girl – his sweetheart'. Her name was Mary Ann Eldred. But although he called at her lodgings, he never saw her that night. He robbed and killed Mr Briggs instead.

It seems that Hoffa had arranged to take over Müller's little first-floor room at the back of the Blyths' house. For he moved there from the Repschs' home on the Monday before Müller sailed. It seems they shared a bed. It was by no means unusual for male members of a family or friends to sleep together then. Travellers staying overnight at an inn were also accustomed to share a bed with total strangers. Hoffa moved in with Müller three nights before he vacated the room. He said later: 'Müller slept with me on the Monday, Tuesday and Wednesday nights.'

On the Tuesday Müller pawned the Albert chain obtained from Mr Death at 21 Minories – he had pawned his own watch and chain a month previously. He received £1 10s for the Albert chain, and then sold the ticket to Hoffa for 12 shillings, which Hoffa borrowed from someone else. Müller said he needed the money as he did not have enough for his passage to America. This he bought, in his own name, for £4 on the Wednesday morning at London Docks. What else he did and how he celebrated his last two days and nights in London is not known. Hoffa said: 'He left me in bed at six o'clock on Thursday morning and said "Goodbye", as he was going to the ship.' Hoffa presumably never expected to see his friend again.

Tanner and Sgt Clarke accumulated most of all this information in the 24 hours after Matthews went to the police (on Monday, 18 July). The known facts and the strong suspicion that Müller was Mr Briggs's murderer were presented to the Chief Commissioner of Police, Sir Richard Mayne, late on Tuesday afternoon, and such was the popular and political concern and interest in the case that he authorised Tanner and Clarke to proceed to New

The Chapel and Visiting-Yard at Newgate. On the right stands the Execution Shed (1898) *(Illustrated London News Picture Library)*

Condemned cell, Newgate (1862) *(Hulton Deutsch)*

(c/o Hulton Deutsch)

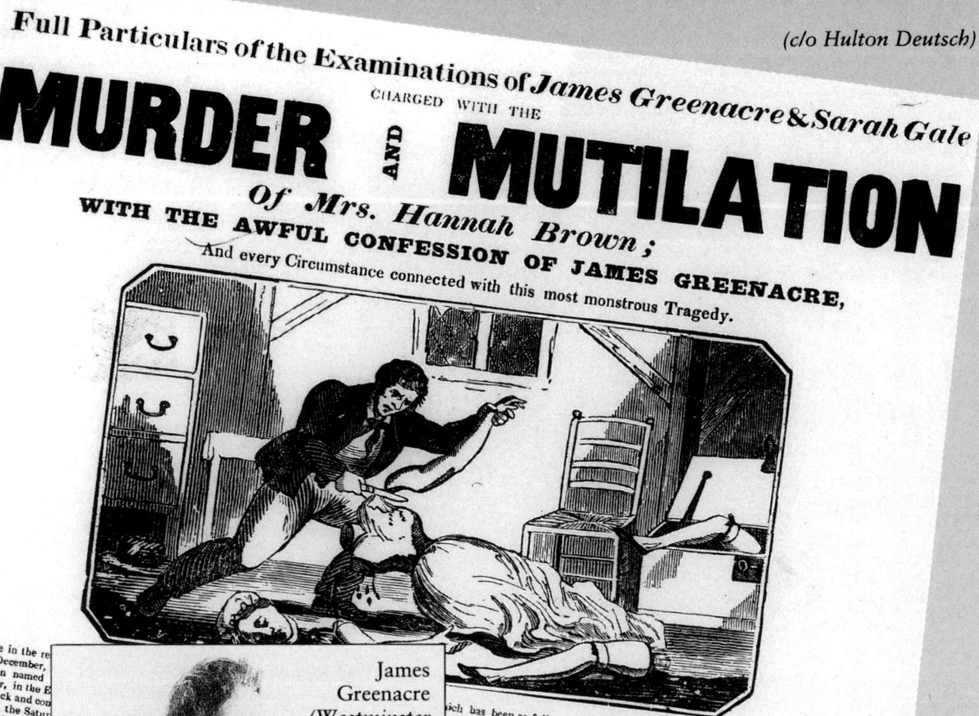

James Greenacre *(Westminster City Archives)*

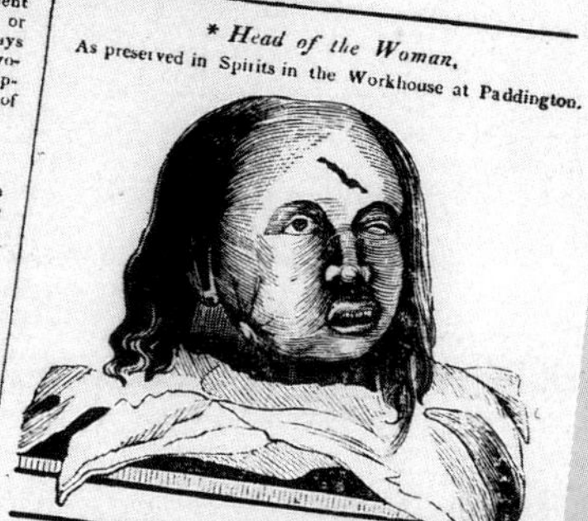

Sarah Gale, also implicated in Mrs Brown's murder *(Westminster City Archives)*

Death's head of Greenacre *(Black Museum)*

Left: Pineapple Gate, Edgwar Road where the trunk of the body was discovered *(Westminster City Archives)*

Wanted Poster for Daniel Good issued by the Metropolitan Police, April 1842 *(Public Record Office)*

METROPOLITAN POLICE OFFICE, 7 *April*, 1842.

MURDER!

A WARRANT HAS BEEN GRANTED FOR THE APPREHENSION OF

DANIEL GOOD,

COACHMAN, who has absconded from his Master's Residence, PARK LANE, PUTNEY, charged with ROBBERY and Suspicion of MURDER: The Trunk of a Female, without the Limbs and Head, has been found by the Police in one of the Stalls of the Stable, some of the Bones of which were in the Harness Room, nearly consumed by Fire, and are now in possession of the Police.

Description of Daniel Good.

He is an Irishman, aged about 46 years, 5 ft. 6 ins. high, very dark complexion, black hair, long features, and bald at the top of the head; walks upright; was dressed in a dark Great Coat, Drab Breeches and Gaiters, and Black Hat.

Information to be given to any of the POLICE STATIONS in the ETROPOLITAN POLICE DISTRICT.

ROEHAMPTON MURDE

EXAMINATION OF GOOD

BOW STREET.—Yesterday morning the great
cinity of this Court, it be
s evening that *Daniel*
Tonbridge-wells for the
veyed to town for the
before the Magistrate
f the journey in a
ich, where he was pl
on van, and conduc
ning. Previous to
d to be allowed
reasons was refus
house of the F di
emain with him
mself very quiet
rsation.
had been disp
should dispose
to enable the
accommodated
brought in t
he bench we
Lennox, Mr. R. C. Dawson, of the
Rev. T. B. Whitehurst, a Magistrate
ford; the Rev. Dr. Pinkney, of
M.P.; Sir Charles Aldis, Lord M
barrister; Lord Faversham, Dr. B
Cottingham, Magistrate of Union-
Precisely at half-past ten o'cl
at the bar. He was attired in
and blue handkerchief and bla
a grab-coloured cap, simi

Death's head of Good *(Black Museum)*

GOOD THE MURDERER.

HIS APPREHENSION AT TUNBRIDGE, AND ARRIVAL AT BOW-STREET.

Information having reached town on Saturday evening, that the murderer Good had been apprehended on that morning at Tunbridge, we made inquiries on the subject, and having reason to believe that such report had some foundation in fact, we at once dispatched our reporter to that place; and from the information which he was enabled to collect on the spot, and which follows, he has no doubt that the miscreant murderer is at this moment in the hands of justice, and locked up in Maidstone gaol. Should he turn out to be Good, the murderer and mutilator of the unfortunate woman, whose body had been found on the premises of Mr. Shiell—and of this, we repeat, there can be but little doubt—his apprehension, it will be seen, is not less singular than that of the discovery of the murder itself.

It appears that about half-past five o'clock on Monday morning last, a man with a fustian jacket and trousers, with a dark waistcoat, entered the Angel public-house, at the southern extremity of Tonbridge, with a hod, in which was found a small bundle, and addressing Mr. Adams, the landlord, asked him if he could assist him to a job as a bricklayer's labourer. Mr. Adams told him that there was a good deal of building going on in the neighbourhood, and it was very likely he would get something to do. The man upon this observed that if he procured work he would come to lodge at his house, and he then called for a penny loaf and half a pint of beer, which he had.

The appearance of the man was such as to raise considerable suspicion in the mind of Mr. Adams that he was not what he represented himself to be, and the suspicion was considerably heightened by the fact of his having a perfectly new hod, a circumstance of not very frequent occurrence among this fraternity, particularly in such times as the
his attention was at the time
other customers

The High Street, Rugeley, showing William Palmer's house and the Talbot Arms where Cook died *(from* The Life and Career of Dr William Palmer of Rugeley *by George Fletcher)*

Below left: The trial of William Palmer at the Central Criminal Court, May 1856 *(Mansell Collection)*

Below: William Palmer (drawing by Joseph Simpson) *(from* The Trial of William Palmer *by George Knott)*

Foot: Letter from Palmer on black-edged paper *(Black Museum)*

Mr. Henry Dorling
Clerk of the Course
Epsom
Surrey

Dear Sir:
Be good enough to enter in the Craven Stakes at Epsom my br. c. "The Chicken" 3 years old. — I have enclosed you a cheque for his Stake & will pay you your fee &c when I come to Epsom. & I am dear Sir,

Yours truly
Rugeley Wm Palmer —
May 17th 1855 —

P.S. I have sent Messrs Weatherby a Cheque for my mare's Stake ("Nettle") for The Oaks —
Wm P.

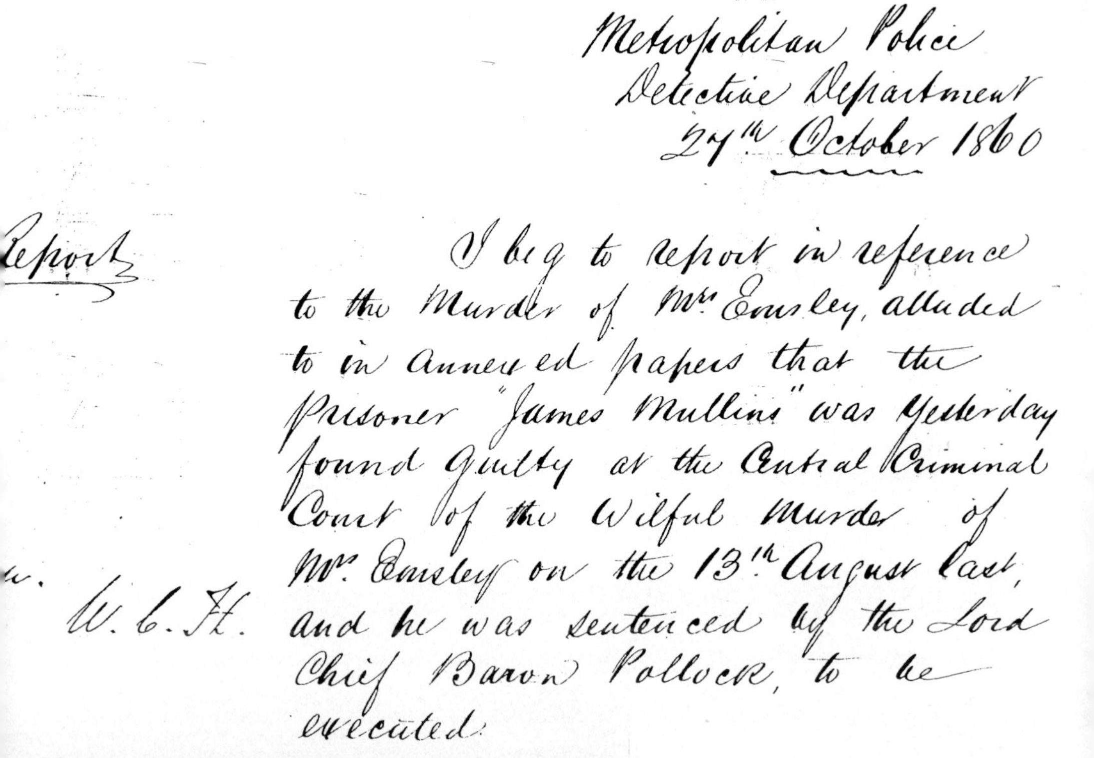

Metropolitan Police
Detective Department
27th October 1860

Report

I beg to report in reference to the Murder of Mrs Emsley, alluded to in annexed papers that the Prisoner "James Mullins" was Yesterday found Guilty at the Central Criminal Court of the Wilful Murder of Mrs Emsley on the 13th August last, and he was sentenced by the Lord Chief Baron Pollock, to be executed.

W. C. H.

S Thornton
Inspector

Above: Police Report on the sentencing of James Mullins *(Public Record Office)*

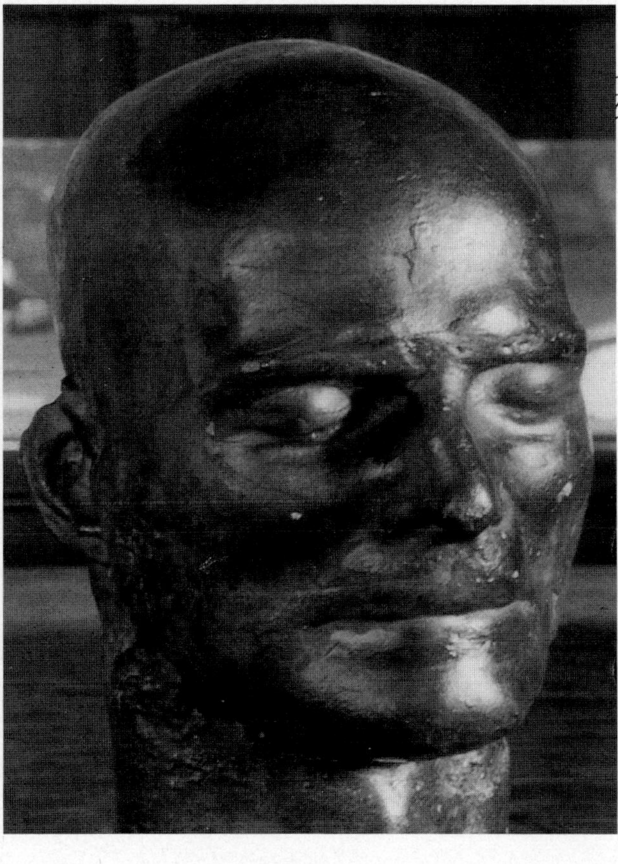

Death's head of Mullins
(Black Museum)

Franz Müller *(Hulton Deutsch)*

Below: Death's head of Franz Müller *(Black Museum)*

Middle picture: The *SS Victoria* *(Hulton Deutsch)*

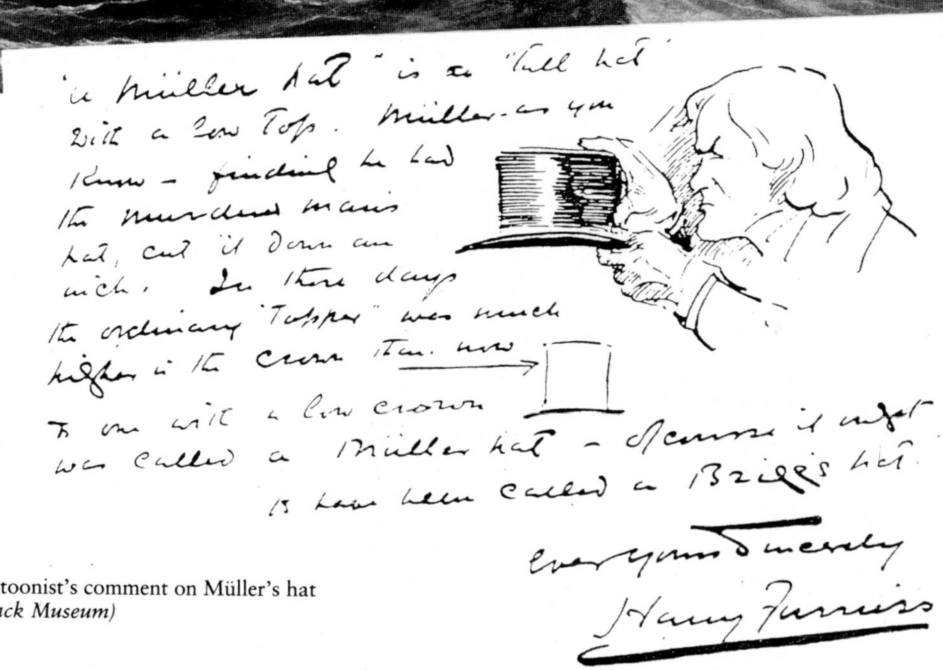

'a Müller hat' is a 'tall hat' with a low top. Müller – as you know – finding he had the murdered man's hat, cut it down an inch. In those days the ordinary 'Topper' was much higher in the crown than now → to one with a low crown was called a Müller hat – of course it ought to have been called a Briggs hat.

Ever yours sincerely

Harry Furniss

Cartoonist's comment on Müller's hat *(Black Museum)*

2 St John's Park, Blackheath, the house burgled by Peace on 10th October 1878 and where PC Robinson was shot *(Black Museum)*

Below: Charles Peace the day before his execution in Armley Jail, Leeds *(Syndication International)*

Foot: Phillips' memoir on Charles Peace with a map drawn by Peace showing the scene of PC Cock's murder *(Black Museum)*

Below left: Charles Peace 's violin *(Black Museum)*

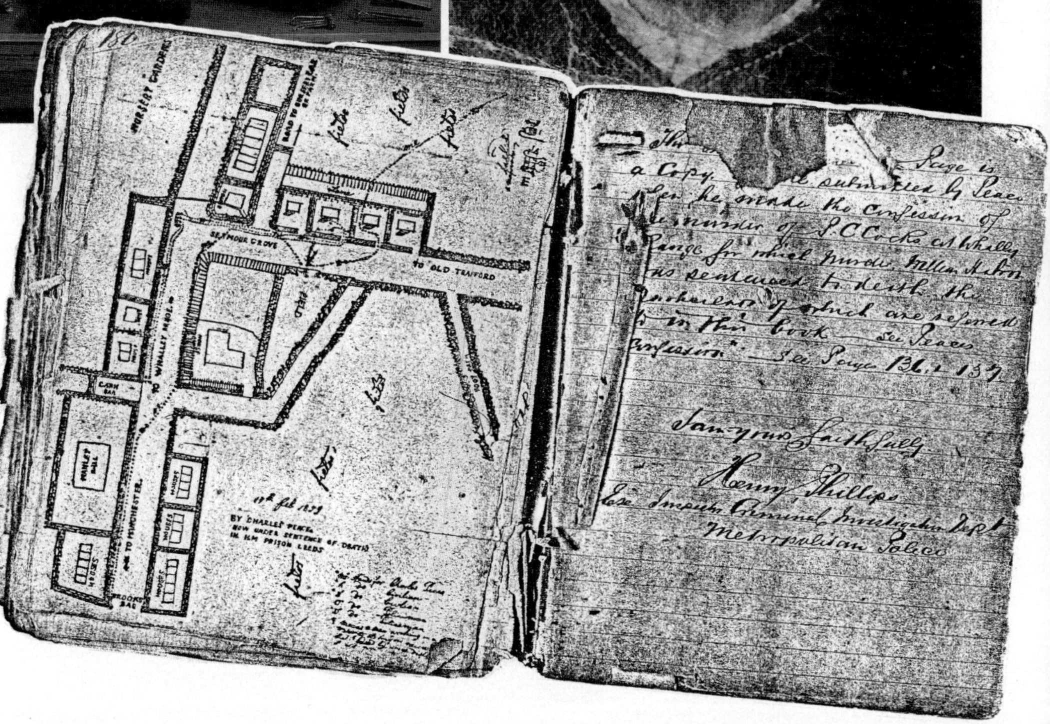

Left: John Lee sketched in court in 1884 *(Torquay Central Library)*

Below: Sketches of Miss Kate Farmer, Miss Keyse, Elizabeth Harris, Eliza Neck, Jane Neck *(British Newspaper Library)*

Above: Babbacombe, showing the Cary Arms and the Glen, where Miss Keyse was murdered *(Torquay Central Library)*

Below: Postcard from Lee to a Miss A. Gibbs (1910) *(Black Museum)*

Lee after his release in 1907, aged 43 *(Torquay Central Library)*

York on a faster ship and arrest Müller when the *Victoria* docked. No expense was spared and no legal chances taken. To identify the wanted man both Robert Death and Matthews were invited to accompany the two detectives, who were armed with all the warrants, letters and other documents necessary for extradition. Matthews's wife (she had four children) was given 30 shillings a week from the Police Fund to compensate for his absence and loss of earnings.

On Tuesday evening, at a private hearing in Bow Street magistrates' court, Müller was charged with murder in his absence and a warrant was issued for his arrest. That night, Tanner, Clarke, Matthews and Death entrained at Euston for Liverpool, from where on Wednesday, 20 July, they embarked on a steamship, the *City of Manchester*, for New York.

While they were at sea, Inspectors Williamson and Kerressey supervised further police investigations in London and unearthed some more facts, via the German authorities, about the unsuspecting suspect on the *Victoria*.

They learned that Franz Müller was born on 31 October 1840 at Langendernbach in the Grand Duchy of Saxe-Weimar. Weimar, a small town in central Germany, was celebrated for its literary associations with Goethe, Wieland and Schiller. Müller had been apprenticed as a gunsmith before getting into some money troubles in Cologne and fleeing from there to London in March 1862. He was 5′ 3″, with light-brown reddish hair and no whiskers, moustache or beard. A New York reporter described him later as having 'small, grey, inexpressible eyes'.

The *City of Manchester* reached New York on 5 August, three weeks ahead of the *Victoria*, which docked on 26 August. All the steerage passengers were summoned on deck and Müller's arm was seized by Sgt Clarke. 'What's the matter?' asked Müller. An American police officer said: 'You are charged with the murder of Mr Briggs . . .' When he failed to remember the details of the charge, Clarke intervened. 'Yes,' said Clarke. 'On the North London Railway, between Hackney Wick and Bow, on the ninth of July.' Müller replied: 'I was never on that line that night.'

He was taken to the saloon and searched, as were his belongings. Among them were Mr Briggs's gold watch and his remade silk hat, reduced by an inch or so when Müller had carefully cut out the inner band, marked with the owner's name. He had then sewn the two parts together. In conversation with the ship's officers, Tanner and Clarke learned that Müller's manner during the voyage had been 'overbearing' and that he had suffered a black eye after calling a fellow-passenger a liar and a robber. Trying to make some money, he had wagered that he would eat five pounds of German sausages. He failed, and paid up with two of his shirts.

On shore Müller was picked out in an identification parade by Death. Presumably Matthews was also involved. But the records never mention him. Perhaps he was taken ill on the voyage.

Extradition proceedings began later that day before Commissioner Newton, who sat in the United States district courtroom in New York in the capacity of a committing magistrate. Müller's extradition was strongly opposed by several German organisations and individuals in the city, who took up his cause and paid lawyers to defend his rights. Other opposition came from Yankees aggrieved by England's support of the Southern States in the Civil War. The prosecuting counsel was provided by the British Consul; Müller's counsel was Mr Chauncey Schaffer, who spoke passionately if not always pertinently and evoked a good measure of partisan applause from the spectators in the court.

He said at the start that there was nothing in the evidence to justify the commitment of the accused on the charge preferred against him. He stated that any man who came to America was presumed to be innocent of any crime. He continued:

> I do not regard the treaty under which it is sought to extradite this man as anything else than a violation of the constitution of the United States, and utterly inoperative . . . The extradition of this man is claimed by virtue of a treaty between this country and England . . . I will show that it is at present suspended after the act . . . A state of war between two nations suspends the operation of all treaties. But it may be said that there is no war between this country and England . . . There does exist what the eminent Groteus terms 'a mixed or unclean state of war' between the two nations . . . and this, as in any war, leads to the suspension of treaties . . . England cannot say she is neutral in this matter when she furnishes our rebellious subjects with vessels of war, mans them, opens her ports to them, furnishes them with arms and ammunition, and sends them forth on their errand of destruction, burning merchant ships and destroying the commerce on the seas of a friendly power. The *Alabama*, built and armed in England, and manned by Englishmen, sank and burned 120 of our ships . . . But when a man is found murdered in London, they pursue the supposed murderer to our shores and cry: 'Treaty, treaty, treaty!' They tore that treaty to pieces three years ago!

Loud applause interrupted this oration. Schaffer went on to assert that the extradition treaty was a dead letter, that 'England, to claim this man, must come into court with clean hands!' He said: 'She must not come here and ask of us to honour her justice when she dishonours her own justice, breaks her treaties, and cries peace and neutrality while at the same time she lets slip the dogs of war!' He concluded by saying: 'The pride and honour and courage of America is at stake!' Again, there was much applause.

Mr Marbury, speaking for the British Government, disposed of this argument as 'immaterial' and 'irrelevant' and suggested that the defence had spoken thus because the case afforded no entertainment – 'which the counsel is always expected to produce whenever he appears in court'. Commissioner Newton's simple conclusion was that there was sufficient testimony to commit Müller for trial. 'It is not necessary for me', he said, 'to determine absolutely that he is guilty of the crime . . . But . . . so clear and distinct is the question of probable cause that I cannot for one moment have a doubt as to the proper course to pursue. Under these circumstances I am constrained to grant the certificate [of extradition], and the prisoner therefore stands committed.'

Inspector Tanner's comments on this are contained in a letter he wrote on 28 August to Sir Richard Mayne. He said:

> It will be seen by the Newspapers which I send, also by the mail, that strong language was used by the prisoner's counsel in references to England ... When the papers are ready, I go on to Washington to obtain the warrant from the President [Abraham Lincoln] to take the prisoner home. I do not know how long it will take but I shall endeavour to leave there by the steamship *Etna* on the 3rd September for Liverpool ... Extraordinary as it may seem, strong sympathy is felt here for the prisoner and it is rumoured that an attempt to rescue him from my custody will be made ... But I shall take such steps as I hope will prevent that.

Marbury also wrote to Mayne saying that Tanner's duties had been discharged 'with such discretion, energy and propriety as to commend my unqualified approbation'.

Nothing evidently happened to interfere with Müller's return to England, and on 3 September Tanner and Clarke embarked on the *Etna* with Müller, Matthews and Death. The prisoner is said to have enjoyed the voyage: the food was superior to that given to steerage passengers on the *Victoria*, and he found time to read and enjoy *Pickwick Papers*, as well as *David Copperfield*.

The *Etna* reached Liverpool on the night of Friday, 16 September. Tanner telegraphed Inspector Williamson in London: 'Cannot come tonight. Will come by nine o'clock train tomorrow morning.' The five men stayed in Liverpool overnight, Müller in a police station. On the Saturday morning Müller set off on his last journey by train.

On his arrival at Euston Station and in London's streets he was reviled and booed by the crowd. After appearing at Bow Street magistrates' court he was removed to Holloway Prison (built in 1850). At Bow Street on 26 September he was committed for trial, a few hours after the jury at the coroner's inquest in Hackney Town Hall returned a verdict of wilful murder. The foreman portentously added: 'The jury ... will take this opportunity of expressing their dissatisfaction with the present state of railway accommodation, as affording facilities for the perpetration of various crimes.'

Before the trial began, German nationals in London and elsewhere were busy on Müller's behalf, disseminating favourable opinions to influence the press and finding evidence and an alibi for his defence, which a well-respected solicitor, Mr Beard, was well paid to prepare. The notable advocate, Serjeant Parry, was employed to defend Müller at the trial, which began in the Central Criminal Court at 10.00 am on Thursday, 27 October 1864 before two judges, the Lord Chief Baron (Sir Frederick Pollock) and his son-in-law, Baron Martin. Sir Robert Porrett Collier (the Solicitor-General) led for the Crown.

Müller, who pleaded not guilty, agreed to be tried by 12 Englishmen; and after the defence had challenged the choice of 16 of the jurors (the prosecution challenged one) the trial began. At that time the jury's names and occupations were published; and this jury included three accountants, a baker, a grocer, and a tobacconist (the foreman, Isaac Moore). *The Times* reporter noted that the accused was 'a short and slightly made young man almost boyish in appearance, and with light brown hair – neatly dressed in a plain, brown morning coat buttoned on the chest – quiet, self-possessed and respectful'. It was difficult to believe that the little tailor could have made such a savage and murderous attack on an elderly man.

In his opening speech, the Solicitor-General said: 'Undoubtedly, the evidence in this case is what is called circumstantial evidence chiefly. But I may remind you that it is by circumstantial evidence that great crimes are most frequently detected. Murders are not committed in the presence of witnesses, and to reject circumstantial evidence would be to proclaim immunity to crime.'

Serjeant Parry did his best to case doubt on that evidence by providing Müller with an alibi and implying that Matthews or some revengeful bank employee killed Mr Briggs. Matthews's alibi, as well as his manner, was somewhat vague. Having been unable at the Bow Street hearing to account for his movements on the night of 9 July, he now said he had made enquiries and established that he was at the cab-stand at Paddington Station between 7.00 and 11.00 pm. The fact that he claimed to have known nothing of the murder until 18 July (when he read the poster) also seemed suspect, especially as his wife said she knew of the murder on 11 July. Matthews's past was also aired in court: in 1850, aged 19, he had spent three weeks in prison for theft (he had stolen a boot and a spur). Parry suggested that Matthews's aim had been to incriminate Müller and at the same time claim the £300 reward. 'Do you expect a portion of the £300?' Parry enquired. Said Matthews, unctuously: 'I leave that entirely to my country – if it thinks I have done my duty.' 'Then you do expect a portion of the reward?' insisted Parry, persisting with the question as Matthews variously replied: 'If they think proper to give it' – 'If they are only satisfied with my conduct' – 'If it had been a shilling, I should have done my duty the same.' To this Parry retorted: 'I do not ask you to compliment yourself.'

Parry also pointed out that no blood-stained clothes had been found on Müller or in his room (although a rag he used to clean his shoes had some blood on it). He claimed that the little tailor could never have assailed and thrown Mr Briggs off the train in three minutes: Briggs was six inches taller and about four stone heavier. He also claimed that Mr Briggs's stick was not the weapon used, and that *two* men had committed the crime – the men seen by Mr Lee in Briggs's compartment at Bow, minutes before the attack.

Lee was, however, unable to identify Müller as one of the two, and Sir Robert Collier was able to impugn his reliability by demanding why he had not spoken to the police for more than a week. Mr Lee said lamely he had thought it 'unimportant' and a 'bother'. He said: 'I only went to Bow for a stroll.' The real reason for his tardiness and confusion was that he had had an assignation with a girl that night and did not wish his actual whereabouts to become known to his wife.

Parry's main effort was expended on an alibi. He produced an omnibus conductor who said that at about 9.50 pm on 9 July a passenger had got on his bus in Camberwell wearing a carpet slipper on one foot. And he called Mrs Jones of Stanley Cottage, James Street, off Vassall Road in Camberwell, to say that Müller was in her house at 9.30 pm: he had gone there (after leaving Hoffa at the Repschs' home) to see Mary Ann Eldred. If this was true, Müller could not have been on the same train as Mr Briggs – it left Fenchurch Street Station at 9.50. 'I had a clock in the kitchen,' said Mrs Jones. 'I looked at the clock, and called out when it was nine o'clock, and then Miss Eldred went out.' Müller arrived after that, she said, and stopped for five or ten minutes to chat.

Unfortunately, the omnibus conductor was unable to identify Müller as the man with the slippered foot. And Mrs Jones, who was 36 and lived with a Mr Kent, admitted that her two female lodgers were 'young women who receive the visits of men'. Mary Ann Eldred was a prostitute. According to the prosecution, Müller, whom Mrs Jones called 'the little Frenchman', would have known that she always went out on Saturday nights. And even if he went to Camberwell, he could easily have got there by 9.00 pm, after leaving Hoffa at 8.00 – with time enough in hand to travel back to Fenchurch Street to catch the delayed 9.45 train.

Mary Ann Eldred, who was also called by the defence, was not a convincing witness, although she supported Mrs Jones's assertion that she left the house at 9.00, before Müller arrived. She had known Müller for a year, she said, and had last met him a week before 9 July, in Cheapside. She revealed that Müller had asked her to go with him to America; he had said he had a sister there.

In his summing-up, the Lord Chief Baron remarked:

> The evidence of Mary Ann Eldred – whom it is impossible to see here without some compassion for the situation of life which she is in – counts certainly very much more in saying what she *cannot* recollect, rather than what she can . . . Then there is the evidence of Mrs Jones. And respecting her husband, I think a man who is living on the profits of such a calling as that pursued by his wife, is about the most infamous of mankind. How far the wife is some shades better than her husband is for you to judge.

Serjeant Parry might have made something of Müller's amazing carelessness in concealing the crime: he assaulted a man to steal a watch and chain but neglected to empty the victim's pockets; he left his hat at the scene of the crime and wore that of the man he had killed; both the hat and the chain he unconcernedly showed to friends; he gave the jeweller's box to the cabman's daughter instead of throwing it away; he booked the voyage to New York in his own name; and he told people the name of the ship. Serjeant Parry could have claimed that such actions were those of an innocent man, not a murderer, who would have sought to avoid, not invite, detection.

It certainly seems that Müller never expected that he would be caught, and that once at sea and then in America he would be safe. It also seems that he never intended to *kill*, but only to incapacitate Mr Briggs, in order to seize the gold watch and chain to pay for his passage to New York. In his own mind he was innocent of any intent to kill.

Parry's speech for the defence, which began on the Friday at 2.30 pm, *before* his witnesses were called, lasted two-and-a-half hours. In it he complained, as others had done, about not having the opportunity to sum up, like the prosecution, *after* all the evidence had been heard. The following year the law was altered, by 'Denman's Act', and the defence was provided with a closing speech, which was made after that of the prosecution and before the judge's summing-up.

This took place on Saturday, 29 October – two days before Müller's 24th birthday. The jury was absent for 15 minutes, returning with a verdict of 'Guilty'. Mr Baron Martin, in passing sentence of death on Müller, said: 'We are perfectly satisfied with the verdict. If I had been one of the jury, I should have concurred with it.' When asked if he had anything to say, Müller responded, speaking softly: 'I am perfectly satisfied with my judges and with the jury. But I have been convicted on false evidence, and not on a true statement. If the sentence is carried out, I shall die innocent.'

The German community now strove even harder to save their countryman from the rope. Petitions were signed, protests made about a miscarriage of justice, and a telegram signed by the King of Prussia and some German princes was sent to Queen Victoria. The Home Secretary, Sir George Grey, was likewise beset. But pleas and petitions all failed. On Friday, 11 November, at 3.00 pm, Müller's solicitor, Mr Beard, visited the condemned cell in Newgate Prison and told Müller he would not be reprieved.

A week earlier a Lutheran minister, the Revd Walbaum, described in *The Times* one of his daily visits to the doomed little tailor:

> He is reserved and uncommunicative, without, however, being in the least morose. He eats and sleeps well. Last evening he had gone to bed about 7 o'clock, and in less than an hour afterwards he was sound asleep. He usually sleeps right through the night and rises about half-past six. He attends the morning service in the chapel daily, and is permitted to take exercise in a yard adjoining his cell, attended by a warder . . . He spends much of his time reading – the Bible principally.

But it was not to the Revd Walbaum that Franz Müller turned in his final days of life. Dr Louis Cappel, pastor of the German Lutheran Church in Goodman's Fields, had also been a regular visitor. An hour and a half before the execution Cappel, while conversing with Müller, in German, urged him to declare finally whether he was innocent (as Müller had always maintained) or guilty. Dr Cappel wrote later: 'With an earnest and passive look he remained one or two minutes silent, standing before. He then suddenly cried out, with tears in his eyes, and throwing his arms round my neck: "Do not leave me! Remain with me to the last!" I judged by this that he had determined to make a confession.'

The execution was set for 8.00 am on Monday, 14 November. Calcraft was the executioner. He had had a busy year: eight people were hanged at Newgate in 1864, out of a national total of 19. This had whetted, not satiated, the appetite of the mob, whose behaviour at the execution was best described in *The Times* by two reports: one outside the prison and the other within. They wrote:

> The barriers to check the crowd were begun across all the main streets which lead to Newgate as early as on Friday last, and all through Friday night and on Saturday and Sunday, a dismal crowd of dirty vagrants kept hovering around them . . . It was, however, different on Sunday night. During the early part of the evening there was a crowd as much of loungers as of drunken men, which stood the miserable drizzle with tolerable patience, while the public-houses were open and flared brightly through the mist. But at eleven o'clock the greater part of the rough mass moved off, leaving the regular execution crowd to take their early places . . . A thick, dark noisy fringe of men and women settled like bees round the nearest barriers, and gradually obliterated their close white lines from view. Many had jars of beer; at least half were smoking, and the lighting of fuses was constant, though not more constant than the cries and laughter . . . Occasionally, as the rain, which fell heavily at intervals, came down very fast, there was a thinning of the fringe about the beams, but, on the whole, they stood it out very steadily, and formed a thick dark ridge round the enclosure kept before the Debtors' door, where Müller was to die . . . Newgate was black enough in its blind massiveness, except at one little point high over the walls, where one window in the new wing showed a little gleam of light . . . Not more than some four thousand, or at the most five thousand, were assembled. Every now and then came a peculiar sound, sometimes followed by the noise of struggling, almost always by shouts of laughter, and now and then a cry of 'Hedge.' . . . Till three o'clock it was one long revelry of songs and laughter, shouting, and often quarrelling. But about three the workmen came to finish the last barriers, and from that time the throng rapidly increased in numbers. Someone attempted to preach . . . Then, again, another man, stronger in voice, began the old familiar hymn of 'The Promised Land' . . . Another and apparently more popular voice gave out some couplet in which at once, and as if by magic, the crowd joined with the chorus of – 'Of, my, think, I've got to die' – till this again was substituted by – 'Müller, Müller, he's the man!' All these vocal efforts, however, were cut short by the dull rumbling sound which, amid cheers, shouts, whooping, clapping of hands, hisses and cries . . . heralded the arrival of the dirty, old gallows . . . The shouts and obscene remarks which were uttered as the two upright posts were lifted into their places were bad enough, but they were trifles as compared with the comments which followed the slow efforts of the two labourers to get the cross beam into its place . . . And then, amid such yells as only such sightseers could give vent to, a strong force of police filed in and took

their places, doubly lining the enclosure round the drop . . . Then, as every minute the day broke more and more clear, the crowd could be seen in all the horrible reality in which it had been heard throughout the long, wet night . . . Among the throng were very few women; and even these were generally of the lowest and poorest classes. The rest of the crowd was, as a rule, made up of young men . . . sharpers, thieves, gamblers, betting men, the outsiders of the boxing ring, bricklayers, labourers, dock workmen, German artisans, and sugar bakers, with the rakings of the cheap singing-halls and billiard rooms, the fast young 'gents' of London . . . Then, as the sun rose clearer, did the mysterious, dull sound explain itself . . . It was nothing more than the sound caused by knocking the hats over the eyes of those well-dressed persons who had ventured among the crowd, and, while so 'bonneted', stripping them and robbing them of everything . . . There were regular gangs, not so much in the crowd itself within the barriers, as along the avenues which led to them . . . Sometimes their victims made a desperate resistance . . . In no instance, however, could we ascertain that 'Police!' was ever called. Latterly, nearly fifty thousand people were crammed between the walls of this wide thoroughfare. Wherever the eye could rest it found the same dim monotony of pale but dirty faces, which seemed to waver as the steam of the hot crowd rose high. At last, when it was near towards eight o'clock, there came shouts of 'Hats off!' and the whole mass commenced, amid cries and struggles, to wriggle to and fro as the bell of Newgate began to toll . . .

Inside the prison the convict had retired to rest at half-past ten, and slept soundly for about four hours, but was anxious and uneasy during the remainder of the night. He rose at six o'clock and dressed. Shortly afterwards, Dr Louis Cappel joined the convict in his cell . . . As the hour fixed for the execution drew near, Dr Cappel administered the sacrament to him . . . The convict frequently clung to him and embraced him, observing, with tears in his eyes, that he was the only friend he had then in the world . . . About half-past seven o'clock the Sheriff of London, Mr Alderman Dakin and Mr Alderman Besley, with the Under-Sheriffs, Mr Septimus Davidson and Mr De Jersey, went from the London Coffee-house, in Ludgate Hill, where they had passed the night, to the Courthouse of the Old Bailey, where they remained until a quarter to eight. There they were met by Mr Jonas, the governor of Newgate, and by Mr Gibson, the prison surgeon, and, forming themselves into a procession, the authorities passed from the sessions-house to the gaol. The way lay through a series of gloomy passages . . . and over the graves of malefactors who had been buried there during the last thirty years. Emerging at length into an open courtyard they paused, until a door was unexpectedly opened and Müller presented himself, attended by a single warder . . . He was pale, but quite calm and collected. A comely-looking young man, he walked with his hands clasped in front of him, looking upward with a touching expression. He was dressed with scrupulous care in the clothes which he wore on his trial

. . . From the courtyard he passed into the press room, followed by the authorities. There he submitted himself to the executioner, and underwent the process of pinioning with unfaltering courage. While all about him were visibly touched, not a muscle in his face moved . . . At this trying moment, Dr Cappel approached and endeavoured to sustain him again and again. Repeating in a docile and affectionate manner words which the reverend gentleman put into his mouth, the convict more than once said: 'Christ, the Lamb of God, have mercy on me' . . . As the executioner was removing his neckerchief and shirt collar, on the arrangement of which some care had evidently been bestowed, the convict moved his head about to allow of that being done . . . Mr Jonas, the governor, approached the convict and asked him to take a seat, but he declined the offer, and remained standing until the prison bell summoned him to his doom . . . One could not help being struck with the appearance of physical strength which his figure denoted, and still more with his indomitable fortitude. Though short in stature, he was compactly and symmetrically made, and there were manifest indications of strength about his chest, arms, hands, and the back of his neck in particular. A signal having been given by the governor, the prisoner was escorted to the foot of the scaffold, the Rev Mr Davis leading the way, and reading as he went some of the opening verses of the burial service.

At the little porch leading to the gallows the Sheriffs and officers stopped. Dr Cappel alone ascended it with Mr Davis and the guilty man. The clergymen at once took their places on the line of sawdust, which had been laid to mark the outline of the drop . . . Close after them came Müller. His arms were pinioned close behind him; his face was very pale . . . He took with a steady step his place beneath the beam, then, looking up, and seeing that he was not exactly beneath the proper spot whence the short, black link of chain depended, he shifted a few inches, and then stood quite still. Following him close came the common hangman, who at once pulled a white cap over the condemned man's face, fastened his feet with a strap, and shambled off the scaffold amid low hisses. While this was being done Dr Cappel, addressing the dying man in German, said: 'Müller – in a few moments you will stand before your God. I ask you again, and for the last time, are you guilty or innocent?' He replied: 'I am innocent.' Dr Cappel said: 'You are innocent?' Müller answered: 'God knows what I have done.' 'Does he also know if you have committed this crime?' Müller replied: 'Yes. I did it' – 'Ja. Ich habe es gethan.' And these were his last words. Almost as soon as these words had left his lips, his kind spiritual guides quitted the platform, and the drop fell . . . So greatly relieved was Dr Cappel by the confession that he rushed from the scaffold, exclaiming: 'Thank God! Thank God!' and sank down in a chair . . . Those who stood close to the apparatus could just detect a movement twice, an almost imperceptible muscular flicker that passed through the frame. This was all, and before the peculiar humming noise of the crowd was over Müller had ceased to live, though as he hung his features seemed to swell and sharpen so

> under the white cap that the dead man's face at last stood out like a cast in plaster. For five or ten minutes the crowd, who knew nothing of his confession, were awed and stilled by this quiet, rapid passage from life to death . . . But before the slight, slow vibrations of the body had well ended, robbery and violence, loud laughing, oaths, fighting, obscene conduct, and still more filthy language, reigned around the gallows far and near.

The body was cut down and stripped, and after a plaster cast was taken of the shaven head, the naked corpse was placed in a rough deal box filled with shavings and quicklime. Franz Müller was buried near Greenacre and Good under the flagstones of a narrow passage within the jail, roofed by a cross-barred grating. An 'M' was carved in the stone wall above his head.

Thomas Briggs junior sent a cheque for £55 to Inspector Tanner via Sir Richard Mayne – 'as a small token of our appreciation of the courteousness and delicacy with which he conducted the case'.

The reward of £300 was eventually (in May 1865) paid to Jonathan Matthews. But most of it went to his many creditors, who had succeeded, a month after Müller's death, in having the cabman imprisoned for debt. Released from Horsemonger Lane Gaol on 17 December, Matthews called on Tanner to complain about the treatment he had received from the Government, who, he claimed, had let his wife and family starve. 'His manner appeared mysterious,' Tanner wrote in a report. 'There does not appear any truth in him.'

Some good was done as a result of this, the first railway murder: corridors were slowly introduced in most carriages and communication cords in all trains. The process was accelerated by the next railway murder, in June 1881, of a 64-year-old gentleman, Mr Gold, who was shot and stabbed on a London to Brighton train by a journalist, Percy Mapleton, and thrown out of a first-class compartment.

Müller's murder also made minor history of another sort – in men's fashion. For a while, the cut-down topper that the little German tailor had made and worn was copied by smart young men in London. It was known as a 'Müller' hat.

In 1866, a Royal Commission, set up to consider the whole question of capital punishment, presented its report. It recommended that capital punishment should only be meted out to those who had committed high treason or murder; that the laws on child murder by women should be changed; that different degrees of murder should be recognised by the law; and that public executions should cease. This recommendation was the only one to be put into effect. And the last public hanging in England – the last in Scotland had happened two years earlier, in Perth – was staged outside Newgate Prison on 26 May 1868, the year in which Sir Richard Mayne, co-founder of the Met, died.

The last man to be hanged in public was Michael Barrett, executed for his part in a Fenian plot to free two prisoners, Captain Burke and his aide,

Casey, from the Clerkenwell House of Detention. The plan was that on 12 December 1867, while Burke and Casey were taking some exercise in the prison yard, an explosion should demolish the prison wall, allowing the two men to escape. It was arranged that Burke should throw a white ball over the wall to signify his presence and readiness. The explosive device, a 36-gallon beer cask packed with about 500 lbs (it is said) of gunpowder, was parked on a dray alongside the wall. When a white ball flew over into the street, the Fenians outside had trouble with the fuse – it failed to ignite. They tried again the following day, Friday, 13 December. In the meantime, the Prison Governor had been warned that an escape attempt was planned, and had kept Burke and Casey locked up in their cells. He also put a temporary end to any prisoners exercising in the yard. At 3.50 pm, although no white ball had flown over the wall, the edgy Fenians successfully lit the fuse and retired. The resultant explosion, which was heard for many miles around, not only demolished the prison wall but wrecked some tenement buildings opposite. Six people were killed, including two children, and many were injured. Michael Barrett, arrested in Glasgow, was the only Fenian to be charged with the crime and was hanged at Newgate in May 1868, still protesting that he neither planted the gunpowder bomb nor lit the fuse.

The Fenian Society was an Irish-American organisation formed in 1848 to promote and accomplish the overthrow of British rule in Ireland and establish the island as a republic. In 1867 an attempt at a popular rising in Ireland against British authority failed and resulted in several attacks and outrages in England. Order was restored, but Fenianism continued to smoulder for many years, and some of the movement's aims and ideals were adopted by Arthur Griffiths, who founded the radical nationalist party, Sinn Fein, in 1902.

CHAPTER 6

Charles Peace

The Murder of Arthur Dyson, 1876

Murder is often compounded with theft or sex – which is to say that it frequently results from a compulsive desire to deprive, or a compulsion not to be deprived of one's desire. Another aspect of the equation is that thieving seems to be related to a low or inadequate sexual appetite or capability and acts as a compensatory surrogate for sex, providing similar thrills. The act of burglary, known as breaking and entering, is a sort of rape, a secretive unlawful penetration of private property made without the owner's consent. The metaphor is enforced by those who take weapons with them, guns or knives. When disturbed, the thief or burglar invariably suffers from instant withdrawal and runs away. But an armed, aggressive and over-sexed thief is more of a danger and has greater problems. He is so highly charged that faced with capture he is likely to explode. Such a one was Charles Frederick Peace.

His story was told in The Murders of the Black Museum, *published in 1982, since when a memoir, written by the Inspector who investigated the case, came to light, containing much original material and information. This first-person account added so much to the life and crimes of Peace that his story was worth revising, retelling and including here.*

He was born in Sheffield on 14 May 1832, the son of a respected shoemaker; he was not a good scholar, but was very dexterous, making artistic shapes and objects out of bits of twisted paper. Apprenticed at a rolling-mill, he was badly injured when a piece of red-hot steel rammed his leg, leaving him with a limp. Later on, his jaw was fractured, and this enabled him to alter his lower features more or less at will. He took part in amateur theatricals, and learned to play the violin with some flair and skill, billing himself at local concerts as 'The Modern Paganini'.

When he was about 18, in search of other excitements and reluctant to earn a living, he began to thieve. He was not too successful at first, and between 1851 and 1866 was jailed for burglary four times, with sentences of one month, four, six and seven years. When he was not in jail he wandered from town to town. In 1859 he met and married Mrs Hannah Ward, a widow with a son called Willie. He returned to Sheffield in 1872. About three years later, he set up shop in Darnall, then a village a few miles east of Sheffield, trading as a picture-framer and gilder. He was also a collector and seller of musical instruments and bric-à-brac.

In 1875 Peace was 43. He was, according to a Sheffield police description issued after the murder of Arthur Dyson – 'Very slightly built, height 5 feet 4 inches, hair grey; lacking one or more fingers of his left hand; cut marks on the back of both hands; cut marks on forehead; walks with his legs wide apart; speaks somewhat peculiarly, as though his tongue was too large for his mouth, and is a great boaster.' He looked about ten years older than his actual age, and apart from being plain ugly, he was as agile as a monkey and very strong. He was also utterly selfish, salacious, mendacious and shrewd.

Towards the end of 1875 or early in 1876 he became involved with his neighbours, next door but one, in Britannia Road, Darnall. Their name was Dyson.

Arthur Dyson, very tall (6 ft 5 ins) and genteel, was a civil engineer, employed by a railway company. He had met his future wife, a young Irish girl called Katherine, when he was in America. She was tall, buxom and blooming, and fond of a drink. They married in Cleveland, Ohio about 1866. Returning to England some seven years later, they lived for a time with Dyson's mother in Tinsley before coming to Darnall. It seems they often had rows.

Peace, commissioned by the Dysons to frame four pictures, including a portrait of Dyson's mother, became familiar with them and was soon enamoured of Mrs Dyson. 'If I make up my mind to a thing,' he once said, 'I am bound to have it.' She unwisely responded to his attentions. It seemed they visited pubs, music-halls and fairs together and that their place of assignation was a garret in an empty house between their two homes. Peace took to calling on the Dysons at any time, including meal-times, until Mr Dyson put his foot down. But Mrs Dyson continued to associate with Peace, sending him notes informing him when her husband was not at home.

In June 1876, Peace was forbidden by Arthur Dyson to call on his neighbours any more. Dyson wrote on a visiting-card: 'Charles Peace is requested not to interfere with my family.' He threw the card into Peace's yard.

Peace was much affronted. He began to harass and threaten the Dysons. 'We couldn't get rid of him,' said Kate Dyson, talking later to the *Sheffield Independent*'s reporter. 'I can hardly describe all that he did to annoy us after he was informed that he was not wanted at our house. He would come and stand outside the window at night and look in, leering all the while . . . He had a way of creeping and crawling about, and of coming upon you suddenly unawares . . . He wanted me to leave my husband!'

On Saturday, 1 July 1876, Peace tripped up Mr Dyson in the street. That same evening he chanced to encounter Mrs Dyson outside her home in Britannia Road as she was complaining to three female neighbours about the assault. He demanded to know if they were talking about him; he was told they were. Asked by him to repeat what she had been saying, Kate Dyson did so. Whereupon Peace pulled out a revolver and said: 'I will blow your bloody brains out and your husband's too!'

The following morning a magistrate's warrant was obtained for his arrest and he fled with his family to Hull, where Mrs Peace found employment as the supervisor of an eating-house.

For a time, the Dysons were, it seems, undisturbed by their former neighbour. But on 26 October, still apprehensive about Peace's reappearance – or perhaps Arthur Dyson was still suspicious about his wife's association with Peace – the Dysons moved to the other side of Sheffield, to Banner Cross Terrace off Eccleshall Road. Their furniture went ahead of them in a wagon, and when they arrived at their new home that evening to take possession of it, Peace walked out of the front door and confronted them. After he and Dyson had exchanged some remarks Peace said: 'You see, I am here to annoy you wherever you go.' Dyson reminded him that there was a warrant out for his arrest. Peace retorted that he cared nothing for the warrant, nor for the police. He then entered a grocer's called Gregory's, next door to the Dysons' house, to buy some tobacco.

A month later, on Wednesday, 29 November 1876, Peace was seen hanging about Banner Cross Terrace between 7.00 and 8.00 pm. He visited Gregory's, asking for Mr Gregory, who was out. He requested a woman in the street to take a message to Mrs Dyson, asking her to come and see him. The woman told him to deliver the message himself. He continued to loiter, and just before 8.00 pm accosted a labourer, Charles Brassington, outside the Banner Cross Hotel and began to malign the Dysons. Brassington moved away. Peace's behaviour may have been connected with the fact, as was later suggested in court, that he had had a rendezvous in the Stag Hotel the night before with Mrs Dyson. The outcome of a murder trial in Manchester was also on his mind. But more of that later.

At about 8.00 pm that evening, Mrs Dyson put her little boy, aged five, to bed. She came downstairs to the back parlour, where her husband was seated in an armchair reading, and about ten-past eight she put on her pattens, or clogs, took a lantern and, leaving the rear door open, went to the outside closet, which stood in a passage at the end of the terrace. It was a moonlit night. Peace later claimed that she left the house when he whistled for her.

Her closet visit concluded, Kate Dyson opened the door. Peace stood before her, gun in hand. 'Speak, or I'll fire,' he said. She shrieked, slammed the door and locked it. Mr Dyson, alarmed, rushed out of the rear door of his house and around the corner of the building. As he did so his wife emerged from the closet. He pushed past her, pursuing Peace down the passage, across a forecourt, down some steps and on to the pavement. According to Mrs Dyson, the two men never came to grips. According to Peace, there was a struggle. He fired one shot, he said, to frighten Dyson. It missed. 'My blood was up,' said Peace. 'I knew if I was captured, it would mean transportation for life. That made me determined to get off.' He fired a second shot, that struck the much taller man in the forehead. The shots were fired in quick succession.

Mr Dyson fell on to his back, and his wife screamed: 'Murder! You villain! You have shot my husband!'

Peace ran across the road, hopped over a garden wall and ran across a field. In so doing he dropped a small packet, containing more than 20 notes and letters and Dyson's card requesting Peace not to interfere. The notes, obviously written by a woman, said such things as: 'You can give me something as a keepsake if you like' – 'Will see you as soon as I possibly can' – 'You must not venture for he is watching' – 'Not today, anyhow he is not very well' – 'I will give you the wink when the coast is clear . . . Will sure tell you' – 'He is gone out, come now for I must have a drink' – 'Send me a drink, I am nearly dead' – 'Meet me in the Wicker, hope nothing will turn up to prevent it' – 'He is out now so be quick.'

Arthur Dyson was carried into the Gregorys' house and then into his own home, where a surgeon, Mr Harrison, found him propped up in a chair, a bullet-hole in his left temple, the bullet being lodged in Dyson's brain. He died at about half-past ten.

From then on Charlie Peace was on the run and wanted for murder, with a reward on his head of £100. He disguised the missing two fingers on his left hand by fitting a tube over that arm, to which he appended an iron hook, so that he appeared to be minus a hand and arm. He acquired the nickname 'One-armed Jemmy'. Burgling as he went, he travelled from town to town, from Sheffield to Bristol, to Oxford, to Derby, to Nottingham and Hull. During an attempted burglary in Hull, in February 1877, he was surprised by the householder, a Mr Johnson, and fired two shots at him, both of which missed.

From Hull, Peace went back to Nottingham, and there he met Susan Thompson, a widow aged about 30, who was also known as Susan Bailey, or Grey. They lived together as man and wife, and Peace supported them by committing several burglaries locally, until one day the police called at his house. He escaped via a back window and fled south, to London, where he found lodgings in Lambeth. Here Susan joined him – and so, before long, did Hannah Ward and her son, whose presence, as the police later believed, 'protected his mother from sudden death'. For Hannah 'possessed the great secret of the Banner Cross murder' – which one day she divulged to Susan Thompson 'in a bad temper'. The two women, sworn on a bible to secrecy by Peace, managed to suppress their mutual animosity and 'act the part of friendship between themselves and the man'.

The Peace household now moved to Greenwich, before settling at 5 East Terrace, Evelina Road, Nunhead, near Peckham. Hannah Ward was installed in the basement with her son. Charlie occupied the other rooms with Susan Thompson – 'a dreadful woman for drink and snuff', according to him – and they passed themselves off as Mr and Mrs Thompson. Before long she bore him a son.

The house was richly furnished, adorned with a quick turnover of other people's possessions and alive with dogs, cats, rabbits, canaries, parrots and cockatoos. As the women were always quarrelling it must have been quite a clamorous household. In the evenings Peace sometimes entertained friends and neighbours with musical soirées, at which he played a fiddle he had made himself, recited monologues and sang.

Meanwhile, he continued his trade, driving around South London by day in his pony and trap, looking for likely 'cribs' to crack, and returning to them at night with his tools concealed in a violin case. He dressed well on these outings – 'The police never think of suspecting anyone who wears good clothes', he said – and looked quite different from his Sheffield self, having shaved off his beard, dyed his hair black and stained his face with walnut juice; he also wore spectacles. He became more successful, more daring than ever, and although his exploits attracted much attention in the papers, no one knew who he was. Every Sunday he and Mrs Thompson went to church.

It seems in the end that someone grassed on him, perhaps one or other of his women. Certainly the police were out in unusually large numbers in the early hours of Thursday, 10 October 1878 in the suburbs south-east of Greenwich Park.

About 2.00 am, PC Edward Robinson noticed a flickering light in the rear rooms of 2 St John's Park. He acquired the assistance of PC William Girling and Sgt Charles Brown, and the latter went round to the front of the house and rang the door-bell, while the other two policemen perched on or by the garden wall at the rear. They saw the roving light within the house go out and a figure make a swift exit from the dining-room window on to the lawn. PC Robinson gave chase, running across the moonlit garden, and was six yards away when Peace turned and shouted: 'Keep back, keep off, or by God, I'll shoot you!' PC Robinson said: 'You had better not!'

Peace fired three times, according to Robinson, narrowly missing the constable's head. He rushed at Peace, who fired a fourth shot that missed, and as they struggled – 'You bugger, I'll settle you this time!' exclaimed the burglar – a fifth shot entered Robinson's right arm above the elbow. Undaunted and no doubt now enraged, Robinson flung Peace on the ground, seized the revolver and hit Peace with it several times. 'You bugger!' said Peace, 'I'll give you something else!' And he allegedly reached for some weapon in a pocket. But by then PC Girling, followed by Sgt Brown, had come to Robinson's assistance and Peace was overpowered.

While he was being searched, Peace made another attempt to escape and was incapacitated by a blow from Girling's truncheon. A spirit flask, a chequebook and a letter case, stolen from the house, were found in his possession, as well as a small crowbar, an auger, a jemmy, a gimlet, two chisels, a centre-bit and a hand-vice.

As Robinson was now feeling faint through loss of blood, the two other policemen took charge of the captive burglar. He was escorted to Park Row police station near the Royal Naval College at Greenwich and not far from the River Thames. There he was charged with burglary and with the wounding of PC Robinson with intent to murder. He gave his name as 'John Ward', and when asked where he lived replied: 'Find out!' Inspector John Bonney, of Blackheath Road police station, was put in charge of the case, and later that morning Peace was brought before Detective Inspector Henry Phillips, local head of the newly formed Criminal Investigation Department of Scotland Yard, the CID.

DI Phillips later wrote a vivid and as yet unpublished memoir of the case. Writing in 1899, he said that Peace's 'repulsive' appearance could be verified by the wax image of him in Madame Tussaud's – where it is to this day.

On the morning of 10 October 1878, DI Phillips and Inspector Bonney tried to elicit information from the bloody-minded burglar, who exclaimed:

'If you want to know where I live, find out! It's your business!' When he became insolent, Bonney threatened to thrash him. 'All to no purpose,' wrote Phillips.

So the two inspectors tried to trap him, using a trick not sanctioned by the police authorities.

> After the prisoner was remanded he was put in one of the Police Cells alone [wrote Phillips]. I then made up a man under my charge, and the Gaoler put him into the Cell with the prisoner. He was pushed in head foremost and very nearly fell on the top of Mr Ward. The newcomer commenced by using abusive and threatening language towards the Police Gaoler. Mr Ward then offered a little sound advice for the benefit of his fellow prisoner. He said: 'Young man, don't never kick up a row with the Police. It's a bad plan and you will always find they get the best of you.'

Unfortunately for Phillips, Peace revealed nothing about his own circumstances, other than that he had been brutally treated by the arresting policemen and charged with burglary.

Peace was then incarcerated in Newgate Prison, where he was visited by Phillips more than once. Phillips wrote later: 'He was very talkative and boasted of his misdeeds as if they were something to be proud of.' He concluded that although Peace could seem 'religious-minded' and a 'nice quiet old man', he was really 'a canting hypocrite'.

The following month, Peace was tried under the name 'John Ward' at the Central Criminal Court in the Old Bailey on 19 November 1878, charged with the attempted murder of PC Edward Robinson. The judge was Mr Justice Hawkins. Mr Pollard was the prosecutor and Mr Montague Williams spoke on the prisoner's behalf.

After a four-minute consultation, the jury found Peace guilty. Asked by Mr Reed, the Clerk of the Court, if he had anything to say before judgement was pronounced, the prisoner made a lengthy, whining speech that apparently impressed most of his listeners, except the judge. Peace said:

> My Lord, I have not been fairly dealt with, and I swear before God I never had the intention to kill the policeman. All I meant was to frighten him in order that I might get away. If I had the intention to kill him I could easily have done it. But I never had the intention to kill him. I declare I did not fire five shots. I only fired four shots . . . If your Lordship will look at the pistol you will see that it goes off very easily, and the sixth barrel went off of its own accord after I was taken into custody at the station. At the time the fifth shot was fired the constable had hold of my arm and the pistol went off quite by accident. I really did not know the pistol was loaded, and I hope, my Lord, you will have mercy upon me. I feel that I have disgraced myself and am not fit to live or die. I am not prepared to meet my God, but I fear that my career has been made to appear much worse than it really is. Oh, my Lord, do have mercy upon

> me, and I assure you that you shall never repent it. Give me one more chance of repenting and preparing myself to meet my God. As you hope for mercy yourself at the hands of the great God, do have mercy upon me, a most wretched miserable man – a man that am not fit to die. I am not fit to live, but with the help of my God, I will try to become a good man [etc].

Peace was sentenced to penal servitude for life.

The judge then called PC Robinson forward, commended his courageous conduct and recommended him for promotion and for a reward of £25. Robinson was duly promoted to sergeant, and for a time a waxwork of him stood in Madame Tussaud's beside that of Peace.

The prisoner was then moved to Pentonville Prison, which in 1878, according to Phillips, was 'a preparatory prison for all convicts sentenced to Penal Servitude. It was here they performed the first nine months of their sentence, under what was known as the solitary system'.

By this time Peace's real identity had been established, as well as the fact that he was wanted for the murder of Arthur Dyson in Sheffield. What happened was that some two weeks before the Old Bailey trial, while Peace was in Newgate Jail, he wrote a letter requesting a certain gentleman, a Mr Brion, to visit him. This Mr Brion did, and was tailed when he left the jail and returned to his home in Philip Road, Peckham Rye. Phillips and Bonney decided to call on him that night (on Saturday, 3 November), although they were 'in some sort of doubt as to who the man was'. He might have been an accomplice of Peace.

'However,' continued Phillips in his memoir, 'we took a straightforward course after inspecting the house in which Mr Brion resided, which appeared to be of a highly respectable appearance and not at all like the haunt of Burglars. We were fortunate in finding Mr Brion at home, and we were still more fortunate in finding we had met with a very respectable man, very willing to assist us in this interesting enquiry.' Mr Brion, a map-maker, had apparently believed 'Mr Thompson' to be equally respectable and had been as surprised as Mrs Brion to hear that their acquaintance was in Newgate. They had believed Peace's story that he was inventing 'an unsinkable boat', and had taken out a patent. He had explained his night-time excursions by saying that he was testing his boat on the Thames at night so that no one could observe him.

The Brions were able to tell the two inspectors where Mr Thompson lived and with whom: Susan Thompson and Hannah Ward. But their house, said Mr Brion, had 'broken up', Mrs Ward having gone to the north of England and Mrs Thompson to Nottingham. The latter, however, who had been staying with the Brions, was expected back very soon. The policemen asked to be informed, by telegram, the moment she returned.

On Monday, 5 November, a telegram came from Mr Brion, and the inspectors returned to Peckham. At the Brions' house they were introduced in the front parlour to Susan Thompson. 'She was a tall, angular-featured woman,' according to Phillips, 'with a certain amount of determination and reserve in her disposition'. She was 'the Key to the whole situation', he wrote. 'But the Key was rusty at first and required some lubrication. First persuasion was used, and then threats.'

> After two hours [wrote Phillips], we were well nigh tired of our work, which seemed so fruitless. We begged of her to tell us who the man was. She refused pointblank. I had been successful in finding a small silver watch in a bedroom she occupied, and this was brought into use when terror was brought to the front. We told her we should arrest her for receiving the stolen watch. Mrs Brion implored her to tell all she knew. She said: 'I cannot tell you. I have taken an oath not to tell you anything.' The torment she was going through began to tell upon her. I pointed out the disgrace she would bring upon Mr Brion if she was arrested at his house. She looked at me with tears in her eyes and said: 'I dare not tell you.' I said: 'You need not tell me one word with your lips – write it.' I pulled out my pocket book and handed her a pencil, and this is what she wrote: *I know that is name is not Ward is Charles Pease of Sheffield.*

Phillips continued: 'The Key had opened the door and now her conscience was relieved as to the Oath. Information as to John Ward's antecedents began to flow freely. She said: "He is the greatest criminal that ever lived and so you will find out. He used to live at Darnall near Sheffield and is wanted for murder and there is a reward for his arrest."'

Susan Thompson eventually received that reward – £100.

Inspector Bonney thought Peace was a most inappropriate name for a burglar and alleged murderer and doubted Mrs Thompson's story. But he and Phillips went off to report to the recently appointed Director of the CID, Mr Howard Vincent, who immediately, to their surprise, sent them north along with Mr Brion, 'at the Public Expense'. Phillips wrote: 'The Director knew nothing of red tape and waited on no occasion for Office rules to be complied with.'

It seems that Phillips had never been north of Finchley, and his experiences over the next few weeks, as well as Peace's character and crimes, left a lasting impression. Over 20 years later, he wrote: 'We went by the Midland Railway, all the way in the dark. The Country looked very dismal, but was lighted up by various bonfires, it being the 5th November. At Trent we separated. Bonney with Brion went on to the town of Nottingham, while I kept on with the Express and soon found myself in Sheffield.' He continued:

> It is a strange feeling of loneliness to be suddenly landed in a great City, having no knowledge of any person within its boundaries. After some enquiry I found myself at the Central Police Office. It was 9.45 pm and an Inspector was then parading the night duty men, very much after the system of the Metropolitan Police. I thought them a very fine body of men. I now introduced myself to the Inspector, and having told him I had come to Sheffield to make enquiries, something like the following

> conversation took place. 'Is there a place near Sheffield known as Darnall?' 'Yes, there is a village named Darnall near Attercliffe.' 'Have you ever heard of the name of Peace as a family living near Sheffield?' 'Oh, yes. We have been looking for a man named Charles Peace for some time – he is wanted for a Murder at Banner Cross near here. But our Chief has received some information that he died in a Coal Pit in Derbyshire.' I said: 'What is your man like? Has he lost some fingers?' 'Yes,' said he. Then I said: ' My friend, you may depend upon it that Charles Peace did not die in a Coal Pit, but is at the present time in Newgate Prison awaiting trial for attempted murder.' He said: 'You had best see Chief Constable Jackson in the morning.'
>
> I asked for a recommendation to some good hotel and I was taken to the Hen and Chickens, kept by one Tingle. Now Tingle was a man anybody could take to because he was homely, and after 5 minutes interview and a Chat, I felt I had known the man for a much longer time. Here I stayed then till after breakfast on the 6th Nov, and upon going to the Central Police Station I had an interview with Chief Constable Jackson, who died in 1898, 20 years after my first introduction to him. A finer stamp of a Police Officer I have never met. No formalities with him. Common sense was his motto before all technicalities. He at first doubted if the man Ward in Newgate was Peace. He put several Photographs of Criminals before me and I was soon able to point out the one most resembling John Ward, and then he told me that that was the portrait of Peace.
>
> However, in order to make matters perfectly clear on this point, he sent off a Police Officer to London, telegraphing to Mr Vincent, and by the time the Officer arrived at Scotland Yard, Home Office Authority had been obtained for the inspection of John Ward, who of course was identified as Charles Peace – much to the discomfort of that person. A telegram soon arrived at Sheffield notifying the result of the interview.

DI Phillips then set out to find Hannah Ward, assisted by an Inspector from Attercliffe. 'A true type of Yorkshireman', wrote Phillips. 'I have never got in contact with such men before. They seemed to have the Knack of making you feel you had known them for years.' They journeyed to Darnall – 'a wild barren-looking country, the more so in November' – and found where Hannah Ward, now aged 50, was staying, in a cottage with her daughter (by Peace) and son-in-law. Phillips wrote:

> As luck would have it she came to the door in answer to my Knock. I told her I wanted to know if she would give up the possession of the house at Nunhead, trying to make her believe that I was Agent for her Landlord. I got inside the house under this pretence and at once noticed a Clock on a Chest of drawers which answered the description of one stolen at Blackheath. The Inspector came up with the Village Constable and then Mrs Peace began to look rather discomfited. I at once arrested her upon the charge of receiving the Clock with a guilty knowledge, and

I searched the house and found property consisting of valuable wearing apparel, such as a sealskin jacket, silver plate and various articles which looked quite out of place in a four-roomed Cottage, whose real occupant was a Collier. Having packed up this property, we set out for Sheffield with our Prisoner and a very heavy bundle of goods which were never expected to find the way back to their owners, but they did.

On 9 November, having heard of Hannah's arrest, Peace wrote from Newgate to 'a gentleman of Sheffield', beseeching him to save Hannah – 'She is inesent, she knows nothing of my doings . . . It is me and not her.'

Hannah Ward appeared before the Sheffield magistrates, was remanded for a week, and some time before Christmas was taken by Phillips back to London on an overnight train and charged by him 'at Bow Street one Saturday morning about 4.00 am'. On 14 January 1879 she appeared at the Old Bailey before Mr Commissioner Kerr, charged with receiving stolen goods. She was discharged, however, on the grounds that she was Peace's *wife* – although this was never proved or established by a search of civil records (as could easily have been done) – and had acted under *his* authority.

Eight days after this, and early on the morning of Wednesday, 22 January, Peace was taken from Pentonville Prison and, handcuffed and attended by two warders, was put on the 5.15 am express from London to Sheffield for the magistrate's hearing. It was very cold: up north there was snow on the ground. Peace was very troublesome, but all went well until the train neared Sheffield.

Peace was well acquainted with the locality [Phillips wrote]. He expressed a wish to pass water, and for that purpose the window was lowered and he faced it. He was wearing handcuffs with a chain 6 inches long, so that he had some use with his hands – and he immediately sprang through the window. One of the warders caught him by the left foot. There he held him suspended, of course with the head downwards. He kicked the Warder with the right foot and struggled with all his might to get free. The Chief Warder was unable to render his colleague any assistance because the Warder's body occupied the whole of the space of the open window. He hastened to the opposite side of the Carriage and pulled the Cord to alarm the Guard, but the Cord would not act. But some gentleman in the next compartment, seeing the state of affairs, assisted the efforts of the warder to stop the train. All this time the struggle was going on between the Warder and the Convict, and eventually Peace succeeded in kicking off his shoe and he fell, his head striking the footboard of the Carriage, and he fell on the line.

The train eventually came to a halt before it reached Kiveton Park, and the two warders ran for over a mile back along the railway line and found their prisoner prostrate in the snow and apparently dead. To their relief he soon recovered consciousness, professing to be in great pain from the bloody wound on his head and dying from cold. A slow train heading for Sheffield chanced to appear and was stopped by the warders. Peace was lifted up and placed in the guard's van. The train proceeded on its way, arriving in Sheffield at 9.20 am.

> An immense crowd had assembled to get sight of this great Criminal [continued Phillips] and the excitement became intense when the 8.54 Express arrived without him. The Guard reported that Peace had escaped. The crowd were unbelieving and they suggested that the statement was a ruse to get the crowd away. But when they saw a sword and a rug and a bag belonging to the Warders brought from an empty carriage and handed to Inspector Bird, it was then generally believed that the statement was true and that Peace had escaped from Custody and that the Warders were on his track.
>
> At the Sheffield Police Court great preparations had been made for the reception of Charles Peace and the Court was crowded. All the persons required to be in attendance were present, except one, and that was the Prisoner. The Magistrate, Mr Welby, was there. Mr Pollard of the Treasury was ready with all his documents to carry out the Prosecution on behalf of the Crown, while Mr Clegg, a solicitor, was there to defend. Mr Jackson, Chief Constable of Sheffield, entered the Court in a state of some excitement and made the startling statement to the Bench that Peace had escaped from the Warders. The ordinary business of the Court proceeded, when it suddenly became known that Peace had been captured and was actually in Sheffield – although it was doubtful if he would be able to attend the Court that day in consequence of his injuries.
>
> On reaching the Police Station Peace was carried to a Cell, where he was seen by Dr Stewart, the Police Surgeon, and a Mr Hallam, a Surgeon of Sheffield. They found him suffering from a severe scalp wound and concussion of the brain. He appeared to be in an exhausted state and vomited freely, and it was with some difficulty that stimulants were administered to him. His wounds were carefully dressed and he was laid in a bed in a Cell and covered with rugs. There the little old man lay, with his head peeping out of the rugs, guarded by two Officers. During the first hour he was frequently roused and he partook of some brandy. At first, force had to be used to get him to take it, but subsequently he drank without any trouble: at the same time he said he should prefer whiskey if he was compelled to take spirit. When he was handled by his Police attendants, for the purpose of giving these stimulants, he ground his teeth, clenched his hands and appeared to be in a fit. But when extra force was used he obeyed the Officers. On one of these occasions a Police Officer who knew him well said: 'Now, Charlie, it's no use. Let's have none of your hanky-panky games here. You will have to take it.' And he did take it (A Coward you see when subdued). He next complained of being cold and extra clothing was provided for him, the object of the Authorities being of course to bring him round as soon as

possible so as to get him before the Magistrate. In a few days the Surgeon certified him as being fit to attend the Court.

In fact, the court went to Peace, and the magistrate's hearing was held on Friday, 24 January by candlelight in the corridor outside his cell.

Swathed in rugs and bandages, he cursed, groaned, complained and endlessly interrupted. 'What are we here for? What is this?' he protested. The stipendiary replied: 'This is the preliminary enquiry which is being proceeded with after being adjourned.' Said Peace: 'I wish to God there was something across my shoulders – I'm very cold! It isn't justice. Oh dear. If I'd killed myself it'd be no matter. I ought to have a remand! I feel I want it, and I must have one!'

The hearing was attended by Mrs Dyson, who had been brought back to England from America, whither she had gone after her husband's death. As the prosecution's principal witness she seemed to enjoy the drama of her situation and was evidently not put out by Peace's presence, appearance and his aspersions. When she took the oath without lifting her veil, he exclaimed: 'Will you be kind enough to take your veil off? You haven't kissed the book!' At one point he put his feet on the table. At the end of the hearing, he was carried back into his cell blaspheming.

Committed for trial at Leeds Assizes, he was taken by train to Wakefield Prison. A large crowd again assembled at Sheffield railway station to witness his departure. Professing to be helpless, he was carried from the police van by prison warders. He looked pale and haggard, despite his brown complexion, and had a white bandage around his head. 'He wore his Convict suit,' wrote Phillips, 'and very comical he looked in the cap surmounting the bandage and appeared as feeble as a Child.'

When Peace arrived at Wakefield, less sympathetic, or more astute, officials compelled him to walk unaided to his cell. There he spent the next few days dictating penitential and moralistic letters. One, on 26 January, was to Mrs Thompson.

> My dear Sue. This is a fearful affair which has befallen me, but I hope you will not forsake me, as you have been my bosom friend, and you have oftimes said you loved me, and would die for me. What I hope and trust you will do is to sell the goods I left you to raise money to engage a Barrister to save me from the perjury of that villainous woman Kate Dyson. It will have to be done at once . . . as the Assizes commence on January 28th. I hope you will not forget the love we have had for each other. Do your best for me. I should like you to write or come and see me if you can. I am very ill from the effects of the jump from the train. I tried to kill myself to save all further trouble and distress, and to be buried at Darnall. I remain your ever true lover till death.

Sue Thompson replied:

> Dear Jack, I received your letter and am truly sorry to receive one from

you from a Prison, and in regard to what you ask me I have parted with all the things in my possession. I sold some of the goods before Hannah and I went away and I shared with her the money that was in the house, and what I had, had to be sold for my subsistence as you well know. I had nothing to depend upon, and have not a friend of my own, but what have turned their backs upon me, my life is indeed most miserable. I have 2 friends who have not turned upon me for which I am most grateful. I am sorry you made such a rash attempt upon your life, for your sufferings are greater than they would have been . . . You are doing me a great injury by saying I have been out to work with you. Do not die with such a base falsehood upon your conscience, for you know I am young and have my home and character to redeem. I pity you and myself to think we should have met. In conclusion, I hope and trust you will be very penitent and that we shall meet in Heaven. Yours, etc – Sue.

On Tuesday, 4 February 1879, Charles Peace was put on trial at Leeds Assizes before Mr Justice Lopes. The prosecutor was Mr Campbell Foster, QC, and the accused was defended by Mr Frank Lockwood. The Mayor, the Sheriff, MPs and a peer were present, and the court was packed, many of the women being armed with opera glasses. Peace, wizened, but wiry and unshaven, his scarred head and hollow features bristling with thin grey hairs, sat in an armchair within a semi-circular spiked enclosure.

Mr Campbell Foster contended in his opening remarks that the shooting of Arthur Dyson was premeditated and committed 'with malice aforethought'.

The prosecution's chief witness, Mrs Dyson, although evidently embarrassed by the implications of some of the defence's questions in cross-examination, behaved with a degree of flippancy, even levity. When asked by Mr Lockwood how wide the passage was outside the closet, she replied: 'I don't know – I am not an architect.' Lockwood, bent on getting her to admit that Dyson and Peace had come to grips before the shots were fired, quoted what she had said before the magistrate – 'I cannot say whether he, that is my husband, attempted to get hold of him or not'. She now declared: 'He never touched him. He did not get close enough.' She was obdurate, although badgered by Lockwood on this point for some time. She was shown her signed deposition and he read from it: 'I cannot say my husband did not get hold of him.' 'He did not try to get hold of him,' the witness responded. 'Do you remember saying what I have read?' demanded Mr Lockwood. Mrs Dyson: 'I said he did not try to get hold of him.' Lockwood: 'Do you remember saying the words I have repeated to you?' Mrs Dyson: 'Yes. I do remember saying it, but the word "try" is left out.' 'Do you remember?' 'I can't say I do.' 'Will you swear that you did not?' 'I won't swear I did *not*, because it is written down.' 'Will you swear your husband did not get hold of him?' 'I say he did not, because he was not near enough to him.' 'Did you give that as the reason when you were before the magistrate?' 'Yes. They did not press me so hard – not as hard as you!' There was laughter in court.

Mr Lockwood pressed on regardless until the judge intervened: 'Whatever you said before the magistrate is correct?' 'Yes,' Mrs Dyson replied. But Mr Lockwood would not let go. To his question 'Did this man touch him with his fist?' she replied: 'No, the *bullet* touched him.'

He was more successful in implying that Mrs Dyson had had an association with Peace, that he gave her a ring, that she continued to meet him after her husband had expressed his dislike of Peace and had been photographed with him at the Sheffield Summer Fair in 1876. She denied that letters and notes referring to assignations were in her handwriting. She was forced to admit, when confronted by witnesses, that she had gone with Peace to a pub called the Marquis of Waterford in Russell Street, Sheffield, to the Norfolk dining-rooms in Exchange Street, and to the Star music-hall. But she denied that she bought drink at the Halfway House in Peace's name, that she gave a man called Kirkham notes for Peace, that she was ever evicted from a pub for being drunk, and that she was with Peace in the Stag Hotel the night before her husband was killed.

Throughout Mrs Dyson's cross-examination, Peace leaned forward looking at her, occasionally summoning his solicitor and whispering.

Mr Lockwood, in his speech for the defence, proposed that the shooting was accidental, that Peace's threats were meaningless and that the prosecution's principal witness was unreliable and her evidence tainted and uncorroborated. The prosecution, he said, had not established their charge. In conclusion, he urged the jury not to lay themselves open to the reproach that they had 'wrongfully taken away the life of a fellow man'.

The judge told the jury that the plea of provocation failed altogether 'where pre-conceived ill-will against the deceased was proved'.

The jury took 15 minutes to reach a verdict of guilty of wilful murder and Peace was sentenced to death. On being asked if he had anything to say before sentence was passed, he muttered: 'Will it be any use for me to say anything?'

Peace was removed to Armley Jail in Leeds where, playing the penitent, he made a full confession of all his crimes to the Revd Littlewood, vicar of Darnall. He revealed that four months *before* the killing of Arthur Dyson he had also shot and killed a police constable, in Manchester.

At the time, in 1876, two young Irish brothers, called Habron, had been accused of the constable's murder and one had been sentenced to death. Their story was also told by Inspector Phillips in his 180-page memoir on Peace.

> About 1870, four young labourers named Habron left their village home in County Mayo and in a suburb of the City of Manchester they settled down. Thomas Habron went into the service of Mr Grealey, a Farmer. The others, William, John and Frank were engaged by Mr Francis Deakin, Farmer, and there the brothers remained without further notice until the summer of 1875. They bore excellent characters on the whole and regularly remitted a portion of their earnings to the old folks at home. All that stood to their disadvantage took the form of

3 summonses for drunkenness. Two were issued in July 1876 at the instance of a young Constable, Nicholas Cock, who however seems to have made a mistake and the summons were dismissed on the 1st August 1876. John and William went to a Beer house known as the Royal Oak where they were regular customers. John drank to his safe return, while William was heard to say: 'Here's Damn the Bobbies,' adding if the Bobby did him, he would do the Bobby. John, contending that the Constable had no right to summon him, said: 'If he does, by God we will shunt him!' The landlady said: 'Why, Jack, what do you mean?' And the reply was: 'We will shift him. We will get our Gaffer, Mr Deakin, to shift him.'

The night was a dark one, and the well-to-do neighbourhood of Whalley Range with the great houses and large gardens seemed more than ordinarily deserted, and while the 3 brothers slept as was their wont in the outhouse in Mr Deakin's premises, the object of their spleen, Police Constable Cock, commenced his beat from Charlton Village along Chorley Lane to West Point, where he was due at midnight. In Charlton Lane he was met by a pedestrian, a Mr Simpson, and at West Point they were met by PC Beanland. Immediately after, the figure of a man was seen moving along in the shadows towards the garden of a house that had been in the occupation of a Mr Gratrix, and when Mr Simpson had said: 'Goodnight, Beanland,' he went into the garden where the mysterious figure had apparently disappeared and examined the door of the house. He had barely turned away again when 2 shots fired in rapid succession were heard. Hurriedly retracing their steps, Beanland and Simpson were horrified to find Constable Cock lying in the roadway, shot through the right breast. The sound of wheels was heard and a night-cart coming along, on this rude vehicle the body of the insensible Policeman was conveyed to the nearest surgery. The wounded Constable did not live long.

The local Superintendent immediately suspected the Habrons, and within an hour, in company with some Constables, had taken possession of the outhouse where the brothers slept. Promptly bidding the brothers to get out of bed, he instituted a rigorous search, ordering each man to put on the clothes he was wearing yesterday . . . By 3 am the 3 Habrons were in the cells at Northumberland St Station.

The charges against Frank Habron were dropped through lack of evidence. But John and William (the youngest brother) were sent for trial at Manchester Assizes on 27 November 1876.

The prosecution implied that Cock had been shot by one or other of the Habrons out of spite and in revenge. Various witnesses recalled various threats the brothers had made, that William had inspected a revolver in the ironmonger's, and that John had said 'shoot him' not 'shift him'. *Two* men were alleged to have been seen lurking near the scene of the crime, one of whom allegedly wore a coat and hat similar to those worn by William Habron. Although Mr Simpson described the mysterious figure he had seen as 'elderly and with a stooping gait', PC Beanland was positive that the man had walked erect and definitely resembled William Habron. Footprints found near the scene allegedly matched those made by the boots of the accused, and some percussion caps were found in a waistcoat pocket worn by William. Mr Deakin, convinced his employees were innocent, explained that he had given the waistcoat to the accused and had probably left the caps in the pocket himself.

On 28 November, the jury, having consulted for two and a half hours, found John not guilty and William guilty, adding a recommendation for mercy 'on the grounds of his youth'. William was 19. Mr Justice Lindley, who had summed up in the prisoners' favour, observed in passing sentence that he did so in the execution of his duty.

Peace had watched the whole trial from the public gallery. He kept silent. 'What man would have done otherwise in my position?' he later demanded.

The following night, in Sheffield, on 29 November, he shot and killed Arthur Dyson.

For three weeks William Habron was confined in the condemned cell. But on 19 December, the Home Secretary, Mr Cross, granted a reprieve and the sentence was commuted to one of penal servitude for life. William Habron was sent to Portland Prison as Convict 1547, where he remained for over two years – until Peace, now under sentence of death himself, chose to confess. He told the Revd Littlewood that he thought it right 'in the sight of God and man to clear the young man'.

Peace's written confession, dated 17 February 1879, and reprinted in Phillips's memoir, said that all the witnesses who appeared for the prosecution perjured themselves, except one (presumably Mr Simpson). A detailed map, drawn by Peace, was included in the confession, indicating with dotted lines the movements of the main protagonists. Peace said that about midnight, as he entered Seymour Grove, he saw two policemen and two civilians standing near a duck-pond. He crossed the road, hurried away from them and slipped into the garden of a house by the gate. When Beanland followed him in and tried the front door, turning on his bull's-eye lantern, Peace returned to the road via the garden wall, crossing the road to the other side. Cock must have seen him, for he came down the road towards the burglar, shouting at him to stand where he was.

> This policeman was as determined a man as myself [Peace admitted later], and after I had fired wide at him, I observed him seize his staff, which was in his pocket, and he was rushing at me and about to strike me. I then fired the second time. 'Ah, you bugger,' he said, and fell. I could not take as careful an aim as I would have done, and the ball, missing the arm, struck him in the breast. I got away, which is what I wanted.

At the confession's end Peace wrote: 'As a prouff of his [Habron's] inescence you will find that the ball that was taken from Cox's breast was one of Haley's No. 9 Pinfire cartridges, and was fired out of my revolver now at the

Leeds Town Hall.' He ended: 'What I have said is nothing but the truth and that is my dying words. I have don my duty and leave the rest to you.'

On 19 March 1879, William Habron was moved from Portland to Millbank and then set free with a full pardon. Mr Deakin was there to meet him, with the news that William's father had died six months earlier 'of a broken heart'. He was given £1,000 in compensation 'to ease his pain and anguish'.

Years later Phillips wrote: 'No part of the case gave Bonney and myself so much satisfaction as the release of the Convict William Habron, an innocent man.'

Charles Peace was hanged at Armley Jail in Leeds at 8.00 am on 25 February 1879.

His last days were spent in interminable letter-writing and prayer and the Christian exhortation of others. But his real reprobate self prevailed. Of his last breakfast, he said: 'This is bloody rotten bacon!' And when a warder began banging on the door as Peace lingered overlong in the lavatory on the morning of his execution, he shouted: 'You're in a hell of a hurry! Are you going to be hanged or am I?' On the scaffold he refused to wear the white hood – 'Don't! I want to look' – and insisted on making a speech of forgiveness, repentance and trust in the Lord.

Four journalists who were present wrote down his last words, spoken as his resolution left him: 'I should like a drink. Have you a drink to give me?' As he spoke, William Marwood, the executioner, released the trap-door. Peace fell: the vertebrae at the base of his head fractured and dislocated, and his spinal cord was severed. A doctor wrote on his death certificate: 'Hanging by virtue of a sentence of law.'

Peace wrote his own epitaph for the memorial card which he himself printed in jail: 'In memory of Charles Peace who was executed in Armley Prison, Tuesday, February 25th 1879. For that I done but never intended.'

In due course DI Henry Phillips donated the tube that Peace had used to cover his arm, a crucible and a collapsible ladder to the Black Museum at Scotland Yard. A hundred years later, Phillips's very informative, handwritten memoir was in turn donated to the Museum by lorry-driver Peter Coyle on behalf of Phillips's great-niece, Mrs Bell.

The Criminal Investigation Department at Scotland Yard was created in 1878. Its first Director was Howard Vincent. Under his successor, James Monro, the CID was put under the nominal control of the Commissioner and Monro became the Assistant Commissioner. To cope with the Fenian outrages in 1883–5, Monro set up the Special Irish Branch.

CHAPTER 7

John Lee

The Murder of Emma Keyse, 1884

Hanging was hardly ever an instantaneous method of execution until William Marwood, public executioner from 1874 to 1883, developed a system of execution involving a sudden drop or fall, calculated to break the victim's neck. The fall could vary in depth from 5 to 15 feet, depending on the weight, age, sex, height and physical condition of the condemned person. Previously, he or she was hoisted off the ground or platform with a noose around the neck, or left dangling when whatever supported the feet was removed. As a result the condemned were slowly strangled or suffocated, hanging by the neck until they were dead. Sometimes executioners, or even relatives or friends, hung on to the hanging man's legs to hasten the process. Some were difficult to hang; and some were cut down too soon and found to be unconscious but alive. Whereupon they were hanged again. Sometimes relatives paid large sums of money to the hangman for a quick cutting-down and permission to acquire the body straightaway. Whereupon it was secretly restored to life. Some were thus saved; others, at the last hour, were reprieved. But one man entered local and criminological legend as the Man They Could Not Hang. He was saved from death by a structural fault. Or, as he believed, by God.

Babbacombe was a small fishing village in Devon, about two miles northeast of Torquay. The largest buildings, situated between a hillside and the beach, were an inn, the Cary Arms, and the Glen, a spacious two-storey house (in those days termed a villa) with a high thatched roof, shuttered windows and a long, low colonnade or verandah facing the sea. Lawns, bowers and gardens surrounded the house, which was full of old paintings and furniture and was valued in 1884 at £13,000. But, according to the *Torquay Times* of November that year, 'the spot is a weird and lonely one in the winter, and especially unsuitable for the living-place of an aged and solitary female. The approach to it is such that no vehicles can be got near it, and the occupant has to mount a very rough and steep hill in order to reach the high-road'.

The owner was a 68-year-old spinster, Miss Emma Anne Whitehead Keyse. Her father had died when she was very young and her mother had remarried a Mr Whitehead, by whom she also had some children. There seems to have been a Scottish connection, as Miss Keyse's sister, who lived a few miles inland at Compton, was called Mrs Maclean, and a step-brother, Mr

George Whitehead, lived in Edinburgh. It seems that Miss Keyse, who had once been one of Queen Victoria's Maids of Honour (or lady-in-waiting), was a very proper, religious woman, severe, though well regarded socially, and strict with her staff. Nonetheless, she had sufficient vanity to have her grey hair dyed a reddish hue.

Two of her servants, Jane and Eliza Neck, who were both in their late sixties, had served the family for well over 40 years, Jane, the parlour-maid, since 1836. The cook was a young woman called Elizabeth Harris, who at the time of the murder was pregnant though unmarried and none too well. Her half-brother, a sturdy, not unattractive young man, was the only other servant. Said to have been a footman, he was more of a gardener and general dog's-body. He was 20 and his name was John Henry George Lee.

Baptised on 4 September 1864, the son of a yeoman farmer, John Lee had lived in a lowly cottage in Abbotskerswell, two miles south of Newton Abbot and not far from Babbacombe, until he was 15. At that age he was first employed as a servant by Miss Keyse and went to work and live in the Glen. But in due course a nearer acquaintance with the sea, with fishermen and seamen – Torquay's development was partly influenced by the use of Torbay as a naval anchorage during the Napoleonic wars and the building of accommodation for officers' families on the shore – persuaded the teenage Lee to join the Royal Navy. However, after a year and a half, he was invalided out, apparently because he had a weak chest. Bad company or example on board ship or ashore, or a criminal bent, prompted him to steal from his next employer, a Colonel Brownlow, whom he served as a footman, and he was sentenced to six months' hard labour. Hearing of this, Miss Keyse wrote a well-meaning but fatal letter to the Governor of Exeter Prison, proposing that her house would be a better environment than the jail for the youth's improvement and correction.

So it was that Lee re-entered her service in January 1884 and returned to the Glen, where he was paid 2s 6d a week.

The house's regimes revolved around religious observances and the exercise of thrift, especially in heat and light and probably food. No oil-lamps were lit where a candle would do, and no fires blazed in any grate except in the kitchen. At night the house was dark and cold. Twice a day there were prayers for all in the dining-room, and apart from attending church every Sunday, Miss Keyse also went there on Fridays; and every night, when she filled in her diary, she invariably included some religious observation or text.

There was nothing odd that we know about Friday, 14 November, except that the cook's pregnancy was making her ill and upsetting routines; that most of the household were late to bed; and that, possibly after some slating or reprimand from Miss Keyse, her young male servant was contemplating her death. Elizabeth Harris, the cook, said later:

> I saw Miss Keyse for the last time in the morning at 10.30. This was at prayers in the dining-room. Eliza and Jane Neck and me were there . . . I heard Miss Keyse's voice during the day. She was in and out. She went to church as she always does on Fridays . . . I went to bed about five

o'clock as I was ill . . . I have not been ill long. I asked Jane not to say anything to Miss Keyse about my illness as she might think more of it than was necessary . . . I fell asleep until nearly 11 o'clock. At that time one of the other servants, Eliza, came to me before she went to bed to see if I wanted anything. I stayed awake a little while longer and then went to sleep.

Jane Neck was on her feet until late that night. She filled the oil-lamps before dusk and later went around the house closing and fastening all the internal shutters and bolting the windows and doors. It was a windy night, with a strong easterly wind blowing off the sea against the front of the house. When Miss Keyse was ready – she had no supper that night – Jane summoned her sister and John Lee for prayers at about half-past ten. He had gone out, as was usual, about 6.30 or 7.00 to post some letters, and stayed out, as usual, until 10.30 or so. He said later he returned at eleven. After prayers Miss Keyse had some tea and toast, made by Jane, and at about 11.00 pm she noticed that John was in his bed and apparently asleep. He said later that he went to bed at midnight.

Lee slept in a pull-down bed in the pantry, a narrow room in a passage near the foot of the hall stairs and within sight of the dining-room door. It was separated from the passage by a partition which had a 1′ 10″ gap at the top, through which any sound, or smoke, would easily penetrate. It seems that Jane Neck entered the pantry to collect or deposit something, or to give John a message. But as Eliza also saw him in bed they may have glimpsed him through the pantry door, which was always open.

A note from Miss Keyse was later found on a table in the pantry. But it is not known who left it there or gave it to Lee. It said: 'John – You had better do some raking of the paths first and go to Compton afterwards.' This referred to a package that Miss Keyse had put together that night for Lee to take to Mrs Maclean the following morning.

Jane still had some other little domestic jobs to do, like putting a hot-water bottle in Miss Keyse's bed; she also put the house-keys on a bedroom seat. It seems that she and Eliza sat with Miss Keyse for a while, possible sewing. At about 12.30 Jane went to make Miss Keyse some cocoa, which as usual she left on the kitchen stove. It was 12.40 when she returned to the dining-room to wish Miss Keyse goodnight, and left her writing in her diary in the light of a single lamp. Just before Jane went upstairs she heard Lee coughing in the pantry.

Jane Neck and her sister slept in a bedroom on the first floor, adjacent to Elizabeth Harris's room. They were both in bed before 1.00 am, and soon asleep. 'I was not long awake when I got into bed,' said Jane.

Not long after this Miss Keyse, it seems, left the dining-room and went upstairs. Having changed into a flannel nightdress, she donned a woollen jacket and, as was her wont, came downstairs to the kitchen carrying a candle (she would have passed the pantry), and after warming the cocoa took a cup of it and a plate of biscuits up to her bedroom. She had drunk but half of the cocoa when for some reason she ventured downstairs again.

Was it then that she left the note for John Lee on the pantry table? Or was there some minor domestic matter that sprang to mind and required her attention? She was in the hall at the foot of the stairs when a hatchet struck the back of her head.

Some two hours later, at about 3.30 am, Elizabeth Harris awoke. It was fortunate that she had been in bed since 5.00 pm the previous day and was not as tired, or as old, as the Necks. Otherwise, she and they might have perished with Miss Keyse, and the murder, as was intended, never discovered. She said later: 'I was awakened by the smell of smoke. I was not woke up by a noise. There was no sound of anything but the wind. So far as I can say there was no smoke in my own room. I thought at first I would not take any notice of it. But afterwards I smelt it stronger, and struck a light. I called to Jane and Eliza three or four times before I could make them hear.'

She was slow getting dressed and out of her room. The Neck sisters were more quickly alarmed and on their feet. Pausing only to light a candle, and calling 'Miss Keyse! Miss Keyse!' they hastened in their nightdresses to her bedroom – to find a sofa, the curtains, the bed canopy and a corner of the bed ablaze. Jane Neck, thinking Miss Keyse was in the bed, tore back the bedclothes, exposing the hot-water bottle but no sign of Miss Keyse.

What happened next is confused, as is the evidence of the sisters, especially Jane's. At some point, dense smoke snuffed out the candle held by Jane. Eliza was the first to feel her way downstairs: part of the bottom steps and the banister were smouldering and on fire. But the worst blaze was in the dining-room, whose door was open, although the flames were largely obscured by the smoke. 'What's the matter?' she heard Lee say from the direction of the pantry. It seems she fetched some water from the kitchen and threw it on the dining-room flames. In doing so she stumbled on Miss Keyse's body, scorched and nearly naked, lying on its back near a couch with the fingers clenched. 'Here is Miss Keyse!' she cried. Although most of the nightdress, stockings and jacket had burnt away, the face and hair, though bloody, were untouched. Charred heaps of paper lay about and there was a smell of paraffin oil.

Meanwhile, Jane had abandoned any attempts she might have made to extinguish the bedroom fire and had retreated to the landing, doubtless coughing and choking. She saw John Lee, who was wearing (although unnoticed by her then) a blue collarless shirt, socks, and trousers with the braces hanging down. He supported her to the balustrade. 'He seemed frightened at the fire,' she said. Later, she would find that the upper part of her nightdress was smeared with blood.

Elsewhere, Elizabeth Harris, who had remained on the first floor, was throwing water on the flaming walls of a guest bedroom called the Honeysuckle room above the dining-room. She saw John Lee but said nothing to him. This room, where the bed was also badly burned, was set alight by the fire below. The police later deduced that there were five separate seats of fire: the dining-room, the two first-floor bedrooms, the hall carpet and the stairs. At the magistrates' court the prosecution would say:

In the dining-room heaps of charred paper were found under the sofa and on an arm-chair. But it was apparent that the fire could not be got to burn, and as a last resource paraffin was obtained and used, being poured over the carpets, over the table, and various parts of the room and then ignited. More paraffin was poured over the carpet in the hall . . . and over the first two stairs, which places were also set on fire.

The police superintendent would say that the dining-room was set on fire an hour before Miss Keyse's bedroom – where some paraffin oil was also scattered about. It seems clear that because the windows were all closed and shuttered and the air in the rooms so still, the flames were slow to spread and most burning items smouldered. If doors and some windows had been opened, and the wind let loose in the house, the fires would have become a conflagration and burned the Glen to the ground.

Apparently the female servants and Lee tried haphazardly to dowse the flames for as much as 20 minutes (according to Jane), before Eliza unbolted the kitchen door and sent John Lee into the windy night to fetch some help. Thinly dressed as he was he ran to the nearby Cary Arms and to Beach Cottage, calling out: 'Miss Keyse's house is on fire!'

The landlord of the Cary Arms, William Gasking, and his niece, were the first to respond. Gasking dressed himself, and equipped with a lantern, made for the Glen, from which billowed volumes of smoke. 'Well, John – what's the matter?' asked Gasking. Lee replied: 'Oh, Mr Gasking, Miss Keyse is burnt to death!' 'Where to?' enquired Gasking, and Lee led him to the dining-room. Gasking took charge. He said later:

> I went to the left-hand side of the body and said: 'Help me to get her out of this.' He began to talk about some other matter and I said: 'Hold your tongue, John! I don't want to hear anything about that.' I also told him to 'Come on!' And then he helped me to move her. John put his left hand to her arm and his right hand under her right thigh. The legs dropped down because they were limp. We took her as far as the kitchen door and then I sent John to get a carpet. I saw the wounds on the body. Her right foot was the portion most burnt. The features of the deceased were not disfigured, but all about the cut in the throat was burned.

Lee managed to drop her body in the hall, where Gasking noticed a pool of blood near the stairs. While he waited for Lee to return, a fisherman, Richard Harris, arrived at the kitchen door, followed by his wife, sister and son.

He said: 'I got there about five minutes to four . . . I asked whose the body was, and Gasking said it was Miss Keyse. I did not notice at first that the lady's throat was cut. I thought it was a burn . . . I made use of the words "What a wonderful burn in her throat," Lee being present at the time.'

He and Gasking placed the body on the piece of carpet, folded over the sides and carried it to an outhouse. 'When I left John,' said Gasking, 'I told him to look sharp and get some water.'

It was probably about now that Jane Neck opened the shutters and the french window in the dining-room and went out on to the lawn. The evidence she gave in court is confused, as she went outside more than once, but she stood there or ran about shouting 'Fire!' until Lee led her back inside. It was about then that he cut his arms deliberately by smashing some panes in the window.

Jane said later: 'The first place I saw John was on the landing. I had no conversation with him until I had been out on the lawn. He did not tell me he had cut his arm until after I had been on the lawn. He also told me he had broken the window to let out the smoke . . . I noticed that his arm was bleeding when he called my attention to it.' Lee's intention was to account for the blood-stains on Jane's nightdress, caused when he took her arm earlier on the smoke-logged landing. He must have noticed the stains and was afraid that others, apart from she, would wonder how they got there. It was of course Miss Keyse's blood, that had soaked his shirt and trousers when he cut her throat, which he tried to conceal by setting paper alight on her throat to obscure the wound. On the lawn he took Jane's arm once again, now smearing *his* blood on her nightdress. The blood-stains on his blue shirt and plaid trousers were probably not evident in the smoke and darkness to Gasking and Harris. But Lee's bare arms, with the sleeves rolled up, were more in view.

When and *how* the nightdress became blood-stained, as well as *when* the dining-room window was broken, were matters much questioned at the various hearings. Gasking later told the inquest: 'When Lee helped me out with the body I saw no stain of blood on his arms. I have examined the clothes I was wearing and can't find a trace of blood on them. If blood came off Miss Keyse's body it would have stained me as well as him. The body was as dry as a horn.' 'I did not notice any blood about her,' said Harris. Nor did he notice any blood flowing from John Lee's arms. Both men also swore that the dining-room shutters were closed when each arrived. Said Gasking later: 'I went around afterwards to the dining-room window, and saw that one of the panes of glass was broken. The outer shutters were opened and fastened back . . . Had the inside shutters been open the wind would have blown in violently . . . I asked Lee when he broke the glass and he told me it was before he called me up. I also asked him how he did it, and he said: "With my fists."'

In fact he must have cut his arms *after* Gasking's arrival. And several panes of glass were broken, not one. Lee probably closed the *inner* shutters, allowing some smoke to escape, when he took Jane back to the dining-room.

By this time, further helpers had arrived, including four coastguards and some fishermen. Firemen from the local volunteers were prevented from bringing their equipment to the scene because of poor access and the steep hill behind the house. Water was collected from a well, from taps and the water-butt; and a pole was used to bring down smouldering sections of ceiling. This, and a handspike, were fetched from a woodshed by Lee. He also produced a hatchet on request. Witnesses would later aver that the hatchet appeared very quickly – the implication being that it was already in the house.

By 5.00 am the various fires had been extinguished and about this time the police began to arrive, some summoned by Lee. The ensuing investigation was conducted by Police Sergeant Nott, assisted by three PCs.

Their arrival may have prompted Lee's departure from the Glen at 5.15 am, although he had already been told to go to Compton House by Jane Neck, to tell Mrs Maclean about her sister's death. Whether he took Miss Keyse's package with him is unknown. He put on an overcoat, which was marked by his bleeding arms, and, carrying a lantern, set off up the hill.

On the way he encountered an elderly chimney-sweep, George Russell, who thought at first, as he told the inquest, that Lee was a policeman. Russell was heading for Sir Frederick Ryden's house and later recalled the ensuing conversation.

'Holloa!' called Lee, holding up his lantern. He told the sweep he was going to Captain Maclean's house to tell them Miss Keyse had died. 'Is she really dead?' asked Russell. 'We should all have been burnt to death,' said Lee, 'if it hadn't been for my sister.' 'How did she know about it?' 'She smelt smoke, came downstairs and saw the sofa afire in the dining-room.' 'Is that all?' queried Russell. 'Was there any lamp capsized?' 'No,' replied Lee. 'There was no lamp or candle . . . I'm very sorry for it. But as she's dead we shall never know how it occurred.' The two then continued on their separate ways.

Some time after half-past five, Mrs Maclean's maid, Mary Blatchford, heard someone knocking at a door. 'Oh, Miss Blatchford!' called Lee. 'Come down! Miss Keyse's house is burning!' She told the inquest later:

> I then opened the housemaid's door and went into her room and spoke to Lee through the window. I asked him if it was much, and he said the dining-room was burning. I asked him if the engine was there and he said it was sent for. I said: 'Where is Miss Keyse?' and he did not answer me for a moment. But then he said: 'Miss Keyse is hurt.' I said: 'Where is she?' And at last he said: 'Her's dead.' I said: 'No! It isn't possible!' And he said: 'Yes, her is, and you must tell Mrs Maclean.' I said: 'I can't tell her!' And he said: 'You must. Jane told me to come and tell you, and you must tell Mrs Maclean.'

The cook, Ann Bolder, also talked to Lee, who told her: 'Miss Keyse's house is on fire and she's burnt to death.' The cook saw that his arm was bleeding and he told her he had cut himself breaking glass to let the smoke out.

The next person whom Lee spoke to was PC Boughton, who had arrived at the Glen at about 5.30 am and been told to guard the outhouse in which Miss Keyse's body lay. He was there when Dr Herbert Chilcote of St Marychurch carried out an initial examination of the body, concluding that Miss Keyse had been hit on the head before her throat was cut and her body partly burnt after death.

Boughton said later:

> At 6.15 I saw John Lee coming down the hill towards the house. I asked him where he had been and he said: 'I've been to Compton. Isn't this a bad job?' I said: 'Yes, it is.' Lee said: 'Isn't my arm bad?' I said: 'What's the matter?' And he replied: 'I cut it in breaking the dining-room window to let out the smoke.' I told him it was a foolish thing to do, and he

> said: 'I was obliged to do it. The smoke was so thick, I couldn't find my way back to the door.' At nine o'clock I saw him again. He was shaking very much and I said: 'Hallo, old man – you're feeling the cold.' He replied: 'So would you if you'd been running about all morning with only your shirt and trousers on.' He added: 'Good God! That ever such a thing should happen! I've lost my best friend.' I said there was no doubt about that, and asked him if he had heard anything during the night. He said: 'No. I was dead asleep, and the servants had great trouble to wake me . . .'

This was not what Jane and Eliza Neck would tell the inquest. But it was probably what Lee told the police superintendent, Captain Douglas Barbour, who began his investigation of the premises and of the circumstances surrounding Miss Keyse's death, when he reached the Glen at 7.00 am on the Saturday morning.

At 8.00 am Dr Chilcote, back in his St Marychurch surgery, was visited by the injured John Lee, whose cut arms had by then been washed and bandaged at the Glen by his half-sister, Elizabeth Harris. Chilcote noted that Lee's right arm was punctured, and that there were two circular wounds 'about the size of a florin' on his left forearm. He opined later that 'they might have bled a good deal'.

Captain Barbour also inspected John Lee's injuries, as well as his bloodstained clothing. An attempt had been made to wash out blood-stains on Lee's trousers. Apart from the pool of blood in the hall, there was blood on the handles of two hall doors, on the glass of the broken windows, and blood smeared or spattered elsewhere, in and out of the house. There were marks of blood on the hall carpet near the stairs, as if a knife had twice been wiped on it. There was blood on an empty oil-can found in a pantry cupboard, to which access was limited when the bed was pulled down. The can's cork lay on the pantry floor. And there was blood on a knife in a pantry drawer. The knife had been used by Miss Keyse when gardening and had been kept in the hall by a small whetstone. It transpired that she must have sharpened the blade that would be used to cut her throat.

In her bedroom Sergeant Nott found a match on the carpet, similar to those in a box of matches found on Lee, along with some letters, when he was searched. Most damning of all was the smell of paraffin which the police noticed, as others had done before, emanating from various items, like the hall carpet and some dining-room furniture; from the burnt shreds of Miss Keyse's nightdress; and from the trousers and socks of John Lee.

Apart from all this, it was evident that none of the windows or shutters or doors had been forced open by an intruder. The arson and murder had been committed by someone within the house.

That morning, when the police investigation ended, Captain Barbour and Sgt Nott cautioned Lee in the pantry where he had been detained, guarded by a policeman. Lee was informed that he would be taken into custody on suspicion of murder. 'Oh, on suspicion?' he said. 'Aye. That's all right.'

The arrest and the crime created an immediate sensation in Babbacombe, in Torquay, in Exeter and beyond.

The inquest, before a jury, opened on Monday, 17 November in the music room of the Glen at 11.00 am. The room, said the *Torquay Times*, was 'a pleasant apartment, overlooking the sea and furnished with rare pictures and old china'. The county coroner, Sidney Hacker, addressed the jury, who were then shown over the house by Sgt Nott and were also allowed to view the body of Miss Keyse laid out in a bedroom. Everyone then moved to the town hall in St Marychurch and the inquest resumed at about half-past twelve. The room was crowded; few spectators had seats, these being reserved for the coroner, certain gentlemen, clergymen, local dignitaries, and the witnesses. Lee was brought from Torquay police station in a cab. 'He was trembling violently, and looked pale and distressed', said the *Torquay Times*.

The evidence of the first witness, Elizabeth Harris, was interrupted by the arrival of George Whitehead, Miss Keyse's step-brother, from Edinburgh. Throughout the inquest, John Lee was allowed to question witnesses, which he did with some vigour, concentrating on Elizabeth Harris and William Gasking, and disputing minor facts. Jane and Eliza Neck answered the coroner's many and confusing questions as best they could; Jane said Miss Keyse had encouraged Lee to emigrate and had lent him some money. The sisters were followed by Dr Chilcote. He reported on the post-mortem examination of the body that had been carried out that morning by him and Dr Steele. Chilcote said the skull was fractured in two places, that the body was scorched mainly on the feet, chest and hands, and that the throat had been cut with great force, so much so that the knife had notched the vertebrae. He thought a hammer or knob-stick might have caused the blows on the head. At half-past seven the inquest was adjourned.

It resumed on Tuesday at 11.00 am. The *Torquay Times* reporter noted that the prisoner 'smiled ostentatiously and tripped up the steps with a jaunty air. Sgt Bastin had him in charge. The prisoner's sweetheart, Kate Farmer, was sitting near the jury'.

This time, Gasking and the other fire-fighters gave evidence, as did the chimney-sweep, Mrs Maclean's maid and cook, and Dr Steele, who deemed that Miss Keyse died from loss of blood and was 'not quite dead' from the blows on her head when her throat was cut. If this had happened first, he said, her blood would have spurted, instead of flowing out 'quietly'. He found *three* wounds on the head, two of which had fractured the skull. The third, he said, was 'a large square wound', which was probably effected by the base of a hatchet he had previously seen. It was shown to him again. The blade had, he thought, caused the other two wounds. This contradicted some of Dr Chilcote's evidence. But Steele was believed, and the hatchet, along with the clothes that Lee had worn, were sent to London to be examined by experts.

A surprise witness was a postman, William Richards, who had known Lee for six years. He revealed that two months earlier he had spoken to Lee in the grounds of one of Miss Keyse's other properties. Lee had a rake in his hands.

'Hard at work?' asked Richards. Lee said he was tired of his job. He said: 'If the Missis doesn't get me a good job soon, she'll bloody soon wish she had.' He added: 'I will put an end to one in the house before I leave.' 'You had better be careful, Jack,' said the postman. 'If anyone gets hold of your words, you'll be locked up.' 'I don't care,' said Lee. On another occasion, when the two of them met at the Glen's back door, Lee was carrying a stick with a black knob at one end. 'You might as well give me that,' said Richards. 'No,' replied Lee. 'It's the one I carry. It would give anyone a hit on the head, wouldn't it?' 'I shouldn't like to have one from it,' the postman replied.

John Lee stood up to question Richards about these remarks, demanding: 'Are you certain these words were spoken?' To which Richards said: 'Yes.' Lee put other questions about the stick, concluding: 'Well, I threw a stick into Mr Horne's garden when I was walking out with a young woman, and if they find the stick, you'll be able to know whether it was the one or not . . . Are you certain of the words?' 'Yes.' 'Very good. They weren't spoken by me.'

He sat down, and the inquest was adjourned until the Friday of the following week.

On Wednesday, 19 November, the magistrates' hearing at Torquay Police Court began and was adjourned for six days. A solicitor, Mr R. G. Templer, appeared on Lee's behalf. Much of the hearing was taken up by the two doctors' evidence, concerning wounds, weapons, clothing and paraffin oil. That afternoon Sgt Nott visited Lee's girlfriend, Kate Farmer, at Ellacombe. She had been seen wearing a diamond ring; and a valuable diamond ring had vanished from one of Miss Keyse's fingers since the fire. But it was soon proved that the ring being worn by Kate Farmer had belonged to her mother, who had recently died. Kate was still in mourning and wearing black.

So were those who attended the funeral of Miss Keyse on Thursday afternoon. Mr Gasking was the undertaker. The remains were enclosed in three coffins: what was called a shell, then a leaden coffin, and a coffin of polished oak, bright with brass fittings. The *Torquay Times* reported:

> A strong body of bearers conveyed the coffin up the ascent, and placed it in the hearse . . . Numerous crosses and wreaths had been sent to the house, and these were laid upon the coffin . . . They were mainly composed of white chrysanthemums and dahlias and arum lilies . . . At the head of the procession were a number of Babbacombe and St Marychurch tradesmen, and next in order were 16 bearers – fishermen and others, four coastguards . . . Some 30 carriages composed the main body of the cortege, at the sides of which hundreds of the general public walked. The blinds of all the houses were drawn.

Mr Whitehead, Jane and Eliza Neck led the mourners at the church, and after 'a solemn choral service', Emma Keyse was laid to rest in the family vault.

The inquest resumed on Friday, 28 November. The magistrates had intimated that the coroner was turning his inquiry into an unnecessarily lengthy judicial investigation – a point that also aggrieved Lee's solicitor, Mr Templer, who suggested that the object of the inquest was only to ascertain the cause of death. Mr Hacker was unmoved, and responded by saying that as the Government analyst, Dr Stevenson, could not come to St Marychurch until Monday, he would continue with the inquest then. In the meantime he questioned Sgt Nott, Captain Barbour and PC Boughton in some detail. Lee was not present, to the disappointment of the large crowd outside the town hall. His behaviour had been so indifferent and disrespectful ten days earlier that he stayed in jail – partly for his own safety, as he had also antagonised the crowd by making faces at them through an ante-room window, and even looping a window-cord around his neck.

Mr Hacker also had an ace up his sleeve, and was determined not to be deprived of the pleasure of playing it. He recalled Elizabeth Harris. Questioned by him, she said:

> Some months ago I had a conversation with John Lee. We were talking and reading in the kitchen. I said: 'Suppose Miss Keyse won't give you a character.' He said if she wouldn't, he would level the place in ashes to the ground. I said: 'Don't burn me with it,' and he said he would let me know . . . On 28 October I had another conversation with Lee in the kitchen. He came in and sat down crying. I asked him what he was crying for and he made no answer. He afterwards said that Miss Keyse was only going to pay him two shillings a week. I said I thought the agreement was for 2s 6d and he said there was no agreement. He grew very angry and said he wouldn't stay there another night . . . He said he would have his revenge, and that on another occasion, when Miss Keyse had been grumbling at him, if she had been near a cliff, he would have pushed her over.

This caused a sensation. When the coroner asked the pregnant young cook why she had not said this before, she replied: 'I tried to screen him. Now I've told the whole truth.' She revealed, with apparent reluctance, that Lee had said something about setting the house on fire and going up on the hill to watch it burn.

On the fourth and final day of the inquest, on Monday, 1 December, the medical expert from Guy's Hospital in London, Dr Stevenson, gave a detailed description of his findings, with regard to the articles sent to him for analysis; the hatchet, the gardening knife, the oil-can, Jane Neck's bloody nightdress, Lee's blood-stained shirt, trousers and socks, a lock of the victim's hair. He had found blood on all the items, and mineral oil on Lee's clothes. Grey hairs with a reddish tint found on his socks matched the piece of Miss Keyse's hair.

Sgt Nott and Jane Neck were briefly recalled and the coroner then indulged himself with an extensive summing-up, lasting over an hour. The jury retired at 2.20 pm. Half an hour later they returned and the foreman declared: 'We find unanimously that the deceased . . . was murdered . . . by the prisoner, John Lee, by striking her on the head with some blunt instrument and afterwards cutting her throat with the knife found in the pantry drawer, which is stained with human blood.'

Twenty minutes later, Dr Stevenson, who had to return to London, repeated his evidence before the magistrates in Torquay. This hearing was resumed on the Tuesday, with an opening by Mr Isidore Carter for the prosecution, followed by frequent cross-examining of witnesses by Mr Templer, who also objected to an artist sketching the accused. Lee glared at Elizabeth Harris when she repeated her evidence; and when she sat down after signing a transcript of what she had said, Lee stared at her 'with so stern an expression on his face that she burst into tears and had to leave the court'.

On the third day of the hearing, John Lee was committed for trial at the next Devon Assizes on two charges, of arson and murder. As he was removed from the court, he laughed.

Many years later, PC Boughton would recall the journey he made with Lee and another policeman from Torquay to Exeter Prison, setting off at 6.00 am. He told a reporter:

> The police feared that there might be a disturbance if he was seen by the public, and consequently we did not go by the railway to Exeter. Instead, we drove the whole distance in a carriage drawn by a pair of fine horses. I remember well it was a beautiful morning: the air was fresh and invigorating, the sky a lovely blue, and all around was a splendid picture, even though we had reached the winter . . . We had a drive which in any other circumstances would have been the most delightful conceivable, right away over Haldon, through Chudleigh, into the city. We stopped at Chudleigh for refreshment, but no one knew that Lee was one of our number . . . On reaching Exeter we had to pass along High Street. There we saw the newspaper placards, and the accused man, looking out of the window, read them aloud – 'Babbacombe Murder: Prisoner before the Magistrates' – without the slightest comment upon them. That was the only reference he made to the crime . . . He was a powerful young fellow . . . He gave us no trouble at all.

The trial of John Lee was held in Exeter Castle before Mr Justice Manisty, with Mr Collins, QC, and Mr Stonehouse Vigor prosecuting, and Mr Molesworth St Aubyn leading for the defence. The trial began on Monday, 2 February 1885.

The *Torquay Directory* said that the prisoner 'wore his usual air of indifference. His appearance was somewhat improved; his hair was brushed and trimmed, and he wore a coat of a dark grey mixture'. Elizabeth Harris, looking 'much careworn', was offered a chair but did not take it. As with other witnesses, her evidence was a repeat of what had been said before. The jury were lodged in the White Hart Hotel overnight, and when the trial resumed on Tuesday, Lee resumed his place in the dock with 'almost serene indifference', although on the Monday he had occasionally appeared uneasy at some things that were alleged and had sourly smiled when some witnesses contradicted themselves. Sgt Nott was the first to give evidence, for nearly three hours, and it was he who read aloud the contents of two letters, written by the accused and his girlfriend, Kate Farmer, who was not at the trial, although she attended the inquest. The letters are remarkable for their literacy and the honesty of the sentiments expressed.

Lee wrote from the Glen on Friday, 10 October:

> My dearest Katie – I write to tell you I am very unsettled in what I am going to do in my future life. I am tired of service, and I am going to look out for something else to do, which might not be to your liking. And, my dear, don't let me keep you from going anywhere that will be for your good. My dear, you may get a better chance going away, and we may not be always the same as we are now, in love. I implore you, if you think we shall not come together, let us break off our engagement before it is too late. I am beginning to love you so much that it will break my heart if we should leave in time to come. So let us break it off at once. My dearest, let what we have going by die out of our thoughts, but our love never can. My dear, you have been the kindest I ever met with in my love and all things . . . If I had kept your company when first I seen you, I would have married you and made you happy. But I am unsettled now, and don't know what my fate may be. Goodbye, my sweetest love, from one who will ever love you the same. John Lee.

She replied on Tuesday:

> My dearest love – Your letter to hand, which has caused me the greatest pain and grief. What can you possibly mean by telling me one time you will leave me, and then writing to know if I wish to break off the engagement? I cannot make it out, as you are undecided as to what you intend to do for the future. Are you also undecided about me? I tell you now . . . that our engagement shall not be broken off with my consent. As to what you intend to do in the future, if it was your lot to crack stones in the street, and would ask me to be your wife, I would not say no. Have a little pity for me, and think how dearly I love you. Perhaps if I had loved you less you might have valued me a little more . . . Do you think I wish you to marry me before you see your way clear? No, my darling, I am quite prepared to battle my way in the world till you think fit to make me your wife. I will never be the one to grumble at waiting for you . . . Jack, I think if we part you would be the cause of grieving me to death and breaking my heart. After what you said on Sunday I never dreamt of your writing me now in the same strain as your last letter was written in. But never mind, I freely forgive you. At the same time I will not give you up. My mother will naturally come into your mind. Would to God it had been my funeral you went to instead of hers. Then I should never have got your letter, and you would never have written it. She was my only friend, but I have always depended upon you to be something more than a friend. You have been my chief support in all my troubles

> . . . Grant my last request by coming down tomorrow evening. Accept my fondest and truest love, and believe me ever your true love, Katie Farmer. Please excuse this scrawl, as I am very unwell today.

The trial ended on Wednesday, 4 February. Mr St Aubyn, for the defence, suggested that the cook's lover might have been the murderer and that she would have had the greatest inducement to protect him and blame someone else. John Lee was found guilty and sentenced to death. The judge remarked on his calmness. Lee replied: 'Please, my lord, allow me to say that I am so calm because I trust in my Lord, and He knows I am innocent.'

In the condemned cell in Exeter Prison, Lee continued to confuse people by his apparent indifference. The *Western Morning News* reported:

> His health was not visibly affected either by his confinement or the anticipation of his fate. He partook of his meals with heartiness and regularity and, in short, evinced little of the depression which would be naturally looked for in the case of one so situated. When visited by his mother and other relatives his demeanour was by no means indicative of a man who realised, much less dreaded, the approach of death by hanging. While persistently asserting his innocence he assumed a cheerfulness, and even a jauntiness of manner, which to his Friends was not less painful than surprising. In bidding his last farewell he betrayed not the slightest emotion – not even when his grief-stricken mother finally embraced him and reluctantly withdrew from his cell.

The execution was fixed for Monday, 23 February. On the Friday before this, the new public executioner, James Berry, travelled from his home in Bradford to Bristol, where he lodged overnight, and on Saturday morning entrained from Bristol to Exeter. Arriving at the prison at noon, he signed the Register Book, saw the Governor and had lunch in the town before being shown his bedroom, a room in the prison hospital. Accompanied by two warders, he then made his inspection of the place of execution. It was a coach-house, in which the prison van was usually kept. From a high beam and a bolt hung an iron rod with a hole at the end, to which the rope would be attached. Below, a double trap-door in the stone-flagged floor opened on to a pit about six feet wide and eleven feet deep. A lever, when pulled, drew back the bolts that held the trap-doors in place, releasing them to fall down against the walls of the pit. Berry tested the apparatus twice and was satisfied that it worked, although he complained to the Governor that the trap-doors were only an inch thick instead of four, that the ironwork was frail, and that springs should be fixed in the pit to prevent the fallen doors from rebounding. The Governor agreed to put these matters right.

We do not know where Berry went or what he did in the way of pleasure on Saturday night. Sunday he spent within the prison, mainly in his room, going to bed at about 9.45 pm. That night it rained, as it had on Saturday night.

On the Monday morning, Berry rose at 6.30 and an hour later entered the coach-house, where he tied a suitable length of rope to the overhead rod and made other preparations, like positioning the white cap and straps to pinion the condemned man's legs. He did not try the trap-doors again, as they had functioned adequately in his Saturday afternoon tests.

Berry has left us two accounts of the execution, in a letter to the Under-Sheriff of Devon, Henry James, dated 4 March, and in his autobiography. But his descriptions are somewhat partial and compressed. The fullest and most objective account of what happened is probably that of the *Western Morning News* reporter, who witnessed the extraordinary and harrowing events of the attempted execution of 20-year-old John Lee.

> At five minutes to eight the reporters, ten in number, were stationed within the main corridor of the building at a point to be passed by the culprit . . . A few seconds later the procession, headed by the Chief Warder [Mr Rainford] entered the corridor. The Chaplain [Revd J. Pitkin] and the Schoolmaster [Mr Libby] came next and were immediately followed by Lee, who walked with pinioned hands between a couple of warders. The Prison Surgeon [Mr Caird] and the Governor [Mr Cowtan] also accompanied the procession, while other warders, and beside them Berry, the executioner, brought up the rear. The slow and deliberate tread of Lee and his companions, the tolling of the prison bell, added to the impressive tones of the chaplain as he repeated portions of the burial service, combined to make the occasion one of deep solemnity. The look of the doomed man . . . bore no signs of anything like fear. He walked with firmness and with head erect . . .
>
> The scaffold, which was the same as that employed in the execution of Anne Tooke about five years ago, had been removed to another part of the building. It was sunk into the ground and formed, in fact, the flooring of a small brick shed . . . The gloomy and repulsive character of the gallows was, if possible, intensified by its enclosure within brick walls. As Lee walked into the building and . . . placed himself on the fatal planks, there was no faltering or sign of fear. He cast a glance at the rope above him, as if to assure himself that its fastenings were perfectly secured, and then inaudibly muttered something to Berry as the latter functionary adjusted the noose around the culprit's neck. There was even a dash of bravado in the unhappy man's demeanour as he glanced at the ghastly paraphernalia of death. A white cap was, in the usual manner, placed over the head and face of the convict, and as the closing words of the burial service died away on the lips of the chaplain, Berry, at a given signal, drew the lever. The only response was a grating sound and a slight movement of the trap . . .
>
> A second and third attempt were made to draw the bolt, but with no more success than attended the first effort. Something was evidently wrong, and Berry, assisted by some of the warders, made an examination of the apparatus, having in the meantime withdrawn the rope and cap from the culprit's neck and face and moved him a little forward. In this terrible position Lee never flinched, but stood erect as before . . .

Not so with the officials, whose hurried movements and pale faces betrayed signs of deep anxiety and even terror. The apparatus having again been prepared, Lee's legs were once more pinioned and the rope and cap adjusted. Again the fatal signal was given, and the loud click of the lever once more startled the witnesses to this terrible scene.

The bolt having once more defied the repeated efforts of the hangman, Lee was freed from the fatal noose and removed, this time to the back of the building . . . By this time the convict had become an object of the supreme sympathy of every man present. Still seemingly unmoved . . . the condemned man surveyed the preparations which were going on before him. After a suspense of several seconds he was once more placed, and Berry ran hurriedly to the back of the shed to drop him. As the bolt again and again refused to yield, Berry made a desperate effort to force the trap down by stamping it with his feet . . .

As the convict had once more to be set aside, a feeling of inexpressible horror . . . seemed to seize everyone present. After a hurried conference of the officials he was conducted to the interior of the prison. In the meantime the services of a carpenter were procured, and by the process of planing, it was sought to remedy the cause of previous failures. This occupied something like five minutes, when for the fourth time the condemned man was placed in readiness for execution . . . The apparatus seemed, if possible, more rigid than ever . . . and Lee was accordingly returned to the cell from which he had been taken . . . The great strain upon him . . . was followed by a certain amount of physical prostration. The Governor assisted him to his cell and offered him stimulants, but he pointedly refused.

So began the legend of The Man They Couldn't Hang. A white dove was said to have perched on the scaffold before the execution began. Lee is said to have cried: 'Oh, God – help me!' He himself claimed to have dreamed the previous night that he would not be hanged and that what happened was a miracle. His incredible survival was also seen as a sign of his innocence.

What was extraordinary – as revealed in Berry's account – was that when Lee was removed from the trap-doors they functioned well enough. Berry wrote: 'I worked the lever after Lee had been taken off, drew it, and the doors fell easily. With the assistance of the warders the doors were pulled up, and the lever drawn a second time, when again the doors fell easily.' He also said: 'It was suggested to me that the woodwork fitted too tightly in the centre of the doors, and one of the warders fetched an axe and another a plane.' A crowbar was also brought. Berry said the Governor and Mr James were 'almost frantic'. The chaplain fled, it seems, after the third attempt. He said later: 'A great noise was heard, which sounded like the falling of the drop. But to my horror, when I turned my eyes to the scaffold, I saw the poor convict standing upon the drop as I had seen him twice before. I refused to stay any longer.'

Legend and most writers say that three attempts were made to hang John

Lee. Berry implies there were two attempts. But the reporter's account indicates *four*. Legend, however, likes the number three.

The distraught officials decided to defer the execution while the Home Secretary's instructions were sought, and the reporters left the prison to tell their astonishing tale to the crowds of people still outside, who had wondered why no black flag was raised half an hour ago. That night a reprieve was granted on humanitarian grounds, and as 'it would shock the feelings of everyone if a man had four times to bear the pangs of imminent death'. Lee's sentence was commuted to penal servitude for life.

What happened that morning, other than a miracle? Berry blamed the mishap on defective ironwork and on the doors, which should have been heavier, he said. He discounted the supposition in the prison that the woodwork had become swollen in the damp produced by two nights of rain, and that the doors jammed when stood upon. None the less, this seems the most reasonable explanation. Although the coach-house had a roof, it may well have leaked and the stone floor may have been flooded by the rain. What was probably crucial was Lee's weight – enough to compress and wedge the doors, but not enough to pitch him eight feet into the pit.

After spending nearly 23 years in jail, John Lee was released from Portland Prison, where he was something of a hero, in December 1907, by which time the Glen had long been razed to the ground. Lee was now 43. Travelling from Weymouth to Newton Abbot by train, he took a cab from there to his mother's cottage at Abbotskerswell. They were besieged by reporters, but both had nothing to say.

One reporter traced Kate Farmer, who now lived in Plymouth. Lee had been in prison for less than a year when she married a man called Parrish and left Torquay. Four years later she left her husband, taking her daughter with her, who was now 21. When interviewed, Mrs Parrish said:

> He has suffered. I hope his future life will be happy. His way will not be my way, for I am now settled in life after my vicissitudes. I hope he may be able to prove his innocence . . . I was then a silly sentimental girl, and did not know my own mind. I am wiser now . . . I remember most vividly the last time I saw him. It was at the inquest. I recall he walked with his head in the air, although he was in such deadly peril. He recognised me and smiled, and said: 'Goodbye, my dear.' Those were the last words I heard him utter. He never sent a letter from prison to me, and never asked me to visit him in Portland . . . My friends told me that Lee would be kept in prison as long as he lived, and a life's devotion would be thrown away. So I put him out of my heart.

A life of John Lee was published and his story was much later made into a film. He is said to have become a publican in London, and in the Black Museum there is a postcard, dated September 1910 and showing the Rustic Bridges of Torquay, that is addressed to a Miss Gibbs at 45 High Road, Borough, London SE. This seems to suggest that he was living in London then. Other than that, little is now known about his life after 'life'. But he is said to have been in America in 1932. Did he ever meet up with his Kate again? Did he marry? And when in the end did he die?

Lee's unsuccessful executioner, James Berry, was a thick-set, muscular man with sandy hair; 5′ 8½″ in height and weighing 13 stone, he was born on 8 February 1852 at Heckmondwike in Yorkshire. In 1874, the year that he married (he had six children), he became a policeman in Bradford, and during the course of carrying out his duties met the public executioner, William Marwood, the originator of the long drop. When Marwood died in 1883, Berry, by now an impoverished boot-salesman, applied for the job, among 1,400 others. The post was given to Bartholomew Binns. But Berry was recommended by the English authorities to carry out a double execution, of Robert Vickers and William Innes, in Edinburgh on 31 March 1884. Binns was found to be unsuitable after four or five months, and Berry was appointed in his place.

His first task was to execute David Roberts for the murder of David Thomas at Llanblethian in Glamorgan. Berry miscalculated the length of the drop and Roberts's neck failed to break – he was left struggling at the end of the rope. Those present were asked to withdraw as Berry went down into the pit and, grabbing the struggler's legs, added his 13 stone to that of the condemned man. His failure to execute John Lee followed in February 1885. Later that year, in November, at Norwich Castle, Berry failed again. This victim was Robert Goodale, who had murdered his wife; he weighed 15 stone. Berry reduced the recommended drop for some reason from 7′ 8″ to 5′ 9″, with the horrid result that the sudden jerk severed the head from the body and both parts fell to the floor of the pit. The attendant Governor, already overwrought and highly strung, burst into tears.

Another condemned man, John Conway, was nearly decapitated by Berry in August 1891, after which, at the age of 40, he retired – 'on account of Dr Barr interfering with my responsible duty at Kirkdale Gaol, Liverpool, on the last execution there'. There had been a dispute about the mechanics of the drop. Thereafter, James Berry went on a series of lecture tours, recommending the abolition of capital punishment, and appeared in music-halls. He also wrote a book.

CHAPTER 8

James Canham Read

The Murder of Florence Dennis, 1894

Energy characterises the late Victorians more than their prudery. Those who survived the depredations of disease, pollution and poverty became epitomes of industry, activity and zeal. They worked long hours in badly lit and aired conditions, slept little, ate, smoked and drank a great deal and produced large families. They had stamina, and for the most part, strong constitutions. Their social and charitable concerns were as great as their appetite for the comforts of religion, and sex. They were great believers, and great deceivers. Public morality might rule the middle class, but it was countervailed by rich seams of private vice. Prostitution was rampant, as were many kinds of crime and social abuse. These matters fascinated many, as they did Conan Doyle's Sherlock Holmes, who first appeared in 1887. Apart from Thomas Hardy, the most famous writer of the 1890s was Oscar Wilde, whose cultivation of the aesthetic was satirised by W. S. Gilbert in Patience *as early as 1881. In 1894, Queen Victoria was 75: she had reigned for 57 years. Gladstone resigned, after a fourth term as Prime Minister, and in 1895 the Liberals were replaced by ten triumphant years of Tory rule and imperialism, when the British Empire ruled half the world.*

Although the jury's verdict of 'Guilty' was undoubtedly a proper one in the case of James Read, there was room for doubt – not for the first time, alas, or the last – about the propriety of police methods in obtaining evidence and a conviction. After the trial, the conduct of identification parades, which were being mishandled and abused, was cleaned up and improved. And the centuries-old unjust anomaly of an accused person not being allowed to give evidence, if he or she so wished, was abolished in 1898.

Soon after six o'clock on the evening of Monday, 25 June 1894, the body of a young woman, fully clothed, was found in a ditch by a footpath in fields near the village of Prittlewell in Essex. She had been shot once in the head. Prittlewell, an ancient settlement mentioned in the Domesday Book, was a mile or so north of Southend-on-Sea, which came into being in the reign of Henry VIII and was originally the South End of Prittlewell. It was now a fashionable health resort, known for its dry climate, safe sea-bathing, amusements, and a very long pier, that stretched out into the Thames estuary for nearly one-and-a-half miles.

The dead girl, who had been murdered on the Sunday night, was Florence

Dennis. Aged 23, she was not married, but was heavily pregnant. She had been staying in Southend with a married sister, Mrs Ayris, who had much to tell the police about the likely father of her younger sister's unborn child, and of one of her own.

He was James Canham Read, aged 37, and known as Jim. A third-class clerk, with a first-class character at work, he was employed at the Royal Albert Dock at North Woolwich, on the north shore of the Thames. He had worked there for nearly 20 years and was well paid and trusted, his salary amounting to £14[illegible] year. His home was in Stepney, where lived his wife and their eight children. But he was not at home when the police called, nor was he at his place of work, which he had left on the Monday afternoon, two hours before the body of Miss Dennis was discovered. He took with him £160 of his employers' cash and disappeared.

Within two weeks, however, the police succeeded in tracking him to a small cottage at Mitcham in Surrey, where he was living with a young woman called Mrs Benson, who had a six-month-old baby. Read was posing as Mr Benson. A search of the premises produced £83 in cash. Read was arrested and taken to Southend. On 30 July he was incarcerated in Springfield Jail in Chelmsford, the Essex county jail, and after being remanded in custody six times, he was committed on 7 September for trial at the next Essex Assizes in Chelmsford, some 18 miles north-east of Southend.

The trial began in the Shire Hall on Monday, 12 November 1894 before Mr Baron Pollock. The newly appointed Solicitor-General, Mr Frank Lockwood, QC, MP, led for the prosecution, assisted by Mr C. F. Gill and Mr Stephenson. Mr Cock, QC, led for the defence, assisted by Mr Warburton.

The Pollock family had flourished in the legal profession for over a hundred years; the Pollock features, long, pale and strongly marked, had presided over many trials. Mr Baron Pollock, who was a very pious, just and learned man, was the last judge to bear the title of Baron of the Court of Exchequer, as distinct from those of the Queen's Bench and of the Common Pleas, which merged in 1880. Mr Cock was also the last of the type of QC characterised as having 'lungs of leather and a voice of brass'. Besides being loud, he was a bit of a bully in court, aggressive and blunt. It was said he was better at demolishing the opposition's case than building his own. Mr Lockwood, on the other hand, had a fine voice and presence; he was handsome, charming and frank, with a sense of humour and a penchant for making comical drawings while at work. A Yorkshireman, he was said to look older than his 50 years. In 1879 he had defended Charles Peace.

Baron Pollock arrived in Chelmsford by train from Norwich on Thursday, 8 November, and was accommodated at a house called Maynetrees in New Street. He presided over the trials of 22 persons, mainly charged with stealing, on the Friday and Saturday and attended church on Sunday. On the Monday, after robing himself at Maynetrees, he was taken in the Sheriff's carriage at half-past ten to the Shire Hall. It was pouring with rain. Read was taken there from the prison in a fly at 6.00 am, accompanied by two warders, to avoid the crowds.

Over 300 applications for tickets to the court had been received, and the

Essex County Chronicle reporters noted (there were two): 'Greater interest and excitement were caused by the trial than by any that has taken place at Chelmsford within living memory.' Two things, they wrote, accounted for this: 'One being the great element of mystery surrounding the murder, and the other the strange and unhappy life of sensuality which is alleged to have been led by the prisoner.'

All eyes were on him when he appeared in the dock. He was wearing the light grey suit in which he had been arrested, and a black tie. He looked spick and span: his hair and moustache had been carefully trimmed, as had his beard, which prison regulations had obliged him to grow. He stood erect and seemed confident, saying 'Not guilty' in a firm, clear voice.

Before the murder trial began, he pleaded 'Guilty' to another charge, that while in the service of the London and East India Docks Joint Committee he stole £159 12s 6d from his employers. He then sat between his two warders with folded arms. Outside, the falling rain and grey skies added a certain gloom to the scene within the court.

The Solicitor-General rose to present the prosecution's case, and, after his opening remarks, related the story of James Canham Read's recent life and crimes.

> So far back as August, 1889, the prisoner made the acquaintance [on the pier at Southend] of Mrs Ayris, the wife of John Ayris [a dairy man] and the eldest sister of Florence Dennis. That acquaintance ripened into an intimacy, and there is no doubt that immoral relations existed between the prisoner and Mrs Ayris . . . In December 1889, Mrs Ayris removed [from Clapham Junction] to 189 St John's Hill Road, Wandsworth. The prisoner was then corresponding with her, but not under her own name or at the address where she was living with her husband – this for obvious reasons. He was writing under an assumed name . . . He addressed her as Mrs Neville, and his letters were sent to 137 St John's Hill Road, a stationer's shop . . . We find the prisoner and Mrs Ayris spending a day at Leigh in the spring of 1891 . . . We subsequently find they were staying at Buckingham together. The immoral relations between Mrs Ayris and this man ceased about March, 1892. There was another meeting in March 1894, at Victoria Station, when she told him it was her intention to take a lodging-house at Southend, and asked him to recommend lodgers . . .
>
> In September 1890, on one occasion when Mrs Ayris and the prisoner were out walking [on Clapham Common], they met Florence Dennis, I suggest by chance. Mrs Ayris introduced Florence Dennis [and another sister, Mrs Deed, who was with her], and they passed on . . . Florence [who was not yet 19] was then living part of her time with her mother, but throughout the case you find she has resided alternately with her mother [at Sheerness in Kent] and Mrs Ayris. In May 1892, a child was born – I think it was Mrs Ayris's second child. Florence Dennis went to her sister's. There was a nurse there, a Mrs Schmidt, and she will tell you that during that time . . . she posted two letters for Florence Dennis, at

her request, and both the letters were addressed to Mr Read, at the Albert Docks. One night Florence was absent from her sister's house, and she remained out until late . . .

In 1893 we find Mrs Ayris living at Hanwell, and Florence Dennis at Sheerness, and we find Florence Dennis corresponding with Read, addressing letters from and receiving them at 63 High Street, Sheerness, where a woman of the name of Hughes was manager. Evelina Dennis, a younger sister of the murdered woman, fetched the letters for Florence, and these letters were addressed to 'Talbott' . . . Some of the documents we have are in disguised writing by the prisoner . . . One of the visits paid by Florence Dennis to Mrs Ayris at Hanwell was in October 1893, and when the body of this unfortunate woman was examined, it was found to contain a child that must have been begotten about that time. After Christmas 1893, letters were addressed to the name of Talbott to the Post Office, Sheerness . . . The correspondence ceased in May 1894, and Florence Dennis was murdered in June 1894 . . .

I take you now, gentlemen, to another scene, and introduce you to another name. In 1892 the prisoner made the acquaintance of a young woman named Kempton, who was living in Gloucester Road, at a [confectioner's] shop. The prisoner met her at a railway station [Gloucester Road], and introduced himself as a Mr Edgar Benson, of 16 North Street, Poplar. He described himself as a traveller on behalf of Messrs Peck, tea merchants, of Cheapside. Correspondence took place, and meetings took place, and according to the sad story Miss Kempton will tell you, she was seduced by the prisoner in the spring of 1893. Miss Kempton had a home at Cambridge, but she left there to go to Hallingbury, where she lived under the care of the prisoner. The prisoner explained his absence from her there by stating that his business kept him away. But he was able to spend from Saturday to Monday with her. On 6 January, 1894, a child was born to Miss Kempton by the prisoner. In February, Miss Kempton moved into lodgings provided for her by the prisoner at Rose Cottage, Mitcham . . .

The prisoner has a brother, named Harry Read. The name by which he was introduced to Miss Kempton was 'Mr Edwards,' a friend. 'Benson' told Miss Kempton that he himself had a sister at Canterbury, married to a man named [Walter] Parker . . . Harry Read – 'Edwards' as he was known to Miss Kempton – lived at 16 North Street, Poplar. But he was dismissed from there . . .

In April 1894, Miss Kempton notices that the prisoner is exhibiting considerable anxiety, and he tells her it is his pecuniary position that troubles him. But, gentlemen, what was it really? Florence Dennis conceived her child in October 1893, and by this time, April 1894, no doubt her condition must have been made known to herself, and to the prisoner . . .

I told you the prisoner spent from Saturday to Monday, as a rule, with Miss Kempton. From Christmas 1893 to the day of the murder, June 1894, he never spent one Sunday at his own house, where his own wife and family lived, at Jamaica Street, Stepney. With three exceptions he spent a portion of the Saturdays, and a portion of the Sundays, during 1894 with Miss Kempton at Rose Cottage, Mitcham. Gentlemen, these three dates are 20 May, 10 June, and 24 June . . . He wrote to Miss Kempton to excuse himself for his absence on the first date, and stated that he had gone to Canterbury, on most important business on behalf of Walter [Parker] whose child was ill with bronchitis. Gentlemen, there was no such child ill, and what he said was false. Florence Dennis at this time was living in Sheerness [in Kent]. On Saturday, 19 May, she went out at night and did not return home until about 10.30 . . . I now come to the next date, 10 June. On 8 June he writes to Miss Kempton: 'I am making arrangements to go to Canterbury tomorrow, Saturday, on important business, so let me beg of you to do your best to keep up your spirits until I come back. I do not expect I shall be back before Monday' . . . On 22 June, this is the excuse the prisoner gives for not going down to Miss Kempton: 'I am sure you fully share with me my regret that I shall not be with you this weekend. I have to go to Canterbury on most important business of Walter's. He has asked me to do this, and I cannot refuse . . . If I can utilise this opportunity to lift myself out of my present critical condition I will do so. But if I do not succeed in this, God knows what I shall do. I'm dead broke.' Absolutely untrue! There was no business at Canterbury – he did not go to Canterbury – he had no relations at Canterbury . . . I shall be able, I think, to show you . . . that he was at Southend – that he was at Prittlewell . . .

I will now resume the story of Florence Dennis. In June 1894 she was eight months advanced in pregnancy. A communication was made to her mother, with whom she was living at Sheerness, and on 19 June she was removed to Mrs Ayris's house at Southend. On Friday, 22 June, the prisoner wrote to Miss Kempton to say that he was going on Saturday to Canterbury on most important business. That Friday he was loitering away his time with his brother and a friend named Kendall [they met at 10.05 pm] . . . and another telegram is dispatched to Florence Dennis. I am prepared to show that the telegram is in the handwriting of the man who was in company with the prisoner at the time – I mean Harry Read. Harry Read it was who sent that telegram from a Post Office near Charing Cross [at 9.25 pm] . . . That telegram was received by Florence Dennis on 23 June [Saturday]. You will hear that Florence Dennis went out . . .

All these telegrams were dispatched in a curious way. Instead of being handed over the counter, they were put into the post, so as to give no opportunity of the sender being identified. The prisoner carried about with him, it seems, telegraph forms and stamps . . .

I come now to the Sunday, 24 June, the day on which the murder was committed . . . Florence remained about [her sister's] house until the evening of that day, and an arrangement had been made by her, with her sister's knowledge, that owing to the crowded state of her sister's house, she should pass the night in a room taken for her at an adjoining house.

On that evening she went out to meet somebody – and by any of her relations she was never seen alive again . . .

That Sunday afternoon, a lady named Mrs Kirby met the prisoner in a wheatfield, coming from Prittlewell. The prisoner asked her the way to Leigh. She said she didn't know, and he said: 'Oh, I may as well go back to Rayleigh again.' And he turned back . . . He was not seen again by anyone we are in a position to call until a little after ten, when a man named Robert Dowthwaite, coming from Prittlewell, meets a man and a woman, whom he identifies as the prisoner and – having seen the dead body – the murdered woman, walking arm in arm along an avenue towards the field in which the murder was committed. Another witness, Richard Golding, who with his family had been in a public-house at Prittlewell, came along this same road, and he saw a man coming down the avenue alone – a man whom he afterwards identified as the prisoner. The man who went up the avenue was with a woman – the man who returned was alone . . . But the prisoner is seen again, by a policeman named Daniel, at Benfleet, early the next morning [at 1.15 am]. The prisoner said he wanted the road to London . . .

Later we find him calling at the house of a fellow clerk at Leytonstone, who was ill [at about 9.20 am]. When he called at the house his appearance was not as usual – he had not that smart, dapper appearance which he usually presented. He had no gloves in his hand, and presented a dishevelled appearance. At about ten o'clock [on the Monday] he arrived at his office at the docks, a little later than usual. But that was explained by his call at the fellow clerk's. At 12.30 he went out and got shaved . . . Later, a clerk named Burgess went into the prisoner's room at the office, and found him burning a fire. He asked what it was for, and the prisoner made some remark about foul air. At 3.00 pm, a telegram is received [at the office] by him from Mrs Ayris . . . The telegram was one inquiring: 'Where is Florrie?' The answer was a letter saying that he had not seen Florence Dennis for 18 months.

On Monday, 25 June Mrs Ayris goes round to the house where her sister had been staying the previous day. She is startled to find that Florence Dennis is not there. She waits . . . After waiting some time she gives information to the police, and then telegraphs to the prisoner, asking where Florence was . . . The body at that time had not been discovered. Mrs Ayris did not know that her sister was murdered . . . When [the prisoner] got that telegram from Mrs Ayris he knew perfectly well that the hue and cry had commenced. He knew that Mrs Ayris knew his address in Jamaica Street, and that there he would probably meet an officer to arrest him. He knew that to stay at the Royal Albert Docks was to court apprehension . . . But there was one place Mrs Ayris did not know, a place known only to his brother Harry – viz, Rose Cottage, Mitcham. Therefore you are not surprised to hear he leaves his work earlier than usual, without signing off [and] takes with him a bag, which probably contained the money, to stealing which he has pleaded guilty . . . Why was he fleeing? Because, I say, he was the only man who knew of that murder . . . He goes to the address known practically only to himself and his brother, in whom he has confidence . . . And at 4.30 he dispatches the following letter-card to his brother: 'My dear Harry – Secure my desk contents and report everything to me at M—. In strict secrecy. Will explain when I see you. Allay all fears. JCR' . . .

Well then – between eight and nine o'clock on the Monday night the prisoner arrives at Rose Cottage, Mitcham. He is dressed in a black coat and vest, grey trousers, a light brown hat, and a light coloured tie. He has money with him, and he accounts for that by saying he has borrowed it from Mr Parker. There is some alteration in his whiskers – he has them cut more closely to his face – and this is the commencement of a disguise which he afterwards developed. Miss Kempton remarks on his appearing tired and weary. He accounts for it by saying that he has been to Canterbury. That is untrue . . .

On 26 June the prisoner went to Croydon, where he bought a ready-made suit [light grey], the clothes, I think, in which he now sits in the dock. From that time he no longer wears the clothes he was wearing on 25 June. He leaves off shaving, and when Miss Kempton asks him why, his first reason was that he had no razor with him . . . When Miss Kempton suggested that he should go out to be shaved, he said it was too much trouble . . . He stays indoors much more than usual . . . On 27 or 28 June he is absent from Rose Cottage, and Miss Kempton receives a telegram from him, asking if all is right. On 30 June she receives another telegram asking her to wire if all is well. What was the cause of his anxiety? His anxiety was to ascertain if any person was on his track – if so, he would not return . . .

In July, Inspector Baker and Sgt Marden go to Rose Cottage to apprehend the prisoner . . .

Now how was this young woman, Florence Dennis, killed? Beyond all doubt it was by a bullet wound. Gentlemen, the revolver is not forthcoming but the bullet is . . . Above the left ear there is a circular wound, about a quarter of an inch in diameter. The edges of the wound are blackened and singed, showing that the revolver must have been held very near to the head of that woman, and the conical bullet was found embedded in her brain. What was the weapon used? You may remember in the opening part of my speech, I alluded to an address: 16 North Road, Poplar. That was the place from which Harry Read was discharged at Christmas 1892, for some misconduct. Some time before that Harry Read purchased a revolver. He, at this time, got very low in spirits, and on one occasion threatened to take his own life. The prisoner, who was present at the time, expostulated with him, calling him a fool, and took the revolver away. Mrs Kelly, a sister, took the cartridges away.

In January 1894 this revolver was seen in the house of the prisoner at Jamaica Street, and was afterwards seen also by Miss Kempton, while they were at Hallingbury. In April 1894 the prisoner's daughter [Emma Read] will tell you she saw at the house in Jamaica Street a revolver case

> in the sitting-room – and the prisoner had a pocket made to carry it . . . I can show the bullet was a 7-Eley, was in a pin cartridge, and was of conical shape. This woman's death was caused by a bullet which would fit exactly the cartridges which were used in this revolver, which is traced to the prisoner's possession, and is seen in the prisoner's possession until April 1894, and which has not been seen since.

After conceding that Mrs Ayris had lied to the coroner and magistrates – she said she had *seen* James Read in Southend on the night of the murder – Mr Lockwood brought his opening speech to a well-modulated close by 1.40 pm, when the court adjourned for half an hour for lunch.

All that the Solicitor-General alleged was confirmed and elaborated by the many witnesses he called. Frederick Rush, a local youth, deposed that he had discovered the body (with her hat on her breast) at 6.00 pm on the Monday night. PC Alfred Marden, to whom Rush told his tale, deposed that the body had clearly been pushed through a hedge in the ditch. He also described the prisoner's eventual arrest. He and Inspector Baker observed Read return to Rose Cottage, in a light suit and cap, on 7 July. Baker went to the door and knocked. Miss Kempton appeared, and then the prisoner (who said he was Edgar Benson). Told he was being arrested as James Canham Read for the murder of Florence Dennis, he said: 'You're on the wrong scent.' He added: 'There's a lady living here with me – she doesn't know who I am.' Seized and taken inside, he was searched, as was the cottage. Money was found. During the search, Read remarked: 'Mrs Ayris can tell you where the revolver is.' When he was escorted from the cottage, Harry Read appeared at the gate. He followed the others. Jim Read said: 'Mrs Ayris knows more about this than I do.' Later he said: 'It's all rot about Southend. I was considering whether or not I should offer myself at the coroner's inquiry to be examined.' He said to Harry: 'What do you think of the little milkmaid [Mrs Ayris] now? Isn't she a –?' and he failed to finish the sentence.

Although it was never mentioned in court, Marden and Baker traced Read to Mitcham by closely monitoring Harry Read's movements and possibly intercepting his mail.

Other witnesses were called. Mrs Emma Deed, an older sister of Florence, who was with her when she first met Jim Read on Clapham Common in the autumn of 1890, deposed that her husband put a stop to Florrie receiving letters addressed to 'Talbott' at their Sheerness home. Mrs Sophie Schmidt, a midwife, remembered posting two letters at Wandsworth (where Mrs Ayris had a baby, in 1892), written by Florrie to 'Mr Read, Royal Albert Docks'. Mr Cock, cross-examining, implied that the letters may have been dictated to Florrie by the prostrate Mrs Ayris, and Mr Lockwood enquired: 'Were those letters written on behalf of Mrs Ayris?' Mrs Schmidt answered: 'They couldn't have been, because I had to promise Florence that I wouldn't tell Mrs Ayris about them.'

Julia Price, a stationer in Wandsworth, agreed that letters addressed to 'Miss Latimer' came to her shop. She did not know who collected them. But when Mr Lockwood asked Mrs Ayris to come forward, and said: 'Is that the woman?' the witness flatly announced: 'No. She was a young and nice-looking person.'

The sudden and brief appearance in court of Mrs Ayris was one of several 'sensations' in court. The *Chronicle*'s reporters noted that though she had 'a very sober air' and looked discomfited, she was 'of prepossessing appearance' and was fashionably attired in a dark dress with a high-shouldered and full-sleeved brown jacket, and a stylish hat – 'black straw trimmed with crape'.

The first day's proceedings concluded at 4.30 pm with the evidence of three post office officials and that of Florence Dennis's brother Fred, a seaman, and of her 14-year-old sister, Evelina. Both recalled Florence posting letters in 1893 and 1894 addressed to 'Mr Read'.

Overnight, the all-male jury were lodged in a large room in the Saracen's Head Hotel, attended by two court officials. One part of the room was furnished with 14 beds, the other part was used as a refectory, where the jury shared four bottles of wine during dinner and afterwards were allowed a cigar each and a glass of 'grog'.

The morning of Tuesday, 13 November was fine and bright. The *Chronicle*'s reporters, who occupied seats 100 and 101 in the crowded press gallery, nearest the judge, were pleased to note, after being forced to write on their knees on Monday, that: 'Today there is a desk constructed at seats 100 and 101, where the occupants may write in comfort and ease.'

After further post office evidence, Mrs Emma Dennis, Florence's mother, appeared. Dressed in deep mourning, she shed tears as she disclosed that on 19 June 1894, at her home in Sheerness, she learned that her daughter was pregnant, as well as who the father was, and 'where intimacy took place'. She took Florrie to stay with Mrs Ayris in Southend later that day. Mrs Dennis wept when she identified her daughter's handwriting on some letters, and told Mr Cock: 'Florrie never did anything by way of earning a living.'

The next and principal prosecution witness was Mrs Louisa Bertha Ayris. Attired as on the Monday, and obviously abashed by her exposure as an adulteress, she replied with brevity, mainly 'Yes' and 'No'. She admitted that while on holiday at Southend in September 1889 (two years after her marriage) she had met Read on the pier and had cohabited with him periodically until March 1892, two months before his child was born. He used to write to her, though not to her home, addressing her as Mrs Neville, Miss Harris or Miss Dennis – never as Miss Latimer or Talbott. She was not aware that Florence was writing to Read until September 1892, or that she was pregnant, until 19 June when, advised by Mrs Ayris, Florence wrote a letter to Read, saying: 'Dear Sir – I have left Sheerness and am staying at Southend. Please write me what arrangements you have made. Write to the General Post Office, Southend, in the name of Miss Dennis.' On Saturday, 23 June, Florence received a telegram – 'Meet me tonight. Great Eastern Station, Southend, 9.30.' She left the Ayris home at 24 Wesley Road at about 9.00 pm and it was 'very, very late' before she returned.

On the Sunday night Florence moved temporarily into the nearby house of Mrs Eggers, and was last seen by Mrs Ayris at half-past nine. The following morning, at 7.00, Mrs Ayris, visiting her neighbour, found that Florrie had been out all night and had not returned. She waited for two deliveries of mail to be made before going to the police, whom she provided with descriptions of her sister and of 'someone else'. That afternoon her husband sent a telegram to Read at the Royal Albert Docks – 'Where is Florrie? Telegraph at once'. That night the police told Mrs Ayris that Florrie had been found dead and she formally identified the body. The next morning she received a letter-card from 'J C Read'. It said: 'Dear Mrs Ayris – What is the meaning of your extraordinary wire? Please write fully. I have not seen the young person for quite 18 months, when you were at St John's Hill.'

She admitted that she never saw Read on the Saturday or the Sunday night, and that when she told the magistrates she had, and described his clothes, what she had said then was quite untrue.

This was seized on at once by Mr Cock in his cross-examination, his aim being to present her as a liar and a deceiver. He suggested that *she* was really Miss Talbott and Miss Latimer and that Read was only writing to *her*. He implied she was badgering Read for money or blackmailing him. For she had called at his Stepney home with their baby, and in March 1894, when she asked to meet him at Victoria Station, she told him (alleged Mr Cock) that she was poor and that her sister had 'got into trouble' with a soldier from Hounslow Barracks, near Hanwell. This Mrs Ayris denied. She had no idea, she said, that Florence was pregnant until June, and only sought Read's advice in March about legal and other matters. She knew from the start he was married, she said; Florence thought he was divorced.

Mr Ayris and Mrs Eggers then spoke of events on the 24th and 25th of June, and four witnesses were called to prove that Jim Read was in Southend on Sunday, 25 June. Two were possibly not telling the truth.

An elderly woman, Mrs Kirby, agreed that at about three o'clock on the Sunday afternoon, crossing wheatfields near the scene of the murder, she met a man who asked her the way to Leigh. She said she couldn't tell him, and he said: 'I may as well go back to Rayleigh.' Both villages were to the west of Southend. The man had 'piercing eyes', she said, and a quick walk; he was wearing a hard hat and a light tie. Questioned by Mr Cock, she admitted that she told the police about the encounter *two months* after the murder, by which time Read's appearance and dress had been well publicised. She did not speak to the police sooner, she said, because 'I was not well. I had a bad cold.'

An umbrella-maker, Robert Dowthwaite, said he saw a man and a woman walking arm in arm through the midsummer fields. He saw her face, but not that of the man, who was wearing, he said, a light coat and dark trousers. In the dock, Read chuckled and smiled: Dowthwaite was clearly confused. For Read, according to the prosecution, had been wearing a *dark* coat and *light* trousers that day. The witness added that the man had 'a very smart, genteel walk' and looked 'superior to his companion'. The next witness, a labourer, Richard Golding, deposed that the man *he* saw, about 10.00 pm, wore light trousers, a dark jacket and a hard felt hat. Golding, out for a walk with his wife and children, noticed that the man, appearing behind them, seemed reluctant to pass and eventually turned off the road and walked on quickly towards Leigh.

Presumably, although the midsummer sun had set an hour or so before, the sky was still light and not overcast – for both Dowthwaite and Golding could see the man in some detail, well enough to recognise him later. But this potentially awkward point was never mentioned in court.

The fourth of these witnesses allegedly came across Read much later, at 1.15 am. This was PC Daniel, who was patrolling his beat in South Benfleet (west of Leigh), and no doubt carrying a lantern, when a man approached him from the direction of Southend. 'Hallo, guv'nor!' Daniel called. 'You're up and dressed early this morning.' 'Yes,' said the other man, who was dressed in a dark *suit*, wore a round hat, and carried a *walking-stick*. He asked the policeman: 'Can you direct me to Benfleet?' Daniel retorted: 'You're in Benfleet now. Whom might you want?' 'I want no one here,' said the stranger. 'I want the road to London.' 'Where have you come from?' 'Southend.' Said Daniel: 'You've come a mile or two out of your way.' He put the other man right and they wished each other 'Good morning'.

PC Daniel, at an identification parade in Southend police station on 9 July, had picked out Read, who was wearing the light grey suit in which he had been arrested. Dowthwaite and Golding also correctly identified him, as did Kirby. It wasn't difficult: his description was well known. And Read was the only man in each line-up to be correctly dressed. The others were labouring men.

But, having accepted Daniel's identification and story (and that of the other two men) the police were lumbered with the unlikely hypothesis that, after the murder (the last train from Southend to London having left at 9.19 pm), Read *walked* the 30 miles from Prittlewell to Leytonstone, via Leigh and Benfleet – in the dark night along country lanes. For he was definitely seen at Leytonstone at 9.20 on the Monday morning, when he paid a duty call on Theresa Scannell's sick husband, a former colleague of his. Mr Scannell told the court that Read was dishevelled, carried no gloves (or a walking-stick) and hadn't shaved.

It was then proved in court that at 10.15 am he was back in his office, where he lit a fire (to burn letters?) and left early without signing off. He was carrying a black bag. Between 4.45 and 6.00 pm he posted his letter-card to Mrs Ayris in the EC district, replying to the telegram 'Where is Florrie?' He then took a train to Mitcham.

The evidence of former sweetshop assistant, Miss Beatrice Diva Kempton, occupied most of the afternoon. Dressed entirely in black and, like Mrs Ayris, wearing a black straw hat trimmed with crape, she spoke softly, never once looking at the man in the dock, whom she had known as Edgar Benson. No one doubted the detailed account of her seduction and life with Read. It was obvious he had told her many lies about himself, his absences, his friends and relatives, and his work. Large sections of his loving letters to her – 'My darling Beatie' – were read out in court by Mr Lockwood. Miss Kempton agreed that she had seen a revolver in January 1894 and that she knew Read's brother, Harry, as 'Harry Edwards', and had met him once. Read had produced a fake marriage certificate to silence her parents, and assured her he would marry her after her baby was born.

Miss Kempton's sad story was deeply damaging to Read. All Mr Cock could do was ask whether the accused man had been kind and affectionate. 'Very kind and affectionate,' she replied, with tears in her eyes. 'He seemed fond of me, and was kind to the child.'

On the third day of the trial there was another change in the weather, and high winds blew 'mournfully round the grey Shire Hall'. So wrote the *Chronicle*'s reporters, their fingers stiff and inky with scribbling. They noted that Read 'was paler, and wore a very anxious look. He seemed occasionally to wander into dreamland'. But he must have listened carefully when his brother, Harry, gave evidence. He was preceded by Thomas Gurrin, a handwriting expert, who opined that various telegrams and letters *were* written by the prisoner, although some of the writing was disguised or printed. After him came William Kendall, an artists' colourman, who said he had met the Read brothers at Marble Arch at 10.05 pm on Friday, 22 June. They drank in a public house until 11.30, conversing chiefly about family matters. There was no mention of Jim Read going to Canterbury on important business the following day or anywhere else. Kendall said he had known the prisoner since he was seven years old. They parted at Baker Street Station, Harry going home with Kendall, with whom he stayed until the Monday.

So that was Harry's alibi – if anyone had imagined that *he* shot Florence Dennis on his brother's behalf.

The *Chronicle*'s reporters described Harry Victor Read, when he appeared, as being 'in gentlemanly attire, in a heliotrope tie, and with a white chrysanthemum in his button-hole. He is a good-looking fellow, with a moustache inclined to be sandy'. It seems he may have been a bit of an aesthete and an admirer of Oscar Wilde, then reaching the peak and ruin of his career.

Harry was evasive about letters addressed to him as 'Edwards' and about his brother being 'Edgar Benson'. But he admitted he had no married sister in Canterbury called Parker. He professed not to know what his brother did at weekends, although they were, he said, on very intimate terms. He denied any knowledge of a telegram being sent to Florence Dennis by him or his brother on the night of Friday, 22 June from Charing Cross, although he admitted they got off a bus there before walking to Marble Arch to meet Kendall at 10.05 – and although a violet pencil, such as Harry had, was used to write the telegram. 'Where was your brother on that Sunday?' asked Mr Lockwood. Said Harry: 'I do not know.'

The last prosecution witness was Inspector Baker. A statement made by the prisoner was then read, asserting his innocence, and no witnesses were called by the defence. Mr Cock then applied for his closing speech to *follow* that of the prosecution, saying: 'I am entitled to reply . . . on the rule that was laid down at the meeting of the judges . . . who decided that it was only the Attorney-General, when he appeared in person, who could have the last word.' The point was debated; and lost by Mr Cock. The judge said: 'My ruling must be that the Solicitor-General, appearing here as the representative of the Crown, has the same right as the Attorney-General.'

After the court had adjourned for half an hour for lunch, Mr Cock rose to speak at 1.45. He complained 'of the enormous difficulty of conducting a criminal investigation without the person against whom the charge is made having an opportunity of giving explanations'. He also complained about the biased reporting, the theories and suggestions of the press, and concentrated on Mrs Ayris as the villain of the case, supposing that all the letters that Florrie received were really for Mrs Ayris, and that *she* was not only bent on 'injuring' her former lover, but intent on sending him to the scaffold. To this end Mr Cock interpreted much of the evidence to support his thesis, and implied that Read, wearying of Miss Kempton, was in the arms of a new paramour on 23/34 June, and that either Mrs Ayris or the soldier from Hounslow Barracks had something to do with Florrie's death. He offered no excuses about Read's affair with Miss Kempton or the theft of his employers' money. But these matters were not part of the charge, he said. And he claimed that the police had failed to prove the prisoner was in Southend on the Saturday night. Or on the Sunday. For the witnesses who said they had seen him were unreliable and not to be trusted. Moreover, there was no blood on the prisoner's clothes – no one had heard a shot – and the medical experts had said Florrie died much later (about 1.00 am) than the prosecution averred. 'No fact proved before you,' declared Mr Cock, 'is sufficient to bring home any guilt to this man.' The court adjourned at half-past four.

The fourth and last day of the trial was 'wet and gloomy'. The Solicitor-General dealt smoothly with Mr Cock's 'theories' and criticised him for 'a most bitter attack' on Mrs Ayris. Where was this *third* woman who might have cleared up the mystery of Read's whereabouts on 23/24 June? Where was the evidence that he was tired of Miss Kempton? Who was this soldier who wrote or printed telegrams with such an educated hand? And where *was* the prisoner on the night of the murder? Said Mr Lockwood: 'It is not one hour which is unaccounted for. It is not six hours. It is 36 hours of this man's life which are absolutely unaccounted for except by the prosecution! . . . Why, gentlemen, one poor moment of that time . . . would relieve him from this most terrible charge!'

Dealing with the sound of the shot, Mr Lockwood said the noise of the revolver shot would have carried no more than 200 yards and be no louder 'than the crack of a whip'. He concluded his speech at 11.25.

Five minutes later, during which Read cheerfully chatted with his warders, Mr Baron Pollock began his summing-up.

After urging the jury to omit from their consideration what they had heard 'of immoral and licentious conduct', he provided them with an explanation of Mrs Ayris's only known lie (that she had *seen* Read in Southend) – 'What she probably meant to say was that she had a strong, intense feeling that he was at Southend that day.' Of the four witnesses who said they saw Read in Southend, the judge remarked: 'It may be said that their evidence is not precise enough. But what evidence of this nature would be precise? The fair rule is to take it as a whole, and if you find substantial agreement in what is important to prove – with circumstantial variety as to the colour of the dress, and so forth – that is in one sense the best evidence you can have.' And where was the revolver, known to have been in the prisoner's possession? If he had disposed of it, why was the person to whom he had given or sold it not called? And why was no one called to prove where he was, if not at Southend?

The judge spoke for 80 minutes, concluding at 12.50 pm, when the jury retired. They returned at 1.30.

Their foreman, Mr G. Thorpe Bartram, of Braintree, was very pale and appeared to be suffering from palpitations when he announced the verdict – 'Guilty'. Jim Read, who also paled at the word, soon recovered his composure and spoke clearly and coolly when asked by the Clerk of the Court: 'Have you anything to say why sentence of death should not be passed upon you?'

Read declared:

> I would wish to repeat that I am perfectly innocent of this charge; that it is now two years since I have ever seen Florence Dennis; that I have never written to her; that I have only received one letter from her – one of the two sworn to by Mrs Schmidt. I have received from her one telegram . . . I have never fired a revolver in my life . . . I have never been to Hanwell in my life. It was in March *last* – which Mrs Ayris swore was in the March preceding – that I received from her a letter making an appointment there [at Victoria Station]. I met her . . . She wanted to borrow a sum of £50. I had not 50 pence, and if I had 50 pence I wanted them for my own family . . . In her evidence she told us that the meeting lasted ten minutes. It lasted three hours. The last thing I have to say is that at the time the murder was committed according to the evidence, I was as nearly as possible 50 miles from the spot.

He sat down and watched, with his arms folded, as the judge donned the black cap. Told to stand for the sentence, he thrust his left hand in his trouser pocket, and pulled his moustache with his right.

Mr Baron Pollock, in pronouncing sentence of death, was brisk and brief. 'Amen!' said the chaplain and others. Many of the spectators, especially the women, wept.

But Read was all smiles when he left the courthouse in a prison van. Wearing a white straw hat with a black band, he waved cheerfully at the crowd, who shouted 'Murderer!' and 'You wretch!'

Mrs Ayris now wrote to the *Chronicle*, saying that after Read's arrest, she received a threatening letter, apparently from Read or his brother. It said: 'If he is committed, you are a ruined woman. So beware!' She also revealed – having seen part of Read's petition against his sentence of death – that in it he now claimed he was out with *Mrs Ayris* on the Sunday night (24 June), walking about Southend. She wrote: 'Was anything ever more absurd?'

If this was his plea, which she of course denied, it meant he now conceded that he *was* in Southend, and not '50 miles from the spot'.

While awaiting the Home Secretary's response to his petition, Read wrote several letters from his quarters in Springfield Jail. In one he wrote: 'You may all satisfy yourselves that my murder, which is fixed for a fortnight today, and which I do not fear at all, is the sacrifice of a perfectly innocent life, which I do not now value at twopence since I have learned the value of earthly so-called friendships, and that so-called "divine justice" which permits such an outrage as this.'

A story was published about him serving as a choirboy at St Mary's Chapel-of-Ease in Shadwell, and his agnosticism was attributed to a schoolmaster, a sceptic, who lent the boy books casting doubt on the Bible and urged him to keep an open mind.

On the morning of Friday, 30 November, Jim Read was visited by his wife for the last time. She was accompanied by his brother, Harry, and an unmarried sister, Miss Read. Still cheerful, he maintained his innocence and said he was hopeful of a reprieve. But there were tears in his eyes as he bade his wife and sister goodbye, though all expressed the hope it would not be a final farewell. Mrs Read and Miss Read called on a Catholic priest before returning to London by train.

Harry Read was back in Chelmsford on Saturday afternoon. Jim was full of jokes, and kept repeating: 'I'm sure I shan't be hanged – you see!' Both regarded the long-delayed response to his petition as a good omen. At one point Harry left the prison to buy a new collar for his brother – he wanted a clean one to wear on Sunday – and when eight o'clock had come and gone with still no news from London, the brothers were even more optimistic. They parted, not expecting to hear anything so late at night. 'Goodnight, old chap,' said Harry. 'See you tomorrow.' 'Goodnight, old fellow,' said Jim.

A thick fog hung around the prison. Harry spent an hour in the George Hotel before catching the 9.25 back to London.

The train bearing the Home Secretary's decision, sent by express mail instead of by special messenger, must have passed Harry's train in the fog. Because of the fog, it was late arriving at Chelmsford, and the missive, stamped 'Official' and 'Immediate', reached the Under-Sheriff just before half-past ten. A copy went to the Prison Governor. Dated Whitehall, 1 December, it said: 'Sir – I am directed by the Secretary of State to acquaint you that . . . he regrets that he has failed to discover any sufficient ground to justify him in advising Her Majesty to interfere with the due course of the law . . .' Jim Read was told that night, unofficially, that there would be no reprieve. He would hang on Tuesday.

His brother learned of the decision in the Sunday papers. He returned to Chelmsford on the afternoon of Monday, 3 December. Stopping off at the George Hotel, Harry opened a telegram which had arrived for him minutes before. He showed it to a local reporter. It was in reply to a telegram he had sent to the Queen appealing for clemency, 'as a case does not appear to have been proved against my brother beyond reasonable possibility of doubt'. The telegram said: 'OHMS. Windsor. Your application should come through the Home Secretary. Signed: Private Secretary.'

Harry Read was not discouraged. He said: 'A member of my family and a lawyer are having a private audience at Windsor today.' 'Keep your pecker up!' said a bystander. Harry walked to the jail, smoking a pipe and knocking the ashes out before he entered the visitors' gate.

Jim was dejected. He said he was 'disgusted' at the Home Secretary's decision. But his sister, Mrs Kelly, who arrived soon afterwards, was able to tell him that her letter to the Queen had received a more positive reply: 'Your letter has been sent to the Home Secretary.' But no change of sentence, no news, had reached the prison by the time brother and sister had to leave. Mrs Kelly left first and returned to London. Harry stayed as long as he could, and when he departed, the two men, trying to control their feelings, bid each other an emotional farewell.

At 10.00 pm Harry returned to the prison to see the Governor. But there was no word from Windsor. He spent the night at the George Hotel, and remained in his bedroom, in bed, while his brother was hanged within Springfield Jail.

Outside the jail, a small crowd began gathering in the early morning fog at about 7.00 am. Among them were several reporters, some policemen, a preacher, an eccentric gentleman called 'The Major', who was prepared to act as hangman if Billington failed to appear, and a milkman, who arrived in his milk cart to make his daily deliveries to the jail. Various officials entered the jail, and at 7.45 the funeral bell began to toll.

Within, Read asked for a little brandy and the reassurance that his death would be instantaneous. He looked haggard but remained composed. Asked by the chaplain if he had anything to say, he said: 'Nothing at all – except to thank you and the others.' He had dressed himself with great care, brushing his hair, combing his beard and twisting his moustache. When the officials and hangman arrived he faced them bravely, and having been pinioned, was led in procession from his cell, across a hall, through a passage and across an open yard to the small execution shed. A cross-beam stretched from wall to wall, from which dangled a chain, and the noose. The pit below, some 15 feet deep, was lined with brick. Overhead, a double skylight afforded some illumination. The condemned man weighed 125 lbs, and the hangman had allowed a drop of 7′ 8″. The only sound was the tolling bell and the chaplain's mournful recitation – 'Man that is born of woman hath but a short time to live . . . In the midst of life, we are in death.'

At 7.55 the fog began to clear from the prison, and the black flag was unfurled at 8.03. Voices in the crowd murmured: 'There he goes!' A few seconds later 12 warders emerged from the prison on their way to breakfast. All looked gloomy and sad; some had tears in their eyes.

At 10.30 the inquest on the body was held in the Governor's office. The jury went to view the body, as it lay in a coffin in a storeroom. The face bore 'a peaceful expression', but there was slight abrasion on the neck. Jim Read still wore the light suit in which he had been arrested, tried and hanged. His red socks showed above his tan-coloured shoes, and his body, it is said, was still warm. He was buried within the jail.

Before he died, on the Sunday, Read wrote to his brother, Harry, saying he had written to the Home Secretary asking that his whereabouts in Southend (and his alibi) be checked anew. He said: 'I had beforehand referred him to the medical evidence, which showed the girl was murdered between 12 midnight 24/6 and 5.00 am 25/6.' He added that '4 witnesses at Mrs Clothier's, No. 1 Granville Villas, Southchurch Road, Southend, could answer for my being in bed the whole of that time'.

If this was so, why were these four witnesses never produced in court?

This statement, elaborating his petition's admission that he *was* in Southend, again negated his claim in court that on the night of the murder he was 50 miles away.

One of the *Chronicle*'s reporters investigated, on the very morning that James Read died. He found that Gresham (not Granville) Villas was near the railway station and that the landlady, Mrs Clothier, was not at home. But a coal merchant, Mr Sicely, who was lodging there, stated 'most positively' that Read had breakfasted there at about 7.00 am on the Monday morning and was thought to have left Southend by the eight o'clock train. Mr Sicely had gone to bed at half-past ten the previous night, and heard another lodger, possibly Read, return somewhat later. The reporter checked with the police, who confirmed that after studying Read's petition they had seen Mrs Clothier and established that Read returned to his lodging at 11.15 on the Sunday night.

So it was now confirmed that he *had* been in Southend on the night of the murder. In which case PC Daniel had been mistaken – or was telling a lie. For although it was possible for Read to have walked the eight miles to Benfleet between 11.15 and 1.15 am (when PC Daniel claimed to have met him) and then returned to Southend in time for a few hours' sleep before having breakfast at 7.00 am, it seems most unlikely that he did.

The implication at the trial that Read had *walked* the 30 miles from Southend to Leytonstone now seems even more absurd. He could easily have travelled on the Monday morning to Leytonstone by train, leaving Southend at 8.00 am and arriving at the Scannells' home at about 9.15. But if he was in Southend at Mrs Clothier's on the Sunday night (and on Saturday), why didn't the police find out? Or having done so, not present this damning fact in court?

It seems that the police, having accepted PC Daniel's evidence and being stuck with the consequent conclusion that Read walked back to London via Leigh, failed to enquire whether he might have lodged in Southend – not just on Sunday – but also on Saturday night. But even more odd is the apparent silence of Mr Sicely and Mrs Clothier. How did they fail to report that a stranger, a man answering Read's description, had lodged at Gresham Villas over the very weekend that Florence Dennis died?

There was another death a few days after the execution of James Read. His loyal and loving brother, Harry, shattered by the events of the last six months and without a job, threw himself into the River Thames, and drowned.

Two events occurred in 1895 that would have a far-reaching impact on the world, and on the study of criminals and the detection of crime. A young Italian with an Irish mother, Guglielmo Marconi, who had left his birthplace to pursue his experiments in wireless telegraphy in London, sent his first message over a mile. And in Vienna, Sigmund Freud published his first work on psycho-analysis.

A more immediately important legal event, and long overdue, occurred in 1898, when the Criminal Evidence Act decreed that any person being tried on a criminal charge could give evidence on his own, or her own, behalf. The Act also allowed a husband or wife of the accused to give evidence in court.

The scaffold, described by Billington's successor, Harry Pierrepoint, as 'the finest scaffold in the whole country, being fitted to hang three persons side by side', was moved to Pentonville Prison in 1902, when Newgate Prison was demolished. The first hanging at Pentonville took place on this scaffold on 30 September 1902 – an event that was also marked by the discontinuance of the practice of flying a black flag in London when an execution occurred. Instead, a bell was tolled.

In 1903, the number of people executed for murder in Britain rose to its highest level for over 70 years – 27 people being hanged. This, however, was well below the average for the years between 1811 and 1832, when about 80 people were hanged per year. This in turn was far less than the average rate of executions in the brief reign of Edward VI (1547–53), when about 560 people were executed each year at Tyburn (at Marble Arch).

Once Newgate Prison was demolished, building on the site began in 1903, concluding three years later. Topped by a large bronze figure of Justice, the new and imposing Central Criminal Court rose in its place, to become more familiarly known by the name of the street over which it towered – the Old Bailey.

CHAPTER 9

George Chapman

The Murder of Maud Marsh, 1902

Poison is rightly regarded as a woman's weapon when it comes to murder. Of the 68 women hanged for murder between 1843 and 1955, 37 were poisoners. But certain men of some education and social standing, especially doctors, are also apt to use poison to effect their murderous ends and seem to relish the power it gives them over their victims' lives and the suffering slow poisoning can cause. Such murders, premeditated and clinically performed, are particularly vile, and those who commit them the most callous and cruel of murderers. For they kill without passion, without a blow being struck, with the victim dying before their coldly curious eyes.

His real name was Severin Klosowski. The son of a carpenter, he was born on 14 December 1865 at Nagornak, a village near Kolo, west of Warsaw. Leaving school in 1880, when he was 14, he was apprenticed for four-and-a-half years to a surgeon in the village of Zvolen. At that time, Poland did not exist, having been swallowed up by Russia, Prussia and Austria. Warsaw was in the Russian sector, and it was to Warsaw that young Klosowski went in October 1885. There he was employed as an assistant surgeon until November 1886, during which time he studied practical surgery at the hospital in Praga, a suburb of Warsaw. The following month he received the degree of a junior surgeon. Wherever he went he collected certificates of employment and various commendations, which praised his diligence, zeal and good behaviour. A travel pass issued three weeks before his 21st birthday describes him as 'height, medium; hair, dark; eyes, blue; nose and mouth, medium; chin and face, longish; birthmarks, none'.

The last of these certificates, which were found much later in Chapman's possession and seem to be genuine, places him in Warsaw in March 1887. After that, there is no record of him until he appears in London in 1888. He is said to have joined the Russian army and to have served for 18 months. If so, he would surely have kept his service record (unless it was defamatory and bad). A witness at his trial, Wolff Levisohn, who had served with the Russian army for seven years, said: 'The accused could not have been a soldier, because he was too young when he came over here.' Chapman was 23 in December 1888.

It was Levisohn, a traveller or sales rep in hairdressing supplies, who established the year of Chapman's arrival in London. He told the Police

Court that he first met Chapman in a hairdresser's shop under the White Hart public house, 89 High Street, Whitechapel, in 1888. Chapman gave his name as Ludwig Zagowski. They discussed the efficacy of certain medicines, Chapman speaking a mixture of Polish and Yiddish. He said he came from Warsaw. According to Levisohn, the other man worked as an assistant to the hairdresser in this shop until 1889, when he became the proprietor. He was there until 1890. During this time, Chapman was joined by his wife and two children. But, said Levisohn, 'he did not support them, and now and again I and another man gave the woman some coppers'.

If Mrs Klosowski appeared on the scene in 1889 – with *two* children – she must therefore have married the junior surgeon in 1887, if not before. There seems no reason to doubt the fact that she was his real wife, and a Catholic, and would therefore have never countenanced any divorce. This would explain why Chapman never married his four subsequent 'wives', although he pretended to do so. Mrs Klosowski, like his later 'wives', seems to have been or become an inconvenience and an embarrassment. She disappears from the scene, almost as soon as she appears. Perhaps Chapman poisoned her, and the children. More probably, he disappeared himself, leaving his family to fend for themselves. It is recorded that Klosowski, using his real name, worked as an assistant for five months at a hairdresser's in West India Dock Road in Poplar. But this was, it seems, in 1888.

It is not known why Chapman never worked as an assistant surgeon in England. Historically, barber-surgeons were a joint occupation in England until 1745, serving as primitive doctors and dentists as well as barbers – the red ribbon on a barber's pole signifying the ribbon bound around a patient's arm before blood-letting. The practice may have survived much longer in rural Russian Poland.

The next sighting of Severin Klosowski, as he still called himself, was in the Polish Club in Clerkenwell in 1889. Here he met a Polish tailor, Stanislaus Baderski, who was living with a married sister, Mrs Polacryk. She and another sister, Lucy, used to visit the club on Sunday nights, and about a month after Chapman met Lucy Baderski they 'married', celebrating with a party on August Bank Holiday, 1889. At the time, Chapman had a barber's shop in Cable Street, Whitechapel. Here the couple lived for a few months before moving to Greenfield Street, also in Whitechapel. Another of Lucy's sisters, Mrs Rauch, who came to London from German Poland in August 1889, visited the Klosowskis in Greenfield Street, and when their first baby, a boy, was born, she recalled that the father washed the infant 'just like a nurse'.

In May 1890 the Klosowskis went to America, where it seems the baby boy died. Lucy returned to London, alone, in February 1891, and gave birth to a second child, a daughter, on 12 May. About two weeks later, according to Mrs Rauch, the father appeared and for a time the couple lived together, moving from lodging to lodging. But in 1893, or earlier, Lucy left her 'husband', apparently because of his ardent interest in other women.

He is next heard of in Tottenham, where in 1893 he worked for a hairdresser, Mr Haddin, at 5 West Green Road. Here he was known by another assistant as 'Schloski', and here the ubiquitous salesman, Wolff Levisohn, re-encountered Chapman in 1894, describing him later as 'a la-di-da then, with black coat, patent boots, and a high hat'. Another woman was with him then, and in 1895, when Chapman, using his real name, sublet a hairdresser's shop in High Road, Tottenham for a few months, he 'got a girl in trouble'. He later moved to another High Road shop opposite Bruce Grove railway station.

This woman and girl was Annie Chapman. She met the man who was to assume her surname towards the end of 1893, when he was working for Mr Haddin in West Green Road. She said later: 'I went there one day and made his acquaintance. After that I went out with him for a little while. I think he said he was either single or a widower. He was living at Haddin's, and he proposed I should go as his housekeeper, and after a time I did so. I lived with him as his wife. We passed as Mr and Mrs Klosowski.'

They were together for a year. Annie Chapman moved out in December 1894 when Lucy Klosowski moved back in – 'He brought her to the shop where I was living with him. He said she was his wife . . . That was the reason I left.' But on discovering a month or so later that she was pregnant, she returned to the shop opposite Bruce Grove railway station – 'I went there . . . and asked him to help me in my trouble. I was going to have a baby. I also asked him to give me a reference to get a situation . . . He did not take much notice.' She saw him once again, in February 1895, when he bicycled over to her Tottenham lodging – perhaps to dissuade her from seeing him again, or to exact his 'marital' rights.

It was in 1895, seeking to obscure his Polish origins, to confuse debtors and demanding 'wives', that Klosowski began calling himself George Chapman. Even after his arrest, he refused to acknowledge that he was Severin Klosowski, saying: 'I don't know anything about that fellow.'

As George Chapman he replied to an advertisement for a hairdresser's assistant in 1895, and was employed for about seven months by William Wenzel, whose shop was at 7 Church Lane in Leytonstone. There a customer, John Ward, offered to rent him a furnished room at his home in Forest Road. Mr Ward happened to have another lodger, Mrs Spink, who had been abandoned by her husband. She became Chapman's first victim, dying of poisoning two-and-a-half years after they met.

Her family came from Otley in Yorkshire and her maiden name was Mary Isabella Renton. While living with a cousin, a corn chandler, Joseph Renton, and his grandmother, in Leyton (her parents died when she was in her teens), she married a railway porter at Leytonstone Station, Shadrach Spink. He, according to Mr Renton, 'was not a sober man', and she 'was also intemperate'. They had a son, also called Shadrach, and a few years later, Spink deserted his wife, taking young Shadrach with him. A few months later, Mrs Spink gave birth to a boy, possibly not Spink's. Called Willie, he was five when his mother took a room in Mr Ward's house in Forest Road. By this time George Chapman was 29 and Mrs Spink about 39. Despite her age, her intemperate habits, and her son, she had a certain appeal – her grandfather had left her nearly £600 in trust when he died.

Before long, Mrs Ward complained to her husband about the 'carrying on' between Mr Chapman and Mrs Spink. Mr Ward spoke to Chapman, saying: 'My wife has seen you kissing Mrs Spink on the stairs. We cannot allow that sort of thing to go on in the house.' 'It's all right, Mr Ward,' said Chapman. 'We're going to get married about Sunday week.' And early on a Sunday morning in October, 1895, they went out together, allegedly to a Catholic church in Whitechapel, and returned that night. On seeing the Wards, Chapman announced: 'Allow me to introduce you to my wife!'

The Chapmans and little Willie left Leytonstone in March 1896, moving for some reason to Hastings. They settled in 10 Hill Street, where a family called Helsdown also lived. For a few months Chapman ran a hairdressing business in a poor part of the town. Then in June, the first Mrs Chapman withdrew £195 of her money so that her husband could open a barber's shop in Albion Mansions, George Street, where she acted as his assistant, lathering the customers' faces and occasionally trying to shave them. A small plump woman (5′ tall), with short dark hair cut like a man's, she must have been something of a character and a bit of a laugh. She also played an upright piano in the shop. Chapman had hired it to attract more custom, and business improved: a female hairdresser was unheard of then and 'musical shaves' were a novelty. That summer he also bought a small sailing-boat and, attired in nautical gear, took his spouse for brief cruises along the coast. Once the boat capsized, and both were saved from drowning by some fishermen – saved in both cases for a more dreadful demise.

Meanwhile, little Willie was leading a miserable and neglected life, sometimes sleeping in a cellar or in the shop; and his mother's addiction to drink now led to rows and blows. She told Mrs Helsdown that her husband had smacked her face and once grabbed her by the throat. She also complained of pains in her stomach and sickness, although no doctor was ever called.

In February 1897, the Chapmans moved to new lodgings in 1 Coburg Place. Another lodger, Mrs Greenaway, who only knew the Chapmans for a month, would later remember that Mrs Chapman, who drank, but seemed in good health though 'dazed', said that her first husband had been killed on the railway and that her second husband had a revolver. She also borrowed four volumes of Cassell's *Family Physician* from Mrs Greenaway which were never returned.

A frequent customer at the Albion Mansions barber's shop was a chemist, William Davidson, who had lived in Hastings for 18 years. He and Chapman used to chat about medical matters, and the barber sometimes called at his High Street shop. On 3 April, Chapman bought an ounce of tartar-emetic, a white powder, for which he paid two pence. Davidson entered the purchase in his poison register book – Chapman signed the entry – and on a red label printed *Poison*, which he attached to the bottle, he wrote: '*Dose, $\frac{1}{6}$th grain to $\frac{1}{4}$ grain: to be used with caution*'. He also sold the barber two old medical books.

Tartar-emetic was sometimes used to treat sick horses. It was used before long to make Mrs Chapman ill. In May, the housekeeper at Albion Mansions noticed that the barber's wife was 'vomiting a good deal' and afterwards 'appeared very poorly'.

About this time, a maidservant, Alice Penfold, was accosted one Sunday evening by a man called Smith, alias Chapman, who said he was single and managed a piano shop. She went out with him three times, and on one occasion accompanied him to St Leonards, to view a public house which he said he was thinking of buying. Then she received a letter from him in London, asking her to come and see him. She did not go.

This letter was written at an East End pub, the Prince of Wales, Bartholomew Square, off Old Street. Having sold the barber's shop and all therein, Chapman had turned himself into a publican. But to do so, to buy a lease on a pub – and before he killed off his wife – he required some, if not all, of her money. At her request, the balance of her Yorkshire trust, nearly £300, was sent south and banked in her name in Hastings on 31 August. Two days later, £50 of this was withdrawn in gold and a cheque for £200 was cashed the following week. On 28 September, George Chapman opened a bank account in London with £230, to which he soon added £55. The first Mrs Chapman died three months later, on Christmas Day.

Four women attended her dying, two neighbours, a part-time nurse and the pub potman's wife, Susan Pagett, who helped behind the public bar when Mrs Chapman was confined to her bed. To begin with, Mrs Chapman complained of feeling 'very bad' with 'pains in her head and all over'. Chapman would tell her, when she appeared behind the bar: 'Get out of it! You can't get drunk down here!' He told Mrs Pagett his wife was suffering from *delirium tremens*, and when she queried what sort of medicine he was giving his wife, he said: 'I told you before that she's delirious. You must take no notice of it.' Mrs Pagett replied: 'Delirious or not – I quickly moved in and I can quickly move out.' She did so, as did her husband, who told Chapman: 'If you've no respect for your wife and want to kill her, I have respect for mine. And you won't kill *her*.' Before they left, Mrs Pagett threatened to send for the parish doctor, and Chapman sent a note via her husband to a local doctor, Dr Rogers, who had also been recommended by Martha Doubleday.

Mrs Doubleday was a neighbour, a pub regular, it seems, who became friendly with Mrs Chapman, whom she described as 'a nice, little-built person, with a fresh colour'. After a month or so, Mrs Doubleday noticed the other woman was white-faced and very thin. Two weeks before Christmas Chapman asked her to sit up with his wife, who was now very ill. She agreed. Three days later Dr Rogers's services were sought. Mrs Doubleday said later:

> I stayed with Mrs Chapman every night. She was in bed in the front room on the second floor, all the time I was there. The accused used to sleep on the couch. She was suffering very much – she vomited frequently and had diarrhoea very badly. I had to get her out of the bed. I never gave her any food. After the doctor came, the accused gave her brandy and medicine. He brought the brandy up with him at night. After she had the brandy she vomited. When the accused came into the room he used to lean over her. Once or twice he told me to go outside, and then I would hear her say: 'Pray God – go away from me . . . ' When

> Dr Rogers came, he and the accused talked together in the bar about Mrs Chapman. I asked the accused what was the matter with her. He replied that the doctor said she was wasting away . . . I was only there at night. I saw Mrs Mumford there during the day . . . Towards Christmas she got much worse. Dr Rogers asked me to go and get Mrs Waymark to nurse her, as I could not do it any longer.

When Mrs Mumford, another neighbour, asked Chapman about his wife's illness, he replied: 'She drinks a good deal of brandy.' She saw him reading medical books in the bar: he said he was giving his wife something to cure her of *delirium tremens*. 'She seems very bad,' said Mrs Mumford. 'Oh, she'll get better when she gets on,' he said. He told her he had been a doctor on board a ship. The nurse, Mrs Waymark, later told the court:

> He used to go up to the bedside and feel her pulse. I sometimes said: 'She's very bad', and he would reply: 'Yes, I know what to do.' She used to say: 'Do kiss me.' She put out her arms for him to bend over and kiss her, but he did not do so. He would take her hand . . . She complained of diarrhoea and vomiting, and violent pains in her stomach. I very often saw her vomit . . . She always complained of thirst. She did not take much food, only a little beef tea, brandy, milk and soda, and water. The accused gave them to her. After she had had the drink, she was sick, and then used to go off in a stupor . . . She got worse and worse.

Mrs Doubleday was present when Mrs Chapman died.

> On Christmas morning she got much worse and became unconscious. She had been vomiting very much. A severe flooding came on. I called out for the accused, but he did not come up for some time afterwards. When he did, he only leant over the bed. He shook his head, and then went downstairs without making any remark. Before she died I called him again – 'Chapman! Come up quickly! Your wife is dying!' But he was too late . . . He went to the bedside and said: 'Polly – Polly – speak.' He went into the next room and cried. She died at one o'clock. Then he went downstairs and opened the public-house. I said: 'You're never going to open the house today?' He said: 'Yes, I am.'

The women were shocked when they laid out the body: it was like a skeleton, and the flesh was discoloured and yellow. That night Chapman summoned an undertaker, and Mary Isabella Chapman, aged 41, was buried in a common grave in Leytonstone on 30 December. Dr Rogers, who would die before Chapman was arrested, attributed her death to a consumptive, wasting disease, phthisis.

Throughout this period, Willie Spink had slept in an adjacent room, but not much longer. Chapman tried to put the boy into one of Dr Barnardo's homes, saying he had no relations. The enquiry officer was suspicious, and Willie was not accepted. But in March 1898 he was admitted to Shoreditch workhouse. Chapman told the officials there (truthfully) that Willie's mother, Isabella Spink, was dead and that her husband had deserted her. As references, he gave the names of Miss E. Painter and Bessie Taylor. Both lived at addresses near the Prince of Wales pub, and Willie's address was given as No. 8 Haberdasher Street, the same as that of Bessie Taylor, who was described as Chapman's housekeeper.

Apparently Chapman advertised for a barmaid or housekeeper soon after Mrs Spink died. Bessie Taylor was chosen. Born Elizabeth Taylor, the daughter of a Cheshire farmer, she was a maidservant in London before becoming the housekeeper/manageress of a restaurant in Peckham. In view of the fact that Chapman was evidently acquainted with both Elizabeth Painter and Bessie Taylor in March, it is possible, as the women were friends and were lodging near the Prince of Wales, that *both* assisted in helping Chapman run the pub, and that Painter was the first to be employed. At Chapman's trial she admitted, without saying *when*, that she sometimes assisted behind the bar, and that he kissed her 'once or twice', although 'he never made any overtures to me, nor said I could be Mrs Chapman'. But by Easter it was Bessie Taylor, aged 33, who moved into the Prince of Wales and before long 'married' the owner – perhaps in July 1898, when a £50 cheque, sent to Bessie by her father, was credited to Chapman's account. On 23 August, he closed the account, withdrawing £370 in notes and cash. In that month the Chapmans moved north, to Bishop's Stortford in Hertfordshire, where they leased another pub, The Grapes. Perhaps local gossip about the death of the first Mrs Chapman and the speedy appearance of a second 'wife' in the Prince of Wales prompted the move.

Not much of special interest happened at The Grapes, except that Elizabeth Painter stayed there for a fortnight before Christmas, apparently standing in for Bessie when she entered a hospital for treatment to her teeth: she had 'lumps on her face from her gums'. According to Mrs Painter, Chapman was 'very unkind' to Bessie on her return – 'He carried on at her all the afternoon, and in the evening he frightened her with a revolver.' None the less, Painter later told the court that the Chapmans were on 'very good terms'. She said: 'Most people are changeable, and he was no exception to the rule.'

In May 1899, the ever-mobile publican moved back to London, leasing The Monument in Union Street, in Southwark, where the second Mrs Chapman would die within two years, during which the Boer War was fought in South Africa, and Ladysmith, Kimberley and Mafeking besieged and then relieved.

Bessie Taylor was a charitable, genial woman, well regarded by the customers and by the sisters at the local mission. Like her predecessor she played the piano and she took up bicycling to please her husband. Her parents and her brother, William, who stayed more than once at The Monument, were favourably impressed by Chapman. Bessie's mother, Mrs Taylor, said she 'had never seen a better husband'. So why did Chapman decide to kill her?

It was not for her money. Bessie, alive, a favourite daughter, could expect to inherit a large sum of money when her parents died. So why? Did Chapman tire of her – as he seemed to tire of all his women after a couple of years? Did a younger woman catch his eye and excite his lust? Did he relish the power over life and death that lay in his hands as he dispensed his poisonous doses? Did he seek to relive some of the hospital dramas of his youth? He was clearly a poseur and liked play-acting, pretending to be other, and more, than he was. Did he also like playing the doctor, the husband, the lover, as well as the man of the world?

As the Christmas of 1900 approached, Bessie, who had been out of sorts for several weeks, became seriously ill. She had complained to a neighbour, Martha Stevens, who was a nurse, of being 'fatigued, languid, and having pains in her stomach'. Mrs Stevens recommended a visit to Dr James Stoker, who thought the sick woman had constipation and prescribed a dose of salts. She visited him more than once, and he first called on her at The Monument on 1 January 1901, when he found her to be suffering from pains in the stomach, vomiting and diarrhoea. Mrs Stevens, who had been acting as a day nurse for about two weeks, was now employed on a 24-hour basis, assisted on some evenings by Elizabeth Painter and then by Bessie's mother, Mrs Taylor. Dr Stoker now called on the patient nearly every day.

He said later: 'She used to get better and then go back again.'

Mrs Stevens said:

> She complained a little about her throat burning, and it was very red. On about two occasions I noticed perspiration. When she vomited it was severe, green, thick and slimy. She did not complain much of being thirsty. When she did complain I saw milk, water, brandy and water, and champagne given to her . . . I sometimes prepared the nourishment she had, sometimes her mother, and sometimes the accused. [He] was there during the night until Bessie's mother came, and then he went and slept in the parlour. I went back to my home in the daytime for an hour sometimes. Mrs Taylor did not go out very often.

Elizabeth Painter said:

> She always felt sick, and it always came on after she had had anything to eat or drink . . . When the accused came into her room he felt her pulse with his watch in his hand. After a time I saw medicine bottles in the room. The accused would shake them and then look up to the light through them. I asked him what was the matter with her, and he said it was a complication of diseases. When I went into the bar, I would ask him how Bessie was, and sometimes he would say: 'Your friend is dead.'

But she did not take him seriously. 'It was just his way of putting it,' she said.

On 22 January 1901, Queen Victoria died, and The Monument, like London and the Empire, was garbed in mourning, in purple and black. Bessie's brother, William Taylor, who came to see his sister more than once, said that in February: 'She appeared to be very ill and shrunken . . . thin, like a little old woman.'

Three other doctors were consulted at Mrs Taylor's suggestion. Each examined the patient and came to three different conclusions: that she was suffering from some womb trouble; that she had a cancerous disease of the stomach or intestines; that she was afflicted with a severe form of hysteria, i.e. imagining things and malingering.

One Sunday, Bessie was suddenly better. Mrs Stevens told the court:

> She got up and went about the house, and then sat down and played the piano in the club-room adjoining her bedroom. As she was playing, Dr Stoker came in and put his finger up so that I should not interrupt her. And he then said: 'Capital!' She looked round and discovered him there. I went home to sleep that night. I was sent for again on Monday or Tuesday. Bessie seemed quite prostrated . . . I was with Bessie on 13 February, and at about 1.30 am I thought she was dying. So I called the accused. He looked at her, and I think he said: 'Oh, she has gone!' And he commenced to cry.

Dr Stoker gave as the cause of death 'intestinal obstruction, vomiting, and exhaustion'. He still believed that the primary cause of her illness was constipation. There was no post-mortem. Two days later, Bessie Taylor's body was transported to St Pancras Station. Chapman went with the hearse. At the station the coffin was received by William Taylor, who took it by train to Warrington. He paid all the funeral expenses, as Chapman claimed to be short of money.

Bessie Taylor was buried, aged 36, in the family plot in Lymm churchyard in Cheshire, where a gravestone, presumably raised by William, records that she was a daughter of Thomas and Betsy Taylor, who were to die within two months of each other in 1902. There is no mention of Chapman or how she died. The death of another daughter, Mary, is also given; she died in 1893 aged 28 – presumably she was Bessie's twin.

On a memorial card, a verse was inscribed, possibly composed by Chapman himself:

> Farewell, my friends, fond and dear,
> Weep not for me one single tear;
> For all that was and could be done,
> You plainly see my time is come.

Mrs Stevens remained at The Monument for a week or so until, as she said, 'a woman appeared in response to an advertisement'. We do not know this woman's name, only that Mrs Stevens called her 'Madam'. Whoever she was, she evidently left without agreeing to be the third Mrs Chapman. That fatal role would be assumed by an 18-year-old girl, Maud Marsh.

Some writers have characterised George Chapman as baboon-like, repulsive, illiterate, ugly, of meagre physique and coarse. He was most probably none of these things. He was not illiterate, although his spelling was poor, and he was clearly something of a dandy, making the most of his dress and appearance with his colourful ties and breast-pocket handkerchiefs, his rings, his gold watch and chain, his carefully brushed hair and luxuriant droopy moustache. Although thin of face, even gaunt, and possibly scrawny, he must, after years on his feet as a medic, barber and publican, have been fairly sinewy and fit. He was a keen cyclist: he would bicycle the ten miles from Southwark to Croydon and back, to see Maud's parents, and when licensee of the Prince of Wales he belonged to a police cycling club. He was also a keen photographer, taking photos of himself and his wives and developing the results. Interested in matters criminal, as well as medical, he cultivated the custom and good opinions of the local police – he even possessed a copy of James Berry's autobiography. The pubs he ran were adorned with guns, swords and pistols, flags, photos and souvenirs of his travels. Apparently he used to regale his customers with exaggerated tales of his adventures at sea and in America, and of hunting game. Sometimes he used an American revolver to kill rats lurking in his cellars. He is said to have affected a republican stance and to have pretended to be an American. During the Boer War, whose late peace was concluded in May 1902, he made himself unpopular by siding with the Boers and drinking to their success.

In the spring and summer of 1901, Chapman must have employed one or more replacements for Bessie Taylor as barmaid/housekeeper at The Monument. Whoever these women were, they walked out, or were sacked, the last in August, and thereby possibly saved their lives. Still seeking to employ another 'wife', Chapman replied to an advertisement in the *Morning Advertiser* placed by Maud Eliza Marsh in August 1901.

Maud's father was a labourer, and the family, which included at least four daughters and a son, lived at 14 Longfellow Road, West Croydon. Maud had been working locally as a barmaid since she was 15 and seems to have hankered after a London job. Her mother accompanied Maud to The Monument when a reply to her ad was received, and learned that the publican, Chapman, was a widower and an American, and that a family occupied the pub's top floor – which was untrue. Despite Mrs Marsh's doubts, Maud was employed there and then, and moved in within a few days.

Within a month, in mid-September, when Maud and George Chapman visited Mrs Marsh in Croydon (her husband was ill in a local hospital), she was doubtless surprised to hear from Chapman that he had taken a great fancy to Maud and wished to marry her. Mrs Marsh said she would consult her husband, whom the couple also visited at a later date. It seems that neither parent was keen on the match, although Chapman promised to make a will, leaving £400 and all his furniture, etc, to his 'wife' in the event of his death.

About this time, possibly before the visit, Maud wrote to her mother to say that Mr Chapman had given her a gold watch and chain. Then this letter arrived in Croydon:

> Dear Mother – Just a line to say on the QT Mr has gone out, so I now write this to you to say that George says if I do not let him have what he wants he will give me £35 and send me home. What shall I do? It does

worry me so; but still I am engaged, so it will not matter much, and if he does not marry me I can have a breach of promise, can't I?

Mrs Marsh wrote and told her daughter to come home at once, with or without the £35. Maud refused, and wrote again, more or less refuting the gist of her previous letter. Her father then visited The Monument, and urged his daughter to behave herself – to no avail. When Mrs Marsh paid a visit to the pub on Sunday, 13 October, she saw some confetti lying about and was told by her 14-year-old daughter, Nellie, who was there on a working visit that lasted two months: 'Maud was married this morning.'

This was soon confirmed by the happy couple – Maud was wearing a wedding ring – and Chapman asked Mrs Marsh to stay for dinner and join in the celebrations. The story was that they had married in a Roman Catholic church in Bishopsgate. Although Mrs Marsh asked to see the certificate – and was told by Maud: 'George has got it, and has put it with his other papers' – she was not disposed to believe that her daughter would lie. Chapman himself was welcoming, and, as she said later, treated her nicely. Her husband, who visited the Chapmans just before Christmas, was likewise placated, later telling the court that he and Chapman, whom he found pleasant and agreeable, were on 'the best of terms'. He said: 'I minded his house for him on two occasions . . . He always answered my inquiries about my daughter perfectly frankly . . . and, as far as I could see, she was very happy with him. I thought he treated her very well.'

That pre-Christmas visit was paid to The Crown, Chapman's latest acquisition, at 213 Borough High Street, Southwark. The move was necessitated, in part, by a fire at The Monument, not long before Chapman's lease on that pub was about to expire. Oddly, the Chapmans were not at home at the time, the tills had been emptied, doors were open, and some of the furniture had been removed. Although the Fire Brigade's headquarters were a few minutes away, the pub was badly damaged. Chapman made an insurance claim and sued a newspaper, which voiced suspicions about the fire's cause, for libel. However, he failed to pursue both claims, and no insurance was paid. Even more oddly, as he very probably set fire to the pub himself, no action was taken against him by the police, and he soon acquired the lease of The Crown, some 500 yards away.

He was a litigious man, and the following summer succeeded in a claim of financial deception, although *he* was in the wrong. Interestingly, Arthur Hutton, a tall man who wore a monocle and prosecuted at Southwark on Chapman's behalf, would appear for the defence nine months later at Chapman's trial.

When Chapman and his third 'wife' moved to The Crown, Mrs Marsh received no communications from her daughter, nor saw her, for seven months. However, her son and other daughters were regular visitors at The Crown, and Mrs Marsh heard from them that Maud was happy and well. But a married daughter, Mrs Louisa Morris, neglected to report that Maud had had an abortion in about April or May.

This was induced by Chapman himself, using certain appliances and concoctions. Maud was much upset by not being allowed to have a baby. She wanted a family of her own, and when her sister, Louisa, brought *her* baby to The Crown, Maud would become 'very distressed and cry a good deal'. She complained that George didn't want any children, not until his business and income had improved. She also complained that George was reluctant to let her leave the pub, restricting her to the bar or the rooms upstairs. On one occasion, when the sisters went out for a walk, Maud began to cry. 'You don't know what he is!' she sobbed, and when questioned revealed that George had beaten her more than once, grabbing her hair and banging her head. In retaliation, she said, she had kicked him.

Clearly, Chapman wanted his women to be useful but passive and decorous doormats, submitting fully to his every professional and personal need. Fear and hatred of women were probably deeply embedded within his psyche. But he needed them for domestic and sexual purposes, and to constantly reassert his own, and others', high opinion of himself.

Maud's intractable youth and tears may have shortened her life. Or Chapman, now 36, may have sought more frequent conquests and thrills. But the appearance of Florence Rayner in The Crown in June seems to have been the spur that hastened the third Mrs Chapman's demise. Louisa Morris would later remember a tea-time conversation when Maud remarked, in her husband's presence: 'What do you think? George says I won't live to be 28.' To which Chapman responded: 'No more you won't!'

Florence Rayner, who came from Peckham, was employed locally and became accustomed to dropping into The Crown about mid-day. Happening to mention that she had some previous experience behind the bar, she was asked one day by Chapman to lend a hand, after which he offered her a job as a barmaid at 5 shillings a week, plus board and lodging. She agreed. This was in the middle of June. She used to eat with Chapman upstairs while Maud managed the bar below. Before long he was being very attentive, kissing the barmaid and asking her if she would come to America with him. 'You've got a wife downstairs,' said Florence. 'You don't want me!' He retorted: 'I could give her *that* – and she'd be no more Mrs Chapman.' He said he would send Florence to America, then sell the business and join her there. 'Be my sweetheart, will you?' he asked, and she said: 'No!' One afternoon he entered Florence's bedroom. But we do not know whether Florence said: 'Yes!' However, three weeks after her arival, Maud became sick, suffering from vomiting and diarrhoea.

It seems that Florence then blotted her copybook by becoming drunk on duty one Saturday night, and Chapman threw her out, refusing to give her a reference. Her version was that she departed to avoid his advances. Several weeks later he visited Florence at her next place of employment, The Forester's in Twickenham. He told her that his wife was in Guy's Hospital suffering from constipation, and said: 'If you hadn't been such a fool, you would have been at The Crown now.'

It was not his idea that Maud should be hospitalised. What happened was that her sister, Alice, called at The Crown towards the end of July (after

Florence had gone and after a servant, Louisa Cole, had been employed in her place) and found that Maud was unwell. 'Where's Maud?' she enquired on arrival. Said Chapman: 'In bed. Dying fast.' Going upstairs, Alice found her sister sitting up in bed, sipping some senna tea; she complained of being constipated and in great pain. Alice took charge. She told Chapman: 'I think Maud ought to have a doctor, or go to the hospital.' He said he didn't want her to be messed about. None the less, Alice persuaded her sister to get up and get dressed – she was so weak that this took an hour – and they went out together, to a local doctor. He was out, so they walked on to Guy's Hospital, where Maud collapsed and was admitted, on 28 July. Chapman was far from pleased.

Suffering at first from a high fever (up to 103°), a rapid pulse and such pains in her abdomen that she could not bear to be touched, Maud slowly recovered. The assistant obstetric surgeon at Guy's surmised she had peritonitis. But her husband was opposed to any internal examinations and insisted he could care for her at home. Had he not been a junior surgeon? So when her temperature returned to normal and her health improved, the doctor had to let her depart, on 20 August, prescribing light food, occasional aperients and some opiates for any pain. Chapman fetched her himself, taking her away in a cab. Two months later she was dead.

Although her parents and sisters had visited her in the hospital, it was Maud's older sister, Mrs Louisa Morris, who, apart from the servant, Louisa Cole, and Chapman himself, saw the most of the dying young wife (she was now 19 and a half) from the day Maud returned to The Crown.

Mrs Morris said later: 'She was sitting on a chair in the bar. She appeared very ill, and I told her she had no business there. I made her go upstairs and lie down . . . I had to help her. I visited her subsequently: sometimes I found her well and sometimes unwell. She was generally up. On one or two occasions I found her lying down.'

At some point Chapman remarked: 'She should have done as I told her.' Mrs Morris asked: 'What was that?' He answered: 'She should have took the medicine I give her.' 'She never would take medicine,' said Mrs Morris, adding: 'It's funny the doctor couldn't find out what was the matter with her.' To which Chapman replied, snapping his fingers: 'I could give her a bit like *that*, and 50 doctors wouldn't find out.' 'What do you mean?' demanded Mrs Morris. 'Never mind!' he said and walked away.

None the less, on Friday, 10 October, Chapman decided he needed a doctor to witness Maud's illness and imminent death. He himself called on Dr Stoker, who had been so effectively ineffectual in knowing what was wrong with Bessie Taylor, and would prove so once again.

That night Stoker called on Maud Marsh – Chapman had revealed to him that she was not really his wife – and prescribed a mixture of catechu, bismuth, opium and chalk, and a diet of soda water and milk, boiled milk, brandy, beef tea, and ice. Two days later he changed the medicine to bismuth, morphia and ipecacuanha. The next day Maud was worse. She now suffered from spasms, and the pain in her stomach was severe. He thought she might have gastro-enteritis and stopped any oral intake of food, or medicine apart from bismuth, and told Chapman that the patient must be fed by rectal injections of a mixture of beef tea, milk and egg. A nurse, he suggested, should be employed.

On 16 October, Chapman asked the charwoman, Jessie Toon, if she could do any nursing. She replied: 'It all depends what it is. Is it a miscarriage, or is it premature?' He said: 'No. Nothing of the kind. She's been sick, and the doctor has ordered her to have food injected.' Mrs Toon said: 'I don't understand anything of that kind.' Nevertheless, she was employed, after seeing the patient, who lay in her second-floor bedroom and cried. Maud said if no one could be found to look after her, she would have to go to the hospital, which she did not want. 'I don't understand it, Mrs Chapman,' the charwoman said. 'But would you like me to look after you?' 'Yes, please, Jessie,' sobbed Maud. 'If you will.' She had just been sick. Unknown to Dr Stoker, it was Chapman who would give Maud the injections, using a syringe with a rubber attachment.

Mrs Toon said later:

> The injections didn't stay with the deceased. They came back again quickly, and she was in terrible pain. No one brought anything into the room for her use except the accused. I didn't see where he got what he brought, or how it was mixed. Dr Stoker sent some medicine to be kept by the bed, but she never took any of it. The accused took it into the kitchen with him and brought it back when he came in with the injection . . . When the attacks of diarrhoea came on, I had to help her out of bed. It was as much as I could manage to hold her, there was such dreadful pain. Her limbs would go stiff, and she complained frequently of thirst . . . She said her throat was burning, and that it seemed to be always burning . . . Everything she drank she vomited within a few minutes. The vomit was green.

On Saturday, 18 October, Maud's father, worried by what his daughter, Mrs Morris, had told him, visited The Crown. He sat with Maud for three hours, during which Chapman was 'up and down stairs every few minutes'. The two men said very little to each other, but when Mr Marsh left at about 10.00 pm, he was deeply disturbed and suspicious, although he took no action for two days. When he did, Chapman gave Maud a final, fatal dose.

In the meantime, on Monday, 20 October, both Mrs Marsh and Mrs Morris went to The Crown. They did what they could; Maud was very ill, in a stupor most of the time, and still having rectal injections. She was in pain and vomiting a good deal; Chapman gave her some brandy and water. Mrs Marsh said to him: 'Don't you think you had better have another doctor?' He replied: 'No. It's no good.' That night Mrs Morris and Mrs Toon went home, leaving Mrs Marsh to tend her daughter. On the Tuesday, Dr Stoker called at noon. Mrs Marsh said: 'Is there anything you can give her to stop the sickness?' 'No,' he replied. 'I'm at my wit's end to know what to do.' 'If she dies,' said Mrs Marsh, 'don't you think you ought to have a post-mortem? If you do, I'll pay the expense out of my pocket.' Chapman, when asked, blamed Maud's condition on a rabbit stew that he claimed had also made him sick.

The unexpected arrival of Dr Grapel at about 3.00 pm surprised all those on their feet in The Crown. That morning Mr Marsh had called on him, expressing deep concern about his daughter, and asked him – he was the Marsh's family doctor – to visit Maud. When Dr Grapel arrived, Chapman tried to pretend that Grapel was not only misinformed but at the wrong address. Muttering that a doctor was already in attendance, Chapman sent for Dr Stoker and the two doctors examined the patient. Dr Grapel said later: 'Her skin was sallow, jaundiced and muddy in appearance, tongue coated, her pulse fairly quick, and her breathing shallow. She was in a semi-comatose condition. I examined her stomach and found it was extremely tender to the touch. When I touched it, she groaned and retched.'

After a consultation with Dr Stoker and a private word with Mrs Marsh, Dr Grapel left, convinced that the patient was 'suffering from some acute irritant poison, probably ptomaine'. Arsenic was also in his mind as a cause, and he decided on his way home that an analysis of the patient's excreta might resolve the matter. At The Crown, Mrs Marsh confronted Chapman. 'Dr Grapel thinks Maud has been poisoned,' she said. To which he replied that he couldn't think how, unless it was the rabbit. She said: 'Dr Grapel says you don't find arsenic in rabbits.' He retorted: 'I can't think what it was then.'

That night Mrs Marsh sat in an armchair in her daughter's bedroom after Mrs Toon had left; Chapman lay on a couch. He brought some brandy in a glass tumbler upstairs and placed it on a safe by the bed. For a while, all three slept. About 4.00 am Maud awoke and asked for some liquid. Her mother gave her a tablespoonful of the brandy mixed with soda. Maud was sick. An hour or so later, Mrs Marsh, who had eaten nothing since her arrival and drunk only tea and stout, swallowed some of the brandy to revive herself. She said later: 'After I had taken it I had severe diarrhoea and sickness and pain in the lower part of my stomach, which continued till about 7.00 am. I had about six attacks of diarrhoea and vomiting during that time. Maud's bedroom was on the second floor; the WC was on the first floor. When I had to go there the accused was left with my daughter. He opened the house to the public about 8.00 am.'

It was Wednesday, 22 October. Mrs Marsh sent the servant, Louisa Cole, to fetch Mrs Toon, who arrived about 8.30 am. She asked Chapman: 'What's the matter? Is she worse?' 'No,' he said. 'Her mother is bad now.' 'What's the matter with her?' 'Sickness and diarrhoea,' he replied. She said: 'What! Two of them now!' 'You had better go upstairs, Jessie,' he said. 'And tell her to get to bed out of the way, the old cat.' He also said: 'Be careful, Jessie, what you say to her, and take particular notice of what she says to you . . . The old cat wants to have her cut about and show me up.'

Upstairs, Mrs Toon watched as Chapman brought another tumbler of brandy into the sick room. He poured some water into the glass and gave it to Maud to drink. Mrs Marsh then came in and spoke of her sickness. She said Chapman should send for a proper nurse. He said she was over-tired and he left the room. Maud asked for another drink. Mrs Toon offered her the brandy. But Maud raised her hand, saying: 'No, no, no.' She drank some water instead. Mrs Toon then tasted some of the brandy to test its strength. It burned her throat, and she went downstairs to wash out her mouth and eat some bread.

Maud was dying. At about 9.00 am she had a spasm or fit. Green fluid seeped from her mouth. Her face and hands were discoloured and dark; her lips were black. At about noon Mrs Marsh summoned George Chapman. He stood beside the bed, looking down at Maud. She whispered: 'I'm going, George.' He said 'Where?' She murmured: 'Goodbye, George.' And within a little while she died.

Chapman wept. He was wiping his eyes when Dr Stoker arrived, too late to do anything, but now resolved to do something. They conversed on the landing. Dr Stoker said he would like a post-mortem, as he could not account for the cause of Mrs Chapman's death. 'What use is that?' asked Chapman, adding that she had died of exhaustion. 'What caused the exhaustion?' demanded Dr Stoker. Chapman replied: 'Diarrhoea and vomiting.' Dr Stoker persisted: 'What caused the diarrhoea and vomiting?' To which Chapman made no reply.

The following day, Thursday, Dr Stoker carried out a private post-mortem. Before he began, he received a telegram from Dr Grapel, suggesting that he look for arsenic. Grapel had decided on this course of action after hearing from Mrs Marsh that Maud had died. But Dr Stoker was not a specialist and found nothing that might have caused her death. However, he bottled her stomach and other organs and sent them on Friday to Dr Bodmer, a chemist and the public analyst for Bermondsey. Reinsch's test was made and revealed some evidence of antimony, as well as arsenic. He so informed Dr Stoker, who communicated with the police very late that night and wrote to the coroner's office.

At noon on Saturday, 25 October, Detective Inspector George Godley and Detective Sergeant Kemp went to The Crown, and Chapman was detained, pending further enquiries. Although two full days had elapsed since Maud's death, he had destroyed none of the evidence that would help to convict him: bottles containing brandy and water, medicine bottles, medical books, a diary, memorial cards and undertakers' accounts for Bessie Taylor and Mrs Spink, photographs, a will, certificates and other documents, some in Polish, and even the red label that Mr Davidson had stuck on the bottle of tartar-emetic in Hastings. All these things were seized by Godley, including gold and silver coins and notes amounting to £268.

George Chapman was charged with the wilful murder of Maud Marsh at 10.15 that night. He said: 'I am innocent. Can I have bail?' Godley said: 'No.' Earlier, Chapman had said: 'I don't know how she got the poison.' He told Sgt Kemp: 'I wouldn't hurt her for the world. I've had a lot of trouble with my barmaids. But I took a great fancy to this one. There was some jealousy lately. She said to me: "I've not had a baby yet. If I don't soon have one, you won't have me with you long."'

It was not until 30 October that Dr Stevenson, a Home Office analyst and expert in poisons, made a thorough examination of the body and established that Maud Marsh had been poisoned by antimony.

He later told the court: 'I found traces of arsenic in a small quantity, and I formed the opinion that death had not resulted from it. Arsenic is sometimes found in antimony when it is impure. I came to the conclusion that death was caused by poisoning with antimony in a soluble form – tartar-emetic, or metallic antimony.' 7.24 grains of antimony, representing 20.12 grains of tartar-emetic, were found in Maud Marsh. A dose of 15 grains would have been enough, he thought, to kill her. But a very large amount of what she had been given would have been quickly ejected or purged. He said:

> Vomiting and purging make people waste away. It produces gastro-enteritis, and they also appear to die from failure of the heart. Antimony depresses the circulation and quickens the pulse . . . The effect of the poison itself generally takes a considerable time before it causes death . . . The symptoms are great depression, profuse perspiration, followed by nausea and vomiting. Purging is set up with pain in the abdomen, and usually after a time there is a burning or metallic sensation in the throat and stomach; there is a great thirst. Spasms are quite common, and patients fall sometimes into a comatose state. They are generally very pallid, and sometimes get quite jaundiced and dark under the eyes, and thin and worn.

Dr Stevenson also carried out post-mortems on the bodies of Bessie Taylor and Mrs Spink, who were exhumed, respectively, on 22 November at Lymm, and at Leytonstone on 9 December. Both bodies were remarkably well preserved – a side effect of the antimony that had destroyed them. 3.83 grains were found in Mrs Spink (much would have disappeared after five years underground) and 29.12 grains in Bessie Taylor. Stevenson concluded that she had been given a large dose of antimony not long before her death.

On Monday, 27 October 1902, George Chapman appeared before the magistrates at Southwark Police Court; the coroner's inquest was opened the following day. On 31 December he was charged in the name of Severin Klosowski with the wilful murders of Mrs Spink and Bessie Taylor. 'By what means?' he asked. 'Stabbing, shooting, or what? Who is this other fellow? I don't know the other fellow.' He never acknowledged that he and Klosowski were one and the same.

There were four sittings of the coroner's inquest, the last on 18 December. Police Court proceedings progressed simultaneously, taking place on 14 separate days until 11 February, and so setting a record for the number of appearances by a prisoner before being committed for trial.

This began in Court No. 11 at the Central Criminal Court, soon to be demolished, on Monday, 16 March 1903. The trial lasted four days. The judge was Mr Justice Grantham, an imperious figure, with a resonant voice, whose preconceived ideas about a prisoner's guilt tended not to be concealed. The chief prosecutor was the Solicitor-General, Sir Edward Carson, KC, MP, who had prosecuted Oscar Wilde. He was assisted by Charles Mathews and Archibald Bodkin, both later knighted and successive Directors of Public Prosecution. Mr Bodkin had led for the prosecution when

Chapman appeared at the Police Court. The defence was led by Mr George Elliott, assisted by Arthur Hutton. Mr Elliott tried to prevent the prosecution citing and examining the murders of Bessie Taylor and Mrs Spink – they were separate indictments. He was overruled by the judge. Chapman, who seemed overawed and nervous, pleaded 'Not guilty, sir', thrice. The all-male jury were then instructed to try him for the murder of Maud Marsh. Forty-three witnesses were called by the prosecution; the defence called none.

Both closing speeches lasted less than 15 minutes, the defence arguing, while Chapman wept, that as he was 'a hated alien', the jury might be prejudiced against him.

Summing up, as if in continuation of Sir Edward Carson's closing words, the judge remarked that the case was unique from medical, chemical, legal and criminal points of view. 'It is the first time,' he said, 'in which the antecedents of the prisoner have been investigated in the way in which they have been on the present occasion, and on which it has been found possible, as well as legal, to bring forward evidence of two other cases in which persons have died at the hands of someone . . . and, as it is suggested, by the prisoner at the bar.' He went on to speak scornfully of the apparent stupidity and incompetence of most of the doctors involved. 'It is a very sad thing,' he said, 'that a person who has up to now occupied only the position of a hairdresser, has been able to defy the doctors . . . to baffle the surgeons for five or six long years.'

The jury were out for a mere ten minutes, returning an inevitable verdict of 'Guilty'. Chapman seemed numb with terror, as Mr Justice Grantham, having donned the black cap, pronounced sentence, saying at the start: 'Severin Klosowski – for I decline to call you by the English name you have assumed – the only satisfactory feature in the case we have just completed is that I am able to address you as a foreigner, and not as an Englishman.'

An appeal addressed to the Home Secretary was rejected (there was then no Court of Criminal Appeal).

In prison Chapman was morose and restless. He refused to see anyone except a Catholic priest – not even his first and real Polish wife – and still maintained he was an American, George Chapman. In one of several letters that he wrote he said: 'One thing whod I wish is this to be Remembered as I am an American orphend of good family and I left my foster father, against his wish, and I took to erning my own living at age of ten.' He also wrote:

> Believe me, be careful in your life of dangers of other enimis whom are unnow to you. As you see . . . I was unjustly criticised and falsly Represented. Also you can see I am not Believed. Therefore you see where there is Justice. They can take my life, but they cannot kil my soul . . . As to crime I am innocent . . . Believe me I am werry grievously sorry but it could not be help now . . . Shall be now starting preparing for my Deth.

He was hanged at Wandsworth Prison on 7 April 1903. In his will he left items worth £140 to the surviving family of Bessie Taylor, and a ring and some clothes to the parents of Maud Marsh.

Some writers have suggested that George Chapman may have been Jack the Ripper – a supposition based on vague coincidences, misconceptions and a suppression of logic and facts. The Ripper's five murders were committed between August and November 1888 in the Whitechapel area, where Chapman lived and worked after arriving in London, although it is not known exactly when. It is most unlikely, however, that an insecure young foreigner in a strange city, speaking little or no English and ignorant of social customs and local geography, would have suddenly set about a series of horrific murders involving mutilation – and then stopped, and married (Lucy Baderski) the following year. In May 1889, the couple went to America, settling in Jersey City, where a series of alleged Ripper-like murders is said to have happened at about this time. The actual dates and nature of these killings would need to be known before they could begin to be ascribed to Chapman. It is said that they ceased at the beginning of 1892. If so, Chapman had already been back in London for a year. The evidence of Lucy's sister, Mrs Rauch, is very clear. She said at the trial: 'She came back alone in February 1891. Another child was born on 12 May. When the child was about a fortnight old the accused came back from America, and I then left my sister, as they were going to live together.'

Mrs Spink died several years later, in December 1897. Apart from a generic similarity to two of Sir Melville Macnaughten's main suspects (one was a Polish Jew, Kosminski, and the other a Russian doctor), there is nothing, no fact, to make a reasonable connection between Jack the Ripper and Chapman the poisoner, except that Chapman was probably in London in the latter half of 1888. So were thousands of other male foreigners – with a moustache and of medium height, as the Ripper was described in the only likely, though very doubtful, sighting of him. This man was also said to be 34 or 35, to be well dressed and look respectable. Chapman was then a poor hairdresser's assistant, aged 22.

What is most inconceivable is that one man could switch from a quick series of frenzied, sexual slaughters of prostitutes done with a knife and mainly outdoors, to the slow, secretive, indoor poisoning of 'wives' over several months and separated by more than a year. The only characteristic the Ripper and Chapman shared, as with other lady-killers, was their loathing of the opposite sex.

CHAPTER 10

Paul Hefeldt and Jacob Lepidus

The Murder of PC Tyler, 1909

It takes two to make a murder – that is to say, no one would be a murderer if no appropriate victim was present, nor would someone become a victim if someone else was not in a murderous frame of mind. It also sometimes takes two, or three, to murder someone else – usually during a robbery, when a conjunction of character flaws and personality failures erupts in an explosive display of murderous violence, that destroys not only others but also the despairing, doomed relationship that bound the two, or three, together. There must have been something very amiss with the association of Hefeldt and Lepidus, aside from their social alienation. For they destroyed not only the lives of two others, but also themselves one fatal day. They could have surrendered: they did not need to die. But they did.

Poles, Russian and German Jews had had a bad name in London for many years, mainly because they were aliens. All aliens were generally regarded as 'undesirable', whether they were refugees, immigrants or genuine thugs. Their foreign languages, accents, customs and practices were enough to make them seem suspect to the average Londoner, especially if they were of the lower orders, impoverished and young. Deprived usually signified depraved, dangerous and bad.

Russians were a comparative rarity, and Russia a dark enigma, where amidst thick snow, wolves and bears, a debauched, corrupt and cruel aristocracy, headed by the Czar, was believed to control and crush legions of starving serfs. In between were a few mad revolutionaries, soldiers and students, seeking to overthrow the status quo with bullets and bombs.

Clearly those Russians who came to London, to the East End or to any of the city's sprawling Edwardian suburbs, would not be of the Czarist or peasant class. They were more likely to be of the dangerous, revolutionary kind – anarchists! And so the London papers, who in five years' time would be hailing Russian soldiers engaged in the First World War as 'our gallant allies', were as hyperbolic about Hefeldt and Lepidus, branding them as anarchists and revolutionaries and what they did as 'The Tottenham Outrage – an amazing series of outrages, singularly rare if not entirely without parallel in a civilised country'.

What happened *was* amazing, particularly the amount of bullets that were fired, not only by the villains, but also by the public and the police, who also exhibited an amazing amount of mad bravery, matching that of the villains they chased. Amazing also was the variety of vehicles used.

Not much is known about Paul Hefeldt and Jacob Lepidus, except that they were in their mid-twenties, Russian, and out of work. *The Times* would say later that both came from Riga in Latvia and that they were engaged in conveying revolutionary literature, which was printed in England, to Russia by sea. They belonged to something called the Lettish League. Lepidus had a brother, according to *The Times*, who was a member of one of the 'Terrorist' societies in Paris and had died when a bomb he was carrying exploded. The police said that Jacob Lepidus had worked for a while at a furniture factory in Tottenham, owned by Messrs Lebus & Co. Hefeldt, they said, had been employed at Mr Schnurmann's rubber factory, also in Tottenham, but only for a few days. Perhaps there was a row. Perhaps he was dismissed. But on the morning of Saturday, 23 January 1909 he and Lepidus went to the office of Schnurmann's factory in Chestnut Road to take a kind of revenge.

The day before, there had been a private memorial service at the Frogmore Mausoleum, Windsor, commemorating the eighth anniversary of the death of Queen Victoria and the accession of Edward VII. It was attended by the 67-year-old King and his family. At Horse Guards Parade in London a 41-gun salute was fired. Asquith was the Liberal Prime Minister, and although most theatres were still presenting pantomimes like *Dick Whittington* and *Red Riding Hood, The Gondoliers* was on at the Savoy, *The Merry Widow* at Daly's, *Our Miss Gibbs* at the Gaiety, and at Covent Garden audiences were enjoying Wagner's *The Ring*.

It was dull and overcast that Saturday morning, and there was a cold north-easterly wind. Hefeldt had a mask, probably just a scarf, in case he was recognised by any of Mr Schnurmann's workers. He and Lepidus tried to look unobtrusive as they loitered outside the factory office, waiting for the return of the motor-car that had been sent, as usual, to the London and South Western Bank in South Hackney to collect the employees' weekly wages. It had no guard – only the 17-year-old youth who made the collection and the driver of the car. No one apparently expected that the object of the bank expedition, a canvas bag containing £80 worth of gold, silver and bronze coins in brown paper bags, would become the objective of a daring daylight robbery. For the rubber factory was just off Tottenham High Road, which was busy with Saturday shoppers – Bruce Grove Station was a few hundred yards away. More importantly, Tottenham police station was immediately opposite the factory. Who would dare to carry out a robbery at such a time and in such a place?

The two who dared did so because they had guns – a Browning and a Hauser, with enough bullets, about 100 each, to start a war. Because of this the two Russians must have thought they would have little difficulty in making their escape. The police, after all, carried no firearms, only their 'little sticks', their truncheons. All the robbers had to do was threaten, or shoot, anyone who got in their way. None the less, they seem not to have worked out any plan of escape. There was no getaway vehicle, or car – neither could drive, and cars were still a novelty. It seems they expected to melt away in the crowd. They were simply not prepared, nor was anyone else in the vicinity, for what happened so suddenly, and so thrillingly, next.

It began at 10.30 am, according to the police, and an hour earlier, according to Mr Schnurmann, who was on the look-out for the arrival of his workers' wages – he may have been at the factory door. He was probably rather anxious about the two men 'who had been hanging about all the morning'. Mr Paul, a partner, was not far away.

At last the car, driven by Joseph Wilson, aged 29, arrived, and Albert Keyworth, aged 17, got out, carrying the canvas bag full of cash, and stepped across the pavement to the office door.

What followed is best told in a report headed *Murders, Attempted Murders, Shooting and Arrest of the Murderers* and written two weeks later, which was submitted to the Commissioner, Sir Edward Henry, by Superintendent Jenkins of N Division, Stoke Newington. His report, edited, amended and put together with other eyewitness accounts and statements, now tells the story of the next three extraordinary hours.

Supt Jenkins: Two men of foreign type stood at the entrance of the premises, one at each side. Lepidus seized the boy and the bag and shot at him, but inflicted no injury. There was a momentary struggle. They both fell, but the man got up with the money.

Mr Schnurmann: He was taking a bag of money from the car to the office when two men who had been hanging about all morning made a dash for the messenger. One of the men was wearing a mask, which made it difficult to identify him. They wrenched the bag from the boy, when another man came to the boy's rescue.

Supt Jenkins: The chauffeur, Wilson, went promptly to the boy's assistance. He grasped Lepidus by the throat. Both fell and struggled desperately. Hefeldt shot at the chauffeur repeatedly – his overcoat was riddled with bullets and a slanting shot passed through every garment, including his under vest, in the region of the stomach. Lepidus released himself and discharged his revolver at the chauffeur. In a miraculous and unaccountable way he escaped injury. The chauffeur cried loudly for help, and a man named George Smith, a gas stoker, went and tripped Lepidus and threw him – the bag of money falling upon the pavement. Whilst struggling with Lepidus, Smith was shot in the chest by Hefeldt. Lepidus released himself and took the money, at the same moment discharging his revolver at Smith, whose escape from death was equally remarkable. The assailants then ran off towards Tottenham marshes, proceeding by way of Chestnut Road, Scales Road, and Mitchley Road.

The revolver shots were heard by the police at the Tottenham Police Station situated immediately opposite the rubber factory. PCs Tyler and Newman, who were on reserve duty, ran out. The chauffeur rapidly explained the position of things, and with the latter PC [Newman] got into the car and followed. PC Tyler pursued on foot.

PCs Bond and Fraser, hearing the alarm, jumped through the open boot-room window of the station into Chestnut Rd, followed by other officers, who were aroused from sleep and who hastily put on some clothing and ran out by the front entrance and took up the chase.

Mr Schnurmann: I jumped into the car and several policemen got in with me. We made off after the men. After chasing them for about 200 yards we gained on them rapidly. But one of the robbers turned and fired at the front of the car. The first shot passed through the glass windscreen, hit the body of the car, and grazed the neck of the motor driver. Another shot entered the radiator and disabled the car. The police then took up the chase on foot, and at this point I gave up the pursuit.

Supt Jenkins: PC Newman received a graze on the cheek and a small wound on the lobe of his right ear. A crowd of persons joined in the chase. Among them was Ralph Joscelyn, aged 10, a schoolboy. He was mortally wounded by a bullet wound in the right breast. He was conveyed to Tottenham Hospital, where he was found to be dead. He was subsequently identified by his mother.

After these incidents, the murderers proceeded rapidly in a north-easterly direction to the Dust Destructor, situated on the marshes. Constables Tyler and Newman [who had left the car] crossed in a northerly direction, with a view of heading them off. When opposite the Dust Destructor, PC Tyler was approaching them from the marshland and called upon them to surrender. But the man Hefeldt stood and took deliberate aim and shot him in the head. Constable Newman remained with his fallen comrade. When Sub-Divisional Inspector Large arrived, Tyler was carried into a house nearby. An ambulance was sent for, and he was conveyed with all speed to Tottenham Hospital, and five minutes after admission he died.

The chase, which had now become most desperate, was continued with splendid determination. The murderers proceeded over the footbridge spanning the Great Eastern Railway, then continued in a north-easterly direction to the west bank of the River Lea. They then went north beside the river to Chalk Bridge, which spans the river just beyond the Rifle Butts, and thence onto the Millstream Bridge, where they held the crowd at bay for a considerable time.

Mr Paul: We followed them all the way to the banks of the Lea. After having gone some distance we saw several men on the other side of the river with guns. We shouted to them to try and shoot the robbers, and they fired. But the shots did not carry far enough to take effect. All the way along, people were trying to stop the desperados. But the two men were firing indiscriminately at all who ventured to arrest their progress. We followed till we got to Chingford Rd, where the tramways run.

Supt Jenkins: It was at the Millstream Bridge that PC Nicod went a short distance ahead of the crowd, and knelt down upon the bank with a view of shooting the murderers. But the revolver which he had, a private one, was found to be defective. Before he could beat a retreat, both miscreants fired upon him, and both shots took effect. He was wounded in the calf of his left leg and thigh. Just previously, a lad named

Cyril Burgess was wounded by a bullet fired by one of the men, in the inner side of the right ankle.

The murderers then passed on along a footway on the south side of Banbury Reservoir, and thence northwards through a narrow pathway towards Higham Hill. Sidney Slater, aged 30, a horsekeeper, out of work, rather recklessly followed the men into this pathway and they fired six or seven shots at him. He was hit in the left thigh and disabled. First aid was rendered by the police.

Frederick Easter, aged 27, a single man [and bricklayer], of 1 Billet Rd, had also joined in the chase. In Folly Lane, the murderers turned again and fired upon their pursuers, and Easter was shot. He was also hit in the left thigh, the bullet passing through the fleshy part of his leg.

They now crossed by the base of Higham Hill through some allotments and entered a field where there was a gipsy encampment. In the same reckless way the miscreants fired among the gipsies, fortunately without causing any hurt. They now entered the premises of Salisbury Hall Farm and took temporary shelter behind a haystack. From either side of it they continuously fired upon the pursuers, who were fully exposed to the deadly fire, many saving themselves by lying down flat on the ground. It was during this severe encounter that William Roker, aged 32, a labourer, married, was very seriously injured, being shot in both legs. He was promptly attended to and conveyed to the Walthamstow Cottage Hospital, where he now lies in a critical condition.

The murderers now passed through the farmyard to the Chingford Rd. Without a moment's hesitation they commandeered an electric tram car [Car No. 9] en route southwards to the Bakers Arms public-house, Lea Bridge Rd. The driver [Joseph Slow] and the conductor [Charles Wyatt] were held up at the point of a gun.

Joseph Slow: We were journeying in the direction of Lea Bridge Rd when I saw a crowd of excited people rushing across Salisbury Farm. I did not know what the matter was, but when we reached a spot near the Crooked Billet I heard cries of 'Stop!' – 'Murder!' I immediately pulled up, and looking round saw a man at the back of the car covering the conductor and myself with a revolver. There was a crowd behind and many of them had guns and were firing in the direction of the car. Several bullets whistled past my head, and it seemed to me that death was inevitable. Had I remained at my post I felt that I should be a dead man in a few seconds. I therefore scrambled up the steps onto the top of the car. I crouched down and was not aware of what was going on below.

Charles Wyatt: Suddenly a man who had jumped over a hedge or ditch rushed onto the platform. In his hand he held a revolver, and he was calling to another man who was about 50 yards up the road. The second man also carried a revolver, and as he ran he turned and fired at the crowd who were in pursuit. The first man was apparently a foreigner, about 5 feet 9 inches in height, and was dressed in a dark suit and wore a cap. He was about 27. As he jumped on the car he shouted 'Stop!' and pointed the revolver at my head. I then saw the driver hurriedly leave his place and rush to the top of the car. Then the bullets commenced flying all around us. Some of the pursuing crowd took cover behind the hedges and fired repeatedly with their guns. The man who had cried at me to stop, motioned to me to drive on.

There were three passengers on board, an elderly gentleman [Edward Loveday, a glass merchant, aged 64] and a woman with her child. The elderly man said excitedly that he would get out. But the desperado, placing the revolver close to my temple, said in a determined voice: 'I ask you to drive on!' I said at first I could not. But he looked so determined and held the pistol so near to my face, that I moved along to the front of the car. By this time the second man had come up and jumped onto the back of the car. He still continued to fire his revolver at the crowd.

I started the car and commenced to drive slowly. All this time bullets were striking and whizzing past the car. The woman passenger and the child crouched down, and it is a marvel how they escaped, as several of the bullets crashed through the windows and splintered the interior of the car with glass. I felt that every instant I should be struck. The man who had first boarded the car held the revolver so close to my cheek that I could feel the warm glow of the barrel. At times he would turn the revolver to the side and fire at some passing object which he thought was a pursuer . . . I was apprehensive whether the driver above would do anything that would involve danger to myself. He could, if so minded, have placed his weight upon the trolley bar, cut the circuit, and by so doing brought the car to a standstill. I was sure that had that been done, the ruffian would have come to the conclusion that I had intentionally stopped the car and would have shot me dead. I had, however, to slow down at a loop [at the Victory public-house, St John's Road] to let another car pass. The woman and child scrambled out and apparently escaped unhurt.

Near here, an advertising cart came towards us from behind. It contained, in addition to the driver, a man, who I believe was a policeman, armed with a gun, and another man. These were in pursuit. But before they could come up with us, the man on the back platform of the car brought the pony to earth with a shot from his revolver, and all three occupants of the cart were hurled into the road.

Supt Jenkins: PC Hawkings was following the murderers in an advertisement cart. He was armed with a gun but did not use it. One of the murderers shot the pony, causing it to fall, and Hawkings and the men with him were thrown out. Bullets had passed through the leg and seat of his trousers. He was grazed over the left eye and leg.

Charles Wyatt: There was no lack of ammunition. I thought that surely the time would come when the men would have exhausted their store. But no sooner were the chambers of the revolvers emptied than they dipped their hands into their pockets and brought forward a fresh supply . . . All this time the crowd was in hot pursuit, and scores of bullets flew by me. It staggers me to think how I escaped being hit.

I now thought it best to continue the journey [to Kite's Corner] as quickly as I could, in the hope that on reaching a busy thoroughfare the men might be overpowered. Then another thought struck me. As we approached a turn in the road, I said to the man who still held his revolver to my head: 'You had better get off here, as there's a police station just around the bend.' The man answered gruffly: 'There is not!' I then said: 'All right – we'll go on.' On reaching Kite's Corner, or just before that, the elderly man in the car, who was very excited, came towards me as if to make a plucky attempt to seize my assailant. The latter, however, was too quick for him. In an instant he fired his revolver, and the old man was struck, I believe, in the neck . . .

At Kite's Corner I saw a milk-cart standing at the kerb and the man who drove it coming towards a gate. He was about to climb the gate when the man at the back of the car shot at him. The two assailants then dashed off the tramcar together and, making for the cart, jumped into it, and lashing at the horse disappeared down Kenilworth Avenue, in the direction of Forest Rd.

Supt Jenkins: George Conyard [the milkman], aged 19, who was inside a shop, seeing the horse being driven off, rushed out to stop it. But he was immediately shot down, the bullet passing through his right arm and chest.

Charles Wyatt: My driver then came down from the top of the car, and we drove as fast as we could to the Bell, thinking we might intercept the desperados. But they were too quick for us. When we examined the tramcar we found that it was riddled with bullets. Never have I had such an exciting time in my life before.

Supt Jenkins: They drove down Kenilworth Avenue to Forest Rd. Here they were overtaken by a horse and van driven by Thomas White, greengrocer. [Another version is that the milk-cart the robbers were driving overturned and they then seized White's van.] One of the men pointed a revolver at White's head and he jumped off his seat. The men took possession of the van and drove rapidly [along Forest Road, eastwards] to Wood St. Meanwhile, PC Adams had commandeered a motor car and followed, blowing his whistle.

Fred Williams: I was driving a car, LN 1662, belonging to my employers Ferdinand and Edward Reiss, along Forest Rd at 11.30 am, and when near the Bell public-house I heard police whistles blow and I looked round and saw a crowd and policemen following. Two policemen [one of whom was PC William Shakespeare] got into the car, and told me to follow two men in a van. I did so. When the policemen got in the car, some of the crowd climbed up behind and bent both wings of the hind wheels.

Supt Jenkins: PC Adams attracted the attention of PS Jowitt and PC Francis, on duty at Hagger Bridge. These officers made an attempt to stop the van, and one of the murderers fired at them. The bullet passed between them and broke the glass panel of the side door of a greengrocer's at 849 Forest Rd. But the action of the officers diverted the miscreants' course, and they turned into Kingsley Rd, before driving across wasteland [northwards] to Fulbourne Rd.

Thomas Brown: I heard my son Thomas calling out: 'Dad! Come quick!' I saw him running up Kingsley Rd, and then a PC named Adams [whose vehicle must have been disabled or abandoned] running up Forest Rd. He said: 'Don't go too near! They've got shooters!' I still kept running down Kingsley Rd, and then I saw two men in a van, the one driving whilst the other was at the tailboard with a revolver in each hand, and suddenly he fired at me, the bullet whizzing past my right temple. [He] again fired at me, and this time the bullet passed through the cloth of the right leg of my trousers. I still continued in the chase, following the murderers up Fulbourne Rd. They were still firing at random at their pursuers.

Fred Williams: When we caught them up in Fulbourne Rd they fired upon us with revolvers. I eased up to keep out of range and they went on. I kept about 30 yards behind.

Thomas Brown: They then turned to the left up Brookscroft Rd, still firing, until they reached Beresford Rd. After this they turned into Wadham Rd. Then I went around into Chingford Rd. Here I met a PC who was doing point duty. I said: 'Come with me quick! The murderers are up there!' He and another PC came running along with me, and then we saw a motorcar [driven by Mr North] that was in pursuit. Into this we all got, also a gentleman who happened to arrive with a breech-loading gun. We proceeded along Wadham Rd as quickly as possible, and whilst on our way were firing at our assailants. Soon the gentleman in possession of the breech-loading gun left the car and let me have the use of the gun and some cartridges. I fired at our assailants in Wadham Rd, and the tallest of the two murderers, who held a revolver in each hand, was keeping up a furious fire on us all the time. Soon they were in Winchester Rd, Highams Park. Here Mr North and myself fired on the two men in the van.

Supt Jenkins: Through this part of their route, Lepidus was driving. Hefeldt possessed both revolvers and kept up a continuous fire upon the pursuers. In Winchester Rd they abandoned the van and ran to the River Ching.

Fred Williams: They jumped out of the van near a level-crossing.

Thomas Brown: I noticed the tallest of the two hand his mate one of the two weapons he had been using, and then they made off for a fence that was close by.

Supt Jenkins: They clambered down the narrow bank of the river. Lepidus succeeded in climbing the fence that bounds it. Hefeldt attempted to do so and failed.

Thomas Brown: Here it was that Mr North and myself fired at the tallest of the two. He fell this side of the fence.

Supt Jenkins: He turned round and saw that his position was hopeless. He cried out to Lepidus: 'Go on! Save yourself! I've only got two left!'

He sank upon the ground, and shot himself through the head. He was seized by the police, disarmed, and taken as soon as possible to Tottenham Hospital in a van requisitioned on the spot.

Thomas Brown: One of the PCs picked up the revolver, which had been used by the assassin. I asked the PC, 747, for the revolver. We then continued to chase the murderer who was now alone. He made his way across to a place called Beech Hall Estate. Here they were erecting some houses, and more shots were fired by the assailant, and a plasterer, by name F. Mortimer, was shot in the right breast.

Supt Jenkins: Lepidus was hotly pursued by PC Zeithing, and was within a few yards of him when he turned and fired three shots at him, one of which passed over his left shoulder, and entered the chest of Frederick Mortimer [a master plasterer], aged 38, and came out at the back of him. This man had just thrown a brick at Lepidus. The PC had a very narrow escape, as one or more of the bullets passed through the lapels of his greatcoat.

Thomas Brown: Then he ran across Oak Hill, through the hedge, around the back of the Oak public-house towards some cottages. I then reloaded the gun I had with me. Then I saw our assailant creeping behind a hedge with his revolver in his left hand, and he saw me taking aim at him. Then he made for one of the cottages nearby and admitted himself by the back door.

Supt Jenkins: Lepidus had run across Hale End Rd into a field at the rear of Oak Cottage, Hale End, occupied by Charles Rolstone, a coal porter. He sought shelter in this small house, consisting of four rooms and a lean-to. He first ran to the front room where, judging from the amount of soot which was found lying in the room, he had made an attempt to climb into the chimney. I may say that before entering the kitchen he had peered through a small window in the door of the lean-to. His face was covered with blood, no doubt caused by the small shot from the fowling-pieces of men who had shot at him when he was crossing the fields in the earlier part of the chase. Mrs Rolstone saw him, screamed, and ran out of the place [by the back door], crying: 'Oh, my children!'

Lepidus then shut and bolted that door, also the front door. Charles Schaffer, a baker, who had chased these men throughout, went to the door of the lean-to, and with the assistance of PC Dewhurst burst it open. Both passed into the kitchen and brought the children [a baby and a little boy] out safely.

After failing in his attempt to hide in the parlour chimney, Lepidus went upstairs into the front bedroom. He gave a stealthy look through the window, which was seen by his pursuers. They had now arrived in large numbers and some of them were armed. They at once poured a volley in his direction, shattering most of the contents of the room.

Thomas Brown: I saw him at one of the bedroom windows. Then I fired at him, the shots piercing some of the windows. Then Detective Dixon came through the house and said: 'Don't fire any more, for God's sake! There are three or four of us inside now!'

Supt Jenkins: At this juncture PC Dixon of the CID, PC Eagles and PC Cater rendered good service. [PC Dixon had cycled over from Edmonton.] PC Eagles obtained a ladder from an adjoining premises and placed it against the back bedroom window. He obtained a loaded gun from a bystander, climbed the ladder, opened the window and looked in. PC Dixon had sent a dog up into this room, which Eagles encouraged to go under the bed. He turned and saw Lepidus with the door of the front bedroom ajar, pointing a revolver at him. Finding that his gun was unworkable, through a safety catch which he did not understand, he rapidly descended the ladder. He changed the weapon for a police revolver which PC Dixon had. The three officers then climbed this very narrow staircase, Eagles being in front, Dixon in the centre, and Cater behind. It was perfectly clear that if the miscreant secured the first shot, these men would have been seriously hurt or killed. Eagles fired twice and later once through the panel of the bedroom door.
Thomas Brown: I entered the house and heard Dixon shout up the stairs to the assailant to surrender. But no answer came. PC Eagles fired up the stairs at the door, and soon all was quiet for some seconds. Suddenly a loud report rang out, I then followed Dixon and PC Eagles [up the stairs]. I then saw a man lying on a bed, bleeding from a wound in the right temple, and a revolver lying on the bed by his side.
Supt Jenkins: Eagles asserts that Lepidus opened the door slightly and presented his revolver at him. But in the fearful excitement of the moment, the PC could have been mistaken. Evidence has since proved that a police shot did not despatch this man. He shot himself. Upon police entering the room, Lepidus was found upon a small bed in the corner in the throes of death. Immediately afterwards he expired. The body was carried down into the yard . . . It was then conveyed in a police ambulance to the Walthamstow Mortuary, Queens Rd . . .

I drove to the scene with my groom and a PC in plain clothes armed with a revolver and ammunition, taking a direct course to Woodford, that being the last place where I heard the murderers were making for. When I reached the Napier Arms public-house, Woodford, I was informed by police scouts of the death of Lepidus at the cottage nearby and the arrest of Hefeldt. I proceeded there and took general charge.

Upon Lepidus there were found two paper bank bags, one of which contained £5 in silver, the other being empty . . .

This extraordinary manhunt was carried out over a course extending about six miles. It would be impossible for me to speak too highly of the splendid conduct of the police of N and J Divisions. In response to my call to duty they were most prompt, and in action cool, tactful, and fearless. The conduct of the public engaged was equally praiseworthy and brave.

Paul Hefeldt died in hospital nearly three weeks later. He and Lepidus, apart from killing PC Tyler and 10-year-old Ralph Joscelyn, shot and wounded 18 other people. In addition to the eleven civilians and policemen mentioned above, six others were injured. They were: William Devine, aged 13, shot in the right leg; George Harwood, 26, wounded in the right hand at the railway bridge; George Rawson, aged 40, wounded in the right wrist at the Millstream Bridge; Joseph Ayley, aged 30, wounded in the left knee while tending PC Tyler; George Cousins, aged 29, shot in the left shoulder; and William Edwards, aged 28, shot in the left elbow 'near where PC Tyler fell'. Only four, however, remained in hospital more than a week: George Conyard, the milkman; Edward Loveday, one of the passengers on the tram; Frederick Easter, bricklayer; and Frederick Mortimer, master plasterer. All recovered in due course.

Four policemen were injured through other causes: PC Forde sprained his left thigh; PC Wadden cut his right thumb; PC Brown cut his left hand; and PC Bond 'contracted a chill through taking up the chase partly clothed'.

Another kind of reckoning also resulted. Thirty-two civilians put in various claims for compensation arising out of injuries, damages and distress caused during the chase.

Fred Williams asked for £23 2s 9d for damage to his employers' car. A Mr Rowntree wanted 3/9 for repairs to his bicycle borrowed by PC Hawkings. Thomas Brown asked for 12/6 for damage to his trousers caused by a bullet. G. White, greengrocer, wanted £2 10s 'for loss sustained through having to rest his pony for four days in consequence of the treatment which he alleges it received on the 23rd'. His assistant, Thomas White, was driving the cart when it was seized by Hefeldt and Lepidus. William Roker, a plasterer's labourer and local pugilist, who was shot in both legs and had a wife and three young children to support, put in an unspecified claim. As did someone on behalf of George Dawkins, aged 41, a cart-driver, who 'was terrified by the shooting . . . and has not been right in the head since'.

The most niggardly claim came from Mr F. Thorogood, of Oak Villa, Thackeray Avenue, Tottenham, into whose house PC Tyler was carried after being shot. Thorogood asked for £1 10s – for the damage done to three pieces of carpet, a table cover and an overcoat 'by the blood which came from the officer's wound'.

Six civilians and several policemen received financial rewards for their bravery. The civilians, all married men, were: George Cousins, a labourer; George Smith, who struggled with Lepidus outside Mr Schnurmann's factory; the chauffeur, Joseph Wilson; William Roker; Charles Schaffer, who helped to rescue the children from Oak Cottage; and Mr North, a greengrocer, whose car took Thomas Brown and others as far as the River Ching.

Brown himself received no reward nor, it seems, did the wages-carrier, Albert Keyworth, or the driver and conductor of Car No. 9. Perhaps their temporary local and national fame was reward enough. The police were given amounts ranging from £5, for senior officers, and £2, for PCs. In addition, several were given medallions recording their bravery, and the salaries of PCs Newman and Zeithing were bumped up at once to the highest rate a PC could receive. Five were promoted to sergeant: PCs Nicod, Dewhurst (who helped rescue the children), Cater, Dixon and Eagles.

On 27 January, the 71-year-old Baron (formerly Sir Francis) Knollys, who had been Edward VII's Private Secretary for 39 years, wrote to the Commissioner, Sir Edward Henry:

> My dear Sir Edward – I have shown your letter both to the King and the Prince of Wales, and His Majesty desires me to thank you for sending him such an interesting and graphic account of the tragedy at Tottenham. It is almost inconceivable that such a thing could have occurred in these days on the very outskirts of London. The King thinks the Police behaved with great gallantry . . . He would likewise ask you to express to the Widow and Family of the unfortunate Constable who was killed, his sincere sympathy with them in their great sorrow.

It is not known what official sympathy or compensation was given to the parents of Ralph Joscelyn for the loss of their 10-year-old son. But PC William Tyler's widow received a substantial sum of money from a special fund – £11 was donated by the Wiltshire police alone.

PC Tyler, aged 30, who had been a policeman for seven years (before that he was in the Royal Artillery), was buried after a grand and very well-attended funeral, with honours, at Abney Park Cemetery. A memorial service followed on 18 July at All Saints' Church, Child's Hill, and in October a stone monument, costing £134, was erected in Abney Park Cemetery, with a memorial brass in the village church.

Mrs Tyler later married PC Williams, who died in 1925.

It is not known where Paul Hefeldt and Jacob Lepidus were buried. Their only memorial is the commemoration in the annals of crime of the fact that they shot and killed a policeman and a boy in Tottenham in 1909 – and that their dramatic pursuit across north-east London is remembered, by some, to this day.

There were other more far-reaching events in England that year; old-age pensions began, and Blériot's flimsy monoplane flew across the English Channel. Elsewhere, the Union of South Africa was formed, and Henry Ford began mass-producing cheap motors – the Model T. In 1910, on 6 May, Edward VII died at Buckingham Palace. His eldest surviving son, George V, aged 45, became King.

In the five years before the First World War, eight policemen were murdered in London, two in 1909. The murder of PC Tyler broke a ten-year period (1898–1908) in which no policemen on duty had been killed. The worst year for the murder of policemen was 1876, when six policemen died.

CHAPTER 11

Ernest Walker

The Murder of Raymond Davis, 1922

1922 was a famous year for murder and murderers. On 5 April, Jack Hewett was arrested for the murder of Mrs Blake. On 13 April, Major Armstrong was sentenced to death at Hereford for the murder of his wife. Raymond Davis was murdered on 22 April. And on 28 April, a pantry boy, Henry Jacoby, was sentenced to death for the murder of Lady White. On 5 May, Ronald True was found guilty of the murder of Gertrude Yates, but insane. On 7 May, Thomas Allaway was charged with the Bournemouth murder of Irene Wilkins. And on 5 October, Freddie Bywaters murdered Mrs Thompson's husband, Percy. He and she were both sentenced to death on 11 December 1922.

Bywaters was 19, Jacoby 18, and Hewett 15 when each of them killed. Walker was 17; his victim was even younger.

After Hewett was sentenced at Oxford in June to be detained during His Majesty's pleasure – he had confessed to the killing of Mrs Blake, licensee of the Crown and Anchor, Gallows Tree Common, near Henley and then retracted his confession – the judge said that it was somewhat appalling to consider the number of crimes committed by young people. There were a great many of them, he said, at the present day – crimes of 'motiveless ferocity'. Like that of Ernest Walker.

Soon after 6.00 pm on Saturday, 22 April, a telephone call was received at the District Messenger office in Sloane Street. The caller requested that a messenger boy should be sent at once to 30 Lowndes Square, Knightsbridge.

This was the handsome London home of Colonel Charles Trotter, CB, and the Hon. Mrs Trotter, daughter of Lord Hamilton of Dalzell. Their country home was at Barton in Buckinghamshire. That weekend they were not at their London residence, possibly because it was the end of the Easter week and they were holidaying or staying elsewhere.

Lowndes Square was very near Sloane Street, and the uniformed messenger boy who was sent there happened that evening to be 14-year-old Raymond Davis, a small bright lad, whose home was far removed in appearance from that of the Trotters, being situated near the clangour of trains, the smoke and whistles, of Clapham Junction Station. Raymond had been with the District Messenger service for about two months, and must have been pleased with his smart new uniform, if nothing else: he wore a pillbox hat and a cape and carried a letter pouch. Thus attired, at about 6.15 on a fine but chilly night, he rang the front door-bell of 30 Lowndes Square.

Some two hours later and 30 miles away, at Tonbridge in Kent, PC Sheepwash was proceeding down a street near the railway station when a tall, slim youth approached him and said: 'I want to go to the police station, as I've done a murder in London.' Although the youth looked very pale and ill, he spoke calmly when questioned by Sheepwash, who was sufficiently impressed by the seriousness of the replies to take the confessed murderer to Tonbridge police station. Besides, he had dried blood on his hands.

There the youth was cautioned, and after giving his name and occupation – Ernest Walker, footman – and his address, he made and signed a statement. He said: 'I do not know what made me do it. I did it between 6.00 and 6.30. I hit him with a piece of iron bar. I have felt bad since last Wednesday, and I lost my mother last January, when the flu was about. I came to Tonbridge as it would give me plenty of time to think and tell the police there. I caught the 7.35 from Charing Cross.'

Although Victoria Station was much nearer Lowndes Square than Charing Cross, Walker's home was at Stanford, near Folkestone in Kent, and trains from Charing Cross to Folkestone stopped at Tonbridge. Perhaps Walker thought of going home, then changed his mind.

At about 9.30 pm the Tonbridge police telephoned Gerald Road police station in Belgravia, and in due course DI Hedley and DS Steel visited the scene of the alleged crime. After knocking and ringing to no avail – No. 30 seemed unoccupied – the policemen forced open the area door.

In the basement pantry they saw blood on the floor by a chair. Streaks of blood then led them to a closed door. There was, however, a key in the lock, and on opening the door they were met with a rush of gas. Taking whatever precautions they could to protect themselves and to avoid a gas explosion, they entered the room, and discovered the body of a messenger boy under a table. He was lying face down; he was fully dressed, and his hat and head had been dealt a heavy blow. Near him was a gas radiator; and on the blood-stained floor was an iron bar enclosed in an umbrella-case cover, and a length of rope with a noose. Around the boy's neck was a bloody teacloth, knotted at the back. He was still alive.

He was soon identified and was taken to nearby St George's Hospital. There, briefly regaining consciousness, he managed to say that a tall man had invited him to come inside and wait for a letter. He then remembered waking up in a gas-filled room with a gag in his mouth. He succeeded in removing the gag before passing out again.

The room in which the boy was found was the butler's bedroom. In Walker's bedroom, DI Hedley found several bits of paper covered with a pencilled scrawl, as well as some books, which the coroner would later describe as 'sensational detective trash'.

While Hedley was thus engaged perhaps, at about 10.15 pm, the head housemaid, Clara Miles, returned to Lowndes Square from her Saturday night out.

That afternoon she and the young footman, Ernest Walker, had had tea together in the servants' hall. All the other servants were out or away. He had seemed 'quite all right' to her, and he was not annoyed, he said, at being left alone when she went out. She told him she would be back just after ten. When he remarked that he would like something to read, she had lent him a book by Edward Phillips Oppenheim, one of the most prolific crime and mystery writers of the day.

There was much for Clara Miles to see in London's theatreland that night. George Robey was at the Hippodrome; Harry Lauder at the Princes; and Tom Wallis and Leslie Henson were in a farce called *Tons of Money*. Several plays by Galsworthy and J. M. Barrie were being presented, as was Jerome Kern's *Sally* with George Grossmith and Dorothy Dickson. Other stars to be seen on stage included Matheson Lang, Seymour Hicks, Godfrey Tearle, Owen Nares, Fay Compton and Phyllis Nielson-Terry; while in the few and new picture houses, Charlie Chaplin could be seen in *The Kid* and the Gish sisters in *Orphans of the Storm*.

Just before 6.00 am on Sunday morning, in St George's Hospital, Raymond Davis died. His father, Steve Davis, a railway-carriage cleaner employed by the London, Brighton and South Coast Railway Company, identified the boy's body. Later that day DI Hedley and DI Burton travelled down to Tonbridge, where they told Walker that he was being arrested on a charge of murder. After being cautioned, Walker said: 'Yes, sir. I don't know what made me do it. I don't think I knew what I was doing at the time.'

On the way back to London he began to talk, but was told to say nothing until Gerald Road police station was reached. There, after being cautioned again, he said in a statement: 'I quite understand what that means. But I wish to say that when I hit the boy with the piece of iron, I didn't know what I was doing. I wanted to send a letter to the laundry, and I telephoned for a messenger boy. I had never seen the boy before, and when he came to the house something came over me and I hit him with the iron. I've had a bad headache since last Wednesday. That's all I wish to say.'

On Monday, 24 April, Ernest Albert Walker, aged 17, appeared at Westminster Police Court charged with the wilful murder of Raymond Charles Davis, 14, and was remanded in custody.

At the coroner's inquest, which took place two days later before Mr Ingleby Oddie, the Trotters' butler, James Pallant, was among those who gave evidence. Most of the scrawled notes that Walker had written were addressed to Pallant, and he identified them as being in Walker's handwriting. When questioned by the coroner, Pallant said that the young footman, who had been with the Trotters for 18 months, had spoken about his mother's death in January, and had been very depressed for about a week. So much so, in fact, that Walker, unknown to Pallant, took one of Colonel Trotter's guns and considered shooting himself. 'He was quite a decent young man?' asked the coroner. Pallant said: 'Yes.' 'Morally?' enquired the coroner. 'Exceptionally so, I should say, sir,' Pallant replied.

DI Hedley read out what Walker had written: One note was scrawled on the back of a printed hand-out advertising menswear. It said: 'Mr Pallant. I prepared this in the afternoon. I covered the boy with my [unreadable] then prepared some more effects. Give my best love to Mrs P and R. I have felt queer this week or so, so goodbye all. I am, Ernest. Please let my dad know.' On the small black-edged envelope of a memorial card was written: 'You can have my shirt and bows also collars. My dad is to have the rest. Ernest. I hope Rachael is well.'

Hedley then produced a letter, written in pencil on black-edged notepaper. One wonders whether someone in the Trotters' family had recently died? Or was it paper saved after the funeral of Walker's mother? This letter was headed '30 Lowndes Square, London, SW1' and dated 'The Fatal Day in the afternoon'. It is one of the few accounts of a murder hand-written by the murderer himself.

It said: 'Dear Mr Pallant, I expect you will be surprised to see what I have done. Well, since my mother died I have made up my mind to die also. You know at Barton you said the guncase had been moved you were right it had I had a gun out loaded it made a sling for my foot to pull the trigger then my nerve went and I put it away. The boy here I had for a companion to –'

The coroner here interrupted Hedley's reading of the letter and asked to see it. 'This is curious,' he remarked. 'He's put a dash after the word "to".'

What the dash signified still remains a mystery. Perhaps Davis was to have been a companion in death, and the missing word is 'die'.

Walker then wrote, after the dash:

> I rang up the Sloane St office and said Please send a messenger to 30 Lowndes Square and he came to the front door. I asked him to come in and wait, brought him to the pantry and hit him on the head with the coal hammer *so simple* then I tied him up and killed him. *I* killed him *not* the gas, then I sat down and turned the gas *full* on and passed over the border. I am sane as ever I was and only I can not live without my dear mother. I didn't half give it to the damn boy I made him squeak. Give my love to dad and all my friends, I remain yours truly, Ernest.

He then added, most oddly: 'Minnie Shorts clapper drives me nearly mad also the cold water.'

On another piece of black-rimmed notepaper Walker had drawn up a chilling 14-point agenda concerning the murder and his own suicide, which contradicted his original statements to the police ('I didn't know what I was doing' – 'Something came over me').

1 Ring up Sloane Street
2 Wait at front door
3 Invite him in
4 Bring him downstairs

5 Ask him to sit down
6 Hit him hard on head tie him up
8 Keep him tied up
9 At 10.30 torture
10 11 pm Prepare for end
11 Sit down turn it on
12 Put letter out
13 Sit down shut windows
14 Kens 2059

The telephone number was that of the District Messenger service.

It is clear from the agenda that the killing of the messenger boy was planned and not a matter of mad impulse. Whatever was in Walker's fevered mind at the time, he evidently intended to gas himself, and the boy, after keeping his victim tied up and out of sight in the butler's bedroom or in 'the safe' which is where meat, fish and vegetables would have been stored. Mr Pallant, it seems, was away; and Walker had possibly expected to be alone in the house that night. Perhaps his agenda was spoiled by Clara Miles saying she would return just after ten. Perhaps she was lucky not to have been killed herself. At any rate, it seems as if Walker hit the boy too hard and was then put off by all the blood. Perhaps he thought Davis was dead. Untying him from the chair, to which Davis had been bound after being hit by the coal hammer – or by an iron bar used to break up coal – Walker then dragged the boy to the butler's bedroom, where he turned the gas on, but could not persevere with his own destruction. So he wrote his notes to Pallant, put on his cap and left the house.

How sane was Walker? At his trial, which began and ended at the Central Criminal Court before Mr Justice Roche on Wednesday, 21 June, Walker's counsel for the defence, Mr St John Hutchinson, said that there was no motive for the murder, that the letters were those of a madman, and that at the time of the murder the accused was under the influence of an epileptic seizure.

To this end he called a teacher at Walker's old school, who said that the prisoner had shown peculiar traits: he was absent-minded and weak; he wrote poetry and had an aversion to taking part in games. Walker's father also gave evidence, saying that his son had been prone to have fits since he was five, and that his mother had been a nervous and excitable woman, who thought she would have to go to an asylum. It was also proved that a relative had died in an asylum in 1893; that another relative died in another asylum in 1898; that two others were admitted to asylums and a fifth died of brain disease.

None of this proved, however, that Walker was mad, dangerous or liable to kill. Nor did the defence's contention that Walker was epileptic, although a Harley Street physician, Dr Macnamara, was produced to aver that after studying the prisoner's family history and symptoms, he had concluded that Walker was suffering from 'the condition of epileptic automatism or its psychic equivalent' when Davis was killed. This meant that Walker, who in prison had professed to have an imperfect recollection of what had happened – and denied writing the agenda or the letters – was only partially conscious and not fully aware of what he was doing. Nor would he be able to control his actions at that time.

For the prosecution, which was led by Mr Percival Clarke, Dr East, the medical officer at Brixton Prison, declared that he had observed *no* symptoms of epilepsy, although they might not have been manifest when the prisoner was being observed. He also said he had seen no evidence that the accused might, on the day of the murder, have been suffering from mental disease.

Asked by St John Hutchinson, for the defence: 'It is a very mad murder?' East replied: 'It is a very unusual murder.'

The judge urged the jury not to be influenced by recent discussions in the press about the nature of criminal insanity, which had arisen out of the trials, in April and May, of Henry Jacoby and Ronald True. But doubtless influenced by the fact that Jacoby, aged 18, had been hanged on 8 June, they brought in a verdict, after five minutes of chat, of 'Not guilty' – but insane at the time.

Mr Justice Roche directed that Walker be detained during His Majesty's pleasure, and he was removed – as with True and Jack Hewett – to Broadmoor Criminal Lunatic Asylum, later renamed Broadmoor Institution.

It is not known when, if ever, he was released.

On the afternoon of Saturday, 22 April, a few hours before Walker thought of suicide and Davis was killed, another young man committed suicide most publicly, stepping in front of a car in Piccadilly Circus and then shooting himself. His inquest was held on 25 April before Mr Ingleby Oddie. The young man's name was Martin Bateson. He was 22, and had become a drama student after leaving Cambridge with a first-class degree in Natural Science. His father, Professor William Bateson, had been a Cambridge don, and in May would be elected as a trustee of the British Museum.

Martin died through his unrequited love for a girl, who was already engaged to someone else. He visited her home on the morning of his death. She sent him away and wrote him a letter, in which she said: 'Dear Martin – After your extraordinary visit to me this morning, I have decided to write this to you. You must never come here again, as I shall always be "Not at home" and I shall return any letters unopened. I am engaged, and your persistence annoys me so much that I consider it dishonourable. I am sorry.'

The letter must have been delivered by messenger boy, as Martin shot himself that afternoon. He wrote several farewell letters, leaving all his money to the girl, about £1,000 after some debts were paid. In one letter he wrote:

She is the loveliest child
And her heart is made of gold
Gold that is undefiled
As it was in the days of old

He added: 'I hope she will be lucky, she will be happy. She will be blessed, if my dying wish is of any avail.'

In 1922, T.S. Eliot's poem, The Waste Land, *was published. It begins: 'April is the cruellest month . . .'*

CHAPTER 12

Florence Ransom

The Murder of Dorothy Fisher, 1940

In 1940 Britain was at war. But it was not until April, when Norway and Denmark were invaded by Germany, that the 'Phoney War' came to an end. On 10 May the Germans overran Holland and Belgium. Chamberlain resigned that day, giving place as Prime Minister to Churchill, who on 13 May was speaking to the Commons of 'blood, toil, tears and sweat' and 'victory at all costs'. On 27 May the evacuation of the British forces from Dunkirk began. By the end of June, Paris and France had fallen, and Britons stood alone, facing 'their finest hour'. Invasion seemed imminent, and a German invasion was indeed planned. The Channel Islands were occupied on 1 July and nine days later the Battle of Britain began, although it was not until August that the full-scale bombing of English airfields in Kent ensued, followed by mass air-raids on London in September. It was during the dark uncertainties of that glorious summer that Mrs Ransom went mad.

Mrs Gibbs was 80, and every Tuesday afternoon she expected her married daughter, Mrs Dorothy Fisher, to come and visit her – whether there was a war on or not. Both women lived in the village of Matfield, about five miles south-east of Tonbridge in Kent. Mrs Fisher and her younger daughter, Freda, resided in a two-bedroom cottage called Crittenden, which the family had used as a weekend retreat before the war; since September it had become their permanent home.

Freda Fisher, aged 20, was, according to the local paper, 'a familiar figure in the village of Matfield, being an exotic type of beauty, of striking appearance in her somewhat Bohemian attire'. Her mother, Mrs Dorothy Fisher, was also somewhat unconventional. With the approval and assistance of her complacent husband, she had recently applied for a permit allowing a male friend, a Dane called Westergart, to live near her in Matfield. Such a permit was needed as the district had been declared a protected area, out of bounds to aliens and others who were not service personnel or indigenous. The application had been turned down.

Mrs Fisher, who was 48, had in fact been amicably living apart from her husband, though in the same house in west London, for several years. He had had a mistress and she her Danish lover, until Fisher moved with his mistress to Oxfordshire and she and her younger daughter, Freda, to Kent. The other daughter, Joan, a repertory actress aged 26, had sailed to India two years previously to marry a doctor there. So Mrs Fisher and Freda were left to face the prospect of invasion in their cottage, attended only by a housekeeper, Miss Saunders, who was 46 and had served the Fishers for eight years.

At 5.00 pm on Tuesday, 9 July, old Mrs Gibbs became impatient. Where was her daughter? She began telephoning Mrs Fisher's house, continuing to do so at frequent intervals until half-past six, when, before the wartime black-out became an inconvenient necessity, she sent John Leury, a carter-cowman and her part-time gardener, to Crittenden cottage, to find out what, if anything, was wrong.

He arrived at the cottage at about 6.45 pm and saw a woman's body, that of Charlotte Saunders, lying on the drive in front of the house. Leury hurried off to inform the local policeman, in the person of a part-time Special and a full-time teacher, Harry Crickmay. He inspected the body and the cottage, which was in a state of some disorder, as if there had been a burglary. All the doors were open, and of the other occupants there was no sign. He sent for further police assistance, waiting at the cottage until several other officers arrived. He later found a yellow woman's bicycle lying by a gate with its handlebars bent, about 50 yards away from the cottage on the road to Tonbridge.

Assistance in the form of DI Frank Smeed, DS Smith and PC Donald arrived at about 9.15, by which time it was dark, and because of the black-out the officers had to examine the premises and the corpse by flashlight. It seemed at the time as if Charlotte Saunders had died from severe head injuries. She had in fact been shot in the back of the head.

If robbery had been the mainspring of the murderous assault, as indicated by the mess in the lounge and bedrooms, nothing seemed to have been stolen. Although drawers had been pulled open and papers and clothing scattered about, jewellery and money had not been taken, nor apparently any item of value. Two oddities struck both Smeed and Smith: some letters found in a writing bureau in the lounge bore none of the surnames and christian names of the three women known to have lived there, although Freda was mentioned more than once. And in the kitchen some broken crockery and a tray that lay on the floor, indicated that a *fourth* person had been expected for tea. For among the items, which Smeed pieced together, were *four* cups, saucers and plates.

DI Smeed and the others also searched the three-and-a-half acres of land around the cottage and the outhouses at the rear. There they found a path that led through some undergrowth to an old orchard. In the gateway to the orchard lay the lifeless body of Freda Fisher. A further search revealed that at the other end of the orchard, where the ground rose steeply, lay the corpse of Dorothy Fisher. Both women had been shot in the back. It was PC Donald who found what would be a vital clue: about halfway between the mother and daughter lay a left-hand lady's glove.

At midnight, a medical examination of the three bodies was carried out by the superintendent from the county hospital at nearby Pembury, Dr Grasby. He worked in the light of torches held by policemen and shaded from enemy aircraft by their capes. It was a mild night; the day had been cloudy and warm.

By this time the Kent County Police, based at Maidstone, had summoned the assistance of Scotland Yard.

DCI Peter Beveridge, who that very day had moved from the Flying Squad to the Murder Squad, was having a drink at 11.00 pm with a close friend, Inspector Greeno, when a message about the Matfield murders reached him. Beveridge was a tall, fair-haired, well-dressed man, a disciplinarian and a Scot. In recent years he had supervised raids on illegal gambling dens, on nightclubs and bottle parties. After talking on the telephone to DI Smeed he sent for his favourite sidekick, DS Bert Tansill, a stout and extrovert man, and they drove through blacked-out London to the West London flat of Mr Westergart. There was no point in visiting the scene of the crime until day. Besides, the Dane, Mrs Fisher's lover, was a possible suspect. His shocked reaction to the news of her death was real enough, however, to remove him from the inquiry, especially as his whereabouts that day excluded him from having had the time for a trip to Kent.

Early on the following day, Wednesday, Beveridge and Tansill drove north to the home of another natural suspect – to Carramore Farm at Piddington, an Oxfordshire village between Aylesbury and Bicester. This was where Mrs Fisher's husband lived, although he worked in London. It was his custom to leave the farm at about 8.00 am and drive to Aylesbury, where he caught the 8.43 to Marylebone Station, going from there to his office. He edited a technical magazine, the *Automobile Engineer*. But on this particular morning he was stopped by the police on his way to Aylesbury and invited to return to the farm.

There Beveridge informed Mr Fisher of the death of his wife and daughter. He broke down at the news, and while he recovered, attended by Tansill, Beveridge took the opportunity to examine the house. In the main bedroom he found a woman in one of a pair of beds. On going outside he encountered the foreman, from whom he learned that the woman was 'Mrs Fisher'. She was difficult and dictatorial, according to the foreman. He said that over the past few weeks, the cowman, Fred, had been showing her how to ride a bicycle, as well as how to aim and fire a gun. Beveridge also learned that Fred's surname was Guilford, that his wife, Jessie, was the dairymaid, and that his mother, Mrs Mary Guilford, did the housework at the farm. All three lived in a separate cottage and had been employed by 'Mrs Fisher'.

On returning to Mr Fisher, Beveridge was introduced to his alleged wife. She was a small, slim, over-made-up woman, aged 34, with bright auburn hair, red-painted fingernails and lips, and was dressed in a bright jersey and blue trousers. She turned out to be a friend of Mr Fisher, and was called Mrs Florence Ransom.

Nothing was said to her about the murders at Matfield, and after some comments about the weather and the war, Beveridge and Tansill made their excuses, shook hands with her and left, taking Mr Fisher with them. This was so that he could formally identify the bodies at Matfield and make a statement. But it was a 90-mile drive, traversing wartime London, and Mr

Fisher, who had reason to be deeply uneasy about the murderer's identity, was inclined and willing to talk – about his marriage and his life.

Walter Lawrence Fisher was a dapper, blue-suited businessman, aged 54. Born in London in 1886, he was educated at the Merchant Taylors' School and then at the Guilds' Technical Institute. After being employed by the Standard Motor Company and the Dunlop Rubber Company, he became editor of the *Automobile Engineer* in 1914, a year after his marriage, aged 27, to Dorothy Saunders Pound. She was then 21. The marriage was not a happy one. After the birth of Freda, the Fishers ceased to cohabit, although they continued to live together in a house at Richmond in Surrey. Before long Mrs Fisher met Mr Westergart and he became a frequent visitor to the house. In 1932 the Fishers and their two daughters moved to Rosslyn Road in Twickenham – a year after the cottage at Matfield was bought as a country retreat, where Mr and Mrs Fisher could conduct their separate affairs. There never seems to have been any question of a divorce. Perhaps one or other, or both, were Catholics. At any rate, and with his wife's tacit consent, Mr Fisher was free to indulge in his own lusts and loves, and about 1934 he met a young and exciting widow, Mrs Florence Iris Ouida Ransom.

Her husband, Douglas Ransom, had died in 1930 after five years of marriage. She also became a frequent visitor to the Fishers' family home, and the *ménage à quatre* continued on its loose, liberated way until 1938, when Mr Fisher bought the farm at Piddington. It was a dairy farm, and was managed for a while by a foreman, until, in March 1940, Fisher went to live there with Mrs Ransom (now posing as Mrs Fisher). His real wife and their daughter Freda had already moved into the cottage at Matfield to escape the expected aerial bombardment of London.

At Piddington, Mrs Ransom, acting as secretary/manager, ran the farm, while Mr Fisher commuted every weekday from Aylesbury to London, returning each evening to the farm at about 6.45 pm. About once a fortnight he travelled down to Matfield to see his daughter and his wife, to whom he paid a monthly allowance, and had visited them at the beginning of July, accompanied by Mrs Ransom. The purpose of this visit was to try to assist Mrs Fisher in obtaining a permit for Mr Westergart to come and live at Matfield. All three – the Fishers and Mrs Ransom – drove to Maidstone to see the police. But the application for a permit was refused.

Mr Fisher told Beveridge that although his wife had never visited him at Piddington, his daughter, Freda, had stayed there for a while in June, when Mrs Ransom had given Freda some clothes from her wardrobe. Beveridge also learned that another oddity of the Fisher *ménage* was their liking for nicknames. Mrs Fisher was 'Lizzie' or 'Mrs Kelly'; Mr Fisher was 'Peter'; and Florence Ransom was 'Julie'.

When the police car reached Tonbridge, the widower was left at the police station while Beveridge and Tansill motored out to Matfield. 'Bert,' said Beveridge. 'What do you make of Mrs Ransom?' 'A good-looker but tough,' was Tansill's reply. 'Her eyes are a bit queer. Sort of vacant.'

Newspaper reporters were already at the cottage. First to arrive had been the representative of the *Tonbridge Free Press*, who was also the first to inform many of the villagers about the murders. Even people living in cottages near Crittenden were unaware that something was amiss and none, it seemed, had even heard any shots. The *Free Press* reporter discovered a local butcher who had called at the house, as he did daily, at 9.15 on the morning of the murders when he saw both Mrs Fisher and Miss Saunders. The part-time gardener, John Leury, was also found and questioned by the reporter, who was soon overwhelmed by the arrival of 22 'newshawks' from the national papers. He was proud to reveal later in a *Free Press* exclusive:

> Among the well-known crime reporters who covered the story were Percy Hoskins (author of a number of books on crime), Edwin Tetlow (*Daily Mail*) and Norman Rae (*News of the World*). Just back from the European war-front was O'Dowd Gallagher (*Daily Express* ace war correspondent), who trekked down to cover the murder story at Matfield after having covered the Abyssinian, Spanish and Chinese wars. Ewart Brooks (*Daily Mirror*) only a few weeks ago obtained a temporary commission to take his own motor-boat out to Dunkirk to assist in the evacuation of the BEF.

Thrilled though he may have been by all these 'aces' and by such an assignment, the local reporter was still diligent enough to report on the 'civilian sensation-hunters who flocked to Crittenden on Wednesday'; on the resulting police road-blocks; on the police search for the weapon – they dragged nearby ponds; and their checking up on the movement of vagrants in the district, of gypsies and tramps. And he was sufficiently well informed to write in the *Free Press* on Friday: 'The possibility of burglary is not ruled out, though it is not yet definitely established whether anything was stolen from the house . . . Another theory which is being considered by the police is that the murderer may have attempted to stage a fake burglary in order to cover up the real motive for the crimes. It is thought that the disorder in the house may have been caused deliberately.'

Such had been DCI Beveridge's conclusion after viewing the bodies of the three women and the cottage interior. He noted the broken tea things prepared for four people. He was told about the lady's bicycle found not far away – it was Mrs Fisher's (Freda had another) – and he took possession of the lady's left-hand glove found in the orchard. A light-brown hogskin glove, almost white, it must, he thought, have been dropped by the killer as she reloaded her gun – although no cartridges had been found in the orchard or elsewhere.

It seemed to Beveridge that Freda Fisher had been the first to be shot in the back after she and her mother, both wearing gumboots, had been inveigled outside. Or had they gone for a walk? Mrs Fisher was carrying a handbag. Perhaps the gun had been hidden by the orchard gate. Mrs Fisher, fleeing to the other end of the orchard, had evidently been pursued by the killer, who reloaded the gun and fired again. Miss Saunders, hearing the shots, may have gone outside via the kitchen door and, on seeing the killer approaching with a gun, have tried to escape by darting around the cottage to the drive, where she too had been shot. The tea tray in the kitchen may have been deliberately upset by the killer. On the other hand, Charlotte Saunders may have dropped it in her fright, before fleeing from the house.

The letters that DS Smith had found in a desk indicated that there had been some row or disagreement in June and that relations between the female Fishers and Mrs Ransom had become quite strained. In one, dated 7 June, Julie (Mrs Ransom) had written to 'Dear Mrs Kelly' (Mrs Fisher) to say she was sorry that Freda had felt she must return home. She had been a little upset, she wrote, although Freda had told her she had 'enjoyed herself immensely'. Freda, said Julie, was 'very sensitive, sentimental, and touchy'. Four days later Lizzie (Mrs Fisher) wrote to Peter (Mr Fisher) as follows: 'I have received the enclosed peculiar and I think unnecessary letter from Julie, and I am now sending it to you, as I really do not know how to deal with it. It is obvious to me it was written while under some mental strain caused no doubt by business worries and responsibilities to which she refers. Otherwise why all this fuss?'

Three days later Julie (Mrs Ransom) wrote again to Mrs Kelly:

> I am sorry that you took the trouble to send my letter to Peter, as he already had a copy . . . I am certainly a little worried, but I could not run this place if I were labouring under any mental strain, as you suggest . . . I very seldom write letters, but when I do they are penned after much thought. I also make copies of them which are filed. I think it much safer to do this as people are so careless with words and facts. I may be extremely dense, but there seems to be some mystery about the whole situation which I am unable to solve, mystery not being a strong point with me unless in a cheap detective story. So I fear I must withdraw and leave her to you, as her father seems as mortified as I.

In a letter to Freda, whom elsewhere Julie called 'Freda, my duck', Julie wrote: 'You will remember your little outburst on the Saturday morning before you departed. Owing to that your Daddy and I had a good talk about you in the evening and it was then we made our decision . . . I can assure you we were fully agreed that you should not come again.'

Whatever Beveridge thought of all this he must have believed that Mr Fisher knew much more than he said. And later that Wednesday some leading questions may well have been asked on the two-hour drive back to Piddington. Earlier, Beveridge had sent for the Yard's fingerprint chief, Superintendent Fred Cherrill, and a top police photographer. He also called in the Home Office pathologist, Sir Bernard Spilsbury. The bodies of the three women had by now been removed to the mortuary in the county hospital at Pembury, where Mr Fisher had been taken to identify them before accompanying Beveridge and Tansill back to Oxfordshire.

However, he did not stay at Carramore Farm that night. And it is possible that he never returned to Piddington, but was dropped off instead in London – which would imply he was too upset to face Mrs Ransom. In fact he did not see her again until 12 July.

What did he say to Beveridge in the car? We do not know. But on returning to Carramore Farm on the night of Monday, 8 July (as he later told the court), he had noticed a tobacco tin with cartridges in it beside Julie's bed. The cartridges were those of a single-barrelled 4.10 shotgun, known as a poacher's gun, which he had bought in Bicester some months ago, at the request of Fred Guilford, and given to him. And in the adjacent bedroom was a canvas bag from which protruded the cleaning rod of a gun.

On the day of the murder, Tuesday, he had returned as usual to the farm at about 6.45: Julie was not in the house. This was very unusual and had never happened before. He ate his dinner, served by the older Mrs Guilford, alone. Julie came in, distressed, at about 8.50 pm with Fred's wife, Jessie, and explained that she had seen a lost cat and chased it and had fallen down and bumped her head. She had then gone, she said, to the Guilfords' cottage to lie down and recover; she lay on Jessie's bed. 'She was crazy and bewildered,' Mrs Guilford would later tell the court, and Mr Fisher would say how restless she was, going to bed that night and getting up and spending half the night awake in the bed beside his.

Was any of this disclosed to Beveridge then, or revealed later? Did Fisher tell the other man, as he later told the court, that Julie had had a miscarriage a few years ago and had been very ill – that she had suffered once from a brainstorm and loss of memory? Did he try to protect her, as the Guilfords did when questioned by Beveridge? With every reason, for Mrs Guilford and her son, Fred, were Mrs Ransom's mother and brother, and Jessie was her sister-in-law.

This was something Fisher could never have told Beveridge, because he was totally unaware of this fact – that Julie's maiden name was really Florence *Guilford*, and that her nearest relations were the trio who had worked at the farm for several months.

Beveridge, on his return to Carramore Farm, eventually became aware who the Guilfords were. But first he talked to Mrs Ransom, asking her what she did and where she was on Tuesday. Her manner and answers were imprecise, although she was definite that she had never left the farm all day. Mrs Guilford, she said, would confirm this. She had recently been to Matfield, but not on Tuesday. We do not know what else Beveridge asked her, and what impression she made on him. But at some point he produced the glove that had been found in the orchard and asked Mrs Ransom to put it on. 'Certainly,' she said. 'But I think it's too small.' Without showing a flicker of concern she donned the glove and waved her hand about, before casually removing the glove and, without a word, returning it to Beveridge. He later told the court: 'It fitted perfectly.'

When he interviewed Mrs Mary Guilford she seemed anxious and uneasy, but agreed that she had seen Mrs Ransom on the farm on Tuesday, although the details were vague. The cowman, Fred Guilford, said that Mrs Ransom had been in the farmhouse scullery at about 8.15 am on the Tuesday, when she gave him a note to give to his mother; she said she was not feeling well and was going back to bed. He admitted he had a 4.10 shotgun, which fired single shots and had to be reloaded every time, but not that it had been missing on the Tuesday. He agreed he had been teaching Mrs Ransom to shoot –

to shoot rabbits, he said. Jessie Guilford had not seen Mrs Ransom on the Tuesday until about 8.45 pm, when she appeared at the Guilfords' cottage complaining of having fallen after chasing a cat. She had then been wearing a red jumper and navy-blue bell-bottomed trousers.

It is not clear how or from whom Beveridge elicited the fact that Mrs Ransom was Mrs Guilford's daughter and the sister of Fred. Perhaps a slip of the tongue, or some family resemblance, led to the disclosure. Most probably the information came from the embittered foreman. It is clear, however, that all the Guilfords had conspired to keep Mr Fisher in ignorance of the true relationship.

Beveridge and Tansill returned to Tonbridge that Wednesday night, to meet up with Sir Bernard Spilsbury, who had dined in a local hotel after conducting the post-mortems in Pembury. He was of the opinion that all three women had been shot at close range, that *six* shots had been fired, one at Charlotte Saunders, two at Mrs Fisher and three at Freda Fisher. His interpretation of this was that the two Fisher women had each been shot once, and as they lay dying the killer had gone back to each woman and fired – twice in Freda's case.

Meanwhile, in Kent, DI Smeed, whose promotion to detective superintendent would come into effect the following week, had with local assistance been making further enquiries, which continued on Thursday and were extended to Oxfordshire and Paddington Station.

Witnesses would later say in court that Mrs Ransom had caught the Wolverhampton to Paddington train at Bicester at 8.56 am on Tuesday, 9 July. At 12.45 Miss Fisher and Miss Saunders were seen on the road near Crittenden and heading towards it: Freda was on a bicycle and Miss Saunders was walking beside her. Mrs Ransom was next spotted by a 14-year-old charcoal-burner, William Smith, who was cycling from Matfield to Tonbridge, at about 3.20 pm. He saw a lady's bicycle lying on the ground with one of its handlebars caught in a gate, and further on he passed a woman walking towards Tonbridge carrying a brown paper parcel about a yard long and four inches wide. She was wearing blue trousers, a fawn overcoat, brown shoes with crêpe soles, and a blue handkerchief around her auburn hair. He saw her again later, at Alders Hill. This time she was running towards Tonbridge. At Alders village a labourer saw her, and then at about 3.45 she asked a baker who was loading his van at the family shop for a lift. She wanted, she said, to get to Tonbridge quickly. As the baker and his father, called Playfoot, were going in that direction, they took the woman with them. On the way she told them that she was meeting some friends in Tonbridge, that her husband was in the Air Force, that her children had been evacuated to Cornwall, and that her mother was very ill. She was carrying a long brown paper parcel, which she held on to all the time. The Playfoots dropped her off in St Mary's Road at about 4.10, near the police station, and at about 4.15 a ticket collector at the railway station was questioned by this same woman about the time of the next train to London. Misunderstanding what he said, she rushed out of the station and told a taxi-driver to take her to Sevenoaks to catch a train. Wondering what was in her long thin parcel, he asked her what train she meant, and as she seemed confused, he sought the advice of the ticket collector, returning to tell her that the next train to London left Tonbridge at 4.25. 'You must have misunderstood me,' said the ticket collector when she went back to him. 'I told you the next best train was the 4.25.'

All these witnesses roughly remembered what Mrs Ransom wore and described her appearance, her manner and her parcel. She was evidently so obsessed about returning home *before* Mr Fisher that she made no attempt at concealment or disguise. Her actions clearly show she was deranged and of unsound mind at that time. But this point was never made by her defence.

Armed with most if not all of this information, DCI Beveridge set off from Tonbridge early on the morning of Friday, 12 July to arrest Mrs Ransom, accompanied by DS Tansill, DI Smeed and Mrs Smeed. The latter's presence was co-opted as no policewoman was available.

On arriving at Carramore Farm they discovered that Mrs Ransom was not there. She had caught a train from Aylesbury to London, where, it was thought, she intended to visit Mr Fisher. The police at New Scotland Yard were warned about this, and on communicating with Fisher at his office they learned that Mrs Ransom had telephoned from London about noon to say that she was very worried: the police had been ransacking the farm. She wanted to meet him at the York Road exit of the Underground station at Waterloo at half-past four.

Jessie Guilford, Fred's wife, would later tell the court that early that morning Mrs Ransom asked her if she would come to Oxford with her to do some shopping. But she changed her mind and they went in a van, driven by he foreman, to Aylesbury after Mrs Ransom said: 'We'll go to London. I want to see my doctor.' On arriving in London the two women went by the Underground to Waterloo, where Mrs Ransom telephoned Mr Fisher and her doctor. They then took a train to Wimbledon, where Mrs Ransom left Jessie Guilford for a few hours. The two women were together again when a call was made to Piddington. Fred answered and spoke to Mrs Ransom, who said agitatedly to Jessie: 'Someone's been to the cottage and taken the gun. I must see a solicitor.'

At about 4.00 pm, Mrs Ransom rang Fisher, telling him to meet her at 5.30 pm at a solicitor's in Warwick Court, off High Holborn and near Gray's Inn.

She and Jessie Guilford got there first, and when the solicitor, Mr Manooch, prevaricated, saying that he could do nothing until he had spoken to Mr Fisher, both women left the building. Fisher then arrived. Jessie Guilford returned *without* Mrs Ransom, who had gone shopping, she said. Then Beveridge and the others appeared. Where was Mrs Ransom? Jessie Guilford said they were supposed to have met at a certain shop in High Holborn. Beveridge went below, fearing that Mrs Ransom might have fled. But there she stood outside a shop.

It was 6.00 pm. As she seemed not to know him, he told her who he was and that he was making enquiries into the deaths of three women at Crittenden. 'Oh, yes,' she said. 'But I must first see my husband. He's in an office around the corner.' A meeting was held between Beveridge, Mrs Ransom, Fisher and Manooch, and she was then taken to New Scotland Yard. There, after being cautioned, she made a statement and was detained.

In this statement she denied being anywhere near Crittenden on 9 July. She said: 'If there is any doubt about me or any suspicion that I was concerned with the death of Freda or the others, I am willing to do whatever is asked of me. I can assure you, however, that I am not concerned, and I do not believe that Mr Fisher is either.'

She also denied that the Guilfords were related to her.

In her shopping-bag was a letter (dated 16 June) from Freda Fisher to Julie, in which Freda thanked her for sending a coat and for her 'nice, long letter'. She wondered why Julie and her father did not want her to stay at the farm any more. She wrote: 'I feel I must have offended you. This I have not meant to do, and I am sorry. You say you are mystified. I am, too, and cannot understand why there has been all this trouble. Mummy thanks you for her letter. With love, Freda.'

On Saturday, 13 July, Mrs Ransom was brought from London to Tonbridge police station, and on Sunday the police scoured the town, looking for eight red-haired or fair-haired women, similar to Mrs Ransom, to take part in an identification parade. They were required to wear dark blue trousers and colourful blouses or jerseys. The parade took place on Monday morning, and several witnesses identified Mrs Ransom as the woman they had seen near Matfield on 9 July.

At 3.00 pm that day, in the presence of DCI Beveridge, Florence Ransom was charged at Tonbridge police station by DI Smeed with the murders of Mrs Fisher, Miss Fisher and Miss Saunders. 'I didn't do it! I didn't do it!' she said. 'How could I? No, no!'

When she was examined later by Dr Grasby, bruises were found on both her legs, consistent with a fall from a bicycle. Dr Grasby and Mr Fisher both gave evidence at the inquest, which was held at 4.00 pm that afternoon in the billiard room at the county hospital. Packed with police officers and the press, it was adjourned after the bodies had been formally identified and the cause of death announced.

Mrs Ransom appeared at Tonbridge Police Court at 10.10 am on Tuesday, 16 July, and was remanded in custody for two weeks. The local reporter from the *Free Press* was there. He wrote:

> Assisted into Court, the accused – a red-haired woman of smart appearance, wearing a grey two-piece suit – entered the dock. She was obviously very distressed and in a half-dazed condition. In the dock, accused sat huddled up, with her head against the shoulder of Mrs Millicent Wiffen, wife of the lock-up keeper at Tonbridge Police Station. Mrs Wiffen had one arm around the accused, and once or twice whispered to her.

Afterwards, Mrs Ransom was taken to Holloway Prison in a large black car with its curtains drawn.

Main gate of Springfield Jail *(Essex Record Office)*

Foot: Letter written by James Read in Springfield Jail to a friend *(Black Museum)*

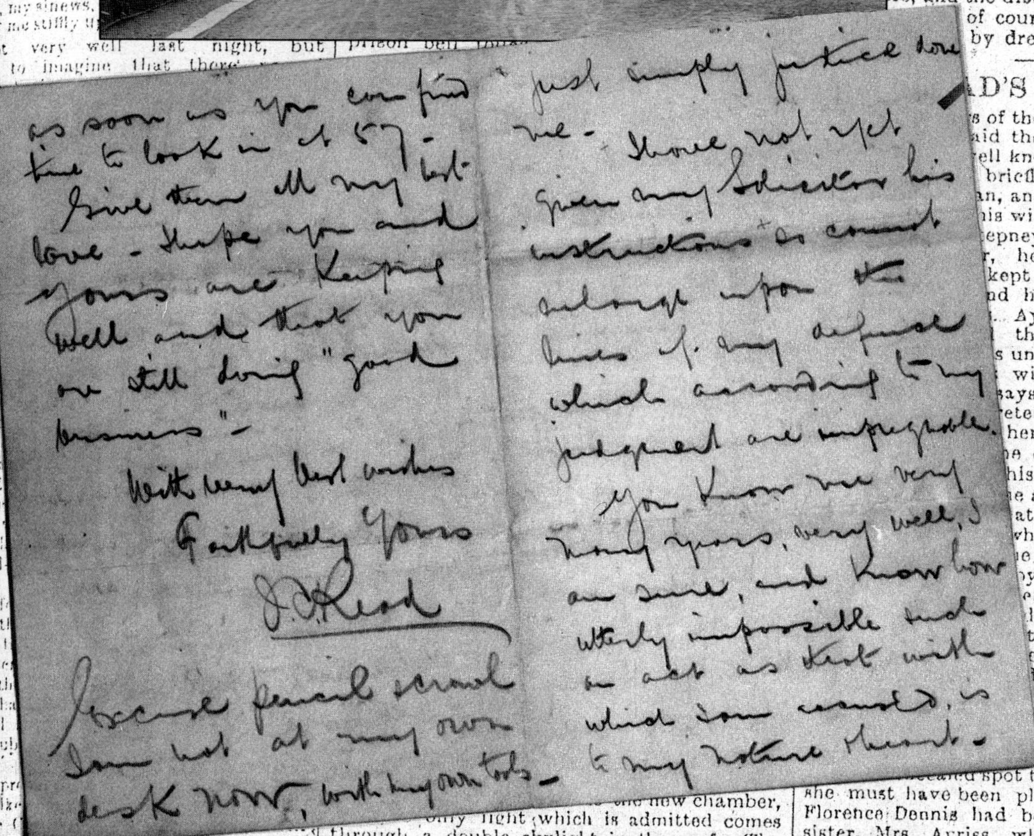

just simply justice done me - I have not yet given my Solicitor his instructions to counsel to enlarge upon the lines of my defence which according to my judgement are impregnable.

You know me very many years, very well, I am sure, and know how utterly impossible such an act as that with which I am accused, is to my nature & heart -

as soon as you can find time to look in at 57 -

Give them all my best love - Hope you and yours are keeping well and that you are still doing "good business" -

With very best wishes

Faithfully Yours

J. Read

Excuse pencil scrawl I am not at my own desk now, with my own tools -

through a double skylight in the roof. The scaffold is over a bricked pit, from 12 to 15 feet deep, and it is so arranged that three culprits can be hanged together, if necessary.

INQUEST ON READ

Main picture: The Crown Inn, Borough High Street *(Greater London Photograph Library)*

Below: Maud Marsh and George Chapman from a photograph taken by Chapman

Right: George Chapman, suspected of being Jack the Ripper *(Hulton Deutsch)*

Right: Bessie Taylor and George Chapman, from a photograph taken by Chapman

(c/o Mary Evans Picture Library)

Below: PC Tyler (Topham Picture Source)

with driver and messenger boy that brought
ages to Schnurmann's factory, Tottenham
Scotland Yard)

Above: Oak Cottage, where Lepidus died *(Mary Evans Picture Library)*

Left: Paul Hefeldt and the bridge where he was shot *(Metropolitan Police)*

Below: Walker's 14-point agenda on black-lined notepaper *(Black Museum)*

Foot: The new Central Criminal Court which now covers the site of Newgate Jail in *The Sphere*, March 1907 *(Illustrated London News Picture Library)*

MESSENGER BOY MURDER.

ACCUSED "INSANE AT THE TIME."

JUDGE AND THE LEGAL DEFINITIONS.

Before Mr. Justice Roche, at t... Criminal Court yesterday, Erne... Walker, 17, footman, was found ... the murder of Raymond Charle... District Messenger boy, in Low... The jury also found that he was i... time and not responsible for his ... Mr. Justice Roche directed ... detained during his Majesty's pl...

...d "Not Gu... and Mr. R... rector of Pu... Hutchinson ... Mr. Prac... n the serv... f Lownde... ootman. ...nd mistre... soner wa... 6 o'cl... et Distr... and the t... half-past ... soner w... bridge ... a murd... were ... dley an... e, wh... in the ... y and ... old th... with ... sir. ... don ... tim... erw...

MESSENGER BOY'S DEA...

ALLEGED CONFESSION BY YOUNG FOOTMAN.

At Westminster Police Court yesterd... before Mr. Chapman, Ernest Albe... Walker, 17, footman, in the employ ... Colonel C. W. Trotter at 30, Lowndes-squa... S.W., was charged with the wilful murde... at that address, of Raymond Charles Davi... 14, a District messenger. The prisoner, a ta... youth of slight build, was defended by M... Ivan Snell.

Detective-inspector Burton said that o... Sunday he went with Detective-inspector Hedley to Tonbridge police station, where he saw the prisoner, who had surrendered to the local police. The witness told the prisoner he would be arrested on the charge of murdering a District messenger boy on Saturday night by striking him on the head with a piece of iron, and cautioned him. The prisoner replied, "Yes, sir; I don't know what made me do it. I don't think I knew what I was doing at the time." On the way to London he spoke again, and the witness said he had better not say anything until he reached the police station.

At Gerald-road police station, added the witness, the prisoner, after being cautioned as before, said, "I quite understand what that means, but I wish to say that when I hit the boy with the piece of iron I did not ... what I was doing. I wante... to the laund...

...ENGER BOY'S MURDER.

...FOOT... OR T...

...GE LET... AT IN...

...ERBY ODD... ting with ... oncerning ... boy, RAYM... s found b... in Low... night. The... murder" ... footman, ... Charles ... ploy of th... ast Railw... as that of ... ed 14. Pellant, h... Lowndes-sq... n footman ... He was ... the slight... m, nor of ... Coroner pr... which he ... of Walker. ...ering the C... so far as h... s once or ... he read tra... ading dete...

...at is this r... —The witn... was in his ... ing he noti... apped. He... tmas time. ...bout it.

...oss-examined by Mr. St. John ... appeared for Walker), the ... ker told him about his mother ... very depressed for about a ... he suggestion is that he t... ther's gun out for the purpose ... self?—Yes, sir. That would be about the same ... ther's death?—Yes, sir. He was in a state of depressio... He was quite a decent young ... Morally?—Exceptionally so, ...

The next witness was Clara ... housemaid at 30, Lowndes-squ... he last to be in the house wi... aturday afternoon. She had t... he servants' hall, and he then ... ll right and was not annoyed ... alone. She said she would be ... 10 and he remarked that he w... thing to read. She lent him a b... Oppenheim.

THE ALLEGED CONFE...

Police-constable Sheepwash ... stated that at 8.30 p.m. on S... Walker came up to him and said, ... I have done a ... to go to the police-station as ... murder in London." After being cautioned, ... "I do ... at 30, Lowndes-square. ... Walker said, ...

... in reply to Mr. St. John ... ON, said that on the prisoner's ... de a relative was in Cane Hill ... 1888 and died there in 1893 ... ease of th...

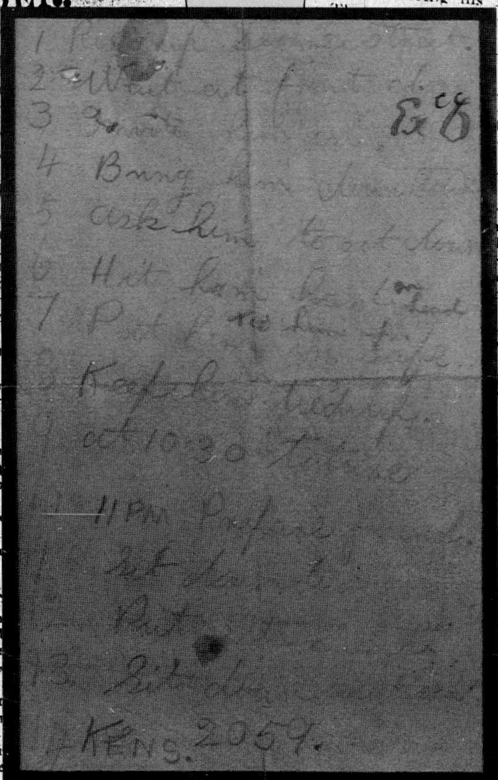

Chief Inspector Peter Beveridge introduces himself to Florence Ransom then arrests her for the Matfield triple murder *(British Newspaper Library)*

Left: Gun used by Florence Ransom *(Black Museum)*

Right: Ruth Ellis in April 1955 *(Topham Picture Source)*

Below: David Blakely *(Syndication International)*

Below left: Gun used by Ruth Ellis *(Black Museum)*

Foot: The Magdala Tavern, Hampstead *(Popperfoto)*

Inset: Ruth Ellis celebrating with friends, Desmond Cussen third from left *(Syndication International)*

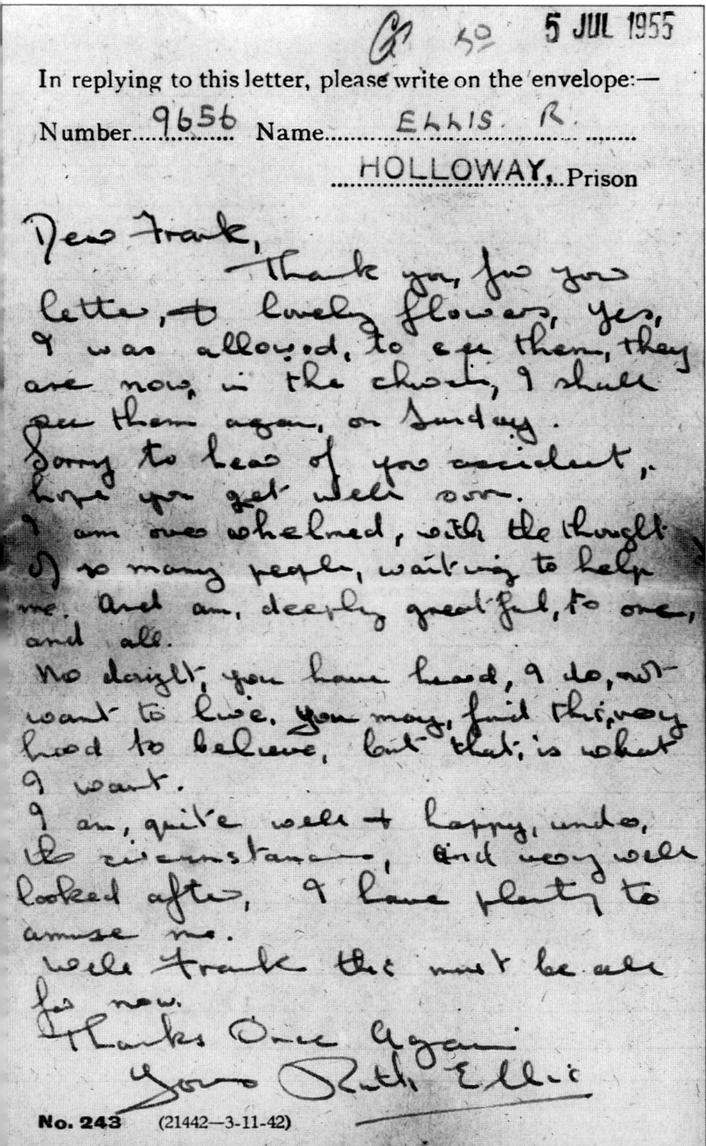

5 JUL 1955

In replying to this letter, please write on the envelope:—

Number 9656 Name ELLIS R.

HOLLOWAY Prison

Dear Frank,

Thank you, for your letter, & lovely flowers, yes, I was allowed, to see them, they are now, in the church, I shall see them again, on Sunday.

Sorry to hear of your accident, hope you get well soon.

I am overwhelmed, with the thought of so many people, waiting to help me. And am, deeply greatful, to one, and all.

No doubt, you have heard, I do, not want to live. You may, find this, very hard to believe, but that, is what I want.

I am, quite well & happy, under, the circumstances, and very well looked after, I have plenty to amuse me.

Well Frank this must be all for now.

Thanks Once Again

Yours Ruth Ellis

No. 243 (21442—3-11-42)

Letter from Ruth Ellis in Holloway prison *(Popperfoto)*

Main picture: Crowds outside Holloway prison the morning Ruth Ellis was hanged *(Syndication International)*

Francis Forsyth, Terence Lutt and Christopher Darby *(Associated Press)*

Below: Forsyth's shoes which killed Allan Jee *(Black Museum)*

Norman Harris *(Associated Press)*

Below: (c/o Hounslow Leisure Services Department)

THE COUNTY OF

Middlesex Chronicle

with which is incorporated the

BRENTFORD CHRONICLE

HOUNSLOW & DISTRICT CHRONICLE
FELTHAM, BEDFONT & HANWORTH CHRONICLE
PUBLISHED AT 136, HIGH STREET, HOUNSLOW, MIDDLESEX
(Phone: HOUnslow 0016-7-8)

TWICKENHAM & WHITTON CHRONICLE
STAINES, ASHFORD & SUNBURY CHRONICLE
SOUTHALL & EALING CHRONICLE
REGISTERED FOR TRANSMISSION BY POST (Postal Rates 23/10 per an

THREEPEN

102nd YEAR No. 5292 FRIDAY, JULY 1st, 1960

BRUTAL MURDER: WHAT WAS MOTIV

Young Man Struck Down In Footpath

ENGAGED TO WED THE DAY BEFORE

S a full-scale murder hunt was launched by police in ... this week for the killer or killers who ... 23-years-old engineer, ... Hall

The funeral of Mrs Fisher and her daughter was held at Paddock Wood the following morning. There were four mourners: Mr Fisher, Mr Westergart, Mr Rainer, a cousin of Mrs Fisher, and Mrs Johnson, a lifelong friend. The floral tributes were few. A cross of red roses placed on the double grave bore a message from Mrs Gibbs: 'To my darling daughter, who was all the world to me. That love will never fade until we meet again – Mother'. Charlotte Saunders was buried in London. It is possible that she was a poor relation of Mrs Fisher, whose maiden name was Dorothy Saunders Pound.

After another remand, on 30 July, there was a two-day hearing at Tonbridge Police Court before the magistrates on Tuesday, 13 August. Mr G. K. Paling, appearing for the Director of Public Prosecutions, attributed the motive for the murders to Mrs Ransom's jealousy – although this is not particularly evident from the letters. He produced the glove, the letters, the bicycle, and Fred Guilford's gun as exhibits. Of the gun he said: 'If this was the gun used, six cartridges were fired, and at least five times did the assailant have to remove the cartridges and put a fresh one in.'

The police never found any of the spent cartridges, nor the right-hand glove. Mrs Ransom must have disposed of both.

At the hearing, the three Guilfords revealed what lies Mrs Ransom had told them about her whereabouts on the day of the murder and what she had persuaded them to tell the police. Mrs Mary Guilford was overcome by emotion when giving evidence: she broke down and wept and had to be given a glass of water. A statement from a gun expert, Robert Churchill, was read. He testified that the wads and pellets removed from the bodies of the three women could have been fired by a 4.10 shotgun, like that produced in court.

Although Mrs Ransom appeared for trial before Mr Justice Hallett at the Old Bailey on 23 September (by which time the Battle of Britain had been won and Hitler's invasion plans abandoned), the trial was then postponed so that the defence, led by Mr Stuart Horner, could have the accused examined by a neurologist and her medical history ascertained. Mr Horner also explained that he had been briefed only a week before.

Mrs Ransom, he said, had been in several hospitals and had suffered from mental troubles for many years. 'Hysteria and a desire for publicity, or what?' demanded the judge. 'No,' said Mr Horner. 'Lapses of memory which may be due to a basic source.' The judge remarked: 'I do not understand lapses of memory. A person is either sane or insane. I am not aware of any third stage.' Mr Horner said this might well be a case of delusional insanity. 'I don't see what lapse of memory has to do with it,' retorted the judge. 'Insanity is not always continuous insanity,' Mr Horner replied, adding: 'One may be insane tomorrow, but perfectly sane yesterday and today. This woman would be prejudiced in her defence if the trial comes on before the defence has had an opportunity to investigate this question of insanity.'

After further argument, Mr Justice Hallett grudgingly acceded – 'So that no one can be given the least possible chance to say he had not been given every chance.'

The four-day trial began at the Old Bailey on Thursday, 7 November

1940, before Mr Justice Tucker. Mr Horner defended, and the prosecution was led by Mr St John Hutchinson, KC, who had been a leading *defence* counsel until very recently – he defended Ernest Walker in 1922. Mrs Ransom was only charged with the murder of Mrs Dorothy Fisher.

The trial made minor legal history as, on account of German air-raids at night, and for the first time in a murder trial, the jury were allowed to go home each night instead of being locked up in a hotel room. During the day 'spotters' on the top of the building kept an eye out for imminent danger during an alert. The court had a glass roof.

Despite the postponement of the trial, no medical expert or prison doctor was produced by Mr Horner, who could only imply that the defendant was unstable, had lapses of memory and might have been epileptic. He also proposed that if the defendant had planned the killings with so much care, as the prosecution claimed, why did she not prepare a better alibi? And there was not one shred of a motive, he said.

The only witness for the defence was Florence Ransom herself. She seemed fairly calm and positive. Guided by Mr Horner, she said that since the age of 16 or 17 she had suffered from a bad memory and had been in hospital many times. Sometimes she had fainted in the street. Later, she suffered from giddiness and had frequently been a victim of such attacks that summer. She sometimes had two or three of these attacks in a fortnight at the farm, and on one occasion had been found, she said, wandering in a lane. Questioned about 9 July, she said:

> I meant to go to London that day. I was worried about my health and wanted an opinion whether I should see a specialist. I remember standing in a field when I saw the 8.27 train – the train I would have caught . . . I must have stayed there a little time because I then saw the 8.56 pass by. I do not remember what happened afterwards until I went back to bed. The next thing I clearly remember is falling in a field and striking my head.

She said that she and Mrs Fisher and her daughter 'were on very good terms indeed'. Asked to examine the off-white hogskin glove, she denied ever owning such a pair. 'I have had only one pair of hogskin gloves in my life,' she said. 'I still have them.' 'Where?' the judged enquired, and Mrs Ransom held up a hand to show the pair she was carrying. They were passed to him and after comparing them with the single glove, he ordered them to be passed to the jury.

Asked by Mr Hutchinson to put on the single glove, she did so and he remarked: 'It fits all right, doesn't it?' She replied: 'Well, it's not a comfortable fit. It's not big enough.'

When handed the shotgun, Mrs Ransom said: 'I asked my brother for lessons ever since he had the gun. I had tried with Mr Fisher's rifle to shoot some years ago. I wasn't even able to hold the gun properly.' She said she returned the gun to her brother after it had remained overnight in the farmhouse. Mr Hutchinson later pointed out that Mrs Ransom received the gun on 8 July, that the women were shot on 9 July, and that she returned the gun on 10 July.

In reply to a prosecution question she said: 'I have never believed that Mrs Guilford is my mother.'

Mr Justice Tucker asked: 'You say you feel quite confident you did not go to Kent on the ninth?' To which Mrs Ransom replied: 'I feel certain I did not. I cannot possibly imagine I could have gone.'

On Tuesday, 12 November, the jury retired for 47 minutes: the verdict was 'Guilty'. Mrs Ransom drooped and shuddered. 'I am innocent,' she said quietly, when asked.

When the judge pronounced the death sentence she collapsed, moaning, and had to be assisted from the dock.

There was an appeal against the judge's directions to the jury about Mrs Ransom's state of mind. It was heard at the Central Criminal Court on 9 December before the Lord Chief Justice, Lord Caldecote, Mr Justice Humphreys and Mr Justice Hallett. Mrs Ransom was wearing the grey costume, blue blouse and grey hat she had worn during the trial – though the hat, as the *Free Press*'s faithful reporter observed, was 'carelessly worn'. He added: 'Two wardresses sat on either side of her, holding her hands and trying to calm her as she rocked in the seat in the dock. Her cheeks were blanched, her lips were pale.' When her insanity was discussed she waved her hands and swayed from side to side. And when the appeal was dismissed, she was heard to mutter: 'I want to go home. I want to go home.'

On 21 December the death sentence was cancelled and Mrs Ransom was reprieved, following a medical inquiry carried out at the request of the Home Secretary, Herbert Morrison. By this time the worst of the London blitz was over, although on 29 December much of the City was set on fire by incendiary bombs: seven Wren churches and the Guildhall were destroyed.

Mrs Ransom was sent to Broadmoor, where later she took part in some of that institution's in-house plays, acting, it was said of one show, 'with an aplomb that would have startled many experienced actors and actresses'.

She was transferred to Whitchurch Hospital in March 1966 and was discharged from there in January 1967, at the age of 60, having been locked away for over 26 years.

It was in 1940 that Albert Pierrepoint, born on 30 March 1905 at Clayton in Yorkshire, became the chief executioner and carried out his first hanging as such, in Pentonville Prison. Following in the footsteps of his father, Harry, and his Uncle Tom, he had been an assistant executioner since 1931, the year James Ellis died.

Two convicted murderers, James Camb and Donald Thomas, escaped being hanged in the spring of 1948. Camb, a ship's steward, had been sentenced to death in March for the murder of Eileen (Gay) Gibson, a first-class passenger on the liner Durban Castle, *en route from Cape Town to Southampton. Her body, which was never found, was believed to have been pushed through the porthole of Cabin 126. Thomas, a young petty criminal, was sentenced in April for the murder of PC Edgar in North London. The Home Secretary had recently ruled that while the House of Commons debated an experimental five-year suspension of the death penalty, no executions would be carried out. So the sentences on Camb and Thomas were commuted to life imprisonment. But in June that year the 'No Hanging' clause, passed by the Commons by 23 votes, was deleted from the Criminal Justice Bill by the House of Lords – by 181 votes to 28. Camb and Thomas were lucky they killed when they did.*

Camb was released from prison in 1959, Thomas in 1962.

The hanging of convicted murderers continued until 1964.

CHAPTER 13

Ruth Ellis

The Murder of David Blakely, 1955

No women were hanged in Britain for over 12 years between the execution of Charlotte Bryant in Exeter Prison in July 1936 for the murder, by poison, of her husband, Fred, and the execution of a 42-year-old lesbian in January 1949 for the murder, with a hammer, of an elderly eccentric, Mrs Chadwick. The last woman to be hanged in Britain was Ruth Ellis, executed for the murder of her lover in July 1955.

Ruth Ellis was born on 9 October 1926 at Rhyl in North Wales. Her real surname was Hornby. But her father changed his name to Neilson for professional reasons, and it was as Ruth Neilson that his fourth child was baptised.

Her grandfather was a Manchester-based musician, who gave piano lessons and played the organ in the cathedral. Ruth's father, Arthur Neilson, was a cellist. He prospered until the dance bands, the palm court players and cinema musicians became less popular and obsolete. He then had to travel further and further afield to get work. His wife, Bertha, was Belgian and a Catholic. She had had a turbulent childhood. Her mother had died when Bertha was two years old and she had been raised by nuns. At the start of the First World War, she was brought to England as a blanket-clad refugee. She had then gone into service, the only available occupation then for an untrained foreign woman.

She and Arthur had six children, spaced over 20 years: Julian, the eldest, was born about 1919; Muriel, born in 1921, would become 'mother' to the younger siblings; the third child, Granville, contracted a disease diagnosed by the family doctor as sleeping sickness and sea air was recommended. As Arthur occasionally worked on liners sailing out of Liverpool, the family moved to the seaside resort of Rhyl in 1926, when Bertha was pregnant with her fourth child, Ruth. Jackie, the fifth child, was born in Rhyl but died 18 months later. The Neilsons' last child, Elizabeth, was born at the outbreak of the Second World War.

The family lived at 74 West Parade, Rhyl, and when Ruth was five she went to the local infants' school. It seems that Bertha was not a good mother and found it difficult to cope with the family and domestic duties; she would often join Arthur on his travels, leaving the responsibility for the younger children and the household to Muriel, who of necessity learned to care for fair-haired little Ruth and the two older boys, making sure that Ruth was properly washed and dressed and that the glasses she wore for her short-sightedness were clean. It was Muriel who protected Ruth from any bullying at school and from their short-tempered father when he was at home.

In 1933 Arthur Neilson obtained work with a cinema band at Basingstoke in Hampshire and the family moved south. Despite a regular pay-packet, he resented the demeaning nature of this employment and vented his frustrations on his family. This worsened when the cinema sacked the band. But he managed to get a job as a hall porter and telephonist at a local mental hospital. It was the end of his career as a musician and he became even more irascible and morose.

Muriel and Ruth went to Fairfields Girls' School, where Ruth learned very little. Her spelling was never good later in life, and when she spoke she dropped her aitches. A short, skinny girl, with straight fair hair and glasses, she was 'as plain as hell' – as she later described herself. She was also head-strong and impudent, and determined to do as she liked. She took to wandering off on her own, appearing later with no explanations and causing further rows at home. Muriel usually took the brunt of her father's anger and, sometimes, his blows.

Bertha Neilson later said: 'Ruth hated us to be poor. She hated boys too at that time . . . But she always liked clothes, and she would borrow mine and dress up in them. She wasn't like my other children. She was so very ambitious for herself. She used to say: "Mum, I'm going to make something of my life."'

Arthur's uncertain temper cost him his post at the hospital in 1939, as the Second World War began. He then obtained a caretaking job in Reading and the family moved again.

Ruth left school in 1941 – she was 15 in October that year. She had already begun to earn some money by working as a waitress in a café. But what she earned she spent on clothes and make-up. Her body had filled out and she was beginning to be aware of the effect she had on the opposite sex. She stopped wearing her glasses and started collecting boyfriends. She was probably still a virgin, as Bertha's religious upbringing meant she was unable to tell her three daughters even the most basic facts of life.

In the middle of 1941, Arthur Neilson obtained a position as a chauffeur in wartime London, in Southwark. He was provided with a flat, and despite the bombing, Ruth and a girl friend of hers called Mac moved in with him, eager to sample the pleasures and thrills of wartime London, and the men. Arthur did some sampling of his own, and Bertha, paying an unexpected visit to Southwark, found him and Mac together in bed. After that Bertha decided to stay with her husband in Southwark. Muriel joined them. Julian and Granville had joined the Army, and were serving overseas.

Ruth was now bleaching her hair and making the most of her appearance: she was 5′ 2″ and had a 34″ bust. She and Muriel, now 20, worked for a while in a munitions factory. At night they went out to local dance-halls, cafés and clubs. Ruth was determined to have a good time, and Muriel had difficulty remembering all her sister's boyfriends. She herself had fallen in love with a young engineer, a Lithuanian, and was waiting patiently to marry him. She could not understand her teenage sister's feckless ways. Once when she remonstrated with her, Ruth said: 'You may be my older sister – but I'm ten bloody years older than you in experience.' She was afraid of nothing and no one. When the Neilsons' home was wrecked by a bomb-blast, Ruth calmly helped to dig her injured father out of the rubble. Arthur was a sick man after that and he never worked full-time again.

The family were temporarily housed in various lodgings until they were reunited in Camberwell, at 19 Farmers Road. They were there when they heard that Julian had been severely injured. The second son, Granville, was also wounded, and captured by the Germans; he became a prisoner of war. Bertha's last child, Elizabeth, had been born at the beginning of the war, and nights spent in air-raid shelters or in the Underground exacerbated the baby's asthma.

Meanwhile, Ruth had left the munitions factory and went to work as a machine-minder in the OXO factory at Southwark. But every night she was out enjoying herself, making the most of being a vivacious, teenage peroxide blonde. London was teeming with servicemen looking for a good time with girls like her, and she was fêted and desired at various dance-halls, restaurants and clubs. For a few months in the spring of 1942 she was stricken with acute rheumatic fever. But she was soon back on her feet, dancing the night away. She was 'dance mad', according to her mother. She was 16 in October.

Ruth was sometimes asked if she was a professional dancer, model, or actress, and she decided to do something about this by leaving the OXO factory (where the other girls thought she was 'stuck up') and then taking some singing, drama and elocution lessons at Richmond, after which her aitches were pronounced – though they tended to disappear when she was excited or drunk. She survived financially during this period by singing with a band in a club, and when that ended she took up various spare-time jobs, one of which was as a photographer's assistant in the Locarno dance-hall in Streatham.

It was there that she met and fell in love with a French-Canadian soldier called Clare (his surname is unknown). Her parents, and Muriel, liked him, and as he was a Catholic, her mother was pleased. In his late twenties, good-looking and mature, he seemed to have plenty of money, was generous with it, with flowers and gifts, and seemed to dote on Ruth. He proposed to her, and her happiness was hardly shaken when she discovered, soon after Christmas 1943, that she was pregnant. Clare said he would ask his commanding officer for permission to wed straightaway.

But permission was unexpectedly slow in being granted. So Bertha wrote to the CO, on Ruth's behalf, explaining the need for haste. He replied that Clare was already married and had three children back in Canada. Clare assured Ruth that he truly loved her and would get a divorce, so that they could marry. But she was unconvinced. She cried a lot and renounced her dancing days, obtaining a humdrum job as a cashier in a café. Although Clare continued to visit the Neilsons, and Ruth, and made regular payments to her out of his wages, the money stopped after he returned to Canada with his regiment in 1945. A society for unmarried mothers arranged for Ruth to have her baby at a nursing-home in Gilsland, not far from the Scottish border and near Hadrian's Wall. Andrea Clare Neilson was born on 15 September 1944, a few weeks before his mother's 18th birthday.

Ruth told everyone thereafter that the baby's father was an American pilot who had been killed in the war. Although she took Clare's betrayal calmly, with assumed indifference, she felt used and abused. She told the *Woman's Sunday Mirror* later: 'I did not feel that anything could hurt me any more, and I had become emotionally rather cold and spent. Outwardly I was the same.'

When she returned to London, she and the baby stayed for a while with Muriel, who had married her Lithuanian and now had three children of her own. She then moved in with her parents. She needed to earn some money to keep Andy, as the little boy was called, and she was loth to work full-time. So like hundreds of girls in her position, she decided to capitalise on her charms. She answered an advertisement for a camera club requiring a model for 'Nude but artistic poses . . . Evening work only'. She got the job.

The pay was very good (£1 an hour) and she eventually found posing easy and agreeable. Ruth said later: 'At first I felt frightfully embarrassed, but I soon got used to it . . . The men treated me very decently. Often, after work, one or other of them would take me to one of the clubs for a drink.'

At one of these clubs, the Court Club, at 58 Duke Street, she met Morris (Morrie) Conley, who owned four nightclubs in central London. He invited her for a drink at one of them in Mayfair.

This was in 1946, and Morrie Conley was on his way to becoming 'Britain's biggest vice boss' – so-called by the *People* nine years later. He was 44, fat and ugly, but affable, shrewd and rich. He was also a convicted fraudster and well known to the police. His clubs were staffed by young hostesses who were encouraged to make men feel welcome and prostitute themselves. As a result they enjoyed a high standard of living in postwar London, where the black market and ration books still survived, thanks partly to the 'overtime' payments from club members who sought and bought their favours. Such a life, of financial security and good times in glamorous Mayfair, was much desired by Ruth, who was eager to escape from Padfield Road, where her parents now lived. And when Conley offered her a job at £5 a week, plus a commission on all drinks she persuaded customers to buy, she agreed.

Soon after starting work at the Court Club, Ruth was earning more than £20 a week – enough to pay her parents' rent, enough to pay Muriel to look after Andy, enough to buy better clothes and make-up and have her hair more expensively done. At the same time she was mixing with 'society', with the occasional titled person and film star, with broadcasters and sportsmen, and above all with men with money to spend. When the Court Club closed at 11.00 pm (it opened at 3.00 pm) she moved on to another of Morrie's clubs that stayed open until 2.00 am. Afterwards, she could choose with whom and how she spent the night – unless Conley decreed she would spend it with him. She aimed to please and was not averse to group sex, or to sex, if required, with other women. 'Specials' earned more, and Morrie's approbation. Sometimes she and another girl, Vicki Martin (who became the girlfriend of the Maharajah of Cooch Behar and was killed in a car crash early in 1955), would go off with some men for a weekend at a country hotel. But she was still a good Catholic, or not very practical, and soon became pregnant again. This time she went to a private nursing-home for an abortion. She would have two or three more.

Then in the spring of 1950, when she was 23, she met George Ellis, a dental surgeon and an alcoholic, at the Court Club. He was 41 and had been divorced the previous year by his wife, Vera, who was given custody of their two sons. He became obsessed with Ruth and badgered her to go out with him. Finally she agreed.

She said later:

> I thought he was rather pathetic: he told such wild tales. I think he really believed them. He used to spend a lot of money and was always good for champagne . . . One particular night [in June], Vicki, Pat and I were in company with some members and George Ellis walked in. He wanted me to join him, but I didn't want to – he used to frighten me with his wild ravings. Vicki and I had planned to go out that night to a party. George Ellis kept pestering me. So to get rid of him, I said: 'You go to the Hollywood and I'll meet you there later.' I had no intention of going there.

But Ellis did, and his face was slashed with a razor when he left the Hollywood with another man's girl. Ruth felt responsible for Ellis's injury and tried to make amends. They went out for dinner at his golf club at Purley Downs, taken there in a chauffeur-driven car – George hired cars and drivers whenever he went out for a drink.

Ruth said later:

> I spent a lot of time in his company. He took me out shopping, bought me lots of expensive things. We ate at the best places – in fact he showered me with everything . . . It was summer holiday time, so we went off to Cornwall. I didn't tell Morrie I was going, so he was rather annoyed. I think we went in July and we came back in September. I don't think Newquay will have forgotten us in a hurry.

Back in London, Ruth moved into Ellis's house at Sanderstead in Surrey, telling people, including George's mother, that they had just returned from their honeymoon. Despite rows centred on Ellis's heavy drinking and spendthrift ways, they were married at Tonbridge Register Office on 8 November 1950.

The following day Ellis entered Warlingham Park Hospital for treatment for his drink problem. This was one of Ruth's conditions, to which he agreed, before she would marry him. Another was that he would sell his practice and house, so that the two of them could start afresh in another town. The proper education of Ruth's son, Andy, who was now six, must also have featured in the arrangement. She did not love Ellis, although she told her sister, Muriel, that this was 'the real thing'. But she was prepared for sacrifices, and toned down her make-up, appearance and dress. For marriage to a well-off, well-educated professional man would give her, apart from some security, a respectable status and, at last, a home of her own. She also expected him to inherit a fortune when his mother died.

Ellis obtained a job, by lying about his recent past and the scar on his cheek, in one of several practices owned by a dentist in Southampton, Ronald Morgan, and occupied the house that went with the job, at Warsash, near Southampton Water. He began work in the New Year – he had already begun drinking again – and within five months he was sacked.

A job in Newquay followed, as did two other drying-out stays at Warlingham Park Hospital. Ruth periodically walked out on her husband, returning to London to lodge with her mother, and the rows, threats and accusations on both sides continued, to which blows were sometimes added. She would throw drink over him and he would hit her. She abused him as 'a drunken old has-been' and he called her 'a bloody bitch from Brixton' – which was where her mother now lived. His dissipation, concerning money and drink, obsessed her less, however, than his imagined infidelity. Once married, and without company when he was at work, she began to suspect him, unreasonably, of having affairs. She knew, from her experience with Clare and the club customers, that married men could not be trusted and easily lied. She began checking up on him, phoning him at work, following him about and visiting him during the day, expecting to catch him in the arms of 'some old bag'. This began at Warsash, and she accused him of having sex with patients and staff – not only there but also at Newquay and Warlingham, where she created a scene, shouting four-letter abuse ('fucking adulterer') at him. She had to be physically restrained and was sedated.

Throughout most of this time she was pregnant. But this failed to impress Ellis or soften his attitude, and a year after their marriage, in November 1951, he tried to obtain a petition for divorce on the grounds of cruelty. The application was refused (they had not been married for three years) and a reconciliation was urged. Ruth would have acceded to this, as in October 1951 she had given birth, with difficulty, to a baby girl, who was called Georgina. Ellis was indifferent. He paid for a layette and undertook to give the mother £4 a week. But he refused to pay for a pram and suggested the baby should be adopted. She returned to Morrie Conley and the only easy way of earning a living she knew. Men, as lovers and husbands, were 'shits', and were only useful as money-machines, to be played for all they could give.

The two children were parked with her parents in South London – they had moved from Brixton to Tooting Bec – and Ruth, now 25, became a hostess once more at Carroll's, which was the new name of the Court Club. It was now open until 3.00 am, and provided a cabaret, dancing and a restaurant. Vicki was still there and now a platinum blonde, as Ruth became from then on. She mocked men and marriage and towns like Warsash – 'In that bloody hick dump you can't even buy a pair of nylons.' But life was pleasant in 1952. Once more she was admired and desired, in control of her men and their money, and of herself. Conley still exacted his pound of flesh, but in return found her a flat in Gilbert Court, Oxford Street (with a Mayfair telephone number), which was owned by his wife. His more superior hostesses were housed therein, paying the rent out of their call-girl activities. Ruth's activities broadened: she dished out cards containing off-key verses and pornographic poses to favoured customers, and advised others on where to purchase specialist rubber, and other, gear.

Early in 1953, she had an ectopic pregnancy (a foetus began growing outside the womb), and was off work for several months. In April, a party was held at Carroll's to celebrate her return. In June the nation celebrated the coronation of Elizabeth II, who was six months older than Ruth Ellis. It was a good summer for Ruth. A regular customer took her on holiday and was so satisfied he gave her a gift of £400. And then the motor-racing gang from the Steering Wheel Club in Brick Street, Mayfair, led by the tall, blond 23-year-old motor-racing champion, Mike Hawthorn (who died in a car crash six years later), chose to spend some of their drinking time at Carroll's. Among them were the two men who would destroy her life two years later – Desmond Cussen and David Blakely.

Desmond Cussen was 33. A director of the family firm, Cussen & Co, who owned several tobacconists in London and South Wales, he had been an RAF bomber pilot during the War, flying Lancasters; after being demobbed, he became an accountant. Unmarried, he lived in a flat in Devonshire Street, London W1, at 20 Goodwood Court. Unprepossessing, short, with a thin moustache, he was unambitious, ordinary and rather shy. He had known David Blakely for about a year, and they shared a common interest in drink, loose women and fast cars – Cussen had a black Ford Zodiac. They were also both strongly influenced (as was George Ellis) by their mothers.

Cussen used to tag along with the motor-racing gang, and it was Blakely who brought him to Carroll's in September 1953. Ruth met him before she met Blakely: she was 26, and Blakely, who had recently celebrated his birthday, in June, was 24.

Ruth said later:

> I was at Carroll's Club, as a guest this time, with the motor-racing boys, including Desmond Cussen, whom I had only just met, when in strolled David wearing an old coat and flannel trousers. I did not like his manner from the start. I thought he was too hoity-toity by far. He greeted the other lads in a condescending manner and was offhand in his acceptance of the proffered drink. He lounged at the bar with his back to the other girls and started making derogatory remarks, referring to the club as 'a den of vice' and jerking his head towards the hostesses' and saying 'I suppose these are the so-called hostesses' and so on . . . I turned to the other boys and in a plainly audible voice, so that he could hear, I said: 'Who is that pompous little ass?' He turned to me and said: 'I suppose you're another of them?' I said: 'No. As a matter of fact I'm an old has-been.' He finished his drink and said: 'Come on, boys. Let's get out of this sink of iniquity', and lounged out of the bar.

She told another hostess: 'I hope I won't see that little shit again.' She did, the following month.

After her 27th birthday on 9 October, when she threw a lavish party at Carroll's Club (*Cocktails and buffet, at 7 pm*), Morrie Conley asked her to become the manageress of the Little Club, a first-floor drinking-club at 27 Brompton Road, Knightsbridge. She was paid £15 a week and given a weekly £10 allowance for entertainment. A two-room flat above the club went with the job, rent-free. Two rooms above this were occupied by a couple of call-girls unconnected with the Little Club. David Blakely was already a member of the club, and on Ruth's first day in charge, he was the first person she served.

David Moffett Drummond Blakely was a Yorkshireman. He was born in a posh Sheffield nursing-home on 17 June 1929, the youngest son of a well-to-do GP, who already had two sons, Derek and Brian, and a daughter, Maureen. His mother was an Irish woman (her father had been a horse-dealer) with blue eyes and considerable charm. David was largely brought up by a nanny, whom he adored, and was particularly close to his sister.

In February 1934, when David was four, his father was accused of murder and acquitted by a magistrates' court. The case was reported in the *Daily Telegraph*:

> After hearing a speech for the defence, the Sheffield magistrates last night dismissed the charges brought against Dr John Blakely, 49, of the murder of an unemployed waitress, Phyllis Staton, 25, and of supplying a certain drug to the girl, knowing it to be intended for unlawful use. The presiding magistrate said the evidence was so weak that no jury would convict. For the prosecution it was alleged that Dr Blakely had procured a miscarriage in such a way that a post-mortem would not implicate him and that a drug had been used.

It was also alleged that the waitress, who died of acute septicaemia, had been the doctor's mistress for at least 18 months.

Although his patients forgave this lapse, Mrs Blakely never did. Appearances were maintained, but there was constant friction and unspoken animosity until she filed for divorce. It was made absolute on 2 December 1940, when David was eleven years old. Mrs Blakely was granted custody of the four children.

Two months later, on 4 February 1941, she married Humphrey Cook, at Caxton Hall in London. Both were 47. He was a wealthy man, the son of a draper, with a passion for racing-cars. They moved to 4 Culross Street, between Park Lane and Grosvenor Square. It was wartime and the two older boys were serving overseas. Maureen was at school and David went to board at Shrewsbury, a public school in Shropshire. He made little academic or athletic impression, but was a member of the Army Training Corps. He got on well with Humphrey Cook and usually spent his holidays with his mother and stepfather. When he was 18 he was called up for National Service and, being ex-public school and a former member of the ATC, he was commissioned as a second-lieutenant in the Highland Light Infantry. Charming, selfish and weak, he was prone to playing silly pranks, getting drunk, and to boasting about his driving and mechanical skills and his successes with women, those who were attracted by his boyish high spirits and eager brown eyes, his long eyelashes and lithe, lean frame – he was 5′ 9″. He also had an uncertain temper and a tendency to sulk; he was cowardly when trouble loomed, hiding or creeping away.

After leaving the Army, his stepfather secured a job for him as a management trainee at the Hyde Park Hotel in Knightsbridge, and a mews flat was found for David, his brother Brian and their nanny at 28 Culross Street. David was too lazy and undisciplined to enjoy hotel work, but he liked pandering to and being flattered by older female guests, while maintaining an association with a theatre usherette, a small platinum blonde who tolerated his erratic and unreliable ways. Women wanted to mother him; he is said to have been an indifferent performer in bed.

The hotel soon realised that David was not cut out for his job, but the management was persuaded by his stepfather to keep him on for a while. As his wages were meagre, his mother made him an allowance of £5 a week, and Mr Cook indulged him by paying some of his debts and giving him loans, which were rarely repaid. For his 21st birthday (in June 1950), Cook bought David a sports car, which soon became David's ruling passion. A good mechanic, he enjoyed tinkering with cars and driving at speed, and accompanied by his stepfather, he attended various racing events in England, entering a few junior races, which he never won. Along the way he chummed up with other racing enthusiasts and he used to meet up with them at the Steering Wheel Club, which was not far from the Hyde Park Hotel. It was frequented by racing-drivers like Mike Hawthorn, Pete Collins, Stirling Moss and Cliff Davis. Even nearer the hotel, virtually across the road, was the Little Club, whither David would vanish during working hours and at nights, for a quick drink and some fun.

David's playboy lifestyle blossomed when his father died, aged 67, in February 1952 and left each of his children £7,000. His hotel work by now ran a very poor third to his racing and social life, and the management fired him in October after a row. Mr Cook may have felt partly responsible for David's failure. At any rate he sent his wife and stepson off on a world cruise. He also bought a small mansion, the Old Park, at Penn in Buckinghamshire, and a separate flat was provided there for his stepson and the nanny. Near Penn was a small engineering company, Silicon Pistons, and David went to work there on returning to England, although he spent most of his time in London. In Penn he started having an affair with a married woman. In London, in 1953, he had an affair with an American model older than him. At the same time he was courting the young, buxom daughter of a Huddersfield businessman, with a wealthy marriage in view.

Ruth Ellis became the manageress of the Little Club in October 1953, and it was in that month that she met David for the second time. Despite her professed poor opinion of him and despite his forthcoming engagement to the

Huddersfield manufacturer's daughter (it was announced in *The Times* on 11 November), she and David began sleeping together two weeks after that second meeting. Later she said that he was playing 'hard to get' and that this was part of his attraction. He began staying overnight in her flat above the Little Club, returning at weekends to Penn. He was overwhelmed by her sexual energy and invention. He told a friend she was 'one of the finest fucks in town'.

In February 1954, she had an abortion, for which she paid. Although David, on being told that he was the father, said that he would marry her, she was still married to George Ellis, and David was still engaged to the Yorkshire girl. Ruth said later, in court: 'He offered to marry me, and he said it seemed unnecessary for me to get rid of the child. But I did not want to take advantage of him . . . I was not really in love with him at the time, and it was quite unnecessary [for him] to marry me.' She called him 'Loverboy'.

Cliff Davis (who was older than David), later said of him and those days:

> Racing-drivers weren't like they are today. You lived at a very fast rate – booze, women, everything . . . I used to see a lot of David. If we'd go to Silverstone we'd have piss-ups in the local pub either before or after a meeting. He liked his booze – he was really a drinker . . . He wasn't averse to poncing, and he certainly ponced on Ruth. His parents kept him and he had a flat just off Park Lane paid for by them. He was looked after by a housekeeper, and his stepfather paid her wages too. I went round there several times, though he didn't encourage too many visitors there. I don't know if he even took the odd bird there . . . [Ruth] was a typical club-girl . . . very attractive [but] too clued-up, too sharp. She'd been around . . . On the other hand, as a woman – not to marry but to fuck – she was wonderful. What an artist! She started at your toes and she went all the way up with her tongue. She gave you the full treatment. Terrific. I only had the experience once . . . But apart from sex, I rated her very highly as a person. As far as I know she didn't take money for sex and she always bought her round. She never ponced on anyone, not once. She had a bloody sight more principles than Blakely – David was a good-looking, well-educated, supercilious shit. But you couldn't help but like him. She was nuts about him . . . I knew he used to knock her around, because she used to have black eyes and bruises. Theirs was the absolute in love–hate relationships. They should never have been allowed to meet . . . They wanted each other, and the feeling was so diabolically strong that it excluded everybody else. If she was talking to somebody else or flirting with someone, it immediately sparked off an explosion. And of course she felt the same over his behaviour. They were usually very good. For after all David was basically a gentleman, although he could be a bastard on occasion . . . The real villain of the piece was Desmond Cusson. He was a snaky bastard. I knew him well. He was well dressed and suave. Not so young as most of us. Thick-set chap. He always used to sit in the corner of the Steering Wheel and drink

> on his own. That is, until he could get somebody to talk to him . . . Cussen was madly in love with Ruth and hated Blakely's guts.

Both Ruth and David liked to display each other to selected friends: he took her to race-meetings; she took him to the theatre and to other clubs. She began, as he did, to neglect her work, although she still performed as a call-girl during the day while Andy, who was nine, was at school. He and two-year-old Georgina were living with their mother in the flat above the Little Club. The bruises Ruth exhibited may have come from clients as well as David. She said in court: 'He was violent on occasions. It was always because of jealousy in the bar. He only used to hit me with his fists and his hands. But I bruise very easily, and I was full of bruises on many occasions.'

She was also jealous – in particular of Carole Findlater, whom David had met in 1951. Carole was then 27, and her husband, Anthony Seaton Findlater (ex-public school, a mechanic and car-engine designer, known as Ant), was 29. They had met during the war, when Carole Sonin (who was Jewish) was in the WAAF and Ant was an RAF sergeant. An interest in cars brought David and Ant together, as well as David's interest in Carole, who was dark, dynamic and wore flashy glasses. She was also a journalist, a sub-editor on *Woman* magazine. David tried to persuade her to leave Ant and live with him. He failed, but the three of them remained friends. And in April 1954, when Carole was eight months' pregnant, David employed Ant, at £10 a week, to assist him on the design and development of a new HRG sports car, which they called the Emperor.

It was in that month, at Ant's birthday party, that Carole and Ruth first met.

The party was held in the Findlaters' second-floor flat at 29 Tanza Road in Hampstead, on the southern edge of Parliament Hill. Carole later said of Ruth: 'She was wearing a black dress with a plunging neckline. She had a small bust, small wrists and ankles – the effect was shrimp-like. She said "Hallo" to me in a tiny voice . . . and then ignored me for the rest of the evening. She spent all her time talking to every man at the party.' Ruth said: 'Carole behaved like the Mother Superior herself, but I took no notice.'

About this time George Ellis reappeared, visiting the Little Club when he was in London – he was now a schools' dentist in Lancashire. Sometimes, drunk, he slept overnight on a divan in Ruth's flat. He took the infant Georgina north with him to be adopted and lodged a petition for divorce in May, soon after Carole Findlater's baby, Francesca, was born.

By now, David's heavy drinking (double gins) and tantrums were becoming a problem for Ruth. She said later:

> I began to think that it was time that the affair ended, because we seemed to be getting too deeply involved. The business at the club was beginning to suffer because of my now frequent absences and the fact that I was being monopolized. Furthermore [Conley] had started charging me a rental for the flat, because he knew that David was living there . . . He had already warned me – he considered it was bad for me and the business.

By now, Ruth was borrowing money from Desmond Cussen, and was puzzled when he apparently expected nothing in return. Spinning tales about her imagined and actual woes, past and present, was a ploy she used to financial and emotional effect. A man-friend said: 'She told me all her troubles . . . I thought I was the only one . . . She used to tell the most awful lies to get money from you.' Deceiving others, and deceiving herself, had become a way of life.

In June 1954, David Blakely took part as a co-driver in the Le Mans 24-hour race and neglected to return to England, although he sent postcards to Ruth, for about three weeks. In his absence she turned to Desmond Cussen, her 'alternative lover' as he was later called in court. She invited him to sleep with her in her flat. Cussen said later: 'I was terribly fond of her at the time.' Ruth told the court: 'I thought that Desmond would tell David we had been intimate, and I thought that would finish it' – the affair with David. Instead, it was renewed with vigour.

The main reason for this was that David's engagement was annulled in the Hyde Park Hotel, on the night of a belated birthday party Ruth gave for him in the Little Club. His fiancée probably broke it off, having heard about Ruth or some other affair. David told Ruth: 'I've got news for you. You're not going to lose me after all.' He asked her to marry him, going down on his knees and in tears. She said later: 'From then on he paid even more attention to me. He literally adored me . . . Now he was free, I'm afraid I allowed myself to become very attached to him . . . I put him on the highest of pedestals. He could do nothing wrong.'

She decided not to prolong her divorce proceedings by claiming maintenance or by defending herself in any way. She was going to marry David, with or without the Cooks' approval, and thus resolved, she became more possessive, and as obsessed as she had been with George Ellis about money, marital security, and other woman, although she humoured and indulged David at first.

In August 1954 he went to a motor-racing event in Holland to drive an MG for a friend. The car broke down. This failure, and the expense of the outing, added to David's financial problems: the money his father had left him was much depleted; the development of the Emperor, which was moved from an Islington garage to one in Culross Street, was time-consuming and costly; and Humphrey Cook, when asked for a loan, had refused to comply. David was still being paid by Silicon Pistons, paying no rent for his accommodation, and receiving his mother's allowance. But his heavy drinking and socialising – he spent his lunch-breaks in a pub at Penn and his nights in the Little Club – drained his income away. He neglected to pay Ant Findlater – who obtained a job selling second-hand cars – and began to rely on Ruth supplying him with free drinks and free meals at the club. She also provided him with cigarettes and clothes. If they went out to eat in a restaurant, she gave him the money to pay the bill. She insisted on accompanying him to other clubs, to keep an eye on him, and again she paid for their drinks. In effect, she was keeping him and in so doing was imperilling her job. There were rows, and sometimes blows: each was jealous of the other's interests and friends. She later told the court: 'He was violent on occasions. It was always because of jealousy in the bar. At the end of the evening when we got upstairs, it was always about the things he had been seeing me do, and so on and so forth.'

All these payments caused Ruth, who was also a heavy drinker (gin or Pernod) and smoker, additional money problems. These were alleviated in part when Desmond Cussen was persuaded to pay the fees for a boarding-school, to which Andy went in September 1954 when he was 10. Spoilt by his mother and undisciplined, he was frequently left on his own and used to roam around London. Now he was out of her way.

In October, Ruth Ellis was 28, and she gave a party at the club. On David's flowery birthday card, sent from Penn, was scrawled: 'Sorry I couldn't find a better card, but in this part of the world they are unheard of. Happy birthday Darling, BE GOOD. Love, David.' He promised to take her to Paris for a weekend, but lied his way out of it. Neither of them trusted the other. Ruth had found out about his affair with Carole Findlater and made him promise never to go to Tanza Road. If he did, he would be banned from the club.

Meanwhile, takings at the Little Club fell, and David's constant drunken, boorish and aggressive presence at the club was making both him and Ruth unpopular. Morrie Conley's business sense overcame his lustful need of her and in December he gave her the sack. Desmond Cussen had already asked her to live with him at Goodwood Court, and now she did, acquiring rent-free accommodation in a prestigious address and an agreeable home for Andy during his Christmas holiday.

David was incensed. But as he had often urged her to leave the Little Club and stop being a hostess, so that she would be more socially acceptable to his family, he could not be angry for long – especially as, she assured him, she would not be sleeping with Desmond and would sleep with him at some hotel as often as he wished. She added that if he really loved her, he would provide her with a home of her own. But of course he had insufficient funds.

None the less, he generally paid the £3 for their nights out at the Rodney Hotel in Kensington, where they stayed on 15 nights between 17 December 1954 and 5 February 1955, posing as Mr and Mrs Blakely. They would arrive about midnight and have breakfast in their room before coming downstairs mid-morning for a drink at the bar. David began taking amyl nitrate capsules to delay his ejaculations, the better to satisfy Ruth. She was becoming very demanding, as well as possessive. A serious crisis loomed.

David told Cliff Davis: 'I'd give anything to get away from her. But as soon as we meet it all starts again.' Ruth told Davis: 'I've given him some money, and he's out somewhere, probably poking the arse off some tart.'

Desmond Cussen had to be satisfied with Ruth's explanations for her absences that she was staying overnight with friends, or visiting them or her little girl, Georgina, up north.

That Christmas, Ruth gave identical silver cigarette-cases to Desmond and David, and as David was in Penn on the 25th, she invited a few friends to Goodwood Court for a party, one being the barmaid at the Little Club, Jackie Dyer. Cussen was at an official function and was unable to be there before 9.00 pm. Ruth put Andy to bed and, leaving a note on the door saying where she was, went off with her friends to a club for a pre-party drink.

Meanwhile, David was becoming bored at Penn; he had been drinking most of the afternoon, and as he also had a present to give to Andy, a toy revolver, decided to call on Ruth. David drove south to London and was vexed when he read the note on the door. He telephoned the club, asked to speak to Ruth and then upbraided her for leaving Andy alone in the flat. Ruth returned with her friends to Goodwood Court and everyone entered Cussen's flat, where a row at once ensued between David and Ruth. He railed at her for being a tart and sleeping with Cussen because he paid Andy's school fees. Ruth swore at him and said that Cussen didn't ponce on her as David did. She accused him of 'poking' Carole Findlater and David retaliated by telling her to go to the Findlaters' home in Hampstead and ask Carole herself. Still furious, they both went out and got into David's car, oblivious of Cussen, who had just arrived and saw them drive away. Cussen also saw how drunk David was and he followed them in his car to Tanza Road. The Findlaters were away in Bournemouth. But David had a key to the flat and went inside with Ruth. Cussen hung about and then drove back to Goodwood Court to play the party host.

At Tanza Road, Ruth and David continued arguing and accusing each other until, exhausted, they went to bed. When she returned to Goodwood Court the following morning, she told Cussen that David had threatened to kill himself if she left him on his own. So she had stayed. Cussen chose to accept her story and others that she later told.

Another night she persuaded Cussen to driver her to Penn to see whether David, as he claimed, would leave his local, The Crown, and go straight home. She watched as David drove to the house of his married woman-friend, whose husband was often away, not leaving until 9.00 am. She then accused David of being unfaithful and tried to stage a confrontation with the other woman. This David succeeded in avoiding, by lying and by taking Ruth to Penn, to The Crown, when he knew the other woman, with whom he used to play darts, would not be there. On another occasion, David happened to see his mother going into The Crown, and insisted on Ruth remaining in the car while he went inside. He brought their drinks out to the car.

On Boxing Day, the day after the Christmas-party row, David, worn out with argument, drink and sex, drove the Emperor in its first race, at Brands Hatch. He came second.

In January 1955, Ruth took some lessons in French, so that she could seem more cultured when she went with David to Le Mans later that year. Her tutor, Mrs Harris (a male tutor was banned by David), remarked on the fact that Ruth was tense, chain-smoked and could not concentrate. Drinks were constantly offered, and Mrs Harris was told that Ruth and her fiancé were continually attending or giving parties or dinners. She had in fact attended the surgery of Dr Rees, who had tried to cure George Ellis's alcoholism. Rees prescribed tranquillisers, which Ruth took from then on to calm her fevered imaginings. She would threaten to visit David's mother in Penn, as well as the married woman, and tell them all about her affair with David. She threatened to call in some of her underworld friends. She told the court: 'The tables had been turned. I was jealous of him, whereas he, before, had been jealous of me. I had now given up my business – what he had wanted me to do – left all my friends behind, connected with clubs, and things.'

Then, on 14 January, a decree nisi was granted to George Ellis, which meant that marriage to David was possible in three months' time. But the irrational pattern of violent quarrels and passionate reconciliations continued, and several hurtful and emotional scenes were enacted requiring the intervention and support of friends. Cussen was co-opted to chauffeur Ruth in pursuit of David, bent on checking where he was and with whom. Cussen himself was checking on *them*. He spotted them drinking together at certain clubs and knew about their assignations at the Rodney Hotel. However, he said and did nothing about Ruth's lies and her pretence that *he*, not David, was the main man in her life.

The worst fight between Ruth and David, involving black eyes, cuts and bruises, occurred in Desmond's flat on the evening of Sunday, 6 February, after a sustained spree of drink and sex. Each accused the other of infidelity. Desmond was out at the time. Ant Findlater and a friend, Clive Gunnell (in whose garage the Emperor now reposed), were summoned by phone to rescue David, who told them Ruth had tried to knife him. Frightened, he wanted to flee, but was prevented by Ruth, who took his car keys – he never thought to leave by taxi or on foot. He told Ant: 'She won't let me go!' And outside, in Devonshire Street, there were more histrionics as Ruth sat in David's car to prevent him leaving and then lay in the road in front of Ant's car. She later complained to Cussen that David had beaten her up, without saying what she had done to him or why.

That same night she ordered Cussen to drive her around looking for David, and early on Monday morning, she was banging on the door of David's flat at the Old Park in Penn. A confrontation between the three took place later that day outside a pub in Gerrards Cross, when Cussen told David ('You gutless little bastard!') to apologise to Ruth. He did so, and fled after she threatened to tell his mother, and the police. Later, a bouquet of red carnations arrived for her, with a note saying: 'Sorry Darling, I love you, David.' A reconciliation followed and Ruth moved out of Cussen's flat.

She moved from Goodwood Court to a furnished serviced room at 44 Egerton Gardens in South Kensington on 9 February. Ruth paid the rent with money she borrowed from Cussen, having told him she was moving out to save him from further embarrassing scenes. A week later she paid 20 guineas to join a modelling course in March. The money was again borrowed from Cussen but soon repaid, evidently from what she earned from clients.

David, absolved from paying for the Rodney Hotel, now lodged at Egerton Gardens overnight during the week, travelling to and from Penn to work and escaping thither at weekends. There he sought the consoling company of his nanny and the married woman, to whom he confided: 'Ruth is madly in love with me, but I hate her guts.' He was also becoming scared of her. There was another violent row about his (and her) unfaithfulness on 23 February. Bruises on her shoulders had to be disguised by Cussen with make-up a few days later before he could take her to a racing-drivers' dance, with David's permission, at the Hyde Park Hotel. That night she said to Cussen: 'I don't know whether I love him or I'm going mad.'

David was also at this dance, with his mother and Humphrey Cook. Ruth danced with both David and Desmond and told them that her divorce had been made absolute that day – which was a lie. She suggested a toast to her freedom. David refused to drink to this and Ruth became alarmed, thinking that he never meant to marry her.

A week's estrangement followed, during which she began attending the modelling course and demanded that David return his set of keys to Egerton Gardens. This was achieved by Cussen knocking him down outside the Steering Wheel Club and Ruth seizing the keys. But several days after this he was waiting outside 44 Egerton Gardens one night when she returned. She wrote later:

> I said: 'What are you doing here?' He said: 'You said if I stopped the affair at Penn, everything would be all right.' I said: 'Have you?' He said: 'Yes.' I believed him. He seemed so genuine and sincere. Later on, he said: 'I've been wanting to come home to you all week. It's been hell. I've missed you so much. I've slept with you so long, I can't sleep without you.' I said: 'That's no excuse for sleeping with somebody else.'

The next day Ruth got Cussen to drive her to Penn at lunchtime. David and the married woman were together in The Crown. Embarrassed, he came over to Ruth, bought her a drink and then left. He said to her later: 'I can't help it if *she* goes into The Crown.'

Ruth now found she was pregnant yet again. This did not endear her to David, who could not be certain the child was his. Nor did it ensure their marriage. When she complained, yet again, about his conduct, he lost his temper. According to her, he hit her face with his fist, grabbed her by the throat and punched her in the stomach. 'Oh God, don't let me do it!' he said (according to her). She choked: 'You're mad – you're stark, raving mad!' He said: 'One of these days I'll kill you!' She said: 'You've done that already.'

She later told the court that a miscarriage followed this scene. She told *Woman's Sunday Mirror*: 'On 28 March, I had an abortion, and I wasn't at all well. David took no interest in my welfare and didn't even bother to inquire if I was all right. I was very hurt indeed about this, and I began to feel a growing contempt for him. The results of my abortion in fact continued until Tuesday 5 April.'

None the less, she would later quote David as saying on Wednesday, 30 March (two days after the abortion): 'I wish we had enough money. We could have kept our little David. I didn't want you to get rid of it . . . No one is ever going to part us. I do love you so much.' And before they left London to race the Emperor at Oulton Park near Chester, Ruth telephoned friends to say matters had improved and that the marriage would soon take place.

Another version of the situation that week is that David was so exasperated by Ruth telephoning him at the garage and pestering him that, in order to get some peace to work on the car with Ant and Clive Gunnell, he agreed to marry her after the race-meeting at Oulton Park.

This took place on Saturday, 2 April. On the Friday, in a practice run in the rain, the car broke down and was withdrawn from competition. Carole Findlater, now woman's editor of the *Daily Mail* (she was writing an article on women's fashion at the meeting), arrived in Chester that night and found that Ant, David, Ruth and Clive were all 'down in the dumps'. David contrived to blame the car's failure on Ruth's nagging and intrusion into his work. 'It's all your fault – you jinxed me!' he said, complaining that he could not afford to get the car repaired. Ruth felt bitter about David borrowing £5 from her to help pay their hotel bill and then paying by cheque. She said later: 'I used to be good company and fun to be with. He had turned me into a surly, miserable woman. I was growing to loathe him . . . He was so much in love with himself.'

She and the others returned to London with the Emperor on the Sunday – a week before David Blakely died.

He and Ruth continued to bicker and battle, publicly and privately, over the next few days. Andy's presence was a strain: it was the Easter holiday and he was sleeping on a camp bed in the same room as David and Ruth, who had a heavy cold. But on Wednesday, 6 April, David was cheerful and optimistic. He talked about getting married and gave Ruth a photograph of himself as a future member of the Bristol team at Le Mans. It was signed: 'To Ruth, with all my love, David'. He also talked about selling the Emperor. When she protested, he said: 'If you can find me £400, I won't need to sell it.'

On Thursday, driven by Cussen, Ruth visited the photographer who had taken the photos for Le Mans to find out whether David had given any to other women. Cussen also checked to see whether David was in The Crown at Penn with the married woman, but he was there on his own. That night, in a cinema, Ruth became annoyed when David talked to her – 'He was telling me he loved me and all kinds of things' – during the film.

At about 10.00 am on Good Friday, 8 April (according to Ruth), David, having spent the night at Egerton Gardens, left in a fairly good mood – 'on the best of terms', she said. He told her he was going to team up with Ant to do some work on the car and that he would be back in the evening at eight and take her out. The Findlaters later said that David arrived at their local, The Magdala in South Hill Park, opposite Hampstead Heath Underground station, complaining about Ruth, saying that she was unstable and violent and he couldn't stand her any longer. 'I want to get away from her,' he said. Ant sympathised and suggested that David spend the Easter weekend with him and Carole at their flat in Tanza Road. He assured David that if Ruth arrived and made a scene, he and Carole would deal with her.

That same Friday morning, Desmond Cussen had collected Ruth and Andy from Egerton Gardens (all week he had driven her to her modelling course) and took them to Goodwood Court for lunch. Afterwards, they went out to a cinema. Then Ruth took Andy home, put him to bed, and prepared herself for David's return. She waited until about 9.30 pm and then telephoned Tanza Road.

The Findlaters' 19-year-old nanny answered and told Ruth that everyone was out and she didn't know where David Blakely was. An hour later, Ruth rang again. Ant answered. Ruth told him she had been waiting for David since half-past seven. Ant admitted that David had been at the flat earlier on, but was not there now. Ruth was not convinced. She said later that she was sure that David *was* at Tanza Road, that the Findlaters would not let him speak to her and were laughing at her behind her back. She kept ringing up. Sometimes Ant would answer and try to placate her; at other times the phone was replaced. Ruth became increasingly frustrated and furious. She tried telephoning Desmond Cussen, but he was out.

Meanwhile, in the Findlaters' flat, David was reacting nervously to the continuing telephone calls. Carole tried to reassure him: she gave him a kiss and told him that if Ruth came after him, she and Ant would protect him and not let her in. Then she took a sleeping pill and went to bed. David was to sleep in the sitting-room on a divan.

Just after midnight Cussen returned to his flat in Goodwood Court. The phone rang – it was Ruth. She asked him to pick her up and drive her to Tanza Road. Cussen did so. David was obviously with the Findlaters as his grey-green Vanguard van was parked outside No. 29. Ruth ran up the steps at the front of the house and rang the street door-bell. She thought she heard a woman giggle. When no one answered, she kept her finger on the bell – 'I just wanted to see David and ask for the keys.'

Inside the house, Ant came down from the second-floor flat to the hall. He listened and was relieved when the ringing stopped and he heard Ruth going down the steps. But she had not abandoned her mission. She went to the nearest telephone box and began ringing the Findlaters' flat from there. Within the flat the receiver was lifted and then replaced. Ruth walked back to the house and rang the door-bell again. There was no response. Now in a fury of rejection and spite – 'rather a nasty mood', she said – she borrowed a rubber torch from Cussen's car and attacked the windows of David's car. She later told the court: 'I knew the Vanguard windows were only stuck in with rubber. So I pushed at one of them, and it came clean out from the rubber. It didn't break, just made a noise. And I did the same with two other windows. I didn't break any – I just pushed them in.'

Ant had seen what she was doing and telephoned the police. He now emerged from the house in pyjamas and dressing-gown and confronted Ruth on the steps. It was about 2.00 am. She demanded to see David, and Ant denied that David was there. He continued to argue with her until a police car arrived. The police officer in charge heard accusation and counter-accusation, vociferously put from Ruth, less so by Ant. Ruth said she had partly paid for the Vanguard, so what she did to the car was nothing to do with the police. Ant insisted that David had no wish to see Ruth or speak to her again. She said: 'I shall stay here all night until he has the guts to show his face.' The policeman viewed the incident as a domestic rumpus. Placatory, he advised Ruth to go home: if she continued to create a disturbance, he would have to charge her with a breach of the peace. He then drove away. But Ruth would not be pacified: she began to shout.

Ant once more rang the police. But Ruth had left the scene by the time the police returned. She walked to the top of Tanza Road, where Cussen had parked, and he drove her back to Egerton Gardens at about 2.45. For over two hours he had sat in his car, making no move to interfere or appease.

Apparently Ruth stayed awake for most of that night, her mind seething with injustice and slighted love. She told herself how much she loved David and how much she had done for him. And how had he repaid her? He had sponged off her and treated her badly, even brutally. Because of him she had lost her job at the Little Club and her security at Goodwood Court. He had promised to marry her, but had failed to do so. He had lied to her, and she was sure he continued to sleep with younger and richer women. She couldn't trust him, and she felt that the Findlaters had pressured him into giving her up.

At about 8.30 on the Saturday morning she rang the Findlaters' flat. The receiver was picked up and replaced. She then got a taxi to Tanza Road and hid in a doorway two houses away from No. 29. She was there for more than an hour. At about ten o'clock Ant Findlater appeared and looked cautiously around. Then he motioned behind him and David emerged. The two men inspected the damaged Vanguard, then got into the car and drove away. Ruth guessed that they would take the car to Clive Gunnell's garage in Rex Place, Mayfair, for the necessary repairs.

She walked to a telephone box and, having waited until she thought they would have reached the garage, she rang its number. Giving a false name she asked for Ant Findlater. When he answered, she thanked him sarcastically for calling the police the previous night. He rang off. She then took a taxi to Goodwood Court and got Cussen to ring the garage on her behalf. Ant recognised his voice and put down the phone. Ruth concluded that by the time Cussen drove her to the garage, Ant and David would probably have left. She heard Cussen telling her that 10-year-old Andy was on his own and would be hungry. She agreed to be driven back to Egerton Gardens, where she gave Andy some lunch. Then they took him to Regent's Park Zoo and left him there, Cussen having given him enough money to enjoy himself and to pay his bus fare home.

At about 2.30 pm, Ruth prevailed on Cussen to drive her north to Hampstead. They saw David's car outside The Magdala pub, but decided to drive on to Tanza Road, intending to confront David there on his return. Some decorators were working on the ground floor of a house opposite No. 29. Ruth went over, and on learning that the flat was up for sale, pretended to be a prospective buyer. From her chair in a front room she could see No. 29, and in due course David and Ant returned from the pub. The nanny was not with them. Ruth made her excuses, left her observation post and moved back to the doorway where she had concealed herself that morning.

Before long she saw David, Ant, Carole, and the fair-haired nanny, who was carrying the baby, leave the house, get into the Vanguard and drive away. Ruth could have spoken to David there, or earlier at the garage, but it seems she was now averse to staging a confrontation and was bent on adding fuel to her feelings of bitter rejection and cold-eyed hate.

She waited for Cussen– he had been driving around looking for her since she had disappeared into the house opposite No. 29. They drove together to The Magdala, but there was no sign of the Vanguard or the others. Cussen persuaded her to return to Egerton Gardens, where Andy, back from the Zoo, was fed and bathed and put to bed.

Ruth had had little sleep for 36 hours, but later that Saturday night she asked Desmond to drive her yet again to Tanza Road. David's car was parked outside No. 29 and a party was now in progress in the second-floor flat. Ruth watched from the road. Someone opened a window and she heard voices and laughter. She said later that she heard David's voice and that when he stopped talking, a woman laughed. She had convinced herself that David was having an affair with the nanny, encouraged by the Findlaters, and her fervid imagination supplied the evidence. When David and Ant emerged from the house at about 9.30 pm with a young, dark-haired woman, she assumed it was the nanny, even though the nanny was fair-haired. At her trial Ruth claimed she heard David say: 'Let me put my arm around you for support'.

She did not see the three again, as she apparently then left Tanza Road to find a toilet. But on her return she again heard giggling and David's voice (the windows were open). Later, at about 12.30, she noticed that the blinds of a front room below the Findlaters' sitting-room were pulled down. She thought this was the nanny's bedroom. Although the party continued above, she could no longer hear David's voice, and imagined that he and the nanny had gone to bed. She told the court: 'I thought David was up to his tricks.' In fact, the nanny's room was at the back of the house.

After about another half an hour of watching and waiting, she let Cussen drive her home, where she spent another sleepless night tormented with jealousy, anguish and hate. When asked in court: 'What state of mind were you in?' she replied: 'I was very, very upset.'

By the morning of Easter Sunday, 10 April, Ruth was emotionally and physically very distressed. She had been on her feet for two days and had probably been drinking heavily and taking drugs. She had also had an abortion less than two weeks before.

At about 9.00 am she dialled the Findlaters' flat. The phone rang for a long time and then Ant answered. Ruth said: 'I hope you are having an enjoyable holiday, because you've ruined mine.' Ant hung up the moment he heard her voice.

In court Ruth was asked how she spent Easter Sunday. She said: 'I have completely forgotten what I did. My son was with us and we amused him in some way . . . About 7.30 I put my son to bed . . . I was very upset, and I had a peculiar idea I wanted to kill him [David].' At some point she took down all her photographs of David and replaced them with some of herself.

Desmond Cussen told the court that he collected Ruth and Andy at about noon and brought them to Goodwood Court, where they all had lunch. He then drove them home at 7.30 pm, and that, he said, was the last he saw of them.

But statements made the day before Ruth Ellis was hanged, corroborated by what she told her friend Jackie Dyer, and others, tell a different story. Ruth's sister, Muriel, who was looking after 10-year-old Andy immediately after Ruth's arrest, claimed she asked him what he had done on Easter Sunday afternoon. According to Muriel, he told her he had seen Uncle Desmond give his mother a revolver, and having oiled it, show her how to use it. And Ruth told a solicitor that after lunch on Sunday, Cussen drove her and Andy first to Hampstead and then to Penn to try to find David. Cussen allegedly stopped the car at Epping Forest (or Gerrards Cross) so that Ruth could walk into some woods and practise firing at a tree. Some of this (not the shooting practice at Gerrards Cross) was confirmed by Andy, who was quoted in the *People* after his mother's death as saying that, on their way back to Egerton Gardens, Ruth Ellis said: 'If I had a gun, I would shoot him.' To which Cussen allegedly replied: 'I've got one – but it's old and rusty and needs oiling.'

Andy was put to bed at about eight o'clock in Egerton Gardens and Ruth then left the flat. According to her, she left with Cussen, who drove her back to Goodwood Court.

The day before her execution she was persuaded by a solicitor, Victor Mishcon, to make a statement, in which she said:

> I had been drinking Pernod (I think that is how it is spelt) in Desmond Cussen's flat and Desmond had been drinking too. This was about 8.30 pm. We had been drinking for some time. I had been telling Desmond about Blakely's treatment of me. I was in a terribly depressed state. All I remember is that Desmond gave me a loaded gun. Desmond was jealous of Blakely, as in fact Blakely was of Desmond. I would say they hated each other. I was in such a dazed state that I cannot remember what was said. I rushed out as soon as he gave me the gun . . . I rushed back after a second or two and said: 'Will you drive me to Hampstead?' He did so, and left me at the top of Tanza Road. I had never seen the gun before. The only gun I had ever seen there was a small air pistol used as a game . . .

In 1977 Cussen told a TV reporter:

> I did not give Ruth the gun. Nor, on that occasion did I drive her up to Hampstead . . . The statement that Ruth gave isn't true in any way. There was no question of us drinking Pernod together. To the best of my recollection, it was a gin and tonic I poured her and she said: 'I don't feel like drinking. I'd rather have a cup of tea.' And she went off and made one. Besides, the police would have smelled Pernod on her breath if she'd been drinking heavily.

He claimed they spent the day listening to the radio, playing records and entertaining Andy, before taking him and his mother back to Egerton Gardens. Cussen added: 'She was a dreadful liar, you know.'

Ruth told the police after the murder:

> I waited all day [Sunday] for David to phone, but he did not do so. About eight o'clock I put my son, Andrea, to bed. I then took a gun which was given to me three years ago in the Club by a man whose name I do not remember. It was security for money, but I accepted it as a curiosity. I did not know it was loaded when it was given to me. But I knew next morning when I looked at it. When I put the gun in my bag I intended to find David and shoot him. I took a taxi to Tanza Road, and as I arrived, David's car drove away from the Findlaters' address. I dismissed the taxi and walked back down the road to the nearest pub [The Magdala], where I saw David's car outside. I waited . . .

David had gone back to The Magdala with Clive Gunnell. They had already been there, at lunchtime, accompanied by the Findlaters and a female friend of Clive. David had cashed a £5 cheque. That afternoon he and the Findlaters had visited the Easter Fair on Hampstead Heath. There was safety in numbers as far as David was concerned, and he walked about with the Findlaters' little girl on his shoulders. Later on, David drove to Clive's home to collect him and his gramophone and some records. Carole went too, and the three of them stopped at The Magdala for a drink before returning to Ant at Tanza Road. They sat around, smoking and drinking and playing records, until about 9.00 pm, when Carole ran out of cigarettes; the party was also short of beer. She asked David to buy some cigarettes for her at The Magdala and get some more beer. Clive went along to give him a hand. They drove the short distance down the hill in David's Vanguard, and parked outside the pub.

It was dead unlucky for David Blakely that he left No. 29 when he did. And if Carole had not run out of cigarettes he might not have gone out at all. Also, if Ruth had ambushed him outside the house, she might well have missed when she fired at him from further away, and he might more speedily have fled.

In the pub, Clive and David bought some beer, in quart flagons and bottles, and Carole's cigarettes. They stayed for a drink. Outside, Ruth watched and waited. She was carrying a .38 Smith and Wesson revolver, and was wearing a pair of black-rimmed glasses. A customer saw her peer through a stained-glass window of the pub.

It was close on half-past nine when Clive and David drained their glasses, picked up their purchases and came out of the pub. Clive walked around to the front passenger door of the car. As David, carrying a flagon, felt for his car keys, Ruth called out 'David!' He ignored her. She took her gun out of her bag and cried 'David!' again. He swung round, saw the gun and as he ran round the back of the car, she fired twice. He screamed 'Clive!' Ruth chased after him. She shrieked at Clive 'Get out of the way!' and fired again. David dodged past Clive, around the front of the car and moved up the hill towards

Tanza Road. Again she fired and he fell, face down. A total of four bullets tore through David: one was fired less than three inches away from his back; another lodged near his tongue.

Of the two other bullets fired from the revolver, one ricocheted and hit a passer-by, Mrs Gladys Yule, aged 53, in the thumb. Another apparently missed. There were clicks as Ruth fired again at David's back. It was later claimed by onlookers that she put the empty gun to her head but then lowered her arm.

She stood on the pavement by David's body as Gunnell ran into the pub. 'She's got him!' he cried. A policeman in plain clothes, PC Alan Thompson, who had been having a drink in The Magdala, went up to Ruth. She said: 'Will you call the police?' He replied: 'I am the police,' and removed the gun. She was taken to Hampstead Police Station on Rosslyn Hill.

At about 11.00 pm three CID officers, DCS Leonard Crawford, DCI Leslie Davies and DI Peter Gill, interviewed Ruth Ellis. She told them: 'I am guilty. I am rather confused.' She then agreed to make a statement, which began with the words: 'It all started about two years ago – when I met David . . .' She gave the police a calm and succinct resumé of the past three days and of the shooting of David Blakely. She blamed no one. Nor did she mention Desmond Cussen. She said that the gun was given to her three years ago 'by a man whose name I do not remember'. As she spoke, she drank some coffee and smoked a cigarette.

A post-mortem was carried out on the body of David Blakely at 9.30 am on Easter Monday. The cause of death was attributed to 'shock and haemorrhage due to gunshot wounds'. Ruth was charged with his murder at 12.30 pm, and after a brief appearance at Hampstead magistrates' court she was removed to Holloway Prison, where she became Prisoner 9656.

She asked for a bible and a photo of David. She told visitors, including Cussen, she was prepared to die. 'An eye for a eye,' she said. 'A life for a life.' Her friend, Jackie Dyer, was asked to check on David's funeral arrangements. Said Ruth: 'Go and see him, and tell me what he looks like.' When David was buried at Penn on Friday, 14 April, she sent a wreath of red carnations, her favourite flower – she had often received them from Clare.

She had already written to David's mother, Mrs Cook:

> No dought these last few days have been a shock to you. Please try to believe me, when I say, how deeply sorry I am to have caused you this unpleasantness. No dought you will hear all kinds of stories, regarding David and I. Please do forgive him for decieving you, has regarding myself . . . The two people I blame for David's death, and my own, are the Finlayters. No dought you will not understand this but *perhaps* before I hang you will know what I mean. Please excuse my writing but the pen is shocking. I implore you to try to forgive David for living with me, but we were very much in love . . . Unfortunately David was not satisfied with one woman in his life . . . I shall die loving your son. And you should feel content that his death has been repaid. Goodbye. Ruth Ellis.

At the time of the murder an industrial dispute had prevented the printing of the national newspapers. It lasted 26 days, ending on 20 April, on the day that Ruth Ellis made her second appearance in the magistrates' court. The following day the murder was front-page news, along with the election of Sir Anthony Eden as the new leader of the Conservative Party for the forthcoming General Election (on 26 May) – 'BLONDE MODEL ACCUSED OF KILLING ACE RACING CAR DRIVER' (*Daily Mirror*) – 'MODEL ON MURDER CHARGE' (*Daily Mail*). She was described as wearing in court an off-white, or grey tweed two-piece suit, edged with black piping, and black high-heeled shoes. Her platinum hair was said to be 'dyed silver-blue' by the *Daily Express*; to be 'ash blonde' by the *Daily Mirror*; and 'dyed silver-grey' by the *Daily Mail*. She was remanded in custody for another week.

At the third hearing, George Ellis appeared in the court's foyer, drunk. He declared: 'Stop this trial! Stop the trial! I want to see my wife's lawyers!' He was taken away.

Witnesses were called at this hearing, among them Ant, Clive Gunnell and Desmond Cussen, who revealed details of Ruth's private life and loves that she had hoped to conceal. The housekeeper at Egerton Gardens, Mrs Winstanley, would later recall Cussen's nervousness in the waiting-room. 'He just couldn't sit still,' she said. 'He was sweating like a pig. I asked him if he was well, but he just ignored me . . . He kept pacing up and down the floor. You could sense that he knew much more than he was ever going to say.'

Cussen showered Ruth with gifts of flowers, make-up, scent and books while she was awaiting trial. He wrote letters and visited her several times. When sentence was passed, all the gifts, letters and visits ceased. It is alleged by some writers that Ruth Ellis made a deal with Cussen – she would say nothing about his actions on the day of the murder, if he promised to provide for Andy after the trial.

In Holloway, she was interviewed by psychiatrists for the prosecution and for the defence. The former concluded that the accused woman was not suffering from any mental illness and knew what she was doing. The latter, Dr Duncan Whittaker, wrote in his report:

> She indignantly denies that her behaviour at the weekend was hysterical, and said that on the whole she is a calm person. Nevertheless, her whole history is that of an emotionally immature person, and her present equanimity is '*la belle indifference de l'hystérique*', whose intolerable problem has been solved at an immature level of behaviour and who is prepared to pay the price for this solution. Jealousy, of course, played a very large part. But it was her incapacity to get out of an intolerable situation which finally precipitated her action . . . An emotionally mature woman would have been prevented from this action by thoughts of her children . . . She told me that she never once thought of them.

Before the trial Ruth Ellis wrote a long account of her life and the events leading up to the shooting for the *Woman's Daily Mirror*. It was heavily edited and rewritten for publication after the trial – partly because her lawyers dared not prejudice a possible reprieve, and also because she wished nothing unsavoury about her past to be known. But her own account of the shooting of David Blakely is worth giving here:

> I felt somehow outside of myself – although I seemed to be registering impressions quite clearly. It did not seem to be me . . . When I got to Tanza Road I saw David's car drive away, and I followed on foot down Tanza Road towards the Magdala, where I saw the car outside. It must have been between 9.00 and 9.30 pm . . . I certainly do not remember looking in the window of the Magdala, and I do not think I did, although I walked down past the Magdala and up again. Anyway, after what seemed to me to be only a few minutes, I saw Clive Gunnell, followed by David, come out of the door of the Magdala. I thought they were both carrying bottles. Clive went round to the nearside door – the car was facing downhill on the same side of the road as the Magdala and immediately outside the [saloon bar] door. David walked up to the door on the driving side. I have a vague impression that he saw me, but went to the door of the car without taking any notice of me. I know I was in a frightful temper, and I think I started forward and took the pistol out of my handbag as I was walking towards him. I believe I stopped a few paces away from him and fired. But what he was doing or whether he was facing me or had his back to me, I cannot say . . . I did not hear him call out. But he started running round the back of the Vanguard. I had no experience in firing a gun before, and I did not think he had been hit, because he was running. I think I followed, and when I was beside Clive I said: 'Stand still, Clive!' or something like that. He was petrified. And then when I got to the front of the bonnet of the car I think I fired again. David was still running and I must have followed, because when I got back to the other side of the Vanguard on the pavement near the rear, he was running along the pavement up the hill towards Tanza Road. He looked round as I shot again, and he fell forward flat on his face. During the whole of this time I felt that I was in a kind of cold frenzy . . . At one time I seem to remember someone saying: 'Stop it, Ruth!' It may have been David – it may have been Clive . . . I do not remember firing any more shots, although the pistol must have been empty. I vaguely remember it clicking. I am sure there were no more shots because I meant to shoot myself. I remember standing there, watching him in a completely detached sort of way. I did not feel anything, except I seemed to be fascinated by the blood. I have never seen so much blood [which flowed down the gutter, mixing with the beer from the burst flagon]. He seemed to gasp two or three times, heaved, and then relaxed. I think that must have been when he died. I saw his outstretched arm, his watch and signet ring. I was rooted to the spot . . . Someone felt David's pulse and said: 'He's gone.' Clive was hysterical and screaming: 'Why did you kill him? Why didn't you kill me? What good is he to you dead? You'll both die now.' Someone said [to Clive]: 'Pull yourself together. You're a

man, aren't you?' . . . I stood beside David, watching him, until the ambulance arrived.

The trial of Ruth Ellis began at the Central Criminal Court on Monday, 20 June 1955 – three days after what would have been David Blakely's 26th birthday. It lasted two days. She pleaded not guilty and spoke in her defence. The judge was Mr Justice Havers, aged 65. The prosecution was led by Mr Christmas Humphreys, a leading Buddhist, aged 54, the son of a judge. He was assisted by Mr Mervyn Griffith-Jones and Miss Jean Southworth. The defence was led by Mr Melford Stevenson, QC, aged 52, with Mr Sebag Shaw and Mr Peter Rawlinson, aged 35.

Ruth Ellis wore a black two-piece suit with an astrakhan fur collar and cuffs and a white blouse. Her hair had been specially redyed. She looked pale, but seemed totally unmoved throughout the trial, except when she was asked in the witness box to identify David's photograph. It was the one on which he had written: 'To Ruth, with all my love, David'. As it was given to her she began sobbing and turned her head away.

Mr Humphreys commenced, on behalf of the Crown: 'Mrs Ellis is a woman of 28, divorced, and in a word, the story which you are going to hear outlined is this – that in 1954 and 1955 she was having simultaneous love affairs with two men, one of whom was the deceased . . .' He ended: 'Whatever may have been in her mind up to the time when she took that gun – if you have no doubt that she took that gun with the sole purpose of finding and shooting David Blakely and that she then shot him dead – in my submission to you, subject to his Lordship's ruling in law, the only verdict is wilful murder.'

None of the first three witnesses for the prosecution, including Mrs Winstanley, was cross-examined by Melford Stevenson, who seemed almost as indifferent to Ruth Ellis's situation as she was herself. Desmond Cussen, who was next, was given an easy time: there were no testing, embarrassing or awkward questions about the relationships between him and Ruth and David; or about her drinking or her taking of drugs; or about her children; or about Cussen's whereabouts on the day of the shooting; or about the gun. The police had found an air-gun and a starting-pistol in a drawer in Cussen's flat, but this was never mentioned in court. All that Melford Stevenson established was that Ruth Ellis had lived at Goodwood Court and had been bruised by David more than once. It seems as if any hint of a conspiracy to murder was deliberately avoided by all the lawyers concerned.

Anthony Seaton Findlater, who followed Cussen into the witness box, was similarly treated, although he was deliberately unhelpful when asked about Ruth's constant phone-calls on the Easter Sunday. He refused to admit she was desperate or disturbed. He said: 'She rang me up, as she had done hundreds of times, and asked if I knew where David was. It was just a telephone conversation.'

Ruth's solicitor, John Bickford, said much later:

Not to cross-examine the witnesses for the prosecution in a derogatory manner was the counsel's decision . . . If they had been cross-examined, that would have caused Ruth Ellis to give her evidence in a very, very different way indeed, and created, I think, an exceptionally good impression. But in point of fact, she was so upset that the witnesses for the prosecution had not been cross-examined that she virtually threw her life away. And as a result her counsel, Mr Melford Stevenson, was deprived of his right to address the jury after the evidence for the defence.

Just one other prosecution witness, Clive Gunnell, was questioned by Melford Stevenson, whose slow and methodical opening address for the defence, conceded that although 'this woman shot the man', she was guilty of manslaughter, not of murder; that Ruth Ellis was 'driven to a frenzy which for the time being unseated her understanding'; that 'the effect of jealousy upon the feminine mind can so work as to unseat the reason'; and that this jealousy constituted 'this defence of provocation'.

His main witness was Ruth Ellis, who spoke in such a toneless and offhand way that she seemed without feelings, morals or remorse. Her apparent coldness made a poor impression on the jury and it baffled the defence. Melford Stevenson's lack of comprehension of the accused's character and background led him to a fatal close. He asked: 'When you say you had a peculiar idea that you wanted to kill him – were you able to control it?' 'No,' said Ruth. Mr Stevenson continued: 'And you went up, and you in fact shot him? Is that right?' 'Yes,' said Ruth.

Christmas Humphreys had only one question to ask after that. 'Mrs Ellis,' he said. 'When you fired that revolver at close range into the body of David Blakely, what did you intend to do?' Ruth matter-of-factly told the court: 'It is obvious that when I shot him I intended to kill him.'

The defence's other witness, Dr Whittaker, was demolished by Mr Humphreys's question: 'In your view, was she at the time, within the meaning of the English law, sane or insane?' 'Sane,' said Dr Whittaker.

Neither George Ellis nor Andy Neilson, who had much useful information to reveal, was called by the defence.

The jury were then dismissed while Melford Stevenson tried to have the charge reduced to one of manslaughter, claiming that jealousy had worked on Ellis's mind to such an extent as to cause provocation. It was a novel defence and it failed. The jealous fury of a woman scorned was no excuse for murder. Nothing in English law allows a defence of *crime passionnel*, and when the court reassembled on Tuesday, 21 June, the judge told the jury, 'the evidence in this case does not support a verdict of manslaughter on the grounds of provocation.' It was murder, or nothing. Melford Stevenson then waived his right to a closing speech, as did Mr Humphreys. The judge summed up and the jury, of ten men and two women, retired at 11.52 am.

One of the jury, a man, said later:

The others were going backwards and forwards to the toilet. I reckon that of the 23 minutes we were out, only about 13 were spent actually

> discussing the case . . . I said she should be found guilty of murder, and this other chap thought we ought to be a bit lenient on her, because of all that she had gone through. The fact was the judge didn't direct us towards leniency. Either she meant to kill this lover of hers or she didn't . . . There was really nothing to argue about. I mean, it was Mrs Ellis herself who admitted she meant to to kill him.

Their verdict was 'Guilty'. Ruth was seen to smile. Mr Justice Havers donned the black cap and told the condemned woman: 'The jury have convicted you of murder. In my view it was the only verdict possible.' He sentenced her to death. A woman at the back of the courtroom sobbed. Her father quietly wept. Ruth Ellis's expression never changed. But as she left the dock she smiled at her parents and friends.

It seemed obvious to those who had access to her in Holloway in the three weeks before her execution that she was shielding someone, but she would say nothing. There were several attempts to get a reprieve. Her MP, George Rogers, co-opted by Jackie Dyer, talked to Ruth about her son's future and persuaded her to let him ask for clemency on her behalf. His first visit affected him deeply. He said later: 'Everything was grey. Everything, even the wardresses . . . Here she was, facing death, and this had stripped her of all feminine vanity and behaviour in the sort of way she must have had it when she was pursuing her normal life in the Club. She was rather thin and very pale. A rather fragile sort of person, with brassy yellow hair. Her eyes were rather shallow, not much depth to them.' He recalled that she had a powder compact that, when opened, played 'La vie en rose'.

Fifty thousand signatures on a petition for mercy were sent to the Home Office. MPs of a liberal disposition raised questions in the House of Commons and, with leading churchmen, wrote to the press. John Bickford sent a letter to the Home Secretary, Major Gwilym Lloyd George, setting out extenuating circumstances. But the most powerful appeal was made in the *Daily Mirror* on 30 June by the columnist William Connor, writing under his pen-name, Cassandra.

He attacked capital punishment as 'this ghastly business, this obscene ritual', and concluded:

> You who read this paper – and millions like you – are the key supporters of this sickening system whereby with panoply and brutality mixed with the very dubious sauce of religion and consolation we bury our worst malefactors in the quick-lime grave . . . The prospect of judicial execution never stopped any murderer. By all the records that have ever been examined, the scaffold does not prevent the use of the gun, the knife, the fatal blow, the strangler's hands or the phial of poison. Ruth Ellis does not matter any more than her two most recent female predecessors to the hangman's noose – Mrs Merrifield and Mrs Christophi. But what we do to her – you and I – matters very much. And if we do it, and if we continue to do it to her sad successors, then we all bear the guilt of savagery untinged with mercy.

The condemned woman, however, continued to tell visitors that she was resigned to her fate and wanted to die. On 5 July she wrote to a friend, Frank Neale: 'I am overwhelmed with the thought of so many people, wanting to help me. And am deeply grateful to one and all. No dought you have heard I do not want to live. You may find this very hard to believe, but this is what I want. I am quite well & happy under the circumstances and very well looked after. I have plenty to amuse me.'

But when on the afternoon of 11 July the Home Office notified the Governor of Holloway Prison, Dr Charity Taylor, that there would be no reprieve, Ruth Ellis reacted far from calmly to the news. She became hysterical and lay on her bed screaming – 'I don't want to die! I don't want to die!'

Yet she said nothing to her mother and Jackie Dyer, who visited her soon after Ruth heard she would *not* be reprieved. Mrs Bertha Neilson, questioned by a reporter on the top of a 629 trolley-bus, said: 'Ruth seemed just the same. Calm as usual.' Mrs Dyer said: 'She was just the same. She said nothing about a reprieve being refused.' But when her solicitor, John Bickford, visited Ruth Ellis she was very abusive, blaming him for the failure of the appeals. She said: 'I know what you've been doing. You've been taking a bribe, in order that I should be hanged and Cussen go free!' She dismissed Bickford and demanded to see her former divorce lawyer, Victor Mishcon. It was Mishcon, on the morning of 12 July (the day before the execution), who persuaded Ruth Ellis to say from whom she received the gun. He argued: 'Don't you owe it to your son to leave behind you a record of the truth?' She said: 'I'll tell you what happened, if you promise not to use it to try to save me.'

She then made a statement. She said: 'It is only with the greatest reluctance that I have decided to tell how it was that I got the gun . . .' She named Desmond Cussen. The statement was signed at 12.30 pm.

Victor Mishcon moved fast. He phoned the Home Office for an interview. Sir Frank Newsam, the Permanent Under-Secretary, was summoned from the Ascot Races. Senior police officers were called in and at 4.30 pm DI Gill and DC Claiden set out to try to find Desmond Cussen. Ruth's brother, Granville, also tried to track him down. But where Desmond was that night has never been revealed. He disappeared. Granville later claimed that he and a reporter tracked Cussen to a flat and found him in bed with a woman. Cussen told them to 'Get lost!' A *Woman's Sunday Mirror* reporter, Duggie Howell, later claimed that Cussen spent that evening with him at his home, drinking.

Meanwhile, shirt-sleeved men and women in cotton dresses were gathering outside Holloway Prison, some with portable radios. There were chants of 'Evans! Bentley! Ellis!' Inside the prison, Ruth Ellis wrote farewell letters, to Jackie Dyer, Frank Neale and George Rogers, who was authorised to take Andy away for a holiday. Andy had been told his mother was on a modelling assignment abroad. Ruth refused to see her brother, Granville, although she saw her parents that afternoon, about the time that the executioner, Albert Pierrepoint, arrived.

At 6.30 am on Wednesday, 13 July 1955, Ruth Ellis was visited by a

Roman Catholic chaplain. She had reverted to that faith and a crucifix had been fixed to a wall of her cell. She knelt before it as the priest administered the last rites. At 7.00 am she wrote a final letter to Leon Simmons, Mr Mishcon's clerk. She said: 'This is just for you to console my family with the thought I did not change my way of thinking at the last moment. Or break my promise to David's mother. Well, Mr Simmons, I have told you the truth and that's all I can do. Thanks once again. Goodbye. Ruth Ellis.'

She was hanged by Albert Pierrepoint at 9.00 am. She had been given a glass of brandy beforehand at her request, and she walked to her death courageously, and without a word.

Outside the prison, about a thousand people, among them Julian Neilson, awaited the posting of the execution notice. At 9.00 am some had wept, some had knelt in prayer, and a musician had played Bach's *Be Thou With Me* on his violin. In Hemel Hempstead, Mrs Neilson prayed in her bedroom as her husband played a solemn lament on his cello below. Ruth's sister, Muriel, ran from room to room in her house, weeping and crying 'No! No! No!'

Granville Neilson identified his sister's body: a scarf had been tied around her neck to hide the marks of the rope. He said later: 'She was laid with a cross at the top of her head and two candles on either side . . . She was made up, with lipstick and powder. I turned around and said to the Governor: "Doesn't she look beautiful?"'

Ruth Ellis's body was interred in the prison grounds until 1970, when Holloway underwent a rebuilding programme. Andy Neilson, her illegitimate son and next of kin, was granted permission to remove the body, which was reburied under her real maiden name of Ruth Hornby in the graveyard at St Mary's Church in the parish of Amersham in Buckinghamshire – a few miles from where David Blakely lies at Penn.

Three months after Ruth's execution, in October, her younger sister, Elizabeth, died from cardiac arrest following an asthma attack. Julian Neilson died in the mid-1960s from wounds sustained in the Second World War. Bertha Neilson's mental state deteriorated rapidly after the execution and she was admitted to a psychiatric hospital, mentally deranged. She died several years after her husband, Arthur.

It is said that Andy Neilson, who was ten years old when his mother was hanged, had not found a satisfactory niche in life by 1977, when he was 33. And his half-sister, Georgina, also found living with her mother's notoriety difficult. At one time she wrote an article on Ruth Ellis for a tabloid newspaper, although she can have remembered little if anything of her mother and nothing of the trial. When a film about Ruth Ellis, *Dance with a Stranger*, was mooted, Georgina applied to play the part of her mother, although she had had no acting experience. Ruth's ex-husband, George Ellis, committed suicide at a hotel in Jersey in the Channel Islands, five years after Ruth's execution. He hanged himself.

Desmond Cussen was last heard of in 1977 living in Perth, in Western Australia, and running a florist shop, *Chez Fleur*. He continued to deny that he ever gave Ruth Ellis a revolver or drove her to Tanza Road on the night of the murder. He told a TV reporter: 'I never thought she would hang, you know. I always thought she would get a reprieve, right up to the end . . . She used to complain when I visited her in Holloway that they'd cut all the reports of her case out of the newspapers she was given to read. She wanted to know the headlines she was making. She loved the headlines. She always wanted to be a star. She achieved that, didn't she?'

The bar-staff at The Magdala public house in South Hill Park, Hampstead, still get the occasional query about the Ruth Ellis murder. Few visitors remember the victim's name.

In 1956, Sidney Silverman's Death Penalty (Abolition) Bill, after being given a second reading in the House of Commons by 286 votes to 262, was rejected in the House of Lords. However, in March 1957 the Homicide Act was passed. The death penalty was now confined to five kinds of murder: (1) committed in the course or furtherance of theft; (2)caused by shooting or by an explosion; (3)committed in the course of or for the purpose of resisting or avoiding or preventing a lawful arrest; (4) of a police officer acting in the execution of his duty or of a person so assisting him; and (5) of a prison officer, or murder done by a prisoner. A previously convicted murderer who killed again on release could also be sentenced to death.

Albert Pierrepoint resigned in February 1956, seven months after the death of Ruth Ellis. The two men who succeeded him carried out 34 executions in the next eight-and-a-half years. Pierrepoint retired to the pub he and his wife Anne had run since 1946. Situated at Hollinwood, south of Oldham, it was called Help the Poor Struggler.

He resigned over a money matter, not through conscience or remorse. What happened was that after making all the preparations to hang a man in Liverpool in November 1955, the condemned man was reprieved. The weather was so bad, according to Pierrepoint, that he was unable to drive the 52 miles back home and stayed in a hotel overnight. In due course he was sent £1 for his pains and nothing for the hotel bill. Highly offended, he sent the money back. The sum of £4 was then sent to him. He sent it back. Eventually the full sum of £15 was sent – the executioner's fee. But as his hotel expenses were not forthcoming, Pierrepoint resigned in disgust at this slight.

In his 25 years in office, as assistant and chief executioner, Albert Pierrepoint hanged over 400 women and men.

He died in July 1992 at the age of 87. His obituary appeared in the national papers on the 37th anniversary of the day on which he hanged Ruth Ellis – on 13 July.

CHAPTER 14

Francis Forsyth, Norman Harris, Chris Darby and Terence Lutt

The Murder of Allan Jee, 1960

Nearly eight years after Derek Bentley, aged 19, was hanged by Pierrepoint in January 1953 for his involvement with Chris Craig in the shooting of PC Miles, four young men were all found guilty of the murder of Allan Jee – although only one of them was responsible for his death. Two escaped hanging, one because he was under 18. But Francis Forsyth, who was *18, was hanged for a murder he did not intend to commit. Norman Harris was hanged for his involvement in the attempted robbery that occasioned the death of Jee, although he struck no blow. Like Bentley, he was hanged because he was there, and because an example, to discourage other young thugs, had again to be made.*

It was Saturday night in Hounslow, a sprawling suburb in western London below the Great West Road. The A315 and A314 meet in Hounslow, which is constantly overflown by planes making their roaring descent to Heathrow Airport. It was 25 June 1960. Allan Jee, aged 23, was walking home. He had said goodnight to his 18-year-old fiancée, Jacqueline Herbert, a hairdresser, who lived in Stamford Brook, and at about 10.55 pm had caught a 657 trolley-bus back to Hounslow. She had walked with him to the bus-stop. That midsummer's afternoon they had been to Richmond and wandered along the riverside before having tea and seeing a film. After that they had returned to Jacqueline's home to watch TV. The day before this they had become engaged, planning to marry in two years' time.

Allan was a pleasant, athletic young man, a good ice-skater, and a trainee engineer. He had lived in Hounslow for most of his life, and had been educated at the Bulstrode Secondary Modern school. For five years he was a choirboy at the Holy Trinity Church. In February 1960 he had been demobbed from the RAF, having spent most of the two years of his National Service in Cyprus during the EOKA troubles. Once he had a narrow escape from death or injury when a booby-trap bomb exploded in a washroom. His mother said later: 'It seems terrible to think that he came through all that trouble safely, only to be killed like this near his home.'

It was about 11.10 pm when Allan stepped off the trolley-bus at the bus station and, taking the usual short-cut to his parents' home at 31 Hall Road, made his way via James Street to a poorly lit footpath that led to a footbridge over a railway line. The footpath was fenced; there was a small park on his right; allotments lay to his left. Ahead of him, where the path turned left, to run parallel with the railway before reaching the bridge, he saw four dark figures: the street-lamp there that lit the corner was out. Perhaps he felt a spasm of doubt or fear. But he was happy and going home, and he strode on hopefully towards the darkness at the bend in the path.

Earlier that night, four local youths, after visiting several pubs, had sat in Joachim's coffee bar. They were Norman Harris, an unemployed driver; Christopher Darby, a coalman; Terence Lutt, a labourer known as Lobe, and unemployed; and Francis Forsyth, known as Floss, a road worker and 18 years old.

Forsyth's fair hair was arranged in a Be-Bop style, rolling on to his forehead; he wore pointed Italian-style shoes. After passing his eleven-plus exam, he had gone for a while to Isleworth Grammar School, where, according to a schoolmate, he was 'touchy and hated to be laughed at'. Sent to an approved school when he was 15, he had two other previous convictions, the first, for larceny, when he was eleven. Norman Harris also had previous convictions and lived around the corner from Forsyth. At 23 the oldest of the four, pale-faced and dark, and darkly suited, he left school at the age of 14 and did his National Service in the Army, serving in Cyprus, like Allan Jee. Like Jee he had been to Bulstrode Secondary Modern, as had Darby and Lutt. Darby was 20, bearded, liked traditional jazz, and as a child had suffered from asthma. Excused from military service, he still carried a spray to relieve any asthmatic attacks. The youngest, Lutt, aged 17, was also the tallest and biggest, with thick, dark greasy hair.

All four lived near each other in West Hounslow, and that night had decided to do some thieving. Harris later told the police: 'I was skint and out of work. I meant to go screwing a shop or house.' Forsyth said a visit to a scrap-metal yard was mentioned. Then one of them said: 'Let's jump somebody.' This was probably Lutt. Forsyth said later: 'Lutt suggested rolling someone. He likes a fight. Come to that we all do when we've had a few shants [drinks].' Harris said: 'We followed some fellow through the path by the park and were going to do him. But some people were coming over the bridge, so we let him go.'

They waited, on edge. Then another man appeared. This was Francis Power, a big, well-built man, who was on his way home, as others were that Saturday night, taking the short-cut across the railway line to Chatsworth Crescent. Power saw four men standing in the dark at the bend in the path, two on each side. He heard their voices, and what sounded like a warning as he approached. They were silent as he passed between them. They refrained from attacking him because of his size, and Power returned safely home. It was now about 11.15 pm. The next person to approach them up the path was Allan Jee.

Lutt punched the young man hard in the face. Jee staggered against the fence, his hands to his face, and Harris caught him as he fell. 'What do you want me for?' cried Jee as Lutt and Harris held him down. Darby later claimed he took no part in the attack. Harris said: 'I put my hand in his inside pocket to get his wallet, but there was nothing in there at all . . . Forsyth was standing above us . . . I saw some blood on my hand . . . I realised Floss had put the boot in.' Forsyth said later: 'Lutt only hit him once. He packs a punch . . . As the fellow came up Lutt struck him . . . He was struggling, so I kicked him in the head to shut him up.'

Forsyth kicked Jee more than once with his Italian-style shoes, until Jee lay bleeding and semi-conscious on the ground. Then Forsyth followed as the others fled.

Although Harris had rifled Jee's other pockets, he had failed to find the small change amounting to 15 shillings, which was all Jee had.

It was over in seconds. The four ran down the path past Anthony Cowell, who was on his way to the main road. He then saw them standing on the corner of James Street. John Summerscale was probably the next to walk up the path; he was taking his mother home. He heard 'muttering and groaning' and saw a man lying full-length on his back. 'I thought the man was drunk,' he said later. Passing on and over the bridge he deposited his mother at her house, and on retracing his steps some minutes later, found an ambulance at the scene.

Meanwhile, a young typewriter mechanic, Douglas Reeve, who lived in the same road as Harris and had just taken his girlfriend home, had paused to peer at the body by the bend in the path and saw it was lying in a pool of blood. He went for help, banging on the door of a house at the end of James Street. It was 11.25 pm. But the occupant, Dennis Kemp, had to see the body for himself before he dialled 999. PC Derek Mizen arrived on the scene at 11.40. He reported later that the injured man was very restless and had to be comforted until an ambulance appeared. He said: 'We had to hold him onto the stretcher, because he started struggling.' Jee was bleeding from the nose and ears.

He was taken to West Middlesex Hospital on the Twickenham Road in Isleworth. A doctor saw him at 12.30 am. Apart from the bleeding, there was an abrasion at the base of his nose and some bruising, as there was around his left eye and ear. X-rays showed he also had a fractured skull.

His mother, Mrs Doris Jee, aged 51, visited the hospital on Sunday; she had last seen her son on Saturday afternoon. She told a reporter: 'He had a terrible black eye, and he lay there, unconscious, having a blood transfusion. I stroked his poor forehead and said: "What have they done to you, son?" I thought while he was sleeping he had a chance. But the hospital said he was critically ill.'

Allan Jee died in the hospital of cerebral contusion at 1.10 am on Monday, 27 June. Mrs Jee said: 'In the middle of the night they came to tell us he was dead . . . I'm sure he must have been attacked without warning. For he was a very fit boy, and would have given a good account of himself, if he'd had a chance . . . We keep asking: "Why, why, why?" And any minute I think that perhaps it hasn't happened and he'll walk up the path . . .'

A full-scale murder hunt was launched, led by Detective Superintendent Fred Hixson. Detectives were called in from other areas; all police leave was cancelled; and appeals were made to the public for any information. Meanwhile, the area around the footpath was minutely searched for a weapon or some clue to the identity of the assailant or assailants. No one imagined the weapon was a shoe. The murder was seemingly without a motive, for no money had been taken off Jee. For a while the police thought he had been attacked at 11.07, for his watch had stopped at that time. Jacqueline Herbert told them, however, that his watch was ten minutes slow.

Scores of people were interviewed – 3,000 in all – including known hooligans and those on police files. And such was the public response that on Thursday, 30 June, the police were able to issue detailed descriptions of three of the four young men seen in the vicinity of the crime on Saturday night. The day before this, Hixson himself interviewed Norman Harris, a known offender, and asked him about his movements on the night of the murder. Harris replied: 'I don't know anything about it, and I can tell you where I was and who I was with. I was indoors before then.' He then made a lying statement about his whereabouts, presumably backed up by Forsyth, and possibly by Darby and Lutt. Hixson told the *Middlesex Chronicle* reporter that there was no immediate prospect of a 'dramatic development'. Extensive enquiries, he said, might take weeks before the killer of Jee was found.

Nearly a fortnight after the murder, on 7 July, Superintendent Hixson was still appealing for people who were in the neighbourhood at the time to come forward. 'It is their public duty to do so,' he said. He added it was vital that the three persons whose descriptions were issued the previous week should be traced and interviewed. Perhaps he already had his suspicions, or was waiting for a lucky break. It came on Sunday, 17 July.

A teenager, Kevin Cullinan, had been feeling uneasy ever since Forsyth told him something of what had happened on the night of 25 June, when he (Cullinan) had seen Forsyth, Harris, Darby and Lutt, all of whom he knew, in Joachim's coffee bar. Forsyth had even revealed that Lutt had grabbed Jee and that he (Forsyth) had kicked him. Then on 17 July, Cullinan went to a pub with Lutt and on the way Lutt asked him who he thought had murdered Jee. Cullinan replied, somewhat boldly, that Lutt, Forsyth and the other two were probably responsible. Lutt was carrying a copy of the *People*, which was offering a reward of £500 for information leading to an arrest. He pointed at this item and said to Cullinan: 'I'll have to watch you now.'

Whether Cullinan then found he had a conscience or lost his nerve is not now known. But on Tuesday, 19 July, Lutt and the other three were taken to Hounslow Police Station for questioning. They were there all day, separately detained and interviewed by a team of dogged policemen. Before long all four began to talk, and by 7.00 pm they had all been charged with the murder of Allan Jee.

It seems that Norman Harris was the first to crack. He asked DI Humphreys: 'What killed him then?' Humphreys replied: 'He was knocked down and kicked on the head while he was on the ground and died from the injuries he received.' According to Humphreys, Harris then said: 'I'll have a fight, but I wouldn't kick a fellow lying on the ground. I didn't know the chap – but I feel sorry for him dying like that.' 'You may have known him,' said Humphreys. 'He went to Bulstrode School at the same time as you. He was about the same age.' 'I can't remember him,' retorted Harris. 'I got thrown out when I was 14 anyway.' Then he added: 'How did his people take it?' Humphreys answered: 'They thought a lot of their son, and they were very upset. In fact the shock's made his mother ill.' Harris was silent for a time, then said: 'I'm the oldest – so it's bound to be down to me.'

Elsewhere, the bearded Chris Darby asked PS Atkins: 'How long do you think we'll get for this?' Atkins replied: 'I'm not in a position to say.' Darby then said: 'It wasn't my idea to roll the bloke.' Ten minutes later he said: 'I didn't kick the chap. It was Floss who put the boot in.'

Harris was now with DS Saxby. According to Saxby, Harris said: 'I've been thinking this over – and if it all comes out, I think I'll dangle.' 'Did you do it?' Saxby asked. Replied Harris: 'If I give out on my mates we'll all dangle together.'

Forsyth was with DC Cowling, whom he asked: 'What am I likely to get for this? I reckon about a fiver . . . Suppose I get five years – what's the remission? I'd do about three years eight months, wouldn't I?' According to Cowling, Forsyth indicated his shoes, and said: 'These are the shoes I had on that night. Look – they're only soft ones. I only kicked him twice to keep him quiet . . .'

DC Barnes was present when Forsyth is alleged to have said: 'I reckon I'll get five years for this. I hope I don't go to the Scrubs . . . Lobe only hit him once . . . Really, it's sort of fading now. It's over three weeks ago. I know I only kicked him twice.'

Harris made a statement, which was shown to Forsyth. Forsyth said: 'That's about right. It was me that did the kicking. I didn't think I'd hurt him that much.' Forsyth then made a statement. Meanwhile, Darby was shown Harris's statement. He said: 'All right – I'll tell you my side of it.' He did so, denying that he had touched Jee. 'I didn't mean any harm to come to this fellow,' he said. Lutt was shown copies of the statements made by both Harris and Forsyth. He said: 'All right. What they say is true.'

Forsyth, Harris, Darby and Lutt appeared at Brentford magistrates' court on Wednesday, 20 July, and were remanded in custody for a week. A crowd of about 100 people, mostly housewives with children, gathered outside. Within, the parents of the four accused were allowed to see their sons in the cells. In the presence of a policeman Forsyth told his mother: 'I'm sorry, Mum. I did it.'

Their next appearance was on Wednesday, 4 August when, after a two-day hearing, they were committed for trial to the Old Bailey, charged with the capital murder of Allan Edward John Jee in the course or furtherance of theft. Another charge was brought against them, of assaulting Jee with intent to rob him. All four pleaded not guilty and reserved their defences. Mr Philip Radcliffe, prosecuting, said: 'They were all agreed to commit some sort of crime by way of larceny. Harris was short of money and his friends agreed to help him. Harris wanted to break into some premises but one of the others, Lutt, was more interested in what actually took place – which was highway robbery.'

Among those who gave evidence were Jee's father, Jee's fiancée, Jacqueline, Francis Power, John Summerscale, Douglas Reeve, and Kevin Cullinan.

Two hospital doctors also spoke, as did several Hounslow policemen, led by Superintendent Hixson.

The trial of Francis Robert George Forsyth, aged 18, and of Harris, Darby and Lutt, began in the No. 1 Court at the Old Bailey on Tuesday, 20 September 1960. The judge was the Hon. Mr Justice Winn, and the chief prosecutor was Mervyn Griffith-Jones. The four accused were represented by Edward Gardiner, QC (Forsyth); Peter Rawlinson, QC (Harris); David Weitzman, QC (Darby); and Victor Durand, QC (Lutt).

In his opening statement, Mr Griffith-Jones said: 'At the very best, it is robbery with violence. Planned and deliberate. The prosecution submit to you that it goes further than that, and on the law as it now stands, is murder.' Of Allan Jee, he said: 'He was set upon. He was knocked to the ground. He was held there, while his pockets were gone through. He was kicked into unconsciousness, and left lying, bleeding, moaning and semi-conscious on the ground, while these four young men made good their escape.' At one point Mr Griffith-Jones held up a black, pointed shoe and said to the jury of nine men and three women: 'The toe, you may think, is almost a lethal weapon.' Later, the pathologist who carried out the post-mortem on Allan Jee, Dr Teare, said he thought the main injuries to the head had been caused by *five* kicks, delivered with 'considerable force'.

At the end of the prosecution's opening speech the charge against Darby was reduced from capital murder to 'simple' murder, as he denied using any violence against Jee. This was accepted by the prosecution – a very fine distinction, as Harris had also committed no actual violence on Jee, and Darby knew that violence was planned 'in the course or furtherance of theft'.

The first witness for the prosecution was Jacqueline Herbert. Another was the director of the Metropolitan Police Laboratory, Lewis Nicholls, who told the court he had found blood-stains on the right sleeve of a jacket belonging to Lutt and on a sleeve of Forsyth's jacket. There were also spots of blood near the turn-up on the right leg of Forsyth's jeans, as well as traces of blood in the welt and on the instep of his right shoe.

Harris and Forsyth both gave evidence. But although an attempt was made by their QCs to minimise the defendants' actions on 25 June and to refute what they were alleged to have said in Hounslow Police Station, their demeanour and replies were unconvincing. Harris said that Jee 'seemed to buckle at the knees and fell towards me . . . I just caught him. I bent down and lowered him to the ground. If not he would have fallen. I went to put my hand in his right-hand pocket. I felt something wet and sticky on my hand. I realised what a senseless thing I was doing and said "Let's have it away" and ran up the alley.' Harris added that he only put half his hand in Jee's inside pocket and touched no other pockets. There was no kicking of Jee when he was there, he said – 'I didn't think he had been seriously injured when I got home.' He was 'very much afraid and upset' when he heard that Jee had died. After giving evidence, Harris appeared to be on the verge of collapse and had to be given some water.

Forsyth, when asked by his QC whether he had intended to rob Jee or anyone else, replied: 'No.' He said that he and the others were chatting in the alley when Jee came along. He heard a whack and realised that Lutt had hit Jee. Forsyth said: 'I moved in to see what was going on and he fell down at my feet . . . He was shouting, and I thought someone might come along, so I kicked him a couple of times to keep him quiet.' Asked whether he intended to cause any serious injury, Forsyth replied: 'No, sir.'

In his summing-up on Monday, 26 September, Mr Justice Winn conceded: 'It is not suggested here that any of these men intended to kill Allan Jee or desired his death.' None the less, the question was whether each of the accused intended to cause serious injury or committed acts which were likely to cause such injury in the course or furtherance of theft – although no money was taken. It was enough that they *intended* to steal. 'One of the vital questions is whether there was a common purpose or design,' said the judge. 'And if so, which of these defendants was party to it, and was ready to give assistance in furtherance of that common purpose.'

After deliberating for 40 minutes, the jury returned at 4.25 pm to deliver verdicts of guilty of murder on all four men. Harris and Forsyth were sentenced to death.

Harris seemed half-dead already: his face was ashen; his eyes were closed; he swayed in the dock. Forsyth stood with his mouth open, swallowing and staring ahead of him; his face was white. Darby, found guilty of simple or non-capital murder, was sentenced to life imprisonment. Lutt, not yet 18, was sentenced to be detained during Her Majesty's pleasure.

Afterwards, Jacqueline Herbert said: 'I have no feeling for them at all. What happened to Allan was so terrible, I have no sympathy for them. They have got what they deserve for the dreadful thing they did.'

Two days later, Norman Harris's father, aged 53, who was seriously ill and knew nothing of his son's sentence, died. The news of his father's death was given to Harris in the condemned cell at Pentonville Prison by the Prison Governor.

Appeals were lodged and dismissed on 24 October by the Lord Chief Justice, Lord Parker, attended by Mr Justice Elwes and Mr Justice Ashworth. It was argued that Forsyth had kicked Jee *after* the failed theft, and *after* the others had fled. Therefore the deed was not committed in the course or furtherance of theft – nor was it part of a common purpose – and should not have been adjudged as capital murder. Nor did the four set out with a weapon, a gun or knife. The jury had been influenced by what they read in the papers and misdirected by the judge.

The Lord Chief Justice concluded his verdict on the appeals by saying:

> This court has spent some considerable time on this case. We have heard the arguments by counsel on behalf of the appellants, and one thing clearly emerges for our consideration, and that is that the learned judge summed up the legal issues not only accurately and perfectly, but with great clarity. The only criticism that can be made is that in one respect [Darby] he was too favourable. There was no miscarriage of justice and no grounds on which this court can interfere.

Petitions against the death sentences were organised, one by Harris's girlfriend, 16-year-old Norma Mackie. She said: 'More people have got pity for Norman than for Floss. And a lot of people were against hanging as a whole. In fact, some people said they had no pity for the boys – but they were against hanging. So they signed.'

The chairman of the National Campaign for the Abolition of Capital Punishment, Gerald Gardiner, QC, wrote to the Home Secretary, R. A. Butler, begging him 'to remember that the existence of capital punishment did not prevent the murder, that the Christian purpose is redemptive, and that a large number of good citizens would be deeply shocked if our society were today deliberately to kill in cold blood a youth of 18, whatever he has done'.

The question of a reprieve for Harris and Forsyth was still under consideration in the first week of November, when a letter deploring the executions, particularly of Forsyth, appeared in *The Times*, signed by 31 distinguished persons, including Kingsley Amis, A. J. Ayer, Hugh Casson, John Freeman, Victor Gollancz, Gilbert Harding, Jacquetta Hawkes, Christmas Humphreys, Julian Huxley, Augustus John, J. B. Priestley, Michael Redgrave, Donald Soper, Stephen Spender, Sybil Thorndike, Leonard Woolf and the Lords Harewood, Harmsworth and Russell.

A letter-writer in the *Middlesex Chronicle* took another view, condemning the 'wicked and wanton crime'. He said:

> With regard to the petition which is circulating in this district to save two young murderers from their very just punishment, a learned QC is quoted as saying that a very large number of people would be 'deeply shocked' if one – or I presume both of them – were hanged. A very larger number of people will be even more 'deeply shocked' if they are not. On what grounds should these killers be pardoned? That they are young? So was their victim. That capital punishment fails to deter? Of course it fails to deter, if culprits know very well beforehand that sentimentalists will rush to their rescue. Their whole attitude, both before and after their trial, indicates, to my mind, only selfish concern for their own skins, a totally unrepentant attitude, and anxiety only to escape the consequences of their actions. The only way to deal with such a petition is to tear it up.

On Monday, 7 November, Harris's mother and Lutt's father took a petition to the Home Office bearing over 1,000 signatures. Forsyth's mother sent a telegram to the Queen. On Tuesday it was announced that there would be no reprieves.

On Wednesday Mrs Ada Forsyth and her 74-year-old husband, Frank, who had been a soldier for 18 years, visited their youngest son in Wandsworth Prison. Afterwards, Mr Forsyth said: 'He was laughing and joking the whole time. He never once mentioned that the reprieve had been turned down. He's a very brave boy. He knows he's got to go, but he's taking it like a soldier, just like his old man.'

At 9.00 am on Tuesday, 10 November, Francis Forsyth, aged 18, was hanged at Wandsworth Prison, and Norman Harris, aged 23, at Pentonville.

Ten years later, in 1970, Christopher Darby and Terence Lutt were released on licence – Lutt in November and Darby in May.

CHAPTER 15

John Hall

The Murders of Inspector Pawsey and DS Hutchins, 1961

Some correlation seems to exist between suicide and murder. Those who kill themselves are said to do so 'when the balance of their mind is disturbed'. This might also be said of those who kill other people. Neither murder nor suicide is, after all, the act of a wholly sane or rational person, but that of someone suffering from much mental and emotional stress; from an excess, or lack, of feeling; from total self-disgust, and/or a total lack of self-respect. Between 1900 and 1949, 29 per cent of those suspected of murder committed suicide; and 21.4 per cent of those found guilty of murder were adjudged to be insane or unfit to plead.

It is also the case that those who murder, sometimes kill themselves soon after, and in many cases, the act of murder can be viewed as an act of displaced self-destruction. The disturbed person, unable to kill himself, or herself, kills someone else instead, someone close. Thus a deeply disturbed woman, wanting but unable to kill herself, or a husband, or lover, will redirect her desire for death, and slaughter someone more vulnerable, like a child, as a substitute. Others, like John Hall, cannot destroy themselves without first killing someone else in an act of sacrificial revenge – a life for a life, a death for a death – so that they do not die alone.

1960 was a time of much social and international unease. The birth of new republics and independent states in Africa, like the Congo, Chad, Togo, Ghana, Nigeria, had been heralded by Macmillan's 'wind of change' speech in South Africa (soon to become a republic itself), and was underlined there by the Sharpeville Massacre. There was trouble in Algeria, the Congo, South Korea, and Laos, and the Cuban crisis loomed. In Britain, the Americans set up a missile early-warning system in Yorkshire, and the Navy's first nuclear submarine was launched by the Queen, a few weeks before John Kennedy became President of the USA. The first Polaris submarine arrived at Holy Loch in March 1961, and the first space-flights were made: that of a Russian dog in March, of Yuri Gagarin in April, and of an American, Alan Shepherd, in May. There were other changes that year: steam locomotives, trolley-buses and trams were being phased out fast; new £1 notes were issued, and the farthing ceased to be legal tender; betting shops were made legal; but homosexuality, despite the Wolfenden Report, was not. The Archbishop of Canterbury visited the Pope and a modern version of the New Testament (the first part of The New English Bible) appeared. In May 1961, the Queen and the Duke of Edinburgh visited the Pope; and in Vienna, on Saturday, 3 June, Kennedy and Khrushchev met.

The previous night, there had been what the police called 'a family dispute' in a house in Tavistock Road, off Romford Road in Stratford. A 30-year-old salesman, John Hall, also known as Helmwig, had attacked his wife, mother-in-law and sister-in-law with a chair. The local police were informed and left a message with the family that Hall, who had temporarily disappeared, should call on them to sort the matter out.

The police learned that Hall had recently remarried – his second wife, Sylvia Roberts, aged 21, having been a friend of his first wife, Joyce, whom he had left two years previously and divorced. The second marriage had taken place at the Forest Gate Methodist church nine weeks before, on Easter Saturday (1 April). There had been 100 guests. After a honeymoon in Spain, the couple had moved into rented rooms in Balfour Road, Ilford.

During his first marriage Hall, who was born in Woodford Green, had run a pet shop for about a year in Cranbrook Road, Gants Hill. For a time he kept two pet ocelots in his garden at Donald Drive, Chadwell Heath, but gave them away to a zoo when he and Joyce moved to Ilford. Neighbours described him later as a quiet, unassuming man, and very fond of animals. He was friendly, they said, but his wife kept herself to herself. However, they were both members of a flying club – Hall had a pilot's licence and had flown 100 hours – and he also belonged to a rifle club and was licensed to carry a gun. In fact he owned several guns.

The 'dispute' in the home of Sylvia's parents in Tavistock Road was apparently caused by her refusal to give him £5 to pay off a loan – he owed the money to the car firm who employed him. Sylvia's mother, Mrs Roberts, told a reporter: 'For some reason he went crazy and began hitting out with a chair. He hit Sylvia and he hit me. I put up my hand to defend myself and a blow broke my wrist. I had 10 stitches in my head and 12 in my arm. Sylvia had 22 stitches in a head wound, and Eileen [Sylvia's sister] was hurt too.'

After the assault Hall visited his parents' home in Empress Avenue, Woodford Green, before staying overnight with a friend.

At 12.05 on the afternoon of Saturday, 3 June, DI George Jones took a telephone call at West Ham police station in West Ham Lane, a few hundred yards south of Stratford Broadway. It was John Hall. He said: 'I understand you want to see me about the affair last night. Can I come and see you? Can I speak to the officer who is dealing with it?' DI Jones indicated that he would be pleased to see Hall and suggested he call at the police station. Hall did so, and arrived there, armed, at 1.05 pm, having driven to West Ham Lane in a red Austin Healey Sprite. He was wearing blue denim trousers and a royal-blue windcheater. John Hall was a tall, thick-set man, 6′ 1″, with fair hair going blond.

After he had reported to the front desk, DI Jones came to meet him and said: 'It's in your favour that you've come here of your own accord. But, as you know, your mother-in-law, wife and her younger sister were badly hurt at Tavistock Road last night.' Hall, interrupting, said: 'I know – and I'm sorry. I went on my knees to them and asked forgiveness. But they started pushing me about. I lost my temper and hit them with a chair. Are they badly hurt?'

Jones took Hall into the CID office, where DS Lewis was sitting at a desk. Also present was DC Walton. Hall was told that he would have to be detained while further enquiries were made. Presumably he was also charged with assault. But, although he may have been prepared to answer questions and to give his address, he was not willing to be detained.

On being told by DI Jones to empty his pockets and put the contents on the desk, Hall produced six bullets from his left-hand trouser pocket and put them on the desk. Then he pulled out a gun.

> It was an automatic pistol [DI Jones said later]. Hall was about a yard from us. As he backed towards the door he had us all at gunpoint. He backed to the door covering us. I told him not to be silly, and he said: 'You're not keeping me here!' By that time he was by the door. He rushed out and down the stairs. An immediate hue and cry was raised, and several other officers joined in the pursuit. Sgt Hutchins and PC Cox were in the chase.

DS George Hutchins was 49. He had joined the police force in 1933 and had been at West Ham for six years. He and his wife, Betty, aged 47, had a 22-year-old son and a daughter, aged 14, and they lived in Elmcroft Avenue, Snaresbrook. PC Charles Cox, who was also married, had two young daughters. Aged 38, he was from Leicestershire and had been with the police since 1947 and at West Ham all that time.

Hall, ignoring his car, ran across the road and into a small park or recreation ground, in which children were playing on slides and swings before going home to lunch. It was a fine, warm, Saturday afternoon and there were quite a few people in the streets. Hall veered to his left, heading for some houses that backed on to Whalebone Lane beside the park. Crossing the lane, he charged through the back garden and back door of 54 Farringdon Road, and exited by the front door. He then made for No. 35, diagonally across the road.

A wood-machinist, Leonard Hilliard, aged 36, was on a ladder painting the front of his parents' house, observed by his father. He said later:

> The bloke rushed into the house, and my father, who is nearly 70, went after him. The man barged into the kitchen and saw my mother was reading to my nine-year-old girl, Vivian. He said: 'I'm wanted by the police!' He tried to rush out of the back door to get into the garden. But my Welsh collie dog growled at him and he turned back. My father caught hold of this bloke, turned him round and said: 'Get out of here!' He did. He was puffing and panting, but he went out without making any fuss.

Hall turned left into Tennyson Road, passing a corner greengrocer's shop with Hutchins and Cox now close on his heels. They were within four feet of him when he turned and fired.

Hutchins fell on the pavement, shot through the stomach. Cox also collapsed, shot in a leg and an arm.

Several people saw it all. Mrs Winifred Norcott, who lived at 71 Tennyson Road, had just shouted to her son, Roy, to come in and have his lunch. Roy Norcott, aged 13, was outside sitting on a wall with his friend, Keith Pearman. He said later:

> I heard my mother shouting to me. I turned round and saw a man running towards me with a gun in his hand. He turned around and shot a man in plain clothes coming after him. This man fell to the ground . . . He fired at a policeman who was also chasing him and hit him too. When he saw us he turned back, but a policeman on a motorbike was coming after him, so he came towards us again. I was scared. I pushed my pal Keith and his mother into the house and we ran into the back garden. Afterwards I heard another shot in the distance.

Mrs Norcott said: 'It was like a television gangster serial. I couldn't believe it was real!'

In the greengrocer's, Mrs Doris Bethell, aged 37, was serving some customers when – 'I heard a schemozzle outside and I went to the door.' She said:

> As I got to the door the man opened his coat and pulled out a long pistol and shot the man. [He] doubled up, clasping his stomach, and fell to the ground. I was terrified. I thought [the gunman] might fire at me. My husband Harry called me back into the shop. I ran back inside to phone the police and then I heard a second shot. My husband came out and saw the two policemen lying on the ground . . . A uniformed policeman was not far from the other man. Blood was pouring from them . . . We got some blankets and put cushions under the two wounded men's heads.

Hall staggered on up the road, pursued now by a helmeted police motorcyclist, PC Leslie England, to whom Hutchins had called: 'Get him, Les! He's got us!' England drove his lightweight machine on to the pavement and cautiously followed. According to what he later told the coroner's court, he was within a few feet of Hall, when Hall turned and fired again – but missed.

According to the civilian eyewitnesses Hall, who said nothing throughout the chase, fired three shots – but none at England. Mrs George Mansfield, who was outside her home in Tennyson Road, said later: 'I screamed, "He's got a gun!" and began to run into the house. The gunman stopped and pointed the gun at another policeman on a motorbike. But he did not pull the trigger that time.' Mrs Florence Carter, aged 52, said: 'I saw him walk up the street with the motorcyclist behind him. Once or twice he turned round. Then at the corner he broke into a run. A moment later I heard another shot.'

This, the third, was probably fired, not at England, but at Inspector Pawsey, who was in a police patrol car. He had driven into Tennyson Road from the Romford Road, in an attempt to prevent Hall's escape.

Pawsey was 40, married, but with no children. He had been at West Ham for five years.

Said PC England later:

> He saw Hall and drove the car across the road and stopped beside him. Inspector Pawsey opened the door of the car, as if to get out, and Hall turned and pointed the gun at him. He did not fire at that second, and Inspector Pawsey shut the door without getting out. He opened the door again, which gave me the impression he intended to get out and tackle Hall. Hall then shot him. He was very close, about three or four feet away, at pointblank range. Hall ran off, and the Inspector said to me: 'Get after him!' The Inspector was sitting and reaching across for the radio microphone. At that time I did not think he was seriously injured. But I knew he was hurt because he did not resume the pursuit. I went after Hall.

David Goddard, aged 11, who was standing in the porch of a house near the junction of Tennyson and Romford Roads, saw Hall approaching him up the road. 'He was lurching as he ran and breathing heavily,' said David later. 'In his right hand, which was pointing in front of him and held straight out, was a black pistol. A helmeted policeman on a scooter was following him along the pavement.' As the gunman passed the porch, Pawsey drove into Tennyson Road and screeched to a halt on the wrong side of the road. Said David: 'The policeman opened the door of the car and was going to get out when the man raised the gun opposite his shoulder and fired at him. The policeman fell forward over the steering-wheel and the horn started to blow.'

Hall now seems to have eluded the police by dodging through another house and more back gardens before crossing Romford Road (the A118) and slipping into a parallel street called Deanery Road. Walking along, he reloaded his gun.

John Wright, aged 13, standing outside his home, called out: 'Is that a real gun, mister?' Further on, another 13-year-old, Janet Bilverstone, was hovering at her front gate. She told a *Daily Telegraph* reporter: 'I saw a tall man – I should think he was about 5ft 11 – wearing a dark jacket, and a white shirt with a dark tie. He was loading a gun. He went past me and then turned on to a bomb-site, jumped over a wall and went into the open back door of a house at the basement. He ran out the other side through the front door and into Romford Road.'

Here he was seen at a distance by DI Jones. Hall got a lift in a red saloon car (perhaps it was someone he knew) and was taken a mile or so east towards Ilford, before asking to be dropped off. He got out of the car and disappeared.

Back in Tennyson Road, Inspector Pawsey, shot in the chest, lay dying in the driver's seat of his car, while a woman vainly tried to send an SOS over the car radio, which was crackling with messages about the shootings and Hall's escape. A man succeeded in operating the radio and told Control: 'A policeman has been shot! Send an ambulance and another police car straight away!'

It was too late. Pawsey died where he was. Hutchins died a few hours later in Queen Mary's Hospital, where PC Cox was also taken, seriously injured, but likely to survive.

Meanwhile, police forces for miles around were mobilised to find and apprehend the gunman. His description was widely circulated and road-blocks set up on major roads to Essex and the south. An all-car alarm went out, and the Commissioner, Sir Joseph Simpson, left Motspur Park in Surrey where he had been attending a police athletics meeting. It was the worst shooting affray involving the deaths of police officers for 50 years – since a jewel robbery in Houndsditch in December 1910, when three policemen were killed and four wounded by a gang of anarchists, two of whom were later trapped and died in the Siege of Sidney Street, in January 1911.

Nothing was seen or heard of John Hall, however, until that night, when he telephoned the *Sunday Express*.

The call was taken at the newsdesk by Nelson Sullivan, who was standing in for an absent colleague on the five-to-midnight shift. Sullivan happened to be a crime reporter, working mainly for the *Evening Standard* in liaison with Scotland Yard. The caller said: 'I'm the killer. I'm the man who killed the policemen.' The caller's voice sounded very agitated and at times incoherent. Sullivan asked for the man's name, and was told it was 'John Hall'. They talked for 14 minutes, while another journalist listened on another line and made notes.

Sullivan later told the coroner's court:

> I tried to quieten him down and told him I would arrange for someone to go to the telephone box and take good care of him. He said: 'I am very sorry, for everybody's sake. I've got a gun pointing at me at this moment.' I asked him to give me the telephone number from which he was ringing. I tried to get the location from him and told him that immediately in front of him there was a panel which gave him the location. He said: 'It's all scribbled. I can't read it.' He then gave a number – Wanstead 4199. Colleagues got through to the police, giving them the telephone number to enable them to trace the call. Hall said he had had some trouble the previous night with his wife and some relatives, and that after the trouble he had to go to the police station. He said he was sad and miserable about what had happened the night before and wanted to shoot himself all night long. Hall broke into uncontrollable sobs and kept saying: 'Tell everybody I am sorry – I didn't mean to do it.'

Hall said he still had the gun at his chest and had 20 rounds left, and Sullivan told the court he expected to hear a shot at any moment. He told Hall not to worry, and that if the police approached the box they would look after him. Hall said: 'If any policeman comes near me, I'll shoot him. I think I can see some police cars coming now. Yes – there are some opposite now. There are police all around. But I'll shoot the first person who comes forward. I expect they'll try to rush the door.' Sullivan said he tried to reason with Hall, who began sobbing again. Hall said: 'There's no one else around. Just police.' He continued: 'I'm terribly sorry. You must understand that. Is there anything else before I go? You'd better hurry up – because I'm going to die. Please don't make me out to be a bad boy. I didn't really mean to give trouble.'

A little later Hall started shouting, 'I am – !' He said no more. Sullivan heard what sounded like scuffling, and voices, and then 'something like a thud'.

The telephone box had speedily been identified as being in Lake House Road, which crossed Wanstead Flats to Aldersbrook and was less than two miles from where the policemen were shot. Empress Avenue and Balfour Road were about as far to the east. Within minutes the box was surrounded and the area cleared. The police closed in, some armed, some with dogs. The women's captain of the Aldersbrook Tennis Club near by said: 'The police formed a cordon across the road and advanced.' Within the box, Hall must have realised that this time there was no escape – from a trap he had made himself. It was a pleasant summer evening and lengthening shadows were being cast by the setting sun.

Colin Harding, aged 30, who lived in Lake House Road, was watching television. He said later:

> I heard the police bells gonging, and I dashed out of the house. There were about 60 police constables charging about; some were hiding behind trees, as if they were seeking cover; and there was one constable behind the phone box near my home . . . I walked towards the phone box and saw a man on the telephone. I tried to move nearer, but I was told to go back by the policeman. I wasn't sure what was going on . . . One policeman was standing just at the back of the box, and two others went up to the door. I heard a shot, and the man fell out of the kiosk just before the police got right up to the door. Suddenly the man fell back, his arms outstretched . . . When this happened, the policemen piled on top of him. I remember the police dogs were snarling on their leashes, but their handlers held them back.

Mr E. F. Lloyd was watching from a window in his house. He said: 'I saw two policemen walking carefully across the grass on the blind side of the kiosk, and as they got near I saw the man suddenly collapse. The door opened with his weight and he slid half out on the ground. As the man fell out of the box he groaned . . . One police officer in a flat cap seized the gun . . . They put him on a stretcher and took him away.'

Hall was still alive: he had failed to kill himself, although the bullet had exploded through his chest below his heart. The gun he had used was a Walther 9 mm automatic of Belgian make. Also retrieved from the telephone box was a copy of the *Evening Standard*, on which Hall had written in large capital letters: I AM SO SORRY.

DI Jones, who was at the scene, took charge, and accompanied the injured man in an ambulance to Whipps Cross Hospital. Hall kept mumbling: 'I'm sorry, I'm sorry . . . Why can't I die?' In the casualty department he appeared to recognise Jones and grasped his hand. 'Say you forgive me!' he pleaded. 'I'm sorry. I want to die.' He was operated on that night, but remained seriously ill.

His young second wife, Sylvia, her head bandaged, was not allowed to see her husband. She left, sobbing, with her father, Mr Roberts, who took her by taxi to Tavistock Road.

The following night, Sunday, President Kennedy and his wife arrived in London and John Hall was taken off the emergency list. He was said to be 'as well as can be expected'. In a private room, D33, propped up on pillows, he was attended at all times by two detectives.

Earlier that day, Mrs Muriel Pawsey was interviewed by reporters at her home in Oaks Lane, Ilford, about a mile from Hall's former pet shop in Cranbrook Road. She was 38, and had been married for 14 years. Her eyes were shadowed with weeping and lack of sleep. She said: 'I had Philip's lunch ready for him yesterday at one o'clock. He was a bit late arriving, but I didn't worry because I thought another job had cropped up.' She continued: 'Phil and I did everything together and had no outside interests. Of course he loved his work and was very thrilled when he got promotion. Then last summer we moved into this police house . . . I never thought anything could happen to us like this. Now I'll have to leave and find a new home.'

The other police widow, Betty Hutchins, spoke to reporters as her teenage daughter sobbed beside her. She said: 'My husband was going to retire in about three years. I looked forward to this so much, because we were going to have some time together.' In Queen Mary's Hospital, Mrs Cox said, after visiting her injured husband: 'He's more comfortable now, but will be in hospital for some time.'

Both widows received a letter on Monday from Mrs Irene Purdy, whose husband, DS Raymond Purdy, had been shot and killed by another gunman evading arrest, Guenther Podola, in South Kensington in July 1959.

On Thursday, 8 June, the Duke of Kent married Katherine Worsley in York Minster, and on the Friday, the funerals of Inspector Pawsey and DS Hutchins took place.

The nine-car cortège made a two-mile detour to pass West Ham police station and Queen Mary's Hospital, where PC Cox was taken in a wheelchair to watch the procession from a window. Two thousand five hundred policemen, including representatives from every force in Britain, lined the route and the road to the grey stone chapel in the City of London cemetery at Forest Gate. Among the dignitaries were the Home Secretary, R. A. Butler, Sir Joseph Simpson, and the Mayor of West Ham. Over 200 floral tributes and wreaths had been sent. That of Hutchins's children, Mark and Sharon, was a policeman's helmet fashioned from blue daisies; their card said: 'To the best Dad in the world. We shall miss you.' Mrs Pawsey's wreath was of red roses, which her husband had grown himself.

On Saturday, 10 June, Sylvia Hall was telephoned at 6.00 am – her husband had taken a turn for the worse. She went to Whipps Cross Hospital with her father. Hall was put in an oxygen tent. But, said Sylvia later, 'he was talking and appeared quite rational.' Her father wept, when Hall said: 'Will you forgive me, Dad?' They left the hospital at 3.00 pm. Sylvia said: 'John was asleep. And that's how I left him. I loved him. And he loved me.'

In Tavistock Road, the telephone rang again at 4.00 pm. Sylvia answered it. Her parents heard her scream: 'He's gone! He's gone!'

So there would now be no trial, and the report on the murders, already compiled at West Ham police station, would never be submitted to the Director of Public Prosecutions. The file was closed.

Sylvia's mother, Mrs Roberts, told a reporter: 'There are no hard feelings. As far as I'm concerned, he was a fine son-in-law, always civil and polite. But he was a sick boy. In a way I'm glad he died. Because it would have been awful if they had got him fit, only to use the hangman's noose on him. Or worse, if they had sent him to Broadmoor.'

The more sensational Sunday papers, cheated of a major trial, set out their findings on 11 June about 'POLICE KILLER JOHN HALL – GUN-CRAZY JOHN HALL'. The *News of the World* revealed: 'He once attacked a motorist, who he thought, had not shown him enough consideration . . . What made him go berserk? Hall's closest friends believe it was his fear of being sentenced for the attack on his family and locked in a cell. He suffered from claustrophobia. Even when he walked into a strange house he would open as many doors and windows as he could. Whenever possible he drove a convertible car with the hood down. When he had to drive a saloon car he opened all the windows.'

The *Sunday Dispatch* said: 'Hall married 21-year-old Sylvia Roberts after a nine-week whirlwind courtship. Each day the 6 ft salesman arrived at her house in a different expensive car. They were all from his car business, which he had been running for a year. Hall was a mental misfit when he was young, and had been in trouble for minor (non-indictable) offences. Juvenile courts had ordered him to approved schools.'

The *Sunday Telegraph*'s crime reporter said that Hall always dressed immaculately and had wealthy friends.

> Flying, fast cars, speedboats, surf-riding and photography were among his hobbies, and he was extremely fond of animals . . . He described himself as a self-employed salesman, but he was a jack of all trades. Among the main jobs he had were lorry-driver, mechanic, traveller, and book-keeper in a furniture store . . . His father, Mr William Hall, 70, is a shoe-shop manager. At the Herts and Essex Aero Club, Stapleford, Essex, which he joined with his first wife, Joyce, in 1955 and where he learned to fly, members described him as 'the best of company, and the last man one would expect violence from' . . . Almost a year after joining the club he crash-landed an aircraft on a golf course on the edge of Epping Forest. He and his passenger escaped with slight injuries . . . He continued flying after the accident, but had not been seen at the club recently . . . Hall had received treatment in a mental hospital. He often

insisted that no one could understand his mind – doctors were sceptical, and he was examined by a number of psychiatrists. He insisted he was in need of mental treatment.

Another paper referred to a medical report, which was said to have stated that Hall had been invalided out of the RAF because of 'mental instability'. If true, and if there had been a trial, it seems unlikely that John Hall would have been hanged, and would, as Mrs Roberts feared, have been incarcerated in Broadmoor.

At the inquest held in West Ham on 22 June 1961, Hall's widow, Sylvia Hall, dressed in a black costume and hat, was invited by the coroner to question, if she wished, any of the witnesses. She asked DI Jones: 'When John took the gun from his pocket [in the police station], did a certain change come over him? Did his eyes go blurry or something?' Jones replied: 'He seemed to develop a temper suddenly. His attitude certainly changed.' Mrs Hall said she asked the question because Hall's eyes 'had gone blurry' when he attacked her and her mother with the chair. She later declined to give evidence against her husband.

The eight-man coroner's jury brought in a verdict of double murder and suicide, and the coroner commended the bravery of all the policemen who had chased after Hall. He said: 'They were all taking their lives in their hands, in accordance with their duty. Each of them did that duty without hesitation.'

In due course, the widows of Inspector Pawsey and DS Hutchins received the Queen's Police Medal, awarded posthumously, on their behalf. It is not known how much they received in financial compensation. Mrs Irene Purdy, whose husband was shot by Guenther Podola in 1959, had received a total weekly income of £10 10s – from his police pension, family allowances and insurance benefits.

Mrs Miles, whose husband PC Sidney Miles was shot by Chris Craig in 1952, only received a police pension of £2 12s 4d a week.

Guenther Podola, who had shot DS Purdy on 13 July 1959, was the last man to be hanged for the murder of a policeman. He was executed at Wandsworth Prison on 5 November 1959.

The last two men to be sentenced to death for murder in Britain and then hanged were both executed on 13 August 1964. They were Peter Anthony Allen, aged 21, and Gwynne Owen Evans (real name John Welby), aged 24, and known as Ginger.

In the early hours of 7 April 1964, neighbours in King's Avenue, Seaton, a village near Workington on the Cumberland coast, heard thuds and a scream. They investigated and called the police. At the foot of the stairs of No. 28, lay the body of John West, a laundry-van driver, aged 53, clad only in a shirt and vest. He had been brutally battered with a cosh and stabbed. West, unmarried, had lived alone in the house since the death of his aged mother the previous year. A raincoat found in the house and not belonging to West led the police to Ginger Evans. He was arrested and implicated Peter

Allen, in whose possession was found a gold watch given to West by the Lakeland Laundry for 25 years' good service. Evans had once worked with West and had gone to his house that night with Allen to borrow some money. They had driven there in a car that also contained Allen's wife and children.

Evans and Allen were tried in Manchester Crown Court, found guilty of murder and sentenced to death. An appeal was dismissed on 21 July by the Lord Chief Justice, Lord Parker, by Mr Justice Widgery and by Mr Justice Winn. And a telegram sent by the mothers of Allen and Evans to the Queen at Balmoral had no effect. The two young men were hanged three weeks later, Evans at Strangeways Jail in Manchester and Allen at Walton Prison, Liverpool – both at 8.00 am. There were no demonstrations, no petitions, no clamour in the press; there were a few ill-attended vigils. Evans and Allen were hanged nine years after the death of Ruth Ellis and the storm of protest that her hanging had caused.

But four months after the execution of Ginger Evans and Peter Allen, Sidney Silverman's Murder (Abolition of Death Penalty) Bill, which suspended capital punishment for murder for an experimental period of five years, was given a second reading by the House of Commons by a majority of 185 votes. The bill did not, however, become law until 9 November 1965.

In August 1992, Harry Allen, the man who had succeeded Albert Pierrepoint as executioner and had hanged nearly 100 people – including Ginger Evans at Strangeways – died aged 80 at Fleetwood, Lancashire, a month after Pierrepoint's death.

CHAPTER 16

Alexander Vanags

The Murder of Eleonora Essens, 1968

Thousands of people disappear every year from their homes, their jobs, and other people's lives. They are mostly reported as missing and quite a few are never seen again. Some without doubt have been murdered, and their bodies have been concealed in cupboards, in attics or under floorboards, or are buried in back gardens, woods and fields, or sunk weighted in rivers and lakes. More murders are probably committed than we would like to think, and will ever know. If the killer is sensible, no one need ever know of his dreadful deed. But a sensible killer is a contradiction in terms.

The murderer's biggest problem, if he wishes to hide the evidence of his crime, is how to dispose of the body. If the murder happens indoors, in someone's home, the killer can either hide the body in the house or bury it in the garden. If it is to be hidden or buried elsewhere, some transport is necessary, and the place of disposal must be at a distance and deep. Dismemberment may seem another necessity, to render a bulky body less obtrusive and more transportable. But even if a murderer manages to hide or bury a body without being seen and with no suspicions being aroused, some mischance, some unconsidered event or act, may expose both corpse and crime. Although Al Vanags did not have a car, he disposed of his body most carefully. But he failed to bury his body deep enough, and forgot about the hungry foxes.

1968 was marked in Mexico by the Olympic Games, in Czechoslovakia by the invasion of Russian troops and tanks, and in America by the assassination of Robert Kennedy and Martin Luther King. In London, Eleanora Essens was murdered.

Three years later, on a fine Wednesday evening in September 1971, Dennis O'Flynn, a dentist from Fetcham in Surrey, near Leatherhead, was playing a leisurely round of golf with a friend, Mike Fisher, on Leatherhead golf course, two miles north of the town and beside the A243, which ran northwards up to Chessington and then to Kingston-upon-Thames. O'Flynn was a 24-handicap golfer, and at about 7.15 pm on the tenth hole he sliced a shot, sending a ball into thick rough by the fairway, not far from the main road. He never found the ball, nor finished the game. For as he poked about, he found something very horrid – a severed female forearm.

He told reporters later: 'I didn't realise what it was at first – it had become quite decomposed. It gave me quite a turn. It was obviously a woman's arm, quite slim, with a silver filigree ring and a blue stone on the wedding finger. The nails were quite long, and it seemed a well-manicured hand.'

O'Flynn and his partner went to a nearby house to telephone the local police, who were able to make a brief search of the area before it got too dark. They discovered part of a leg, much eaten, and a seven-inch bone.

A further search with tracker dogs was carried out the following day, Thursday, 2 September, with policemen waiting quietly as women golfers competing in Ladies' Day played their shots. But no other body parts were found on the golf course, and the police, led by DCI Paddy Doyle from Leatherhead, remained uncertain whether they were dealing with a murder, suicide or grisly prank. It seemed, from the state of the left forearm and hand, that its owner had died within the last two weeks and that she might have been about 25. There were teethmarks on the arm and on the remains of the leg, and it was evident that the leg had been gnawed, as had the bone. Golf-club groundsmen told the police that the limbs had been found on a foxes' trail. But where was the rest of the body? Where did it lie? Or had a fox dug it up? The arm and leg could have been carried by a fox for a mile or more.

The trail was followed up in both directions, one of which took the police away from the golf course and across the Leatherhead–Kingston road. There, in Ashstead Wood and not far from a bus-stop, they found a shallow grave, disturbed by foxes, from which the arm and right leg had been removed and dragged on to the golf course. But the left leg was still in the grave, wrapped in polythene in a hold-all. A dark blue corduroy slipper was still on the foot. It seemed as if a woman's dismembered arms and legs had been buried there together.

This looked like murder, and the Murder Squad at Scotland Yard were called in, led by DCS Peter Shemming. Other searches of the areas were carried out, but by Sunday morning nothing more had been found. It was then decided to seek the assistance of a local recluse. Ted Churcher, aged 71, who had lived in a tent in Rowhurst Woods off the Oxshott Road, for 30 years, was asked to employ his extensive knowledge of the area and look for anything untoward. Called 'Catweazle' after a wizard in a children's TV series of that name, he set to work on Monday, 6 September.

He said later:

> I have been living in these woods in a tent for years and years and I know every square inch of them. I joined the hunt early this morning and went to the first grave. After examining it, I just walked round and round through the thick undergrowth until I noticed this mound of earth, which I know wasn't there the last time I walked through this place. I stuck my hook into the ground and felt something. So I started digging and a few inches down came across this parcel wrapped in polythene. Inside was the torso of a woman. It wasn't a very pleasant sight.

The torso was wrapped in a navy-blue slip and had been buried deeper in the wood than the limbs. Some concentrated digging of the area soon uncovered a third grave a few yards away. PC Duck first of all unearthed the bones of a hand wrapped in polythene, and then below this the victim's decomposed head was found in the remnants of a cardboard box.

DCI Doyle said: 'This is a tremendous break and we owe a lot to Mr Churcher.' DCS Shemming told reporters, before a post-mortem had been made: 'We think the victim was a girl in her late teens or early twenties and about 5ft 4ins tall.'

He was wrong about the victim's age and unaware, like others who had seen the sawn-up remains, that they had been marvellously preserved by the polythene bags in which they had been wrapped, and in which some articles of clothing used to staunch any bleeding were also found. Even after the post-mortem, in which it was revealed that the woman had had a hysterectomy, and had been savagely battered about the head, her age was wrongly given as being from 35 to 45. She would turn out to be 48 – although some newspapers gave her age as 51. She was evidently very well preserved in more ways than one.

But who was she? The police needed to identify the victim before they could begin the hunt for her killer. Dental records checked against her teeth would confirm who she was once a name was produced. The only immediate means of identification were the rings on the wedding-finger of her left hand, which her murderer had failed to remove. It was through these rings that he was eventually caught.

There were two rings – not one, as Mr O'Flynn had thought – and the stone on one was amber in colour not blue. It was surrounded by little *diamanté* stones. The other ring was a plain silver band, unmarked inside but for the number 835. Pictures of the rings were released and published in the newspapers. They produced a good response, and the information was added to the many reports of missing women, over 1,000, that the police were already checking. One of these women was a Mrs Essens from Mansfield. A woman in Mansfield, Mrs Kuicel, told the police that the rings could belong to her 'old friend Nora'. Mrs Kuicel came from Latvia, and so did Mrs Essens, whose first name was Eleonora.

In the meantime, forensic and other experts had concluded that the dead woman had been killed in December 1968 or in January 1969. Tree-roots were adjudged to have been damaged by the grave-digger before the spring of 1969; and part of a newspaper, the *Evening Standard*, which had been used to wrap the remains, was dated 5 December. A drawing of the woman was also made from her skull by a descendant of the 18th-century portrait-painter, Sir Joshua Reynolds.

Roy Reynolds had called at Leatherhead police station in response to a call for information. He said he had seen a man leaving woods near the golf course with a spade – a matter which was later found to have no bearing on the case. But in conversation with the police he mentioned that while working as an artist in Birmingham some time ago, he had drawn several portraits of wanted persons from descriptions provided by victims. He was now asked if he could recreate a human face from the bony proportions of a skull. He said he could, and after five hours of studying and measuring the skull, he went home and produced several sketches, which he showed to the police the following day. The woman's features, he felt sure, had included a long straight nose, a long chin, and eyes slightly recessed.

He told a reporter:

> I used the basic methods of the Old Masters like Leonardo da Vinci and Michelangelo. They sketched the bone structure of human forms, then filled in the flesh around the skeleton. From my measurements and using my training in anatomy, I knew the face muscles could pull the face flesh only in definite directions. That gave me the all-important clues to the shape of the face. It proved to be accurate. It may have come as a surprise to the police, but I was certain from the outset.

For a while DCS Shemming was dubious about releasing the reconstruction – it might have been very misleading. But he took a chance. The picture was publicised, and featured in October, along with more factual clues, on ITV's *Police 5*.

The programme was seen by Mrs Essens's killer and his current girlfriend in his Chiswick flat. 'It looks like your old friend Nora,' she remarked. He shrugged, said nothing and went into the kitchen to do the washing-up.

Among the viewers who responded to the programme was the woman from Mansfield, Mrs Kuicel, who had thought she recognised the rings. She now provided the police with a photograph of Mrs Essens, with her eyes closed (as in Reynolds's sketch), and when it was compared with the sketch the resemblance was seen to be very close. DCS Shemming also had the photo blown up so that, when superimposed on a photo of the skull, there was seen to be an almost perfect match.

This was a significant advance in solving the case, but the police still needed irrefutable proof that the remains buried near the golf course were those of Eleonora Essens.

A dentist had found the severed forearm, and now another dentist discovered among his records a dental chart that matched the teeth of the skull. Clifford Allen had chanced to keep dental records going back for six years – usually they were destroyed after two. Mrs Essens had been a patient of his in Nottingham.

Her husband, Alexander Essens, was traced, and identified the two rings, one of which, the silver band, was a pair with one he wore. They had been made by a jeweller from a silver necklace and were used as wedding rings by Mr Essens and his bride.

The police learned that Eleonora Essens was born in the town of Riga in Latvia on 24 December 1920. She married there and had two children. But her husband and the children were killed in the Second World War when the Germans overran Latvia and the other Baltic states in 1941. The previous year the Russians had occupied the country, incorporating it within the USSR. They succeeded in driving the Germans out of Latvia towards the end of 1944, and it was about this time that the widowed Eleonora met Alexander Essens, who was also from Latvia, in a displaced-persons camp at Lübeck in northern Germany. After the war they both came to England and settled in Nottinghamshire, where Alexander Essens obtained employment as a coal-miner. They married in 1947 and made a home for themselves in a council house in Mansfield. Here they got to know another Latvian refugee, Alexander Leonard Vanags, who also worked as a miner in a Nottinghamshire pit. He first met Mrs Essens, who was seven years older than him, at a party in 1956 – she seduced him, he later claimed.

Like Mrs Essens, Vanags was born in Riga, on 5 August 1927. Like her, he had ended up in England after the war, and had married there in 1948. Like her, his marriage, to a German girl, broke down and he had been living apart from his wife, Ingrid, and their two children, since 1954. Mrs Essens and her husband had, however, compromised: they continued to live together but lead separate lives. In 1956 or soon thereafter, Alexander Vanags moved into the Essens' home. He remained there for several years, still working as a miner, until 1963, when a violent row between Mr Essens and his wife resulted in Mrs Essens and Vanags leaving the council house and setting up house together in Nottingham.

Alexander Essens said later: 'Occasional rows between my wife and I culminated with a fight at Christmas 1963, after which she took me to court for assault. After that I told her to get out, and she left . . . She used to play around and sometimes got drunk. In fights she used her fingernails. Every woman does – it's their only defence.' Essens said that the last time he saw his wife was in 1964 on New Year's Eve, when they met at Mansfield magistrates' court in connection with legal proceedings about maintenance payments.

It was in 1964 that Alexander Vanags lost an eye and injured a shoulder in an accident on a motor-scooter. Thus incapacitated, he was prevented from pursuing his job as a miner. Instead, he found employment at a printer's. In 1967 he and Mrs Essens left Nottingham and went south to London, Vanags having obtained a job as an editor of aircraft books with a publishing company, Macdonalds. The couple moved into rented accommodation in Cheam, on the south-western edge of London, not far from Ewell and Epsom. Cheam was also about six miles from where Mrs Essens's dismembered body would be buried at the end of 1968.

Discontented with her suburban existence, she persuaded Vanags to move closer to central London, and he rented a flat in Chiswick, where she was later killed.

On Thursday, 18 November 1971, the police formally identified Eleonora Essens as the woman whose remains had been discovered near Leatherhead golf course in September.

The following day Alexander Vanags, now aged 44, went to West End Central police station to tell the police that Mrs Essens had disappeared from the flat in Chiswick on Sunday, 28 December 1968, after a row. She never returned to him, he said, although she had telephoned him at his office in January 1969. He told the police that she had walked out on him before, and was in the habit of consorting with Greek and Greek-Cypriot acquaintances in Soho. She was, he said, a terrible flirt, and often stayed out all night. She had several lovers, he claimed, and had left him four times in all. He called her Minky.

While the police checked various Soho nightclubs and restaurants which Mrs Essens was said to have frequented, Vanags was taken to Leatherhead for further questioning. He was detained for 24 hours while his home and his background were checked.

The police found that he had been living since June 1969 with a Guyanese girl, Denise Abbott, now aged 22, in a flat in a large Victorian house called Kendal in Sutton Lane, Chiswick, and that, as he said, he was the technical editor of aviation books published by Macdonalds of Poland Street in Soho. He earned £2,400 a year. He had met Miss Abbott in the Hammersmith Palais, where he often used to go to pick up young girls and bring them home. Some of them, including Denise, featured on a hand-written chart, in which his lovers' attributes were listed and awarded marks from 4 to 10. Mrs Essens (Nora) also appeared on the chart. She had been given the highest marks: her face, legs and figure rated an average of 6, but her bust was given 9–10, and her hair, make-up, conversation, kissing and love-life all scored 10.

Vanags was released on Saturday night. About this time he wrote to Alexander Essens in Mansfield, claiming that Mrs Essens had walked out on him and complaining about the way she had treated him. He wrote: 'It was a dog's life. The devil only knows what for her would have been the ideal man – maybe a lapdog . . . She would never admit that she was wrong. If I had been a strong man I would have shown her the door. But you know I could not do that.'

On Tuesday, 23 November, Vanags told a *Daily Mail* reporter: 'I'm going to hide. I'm going away from London for a while. I can't stand the strain of this inquiry any longer.' Miss Abbott (his fiancée, according to the *Daily Mail*) said: 'This business has turned me into a nervous wreck. The police have been watching Alex's flat, and people have been saying terrible things about him.'

What happened next between Vanags and his girlfriend is not a matter of record; nor is where he went. He was interviewed again by the police on 28 December (the third anniversary of Mrs Essens's disappearance and death).

But it was not until Monday, 10 January 1972 that Vanags was arrested in Chiswick High Road as he returned from work, and then charged on the eleventh with the murder of Eleonora Essens. At first he said: 'I didn't do it.' Then he told DCS Shemming: 'I did kill her. She was horrible to me.'

He made a statement. He said that on the Sunday after Christmas Mrs Essens began tearing up his books; he lost control when she taunted him and he hit her with a pistol-butt. He hit her more than once. When she collapsed, he listened to her heart and felt her pulse: both were very faint. He wrapped a cardigan around her head and sat beside her for a long time, wondering what to do. Then she died. After dragging her body between the two single beds in the room, he covered it up and tidied the flat. He went to work and told people Mrs Essens had gone away. But her body remained on the floor between the beds for three or four days before Vanags resolved to dispose of it by cutting it up. He told the police that Mrs Essens had twice attacked him physically and twice threatened to blind him in his one good eye.

He appeared before Epsom magistrates on 12 January and was remanded in custody. He was committed for trial on 2 March.

The trial began in the Central Criminal Court on 3 July 1972 before Mr Justice Swanwick. The prosecution was led by Mr Richard Lowry, QC, and the defence by Mr Basil Wigoder, QC. Vanags pleaded not guilty to murder, but guilty to manslaughter; his defence was provocation. He wore a smart grey suit, cream shirt, and a wine-coloured tie. He looked straight ahead, with his eyes on the judge. Occasionally he made notes.

Mr Lowry read out the statement made by Vanags to the police, in which he said that on 28 December 1968, just after Christmas and after Nora's birthday on Christmas Eve (when she was 48), she was in bed in the flat in Sutton Lane and he was doing the household chores. At that time he was 41. She began mocking him for his inefficiency, and when he suggested that they go out for a drink she laughed at him and said: 'I'm going out when I'm good and ready.' She also shouted at him: 'I'll see you ruined!'

Vanags's statement continued:

> You couldn't stop her. She would never forgive or forget. She said I was good for nothing and I was no good in bed at all. Later, Nora was shouting and tearing up my books. I couldn't contain myself any longer. I grabbed a pistol and hit her. She screamed at me: 'You're nothing but a bastard!' and 'Your mother was a whore!' I hit her and hit her. I must have gone mad. I sat down and cried. I didn't know what to do. What could I do? I dragged the body, after checking she was dead, and put it between two single beds. I went to work next day without sleeping a wink. I ditched the pistol in a rubbish bin near Chiswick railway station. After three or four days I decided the only thing to do was to dismember her. So I went out and bought a bottle of vodka.

This was either on New Year's Eve or New Year's Day, a Thursday. He drank half of the bottle before cutting Nora up with a hacksaw. First he cut off her head, shutting his eyes as he began. Having done so, he was sick. He wrapped the head up and put it in a cardboard box, which he tied up with string. Having decided, after looking at a map, to dispose of the body in the Epsom Forest area, he took the box to Victoria Station, travelling by tube with the box on his knee. He put the box in a left-luggage locker near the air terminal office. He was glad to get rid of it as he thought of the head as being full of evil. Then he went to Woolworths to buy some large plastic bags. Returning to Sutton Lane he cut off the legs and wrapped them up separately. He did the same with the arms. The torso was too big, he felt, to dismember. After packing the severed legs and arms into a blue hand-grip, he took a taxi to Victoria, where he left the grip in another left-luggage locker and returned to the flat to deal with the torso. This he did the following day. He wrapped up the torso and squeezed it into a hold-all. Thus burdened he struggled with the hold-all up Sutton Lane to Chiswick High Road, where he hailed a taxi and proceeded for the third time to Victoria Station.The hold-all containing the torso was jammed into yet another locker. Mrs Essens was together again in one place, though not in one piece.

Vanags was now shocked to find, on opening his first locker, that it was empty – the head had disappeared. But having gone so far he did not panic and decided to do the obvious thing of enquiring about the missing box at the lost property office. He was told that the box had been removed from the locker, because the time allowed had expired. The box was returned to him and he took it by train to Mitcham. But the ground was frost-hard and he was unable to scrape a hole (he was apparently using a knife). So he returned with the box to London and put it back in another locker.

He needed a spade. He was also needed back at work. He bought a spade in Brewer Street, near his place of work in Soho. Retrieving the hold-all containing the torso from its locker in Victoria Station, he carried it (and the spade) to a Green Line bus-stop on Eccleston Bridge where he got on a bus for Leatherhead. This was probably on the Saturday. Getting off the bus across the road from the golf course, he lugged the hold-all into adjacent woodland, dumped it, and covered it up with branches. Then he returned to Victoria to collect the hold-all containing the legs and arms. He also bought some red roses, which he put inside the two hold-alls before burying them and their contents in separate shallow graves in the wood. Each was marked by a mound. He hid the spade and returned to Sutton Lane.

The next day (probably Sunday) Vanags collected the head from its locker, bought another bunch of red roses and went by train to Ewell, from where he walked for about three miles to his burial ground in the wood, carrying the box and the roses. He dug a hole and buried the box, and stuck the roses in the ground. Near by he carved the letter N, for Nora, on a tree. Then he went home. As if to restore his self-esteem he then embarked on a sexual spree.

All these winter journeys, on foot and by taxi, Tube, Green Line bus and train, were necessitated because Vanags did not drive: he had no car. He had to rely on public transport. But although he showed some resourcefulness as well as grim and dogged determination in disposing of Mrs Essens's remains, he neglected to remove the rings from her left hand or make the three graves deep enough. He also wrapped the remains in plastic bags (which served to preserve them), and in items of clothing (none of which, however, bore laundry-marks). A newspaper, which could be dated, was also used to staunch the blood. Then he marked the burial-place of the head with a small N carved on a young tree. It is not known if and when the police noticed the N and what they made of it when they did. But despite all the errors he had committed in concealing the remains, they would probably never have been found, had it not been for a hungry fox.

For nearly three years Vanags tried to put Nora out of his mind, and perhaps he succeeded – until a fox dug up one of his graves and Dennis O'Flynn drove a golfball into the rough.

The prosecutor, Mr Lowry, chose to take a line that was far from condemnatory and took him into the territory of the defence. He conceded that although Vanags had acted wrongly in killing Mrs Essens and in trying to conceal the circumstances of her death, there *had* been a measure of provocation. Vanags, he said, had been 'led an awful dance' by Mrs Essens: 'She made trouble at Vanags' workplace by ringing up a girl employee and suggesting he was carrying on with her. She came to his office and spied on him and made many nuisance telephone calls.' Mr Lowry went on to tell the court that in September 1967 Mrs Essens attacked Vanags with hot water from a kettle, causing him to have medical treatment; that she accused him of various misdemeanours concerning money and other women; and that in 1968 she rented a room in a house owned by the Latvian Welfare Society and had an affair with a Latvian seaman. According to Mr Lowry, manslaughter was a possible verdict for the jury to think about.

When Denise Abbott entered the witness box to give evidence at the start of the second day of the trial, she became hysterical and ran shrieking out of the court. It was agreed that a statement that she had made to the police could be read aloud instead.

Alexander Vanags also went into the witness box to tell the court about his life with Mrs Essens and how she met her death.

He said that on the day she died he was doing the housework while she stayed in bed, passing all kinds of remarks. She demanded a 12-egg omelette. He made it and brought it to her, but all she said then was – 'You are a fool!' Vanags carried on dealing with some household chores, and after a while he noticed that Mrs Essens had gone to a bookshelf. She began to pull out various books and tear them up. Some of the books were rare editions. She said: 'I'll see all this destroyed – all these damned papers destroyed. That's all you want – papers!' He tried to reason with her. He said: 'Please, please, leave my books alone.' Then he grabbed hold of her hand. She screamed at him and suddenly attacked him, hitting him with her hands. She screamed: 'I'll blind you for good!' He said she scratched him near his right eye and on his cheeks and hand. He seized her wrists but could not subdue her. He was standing by the bookshelf on which lay the broken pistol. He told the court: 'I grabbed it. I just wanted to knock her out. I could not control her.' He hit her once with the butt of the pistol as she faced him, but not very hard. He said: 'She spat in my face and screamed: "You're nothing but a bastard! Your mother was a common whore!" Then I just lost control. I have never ever hit her or lifted my hand against her before. I hit her a number of times. I held her by the dressing-gown and then I just let her drop . . . I had no intention of killing her. All I had in my mind was to knock her out.'

Vanags's virtues and Mrs Essens's awfulness were emphasised by the managing director of Macdonalds, James MacGibbon, who said: 'He was a meticulous worker, even to a fault. He was extremely conscientious, very unassuming and always very helpful. I thought he had a certain lack of confidence outside his professional work . . . Once he arrived at the office with a black eye. His mental distress was often noticeable.' A colleague, Dennis Green, proclaimed: 'He was one of the most gentle men I have ever met – at times almost irrationally calm in accepting what he obviously suffered at [Mrs Essens's] hands.'

Continuing the apparent consensus in court that there should be a sympathetic verdict, Mr Wigoder, in his closing speech for the defence, outlined the sufferings, bravery and honest endeavour of Vanags's early life.

When Latvia was occupied by the Russians in 1940, Alexander Vanags's father, a Latvian air force officer, was arrested by the Russians and executed.

After the Germans overran the country in 1941, the teenage boy and his mother searched for his father's body among the hundreds of corpses disinterred from three mass graves. After three years of privation, hiding and hardship, Vanags, aged 16, volunteered for the German air force in 1944. In March 1945 he was serving on the Eastern front when he was captured by the Russians. In May, the war in Europe came to an end with the surrender of the Germans. Vanags ended up in a displaced-persons camp in Lübeck (at the very same time Mrs Essens was there). But in 1946 he absconded, and made his way to the British zone in West Berlin. He met his future wife, Ingrid, there and came with her to England in 1948.

Mr Wigoder asked the all-male jury to consider the effect of Mrs Essens's abuse and taunts of sexual inadequacy on such a man, described by one witness as 'the gentlest man I know'. He said: 'Imagine yourself in his place, as a child of 14 walking with your mother along a row of recently disinterred graves, inspecting hundreds of dead bodies in order to try to see if you could recognise the body of your own executed father. If someone called you, in those circumstances, a bastard and the son of a common whore, is not that provocation that might make anybody, any reasonable person, see red?'

It was an illogical question, to which the reasonable answer should have been 'No'. But Mr Wigoder continued to paint a very sympathetic picture of the defendant, saying that it was entirely through his own efforts that he had raised himself to a responsible position as a publisher's editor. He had spent many years on research, said Mr Wigoder, and his files represented a lifetime's work. 'Put yourself again in his position,' said Mr Wigoder. 'You suddenly see somebody, for no reason, flaying them, ripping and tearing them up. Provocation? Enough, perhaps, to make a reasonable person see red.' And the prosecution had admitted that there *had* been provocation.

In his summing-up, the judge told the jury that there was no dispute that Vanags had killed Mrs Essens by aiming several blows at her head with a pistol. They would have to ask themselves, he said, two questions: 'Are you satisfied beyond reasonable doubt that when the accused delivered those fatal blows with that weapon, he did in fact intend to kill, or at least to cause really serious injury? Secondly – that provocation is ruled out, either because the accused himself was not provoked by the deceased so as to cause him to lose his self-control and do what he did, or because a reasonable man would not have been so far provoked?' If the jury were satisfied on *both* counts, said the judge, they should find Vanags guilty of murder.

After retiring for 90 minutes on 7 July, the jury found Alexander Vanags not guilty of murder.

Speaking in mitigation before sentence was passed, Mr Wigoder told the judge that there were facts in the case that would enable him to reduce the sentence very substantially. He said of Vanags:

> He has been of real service to this country, especially in the war. He was with the Polish resistance and the French Auxiliary Police in Berlin, and then he came to this country, where he was prepared to take work in a humble way . . . Once in a person's lifetime he is entitled to the credit for

> his past good services and I submit that in this case the occasion is now. This man will never offend again. He is a law-abiding citizen – he always has been and always will be. The jury have found that there was provocation – provocation that might have caused any reasonable person to lose self-control. And unfortunately in this case that weapon was at hand.

Here the judge remarked: 'I do find that a man who has been a miner in the pits could have overpowered a woman without resorting to that.'

Mr Wigoder replied that Mrs Essens was a strong woman, and that matrimonial disputes often took place in the heat of the moment. Vanags, he added, had brought punishment upon himself for the rest of his life – 'For his affections for this woman still remain . . . It would be a waste of human resources if he was imprisoned for a long time.'

In passing sentence, Mr Justice Swanwick told Vanags, who stood before him with his head bowed and showed no emotion:

> I am quite satisfied that the jury have reached their verdict of manslaughter on the grounds of provocation. Nevertheless, this was a very serious assault on this lady despite the provocation. You used a terrible weapon which happened to come to hand. Had you thought about it, I am sure you could have overpowered her manually . . . I bear in mind everything so ably said on your behalf. But it is not a case I can pass over without a substantial sentence.

Vanags was jailed for three years for manslaughter.

On 2 April 1973, aged 45, he was brought from prison to the London Divorce Court and, accompanied by two prison officers, was given a decree nisi because his marriage to Ingrid Vanags had irretrievably broken down. The divorce was uncontested. He was released from prison in 1974 and is believed to have become the editor of a newspaper in South London.

DCS Peter Shemming, commended by the judge for 'the extremely efficient inquiry conducted under your supervision', retired in July 1973. He was 47 and had been a policeman for 25 years. His next job was as joint general manager of a country club, Woolston Hall, at Chigwell in Essex, owned in part by the James Bond actor, Sean Connery, and the former England soccer captain, Bobby Moore.

The Vietnam War was brought to an end in January 1973, and, after Watergate, President Nixon resigned.

CHAPTER 17

Donald Neilson

The Murder of Lesley Whittle, 1975

There was (perhaps still is) a tendency among some senior police officers to bathe in the limelight of a major murder case, and to exaggerate the quality of their efforts and that of the murderer, the more so the longer he evades being caught. The senior officer in charge is said to go without food and sleep for days in his dedicated search for the killer. He holds regular press conferences, makes dramatic announcements and instigates an excess of enquiries. Thousands of statements are taken, and paperwork and information piles up to such an extent that the trees cannot be seen for the wood. In the meantime, the murderer is attributed with demonic cunning and extraordinary powers of prescience, strength and disguise – how else could he outwit the police? He becomes a master criminal, a monster, a fiend.

In fact he is none of these things. He is just the proverbial needle in a haystack and extremely hard to find. If his connection with the victim or victims is obscure, or random, and his basic attempts to conceal his crime succeed, there is every chance he will never be captured – especially when, as is often the case, he is protected, knowingly or not, by a doting mother, girlfriend or wife. He is caught eventually through his own careless acts or talk, misjudgements or sheer bad luck, not through superior police intelligence and detection. And then he goes and confesses. Most murderers – those of whom we are aware – need others to know about the extraordinary thing they have done. They want to exhibit their kill.

Some regional police forces used to be (perhaps still are) not particularly adept at solving all but the most obvious murders – which is why the technical expertise, greater awareness and special skills of Scotland Yard's Murder Squad were brought in to assist. A few regional chiefs could become bogged down by a morass of reports, false trails and hunches, and be bedevilled by blinkered and bureaucratic thinking, as much as by a lack of understanding of murder and murderers. When more than one regional force was involved, the opportunities for blunders and bungling multiplied.

Richard Skepper, aged 18 and still at school, was fast asleep in his first-floor bedroom in his parents' home, a corner-shop sub-post office in New Park, Harrogate, on the York to Skipton road. His older sister and brother were not at home. His father, Donald, aged 54, a Methodist and much respected locally, had been at choir practice earlier that night, retiring at 11.15 pm on

Thursday, 14 February 1974. Young Richard was a heavy sleeper, and at about 4.15 am on the Friday the faint barking of boxer dogs at a public house across the road could not waken him. Nor did the man who quietly entered the bedroom and searched it, rummaging through the pockets of Richard's trousers beside the bed before shaking a shoulder of the sleeping youth. More shaking, and the switching on of the bedside lamp, succeeded in arousing him. Dazzled and startled, Richard saw the twin barrels of a sawn-off shotgun and behind it a man in black, wearing a black hood with a visor-like slit through which dark eyes stared. 'No noise,' whispered the apparition and switched off the light, adding 'Where are the safe keys?' Richard replied that his father kept them on a shelf downstairs. Told to lie face down, he obeyed, and, threatened now by a knife, let his wrists be tied with string behind his back and his ankles to the foot of the bed. A strip of sticking plaster was pressed across his mouth. 'Go to sleep,' the intruder whispered, and left the room.

Ten minutes later he returned. Talking in hoarse African-sounding pidgin English, he said, with the knife held close to Richard's face: 'Can't find keys. Where are keys? You come – show me.' The youth's ankles and wrists were untied and, still gagged, he was taken downstairs. A search was made but no keys were found. In the kitchen the hooded man ripped off the gag and Richard told him the keys might be in his parents' room, in a dressing-table drawer. 'You go get keys,' said the intruder. 'Me watch at door. No noise.' 'They'll wake up if I go into their room,' protested Richard. The shotgun was raised. 'You go,' said the hooded man.

In her bedroom Mrs Skepper was woken by movement on the stairs. Then she heard and saw someone dimly enter the bedroom and creep towards the dressing-table.

'Is that you, Richard?' asked Mrs Skepper. 'Are you all right?' 'Yes,' replied Richard. Then Donald Skepper awoke. 'What's the matter?' he demanded, sitting up and pulling the cord that switched on an overhead light. A dark figure, revealed in the doorway, sprang forward and said: 'Put that light out!' Mrs Skepper screamed. The figure backed away, flicking a switch by the door, intending to kill the bed-light. But the ceiling light came on instead. Simultaneously Mr Skepper demanded: 'What's this? What do you want?' 'He wants the safe keys, Dad!' said Richard. 'Oh, does he?' Mr Skepper exclaimed. 'Let's get him!' So saying, he swung his legs off the bed. There was a sharp explosion as the intruder's gun was fired. This done, he fled out of the house.

Donald Skepper, shot from three or four feet away, fell back on top of his wife, who did not realise at first that her husband was not only injured but fatally so. As Richard dialled 999 downstairs, Joanna Skepper tried to give Donald the kiss of life. He died in her arms, a two-and-a-half-inch hole in his chest. It was her birthday.

Exhaustive enquiries and searches were made in the area involving frogmen and soldiers, as well as the police; shotgun-owners and firearms-dealers were questioned; a £5,000 reward was offered by the Post Office for information; and some 30,000 people were interviewed over the following year. Seven months later, another sub-postmaster was killed.

It happened not in Yorkshire but in Lancashire, at Higher Baxenden near Accrington, at about 4.00 am on Friday, 6 September.

Derek Astin was 43, an ex-Royal Marine, and was recovering from an operation to amputate a big toe. He and his wife, Marion, were woken by someone moving about their bedroom in the flat above their shop. Despite his bandaged foot, Mr Astin hurled himself at the intruder, forcing him out on to the landing, into a bathroom, and blocking his escape. Mrs Astin had picked up a vacuum cleaner. 'Hit him with this!' she cried. There was a loud bang as a shotgun was fired at point-blank range, tearing a hole in Derek Astin's upper left arm and shoulder. He staggered back and the gunman pushed past. But somehow Mr Astin succeeded in grabbing and unbalancing his assailant, who tumbled down the stairs. As Mr Astin clutched the banisters at the top of the stairs, sagging against them, a second shot was fired, from below, this time from a .22 pistol. The bullet ripped through his buttocks and stomach. He collapsed on the landing, bleeding profusely. The intruder fled.

The Astins' 13-year-old daughter, Susan, tried to help her mother staunch the flow of blood, before running from the house, with her 10-year-old brother, Stephen, to summon help – the telephone wires had been cut. Derek Astin died in the ambulance taking him to Blackburn.

Another reward of £5,000 was offered by the Post Office and another major police investigation began. The Yorkshire CID chief hunting for the Harrogate killer, hearing of the Baxenden shooting, liaised with his Lancashire counterpart, and they concluded that the similarities of each murder, of time, method, weapon and costume, meant that they were after the same man. Similar descriptions of the gunman were provided by the widows and children, and his method of entry had also been the same. He had used a brace-and-bit drill to bore holes in wooden window frames, through which a piece of wire could be passed to dislodge the catch.

Details of other brace-and-bit burglaries involving sub-post offices in the region were studied by the police and 18 such raids, not all productive, and including those at Harrogate and Baxenden, were eventually attributed to Donald Neilson.

All but one, that at Harrogate, were south and west of Neilson's house on the edge of Bradford, in an area bounded by Preston, Birmingham, Mansfield and Leeds. They began in January 1971, at Jump near Barnsley, and ended in November 1974, a period of nearly four years, during which Neilson stole postal orders, cash and stamps worth a total of £30,000, his biggest haul being £4,400 from a sub-post office in Staffordshire.

An unsuccessful raid on a sub-post office in Nottingham in September 1967, when the intruder was tackled by the postmaster, routed and fled, was also pinned on Neilson. It seems most unlikely, however, that Neilson would have embarked on his first raid so far from his home and then lie low for over three years. He himself said his post-office raids began in 1971. After the raid at Jump in January that year, his profitable outings averaged three a year.

His last raid and third murder occurred on 11 November 1974 at a sub-post office at Langley, near Oldbury and west of Birmingham, which was run by Sydney Grayland, aged 56, and Peggy, his wife. They lived on a nearby council estate with Peggy's brother, Geoff. Sydney's health was not too good – he had been a prisoner-of-war of the Germans for several years. But since 1972, when his wife was appointed sub-postmistress, he had given her a hand. The post office was in a semi-derelict street which was about to be demolished. Every evening the Graylands would close the counter at 5.30 pm, after which the mailbags were collected by a van, the accounts completed and the place locked up. At about 6.00 pm Mr Grayland would make his way through a storeroom at the rear (which had no light) to fetch his car from a lean-to garage in the yard. He carried a torch.

What exactly happened that night is unclear, but it seems he came face to face with an intruder at the back door. Mrs Grayland said later: 'I heard a noise coming from the storeroom, and I thought it was caused by my husband tripping over. I went in to see what had happened . . . I saw my husband on the floor.' She also saw another man, and she saw his face. She continued: 'I was so terrified I can't say what he was wearing or what he looked like. I got down on my knees to my husband. He said: "Watch it, Peg. I've been hit." Probably I was hit afterwards. I next remember waking up in hospital.'

According to Neilson, he entered the storeroom wearing a hood and carrying a .22 gun, as well as a torch to which a small bottle of ammonia was taped. He had planned to surprise the man who worked there. But he was taken aback when this man appeared, shone a torch in his face and then grabbed *his* torch. In doing so the ammonia was squirted over Neilson's hood and into his eyes. Blinded by the other torch and the ammonia he fired the gun, lashed out with his foot and pulled the hood off his head. He turned to get out, but blundered into something and was then assailed by another person whom he struck with his gun. This person (Mrs Grayland) fell, but resisted when he tried to tie up her hands. She struggled and he hit her again and again. Having incapacitated her, he dashed into the shop and (despite the ammonia in his eyes) managed to steal £861 in cash and postal orders and get away.

Sydney Grayland was shot and killed by a single bullet that entered his right side and severed the abdominal aorta. Death was caused by haemorrhage and shock. Mrs Grayland, whose head was badly battered, suffered three depressed fractures of the skull.

The couple were not found until about 10.55 pm, when two PCs in a passing panda car noticed that the lights were still on in the shop. They investigated. Mr Grayland lay on the floor near the storeroom's back door, which was ajar: he was dead. His wife, her face a bloody mask, was discovered under a pile of cardboard boxes in a corner, her hands tied in front of her with a cord 25 yards long; a metal coat-stand lay across her. She survived the attack, but was unable to make a statement to the police for another month. On the floor the finger-tip torn from a black rubber glove was found, as well as a footprint made by a rubber boot, a chip of wood snapped off the handle of a .22 pistol, six .22 bullets, and five spent cartridges. A woman motorist would later say that she heard a series of cracks like fireworks as she drove past. Four of the missing bullets were never found: the fifth was in Mr Grayland.

When Peggy Grayland's condition improved she was told not only of her husband's death but also of that of her 45-year-old brother. Shattered by events, he had died of a heart attack.

Despite the fact that forensic tests proved that the bullets that killed Mr Astin *and* Mr Grayland came from the same .22 pistol, the three post-office murders were not linked in the press; neither did they attract much attention. This was partly because three regional police forces were now involved and because some police officers were bemused by the *modus operandi* of the Langley murder, which was different from the two earlier ones. But the National Federation of Sub-Postmasters was up in arms, demanding danger money for their 21,000 members as well as better protection and better pay, which ranged from about £8 to £19 a week. The Post Office promised some improvements and, with the Federation, upped the reward for information about the three murders to a record £25,000.

That November and over Christmas the West Midlands police were preoccupied with the hunt for the IRA terrorists whose bombs in two Birmingham pubs had killed 21 and injured 166. Mrs Grayland was able to leave hospital just before Christmas and she compiled a Photofit picture of her assailant. Then, two weeks into 1975, in a Shropshire village called Highley, 15 miles west of the sub-post office at Langley, a girl called Lesley Whittle disappeared.

She was born on 3 May 1957, when her mother, Dorothy, was 40 years old; she had an older brother, Ronald. Her father, George Whittle, a former bus-driver, ran a prosperous coach and rural bus firm which when he died, aged 65, in 1970, was worth some £106,000. Dorothy Whittle was not, however, his legal wife. His first and only wife, Selena Whittle, had parted from him nearly 30 years ago, in 1941; and although a divorce was discussed, no action was taken. While Dorothy moved into his home, Selena Whittle moved to Coventry, where she survived on her wages and a maintenance allowance of £2 a week and, when these came to an end, she got by on her pension and social-security benefit. In 1970 Selena was aggrieved to read in a local paper that in addition to a £63,000 net estate, George had already settled gifts of £107,000 on his son, and £82,000 on his daughter, Lesley, while Dorothy, who had changed her surname to Whittle, had received three houses and £70,000. Selena Whittle received nothing in her husband's will – George had always told her he could not afford to increase her allowance. She took legal action, and in May 1972, a High Court judge awarded her £1,500 a year for life, backdated to her husband's death.

George Whittle's riches and meanness towards his wife made headlines in the *Daily Express* of 17 May. The item was read by Donald Neilson. That month he also read an article in *Reader's Digest* about the kidnapping in America of Barbara Mackle, a student heiress, who was held captive in an underground cell. The sensational kidnapping in Wimbledon in December 1969 of Mrs Muriel McKay, wife of a *News of the World* executive, was likewise known to him. She was snatched from her Wimbledon home by the Hosein brothers, who demanded a ransom of one million pounds. Her body was never found, but the Hoseins were caught and imprisoned for life for her murder. This particular crime was the first kidnap-and-ransom case perpetrated in Britain – and an unhappy example of muddle, mistrust and lack of co-operation between the family, the police and the press. Neilson said later: 'I studied the McKay kidnap closely. The police made such a balls of it, and I worked on the principle of learning from their mistakes.'

He originally planned, he said, to kidnap Ronald Whittle, or his mother, on a moonless night in January 1974, when the hours of darkness were also very long. Much of 1973 was spent in lengthy and detailed preparations. But the fuel and energy crisis that arose that winter, culminating in a three-day working week, petrol coupons, lower speed limits and less traffic on the roads at night, meant he would expose himself, in travelling at night, to extra risks of detection. So he deferred his kidnap plans for a year – until January 1975, when circumstances, including maximum darkness, would again be right.

In the meantime, he continued with his post-office raids, and in doing so shot three men. If it had not been for the miners, Mr Heath and the three-day working week, none of the sub-postmasters would have been killed. Nor might Lesley Whittle have died.

'I shelved [the plan],' said Neilson later. 'And went on with the post offices. And everything went wrong.'

Most things had gone wrong for him since he was born; little went right. For a start his real name was Nappey.

He was a Yorkshireman and was born on 1 August 1936 in Morley, a bleak little industrial town south-west of Leeds and south-east of Bradford and less than eight miles from both. His father, Gilbert Nappey, worked in a woollen mill, and his mother, Phyllis, in a textile factory. They lived in a close, working-class community, in a one-up, one-down terraced house at 20 Henry Place, behind Morley High Street: the site is now a car-park. A daughter, Joyce, was born when little Don was four and both grew up during the black-outs, shortages and occasional dramas of wartime England, succeeded postwar by rationing and social austerity.

Don Nappey was a slight, short and scruffy boy, plagued with spots and ragged at school, being derided as 'Dirty Nappey'. He often played truant and, though protected by his mother, was periodically punished for various misdemeanours by his strict, teetotal father. 'I always seemed to be getting into a bother,' said Neilson. 'I used to get a fair few hidings.'

Early in 1947, when he was ten, his mother died of breast cancer. She had been ill for several years and latterly neighbours could hear her agonised screams. Henry Place was deep in snow when her coffin was taken from the house, and her inconsolable son sobbed for days. Not long after this he was caught by the police breaking into a Co-op. He was let off with a warning and vowed never to be caught again.

Domestic drudgery was now added to his woes. For although a grannie came in for a while to do the cooking, washing and shopping, these devolved as a duty on the reluctant boy, who was eventually laden with all the household chores, with making breakfast for his little sister and father, as well as the evening meal. He also baked cakes. This regime became increasingly unsatisfactory to all, and Mr Nappey acquired a succession of housekeepers to take the place of his teenage son. When Mr Nappey considered marrying one of them, Don left home. He was now 16, an apprentice joiner, and he became a lodger with the Corfields – a family in Tingley who had once been neighbours – sharing a room with the son, Gerry. He stayed there for over two years. Joyce went to stay with relatives when her father moved south and disappeared.

Gerry Corfield said later: 'Although he would sometimes come around with our group of youngsters, he was not one of us. He was a loner, the odd one out, and thought he had to prove himself by doing daredevil things, like jumping off high walls or riding a bike at breakneck speed. He was not very easy to get on with and girls always seemed to shy away from him.' Mrs Corfield said: 'He was a shy person, very much within himself. You could not seem to get through to him. But he never gave any trouble at home. He never shrank from hard work and would work overtime whenever he got the chance.' Neilson said of himself then: 'I never had a mate of my own age . . . People never thought the same way as I did. I never seemed to understand why.'

With the money he saved from working overtime, Don bought a 125 cc motorcycle and used it to roar into Bradford, where his main pastime – for he neither smoked nor drank – was to go ballroom dancing. He was good enough to win some medals. It was in a Bradford dance-hall that he met his only girlfriend and future wife, Irene Tate. She was a millworker and two years older than he. She had a twin sister called Hilda, who remembered: 'They would dance with different partners during the evening but always go home together . . . I never got on with Don very well. You couldn't speak to him or hold a conversation with him.' Of Irene, she said: 'Although we were twins, you couldn't say we were close. Irene went her way, I went mine. She preferred to be with the boys. She would sooner go off down the road and play football and cricket with the boys than be with me.'

In this period Don changed his job as an apprentice joiner three times, unhappy with the attitudes and demands of his bosses. Then on 6 January 1955, when he was 19 and a half, he was called up to do his National Service, serving with the King's Own Yorkshire Light Infantry for two years. But he was such an indifferent soldier, surly, scruffy and a poor shot, that he was back-squadded after eight weeks of basic training and had to repeat the whole process. At the end of this double dose of training he married Irene Tate at St Paul's in Morley, on 30 April 1955.

Neilson wore his battledress and a big white carnation; she a white wedding-dress. He was three months short of his 19th birthday; she was 20. His occupation was given as 'joiner' and his address as '20 Henry Place'. Hers was on the Leeds Road east of Bradford. There was no reception, no guests or relations, apart from an aunt and uncle of his who had been asked the day before to act as witnesses. It was several months before Irene's mother and her twin, Hilda, learned that Irene was married. Some of the Tates believed that Don married her to acquire an Army marriage allowance, which she was told to save, while living off her wages and staying at her older sister's place. A fellow-conscript said of Don: 'I never saw him buy anything, not even a cup of tea.' Even then he was money-conscious and mean.

An overseas allowance was also added to his pay, and while his bride languished in Bradford, Private Nappey was posted to Kenya, then to Aden and Cyprus. He was promoted to Lance-Corporal before being demobbed on 27 January 1957 – three months before Lesley Whittle was born.

His two years in the Army shaped his life, giving him interests and excitements unknown before: the peculiar pleasure of jungle warfare and survival skills, of the power of weapons, of fitness and self-reliance. He relished the hide-and-seek thrills of security patrols, dealing with Mau Mau gangs on Mount Kenya, EOKA guerillas in Cyprus, and Arab nationalists in Aden. A soldier in Kenya said: 'After Morley it was a bit like paradise. The sun was always shining . . . I wouldn't look any further than Kenya to work out how Nappey learned the tricks of his trade . . . In a way it's not surprising that one of our number used his training for illegal purposes in later life. The only surprising thing is that it was Nappey. He wasn't really very good at it.' Neilson said of himself: 'I never saw any blood, guts hanging out, or owt like that. I enjoyed my time in the Army. But I never admitted owt about it . . . It's possible to be afraid and at the same time to enjoy oneself.' He thought of joining the SAS. When his National Service came to an end, he cried.

Back in Bradford he joined Irene in her eldest sister's home, working for a while as a joiner, then as a door-to-door salesman, selling brushes. On 12 January 1960, the Nappeys' only child was born – Kathryn.

Soon after this, they moved to a terraced house on the main road to Leeds, the A647, to Grangefield Avenue. Various conversions were carried out on the house by Don, who was full of ideas and restless energy. He turned the roof space into an attic bedroom, paved the small front garden, concreted the back yard, constructed a garage and installed washbasins in the two front rooms, which were let to lodgers to supplement the family's income. He was always busy at something, repairing his car or repainting his home, which was smart to look at, but untidy within; his wife was also very casually dressed. Averse to anyone in authority, he never settled in any job. From 1962 he was self-employed, experimenting with several ventures, like wastepaper collecting, scrap-metal dealing and window-cleaning. He said later: 'Working for somebody else were no way to make out. The only way was being self-employed. That way you got everything – the wages, the profits, but also the losses . . . I got satisfaction out of working hard and completing a job. But then it was spoiled by people not wanting to pay for it.' In 1965 he became a mini-cab driver, using a Morris Oxford of his own and renting a radio. This lasted for three years, after which he set up as a joiner and carpenter, specialising in repairs, in building house extensions and garden sheds. He had an IQ of 119.

It was about this time that he changed his surname from Nappey to Neilson, so that Kathryn would not be teased, as he had been, when she started school.

One of the women lodgers used to act as a babysitter. She said later: 'Both Mr and Mrs Neilson used to go out in the car. Usually it was about 10 pm or 10.30 pm, and I would look in at Kathryn about 11.00 pm before I went to sleep. I have no idea what time they used to get back or where they had been

. . . I always wondered why no relatives visited them. Even Kathryn, whom they doted over, never seemed to have a friend around.'

A neighbour said: 'He always seemed rather secretive, and in the ten years I lived next door I only went into his house twice. He said nothing about himself, and if he had been working away from home and I asked him where he had been, he would just say "Here and there". He looked every inch a part-time paratrooper. We called him "Castro" because he always wore battle-dress and *marched* down the street. He even bought his own jeep.'

There was a reason for this. Wearing bush hats and camouflage gear, Neilson, his wife and daughter periodically carried out mock military manoeuvres and operations on moorland or in woods, armed with home-made weapons and guns. They ambushed each other and went on patrols; they pretended to shoot and kill, and to die. These war games, which seem to have faded out in 1973, were an outdoor expression of Neilson's military mania. Indoors, an attic hideaway was stuffed with all manner of military gear; and the bookcase in the lounge was full of works on warfare and tactics, survival, keep-fit and kindred topics. Kathryn, as she got older, was taken on runs and often went swimming with her father at the local baths. Her hair was kept short, as was her mother's, and she was treated and disciplined like a boy, being confined to barracks (forbidden to leave her room or the house) or punished with hard labour (cleaning paintwork or doing menial tasks) if she did anything wrong. Neilson was also very possessive and jealous, always wanting to know what she was doing, with whom and where. She was his playmate, the son he wanted but never had; Irene was more a mate than a wife. He said of her, after admitting he treated her badly: 'She isn't bad-tempered; she's rather a happy person. But I was the boss at home.' It seems they seldom had sex. His pleasures were chiefly solitary and secret, and he found that breaking and entering houses provided the greatest excitement of all.

His venture into petty crime was a considered career move. He told a Bradford psychiatrist, Dr Hugo Milne:

> I've always worked hard and I thought I would have made a lot of money from my work. But I didn't. I was just banging my head against a wall. I never had enough capital for big jobs, although I've never gone bankrupt. So, there was only one thing left for me. There was no other way than crime . . . It's no fault of mine I haven't made any money. I didn't turn to crime to get a flashy sports car. I never even had a decent holiday until I turned to crime. When I thought about what I was earning and what others were getting for doing no work at all, there didn't seem to be any sense in it. There was no point in being honest.

He began burgling middle-class homes in the latter half of the 1960s, infrequently at first and during the winter months, when outdoor work and pursuits were reduced and the nights long and dark. He only took cash, so that no middlemen or 'fences' were involved, and he used public transport, as cars could be readily spotted and traced. He studied police routines and methods, as if they were the enemy in a one-man war, and varied the pattern and direction of his raids. He always had a bath beforehand and donned clean clothes which were splashed with disinfectant, so that any police dogs would be confused – as would the police themselves by his criss-crossing of district and county boundaries. If he lost control of a situation, or something went wrong, he abandoned the raid. Although he carried a gun, his maxim was: Never threaten to kill – Tell them 'Do as you're told and you won't get hurt'.

Long before he became notorious as the Black Panther, a title whose coining was claimed by the Post Office, police and the press, he was known by local police teams as the Red Shadow (sometimes he dressed all in red), the Phantom, and Handy Andy. His happiest moment was when he burgled what happened to be a policeman's house, and stole his whistle.

He told Dr Milne:

> I was scared to death when I was breaking in anywhere. But I enjoyed the freedom of being out at night: the freedom to go anywhere I wanted, the thought that nobody was interfering, that nobody knew. There was a satisfaction in breaking the system . . . Having started on houses, post offices were just the same . . . No problem. The financial gain was greater. The money I took was Government money. As far as I'm concerned, I've never robbed anybody. I didn't want to rob old-age pensioners. If I'd thought like that, I could have bashed old people on the head, like some lunatics do . . . Everyone says a burglar is cowardly. But to wake somebody at night is not something cowardly. My thinking is that you've got a bloke in a detached house in bed at a psychological disadvantage – plus the time of two or three in the morning. He's only in his pyjamas or naked. He thinks of getting dressed, and you're away . . . When I put on a mask, I adopt a different personality. People saw me as the Black Panther, and I didn't speak in normal voices. It wasn't me . . . It's the same as in a play. It's an act – and I'm the principal actor. I've got to convince them I'm in control.

His decision to kidnap someone was to have been the climax of his criminal career, the greatest test of his skills and his final battle and triumph over the police. And with the large amount of money he expected to gain, he intended to set himself up with a permanent business.

The idea came to him after he read a copy of the *Daily Express* in May 1972.

Neilson later told the police:

> The idea and information of victim and victim's home and reason for crime I obtained from a newspaper report on Whittle's will. From the newspaper I got the address and bought maps to enable me to find [the] address. From the amount of will and income from existing business I estimated that £50,000 would be sufficient and would not be too great a loss . . . I reckoned the mother would immediately pay a ransom of this

amount for the son, or alternatively the son for the mother. From the maps I found location of business and house in summertime and also looked for a place where ransom could be collected. I pulled into the car park at Dudley Zoo and went into the Zoo. From the hill at certain places I saw a clear view over a large empty area. I reasoned that with a good pair of binoculars I would be able to see anyone walking at dusk or on a clear night . . . I would be far enough away on the hillside to make good my escape, if I saw instructions were not carried out correctly. Several routes were available through the woods to the rear of Zoo. Expecting the first collection to be in doubt, I then required a second collection point in a different area. I decided for a second collection to be dropped from a train. I needed a railway line in a large open space, with possibly a tunnel. From a map I followed the line of the railway, and went by car to a parking place at the opposite end of Bathpool Park [at Kidsgrove]. I left the vehicle and walked the footpath alongside the railway. The path went past a concrete drain area, and I came to an electricity sub-station. As I approached this I heard a roaring noise underfoot. I found the noise came from a slightly raised manhole cover. I raised the cover and saw a large ladder going down into a shaft. I returned at a later date with a torch and went into the drainage system. After exploring the full complex, I decided this would be used in some way for the collection . . . Next I found telephone boxes on a chosen route to be used in leaving instructions for deliverer of ransom. I then purchased several items of equipment . . . Over a long period of time I visited all areas mentioned earlier to familiarise myself with the areas.

It was well over two years before the kidnap plan, having been postponed for a year, was put into effect, by which time the three sub-postmasters had been killed. Although Neilson later claimed that he kidnapped Lesley in error, it is inconceivable he was unaware where Dorothy Whittle and her daughter slept and that Ronald was living elsewhere. Besides, mother and son were more likely to be troublesome, to resist, to faint or fight. Lesley was smaller than Neilson and more suitable for concealment underground. Like his own daughter, she would also be more easy to control.

On 12 January 1975, Kathryn Neilson was 15, and by now was finding life with her father increasingly restrictive and irksome, even intolerable. It is said that she had begun to hate her father. Two days after Kathryn's birthday, Lesley Whittle, who by then was 17 and a half, disappeared from her home.

Highley was a nondescript sprawl of a village on the crest of a hill. At one end of the High Street was a large white house called Beech Croft, designed in the 1930s Odeon-cinema style. Lesley lived there with her mother – Ronald Whittle, who was 28, having moved out when he married his wife, Gaynor. They lived not far away, and modestly enough, although the family firm, now run by Ron, who sported a trim beard, possessed 56 coaches and employed as many people. He said later: 'We've always ploughed our money back into the business. In terms of personal wealth, as opposed to business assets, you could almost say we are relatively poor. There must be many families richer than we are in the area.' Nor was Lesley wealthy. Her inheritance, held in trust, was not hers until she was 21. In the meantime, she was studying for three A levels, in geography and in pure and applied mathematics, at the Wulfrun College of Further Education in Wolverhampton, whither she travelled each day, via Bridgnorth, by bus.

On the night of Monday, 13 January, Dorothy Whittle went out to visit some friends. Lesley stayed at home. Small and slim – she was only 5′ 2″ – she watched TV ('Alias Smith and Jones'); made and received some phone-calls; altered a pair of jeans; washed her long brown hair, and before she went to bed opened the garage door and left the lights on downstairs. An untidy girl, she scattered her clothes on her bedroom floor. In the bathroom was £300 in cash in a leather briefcase, takings from the family business to be banked the following day.

Dorothy Whittle returned at about 12.45 am and pottered about for half an hour before turning out the lights and going upstairs. She checked that Lesley was in bed and asleep and, having taken a sleeping-pill with her Ovaltine, was soon asleep herself, despite high winds buffeting the house. She was up early the following Tuesday morning to get Lesley off to college, and took a breakfast tray up to Lesley's bedroom at 7.00 am.

The bed was empty – nor was Lesley anywhere else in the house. Could she have gone for a walk? Or gone early to college? But her clothes, both cast-off and clean, were still in her room. It was inexplicable. When Dorothy Whittle tried to phone her son Ron and found the line was dead (the wires had been cut), she began to panic. She rushed out of the house in her dressing-gown and drove to Ron's house, where he and his wife tried to calm her down. As Ron scoured the village in his car in case his sister had had an amnesiac fit or a nervous breakdown, his wife Gaynor, who was expecting a baby, went to Beech Croft to check the house for herself. A search confirmed that Lesley had disappeared and that the inner garage door that led into the house was open.

Then in the lounge she noticed something odd. A large vase had been removed from its usual place and stood on the hearthrug. On top of the vase was an open box of Turkish Delight, among which lay four curled-up strips of red plastic tape. Gaynor nearly fainted when she read the message, punched on each strip by a Dymo-tape machine:

> NO POLICE £50,000 RANSOM BE READY TO DELIVER FIRST EVENING WAIT FOR TELEPHONE CALL AT SWAN SHOPPING CENTRE TELEPHONE BOX 64711 64611 63111 TO 1 AM IF NO CALL RETURN FOLLOWING EVENING WHEN YOU ANSWER CALL GIVE YOUR NAME ONLY AND LISTEN YOU MUST FOLLOW INSTRUCTIONS WITHOUT ARGUMENT FROM THE TIME YOU ANSWER THE TELEPHONE YOU ARE ON A TIME LIMIT IF POLICE OR TRICKS DEATH . . . £50,000 ALL IN USED NOTES £25,000 £1 £25,000 £5 THERE WILL BE NO EXCHANGE ONLY AFTER £50,000 HAS BEEN CLEARED WILL VICTIM BE RELEASED . . . DELIVER £50,000 IN WHITE SUITCASE . . . SWAN SHOPPING CENTRE KIDDERMINSTER.

Gaynor took the tapes to her husband before telling her mother-in-law. He was in his office. 'Lesley's been kidnapped!' she cried. At 9.45 am Ron Whittle telephoned the police.

The head of West Mercia CID, DCS Bob Booth, took charge of the kidnap inquiry, detaching himself from a murder investigation at Wellington in Shropshire – the naked body of a girl, stabbed to death, had been found in a ditch. He gave orders that the inquiry was to be very low-key and cautious: officers were to wear plain clothes and try to be unobtrusive; they were also to note the number of every car that passed Beech Croft and investigate the Whittles' lives. A news blackout was also imposed.

To begin with, the police were puzzled by various odd and amateurish aspects of the case, suspecting a hoax, or a student prank, or that Lesley had disappeared of her own volition. There were footprints outside the house and a trail of earth within; a few screws had been removed from the garage inner door although it had not been locked; and £300 lay untouched in the bathroom. Lesley's jewellery was missing, but she wore these items, her rings, bracelet, watch and a silver chain, in bed. Also missing was her long blue candlewick dressing-gown, and a pair of her mother's slippers. Presumably she had put these on before she left, as she slept in the nude.

What was also odd was the modest and casual nature of the ransom demand. Why only £50,000? And why pick on Lesley Whittle, when there were many other girls with far wealthier, better-known families and far more imposing homes? The plastic tapes were also addressed to an unspecific 'YOU' and made no mention of Lesley's name. 'KIDDERMINSTER' had apparently been added to correct an earlier omission, and 'IF POLICE OR TRICKS DEATH' seemed somewhat melodramatic, even juvenile. Could it be a student rag?

Lesley's college friends were questioned, including her rugby-playing boyfriend, who was now in his first year at Sheffield University. His alibi and his non-involvement in her disappearance were verified. He was clearly very upset at the news of what had happened. Enquiries concerning the Whittles themselves established that mother and daughter were close, but that brother Ron had had rows with his sister. He admitted that if anything happened to Lesley her money would pass to their mother and himself. His manner was too calm and businesslike, and he seemed very self-possessed. At the time, and for some weeks later, he was suspected by some of having organised his sister's disappearance.

Meanwhile, with DCS Booth's approval, Ron Whittle withdrew the required sum of money in notes from a Bridgnorth bank. But *two* suitcases were required to accommodate all the notes. Booth was willing that the Whittles should be seen to co-operate with the kidnapper's demands (if they were genuine). He knew that most kidnap victims seldom survived for more than 48 hours. He had also received an offer from Scotland Yard of the assistance of 12 'experts', some of whom had been involved in the botched hunt for the kidnappers of Mrs McKay. This was accepted, along with some surveillance equipment, and arrangements were made to reconnect and tap the Beech Croft phone, as well as the three call-boxes at the Swan Shopping

Centre. Full surveillance was also arranged. Operation Basket – 'We'll soon have him in the basket,' DCS Booth had said – was under way.

Kidderminster was about eight miles south-east of Highley and in another county, Hereford and Worcester. Ronald Whittle drove there in his Scimitar sports car, with the two suitcases on the passenger seat and DC Woodwiss, armed with a pistol, crouching on the floor behind him. They reached the shopping centre at about 6.00 pm. Ron Whittle took the suitcases out of the car and waited with them by the call-boxes, observed by about 40 police persons pretending to be anything other than what they were. Whittle and the others, including cramped DC Woodwiss, were prepared to wait, as instructed by the tapes, until 1.00 am. But now things began to go badly wrong.

Someone at Kidderminster had informed a local freelance journalist, Bill Williams, that a major police operation involving a kidnap was afoot, and where. He checked the information, and although a senior police officer at Kidderminster refused to confirm or deny the story (or say there was any embargo) Williams was sufficiently sure of his facts to feed them to the *Birmingham Post* at about 7.00 pm. He then telephoned the BBC newsroom at Pebble Mill. It seems that not one of the news editors who now became involved was told by the police officials they contacted *not* to publish the story. The news of the kidnapping of a young heiress, Lesley Whittle, was accordingly broadcast on local radio, BRMB, at 8.00 pm, and on the BBC TV News at 9.00.

From about 7.20 pm, both the Whittle homes in Highley were bombarded by telephone calls from various journalists. DCS Booth, now at Beech Croft, was furious and aghast. Operation Basket was blown. Soon after 9.00 pm Ron Whittle was recalled to Highley and his undercover back-up disbanded. It was felt that the kidnapper would make no move, now that details of the kidnap and of police involvement were known. The possibility that the kidnapper might *not* be near a radio or TV set seems to have been disregarded, and apparently the call-boxes at the Swan Shopping Centre were left unattended. Instead, Bob Booth gave a press conference at 10.30 pm at Kidderminster police station, in which he provided further details about the kidnap and remarked that it was 'just like an episode from "Kojak"'. Although he said, 'I am not too happy that someone saw fit to release information about police activities', he apparently refrained from telling the press to stay away from Highley and not imperil Lesley's life.

At midnight, as senior police officers planned their next move, the telephones in the three deserted call-boxes at Kidderminster began to ring, one after the other. The phone-tappers heard them, but no one was there to reply – although a passer-by picked up one phone and said: 'Who's this?'

Engineers traced the incoming calls to the exchange at Dudley, about 15 miles east of Highley; and on the following day, Wednesday, 15 January, DCS Bob Booth decided to comply with the kidnapper's demand – IF NO CALL RETURN FOLLOWING EVENING.

Very few people knew of this decision, and to divert the press from Kidderminster, Booth told reporters that no further contact had been made.

Unfortunately, reporters, including Bill Williams, now felt free to identify the Kidderminster call-boxes, and photos of them, plus full details, appeared in some local papers that afternoon. Part of the Dymo-tape ransom demand was also shown.

This time the press were rebuked. But there was now no holding them back as they vied for 'exclusives' and information. That night, when Ron Whittle returned to the call-boxes with a single, bigger suitcase and an armed guard in his car, reporters, photographers and a small crowd of curious spectators joined police undercover observers at the scene. Although the police tried to keep the unwanted observers away, the press and other bystanders were loth to miss the spectacle of Ron Whittle receiving the kidnapper's call. It never came, although he and his audience lingered there for six hours, until after midnight – when a man rang Beech Croft, saying that the ransom was to be taken to a subway in a park at Gloucester. If it was not delivered in 90 minutes, he said, Lesley would be killed.

Ron Whittle was diverted from Kidderminster via Highley to Gloucester, 50 miles to the south. Security was now very strict, and the reporters tailing his Scimitar car were successfully lost. Arriving at 2.15 am, he walked to the subway with the suitcase. He waited, and becoming impatient, shouted: 'Come and get it! I'm not leaving the case until I see my sister!' Nothing happened, except that a man and a woman walking their dog passed by. Frustrated and disappointed, Whittle and his attendant posse of policemen drove wearily back to their respective homes.

It later transpired that the couple with the dog, who lived near by, had made the phone call after seeing the Whittles' telephone number on TV – it had been broadcast to encourage the real kidnapper to telephone the Whittles' home. The couple were in urgent need of money, but decided not to collect the case when they caught sight of detectives hiding in bushes in the park. Although the man was never caught – he had fled – the woman was sentenced in July 1975 to four years in prison for demanding £50,000 with menaces. This setback was observed by some of the expert helpers from Scotland Yard.

Earlier that same Wednesday night, in what seemed to be an unconnected incident, a man was shot outside a Freightliner terminal at Dudley. Although he died 14 months later, the gunman, Neilson, was never charged with this murder. For if a victim does not die within a year and a day of an assault, the law is that a murder charge cannot be made.

Gerald Smith, aged 44, and married with two teenage children, was the overseer of the night-shift at the depot. He was walking across the main yard at about 10.15 pm when he noticed a suspicious-looking character lurking in an approach road near the car-park of Dudley Zoo. Concerned about his company's security and aware of recent IRA activities in the Midlands, he investigated, and suddenly encountered a man between two lorries. It was a cold, dark, murky night, but he saw that the other man, who was wearing a flat cap, a raincoat and a rucksack, was short and scruffy and carried a plastic bag. They exchanged a few words, Smith demanding to know what the stranger was doing there. Unsatisfied by muttered replies, he turned, intending to return to his office and phone the police.

As he walked away, Neilson shot him with a pistol in the left buttock. Smith began to run, but Neilson now shot him in the back. Smith shouted: 'You idiot! What are you playing at?' Neilson shot him four more times, before levelling the pistol at Smith's head – he was now on his knees. Smith stared up into the muzzle of the gun. But there was just a click – the pistol misfired. Neilson turned and ran.

Despite his wounds, Smith walked back to the depot. 'Get the police!' he said. 'A bloke out there just shot me. He emptied the gun at me from point-blank range!' It was not until he was taken to hospital that his serious internal injuries were revealed, necessitating the removal of a kidney and other operations; he nearly died. But he was able to give the police a good description of the assailant, although he inadvertently misled them by avowing that the gunman had a local accent, even ascribing it to Tipton, two miles from Dudley.

The police were mystified by this violent and unprovoked attack. They were amazed when empty .22 cartridge cases found in the Zoo car-park proved on Thursday to have been fired from the pistol that had already killed Derek Astin and Sydney Grayland. The Black Panther had struck again. But what was he doing in Dudley? And why had he tried to kill Gerald Smith?

No senior policeman, as far as it is known, connected the random shooting in Dudley with the kidnapper's phone-calls from Dudley the night before. And although lorry-drivers and others were questioned and the area searched, no one checked out a dark green Morris 1300 saloon, which stood in a car-park opposite a bus garage about 200 yards away. It had false number-plates and its tax disc number had been altered. It had been stolen from West Bromwich in October, three weeks before the murderous assault on the Graylands at Langley, and had been used in the kidnapping of Lesley Whittle in the early hours of Tuesday, 14 January.

Neilson had abandoned the car. He never returned to it or drove it away, believing the police would soon find it and be watching and waiting for his return. Journalists later surmised that if the police had found the car that Thursday, Lesley Whittle might not have died.

On the night of Thursday, 16 January – the second night after the kidnapping and the night after the shooting of Gerald Smith and the abortive journey to Gloucester – the transport manager of Whittle's Coaches, Len Rudd, was manning the Whittles' phone. The lines to their home had been put through to Mr Rudd's extension (the home and business lines were connected) and no policeman was present to monitor the calls although the lines were still being tapped. Mr Rudd was in his pyjamas. It was about 11.35 when his telephone rang.

He heard the bleeps of a coin-box call and then Lesley's voice. He tried to talk to her, and then realised that her words, repeated three times, had been recorded. He wrote down her message – 'Mum, you are to go to Kidsgrove Post Office telephone box. The instructions are inside, behind the backboard. I'm OK. But there's to be no police and no tricks. OK?' She sounded quite calm. Engineers would later trace this call to a telephone exchange in Staffordshire that included Kidsgrove.

Rudd telephoned Ron Whittle, who in turn rang the incident room at Bridgnorth. He was told to wait. This he did, with increasing impatience, until after midnight. Then he rang Bridgnorth again, and was told to report there for a briefing. He was fitted up with a one-way radio, and another was put in his car. No electronic bug, however, was put in the car or in the suitcase. Through the radio he could talk to the police in an emergency, but they could not communicate with him. He waited while lengthy arrangements were made for undercover surveillance in Kidsgrove. The Staffordshire police were told something was going on, but given no details. They were asked to stay out of the way.

It was not until 1.30 am, two hours after the one and only call the Whittles ever received from the kidnapper, that Ron Whittle set off in his Scimitar on the complicated 50-mile northward drive to Kidsgrove. This time he was without an armed guard. He was tired, alone and afraid.

Twice he lost his way, and it was 3.00 am before he found the designated call-box. But he could not find any Dymo-tape. The police listeners heard him say: 'I am searching behind the backboard . . . I am searching the ledges . . . Now I'm examining the floor . . . There's nothing here!' He went out to see if there was any other call-box near by, and in desperation rang the West Mercia police HQ. He was told to stay where he was and continue searching. Eventually he located the Dymo-tape, which had fallen down, or been pushed too far, behind the backboard. More minutes passed as he struggled to get it out. When at last he succeeded, instructions on the tape directed him to Bathpool Park.

The park, a large area reclaimed from mining wasteland, was a muddle of mounds, tracks, trees, tennis courts, football pitches and a ski-slope. Its main feature was a reservoir with an extensive overflow system underneath the park; and a railway line connecting Stoke-on-Trent and Manchester ran through a long cutting beside it.

Ron Whittle entered the park via Boathouse Lane at about 3.30 am, but failed to see the low wall where he was supposed to stop. The message had said – DRIVE PAST WALL AND FLASH HEADLIGHTS LOOK FOR TORCH LIGHT RUN TO TORCH FURTHER INSTRUCTIONS ON TORCH.

He drove about, flashing his headlights, to no avail. He left the car and shouted into the darkness: 'This is Ron Whittle! Is anyone there?'

After half an hour, during which he kept up a frustrated monologue on his radio, he left the park, met up with the police and drove back home.

According to Neilson, Lesley Whittle, held captive in the drainage system, died accidentally about half an hour before her brother reached the park.

She may, however, have still been alive when the park was searched the following day. This is said (by DCS Booth) to have been done by the few officers from Scotland Yard – who later denied that they were solely involved, if at all. No comprehensive search was apparently made, as the kidnapper was supposed to think that Ron Whittle was acting on his own – a strange pretence when the media had trumpeted that the police were fully aware of what was going on. If the park had been thoroughly searched, several objects that Neilson had left scattered about that night and previously might have been found – in particular a torch placed at the top of a drainage shaft and bearing a Dymo-tape message DROP SUITCASE INTO HOLE. It seems unlikely that a comprehensive search was made, in view of the fact that nothing was found. To some observers it would later seem that a lack of consultation and communication, combined with inter-force suspicion, rivalry and carping contempt, may have combined to ensure that Lesley Whittle, dead or alive, was not found that day. Nor Neilson caught for nearly a year.

As a result, many months, and many man-hours of police time were wasted in fruitless enquiries and paperwork. The hunt for Neilson would become the most expensive in the annals of murder, costing the taxpayer well over £1 million.

For seven days after Ron Whittle's journey to Bathpool Park, he and the police waited for the kidnapper to make contact. He never did, although hoax calls continued to be made. The shooting of Gerald Smith in Dudley, though now attributed to the Black Panther, was still not connected with the kidnapping of Lesley. Then on Thursday, 23 January, the various police investigations meshed and merged.

A man told the police in Dudley that a green Morris 1300 had apparently been abandoned in a car-park. The police investigated and not only found that it had been stolen, but also that it contained a plethora of Black Panther clues, including 90 feet of rope; black plastic sheeting; a yellow foam-rubber mattress; a torch; batteries; a bottle of Lucozade; cooking equipment; men's clothing; four brown envelopes and a tape-recorder containing a cassette.

In the envelopes, each numbered and labelled by hand (eg – 'At 55719 for street light'), were four strips of Dymo-tape. They were the instructions, the ransom trail that Ron Whittle should have followed on the Tuesday and Wednesday nights, taking him from Kidderminster to call-boxes in Wolverhampton and Dudley, and then to a streetlight in the road leading to the Freightliner terminal.

The police were elated, astounded and dismayed – the Black Panther, their most wanted man, who had already killed three and seriously injured others, had kidnapped Lesley Whittle. They surmised that he had been laying the ransom trail when interrupted by Gerald Smith. The tape cassette, which was not played until after midnight, clinched the inescapable fact that Lesley was in the hands of the Panther. Assembled senior policemen heard her say three times, as if in an empty room: 'Go to the M6 north to junction 10 and then on to the A454 towards Walsall. Instructions are taped under the shelf in the telephone box.' She then added: 'There's no need to worry, Mum. I'm OK. I got a bit wet, but I'm quite dry now. I'm being treated very well. OK?'

This message was clearly meant to have been played, from Dudley, when the Panther telephoned the call-boxes at the Swan Shopping Centre at midnight on the Tuesday. It was also to have been used on the Wednesday night. The four Dymo-tape messages would then have led Whittle to the ransom drop. But where was that? The fourth message referred to instructions taped to a streetlight. As this fifth message was not in the car, the police assumed it was already in place, or had been dropped when the Panther fled after shooting Gerald Smith. They looked for a piece of red tape in the Freightliner terminal area, but found nothing. None of the call-boxes specified in the other messages was checked, although a watch was kept on them, as the police assumed that the tapes contained in the envelopes had not been placed. Yet some tapes must have been in position on the *Tuesday* night.

In fact, the tapes in the envelopes were *duplicates*. But this was not realised until 3 February, when a 17-year-old youth found a strip of black Dymo-tape in a call-box outside the bus garage in Dudley (where the Morris had been parked). It was the fourth message. The police then searched the other relevant call-boxes and found three more black tapes. A fifth was found on a lamp-post in the Freightliner road. Like the others, this was a strip of black Dymo-tape on black adhesive tape and was very hard to spot. Ron Whittle could never have seen it at night, and there were five lamp-posts in the road.

The message on this tape was – CROSS ROAD AND CAR PARK GO RIGHT TO GATE NUMBER 8. But it would have been impossible for Whittle to comply. There were many gates in the walls around the adjacent Zoo and none was numbered. It was not until 8 February that a policeman found a black strip of Dymo-tape by the perimeter wall near an iron-barred gate seven feet high. This one said: INSTRUCTIONS AT END OF ROPE. Two hundred and fifty feet of rope had been found near by on 18 January by a policeman on another inquiry. Although no taped instructions were ever found with this rope, the police concluded that the Panther's final instruction to Whittle had been for him to tie the suitcase to the rope. Whereupon it would have been hauled over the wall by the Panther and seized. He would then have made his escape within the Zoo.

Having abandoned this ransom trail and drop as well as the Morris car, the Panther had been forced on the Thursday to make another tape-recorded message with Lesley and improvise another ransom trail, taking Whittle to the Kidsgrove Post Office and thence to Bathpool Park.

Senior officers of the West Mercia and West Midlands police forces kept the discovery of the Morris car's contents and their knowledge that the Black Panther had kidnapped Lesley Whittle to themselves. Junior police officers and other forces were not told. A news black-out was imposed on the press on 27 January. It lasted a fortnight and ended with a press conference in Dudley, during which DCS Bob Booth revealed the identity of Lesley's kidnapper. He said: 'This man is the most dangerous criminal at large in this country today.'

The public's assistance was now officially sought, and alleged sightings of the Morris car over the previous winter, as well as of the Panther, whose Photofit pictures misled many, poured into police stations all over central England. Hoax calls continued, and for a time two men, with local regional accents, were imagined to be the Panther himself. House-to-house enquiries were made at Highley and Dudley, and Dudley Zoo was searched (Lesley's body was imagined by some to have been fed to carnivores there), as well as many acres of woodland, mine-workings and wasteland, where suspicious persons were said to have been seen. Lorry-drivers, coach employees, post-office employees and known criminals were questioned. Radio broadcasts and television appeals, involving Ron Whittle and DCS Booth, were made.

Press conferences were held every day. But it was not until Tuesday, 4 March, when the pretence that Whittle and the police were not allies was abandoned, that media and police attention concentrated on Bathpool Park.

Now some schoolboys came forward. Back in January one pair had found a Dymo-tape with the message DROP THE SUITCASE INTO HOLE. Another pair had found the torch to which the tape had been attached – within the bars of a concrete pillbox capping a deep shaft in the park.

On 6 March, DC Phil Maskery went down the shaft carrying a torch. At its foot was a five-foot-wide tunnel through which a few inches of water ran; and in rubbish below the shaft lay a Dymo-tape machine. Another shaft was inspected, and then a third, the deepest at 62 feet – but not before a safety check for dangerous gases had delayed further searching for a day.

At last, on the afternoon of Friday, 7 March, Lesley Whittle's body was found, nearly two months after she had been taken from her home.

DC Maskery descended the shaft down a steel ladder encased for 45 feet by a safety cage. The shaft was six feet across. There was a metal platform at 22 feet and another as far below, near which was the mouth of a small, dry tunnel. A third ladder, unprotected, took him down another nine feet to a third platform, five feet long and two feet wide, on which lay a yellow foam-rubber mattress and a folded maroon sleeping-bag that had been used as a pillow. By the light of his torch he saw below the platform part of a blue dressing-gown dangling from a metal projection. He also saw a piece of taut wire, clamped at one end to the ladder. The other end led over one edge of the platform, below which hung the pale, naked body of Lesley Whittle, still wearing her silver trinkets, and with a wire noose around her neck.

She had died almost immediately, and, in effect, of fright. An autopsy revealed that she had not been strangled by the wire noose, which had been clamped around her neck like a collar and padded with Elastoplast. The cause of death, given as 'vagal inhibition', meant that sudden pressure on the vagal nerve and carotid artery in her neck had caused her heart to stop. Although the pathologist could not establish an exact time or day of death, it was evident she had not eaten for two or three days – or even more. There were some minor bruises on her body, which was very thin and weighed seven stone. But there were no signs of sexual interference or violence, nor of any abrasions that might have been caused by the metal lip of the rusty platform. It seemed that she must have been enclosed in a sleeping-bag when she fell (or was pushed) off the platform. For a zipped-up sleeping-bag was discovered in an underground canal, whither it had been swept by rainwater flooding through the tunnel below the platform. It could have slid off her. Also found in the canal were her mother's bedroom slippers, a half-bottle of brandy, a flask, a polo-neck jumper, trousers, socks, strips of Elastoplast that had been used to cover her eyes and mouth and bind her wrists, and some unused Dymo-tape.

The length of steel wire used to tether her to the ladder was five feet long. It had snagged on a metal projection, like the dressing-gown. As a result, the full vertical drop had been reduced, leaving Lesley suspended below the platform with her toes about seven inches from the tunnel's floor. If the wire had *not* snagged, her feet would have touched the ground – and she might never have died.

At the time all these details were not known or understood, and the imagined manner of her death was viewed with horror. It seemed that the Panther had deliberately hanged his victim in her cold, dark tomb.

But who was he? Where was he? The answers to these questions were now being sought by Commander John Morrison, aged 55, the head of New Scotland Yard's Murder Squad, who had been brought in by the Chief Constable of Staffordshire to solve the murder of Lesley Whittle. Resentfully, DCS Booth told reporters: 'Staffordshire have got our body.' His final assertion, made before it was decreed that Morrison alone would in future make statements and hold press conferences, was that the kidnapper would be arrested within 24 hours. It took another nine months.

Meanwhile, every effort was made to trace the owner of the many items found in the green Morris, in the drainage system and in the park, where articles abandoned by Neilson continued to be discovered or returned by schoolboys and others, and not by the police. But not one of these items, most of which had been bought at chain-stores with cash, gave the police any leads. They knew the Panther's probable age, his height, his measurements, and the size of his shoes. They knew he was very fit, skilled in mechanical matters, in outdoor pursuits, and had probably undergone some military training. They surmised he was a tradesman, a loner, obsessed with details, and that he probably had a wife – for a pair of unglamorous women's panties were discovered in the Morris doing service as a duster. The police even had examples of his handwriting on the envelopes, and partial fingerprints on a notepad. But an exhaustive check of prints kept in criminal records drew a blank.

A reconstruction was staged in Bathpool Park in April, a local repertory actor posing as the Panther. Hundreds of men, suspected of being the Panther and named by workmates, neighbours and wives, were interviewed by the police, as were over 3,000 men who had been employed in the two-and-a-half-year construction of the Bathpool drainage system. And three men who resembled the Panther Photofits were arrested at other times, one in Shropshire and two in Leeds. Many theories and avenues of enquiry were tried and tested, and police forces elsewhere had to deal with three copy-cat kidnappings, all unsuccessful.

Then in Leeds, in October 1975, the Yorkshire police were faced with the hunt for a killer that would endure for over five years. His first victim was a prostitute, Wilma McCann. Thirteen women, in all, were murdered and seven maimed before the Yorkshire Ripper, Peter Sutcliffe, was caught, by chance, in January 1981.

And it was by chance that Donald Neilson was caught, on Thursday, 11 December 1975.

It happened in Mansfield Woodhouse, a Nottinghamshire mining village off the M1. PCs Tony White and Stuart Mackenzie were sitting in a parked panda car at about 11.00 pm, looking out for troublemakers and drunks, when Mackenzie, the driver, noticed a short, scruffy man, carrying a hold-all, hurrying along the other side of the road. The man averted his face as he passed. 'He looks worth a check,' said Mackenzie. They did a U-turn and stopped beside the stranger. PC White, in the passenger seat, asked for the man's personal details. He said he was a lorry-driver, John Moxon, from Chapel-en-le-Frith. White turned to write this down on a clipboard. 'Don't move!' said the man, suddenly pointing a double-barrelled sawn-off shotgun at White through the open window. 'You! Into the back! No tricks. Or you are dead.' White scrambled over his seat into the back of the car behind Mackenzie. The gunman got into the passenger seat, the barrels of his gun in Mackenzie's left armpit. 'Drive!' said the man.

Why Neilson did not shoot and run, as was his wont, is a mystery. But, taken by surprise, he had no plan and no escape route. He probably needed time to think.

He directed them southwards to a village called Blidworth. Both policemen pretended to be cowardly and obsequious, calling the gunman 'Sir' and going on about their wives and children. 'Shut up and sit still!' the gunman said. He asked for some string, obviously planning to tie them up. There was none in the car. 'Sorry, sir,' said White. They were now heading for Sherwood Forest, but first had to pass through another mining village called Rainworth. They approached a Y junction. 'Which way?' asked Mackenzie, and as the gunman looked ahead to read the signs, White lunged forward. He seized the muzzle and wrenched it upwards. Mackenzie braked hard. The gun exploded, tearing flesh from White's right hand. With his left he seized the gunman's head in a stranglehold. Mackenzie, who had dived out of the car, raced around to the other door, yelling to the customers in a fish-and-chip shop called the Junction Chippy to come and help. Four did so, including a man who had once been picked up by the police as a suspect in the Panther inquiry. After a violent struggle, in which the gunman's face and body were battered, he was overpowered and handcuffed to some railings near the chippy, where he collapsed.

A body search produced a belt of 12-bore cartridges and two knives. In the hold-all was a quantity of house-breaking equipment, including two hoods and a bottle of ammonia. It later transpired that Neilson had reverted that year to burgling people's homes.

He was taken to Mansfield police station, stripped and, garbed in a blanket, was interviewed for six hours overnight by DCS John McNaught. Neilson refused to give his real name and said very little. He had a black eye and his face was cut and bruised. When accused of being the Black Panther he replied: 'Not true. I no shoot anybody . . . I shoot dog, but no policeman. I no Black Panther. When Black Panther work, he shoot to kill . . . If you say I am Black Panther they lock me up and throw away the key.'

By Friday morning, word had spread, and the media besieged the police station. When Neilson's fingerprints were taken, they were found to match the partial print the Mansfield police had on file. McNaught rang Staffordshire CID. 'I think we've got your man!' he said. Commander Morrison and other senior officers drove to Mansfield. But it was not until Friday night that Neilson provided DCS Roy Readwin, head of the Nottinghamshire CID, with his real name and address, so that his wife could be told where he was.

He was taken at midnight under heavy guard to Kidsgrove, 70 miles away, as the police searched his home in Grangefield Avenue, Bradford. The house was up for sale – Neilson was planning to move away from his coloured neighbours and buy something cheaper, in Pudsey.

They found an arsenal of assorted weapons in the attic of the house, along with masses of survival equipment, anoraks, hoods, shoes, radios, torches, car keys, ammunition, ropes and wire. Mrs Neilson and Kathryn, in their night clothes, were in tears. A notebook containing sketches, addresses and plans of future raids was found in the living-room, and a small model of a black panther was discovered hidden in a sideboard. Mrs Neilson said it had been bought in Blackpool two years ago as a present for Kathryn.

At 7.00 am a police van arrived to transport over 500 potential exhibits that the police removed from the house. In garages in Northampton two stolen cars were later found.

Meanwhile, in an office at Kidsgrove police station, at 2.15 am, Neilson, now wearing a boiler suit and socks and handcuffed to a chair, faced John Morrison. The head of the Staffordshire CID, DCS Wright, and DCI Wally Boreham from Scotland Yard were also present. When Morrison asked Neilson if he could help them about Lesley Whittle's death, he replied, after a long silence: 'No, sir. Not me. Not Lesley Whittle.'

Every question was met with long silences, as much as 15 minutes. He explained: 'I'm thinking, sir.' When at last he revealed some details about his age, occupation and National Service, the interrogators left, returning at 5.20 am. Now Neilson began to sob, and when asked whether he had been to Highley and Bathpool Park he replied: 'I don't know, sir. I've been lots of places.' Asked directly whether he had murdered Lesley Whittle, he wept and said: 'No sir. Not me. Not murder the young girl.'

The interview was curtailed at 6.40 am on the Saturday morning and resumed at 3.15 pm. Slowly, Neilson began to admit that he had been to Highley, Bathpool and Dudley. After one 20-minute silence he said: 'I didn't murder her. I didn't even known who I was going to get from the house.' Morrison cautioned Neilson, who said: 'The papers don't tell the truth. The Black Panther, so-called – they tell lies about him. He is not like they say . . . I want to make a statement. I want everybody to know the truth.'

He was now asked about the sub-postmaster murders, and after further silences he said – of Harrogate: 'I'll tell you about it' – of Accrington: 'These look bad for me. But I must let the people know the truth. I did that' – and of Langley: 'My God, this is a bad one.You might as well know it was me.' Once again he wept. Of the shooting of Gerald Smith, he said: 'Yes, all right. I did all these things . . . I want to make statements about them all. It was not how people said.'

At 7.00 pm on 13 December, Neilson began talking about the kidnapping of Lesley Whittle. DCI Boreham, on Neilson's insistence, wrote down his exact words, some of which he corrected himself and initialled. At 8.25 pm, there was a break as he ate two sandwiches. At five to eleven he was given two bags of crisps, and an hour later the session was adjourned. It was resumed at 2.05 on the Sunday afternoon and ended at 5.50.

After beginning with an account of how he conceived and planned the kidnapping, he went on to give his version of the last three days of Lesley's life.

He said: 'One night I set off to go to Highley. I arrived late at night. I went through back door of garage to inner back door of house. I removed outer handle and turned spindle with pliers to enter.'

He later told the court that he had arrived at about 2.00 am on the night of a new moon. He was wearing a dark blue hood. On entering he went first to the kitchen to check if there was any dog food or a dog bowl – if there had been, he said, he would have left. Then he cut the telephone wires. He said that if his victim had screamed or shouted he would have abandoned the whole plan. His statement to the police continued:

> I went upstairs, floorboards at top of landing made loud creaks. I went into first bedroom on right. There was someone in bed. I awoke the person and said: 'Don't make any noise. I want money.' The person replied: 'It's in the bathroom.' I said: 'You show me.' A girl got out of bed. She was naked. I said: 'Put on some clothes.' She took a light coat from the bed and put this on and led towards the bathroom. The boards on the landing creaked loudly. At the same time I heard a sound from a bedroom at the end of the passage at the top of the stairs. The door was open. I pushed the girl on to the top step, off the creaking boards, and motioned her to go down the steps quickly, as I thought someone may be coming from the bedroom at the end of the passage. We went quickly downstairs and out towards back door. I forgot to mention that she had put a pair of slippers on. I also carried a shotgun. We went out of the back door through the garage and up to near a clothes post in the garden. I then said, again: 'Where's the money? How much?' She said: 'In the bathroom. In coin, £200.' It was cold and she shivered. I said: 'You wait in car while I go fetch money.' She said: 'All right.' I put sticking-plaster to keep hands together, also a strip on her mouth. I then carried her to the car, which was parked in a lane [it was facing downhill], down some steps running along the side of the house. At the same time as I put sticking-plaster on her mouth I put sticking-plaster on her eyes. She climbed on to the back seat beside some sponge mattresses. I said: 'Don't make a sound and you OK.' She nodded. I closed the door then ran back to the house and left a Dymo-tape with instructions and ransom demand on it and ran back to the car. I sat in the driver's seat and lifted the sponge mattresses, which were rolled up. Told her to lie on back seat and rested sponge on top so she would not be seen. I then drove down the road, turned round and came back down the road and down through Highley going to Bathpool. When I pulled on to the main road I pulled off my hood which had been on since I entered the back garden for the first time. The girl could not possibly see my face, as she was laid on the back seat facing towards the back of the car with two pieces of foam mattress on top of her. I drove fast down the road, and after a short time the girl started struggling and making a noise. She could not get up because of the sponge mattresses. After we were clear

of houses and streetlights I pulled on my hood. Stopped the car and pulled the sponge up. She was trying to speak behind the plaster. I removed the plaster from her mouth and said in an un-normal voice: 'You have been kidnapped. Be quiet and you will not be harmed. If you do not behave I will put you in the boot. If you good, you can stay there.' She said: 'I'll be quiet.' I said: 'Are you warm enough?' She said: 'Yes.' I checked the heater was on warm and drove off to Bathpool. We arrived at Bathpool early morning while still dark. In the car earlier I had put sponge mattresses, sleeping-bags, tape-recorders, torches, batteries, bottle of brandy, Dymo-tape, writing-pads, pens, polythene bags, paint and brush, survival blanket, black plastic sheet, length of wire, fasteners, socks, flasks and food and spanners. Leaving the girl in the car I took sponge mattress and sleeping-bag down shaft and through tunnel. I was carrying a torch. I left the mattress and sleeping-bag in the short dry tunnel. I then went back to the car for the girl and we went down the ladder and through to the sleeping-bag and mattress. I placed the mattress on the steel platform, sleeping-bag on top. Removed sticking-plaster from girl also dressing-gown which had become wet getting there. The girl dried herself with top half of dressing-gown and got into sleeping-bag. I put on hand lantern left previously. I reassured girl and went to collect other equipment from car. By the time I had got equipment below ground it was getting light. I had to move the car a short distance. Then went back to equipment and took all equipment to far end of tunnel where girl was. Put girl in another sleeping-bag on top of first. I gave her survival blanket and bottle of brandy and tape-recorder and flask of soup. Then sorted out equipment and Dymo-tapes. During the day I made all Dymo-tapes as required, and the girl taped message on tape-recorder for telephone by reading what I had written in capitals on writing-pad. During some of this time I conversed in un-normal voices, whilst she talked normally. At approximately 4.30–5.00 pm when dark I went out and took car to Walsall to commence putting out instructions for collection of ransom. All these were taped in telephone boxes. The last telephone box was outside the bus garage at Dudley. After completing laying instructions at Dudley Zoo I went back to the telephone box at bus garage, with taped instructions on tape cassette that girl had made earlier that day with the ransom message to her mother. I dialled the three telephone boxes alternately at Swan Shopping Centre, Kidderminster, at approximately midnight. As near as I can remember. At first the telephones rang at the other end normally, but with no reply. After a few times dialling, all three dialling tones at other end went different, a kind of discontinued or engaged signal. Then I dialled for last time and someone answered and said: 'Who is this?' I then rang off . . . I suspected a trap and returned to Bathpool, parking on estate road at top of footpath down to Bathpool. I returned to girl and made soup, using stove from car, and we had some. I explained there would be delay.

The following evening I left to phone again from Dudley. I left the car abandoned in the car park [after he had shot Gerald Smith] . . . I made my way back to Bathpool. It was dark when I got back. I went back to the girl and explained that there would be a delay, as the tape-recorder had broken down and I couldn't send the message. During the period from then until the time I left to make final telephone call, we made new instruction tapes on the Phillips tape-recorder, and new Dymo instructions. I left to make final telephone call, arriving at telephone box at approximately midnight. I made the call and played the tape into the telephone. I thought at the time it was a male member of the Whittle family, and the voice stated positively there would be no tricks. From the sincere tone of the voice I fully believed that the instructions would be carried out . . . I walked back through the woods. On the path going through the woods, I broke up the Phillips tape and left it in the mud. As I got to the top of the hill overlooking Bathpool I saw a police car approach from the far end of Bathpool and check a courting couple parked in the car park. As this was only approximately 20 minutes from the time I had made the call I did not suspect a police trap. The police car and the other car left almost immediately and I could see no other vehicles near the area. I returned to the girl and told her they were bringing the money and it would take about two hours for them to get there, then she would be going home. She wanted to come with me then, but I explained she would be better waiting there just a little while longer, until everything was finalised. I explained I had to go get ready to collect the money, so that no one would be seen and they would not be able to set a trap. I then went up and removed a metal grill to enable me to descend into the drainage system without anyone being able to follow. I had presumed it possible they would have put a bug in with the money.

The depth of the drain underground would have made it not possible for them to follow the bug. The tunnel runs into a disused canal system. There is also a disused rail tunnel approximately on top of the drainage system. I reckoned with the many different entrances to all these tunnels and they not knowing location of same, this would give me ample time to return with the money to the girl, smash the bug, and take out the girl with me and for her to wait for them to find her. Alternately, there is a telephone box a short distance away up the path . . . At no time did the girl see me. She could not possibly have recognised me by sight, description, or from voice. There was positively no reason that the girl could not return to her family and give her family and the entire British police force every co-operation in trying to find me. So there was positively no reason to do the girl any harm, even if the ransom was not paid . . . The girl could have been left where she was, or left at the top of the drainage system, whether or not the ransom had been paid, and I would have made my escape to safety, leaving the girl to be found in a very short time by her family or the police.

I went and removed the grill on the top of the shaft. It was a cold, slightly frosty, clear night. There was no fog or mist, and visibility through my binoculars was excellent. From the top of the drainage cover I could see the point where the instructions said the car had to stop. I could also see if there had been anyone on foot. From memory I waited approximately one-and-a-quarter hours. Then a car drove into Bathpool from the direction of the instructions. The car stopped and turned lights out. From the time-lapse it could have been a car sent by the police if there had been a phone-tap on the Whittle phone. Or it could have been a courting couple, whom I have seen on other nights come into Bathpool as late as 4.15 am . . . On this night the car that entered could have been either police or a courting couple, either of which did not disturb me. I waited, and a few minutes later a car came into Bathpool Park and drove in the direction of the instructions I had phoned. It did not, however, carry out the instructions. It then reversed quickly and went past the first car that had pulled in and drove along a dead-end track which runs parallel to the railway. At this point I had a doubt as to if a police trap was in progress. From my position I fully believed I had no cause for alarm. My safety was not threatened in any way. I waited, and began to doubt the sincerity of the man who answered the phone-call.

Approximately 45 minutes later a helicopter passed overhead, nearly directly over me. It approached from the opposite side of Bathpool to the ski-slope, travelling at right angles to the railway line . . . It must have gone some distance, then turned south. It came round in half a circle and hovered some miles to the south of me. Its lights were in plain sight to the naked eye, as there is total blackness and could be identified with binoculars. It seemed obvious from this there was a police trap in operation. I was not panicked. In the next few minutes the car that had driven along the dead-end track returned and went out of Bathpool. At this point I realised the money was not going to be paid. Minutes later the first car that entered Bathpool followed the dead-end track car out of Bathpool. I decided there was no point in waiting further. I entered the shaft through the grill opening and went along the tunnel. After climbing into the short pipe leading to the platform, I saw the light from the other side, as the girl had on her torch. As I came down out of the short tunnel on to the platform, the girl moved to her right, to allow me on to the platform beside her. As I stood on the platform she went over the side and was suspended from the wire . . .

I moved to the side of the platform that she had gone over. Her head was below the level of the platform. I saw her face. Her eyes seemed to be half closed and stopped moving. I froze, then panicked. The next thing I remember is shoving the cover up to get out. I then closed the cover. I stopped there for some moments unable to think what to do. A car came up the road and into Bathpool. I started to dash from the top of the mound down towards a disused railway line. I fell, and a bag I had in my hand spilt its contents. I lay still for some moments. Then along a track which runs near the bottom of the ski-slope I saw the lights of a vehicle slowly moving towards this end of Bathpool. A car drove out of Bathpool down the road towards Kidsgrove. I think the same car came

> back seconds later with no lights on. At this point I thought I was near to being surrounded. I started to collect the things and put them back into the bag. I heard the sound of dogs coming from as near as I could tell the dead-end track. I panicked and fled in the opposite direction.

After this statement, Neilson made others, more briefly, about the sub-post office shootings. The police later denied that a helicopter had flown over the park, or that any police cars drove into it. However, a courting couple noticed a panda car, with lights on – also someone (Neilson) flashing a torch.

Neilson was charged on Monday, 15 December at Newcastle-under-Lyme magistrates' court with the murder of Lesley Whittle. Other charges, of murder and attempted murder, followed on the Friday. He was remanded in custody 18 times.

Gerald Smith died on 25 March 1976, and on the day of his funeral, Neilson was committed for trial on nine charges at Stafford Crown Court: 245 statements were formally entered as well as 848 exhibits. At a pre-trial review in Birmingham in May, the venue was moved to Oxford, where an unprejudiced jury was more likely to be found than in the Midlands.

The trial began on Monday, 14 June in Oxford Crown Court, a hot, sweltering day in a summer that would become the hottest in Britain for 250 years.

The judge, Mr Justice Mars-Jones, decreed that jurymen could remove their jackets and ties and counsel their wigs. Neilson, tense and tight-lipped, wore a black tie and dark green suit. He was defended by Gilbert Gray, QC, a skilled and humorous orator. The prosecution was led by Philip Cox, QC, whose chambers were in Birmingham. Before the jury was chosen, Mr Gray succeeded in getting the charges relating to the shootings at Dudley and Rainworth removed from the indictment. They would be dealt with separately, as would the sub-post office charges. Donald Neilson would now only be tried on three charges relating to the kidnapping and murder of Lesley Whittle. This trial lasted until 1 July.

He pleaded guilty to the kidnapping and blackmail charges and not guilty to murder. The prosecution had earlier refused to consider the defence's proposition that the murder charge should be reduced to manslaughter. The central issue was whether Lesley *fell* off the platform – or was pushed – and Mr Cox contended that she was killed because she would have been able to identify her kidnapper. Mr Cox asked: 'Was he hooded *all* the time he was in that drain? Or did he relax his precautions of attempting to keep his identity from the girl?'

When a tape of Lesley's voice was played, Neilson sobbed into a large white handkerchief. He also tended to weep when his wife and daughter were mentioned. Most of the evidence of witnesses, including Neilson's statement, was read out in court. But Ron Whittle and DCS Bob Booth both made an appearance, the latter being openly critical about alleged procedural failings committed by the Staffordshire police and the team from New Scotland Yard. 'I was disgusted,' he said. For this he was later rebuked by the judge, who remarked: 'I do deplore the fact that he took advantage of the opportunity of appearing in the witness box to launch a bitter attack . . . on fellow-officers.'

Neilson himself gave evidence, standing at attention and gazing straight ahead as if he were at a court martial. In prison he had been doing 200 finger-tip press-ups and running round the exercise yard every day. He addressed the judge and counsel as 'Sir' and was both precise and prolix in his replies. He seemed determined that the court should know all about his plans and applaud his commitment, fitness and skill. He spoke for 20 hours over a period of four days, fascinating his audience by the most detailed account ever heard in a court of the genesis, preparation and execution of a crime.

He told Mr Gray: 'I needed somewhere which was soundproof. In that way the person didn't have to be gagged. I needed somewhere that a person would be able to move about. In that way they would not have to be bound. I needed somewhere where there could be light that wouldn't show out when I wasn't there.' He had thought of building a soundproof room in a garage, or of using a boat in a disused canal tunnel. 'Eventually I realised that the ideal place to cover any eventuality would be at the bottom of the main shaft at Bathpool, where there was an ample supply of fresh air.' Still maintaining that Ron Whittle was one of his main targets, he said of the wire tether: 'The only way to guarantee that he could not leave was to put steel cord round his neck . . . If I put it round the ankle, wrists or waist, he could work it with both hands on the edge of the concrete, chafing it. It was also possible to slip if off a wrist or ankle made soft and slippery by water.' He told how he coaxed, assisted and carried the blindfolded girl in the drainage system. He said: 'I lifted her by one hand under her bottom into the dry pipe.' On the platform he removed the wet dressing-gown so that she could dry herself. He said: 'I didn't look at her in the sense of what is meant when you say to look at somebody. I saw what there was to see . . . My feelings throughout the time I was with her were feelings of professional detachment.' Of his disguise he said: 'To me, having gloves and hood on were the same as wearing trousers and boots.' But at one point, when explaining how he was worried by something that had occurred, he said: 'There must have been something in my face, in my expression.' This seemed like an admission that Lesley *had* seen his face. Mr Gray tried to correct this error. He asked: 'But did you not have your hood on at the time?' To which Neilson replied, nodding: 'It must have been my manner.'

He went on to reveal that the script of the messages Lesley recorded had been written out on an 8″ × 5″ card which was taped on to his chest and under his shirt. He said her hands and feet were free, and that when he secured the wire with clips around her neck 'she made no protest and showed no signs of fear', and that she was then in the sleeping-bag with her head against the ladder. When Ron Whittle failed to appear in Bathpool Park in the early hours of 17 January, he said he decided to abandon the kidnap operation, to 'release the girl and make good my escape . . . It was obvious to me that there would be a thorough police search at Bathpool at first light . . . My last act would be to ensure that she understood fully what was happening and make sure she was on my side . . . Throughout the plan she was my ace, because when she was released she would have to tell them of my behaviour.' As she had not been ill-treated, he expected the subsequent hunt for him to be less hostile. He said: 'It was essential for the plan that my conduct should be proper and correct at all times, and hers certainly was.'

Neilson now gave the court a more detailed account of Lesley's death:

> I descended the ladder about three rungs at a time. The time to stop, the time to rest, was after I got to the bottom of the ladder. As I came out of the dry culvert, I looked down and saw she was there in the normal position. At a glance down I saw she started to move, as she normally did, to allow me to get on to the platform beside her. She moved away from the ladder and to her right. As I took my foot off the ladder and turned to face the front, I look round and she went over. The lantern was still lit, and I grabbed this and stepped across the other side of the landing and put my foot down on the concrete ledge and went down, as it were, into a crouching position . . . I held my left hand down and towards her with the intention of pulling her back up . . . Her right hand was stretched out behind her, moving. Her other arm was bent at the elbow. Her fists were clenched . . . The torch was pointing into her face. Her eyes flickered and stopped. Everything stopped . . . It was then I realised she was dead . . . She was dead. There was absolutely nothing I could do . . . She did *not* take minutes to die. She was dead in seconds. She was dead before I left.

There were tears in his eyes and his voice had risen as he spoke.

His cross-examination took two days. Mr Cox's questions were aimed at discomfiting Neilson and implied he always had Lesley's murder in mind: 'You had planned her death, hadn't you?' – 'You did not care whether she saw your face or not, because you knew from the beginning you were going to kill her?' – 'If she had seen your face, she would be able to recognise you on a subsequent occasion?' – 'You couldn't allow her to live?' Neilson was emphatic in his replies, though he often paused to think. He was also indignant, even angered. He said 'Rubbish!' more than once.

Mr Gray, in his final speech for the defence, argued that if Neilson had meant to kill Lesley Whittle, he need never have taken so many precautions about disguise or about her well-being and comfort. He said that her death was an 'unlooked-for misadventure'. It was 'unplanned and undesired' – 'Neilson started something which went hideously wrong.'

The judge pointed out that Lesley died after Neilson abandoned the kidnap plan, believing the police were closing in. But he went on to say: 'There is no direct evidence that Neilson pushed her over the side. There is a lot of evidence to show that he did not. Otherwise you would have expected certain results, which do not appear . . . He has always denied any such thing . . . The prosecution's case depends very largely on circumstantial evidence.' It seemed he favoured a verdict of manslaughter, rather than one of murder.

But the jury, who were out for less than two hours, returned a verdict of 'Guilty'. There was some applause in the court and cries of 'Good!' Sentence was deferred. Taken below, Neilson burst into tears.

Sunday Dispatch

June 4, 1961

TWO POLICEMEN DIE: THEN THE BIGGEST MANHUNT

A call from WANstead 4199, a shot, a scream—and it is all over

LONDON GUNMAN SHOT IN PHONE BOX

Above: Telephone box in Wanstead *(Topham Picture Source)*

bove: Inspector
wsey, DS Hutchins
d PC Cox *(Associated
ess)*
p: John Hall
ssociated Press)
ght: Tennyson Road,
ere John Hall shot
pector Pawsey and
 Hutchins *(John
st Historical
wspaper Service)*

Left: The house in Sutton Lane, Chiswick, where Mrs Essens was murdered *(Black Museum)*

Main picture: Ashste Wood by the A243, where Mrs Essens's dismembered corpse was buried *(Black Museum)*

Reynolds's sketch, compared with a drawing of Mrs Essens *(Press Association)*

Left: Donald Neilson, *Daily Mirror*, 22 July 1976 *(Syndication International)*

Below: Lesley Whittle's home in Highley *(Syndication International)*

Inset: Ronald Whittle, Lesley's brother *(Hulton Deutsch)*

Main picture: Aerial view of Bathpool Park after the discovery of Lesley's body, March 1975 *(Syndication International)*

Below left: Lesley Whittle at her brother's wedding in 1972 *(Syndication International)*

assassin's tiny killer

PINHEAD PELLET OF DEATH

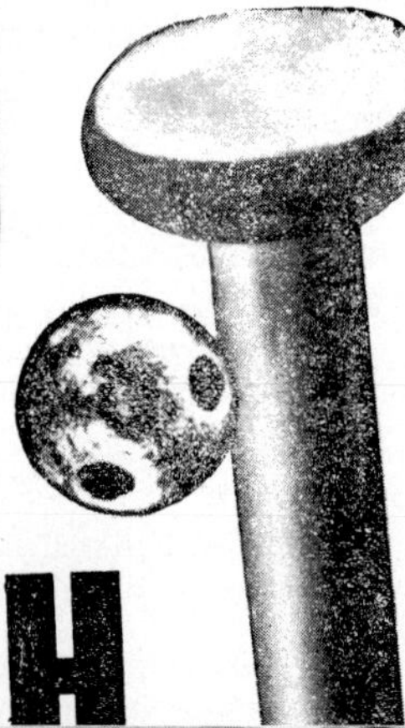

AN incredible micro-killer—half the size of a pinhead—is the latest " James Bond " weapon in the hands of Communist assassins.

The tiny pellets of death, containing ...

'stronger th... cobra veno...

By GUY ...

A METAL pellet cont... deadly as cobr... Georgi Markov, 49, t... who "hated the regim... inquest decided yeste...

The poison was ricin, ... castor oil plant. The p... fractionally larger than a... pinhead.

Mr Gavin Thurston, the ... Inner West London Coroner ... decided that Mr Markov, who ... regularly broadcast to Bul... garia on the BBC's Worl... Service, was "killed unlaw... fully."

Mr Markov died four da... after telling how he was jabb... in his right thigh with an u... brella while waiting for a b... on Waterloo Bridge.

Among the witnesses yest... day was Commander Ja... Nevill, head of Scotland Ya... Anti-Terrorist Squad, who ... that during investigati... police officers had travelle... France, Italy and Germany ... quiries had also been mad... America.

"But we still have n... dication who was respon... or how the pellet was ad... stered."

Test on pig

During the two-hour i... at Battersea, a patholog... the Government research ... at Porton Down, Wilts, ... pig, injected with a ... amount of ricin, died 2... later.

The first witness... Markov's widow, Annabel, dark-haired and attractive, told of their first meeting in 1974 ...

The highly magnified ... pellet and the two minute holes drilled through it.

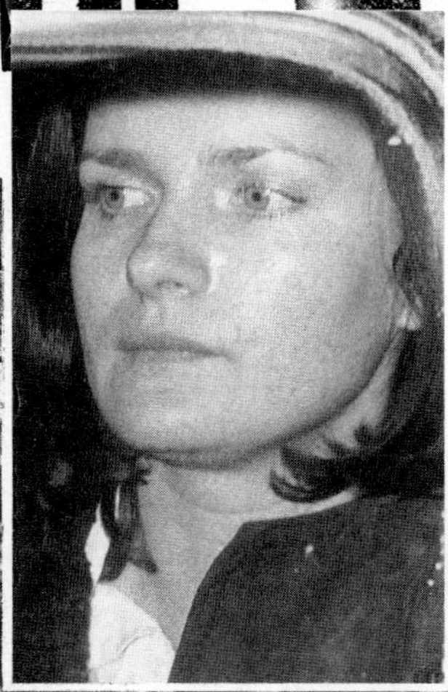

Left: *(c/o John Frost Historical Newspaper Service)*

Inset: Annabel Markov leaving Battersea Coroner's Court, 2 January 1979 *(Press Association)*

Below: Markov, 13 September 1978 *(Topham Picture Source)*

Above: Simon Tipper and his bride *(with thanks to Lt.-Col. Parker Bowles)*

Main picture: Lt.-Col. Parker Bowles (top right) at the scene of the car-bomb explosion *(Topham Picture Source)*

Far right, above: Lt. Daly *(with thanks to Lt.-Col. Parker Bowles)* and *below*: Nichola Daly and her sister at Hyde Park *(Syndication International)*

Right: SQMC Roy Bright *(with thanks to Lt.-Col. Parker Bowles)*

Left: Dennis Nilsen *(Express Newspapers)*

Below, from top to bottom: Martyn Hunter-Craig *(Syndication International)*
Douglas Stewart *(Syndication International)*
Trevor Simpson *(Press Association)*
Carl Stottor *(Rex Features)*

The house in Melrose Avenue, Kilburn *(Topham Picture Source)*

Left: Dennis Nilsen's flatmate, David Gallichan *(London News Service)*

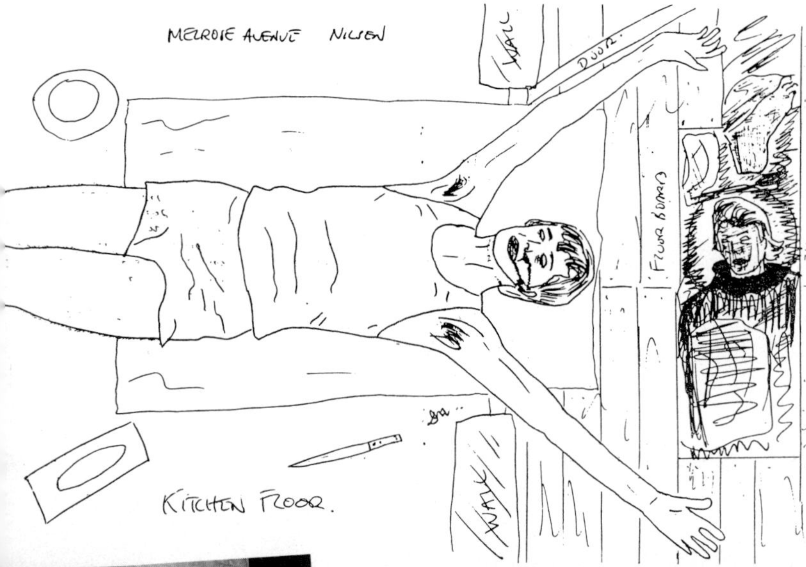

Left: Drawn by Nilsen *(Killing for Company)*

Below: The police search for remains in the back garden of 195 Melrose Avenue *(Topham Picture Source)*

Foot: Bleep *(Press Association)*

bove: Mike Cattran t the manhole by 23 ranley Gardens *Syndication nternational)*

ight: Nilsen's mother etty Scott and her econd husband Adam *Photograph by Tony rossley, Camera Press)*

Left: *(c/o Hulton Deutsch)*

Below: William Calcraft *(Hulton Deutsch)*

William Marwood *(Hulton Deutsch)*

Left: James Berry *(Hulton Deutsch)*

Below: Pierrepoint *(Hulton Deutsch)*

On Monday, 5 July, the same judge, counsel, and accused assembled in the same court for Neilson's second trial – on nine charges connected with burglary, the sub-post office murders, and the attempted murders of Mrs Grayland and PC Mackenzie. The three widows were among those who gave evidence, as did Neilson, who again gave the court a detailed dissertation on his criminal operations and plans. He maintained that all three deaths were accidental, that he never intended to use violence or to kill. He said: 'Violence never has been part of my plan.'

The trial lasted 12 days. The jury were out for over five hours, returning with verdicts of guilty to the three murder charges. But the attempted murder charges were reduced to one of inflicting grievous body harm in the case of Mrs Grayland, and of possessing a firearm with intent to endanger life in the case of PC Mackenzie.

Before passing sentence, the judge told Neilson:

> The enormity of your crimes puts you in a class apart from almost all convicted murderers in recent years . . . You were never without a loaded shotgun or other loaded weapons when you went out on your criminal expeditions. And you never hesitated to kill whenever you thought you were in danger of arrest or detection. You showed no mercy whatsoever . . . In my judgement such is the gravity and the number of offences, and the danger to the public when you are at large, that no minimum period of years would be suitable. In your case, life must mean life.

Neilson was given five life sentences, plus one of 21 years in prison, and four of ten years.

His appeal, against his conviction for murdering Lesley Whittle, was heard in July 1977 and dismissed. Lord Justice Lane said: 'If ever there was a proper decision by a jury, it was this.'

However, it now seems more than probable that Neilson never murdered Lesley Whittle – and that he should never have been convicted of murder, or even of manslaughter. There was no proof to substantiate either charge and the circumstantial evidence was very thin. The Bradford psychiatrist, Dr Milne, who interviewed Neilson for 16 hours and deemed that he was a 'classic obsessional personality with paranoid attitudes', concluded: 'What Neilson told me, as far as Lesley was concerned, I felt rang true. His version of what took place during the post office shootings did *not* ring true . . . Even though he is obsessional, with an aggressive character, this is under a very considerable degree of rigid control. I found him to be most likeable and easy to talk to.'

Neilson only killed when his immediate escape was threatened, when he had no time to think. The four men he shot were also total strangers. Killing Lesley, whom he treated with comparative consideration for three days, almost like his daughter, would have been a coldly premeditated act. When things went wrong, his maxim was: Leave at once.

It is likely that he abandoned Lesley as he abandoned the Morris 1300 –

that he never went back down the shaft when his plans went awry on the night of the 16th, that he panicked, and fled.

Commander Morrison, who referred to Neilson as a 'diabolical genius', said: 'I am convinced Neilson pushed Lesley off.' But in *The Capture of the Black Panther*, Harry Hawkes concludes:

> The probability is that Neilson was not even present when Lesley died, and never saw her hanging there. For a man obsessed by detail, his statement, when analysed, is suspiciously vague and lacking in actual facts about her death. His scant account mentioned nothing about the girl being inside the sleeping-bag when she went over the side and – even more telling – there is no reference to the crucial snagging of the wire . . . Had he been there it would have been simple to unsnag the wire.

Neilson evidently expected, as he did with the Morris, that the police would find Lesley the day after he abandoned her. He might also have suspected that the police, having found her, would keep quiet about it and set up a trap. Perhaps he *did* go back down the shaft – but not for a few days or weeks – only to discover that she was dead.

It is possible that Lesley Whittle, alone at the bottom of that cold, dark shaft, imagined that Neilson would never return, and in her panic and terror, while trying to free herself from the wire, rolled off the platform to her death. She must have been inside the sleeping-bag at the time, for her body was unmarked. Or did she roll off in her sleep, during a nightmare?

Or was Neilson, in this one respect, telling the truth?

PCs White and Mackenzie were each given the Queen's Gallantry Medal, and two of the men who helped to subdue Neilson received £250. But the Post Office's £25,000 reward was never paid, as no actual information was received leading to Neilson's arrest. Kathryn Neilson is reported to have been paid a large sum of money by the *Sunday People* for her exclusive story. This sum, it seems, was originally offered to Irene Neilson. She, however, had been charged with dishonestly cashing postal orders, stolen by Neilson, along with a date stamp, from Tittensor Post Office in Staffordshire in March 1974. When the police searched the Neilson home on 13 December 1975 they discovered that Mrs Neilson had burnt about 50 postal orders from Tittensor. In August 1976, a month after Neilson was sentenced, his wife pleaded guilty at Eccleshall magistrates' court to six charges of cashing stolen postal orders and asked for 76 similar offences to be taken into consideration. Using false names and driven about by Neilson, she had cashed the postal orders in several northern towns between October 1974 and March 1975, netting £580. It was in November 1974 that the Graylands were attacked in Langley and Mr Grayland shot and killed. Although Neilson had been raiding post offices since January 1971, and burgling homes for several years, disappearing from home for many hours overnight, Irene Neilson said she knew nothing about his criminal activities until 1975.

She was sentenced in September 1976 to a year in jail; she served eight months in Strangeways Prison.

Donald Neilson, 57 in August 1993, is still in prison and 'unlikely to be released in the foreseeable future'.

The summer of 1976 was the hottest in Britain for 250 years. It was also a year of leadership changes. Harold Wilson resigned as Prime Minister and was replaced by James Callaghan; and Jeremy Thorpe, who resigned as leader of the Liberals in May, was replaced by David Steel. In September, Mao-Tse-tung, the leader of Communist China, died, and in November, when the Sex Pistols hit the charts, Jimmy Carter was elected as President of the USA.

1977 was notable in Britain for the celebrations of the 25th anniversary of the accession of Elizabeth II. Red Rum also won the Grand National for the third time; Virginia Wade won the women's singles at Wimbledon; and in August Elvis Presley died.

In 1978 two Popes died; Paul VI and John Paul I, who was succeeded by the first non-Italian Pope for 400 years, the Polish John Paul II. In Iran, millions demanded the abdication of the Shah and his replacement by the Ayatollah Khomeini. Mrs Thatcher, the Conservative leader since 1975, was about to cash in on an industrial winter of discontent.

CHAPTER 18

The Murder of Georgi Markov, 1978

Political figures, statesmen and kings, have been the objects of assassination since civilisation began. But it is only recently, with the spread of terrorism and effective armaments, that less distinguished, ordinary persons have been pointlessly slaughtered for the sake of some manic, misguided ideal, or in revenge. Terrorism has become the blind reaper of the last quarter of the twentieth century, and terrorists the most pitiless, callous and calculating of all killers. For they mainly kill and maim unprotected, innocent strangers, from afar, with steely premeditation and ice in their hearts.

In 1971, there were 17 known political assassinations of individuals throughout the world. In 1980 there were well over 1,000. The 1970s were in fact disfigured by over 3,600 terrorist actions – bomb explosions, fire-bombs, kidnaps and hijacks – one for every day of the year. These were caused by a tiny minority, belonging to about 140 terrorist groups. Meanwhile, hundreds of thousands, even millions, of other people died through the actions of military regimes and dictatorships, of counter-revolutionaries and the secret police, in Communist countries and elsewhere. The order for the murder of Georgi Markov came from over a thousand miles away, and was as much an act of fear and loathing, as of political retribution and spite.

Georgi Markov was a Bulgarian. A popular and successful novelist and playwright, he defected from Bulgaria in 1969. His brother, Nikolai, had defected a few years before this and settled in Italy, to where Georgi fled before coming to London in 1971. Like many other talented emigrés, he obtained work as a radio presenter and newsreader with the BBC World Service, based in Bush House and situated at the foot of Kingsway between the Aldwych and the Strand. In 1974 he met Annabel Dilke, who was also working in Bush House. She came from Dorset. They married the following year.

In Bulgaria, Markov had been for a while the 'cultural representative' of the Communist regime and was esteemed by the nation's despotic president, Todor Zhivkov – to such an extent that the two men would walk and talk together in the countryside, and on one occasion Markov spent a weekend at Zhivkov's hunting-lodge on Mount Vitosha, outside Sofia, where he was also welcomed at the country retreats of other party leaders. Originally a chemical engineer, his first literary success was a book of short stories published in 1961. His writings were received with official approval while they dealt with non-contentious matters and were agreeably full of Eastern European introspection, artistic expression and angst. But increasingly he found it difficult to conceal his impatience with the regime, and his talent for satire found ample fodder. The Bulgarian army was targeted in one of his plays and a general portrayed as a clown. It was called, ironically, *The Assassins*.

Zhivkov's regime became even more corrupt and oppressive after the Russians and other Warsaw Pact forces entered Czechoslovakia in August 1968: the country was taken over and divided into a two-state federation, and in April 1969 the First Secretary, Mr Dubček, was replaced by a Soviet dependent, Dr Husák. That year Markov, now an unabashed dissident, wrote a play *The Man Who Was I*, which displeased the cultural committee when they were given the obligatory preview in the Satire Theatre, Sofia. During the performance Markov was told he was 'in trouble'.

Being one of the Communist Party's literary élite in Sofia, he not only had a passport but superior accommodation and highly privileged transport – a BMW. He went home, packed a suitcase, gave a cousin some money to drink his health, and drove across the frontier into Yugoslavia. From then on, as far as the Bulgarian regime was concerned, he was a non-person. His name was deleted from records, his writings banned, and in his absence he was charged with fraud.

But in England he continued to write, producing three novels: *The Great Roof*, *Women of Warsaw*, and *Portrait of my Double* (none of which was apparently published here), and two plays (one of which, *Let's Go Under the Rainbow*, won an award at the Edinburgh Festival Fringe). A former colleague in the Bulgarian Writers' Union later claimed that Markov was 'a very ambitious man' and thought that by going to England he would become 'another Joseph Conrad'.

In the meantime, through the medium of the BBC's World Service, he began to exercise his new-found freedom by mocking the mediocrity of President Zhivkov and his subservience to Moscow. These broadcasts, which were transmitted to Bulgaria by the BBC, further antagonised the Communist authorities, and when he tried to re-enter Bulgaria to see his dying father, permission was refused. This added an edge of bitterness to his views and he became a more outspoken and constant critic of President Zhivkov and his regime.

Markov also provided weekly scripts for Radio Free Europe, based in Munich. These were also highly critical of Zhivkov – as were his memoirs, which were serialised chapter by chapter from Munich and transmitted to Bulgaria. They were not vituperative. But his wife, Annabel Markov, said later she believed the memoirs led to his death – although she admitted: 'When you read them now, they are so mild you cannot believe that they were enough to get someone killed. They are not a polemic against Zhivkov . . . It wasn't that he was attacking Zhivkov, but that he was laughing at him. That was what was unforgivable.'

Markov had also written a political satire with another author, David

Phillips. Called *The Right Honourable Chimpanzee*, it was about to be published, under a pseudonym, by Secker & Warburg, towards the end of 1978.

This constant verbal and impenitent assault must have irritated and angered Zhivkov and other Communist party leaders. But authors are very seldom murder victims and writers are seldom killed on account of what they write. There may have been an additional and more potent political reason for Markov's death.

In June 1977, the head of the Paris bureau of the Bulgarian Radio and Television network, Vladimir Kostov, aged 48, defected and sought political asylum in France. With his wife and two grown-up children he disappeared from Paris and sought a safe and secret lodging with friends in the South of France. His defection alarmed the Zhivkov regime much more than that of Georgi Markov. Kostov, a television commentator of some repute and great popularity – he is said to have been the Robin Day of Bulgaria – had an intimate knowledge of the inner circles of the regime, and how it worked, at home and abroad. As a senior television journalist he had also travelled widely in Europe, Russia and the Middle East. The information he had was much more extensive and up-to-date than Markov's and his defection a much greater and more dangerous loss. The Bulgarians tried to persuade the Kostovs to return by flying both their mothers to Paris. But they suspected a trap and no meeting of the families took place.

In August, Nikolai Markov, Georgi's brother, who was a stamp-dealer in Bologna, telephoned London to tell Georgi that he had been visited by a Bulgarian official and told to pass on a warning – Georgi was being blamed by party chiefs for Kostov's defection and they were bent on revenge.

Markov later denied that he played any role, let alone a crucial one, in Kostov's decision. But he was sufficiently concerned to tell some Bush House colleagues of the threat and postpone a trip to Munich. Then a Bulgarian in West Germany warned him of a plot to kill him, and it is said that while on holiday in Italy he used to stand with his back to the sea. Nothing sinister occurred, however, for nearly a year.

Then on 24 August 1978, as Kostov was ascending an escalator in the Paris Metro, he felt a stinging sensation in the lower right of his back. Later, he said he also heard a muffled crack, like an air-gun report. The wound was slight, somewhat like a bee-sting, and hurt as much. So he and his wife went to a clinic near their home in Nanterre and a male orderly tended the 'sting'. It had produced a small swelling and was exuding what looked like microscopic 'metallic crumbs'. The orderly bathed the area, wiping the crumbs away. He applied a dressing and Kostov departed, soon none the worse. He never knew what hit him – not for another two weeks, when something similar happened to Georgi Markov, on Thursday, 7 September 1978, Zhivkov's birthday.

Markov was a thick-set man, six foot, nearly 14 stone, and 49 years old. What happened to him about 6.35 that Thursday evening is uncorroborated and relies only on his own reported accounts; and there is some confusion about *where* he was attacked.

According to the *Sunday Times* Insight team:

> Markov was a man of habit. Once a week, in the early afternoon, he would drive from his home in Clapham to a car park on the south side of the River Thames near Waterloo Station; he would walk the half mile across Waterloo Bridge to Aldwych and the Bush House headquarters of the BBC External Services, to begin a 12-hour shift; at 6.30, when parking restrictions in Central London end – and after reading the early evening news – Markov would go back across the river, pick up his van, drive it to Aldwych, park and then stroll back to his office in ample time to prepare the 9.30 news bulletin.

The Insight team, writing on 17 September 1978, implied that Markov was attacked as he was 'walking down the south side of Aldwych' past a bus-stop.

Mrs Markov, appearing before the inquest three-and-a-half months later, told a different story. She said her husband told her that

> while waiting for a bus on the south side of Waterloo Bridge he had felt a jab in the back of his right thigh and, looking around, saw a man drop an umbrella. [She continued:] The man said he was sorry, and Georgi said he got the impression that he was trying to cover his face as he rushed off and hailed a taxi. Georgi told me he thought the man must have been a foreigner, because the taxi-driver seemed to have difficulty in understanding him.

If Markov was waiting for a bus on the *south* side of Waterloo Bridge, he was clearly heading, without his van, for the north side, for the Aldwych and Bush House. For he was in Bush House at about 7.00 pm, talking for an hour with the head of the BBC's Bulgarian Service, David Buckley. They discussed folk music. When Markov got up to leave, he complained that his leg was stiff. He told Buckley: 'I must have bumped into something. Or perhaps it was the chap who bumped into me.'

He then, it seems, asked a friend in the office, Ted Lirkoff, another Bulgarian exile, to have a look at the back of his leg and see if it was marked. Markov undid his jeans and Lirkoff peered at his thigh. He later told the inquest: 'On his leg was a little red spot, like a puncture, about one-and-a-half millimetres across. He told me there was some pain. But I got the impression that it was not a very big pain at the moment.'

Lirkoff had been much vaguer when talking to the Insight team three months earlier. Understandably apprehensive at the time, he had told them he could remember little about that Thursday night, except that Markov had said he had been 'stabbed with an umbrella while passing a bus queue, by a well-built man who had apologised in a heavy foreign accent and then fled'.

Later on that night, Markov returned to his home in Lynette Avenue, on the south side of Clapham Common, at about half-past ten. He said nothing to his wife about the umbrella attack and bedded down in his study, as he was on an early-morning shift and did not want to disturb her when he got up. But at about 2.00 am Annabel Markov was aroused by sounds of him moving about.

She later said: 'I was worried and called out to him. I got out of bed, and when I saw him he had been sick and was lying on the floor. I took his temperature, and it was 104°.' She telephoned her doctor and he told her it could be influenza and advised her to keep her husband cool. 'I stayed with him all night,' she said later. 'And it was then he told me about the attack. He said: "I have a horrible suspicion that it might be connected with something that happened today." . . . He showed me some blood on his jeans and a mark like a puncture, about the size of the tip of a ball-point pen, on the back of his right thigh.'

The next morning she went to work at 10.30, taking their two-year-old daughter, Sasha, with her, so that her husband could sleep. She told the inquest: 'I don't think either of us believed this could be what we feared – that he had actually been attacked by members of the Bulgarian Secret police.' When the doctor called that afternoon he recommended that Markov enter a hospital, and about 24 hours after Markov was attacked he was admitted to St James's Hospital, Balham, suffering from an unexplained high fever.

The house physician, Dr Bernard Riley, found a circular area of inflammation on the rear of Markov's right thigh, with a central puncture mark about two millimetres wide. He doubted whether the puncture had been caused by an umbrella, as he thought it was too small.

By Saturday, 9 September, Markov's white blood-cell count had risen from 10,600 cells on admission to 26,300 – 'astonishingly high'. It reached 33,000 – the normal count ranges from 5,000 to 10,000 – and Markov's condition continued to deteriorate, despite massive injections of antibiotics. When his temperature and blood pressure plunged, Dr Riley diagnosed septicaemia. By the morning of Monday, 11 September Markov had become 'violent and confused'. He died before mid-day of cardiac arrest, apparently caused by acute toxaemia (blood-poisoning).

It was then no more than a 'suspicious death'. But Markov's background and assertions that he had somehow been poisoned by an umbrella, attracted some high-level police interest, and his autopsy was attended by the head of the Anti-Terrorist Squad, Commander Jim Neville.

X-rays showed that a speck of 'high metallic density' like a pin-head, lay beneath the skin of Markov's thigh. Extracted, it was found to be a tiny metal sphere, 1.52 millimetres in diameter. It had two holes, .35mm wide, bored into it, which met in the middle and crossed, and it was made of an alloy composed of 90 per cent platinum and 10 per cent iridium. But what had it contained?

The pellet was sent, with some of Markov's skin from both of his legs, to the government's Chemical Defence Establishment at Porton Down, a few miles from Salisbury in Wiltshire, where highly secret research into biological warfare was carried out. The pathologist there who examined the pellet, Dr David Gall, concluded that the quantity of poison contained within the pellet (which would then have been coated and sealed with some substance that would dissolve on entering the skin) must have been so small that it would have to have been exceedingly toxic – more so than the majority of poisons produced by chemicals, reptiles, sea creatures, or plants.

In narrowing down the field of possibilities, Dr Gall injected a poison called ricin into a pig – a slightly larger dose than Markov would have received. The pig developed a fever, like Markov, and symptoms almost identical to his. A day later it died.

Meanwhile a minor operation was carried out, at Scotland Yard's request, on Vladimir Kostov in Paris, and a small metallic sphere, identical to the one found in Markov's thigh, was discovered in Kostov's back. It was thought he survived the attack on him because the encapsulated poison had somehow escaped and not entered his body. Or that the pellet had been fired from too far away and had not penetrated deeply enough. Experts concluded that the umbrella used to kill Markov had either injected the pellet when he was stabbed with its point, or had been converted into a gas-gun which, when fired at point-blank range, would send a pellet into his flesh.

All this was sensational stuff to the press. It was better than James Bond or any spy-fiction – this was real. The police were also very intrigued with the case, and detectives travelled to France, Italy and West Germany in pursuit of their investigations. Enquiries were also made in America. Although the Bulgarians offered their assistance, this was not taken up. *Their* view was that Markov had been killed by Western agents, to discredit Bulgaria's international image, and to get rid of an agent for whom they no longer had any use. The Bulgarians said it was absurd to suggest that *they* had had a hand in killing Markov ten years after his defection.

Georgi Markov was buried on Saturday, 14 October, in the ancient churchyard of Whitchurch Canonicorum, a Dorset village near Lyme Regis, far from his Bulgarian home. Sea-fog swirled around the mourners, who included Markov's mother, Raika, his brother Nikolai, and several colleagues from Bush House and Radio Free Europe; many wept. Scotland Yard detectives stood apart, and one took photographs of the mourners. Among the wreaths was one from Vladimir Kostov. It bore the message: 'In honour of Georgi's cause and sacrifice.'

Later, Annabel Markov had an inscription written in Bulgarian on one side of his gravestone and in English on the other: *He died in the cause of freedom.*

The inquest was held in Battersea on Tuesday, 2 January 1979, before the Inner West London coroner, Gavin Thurston. More snow was forecast for London that night after one of the worst winters in parts of northern Europe for 80 years. The day before, most train services in the south and east of England were curtailed or cancelled. The temperature at Linton-on-Ouse in Yorkshire fell to minus 17° Centigrade on Monday night.

Mrs Markov, described by the *Daily Telegraph* as 'dark-haired and attractive', was the first witness. She said that her husband had defected from Bulgaria 'because it was intolerable for him to remain any longer', and she described what happened on the five days before his death.

Dr Riley, the house physician at St James's Hospital, told the coroner that the fatal pellet might possibly have been pushed into Markov's thigh by the tip of the umbrella. The pathologist who carried out the post-mortem, Dr Crompton, said that ricin was a vegetable toxin and extremely rare. It was extracted from castor-oil plants, and there were some cases of people being poisoned after handling these plants. He agreed that a modified air pistol or gas-gun might have been used to fire the pellet and that Markov was unlikely to have inserted the pellet himself. 'It was in an awkward place,' he said. Asked who might have made the pellet, he replied: 'Somebody with precision tooling equipment. I would hazard a guess at a watchmaker or a surgical instrument maker.'

Dr Keeley, of the Metropolitan Police laboratory, said that a high-temperature furnace and special drilling equipment, as well as specialist skills, would have been needed to make the pellet. The two pellets found in both Markov and Kostov were identical, he said.

Dr Gall, of Porton Down, stated that ricin was twice as poisonous as the venom of a cobra. Combined with human tissue, it could be broken down by the body's natural protein-making cells and was very difficult to detect. It came from the seed of the castor-oil plant, he said, and a toxic residue was left after the oil had been extracted. The plant was grown in a number of countries, particularly in India and Italy. It also grew freely in Bulgaria. Much of the world research into ricin had been carried out in Czechoslovakia and Hungary, he said. There was no known antidote. The coroner asked: 'Does ricin have any legitimate use?' Dr Gall replied: 'There is no legitimate use for it.'

After two hours of question and answer, the coroner recorded a verdict that Georgi Markov died of toxaemia caused by the implantation of a metal pellet containing ricin. He said: 'I have no doubt it is a case of ricin poisoning, and that he was killed unlawfully.'

Although some of the investigators working on the case believed that an umbrella had been converted into a lethal weapon, others thought the umbrella had been employed as a diversion, and that, as with Kostov, someone shot at Markov with a gas-gun.

The following month (February), one of Markov's plays, *The Archangel Michael*, was given a series of rehearsed readings at the Royal Court's Theatre Upstairs in London. It was later staged at the Crucible Theatre, Sheffield, in March. In April, his life and death were the subject of a 'Panorama' TV Programme on BBC1.

His memoirs, *The Truth That Killed*, were eventually published by Weidenfeld & Nicolson in 1983. But it never seemed as if the truth would ever be known about who killed him – not until the Soviet leader, Mikhail Gorbachev, announced a wide range of domestic reforms and the Iron Curtain began to lift. A pent-up flood of democratic feeling and ideas swept across the Soviet Union and its satellite states. Peace broke out in the nuclear arms race; the Russians withdrew from Afghanistan; Germany was united; the Berlin Wall was brought down and the Cold War came to an end with the cataclysmic collapse of Communist regimes in Eastern Europe and the USSR.

In Bulgaria, President Zhivkov was ousted from power in November 1989. A few months later, in January 1990, Annabel Markov, now 47, flew to Sofia for a week, the first of several visits. Bulgaria was still a Communist state, but the new leader, Petar Mladenov, had agreed to an inquiry being made into the death of Georgi Markov, and the rehabilitation of his name and works had begun. His widow met Alexander Lilov, secretary of the general committee. She said later:

> Lilov told me that he was a great admirer of Georgi's work, and that he had read all of it and that the inquiry should take place as soon as possible. He told me it was very important that people should read Georgi's memoirs and his record of the awful years of the Zhivkov regime. He said that if Bulgaria were really to have a democracy, people ought to know the truth. I was absolutely astonished. It's more than I ever dreamed of. Perhaps they will find out the truth about his death and perhaps not. But at least now his work will be available again.

Suddenly Markov was transformed in Bulgaria from a traitorous dissident to a national hero. He and his writings were praised by the newspapers that had once denounced them. His plays and novels were to be revived. Mrs Markov met members of the Bulgarian Writers' Union. She said: 'I went to lunch at the Writers' Union and all they wanted to know about was Georgi's death. I had to tell the story again and again. They knew nothing. I couldn't believe it. In the West, the manner of Georgi's death had become a *cause célèbre*. Yet here, in his own country, they were completely ignorant.'

She returned to England on 13 January after what she called 'the most extraordinary week of my life'. She said: 'I am not embittered . . . I don't suppose I will ever get an explanation of what happened. But I am grateful that it is out in the open, that people are beginning to realise who Georgi was, what he did, and what he stood for.'

By 1991, the Communist Government had resigned. All Markov's works were again in print, his memoirs published, and his name restored to the Writers' Union. As if in recognition of all this, the new head of state, President Zhelev, on a visit to England, laid a floral tribute on Markov's grave at Whitchurch Canonicorum on 21 February 1991.

The brief ceremony was attended by Annabel Markov and her 14-year-old daughter Sasha, who as a baby had been christened in the church. Mrs Markov said: 'President Zhelev was a dissident writer himself and he deeply admires Georgi's works. He suggested that he make the visit . . . It's a kind of recognition of what was done by the old regime. It's a political and at the same time a very personal gesture by the President of Bulgaria, who is saying in effect – "The bad old days are over."'

It seemed so when in June 1991, the Bulgarian Interior Minister, Khristo Danov, admitted that the country's secret police had been involved in the murder of Georgi Markov. But the relevant files had been destroyed. The man charged with being responsible for this, General Savov, who was the former deputy minister in charge of foreign intelligence in 1978, was found shot dead in January 1992, the day before he was due to go on trial. His body lay in front of a memorial to anti-Nazi resistance fighters in his village. No bullet was found, and a villager claimed later that no pistol lay beside him – although a Colt was later produced by the police. A suicide note was said to be strangely impersonal and possibly forged.

There were other deaths in suspicious circumstances of some of those who had worked with Savov, like General Kotsev (in a car-crash), and it seemed that the real perpetrators of Markov's murder were still trying to cover their tracks. But they could not gain access to the KGB archives.

In Moscow, a former KGB general, Oleg Kallugin, bluntly declared: 'Todor Zhivkov was the organiser of the murder of Georgi Markov. No doubt about it.' He and his Interior Minister, Dimiter Stayanov, were said to have sanctioned a plan to 'neutralise enemy emigrés'. This was accomplished by the Bulgarian secret police in collaboration with the KGB. According to a KGB defector, Oleg Gordievsky, the umbrella was obtained by the KGB in Washington and converted into a weapon by the Moscow KGB, who also manufactured the pellet.

Meanwhile, in Bulgaria, two journalists identified the man who actually assassinated Markov as a retired Bulgarian diplomat, now living on a pension in Sofia. They also claimed that before he defected, Markov had been a womaniser and gambler – and worked for the secret police.

It was also revealed, in 1992, that General Kotsev, who in 1978 was in the Interior Ministry at the same time as General Savov, came to London to see the head of the Bulgarian intelligence service there – just before Markov died.

Did Kotsev bring an umbrella with him? And did he give it to someone in the intelligence service to use – someone who now lives comfortably in Sofia, 15 years after he shot or stabbed Georgi Markov on Waterloo Bridge?

Zhivkov, now aged 80, was put on trial on corruption charges in 1992. 'How can you imagine,' he protested, 'that I, Todor Zhivkov, would hand out cars to his colleagues?' He was convicted in September 1992 and sentenced to ten years in jail.

No charges relating to the murder of Georgi Markov have, so far, ever been made.

In May 1981, a Turkish gunman among the crowds in St Peter's Square in Rome, fired five bullets into Pope John Paul as he was carried across the square. The Pope survived. His assailant had spent a month in Bulgaria before the assassination attempt. President Reagan also escaped an attempted assassination. Other assassins succeeded in killing the Presidents of Bangladesh, Iran and Egypt that year. Even the Queen was shot at in the Mall, as she rode to Trooping the Colour in June. But this gun only had blanks. The most cheerful national event that year was the wedding, in July, of Lady Diana Spencer and Prince Charles.

CHAPTER 19

The Murders of Lt. Daly, SQMC Bright, L/Cpl. Young and Trooper Tipper, 1982

The IRA is a segment of the oldest terrorist organisation in the world. Nationalists opposed to English rule in Ireland began a long war of underground resistance when the English invaded Ireland in 1169 and took possession of the whole island for over 800 years. In the 1850s that resistance found expression in the Fenian Society, an Irish-American movement aimed at the overthrow of British rule and the establishment of a republic. The Fenians' ideas, centred on independence and unity for Ireland, were largely adopted by the radical nationalist party, Sinn Fein, founded in 1902. A more extreme group, the Irish Republican Volunteers, refused to fight for the British in the First World War and organised the Easter Week Rising in 1916 and proclaimed an Irish Republic. This did not in fact become reality until 1922, when the Irish Free State was born. Its name was later changed to Eire. The six counties of Northern Ireland, or Ulster, predominantly Protestant, chose to remain part of the UK, though with their own Parliament. The IRA, as the IRV had now become, refused to accept this partition of the island and of continuing British rule in Ulster and, though declared illegal, began a series of campaigns to oust the British from Northern Ireland and unite the North and South.

The present 'Troubles' began in 1969, when British troops were deployed in Northern Ireland after severe sectarian fighting. Further outbreaks of violence and rioting occurred in Londonderry and Armagh in 1970, and in August rubber bullets were first used by British soldiers in Belfast. The first British soldier was killed in February 1971. Suspected IRA terrorists were then interned without trial, and murders and bombings increased. After Bloody Sunday in January 1972 – when 13 people were killed by the Paras in Londonderry – direct rule from London was imposed on Ulster, in March 1972. A bomb explosion at the Parachute Brigade headquarters in Aldershot in February, which killed seven people, including five women and a priest, was the prelude to a bombing campaign in England that lasted for two years. Letters and parcel bombs damaged and maimed, while car-bombs and time-bombs killed and injured. In March 1973 one person was killed and 244 injured by car-bombs in the Old Bailey and Whitehall; and 72 were injured by seven explosions in the week before Christmas. In January 1974 there were further explosions: 12 people were killed when a suitcase bomb blew up on a coach on the M62, which was carrying servicemen and their families, and six people died when two pubs in Guildford, used by soldiers, were wrecked by bomb blasts in October. A bomb explosion killed two near Woolwich barracks in November. Then 21 people died when bombs exploded in two crowded Birmingham pubs.

In 1975, when Mrs Thatcher became the Tories' leader, a bomb blast at a pub in Caterham injured 33. In September, there was a series of explosions in or near restaurants and hotels in London: five died and 100 were injured. In October, a cancer surgeon, Gordon Hamilton Fairley, was killed by mistake by a car-bomb; and in November Ross McWhirter was shot dead outside his home. The Peace Movement launched in Ulster in 1976 coincided with comparative quiet on the English mainland for the next five years, during which, in 1977, the Queen celebrated her Silver Jubilee. Mrs Thatcher won the General Election in May 1979, and in August that year Earl Mountbatten, holidaying on a boat off north-west Ireland, was killed, along with three others, when the boat was blown up by a bomb.

The next bombing campaign began in October 1981, when a laundry-van packed with explosive, nails and bolts was detonated by remote control as a coach containing Irish Guards returned to Chelsea barracks: 37 guardsmen and civilians were injured and two civilians were killed. A week later, the Commandant General of the Royal Marines, Lieutenant-General Sir Steuart Pringle, was maimed by a car-bomb; and an explosives expert, Kenneth Howarth, died trying to defuse a bomb in Oxford Street. The Wimbledon home of the Attorney-General, Sir Michael Havers, was blasted in November. There were other, minor bomb blasts in December and January. Then there was a six-month lull.

Meanwhile, in Ulster, some of the IRA were on hunger-strike in prison: ten, including Bobby Sands, were to die as a result. A hiatus was caused by the IRA's attacks in London by increased police activity and by the Falklands War, which ended in June 1982. But a renewal of the bombing campaign was being planned – a special double event for central London on 20 July. A week before this, Gerard Tuite was jailed for ten years in Dublin for possessing explosives in London between 1978 and 1979. During his trial a cassette tape was played in court outlining IRA surveillance carried out in London on various Army barracks.

Since 1969, over 60 people had been killed in England by the IRA and hundreds injured, and 33 alleged members of the IRA had been given prison sentences ranging from 20 years to life – although nearly half of these sentences were eventually quashed. Many more had died in Ulster. From 1969 to August 1992, over 3,000 people – soldiers, policemen, civilians, and members of sectarian factions – have been killed by bullet and bomb: an average for those 23 years of over 130 a year.

Sunrise was at 5.08 on the morning of Tuesday, 20 July but, concealed by thin cloud, the sun was not apparent at first. It was bright and sunny later, with a slight breeze, and the temperature rose to 23°C.

At 6.51 am, a blue four-door Morris Marina, which had been left for two nights in a car-park under the Royal Garden Hotel, at the western end of

Hyde Park, was picked up and driven away. The car had been bought by a man at an auction at Enfield in north London on 13 July. Its registration number was LMD 657P. Some four hours after the blue Marina was collected from the hotel, at about 10.00 am, it was seen being parked by a man on the South Carriage Drive in Hyde Park. The driver was lucky to find a space in the line of vehicles on the right-hand side of the road, left there by shoppers and office workers in nearby Knightsbridge. Perhaps he had tried, and failed, to park the car outside or near the Hyde Park barracks, home of the Household Cavalry and further up the road.

The car faced west; on its left a grassy bank topped by a large plane tree sloped down to the start of Knightsbridge; on its right was the south-eastern section of Hyde Park and Rotten Row. A few hundred yards away, behind the blue Marina, was Hyde Park Corner, Park Lane and the Hilton Hotel. In front of it stretched the South Carriage Drive, a wide avenue skirting the park, passing a tall red-brick block of mansion flats and the French Embassy at Albert Gate, beyond which were the Royal Thames Yacht Club, the Hyde Park Hotel, the huge office block of Bowater House straddling Edinburgh Gate, and the long red-brick and concrete monoliths of Hyde Park barracks, dominated by an ugly, 28-storey tower of flats for married NCOs and troopers. Designed by Sir Basil Spence, the barracks was formally opened by Field-Marshal Sir Gerald Templer and Admiral of the Fleet, Earl Mountbatten, in October 1970.

The blue Marina had been parked half a mile from the barracks' main gate. In its boot – on the right-hand side nearest to the road – was a 25 lb gelignite bomb, radio-controlled. Packed around it were 30 lbs of six- and four-inch nails.

It had not been entirely abandoned. Someone watched and waited in the park – perhaps near the bandstand, not far from a statue of St George on his steed, triumphing over a slaughtered dragon, which served as a memorial to 'the Cavalry of the Empire'. Perhaps he sat on a park bench, keyed up and ready to kill, and keeping the blue car in view through the trees. He held or carried a remote-control device that would be triggered as the standard-bearer of the mounted Queen's Life Guard crossed the line of sight between him and the car.

Men of the Household Cavalry had gone on guard at Horse Guards in Whitehall since 1751, apart from a brief interval during the Second World War. These duties now alternated between mounted squadrons of the Life Guards and the Blues and Royals, both based at Hyde Park barracks. Every morning, at about half-past ten, a ceremonial unit of mounted soldiers would set off from the barracks, via Hyde Park Corner, Constitution Hill and the Mall, to Horse Guards Parade, timing themselves en route so that they arrived at the central arch of Horse Guards as the clock above it struck eleven. It was a 24-hour guard duty, and the ceremony of Changing the Guard took place every weekday at 11.00 am. If the Queen, their Colonel-in-Chief, was residing in London, the Guard was 16-strong; if she was away, it numbered 12, and was without a trumpeter, standard-bearer and officer. On Tuesday, 20 July the Queen was at Buckingham Palace, so a full Guard was mounted that morning; and that morning it was the turn of the Blues and Royals to relieve the detachment of the Life Guards on duty at Whitehall.

The Blues and Royals had been formed 13 years earlier by the amalgamation of the Royal Horse Guards (the Blues) and the Royal Dragoons (First Royal Dragoons). They were an armoured-car regiment (their main military role), and had served in Northern Ireland. Twenty-one of them had recently returned from the Falklands War and paraded through Windsor, their regimental home.

The Household Cavalry's Commanding Officer was Lt.-Col. Andrew Parker Bowles, aged 42, who had served with the Blues and Royals. The previous November, the managing director of a small security firm in London, Mr Wynne, had written to him, drawing attention to the vulnerability of the barracks' mess and advocating the installation of certain safeguards. Wynne wrote: 'The real risk to my mind is the way in which large groups of your horses walk or trot along the same route on an almost daily basis. If I were the IRA, I would only require a shovel, explosives and remote detonation facilities to wreak desperate havoc with little or no risk involved.' Lt.-Col. Parker Bowles replied: 'We are very aware of our vulnerable position.' Action to improve security, he said, was taken 'within financial restrictions'. He later told reporters:

> Without taking the cavalry through even busier streets than now, and by very roundabout routes, there is very little more that we can do. There are very few variations. If you think about it, there is a maximum of three routes by which you can get from the barracks to Horse Guards Parade. We do change the route every so often. But if you want to have a Queen's Life Guard, then I'm afraid we are vulnerable to a bomb or even to anyone who carries a gun. There are certain risks we have to take.

On that Tuesday morning the troopers and NCOs of the Blues and Royals were up early, preparing their uniforms and horses for inspection by the Adjutant at 10.00 am. Some of them had never ridden a horse before they volunteered for this three-year tour of ceremonial duty, which was prefaced by five months of riding instruction. The horses were also intensively trained and carefully chosen. Geldings or mares, most of them came from Ireland, and were selected in accordance with certain requirements: they had to have the right colour (black), the right height (16.2 hands minimum), and the right temperament. The troopers were encouraged to form strong bonds of care and understanding for their horses, which were almost as well housed as the men, with central-heating, spacious stalls, good feed and clay-brick floors.

Men and horses began lining up in the yard for inspection at 9.50 am, the men wearing black thigh-boots, white breeches, blue tunics, gleaming cuirasses (breast- and backplates), white gauntlets and silver-plated helmets with red horsehair plumes. The red and gold tasselled standard was to be borne by SQMC (Squadron Quarter-Master Corporal) Roy Bright, aged 36, who had joined the Blues in 1964. A keen sportsman, fencer and pentathlete, he had met his wife in Germany when they were both 20 and she was a military nurse. They now had two teenage children. Every weekend he drove the 150 miles to his Shropshire home to be with his family, leaving at 4.00 am every Monday morning for the long drive back to work.

Some of the troopers were very young: the trumpeter, Stephen Sullivan, the only one to ride a grey horse, was 18. Simon Tipper was 19; he had only been married for two weeks and was now living in Putney with his young wife and mother-in-law. L/Cpl. Jeffrey Young was also 19. Married at the age of 17, he already had two children, aged three and 22 months. Corporal of Horse, James Pitt, a Scot, aged 28, was soon to be married; his horse was called Eclipse. Lance-Corporal Michael Pedersen's horse, Sefton, aged 19, was the oldest horse on the parade.

Two of those in the Guard that day should not have been there. Trooper Ian Smith, aged 23, whose fiancée was expecting twins, had stood in at the last minute for a sick friend. And the officer in charge of the new Guard, Lt. Anthony Daly, also aged 23, was likewise standing in for a friend. He had then tried to exchange his duty with a senior officer, Major Henry Hayward. But the Major had engagements that afternoon and was unable to comply.

In view of the fact that Lt. Daly would definitely be Captain of the Guard, his mother had arranged to bring an Australian friend to watch the Changing of the Guard at Horse Guards Parade that morning. She was now waiting there in the officers' quarters for her son and the Guard to arrive.

Anthony Daly, born on 27 January 1959 and educated at Eton, had followed his grandfather and father into the regiment and joined the Blues and Royals in January 1977. In 1979 he served in Northern Ireland for four months. He excelled at several sports and captained regimental rugby teams, playing alongside Bright and Young. He had also run in the London marathon earlier that year. Earlier that month he had returned to London from his honeymoon in Bermuda, having married Nichola Barcilon, the daughter of an RAF group captain, at the RAF church, St Clement's Danes, in the Strand less than four weeks before.

The full Guard, once the inspection was over, formed themselves into a processional column and as the trumpeter sounded the advance they moved out of the yard just after half-past ten. With a clatter of hooves, swords at the slope, and harnesses jingling they passed through the main gate into the road and turned right. Two mounted policemen attached themselves to the column, one at the front, the other at the rear, and the sun flared over them briefly as they set off down the road towards Hyde Park Corner – at the trot, as their inspection had delayed their departure by a minute or so.

Major Hayward, aged 34 and HQ Squadron Leader, had been exercising his charger, Yukon, in the park. He returned to the barracks as the Queen's Life Guard left. Reining in his horse he saluted the standard as it passed before him. Then he rode into the yard.

The Guard trotted on down the South Carriage Drive. Lt. Daly rode on the right of the standard-bearer, SQMC Bright, with a trooper known as a 'coverer' on the standard's left. These three were in the middle of the column, which was led by the trumpeter, Trooper Sullivan, out on his own, behind a mounted policeman. Then came six troopers riding in pairs. Another six followed the standard. The position of the men in the column would in minutes be a matter of life and death, or injury – depending on whether they rode on the left, or right, and on exactly when the man who watched their approach from the park activated the bomb in the car.

The column passed Bowater House, the Hyde Park Hotel and the Royal Thames Yacht Club, opposite which, on the edge of the park, a small copse of flowering trees had been planted and dedicated by Prince Charles seven months previously, as a memorial to the former Commodore of the Yacht Club, Earl Mountbatten, killed by an IRA bomb in August 1979.

They trotted past Albert Gate and the French Embassy, and the large mansion block of apartments, the last of the buildings on their right. Now, in full view of the five-arched gate at Hyde Park Corner, through whose central arch they would ride, there was nothing on their right but a stretch of grass and some trees and a line of parked cars.

People who happened to be out walking stopped to watch and admire the colourful pageant of horses and men. Among them was a Canadian, Mrs Diane Elder, and a family with the same surname as that of Lt. Daly. Back at Albert Gate, a car driven by the *Daily Star*'s royal reporter, James Whitaker, was brought to a halt by traffic lights switching to red.

The trumpeter passed the blue Marina, and for some reason Trooper Simon Tipper, riding behind the standard carried by SQMC Bright, turned his head to the right.

The Marina exploded – and in that instant Simon Tipper died.

James Whitaker, sitting in his red Ford Cortina at the traffic lights, saw it all. He wrote later:

> The moment that will haunt me for the rest of my days arrived at 10.40 and 23 seconds. I am so precise because my first, unthinking reflex was to look at my watch. Seconds before, it had been a beautiful summer day, and I had been driving to work down the South Carriage Drive. Then the traffic lights changed to red, and I slowed to a halt. Idly, I watched a detachment of the Household Cavalry clip-clopping down the road 100 yards ahead of me, plumes dancing, cuirasses gleaming in the sun, their black horses well-groomed. A ball of flame shooting into the air was the first sign of the catastrophe. This was followed almost instantaneously by an ear-splitting thud and a column of black smoke. My car shook, as if the earth trembled beneath me, and it was at that moment I looked at my watch. And at that moment everything went into slow motion. But it was what I witnessed next that will live with me forever. I saw bodies licked with flame, mis-shapen masses, tumbling down from the sky – horses, and their riders coming down after them. I drove towards the scene and got out of the car, and there was this terrible, total silence, a complete vacuum of noise. Not one horse made a single sound. No whinnying. No snorting through their nostrils. The great beasts lay on their sides or half sitting-up looking pitiful, their eyes half staring out of their sockets. One or two had somehow remained on

their feet and looked around with almost human panic and shock in their dark brown eyes. One or two of the riders, their bright uniforms shattered and scorched, stood dazed, or wandered among the stricken animals. Some lay dreadfully still. A car burnt furiously by the road. Others were wrecked. The column of evil black smoke coiled into the sky, turning the sun blood red, and a woman began to scream. Now I saw more red, the glistening red of the blood that started to seep and sometimes spurt from the glossy black coats of the horses. Then the less seriously injured troopers staggered to their feet. I watched, mesmerised, as every single man who could walk began to look around for his horse, to see if it was all right, to catch the ones that had struggled up. Instinctively, the troopers cared more for their terribly wounded, muted horses, than for themselves. By now, and only a few minutes had passed, I was beginning to cry. Then two policemen ran up the road, shouting that there might be another bomb and telling me and others to move away. I ran around the corner to the Hyde Park Hotel, to phone the office and get some help. But I was not very coherent, gasping, and it was difficult to make myself understood.

The Times reported:

> The nearest soldier was about eight feet from the bomb. The force of the explosion catapulted another parked car on to the roof of a vehicle nearby. Nails and wreckage were sent flying over a 250-yard area. The windows of shops in Knightsbridge, including Barclays Bank and the National Farmers' Union, were blown out, and pieces of the booby-trapped car were found embedded in partition walls on the second and fourth floor of the NFU building . . . Hundreds of people were in the park at the time.

Bits of the car and dozens of nails had scythed through the centre and rear of the mounted column. All the Blues and Royals were injured, though some, like trumpeter Stephen Sullivan, were not seriously hurt. He said later: 'I just remember coming to and seeing soldiers and horses everywhere.' The worst injured were Lance-Corporal Young and the standard-bearer, Roy Bright. A nail had torn into Bright's neck and upwards into his brain. Trooper Ian Smith and Corporal of Horse James Pitt were also injured. Pitt said: 'It was carnage. There were horses trying to stand up, and they couldn't understand why they couldn't do so with only three legs. I never thought they would go for the animals. My horse, Eclipse, took the blast that was meant for me. That horse saved my life.' Mike Pedersen, riding Sefton, was wounded by a piece of metal that sliced into his right hip; and his little finger was transfixed by a nail. He said:

> I didn't know what had happened. I was just in a daze. There was a huge noise and I was deaf. I saw a large cloud of smoke and vaguely saw soldiers and horses on the ground. It never occurred to me it was a

> bomb. Sefton's legs were outstretched and braced. He didn't try to bolt or dump me and I stayed mounted, although I didn't have any reins – they'd been blown away. I don't know if it was him or me, but between us we turned round and walked back towards the barracks. We didn't get that far before a soldier came running to meet us. He lifted me off Sefton's back, and someone else stuffed his shirt into Sefton's throat to stop the bleeding. When I found it was an IRA bomb, I couldn't believe anyone would do that to a horse.

Major Hayward was in the barracks' yard, talking to another officer. He said later:

> When I heard the bang, along with everyone there, I went to the Knightsbridge side of the barracks. The sound seemed to come from there. For some reason I then turned round and saw a woman at the Ceremonial Gate. She had got out of a taxi. She was hysterical and saying something to the guard at the gate. He signalled to me to come over and I did. She was in tears and said something like: 'It's terrible! There are horses everywhere! Why aren't you doing anything about it? They need help.' It was difficult to understand what she was saying. I stepped out into the road, looked and saw the smoke. The traffic had stopped. I realised it was the Guard. I ran back into the yard, shouting at the veterinary officer, Major Carding, telling him what had happened. I ran upstairs to Andrew's office and barged in. He was in conference. I said: 'Colonel – that bomb was the Guard!' We rushed down to the yard, where we got a staff car to take us to the scene. Troopers ran down the road. Quite a few people were there already, including an ambulance and the police. We could do little. There was this mass of bodies, horses and men, in the middle of the road. Blood everywhere. The wounded horses were being shot. Some of the men were standing up, holding their heads. Cpl. Pitt's face was covered in blood. I remember seeing L/Cpl. Young lying in the road, bleeding and badly injured – he had been crushed by his horse. Anthony Daly seemed unmarked. But he was dead. It could have been me.

A policeman on diplomatic duty outside the French Embassy had run up. Armed with a revolver, he began shooting the injured horses. One was already dead. But as he aimed at their chests, intending to hit their hearts, he failed to kill them straight away. They reared as he shot them, and lunged. He managed to kill two or three before a farrier from the barracks took the gun off him and shot the remaining injured horses in their foreheads, between their eyes. Six horses were shot.

One of the mounted policemen, John Davies, aged 24, was injured, as was Echo, his horse. Of the civilians in the area, five were hit by flying metal, nails and broken glass.

Thomas Daly, a milkman, was further up the road with his wife, Pauline, and their two-year-old son, Thomas, who was in a push-chair. Mr Daly pulled the chair back off the road between two cars as the Guard approached. His wife remained on the road. Mrs Daly said later: 'There was a tremendous bang. I was aware of something hitting my leg. I must have passed out. The next thing I knew I was lying in the road. I couldn't hear anything at first, because of the bang.' She was also unable to hear herself screaming. But she was out of hospital in 24 hours. Her son was not hurt.

Mrs Elder, standing on the grass near the plane tree, was less fortunate. Peter Anderson, aged 22, was working in Knightsbridge. He said: 'I ran outside and saw a fireball. I got up the bank and all I could see was devastation and carnage. The first thing I saw was a middle-aged lady. She was on her hands and knees screaming, with part of her foot blown away.' Kelly Scales, a waitress, said: 'It was horrific. I've never seen anything like it. One woman was sitting on the bank bleeding, with half her foot hanging off.'

A hairdresser, Tony Tenconi, said:

> There was this massive noise and a great heat. Glass was falling from the flats above, and I thought it might be a gas explosion, until I saw a ball of flame over in the park. I ran across and it was just a carnage of horses, with blood spurting from their wounds. I ran back to the shop, grabbed a handful of towels and screamed to the girls to wet them with cold water. As I ran back there was a woman screaming 'Help me!' There was also this soldier with blood pouring out of his head. I pressed his wound together until the ambulance men arrived. I saw a soldier walk away and then just collapse. Horses lying around were twisted with pain, some trying to get up. They were slithering about and sliding into the helpers. A policeman produced a revolver and began shooting the horses around me. They were still writhing after they were shot. An officer shouted: 'Shoot them again!'

'It was a scene of sheer horror,' said a businessman, John Marriott, who lived near by. 'I saw one trooper with his head blown off. A horse was lying on top of one of the injured men and a mounted policeman covered in blood climbed on to the horse to stop it moving about and causing the soldier more harm.' Ray Ashley, a workman, said: 'There were two troopers trapped under the bodies of their horses. A policeman was shooting injured horses as they tried to get up. I had to look away. I saw one horse trying to get up on the one leg it had left. It was dreadful.' Another workman, John Marshall, said: 'One of the soldiers got up off the ground. The metal on his uniform was all twisted out of shape and his helmet was battered. He took it off and kicked it down the road.'

James Whitaker, returning to the South Carriage Drive, encountered two young troopers, in tears, leading an injured horse back to the barracks. He wept himself as from the park (the road had been cordoned off) he saw the last of the horses being shot. He wrote later: 'I have seen men die like animals, and animals die like men. And nothing, ever again, will seem the same.'

No responsibilities were greater, graver, or lasted longer than those of Lt.-

Col. Parker Bowles and his 2IC, Major Hayward, who had to deal with the effects of the bomb explosion on the men under their command, on those who survived, on the families of the dead and injured, as well as with the police, security officers and the press. The Life Guards on duty at Horse Guards Parade remained there without a change of guard for another 24 hours.

Major Hayward commandeered the staff car of a senior officer in the Royal Green Jackets who had happened to stop in South Carriage Drive. With a police escort he drove to St James's Street, while Parker Bowles returned to the barracks. Hayward said:

> I knew where Lt. Daly's wife worked. It was in an optician's. When I saw her I said: 'Something has happened,' and asked her to accompany me back to the barracks. I didn't tell her Anthony was dead. I just kept her talking. When we arrived, using the Knightsbridge entrance, I took her up to Andrew's office. The regimental medical officer was already there, with his wife . . . I then had to find Trooper Tipper's wife, and tell his father that his son had just got married – he didn't know – and now was dead.

Anthony Daly's mother, at Horse Guards Parade, heard the bang of the explosion. But it was not until eleven o'clock struck, when the Guard failed to arrive, that she realised something was dreadfully amiss. She was told of her son's death by the major-general commanding the Household Division.

The injured were taken to Westminster Hospital. Ten wounded horses, including Eclipse, aged 7, Copenhagen, aged 10, and the police horse, Echo, were brought back to the barracks, leaving a bloody trail for 400 yards down South Carriage Drive.

Major Noel Carding, the regimental vet, said of 19-year-old Sefton: 'These are the worst, the saddest, most dreadful injuries I have ever seen inflicted on a horse.' Sefton had sustained 38 wounds caused by shrapnel and nails; his jugular vein had been severed; his right eye and face were also scorched. Major Carding said: 'He has lost a great deal of blood and is in deep shock. He is deadly quiet. I've not been able to get all the lead out of him, but I hope he will survive . . . These are magnificent horses, so stout-hearted. They bear their suffering in silence.'

The horses which died were Cedric, Epaulette, Falcon, Rochester, Waterford, Yeastvite and Lara. Their nameplates were removed from their empty stalls the following day.

Their bodies, however, remained out on the road that Tuesday afternoon for two hours, covered by tarpaulins, as transport was organised to take them away. The area had been cleared by the police, who feared that a second bomb might have been placed in another parked car. They were right about the second bomb. But it was not in Hyde Park.

At 12.55, as the dead horses were being removed, a distant boom was heard coming from Regent's Park.

The band of the 1st Battalion Royal Green Jackets were giving a lunchtime concert on a bandstand in the park. It was thought to be safe for them to perform in London rather than in Ulster, where their battalion was currently based. The band, numbering 30 in all, had left Winchester that morning by coach, arriving in London at half-past eleven, some 50 minutes after the car-bomb explosion in Hyde Park. The bandmaster, David Little, heard about the bomb attack on a radio as he drank before the concert with other bandsmen in a pub. He then checked the bandstand himself.

He later told an inquest: 'I walked round the bandstand and checked the floorboards. The band would have checked the bandstand earlier anyway, as we've done over the years since another band nearly got it in Brussels. I found nothing out of place. I asked a colleague to make a further check.'

The bandstand was situated on the south-western rim of Regent's Park, by a lake full of ducks, geese and swans and not far from the top of Baker Street. About 100 people listening to the music reclined in deckchairs all around the bandstand or sat on the grass. Hidden under the floorboards was an IRA bomb. There had apparently not been enough space to include a briefcase full of nails, which was found later by divers dumped in the lake. If the nails had been packed beside the bomb, the casualties would have been much greater. At 12.30 the band began to play.

At 12.55, as the band played a selection from the musical *Oliver*, the bomb exploded, triggered by remote control or by a timing device. A sheet of flame shot upwards, as did the blast, hurling bandsmen, their instruments, music stands and spears of wood into the air. The bandstand's iron cupola and supporting pillars withstood the blast.

'I remember the explosion,' said Bandmaster Little. 'And the whistling in my ears. The next thing I knew I was facing the audience with my back to the bandstand.' Cpl. John Mitchell said: 'We were playing away and bang – that was it. People were mutilated. There were bodies everywhere. They were all my friends. I've been working with them for ten years.'

Simon Braidman, a student, was sitting on the grass with his sister and another girl. He said: 'There was an enormous explosion. The sky was full of debris. I was hit by a piece of wood. I saw it falling, but I was so shocked I just couldn't move out of the way.' A pensioner, Benjamin Morris, said: 'I saw a lot of soldiers blown out of the bandstand like dummies. It was like wartime. Some were dead, lying on the grass. One soldier came up to me crying, with blood pouring down his face.' Another pensioner, Miriam Sheridan, said: 'I saw the soldiers lying on the grass with some of their intestines hanging out. Two soldiers were walking around with blood pouring from their heads. I stroked one of the soldiers' heads. He was very young, and I held his hand and I told him help would soon arrive.' A building worker, Donald McCulloch, said: 'One soldier reached out his hand for help, but his body had been blown in half. He was completely cut in two. He was still alive.'

The bandsmen's injuries were horrific: one was grossly mutilated, some lost limbs, or suffered compound fractures and burns. One bandsman died of cerebral lacerations and a fractured skull; another had both an arm and a leg torn off.

Six bandsmen died in the park, and a seventh would die later of pneumonia brought on by his multiple injuries. They were: Warrant Officer Graham Barker; Sgt. Robert Livingstone; Cpl. John McKnight; Bandsmen John Heritage, George Mesure, Keith Powell and Laurence Smith. Thirty bandsmen and civilians were injured by the bomb. Since 1969, 28 men of the Royal Green Jackets, including two officers, had been killed in Northern Ireland, five dying there in 1981.

There were shocked gasps in the House of Commons later that afternoon when the Home Secretary, William Whitelaw, revealed that in addition to the two Blues and Royals who had died in Hyde Park, six Green Jackets had now been killed in Regent's Park. The leader of the opposition, Michael Foot, declared that no political question would be settled in democratic Britain by a resort to 'pitiless barbarity'. Mrs Thatcher denounced the bomb explosions as 'these callous and cowardly crimes, committed by evil and brutal men'.

A garden party at Buckingham Palace that afternoon went ahead, amid unprecedented security checks, including the closure of the Mall. The Queen was said to be visibly distressed when she spoke of the bombings to some of the guests. It had already been a stressful month for her: an intruder, Michael Fagan, had entered the palace on 9 July and found his way to the Queen's bedroom before he was arrested. Then the senior policeman on the Palace staff, Michael Trestrail, resigned after confessing to a relationship with a male prostitute. And the Falklands War had only ended a month before.

The Queen sent a telegram to Lt.-Col. Parker Bowles which said: 'I was deeply shocked and distressed to hear of the dreadful tragedy suffered by the Queen's Life Guard today. The Duke of Edinburgh and I send our heartfelt sympathy to the families of those who died, to the injured and to the Mounted Regiment itself. Elizabeth R.'

That night, during the Royal Tournament at Earl's Court, which was attended by Prince Charles, there was a minute's silence for the victims of both bomb explosions and a trumpeter played the Last Post.

An hour before the sun set on that Tuesday there was a partial eclipse of the sun.

The following morning, Wednesday, 21 July, the newspapers carried headlines like – 'IRA MASSACRE – THE IRA BOMBERS ARE BACK'. The *Mirror* said: 'The IRA returned to London yesterday, killing without warning and without pity. They bombed not only soldiers but innocent passers-by. Year in and year out, they are the most consistently wicked gang of killers in the Western world.'

The IRA had already issued a statement in Dublin and Belfast, admitting responsibility for the bombings and comparing their situation to Britain's against Argentina in the Falklands War. They said: 'Now it is our turn to properly invoke Article 51 of the UN Charter and properly quote all Thatcher's fine phrases on the right to self-determination of a people. The Irish people have sovereign and national rights, which no task or occupational force can put down.' They justified the bombings as acts of self-defence.

A headline in the pro-IRA weekly, the *Republican News*, said: 'IRA ROCK

ENEMY MORALE'. The bomb operations in London were said to have been 'brilliantly executed', although 'regrettably there were injuries to several civilians'.

On that Wednesday morning the Duke of Edinburgh visited the Hyde Park barracks before a detachment of the Life Guards set out for Horse Guards Parade to relieve the unit from their own regiment who had now been on duty for nearly 48 hours. As Lt.-Col. Parker Bowles explained later: 'It will take more than a cowardly attack like yesterday's to stop us doing our duty. We are all determined to carry on and will continue to mount a guard as we have done for 300 years. My men would be most disappointed if we did not. I know it is what my men expect and want to do.'

The Duke inspected the new Guard and spoke to five survivors of the bomb-blast who were out of hospital and on their feet. Among them were Cpl. of Horse James Pitt and Trooper Sullivan, both of whom, with Lt.-Col. Parker Bowles and Major Carding, talked later to the press.

Reporters were also allowed to view the injured horses in the stables, and pictures of Sefton soon featured prominently in local and national papers. Major Carding said: 'Everyone is disgusted and horrified at this cowardly attack on both men and horses.' A Corporal of Horse was quoted as saying: 'Those horses are the pride of Ireland. The men who injured them are its shame.'

The new Guard of 16 men left the barracks a few minutes late and trotted up the South Carriage Drive, now cleared of cars, towards the scene of the explosion. Spectators applauded; some cheered. As the Life Guards approached the scorched and riven plane tree and passed over the patches of sand spread over the blood-stained road, they held their swords erect, at the carry, and the Captain lowered his, in honour of their dead and injured colleagues in the Blues and Royals. The spectators were silent here. Below the tree someone had left a posy of pink carnations, with a message that said: 'In loving memory. Father forgive.'

L/Cpl. Jeffrey Young died in hospital that day: he would have been 20 the following week.

Messages of sympathy, good wishes and greeting cards had already begun to arrive at the barracks, including bags of sugar lumps and carrots for the injured horses, for Sefton in particular. Eventually, one side of his stall was covered in Get Well cards. Lt.-Col. Parker Bowles received a telegram from the Prince and Princess of Wales, whose first son, Prince William, had been born in June. It said: 'We were both utterly appalled and sickened by what happened in Hyde Park yesterday and felt heavy at heart throughout the rest of the day. Please would you convey our very deepest sympathy to the families of those who lost their lives so tragically and to the troopers who looked after the horses that were killed – Charles and Diana.'

On the morning of Thursday, 22 July, the Blues and Royals rode out of the barracks once again, bearing the torn and bloodied standard that had been torn from the grasp of SQMC Bright. The sun shone, and all along the route people applauded and cheered at windows and in the street. Among them was Nichola Daly. She stood with her younger sister opposite the place where her husband had died. Her sister, Rae-Louise, who had been a bridesmaid at the Dalys' wedding, wept as the Guard rode past. Mrs Daly called out: 'Well done, Guard! Well done!'

Roy Bright died in Westminster Hospital the following night. Brain-dead since the explosion, he had been kept alive for three days by a life-support machine, until, with the approval of his wife, Marion, arrangements to transplant his kidneys to save the lives of two middle-aged women could be made.

'He would have been the first to applaud that decision,' said Mrs Bright weeks later – she had been with her husband, as was his widowed mother, when he was allowed to die. She said:

> With his brain gone, there was no sense in denying a chance of life to others ... Doctors had told me that early tests had shown no sign of brain activity, and these tests had to be repeated before any final decisions were taken. I'll never forget Roy's face as he lay there. Once the second tests proved negative, I didn't want him to be kept alive. I couldn't imagine him living as a vegetable. Not Roy. He was always so full of life ... Everything he did, he did with enthusiasm. We went walking, camping, caravanning, boating. He was always an outdoor man and had loved horse-riding ever since he was a boy. Apart from his family, the men and horses in his regiment were the great love of his life. He'd do anything for them. If any horse was awkward or difficult to manage they'd say 'Give it to Roy – he won't fail.' And he never did ... He was such a strong, fit man. I didn't believe that anything could destroy him.

The biggest security operation in central London since the wedding of Prince Charles and Lady Diana Spencer took place on Monday, 26 July, when the nation paid homage in St Paul's Cathedral to those who had died in the Falklands War. The Last Post and Reveille, which were played during the service, would be heard in eleven churches elsewhere, as the Blues and Royals and Royal Green Jackets who had died on 20 July were buried over the next two weeks.

On 27 July, L/Cpl. Jeffrey Young was buried, on his birthday, at Tonyrefail, a mining village in South Wales. The funeral of Lt. Anthony Daly was held in the Garrison Church at Windsor the following day. His flag-draped coffin was carried by ten men from the Blues and Royals, including some who had been part of his last Guard. His father, Lt.-Col. Dennis Daly, was there, as well as his mother, sister and younger brother, Christopher, aged 18, who joined the Blues and Royals in 1987. During the service, Nichola Daly wept silently on the shoulder of her uniformed father, Group Captain Barcilon.

Simon Tipper was buried at Swinford, near Stourbridge in the West Midlands, and Roy Bright at Broseley in Shropshire.

By then, the death toll from both bomb explosions had reached eleven, with the death on 1 August in St Mary's Hospital of Bandsman John Heritage, a 29-year-old drummer from Banbury, who was married with two young children. By then only one of the wounded Blues and Royals was still in hospital, although ten bandsmen were still receiving hospital treatment.

In the middle of August the injured horses were put out to grass at the Army Veterinary Centre at Melton Mowbray in Leicestershire. But it was not until 28 September that Sefton was reunited with his rider, Mike Pedersen, and returned to work for another two years, retiring in August 1984. A painting of Sefton, auctioned in London, had raised £12,500 for the appeal funds set up for the dependants of the victims of the bombs, and £50,000 was donated by people in the Irish Republic. Each of the four widows of the Blues and Royals eventually received about £25,000.

The inquest into the deaths of the eleven soldiers was held at Westminster on Thursday, 21 October, the coroner recording a verdict of unlawful killing on all of the men. The head of the anti-terrorist squad at Scotland Yard, Commander Bill Hucklesby, said afterwards: 'The police are very grateful to numerous members of the public who offered information concerning these crimes.' He said 6,000 telephone calls and 400 letters had been received, and 1,200 statements taken. He added: 'I am hopeful and determined that our investigations will result in the prosecution of the criminals responsible for these bomb outrages.'

These investigations were not brought to a conclusion for five years, until 27 October 1987, when Gilbert McNamee, aged 27, was convicted on fingerprint evidence of conspiring, between January 1982 and January 1984, to cause explosions likely to endanger life or cause serious injury to property.

McNamee, known as Danny, came from Crossmaglen in County Armagh. He was one of eight children. His mother died when he was five, and when he was 14 his father was killed by an IRA bomb, meant for a passing patrol, which exploded in a Crossmaglen pub. Two of his cousins were shot by the IRA who thought they were police informants. Despite all this he went on to achieve eleven GCE 'O' Levels and three 'A' Levels and studied physics at Queen's University in Belfast. He graduated in 1982 with a pass degree, and went to work in Dundalk in Ireland as an electrician at a factory which made parts for CB radios and gaming machines. The brothers who ran the business, George and James McCann, were both members of the IRA. George McCann was later arrested in France and jailed for smuggling arms for the Irish National Liberation Army. In 1984, McNamee was himself arrested by the Irish police and charged with possessing micro-circuitry for use in explosive devices. But an Irish jury concluded that the circuits were for use in anti-theft devices in gaming machines. He was released, and returned to Crossmaglen. In January 1986, his fingerprints were routinely taken by an RUC patrol in Northern Ireland. Later that year they were found to match prints on two IRA arms caches discovered in England. He was arrested at his home in Crossmaglen in August 1986.

The trial of Danny McNamee – 'a slightly built man with thick-lensed glasses', according to the *Daily Telegraph* – began at the Central Criminal Court in London on 12 October 1987. He pleaded not guilty. The judge was

Mr Justice McCowan, who was provided with a bodyguard throughout the two-week trial. The prosecution was led by Roy Amlot, QC, and the defence by Richard Ferguson, QC.

Mr Amlot claimed that McNamee's fingerprints were on a Duracell battery attached to a bomb defused in London in December 1983, as well as on tape on two encoders, components of radio-controlled bomb mechanisms, found in two large arms caches, one of which was unearthed in an Oxfordshire wood in October 1983, and the other in Salcey Forest in Northamptonshire in January 1984. According to the prosecution, McNamee made the bombs that IRA units used in England. He was linked to the Hyde Park bombing, it was said, by fragments of a circuit board that matched similar components in one of the arms caches. 'It is not suggested,' said Mr Amlot, 'that McNamee was present in Hyde Park when the bomb went off. The crown's case is that he was the bomb-maker . . . who worked in Ireland for the Provisional IRA.'

He went on to tell the court that McNamee's alleged co-conspirators, Paul Kavanagh, Thomas Quigley, and Natalino Vella, had already been convicted, in 1985, of explosives offences. Kavanagh and Quigley had each been jailed for 35 years.

McNamee was also said, after his arrest, to have offered the police an innocent explanation for the presence of his fingerprints on the battery and encoders – 'I work with electrical equipment a lot and repair many things. If my fingerprints are on it, it must have been that I was repairing something.'

During the trial he gave evidence in his own defence and denied being involved in any way in bombings. He said that although he was an Irish nationalist, he abhorred violence. Members of his own family had been killed by the IRA, he said, and it was unthinkable that he would be one of their number or work for them.

Danny McNamee was found guilty of conspiring to cause explosions and sentenced on 27 October 1987 to 25 years in prison. He was sent to Parkhurst Prison on the Isle of Wight.

The police believed that he was 'the IRA's master-bomber' and responsible in part for the murders of at least 30 soldiers, policemen and civilians in Northern Ireland and England from 1981 to 1986, a period which included the Hyde Park and Regent's Park bombings, the bomb explosion by Harrods in December 1983, which killed six people, and the explosion that killed five in the Grand Hotel in Brighton, where Mrs Thatcher and her ministers were staying during the Conservative Party Conference in October 1984. Some policemen believed that McNamee had a hand in the manufacture of up to 80 bombs and the consequent deaths of as many people. If so, he would be the biggest mass-murderer in British criminal history. But murder is not something with which terrorists are usually charged. Their offences come under the Prevention of Terrorism Act.

An appeal against McNamee's conviction was heard before the Lord Chief Justice, Lord Lane, Mr Justice Kennedy and Mr Justice Judge in December 1990. Richard Ferguson, QC, told the court that there was not a shred of evidence to link McNamee to the Hyde Park bombing, which had only been included at the last minute in the charges against him. The indictment had been altered twice, he said – ten days before the trial and again at the end of the trial after the closing speeches, when the charge was amended to 'within the UK and elsewhere'. Mr Ferguson claimed that the judge had also misdirected the jury and misrepresented McNamee's defence. The Old Bailey trial was 'unfair', he said. He cast doubt on the validity of the forensic and fingerprint evidence, and protested at the way the police had used the press to vilify McNamee.

Lord Lane and his two Appeal Court judges dismissed the appeal; also dismissed was a later application to appeal to the House of Lords. McNamee is still in a high-security prison and unlikely to be released for several years.

A small memorial stone to the four Blues and Royals who died in the Hyde Park bombing was dedicated in the presence of the Queen Mother in October 1983. It lies on the north side of South Carriage Drive opposite the scene of the explosion, which is marked now only by a kerbstone with a chipped and damaged edge. But when the road is wet with rain or damp with dew, a scorchmark like a black stain still appears.

The bombings did not cease with McNamee's arrest, although there was a long lull, punctuated by a bomb blast at the Mill Hill barracks in north-west London in August 1988, in which a man was killed, and by a large explosion a year later at the Royal Marines School of Music at Deal in Kent, when ten soldiers died. But in the first six months of 1990 there was a series of explosions at military offices and establishments in and around London, caused by parcel-bombs and car-bombs. These culminated in blasts at the Carlton Club, at the Stock Exchange, and in the death of MP Ian Gow.

Two bombs were directed at the band of the Blues and Royals in 1991. A bomb found outside the Beck Theatre at Hayes in West London in June, where the band was playing, was defused. In November, another small bomb, outside a concert-hall in St Albans where the band was due to play, blew up accidentally and killed the man and woman who had brought it there.

In April 1992, a 200-lb car-bomb exploded in the City of London, devastating the Baltic Exchange and several buildings, including two office tower-blocks, and causing damage costing billions of pounds. It was the worst single explosion in London since the Second World War: three people were killed and 91 injured. A few hours later another car-bomb wrecked a fly-over at Staples Corner on the M25.

The bombers were back once again with another double event. The murderous war being waged by the IRA to achieve the unification of all Ireland still goes on.

CHAPTER 20

Dennis Nilsen

The Murder of Stephen Sinclair, 1983

The disintegration of modern life, of the controlling influence of the family, religion and social standards, along with the general excesses of sexual expression, the wide availability of guns and drugs, and the everyday unsettling television images of affluence, disaster and death – all these have contributed in some way to an increase in murder, and especially to the modern phenomenon of the mass murderer known as the serial killer. There have always been mass murderers, like William Palmer, the poisoner. But they were very rare, and their victims rarely exceeded seven or eight. Since the 1970s, this kind of killer has increased, exacting a bloody revenge on society; some effecting a massacre of total strangers by gun, and others killing strangers to satisfy perverted sexual desires.

One of the first killing sprees of this sort, involving guns, occurred in August 1966 in Austin, Texas, when Charles Whitman, aged 25, stabbed and shot to death 21 people in less than 12 hours, killing most by sniping at them from a university tower. More recently, another 21 people were shot and killed by a gunman in and near a McDonald's in San Ysidro, California, in July 1984; and 22 were shot, again in Texas, in 1991. In England, Michael Ryan, aged 27, shot and killed 15 people and then himself in Hungerford, Berkshire in August 1987.

A more discriminate kind of slaughter, that of the sexual murder of young women, men and boys, escalated in America in the 1970s, prefaced by the murders committed by Charles Manson and his Family: he himself claimed to have murdered 35. Dean Corll, aged 33, together with two younger associates, raped and killed at least 27 boys in Houston, Texas, before he was shot and killed by one of those associates in 1973. In Florida, Ted Bundy was sentenced to death in 1979 for raping and killing at least 18 girls. In 1980 John Wayne Gacy, a twice-married contractor in Illinois, was sentenced to life imprisonment for the rape and murder of at least 32 young men and boys.

Also in that year, in England, Peter Dinsdale, known as Bruce Lee, was charged with the manslaughter by arson of 26 people in Hull; and another arsonist, John (Punch) Thompson, aged 42, caused the deaths of 37 people in two Soho drinking-clubs at 22 Denmark Place in August 1980 – when Dennis Nilsen was working around the corner in Denmark Street. The clubs were mainly used by Spaniards and South Americans. Thompson, the biggest mass murderer in British criminal history, was said to have argued with a barman about being overcharged, then obtained a can of petrol and set the house alight.

Dennis Nilsen, the first known homosexual serial killer in the UK, murdered and attempted to murder 22 young men in London in just over four years. His first victim died on New Year's Eve 1979, almost two years before Peter Sutcliffe, the Yorkshire Ripper, killed his last, in November 1980. Sutcliffe was arrested on 2 January 1981. Nilsen was arrested two years later, a fortnight after he had killed and dismembered his fifteenth victim, and his last.

Stephen Neil Sinclair was Scottish, like Nilsen, and like him a psychopath. In later years, if he had lived, he might have become a murderer himself. His real surname was Guild. Born in Perth on 20 February 1962, he was less than a month from his twenty-first birthday when he met the tall, stooping, studious-looking, bespectacled 37-year-old man, who called himself Des, on Wednesday, 26 January 1983. Des had grey-blue eyes and was 5′ 10″. They coincided in a Soho pub called the Royal George in Goslett Yard, near the Jobcentre in Denmark Street where Nilsen used to work as a clerical officer, finding jobs for the unemployed. Nilsen probably told Sinclair about this, and about his childhood in the north-east of Scotland, his years in the Army, mostly in the ACC (Army Catering Corps), and his year as a police constable with the Metropolitan Police. He now worked at the Jobcentre in Kentish Town.

Sinclair was about 5′ 5″, with ginger hair bleached blond. He was wearing a leather jacket, jersey, a blue and white football scarf and black jeans. A drug addict, who had attempted suicide more than once by slashing his arms and wrists, he had been destitute in London for several years, sleeping rough, usually in squats or derelict buildings, easing the pain of his existence with punk music, barbiturates, drugs and drink. A social worker who knew Sinclair, said: 'He was a very lonely, depressed and isolated guy, who could only get on with people on the surface . . . As far as I know, he had no friends whatsoever . . . Exactly a year before he was killed, his only friend, another punk, was stabbed in Green Park, near Piccadilly . . . He didn't have much to live for.'

Rejected as a baby by his parents, Stephen was fostered and then adopted, aged two, by the Sinclairs of St Martins, a small village in the heather-clad hills north of Perth. The father, Neil Sinclair, was a former Army officer and a driving instructor; his wife was a domestic science teacher; they already had three daughters. The little boy became uncontrollable, destroying all his toys, thieving, lying, setting things on fire, causing trouble every day, and every night wetting his bed until he was well into his teens. He had seizures, was violent, and showed no feeling for animals, the young or old. Mr Sinclair said: 'There was absolutely no love in him: he never cried at night . . . It was no use spanking him . . . Morally, he was like a one-and-a-half year old, even in his teens. He couldn't discern right from wrong.'

The Sinclairs gave their adopted son to the social services when he was about 13. After a spell in an approved school, whither he was sent for stealing, he was fostered by a Mr and Mrs Donald. He continued to steal, to lie, to misbehave and to wet his bed. His strangeness and moods began to alarm the Donalds, who returned him to the social workers within a year. He was soon in prison; he came to London; he contracted hepatitis B. The one night he spent with Dennis Nilsen was the end of the road for them both.

There are two main accounts of what happened that night and thereafter. Both are by Nilsen. Even so, the details within them do not tally. For it seems that Nilsen sought to conceal, as much as wished to reveal what he did. He wanted to share, to proclaim his terrible secrets, but not what was really in his mind and not what he really did.

He told the police, a fortnight after the event: 'We were having a good drink at the George and later I said: "You don't mind coming back to Highgate?" And he said: "Okay." We went to an off-licence in Greek Street, and I got a bottle of whisky and about six bottles of lager. It must have been after 9.00 pm when we got to my flat at Cranley Gardens.' In another, later account Nilsen said that he bought Sinclair a hamburger at a McDonald's in Oxford Street and that the drinks were purchased at a Shaftesbury Avenue off-licence.

They would then have taken the Northern line tube to Highgate and walked the half mile from there to Nilsen's flat up Muswell Hill Road, passing between Highgate Wood and Queen's Wood.

The flat was in the attic of 23 Cranley Gardens in Muswell Hill, a leafy North London suburb. The semi-detached house, owned by an Asian woman, was shabby and in need of repair: all the woodwork, painted pale blue, was peeling; roof tiles had slipped. Three flights of stairs led to Nilsen's door, which opened on to a cramped space containing a gas-cooker, water-heater, sink and kitchen cupboards. The bathroom was beyond. Another door led to a messy, foul-smelling front room, containing two wardrobes, two armchairs, a tea-chest, heaps of belongings and bits of brown carpet; the windows were wide open. Nilsen slept and ate in the back room, which was furnished with a low double-bed, tables, an upright chair, a sofa, TV set, stereo system, posters and some plants. The rooms were cold and squalid and every ceiling sloped. They were also occupied by Nilsen's only regular companion, a shaggy black and white mongrel bitch called Bleep, who had a bad eye. She had already witnessed 14 murders, and the dismembered remains of Nilsen's two most recent victims were packed in the tea-chest and in one of the wardrobes in the chill front room.

Bleep greeted her master enthusiastically when he and young Sinclair entered the flat. Nilsen later told the police:

> I remember the 9.25 episode of 'Boys from the Blackstuff' was on TV. I let the dog out straight away. Right away. I said: 'This is a fantastic programme – we've got to watch this.' We started to drink. Whisky and then lager. I then let the dog into the front room and she curled up by a chair. He [Sinclair] went out of the door at one stage and into the bathroom. I realized afterwards he was probably injecting himself with drugs. I saw a tin in his hand. He was later sitting in the lounge and started to nod off. I sat with the headphones on listening to music, to the

rock opera, *Tommy*. I heard the whole of it. God knows what time it was. I can't remember anything else until I woke up the next morning. He was still in the armchair and he was dead. On the floor was a piece of string with a tie attached to it . . . I know I must have killed him . . . I must have made up the piece of string that night. I don't know if he struggled. I would have thought it was quick . . . After I found him in the chair, I listened to LBC radio . . . I left him in the chair. [That] morning I was slightly late getting in to work. When I came home in the evening I examined him and rigor mortis had set in.

That is what he guardedly told the police after his arrest, and that is what was read out later in court. What Nilsen wrote about that night in an exercise-book *after* his trial paints a different, detailed and more terrible picture, indicating premeditation and what thrills and pleasures he derived from killing and then caressing a corpse.

I am sitting cross-legged on the carpet, drinking and listening to music. It finished with the theme from *Harry's Game*. I drain my glass and take the phones off. Behind me sits Stephen Sinclair on the lazy chair. He was crashed out with drink and drugs. I sit and look at him. I stand up and approach him. My heart is pounding. I kneel down in front of him. I touch his leg and say: 'Are you awake?' There is no response. 'Oh Stephen,' I think. 'Here I go again.' I get up and go slowly and casually through to the kitchen. I take some thick string from the drawer and put it on the stainless steel draining-board. 'Not long enough,' I think. I go to the cupboard in the front room and search inside. On the floor therein I find an old tie. I cut a bit off and throw the rest away. I go back to the kitchen and make up the ligature. I look into the back room and Stephen has not stirred. Bleep comes in and I speak to her and scratch her head. 'Leave me just now, Bleep. Get your head down. Everything's all right.' She wags her tail and slinks off into the front room. Her favourite place is on one of the armchairs in there, where she curls up. Looking back, I think she knew what was to happen. Even she became resigned to it. If there was a violent struggle, she would always become excited and start barking . . . I walked back into the room. I draped the ligature over one of his knees and poured myself another drink. My heart was pounding very fast. I sat on the edge of the bed and looked at Stephen. I thought to myself: 'All that potential, all that beauty, and all that pain that is his life. I have to stop him. It will soon be over' . . . I did not feel bad. I did not feel evil. I walked over to him. I removed the scarf. I picked up one of his wrists and let go. His limp arm flopped back onto his lap. I opened one of his eyes and there was no reflex. He was deeply unconscious. I took the ligature and put it around his neck. I knelt by the side of the chair and faced the wall. I took each loose end of the ligature and pulled it tight. He stopped breathing. His hands slowly reached for his neck as I held my grip. His legs stretched out in front of him. There was a very feeble struggle. Then his arms fell limp down in front of him.

I held him there for a couple of minutes. He was limp and stayed that way . . . I spoke to him: 'Stephen, that didn't hurt at all. Nothing can touch you now.' I ran my fingers through his bleached blond hair. His face looked peaceful. He was dead. The front of his jeans was wet with urine. I wondered if he had defecated as well. I got up and had a drink and a cigarette . . . I had to wash his soiled body. I ran a bath. I kept the water in it hand-warm and poured in some lemon washing-up liquid. I returned and began to undress him. I took off his leather jacket, jersey and T-shirt. Then his running shoes and socks. I had difficulty with his tight wet jeans. He still sat there, now naked, in the armchair. He had only urinated. He obviously had not had a square meal in a couple of days. I had not really known that his hair had been bleached until I stripped him. I discovered that he had ginger pubic hair. Otherwise his body was pale and hairless. He had crepe bandages on both forearms. I removed these to reveal deep, still open, recent razor cuts. He had very recently tried to commit suicide . . . I picked up his limp body in my arms and carried it into the bathroom. I put it into the half-filled bath. I washed the body. Putting my hands under his arms I turned him over and washed the back of his body. I pulled him out. He was very slippery with all that soap. I sat him on the loo and towelled the body and his hair as best as I could. I threw him over my shoulder and took him into the back room. I sat him on the white and blue dining-chair. I sat down, took a cigarette and a drink and looked at him. His head hung back, with his mouth slightly open. His eyes were not quite closed. 'Stephen,' I thought. 'You're another problem for me. What am I going to do with you? I've run out of room.' . . . I laid him on top of the double bed. It must have been well into the next morning of 27 January. I lay beside him and placed the large mirror at the end of the bed. I stripped my own tie, shirt and grey cords off, and lay there staring at both our naked bodies in the mirror. He looked paler than I did. Being ginger-haired, he would anyway. I put talcum powder on myself and lay down again. We looked similar now. I spoke to him as if he were still alive. I was telling him how lucky he was to be out of it all. I thought how beautiful he looked, and how beautiful I looked. He looked sexy, but I had no erection. He just looked fabulous . . . Soon I felt tired. I got in between the sheets, as I was starting to become cold. He still lay there beside me on top of the bedclothes. I knew he would become cold very soon, and I did not want to feel his coldness actually in bed with me. The coldness of a corpse has nothing endearing in it. Bleep came into the room and jumped up on the bed beside me. 'Come on, old girl. Get your head down. Stephen is all right now. He's okay.' She settled down at the end of the bed, stopping only to sniff once near Stephen's leg. She knew that the warm, friendly Stephen was no more, and ignored his body completely. I turned his head towards me and kissed him on the forehead. 'Goodnight, Stephen,' I said.*

* This and all the ensuing quotations from Nilsen's journals are reproduced by the special permission of Brian Masters, author of *Killing for Company*, who retains the copyright of these journals.

In a third account, written *before* the trial, in which the murder is not even mentioned, details vary: the body is dried on the edge of the bath, not on the loo; talcum powder is put on the corpse, not on Nilsen, who now has an erection. In this account, his tendency to sanctify horrific scenes is given rhapsodic expression: 'A great peace came over me. I felt that this was it, the meaning of life, death, everything. No fear, no pain, no guilt . . . No sex, just a feeling of oneness.'

The reality was probably even more gross. For Nilsen clearly exalted in the possession of the young man's completely helpless, naked body. He told a psychiatrist that he masturbated beside, or on, Stephen Sinclair's corpse. He probably did so more than once. What else he did with it over the next eight days we do not know, though Nilsen wrote: 'Afterwards, I dressed him in my clothes.' After what? And when? He told the police: 'I put the body in the cupboard.' But when was that?

The probability is that during the nights and the weekend following Sinclair's murder his body was taken out and used and abused as Nilsen wished – until it was rendered obnoxious by decomposition and became offensive as a plaything. Now it had to be destroyed, although its parts would be kept, as were those of his two other broken and rotting male toys, crammed in black plastic bags.

Although Nilsen was apparently outspoken about his murders, and unusually so, his memory was very selective, and erratic, and very little could be verified about what he said. He probably hid much more than he revealed, as had been his habit for much of his life. For years he had lied to his family and friends, and to himself, about himself and his homosexuality (he told the police he was bisexual), and acquaintances were told things about his past life which were not true. He was inured to deceive others, and especially his victims and himself. He also, as with other murderers and most of humanity, wished people to think well of him, to be socially acceptable, despite what he had done. At the same time, he needed people to know just how unique, how special he was, how different from the rest – but not that he was a necrophiliac, indulging in vile and unnatural deeds.

He was not ashamed, however, to tell the police about his dismemberment and disposal of the bodies. After all, this showed some expertise, as well as enterprise and resolve. As a former Army cook he was used to chopping, carving and gutting meat, and when dealing with humans, was unconcerned by any concept of desecration or violation. 'I can never understand a traditional and largely superstitious fear of the dead and corpses,' he wrote. Killing, he thought, was a much more dreadful act than cutting up a corpse. That was merely distasteful and hard work. He wrote: 'The victim is the dirty platter after the feast, and the washing-up is a clinically ordinary task.'

He told the police:

> 'On Friday night [eight days after Sinclair was killed] I thought I might as well start doing what I had to do . . . I took a plastic bag and sliced it into a sheet. I put it in the middle part of the front room and took the body from the cupboard and laid it on the plastic sheet, face up, and got

> the long kitchen knife with the brown handle and sharpened it with the sharpener. I cut the head off and got the pot out of the bathroom. There was a fair amount of blood, and some of it spilled out on to the carpet. I put the head in the pot and filled it with water. I put the lid on, lit the stove, and lit the front and rear burners and one at the side. I thought – I've got the whole weekend – and got fed up. I thought I'd go and get a bottle. Then I moved the body on to another sheet, which I laid beside the original one because there was a sizeable pool of blood on the first sheet. I tried to pick up the sheet and moved through the door, and a big drop of blood splashed on to the white carpet by the bathroom door. I got a couple of paper kitchen towels and tried to soak it up. But it had soaked right into the carpet. When the head was coming to the boil, I turned the gas down to simmer, and I said: 'Come on, dog.'

He took Bleep on a lead to a supermarket in Muswell Hill Broadway, where he bought some Marlboro cigarettes, a bottle of Bacardi and some Coca-Cola. Back in the attic flat, Nilsen listened to music on his headphones and watched TV, while Sinclair's head continued to simmer in the pot. He drank most of the bottle of rum, diluted with Coke, and then went to bed, having switched off the gaslights on the stove. Overnight the head cooled in the pot and the headless corpse lay in the front room, the windows open wide.

'I did not get up until 11.00 am on the Saturday,' Nilsen said. 'The place was looking untidy, and I thought I would clean it up. I took the dog out. There was a note on my banisters – *The plumber has been. Don't flush the loo.* On the way back I saw one of the girls. She asked me if I had got the note.'

This was a barmaid, Fiona Bridges, who lived with her boyfriend, Jim Allcock, on the ground floor. They, and the two girls who shared another ground-floor room (the first-floor rooms were empty), had been inconvenienced since Thursday, 3 February, by toilets which would not flush. At this time there was a water-workers' strike in England: many areas were without any water; stand-pipes for public supplies were in use; and mains pipes had burst. The cold spell made it worse. On the Friday, Jim had contacted a plumber and Fiona had asked Nilsen, when he returned that evening from the Jobcentre at Kentish Town, if there was anything wrong with his toilet. He replied in the negative and proceeded upstairs, where a few hours later he cut off Sinclair's head. The plumber arrived on Saturday morning, while Nilsen was still in bed. But his efforts failed to solve the problem and the landlord agreed to call in Dyno-rod – but not until the Monday. Allcock left a note for Nilsen, whom the other tenants knew as Des, and Fiona explained the situation to him when he left the house to take his dog for a walk. 'I began to realise that it could be something to do with my activities,' he told the police.

His activities, apart from the stench they caused in his flat (which, however, he was used to), had alarmed him earlier that afternoon, when a friend, Martyn Hunter-Craig, visited him unexpectedly and knocked on his door. According to Nilsen, he silenced the TV and his dog, and said nothing.

According to Hunter-Craig, Des shouted something like: 'You can't come in! I'm tied up with someone.'

Though advised about the visit on Monday of the Dyno-rod man, who might require to examine the bathroom in the attic flat, Nilsen did nothing about the severed body of Stephen Sinclair, nor anything about the other remains, until the Sunday. He might have removed the stinking contents of the tea-chest and the wardrobe later that night and dumped them elsewhere, in Highgate Wood, or in any of the other woods, parks and playing-fields that lay within half a mile of Cranley Gardens. Instead he stayed in and watched TV, with the headless, naked corpse on the front-room floor. When he took some action, it was only to hide Sinclair's body and head. 'I anticipated that on Monday somebody in authority might be coming round to ask questions. I got the knife out again, I sharpened it, and I dismembered the body.'

This operation occurred on Sunday afternoon. He cut the body in half at the waist, and then separated the two arms from the torso. All the various sections, including the parboiled head, were stuffed into two black plastic sacks and put in the bigger wardrobe – apart from Sinclair's packaged lower half, which was jammed into the wall-space at the foot of the bath. To do so, Nilsen first had to move another black sack containing other remains – those of Graham Allen, slaughtered five months before – and transfer them to the wardrobe. This done, he put a deodorant block on top of one of the bags and locked the wardrobe's doors. Another deodorant stick already stood on a table in the bathroom. On Monday morning, 7 February, Nilsen set off as usual for his place of work.

He was short-tempered at work that Monday, excusing himself by saying he was under great pressure. When he returned to Cranley Gardens he was probably relieved to learn that no one from Dyno-rod had called. Again he did nothing about disposing of the remains of three young men in his flat, and on Tuesday morning he again went to work.

Dyno-rod, in the person of 30-year-old Mike Cattran, turned up at 23 Cranley Gardens at 6.15 pm on Tuesday, 8 February. Accompanied by Jim Allcock, who held a torch, Cattran investigated the manhole by the side of the house that led to a sewer and into which the waste from the household drained. A nauseating, cloying stench assailed them as the manhole cover was raised. Using the iron rungs in the manhole wall, Cattran climbed down the 12-foot shaft, until he stood at its base, where his torch spotlighted the soggy pile of over 30 pieces of grey, rotting flesh on which he now stood. He moved and another piece flopped out of the exit-pipe from the house.

He told reporters later: 'I was formerly a lifeguard in Cornwall, and I'm well aware of what decomposing flesh is like . . . It wasn't a carcass, but bits of chopped-up flesh. Enough to fill two four-gallon buckets.'

He told the *Daily Mirror*:

> When I got down there I couldn't believe it. I pulled out lumps of flesh the size of my fist, and strips of flesh that looked as though they'd been cut from an arm. After a few minutes I came up for a rest and to get some fresh air. Then I went down again with a plunger. As I pushed it down

> towards the mains, the whole lot moved and my bottle went. There was a bit with hair on it . . . I was trying to think what sort of animal it could be . . . Eventually I got to thinking that it had to be a body.

Saying nothing of his fearful thoughts to the tenants, Cattran went inside the house and asked them if any of them had flushed meat from a freezer or dog-meat down their toilets. Nilsen said he had a dog, but fed it on tinned meat. He expressed his concern about the situation and left the house with Cattran to examine the shaft and its contents for himself. As Cattran shone his torch down the shaft on the pale porridge of flesh, Nilsen questioned him about how the drain would be cleared (with a machine), and when. 'Tomorrow morning,' said Cattran, and at 7.00 pm he telephoned his boss, who was at home, about his difficulty, using a pay-phone on the first-floor landing of the house. Then he left.

Nilsen went back upstairs and wrote a letter to the landlord, complaining about standards of maintenance, about the state of the roof, the poor lighting on the stairs, and the drains. He wrote: 'When I flush my toilet the lavatory pans in the lower flats overflow (since Friday 4 Feb 83). Obviously the drains are blocked and unpleasant odours permeate the building.' Alone with his corpses, with Bleep by his side and a rum and coke in his hand, he then wrote a poem and considered what to do.

He thought of replacing the pieces of flesh in the manhole with pieces of chicken. He thought of running away, of suicide. But he felt he had to face up to what he had done, and that what he had done should be known – 'Someone's got to know the truth about what happened to them.' He wrote later: 'I could not guarantee that another death would not occur at some future time. I was sickened by the past, the present, and a doubtful future . . . I thought of dumping the remains left in my flat, but decided to leave everything where it was.'

None the less, after midnight, he went downstairs with a torch and a large plastic carrier bag. He entered the manhole, climbed down the shaft and put all the pieces of flesh he could find in the bag, which he dumped over the back garden hedge. As he re-entered the house, with his sleeves rolled up, he encountered Jim Allcock, who had been shaken awake by a frightened Fiona and urged to investigate the sounds and movement near their bedroom window. 'There's somebody having a go at the manhole,' she had whispered. 'I bet it's him upstairs.' Nilsen looked at Allcock. 'Just went out to have a pee,' he explained, and went back up to his flat.

On the cold and frosty morning of Wednesday, 9 February, about 8.30, Nilsen and Allcock went separately to work. Nilsen was wearing Sinclair's blue and white football scarf. At 9.15 Cattran returned to No. 23 with his boss, Gary Wheeler. Cattran saw that the oblong manhole cover behind the wooden passageway gate had been moved. He lifted the cover, shone his torch down the shaft. 'It's all gone!' he cried. He scrambled inside, and poking about with his hands, retrieved a pallid chunk of flesh from inside one of the drains. Then he discovered four small bones. He laid his finds on the rough path by Wheeler's feet. The two men were joined by a nervous Fiona

Bridges, clutching her dressing-gown about her. She told them what she and Allcock had seen and heard that night. Wheeler made up his mind. He told her: 'Call the police!'

DCI Peter Jay, the tall chief of Hornsey police station's CID, arrived at Cranley Gardens at 11.00 am. The flesh and bones were taken in a plastic bag to the Hornsey Mortuary and thence to Charing Cross Hospital, where they were examined that afternoon by a pathologist, Professor Bowen. He pronounced the flesh to be human, and that the bones came from a man's hand. DCI Jay headed back to Cranley Gardens at about 4.30, with DI Steve McCusker and DC Jeff Butler, to await Nilsen's return.

At work, Nilsen tidied up his desk and left a note in a desk drawer, saying that if he was arrested the police were not to be believed should they claim he committed suicide in his cell. He told an assistant: 'If I'm not in tomorrow, I'll be either ill, dead or in jail.' About 5.15 he left the Jobcentre in Kentish Town (since closed) and, wearing Sinclair's scarf, set off home by Tube. He wrote later:

> I was sure I would be arrested when I came home, or sometime that evening . . . I was totally resigned to this inevitability. I was worried about what was going to happen to Bleep . . . My heart began to beat very fast as I walked down Cranley Gardens. I approached the house and knew instinctively that something was out of place, ie, that nothing seemed out of place. The house was almost in total darkness. I opened the front door and stepped into the dark hallway. On my left the front room door opened and I could see three large men in plain clothes. That's it! My mind began to race in all directions . . .

'Mr Nilsen?' Jay enquired. 'Yes,' replied Nilsen, and Jay said, after introducing himself: 'I've come about your drains.' 'Why should my drains be of interest to the police?' demanded Nilsen and asked if the other two were health inspectors. Jay said they were police officers and provided their ranks and names. All four then ascended the stairs to the attic flat. Nilsen led them into the back room. Jay said: 'This morning, Mr Nilsen, we found a piece of flesh in your drains. It's been identified as part of a human body.' 'Good grief!' said Nilsen. 'How awful!' 'Don't mess about,' warned Jay. 'Where's the rest of it?' 'In two plastic bags in the wardrobe next door. I'll show you.' They all moved into the front room overlooking the street. The smell made the policemen grimace. 'In there,' said Nilsen, indicating the larger wardrobe and offering his keys. Taking them, Jay said he would open the wardrobe later. 'Is there anything else?' he asked. 'It's a long story,' said Nilsen and suggested that he would tell them everything at the police station, not in his flat. Whereupon he was formally cautioned and arrested on suspicion of murder, although the police had no idea of the victim's identity – or that more than one body was involved.

DC Butler was left to guard the flat, while DCI Jay and DI McCusker took Nilsen to Hornsey police station by car. Nilsen sat in the back with McCusker, who enquired as they left Cranley Gardens: 'Are we talking about one body or two?' Nilsen, looking straight ahead, replied: 'Fifteen or sixteen. Since 1978.'

The two policemen were stunned into silence until they reached the police station in Hornsey Road. There Jay, still incredulous, asked: 'Are you telling us that since 1978 you've killed 16 people?' 'Yes,' replied Nilsen, without any sign of emotion. 'Three at Cranley Gardens, and about 13 at my previous address, 195 Melrose Avenue, Cricklewood.' He wrote later: 'That was the end of the beginning, and the end of the killing . . . It was all out.' It was also 'the day help arrived'.

But it would take 30 hours, in interviews spread over the next ten days, before Nilsen finished telling his story. In the meantime, DCS Geoff Chambers, head of Y District CID, took charge of the case.

That night the two plastic sacks in the wardrobe were removed and examined by Professor Bowen. They were stuffed with smaller shopping-bags, which contained the three upper sections, innards and the almost featureless and hairless head of Stephen Sinclair, as well as another boiled head, and a gutted male torso with arms but no hands or legs. These were some of the parts of Graham Allen, killed five months ago. The sack containing Sinclair's lower half was retrieved the following day, Thursday, as was the tea-chest in which, under a velvet curtain, sheets, newspapers, air fresheners and mothballs, were the remnants, bones and skull of John Howlett, killed in March the previous year. Bleep was taken to Battersea Dogs' Home (she died in March) and that evening it began to snow.

On Friday, 11 February, the five severed sections of Stephen Sinclair were assembled on the mortuary floor, and when Nilsen supplied the police with the victim's name, they were able to confirm his identity from his fingerprints, which were in police records. Later that day, Nilsen accompanied DCS Chambers and DCI Jay to Melrose Avenue, and indicated where the police might discover the burnt remains of 12 or 13 other men whose bodies had been consumed in bonfires at the rear of the house over the past three years. In some cases he remembered very little about his victims, and eight, in fact, would never be identified or named. Seven other young men, he said, had for varying reasons escaped his murderous assaults.

That evening, at 5.40 pm, Dennis Nilsen was charged with the murder of Stephen Sinclair, and the following morning he appeared at Highgate magistrates' court.

Since Thursday, newspaper reporters had been rabid in pursuit of stories and facts, flocking to both scenes of the crimes and harrying anyone who might have something to say. On the Friday morning, front-page headlines proclaimed: 17 BODIES IN MURDER HORROR *(Daily Mirror)* – SIXTEEN MURDERS *(Daily Express)* – MASS MURDER INQUIRY STARTS *(The Times)*. Later headlines declaimed: HOUSE OF HORROR – HOUSE OF DEATH.

Neighbours at Cranley Gardens were questioned about No. 23. Mrs Peggy Macpherson, 68, said: 'None of the people who lived there seemed to stay very long.' 'Down-and-outs and tramps often visited the house,' another neighbour divulged. 'It was impossible to say who lived there and who was just staying overnight.' A third neighbour added: 'There were lots of parties there . . . Squatters who lived in the middle-floor flat used to have the parties . . . Mainly loud music and getting stoned.' Some had complained about dogs and foul smells emanating the previous summer from the drains.

About 60 reporters, spectators and TV crewmen gathered outside 195 Melrose Avenue, where a squad of policemen in green boiler suits arrived on Friday to pull apart the ground-floor flat and sift through every inch of the rear garden and wasteland. A large blue plastic tent was erected to conceal operations and protect the searchers from the snow. But two young builders, who had been completing the restoration of the flats within the house, were seized on by the press.

Mark Tekinalp, 22, said: 'We've been working on the house since last year, when it was damaged by fire. We've just discovered from the police there was a body stowed under the floorboards in the back room. Apparently it was removed later and buried in the garden along with other bodies. We used to eat out in the garden during the summer. We were apparently sitting on corpses.'

Two of the renovated flats had been sold, but not yet occupied. Diana Keating, aged 27, had bought the ground-floor flat, formerly Nilsen's, for £31,000. She said: 'I just can't believe it's happened. Believe it or not, I had wanted a flat with a garden. I didn't sense anything wrong at all, and I've visited the flat many times. I don't know when I'll be going to the flat again.'

Nilsen's family and schoolfriends in Scotland were sought out. His mother, Mrs Betty Scott (she had remarried), said: 'This has come as a great shock. I've not seen my son for about ten years.' Weeping, she fetched photographs of Dennis and trustingly gave them to a reporter. His older brother, Olav, in Fraserburgh, said: 'I've not seen my brother for about nine years. We had a silly family row.'

Much about Nilsen's background was unearthed by the press. But within a week, any revelations that might prejudice the trial were muzzled by the Attorney-General and the DPP (Director of Public Prosecutions). Nilsen himself could not stop talking. Once a lonely man, with low self-esteem, he was now the awful focus of everyone's attention. He talked at length to everyone he met. He wrote wordy and pretentious letters to all and sundry, explaining, excusing, accusing, complaining. Politics was his chief topic after himself. In Brixton Prison he began filling exercise-books with his partial, consciously literary remembrances and thoughts – writing, as he wrote his letters, from edge to edge of every page. Sometimes he wrote and spoke with wit and a certain graveyard humour. But a police officer, when asked why Nilsen had no friends, replied: 'Because he's a fucking bore.'

None the less, Nilsen's ready co-operation was required if his victims were ever to be traced, his story confirmed, and a strong case against him sustained. So his interviewers, Chambers and Jay, were chatty and matter-of-fact, communing with Des over cups of coffee, tea and packets of cigarettes, and letting him lapse into monologues without interrupting him too much. But the more he said, the less, it seemed, they were able to understand. They found out about the who, and where, and when – but not the reasons *why*.

Nilsen himself said: 'I've killed people. But I can't understand why those people. There's no common factor.' Chambers stated: 'I think you went out looking for these people with the express intention of luring them back to your flat, plying them with drink, and then killing them.' To which Nilsen replied: 'I do go out in search of company. When I voluntarily go out to drink I don't have the intention at that time to do these things. Things may happen afterwards drinkwise. But they're not foreplanned . . . I seek company first, and hope everything will be all right.' He wrote later:

> In none of these cases am I conscious of feeling any hate towards any of the victims . . . I remember going out to seek company and companionship, which perhaps would lead to a personal sexual and social relationship being established . . . I would invite some people back with me, others would invite themselves. Sex was always a secondary consideration. I wanted a warm relationship and someone to talk to . . . Because of the effects of drinking, sex would (or would not) happen the next morning . . . I would never plan to kill anyone . . . I would be a bit dazed, shocked and shaking all over afterwards . . . I suppose I could lie and say they refused to have sex and I killed them. No, that's not true . . . The only similarity was a need not to be alone . . . They were not all homeless tramps, etc. Not all young, homeless men who came to my flat were attacked or killed. Not all were homosexual or bisexual. The reason that some were homosexual was mainly because they would come to the pubs which I frequented. I was approached marginally more often by those liaisons than I approached them . . . I sometimes imagine that I may have felt that I applied a relieving pressure on a life as a benevolent act, in that the subjects were ultimately free from life's pain.

His first solicitor, Ronald Moss, after listening to the detailed catalogue of horrific acts that Nilsen outlined to the police, asked: 'Why?' Nilsen answered: 'I'm hoping you'll tell me that.'

Dennis Andrew Nilsen was born in the north-east of Scotland, in Fraserburgh, a fishing town, on 23 November 1945. His mother, Betty, was the pretty daughter of a fisherman, Andrew Whyte. She had married a Norwegian soldier, Olav Magnus Nilsen, in May 1942. He came to Scotland after the Germans invaded Norway in 1940 and was one of the thousands of servicemen quartered in the district to repel an imagined German invasion of Britain. The marriage was a mistake, although it produced three children, two boys and a girl. The Nilsens never had a home of their own. Betty Nilsen continued to live with her parents, sharing a room with little Olav, Dennis and Sylvia, in the Whytes' cold flat at 47 Academy Road, where drinking, smoking, cinema-going and even the radio were frowned upon; every Sunday everyone went to church. Olav Nilsen was an increasingly infrequent visitor. After the war he drifted away and the couple were divorced in 1948. Dennis was very attached to his grandfather, who died of a heart attack at sea in October 1951 when he was 62; Dennis was almost six. The sight of his grandfather in a coffin was traumatic, according to Nilsen. He wrote later: 'My troubles started here. [His death] blighted my personality permanently. I have spent all my emotional life searching for my grandfather . . . He took the real me with him under the ground.'

Other traumatic events were the drowning of a friend of his brother and, when he was about eight, his own alleged near-drowning (he walked into the sea) and rescue by an older boy, who then masturbated over his unconscious, naked body on the beach. Then when he was nine, the pigeons he kept in fish-boxes on an air-raid shelter were strangled by another small boy. Later, he and a school friend found the body of an old man who had drowned in a river. All these events, Nilsen would later infer, caused him to have an unusual preoccupation with dead bodies and confuse images of death and love.

The young Dennis was kind to animals, caring for any stray dogs and fledglings he found. He had a pet rabbit of his own, Snowy, but one winter it died. Wild rabbits infected by myxomatosis horrified him. To put them out of their misery he killed them himself. As a child he was quiet, shy, introverted, sensitive, secretive, brooding and solitary, tending to wander off on his own.

He became difficult when his mother, after a divorce was obtained, married a builder, Adam Scott. In time they had four children, three boys and a girl. Dennis was bitterly resentful, and he came to the attention of the local police more than once for minor misdemeanours. But in 1955, when he was ten, the family moved seven miles inland to the village of Strichen, to 16 Baird Road, and the discipline of Strichen School helped to sort him out, as well as the rigours of an early morning paper-round. A skinny boy, he was hospitalised with pneumonia and pleurisy when he was eleven or twelve.

It was through an uncle that he acquired interests in argumentative and radical socialism, in classical music and in the making of amateur films. His best subjects at school, where he was an above-average pupil, attentive, hard-working and neat, were art and English; he had little interest in team games or sport. At school he concealed his silent adoration for a younger boy, Adrian, a minister's son, and for a boy pictured in a French book, Pierre Duval. But his actual sexual experience by the time he left school, aged 15, was nil, although he once explored the body of his brother, with whom he shared a bed at home, while Olav was asleep.

Having joined the local Army Cadet Force when he was 14 (he liked the uniform and the acceptable, conformist image it gave him – 'I felt proud and useful'), he enlisted in the Army in August 1961, intending to train as a chef. In September he took an overnight express from Aberdeen to King's Cross Station in London and then made his way to Aldershot.

His next three years as a boy soldier were 'the happiest of my life'. In September 1964 he completed his training and catering courses and joined the ACC (Army Catering Corps). He was posted to Osnabrück in Germany. On leave in Scotland before he went overseas, he was driving a scooter in the rain when he skidded and crashed. He banged his head – but was otherwise uninjured, though bruised. Similar accidental head injuries were also sustained early in their lives by other multiple murderers, like Christie and Haigh. Perhaps there is some connection. Certainly, Nilsen then began the heavy drinking that marked the next 18 years.

From Germany, he went to Norway and then to Aden in 1967, when he was 21. He was attached to the military staff at a prison where terrorists were detained. In June he was posted as a L/Cpl. to Sharjah on the Persian Gulf, where he had his own room and achieved his first sexual experiences, with an Arab boy. He also began admiring his own body, naked, reflected in a mirror by his bed. 'The image in the mirror becomes your only friend and true lover,' he later wrote. In January 1968 he was attached to the Argyll and Sutherland Highlanders, catering for them in Plymouth, then in Cyprus and in Berlin, where he had a series of one-night encounters with male civilians, as well as one session with a female prostitute. Esteemed for his talents as a chef and his capacity for drink, he had several mates, who thought he was eccentric, a bit moody and a bit of an oddball, a loner, rather than 'queer'. Because of his initials, he was known as Dan. Now Corporal Nilsen, he went with the Argylls in 1970 to Fort George near Inverness, and in August he cooked for the Queen's Royal Guard at Ballater, near Balmoral. He spent most of his leave periods in Strichen, parading his uniform, visiting friends and the scenes of his childhood, reading and writing poetry, and devising culinary treats for his half-brothers and sister. He showed an interest in a local girl and sent off a computer-dating questionnaire. But, as his married brother Olav remarked after Dennis's arrest: 'He would have been bored back home. Strichen is no place for a poof on holiday.'

In January 1971, when Nilsen was 25, he was posted to a Signals Squadron in the Shetland Islands. Here he took part in Scottish country-dancing at socials and bought a cine-camera to record the scenery and local life. Here he also fell hopelessly in love with an 18-year-old soldier in the summer of 1972. Nothing sexual apparently occurred. But the intensity of Nilsen's feelings confused the youth and he began to distance himself, causing Nilsen much distress. Nilsen wrote later: 'I knew I was leaving the Army in a few weeks, and would probably not see him again. Every kind of deep emotional pain in those last weeks sorely afflicted me. I wished I were dead.' Before he left the Shetlands he burned all the films he had made, some of which featured the young soldier, and in which he was encouraged by Nilsen to pose as if he were dead or asleep.

After serving for eleven years in the Army, Nilsen left in November 1972. He returned to Strichen, wondering what to do next; he was now 27. There was a bitter row with Olav, after which they never spoke again, and having considered other uniformed, institutionalised careers, as a prison officer or a policeman, he opted for the latter.

In December he joined the Metropolitan Police in London, and after 16 weeks' training at Hendon, he was sent, as PC Q287, to Willesden Green police station – half a mile from Melrose Avenue where, six years later, he committed his first murder and where he would kill a total of 12 young men.

Although he worked hard and well, making several arrests and appearing in court, his left-wing opinions made him uncomfortable with the authoritarian attitudes of the police, and he missed the more relaxed camaraderie of the Army. After duty he frequently found himself on his own, isolated because of his secret homosexuality and consequent indifference to most of his colleagues' diversions. He began frequenting pubs where homosexuals were known to meet. In 1973, while still at Hendon, he had sex with a man he met at The Coleherne in Earls Court. In August, in the Section House where he and other unmarried policemen lived, he had sex with a younger man met in the King William IV. They had anal sex – the only time, according to Nilsen, this ever occurred. He wished to make this relationship more permanent. But the young man, the son of a former colonel, was more interested in sleeping around.

The pressures of his double life and dissenting views caused him to resign from the police after a year, in December 1973. He remained in London, working as a security guard and lodging in a room in Manstone Road, off Cricklewood Broadway. Then in May 1974 he began working for the Department of Employment at the Jobcentre in Denmark Street, off Charing Cross Road. He was there for eight years, interviewing the unemployed and advising them about jobs. Eventually, he became involved with the civil-service union, the CPSA, becoming the branch secretary at his place of work. Over-zealous and outspoken, he attended every union meeting, conference and anti-government demonstration, upsetting his employers and even some of his comrades by his aggressive, barrack-room style. One of his colleagues called him Des, and from then on that was what he called himself.

When not at work he increasingly visited London's gay pubs, picking up young men and boys and taking them home to his new lodging, a room at 80 Teignmouth Road, not far from Melrose Avenue. But this way of life depressed him. He wrote later: 'Anonymous sex only deepens one's sense of loneliness and solves nothing. Promiscuity is a disease.' He also wrote: 'My most fulfilling sexual feasts were savoured with the image of myself in the mirror.' None the less, disapproving and prudish though he was, he continued to search for some loving companion or friend in such pubs as The Coleherne, the King William IV, The Salisbury in St Martin's Lane, the Golden Lion in Soho, the Black Cap in Camden, and The Champion in Bayswater Road.

One 17-year-old, who had called at the Jobcentre, was invited back to Teignmouth Road. Frightened by some act or remark or look of Nilsen, he panicked, causing a scene and cutting himself on some glass. An ambulance and the police were called, and Nilsen was questioned at Willesden Green police station, where he had served for a year in 1973. No charges were brought.

Nilsen was 30 in November 1975, the month in which he met David Gallichan, aged 20, outside The Champion. Gallichan was short, fair-haired, wore ear-rings, was unemployed and rather camp. He went back to Teignmouth Road with Nilsen, stayed the night and was easily persuaded by Nilsen, desperate for some permanent relationship, to move in with him. He stayed for a year and a half. Before Christmas, Nilsen rented a rear ground-floor flat for them both at 195 Melrose Avenue, not far from Teignmouth Road.

He was able to afford the additional expense and the cost of furnishings as his father, after marrying three more times and dying in Ghana, had left him a legacy of £1,000. At the same time Nilsen learned that the real name of his father, whom he had never known, was Moksheim – as should have been his own.

Gallichan, whom Nilsen called Twinkle, came from Weston-super-Mare in Somerset. He was a passive person, seemingly content to be kept, to do the decorating, the domestic chores and tend the back garden, which Nilsen had commandeered for their exclusive use. A high fence was put around it, a plastic fish-pond and path installed, and trees and shrubs, as well as vegetables, were planted. A puppy bought in a pet-shop, which Nilsen called Bleep, and a stray kitten, called Dee-Dee, enhanced the domestic scene, as did reproductions of paintings by Canaletto which hung on the walls. They had separate beds, and sex was sporadic. But they went out to pubs and bars together and Nilsen did his best to keep Twinkle amused, by telling him jokes and playing pranks. Most evenings they stayed in.

> We got as close as anyone could [said Gallichan later]. He was like a teacher to me. He would correct me if I said something wrong or mispronounced a word . . . But he wasn't domineering. I had my life and he had his. He wouldn't go out often, and he never celebrated anything special, apart from Christmas. You could forget birthdays. He never got any cards . . . He never lost control when I was with him. He liked keg beer and whisky and bacardi and vodka. But he didn't drink to excess . . . He had some regrets about leaving the Army, wondering whether he should have signed up for a second term . . . He was neat and tidy in appearance. He mostly wore a tie and always polished his shoes, and took great care of personal hygiene. He had a bath in the morning and a shower in the evening when he came home, and then would have a bath before he went to bed.

In April 1976, Nilsen had a gallstone operation, and at Christmas he boldly took Twinkle to his office party in Denmark Street. But the association was becoming strained. Gallichan, who now had a job in a station buffet, began drifting back to gay bars, oppressed by the older man's autocratic manner and by London itself. Both began bringing different partners back to the flat. According to Nilsen, he once brought a Swiss girl home and they had sex.

Twinkle moved out in the summer of 1977. He said later:

> I told Dennis I was moving out . . . It was the only time I saw a different side of him. He was cold and dismissive. It was as though I had insulted him . . . He said: 'I want you to move out as soon as possible' . . . About six months after I'd moved out, I had drinks with him. He was a lot quieter. There was someone there at the flat at the time. I asked him if he wanted my address, but he said: 'No.' I was a little bit hurt.

Twinkle's new protector, with whom he went to live, was an antique-dealer in Somerset.

Nilsen, rejected, filled his empty days with work and his nights with music, drink and casual sex. He drank for hours on his own, listening to pop and classical music on his headphones. The beds, converted into a raised, double platform-bed, were occupied by occasional pick-ups, one of whom, Steve Martin, moved in for about four months. There were others. But sooner or later, they all walked out on him. On his own, Nilsen's masturbatory fantasies involving his mirror-image and death increased. Once, while three strangers slept, he filled the room with smoke. Their asphyxiation seems to have been Nilsen's intention, for he left the room. When they awoke in some alarm, he made some excuse.

Paul Dermody stayed with Nilsen for two weeks in November 1978. 'He talked at me, not to me,' said Dermody. Soon after he left, the killings began.

Towards the end of 1978, Nilsen's feelings of demoralisation and despair had reached their peak: he had achieved nothing of any importance at work and had no meaningful relationships with anyone – no one on whom to call if in need of help. He felt lonely, unloved, unwanted and no one would care if he died. He spent Christmas alone in his flat with Bleep, drowning his desolation in immoderate drinking, listening to music and watching TV.

On 30 December, full of self-pity and loathing, he forced himself to leave the flat and seek some company in an Irish pub in Cricklewood Broadway, the Cricklewood Arms. After downing several pints of draught Guinness, he began conversing with an Irish lad, aged about 17. 'That night,' he wrote later, 'things began to go terribly and horribly wrong.' He told the police:

> He was much shorter than I was. About 5 feet 6 inches. He was southern Irish and had short, dark brown curly hair. His hands were rough. At closing time he indicated to me that he had too far to travel. We went back to Melrose Avenue and we started drinking. We had a damn good old drink, and later on I remember thinking: 'He'll probably be going soon – another ship passing in the night.' The next morning I had a corpse on my hands. He was dead. I believed I had killed him. Strangled him. I got the impression that he wanted to go and I wanted him to stay. I wanted company over the New Year. There was a desperation for company. My tie was around his neck. I think I started off with about 15 ties.

Nilsen, writing after his trial, revealed much more about what happened that night and thereafter. He and the Irish boy had eventually undressed and passed out in the double bed. Nothing sexual occurred. Nilsen was the first to wake, at dawn that New Year's Eve. He wrote:

> The fire had been on all night, so it was quite warm. I snuggled up to him and put my arm around him. He was still fast asleep . . . I ran my hand over him, exploring him. I remember thinking because it was morning he would wake and leave me. I became extremely aroused and I could feel my heart pounding and I began to sweat. He was still sound asleep. I looked down on the floor where our clothes lay and my eyes fixed on my

> tie. I remember thinking that I wanted him to stay with me over the New Year, whether he wanted to or not. I reached out and got the neck-tie. I raised myself and slipped it on under his neck. I quickly straddled him and pulled tight for all I was worth. His body came alive immediately. We struggled off the bed on to the floor.

With Nilsen on top of him, the Irish boy tried to push himself away, using his feet and knocking over a coffee table, until he backed against a wall. After half a minute his struggling diminished and his arms flopped on to the floor. Trembling, exhausted, Nilsen staggered to his feet. But the boy was not dead. Unconscious, he began breathing in harsh gasps. Nilsen, panicking, filled a plastic bucket with water in the kitchen. He seized the naked boy, draped him face-down over a dining-room chair, raised his head by the hair and then pushed it into the bucket, which overflowed. There was no resistance this time. After two or three minutes the bubbles in the water ceased to rise.

Nilsen picked up the body and deposited it in an armchair. He sat down himself and recovered some of his composure, staring at his now permanent guest and reviewing what he had done and what he would do. He made himself a cup of coffee, smoked several cigarettes and removed the tie from the corpse. He then tidied the room and let Bleep in from the garden. She sniffed at the dead boy's legs. Nilsen dragged her aside and told her to keep out of the way. He decided to give the body a bath. Picking it up over his right shoulder he carried it into the bathroom, washed it thoroughly in washing-up liquid, and having dried it while floppily propped up on the loo, he carried it back to the bed, where he examined and stroked the still-warm, loose-limbed corpse. Then he covered it with the bedclothes, so that the boy seemed as if he were asleep. For a while Nilsen sat and looked at him and thought. Then he dressed and went for a walk. People had seen them together in the pub and then leave together. He expected the police would call. But when he returned to his flat he felt hungover and very tired and wanted to sleep. After dressing the boy in clean Y-fronts, vest and socks from his wardrobe, Nilsen had a bath and went to bed, where he embraced the boy, and removed his pants, caressing him as and where he wished. Sexually aroused, he attempted to penetrate the corpse. But his erection subsided: the body was cooling. He laid the dead youth on the floor, covered him with a piece of curtain, lay down in his bed and fell asleep. He slept all day. Waking that evening, he fed Bleep and the cat, made himself a meal and watched TV, with the curtained corpse on the floor. Deciding now to hide the body in case anyone called, he took up some of the living-room floorboards and tried to push the body underneath. But it had stiffened and was intractable. So Nilsen propped it against a wall: he had read somewhere that rigor mortis was temporary. The corpse stood there all night as Nilsen slept. The following morning, New Year's Day, he succeeded in laying the body in the freezing space under the floorboards, after carefully loosening its limbs and once again closely inspecting and touching every part of the corpse, from head to toe. The cat slipped under the floor and it took ten minutes to coax her out.

Nilsen then ripped up the dead boy's clothes and threw them into a dustbin. A week went by and meanwhile Nilsen went back to work. Then curiosity as much as desire prompted him to play once more with his guest. Nilsen wrote:

> I disinterred him, and pulled the dirt-stained youth up onto the floor. His skin was very dirty. I stripped myself naked and carried him into the bathroom and washed the body. There was practically no discoloration and he was pale white. His limbs were more limp and relaxed than when I had put him down. I got him out of the bath and washed myself clean in the water. I carried the still wet youth into the room and laid him on the carpet. Under the orange side-lights his body aroused me sexually. I knelt over him and masturbated onto his bare stomach. Before I went to bed, I suspended him by the ankles from the high wooden platform. He hung there all night, his fingers just touching the carpet. The next day, while he was still hanging there upside-down, I stood beside him and masturbated again. I wiped him and took him down. I laid him on the kitchen floor and decided to cut him up. But I just couldn't do anything to spoil that marvellous body.

He encased the body in plastic bags and replaced it under the floorboards, where it remained for nearly eight months, until it began to smell too much. The corpse of the teenage Irish boy was burnt in the back garden on 11 August 1979.

Nilsen told the police: 'I did not dismember his body. When I took it up it was remarkable. There was very little decomposition . . . I had built a bonfire the day before. I burnt him at the bottom of the garden about three feet from the fence. It was a relief to be rid of the body. Burnt meat smells. But I had made sure to burn rubber on the fire – it cancelled out the smell.'

Afterwards, he pulverised the bones and raked them into the ground. He would build two more bonfires and kill eleven other boys and young men in 195 Melrose Avenue before he left the house in October 1981. But for nearly a year, he refrained from killing any of his visitors and from having sex with any of them (according to him), although on 13 October 1979, a small Chinese student, whom Nilsen met in a pub near Leicester Square, The Salisbury, had a narrow escape. His name was Andrew Ho.

Nilsen told the police:

> He said he was very short of money and gave me a hard-luck story. He asked me if he could come back to my place and I said: 'Yes.' On getting back to Melrose Avenue I wasn't drunk and he said: 'What are you into?' I said I didn't want to have sex with him – just give him £10 and he could sod off in the Tube. He laid some emphasis on the fact that he could tie me up, and I thought his main emphasis was robbery. I was getting a bit agitated and said: 'I'll tie *you* up.' He said: 'I'm not so keen on that.' I said: 'I'll tie your legs anyway, and see what happens.' I said: 'This is a terrible way of making a living. Fraught with danger.' He lay

> there with this tie around his legs – his arms were free. What I did was use my tie and put it around his neck, and pulled it. I said: 'This is the sort of thing that could happen in your way of life.' I relaxed my hold and he struggled. He was in a hell of a state . . . He threw a brass candlestick at me and hit me right on the head. He picked up a letter opener and said he wanted to get out. He got out and left and I said: 'Let that be a lesson to you.'

Half an hour later the police arrived at the flat. Nilsen denied trying to strangle Ho, and the matter was dropped. He chose to make no charges although *he* was injured, and in the end no charges were brought by Ho. If they had been, another 14 men and boys might have lived. But two months later, Nilsen killed again.

His second victim was a 23-year-old Canadian, Kenneth Ockenden, who had come to London, after completing a welding course in Toronto, to visit some relatives and see something of Britain. He is said not to have been homosexual. Short, fair-haired and likeable, he had toured the Lake District with a former school friend called Larry before returning to London on his own. On Monday, 3 December he telephoned an uncle to say that he was in a hotel at King's Cross and would meet up with him on the 5th. No one ever heard from him again.

That Monday he met Nilsen at lunchtime in a pub in High Holborn, the Princess Louise. Nilsen had the afternoon off and according to him they spent the afternoon sightseeing, walking from Trafalgar Square, where they fed the pigeons, down Whitehall to Westminster Abbey. Ockenden took several photos. He agreed to go back to Melrose Avenue with Nilsen, where they had a meal of ham, egg and chips. As there were some good programmes on TV, they stocked up with rum, whisky, coke and beer at an off-licence – Ockenden insisting on paying half the bill – and returned to the flat, where they settled down to drink, watch TV and listen to music. Nilsen liked Ken Ockenden and brooded over the fact that Ken would be flying to Canada very soon and disappear from his life. He was also now listening to an LSO record through Nilsen's earphones and seemed oblivious of him.

Nilsen told the police:

> I was still drinking and he was drinking. I indicated: 'All right?' And he said: 'Bloody good! Fantastic!' He got engrossed in the records, and I was sitting in the corner, drinking, and I thought: 'Bloody good guest this.' I thought he'd be there all night. He was enjoying it. I turned the TV up loud. I watched TV and was drinking. He kept on listening to his music. It must have been well after midnight. Maybe one or two in the morning. I was dragging him across the floor with a flex around his neck. I was saying: 'Let me listen to the music as well.' He didn't struggle. I was dragging him across the floor. The dog was barking frantically in the kitchen, trying to get in the door. I put the dog out in the garden and said: 'Get out! This has fuck all to do with you!' He was lying on the floor. I untangled the earphones. I must have put half a glass of Bacardi

> in the glass. I put the earphones on and listened to the whole sequence of the records. He was dead. I kept on drinking . . . In the morning the record-player was still going round. The earphones were on the floor and I was in the armchair. I had been asleep.

Ockenden was strangled with the headphones flex. Although Nilsen provided the police with apparently helpful and detailed statements, there are many discrepancies, large and small, between what he told them and what he wrote in his exercise-books. Only the latter contain some descriptions of sexual acts with the corpses. Nowhere, however, does he describe the act of strangulation: the staring eyes, the sounds his victims made; nor what he felt. He could not admit to others that he *enjoyed* killing, and having sex with a corpse.

But in his written account of the killing of Ken Ockenden he felt able to reveal that after stripping Ockenden, who had 'completely messed himself', he cleaned him up with paper kitchen towels, gave him a bath and took the body to bed – 'No sex, only caressing, etc.' Ockenden's clothes, money, passport and films were destroyed (although his camera was kept for a while), and the body was jammed into a cupboard for a night, sitting on the floor, knees up, until rigor mortis had passed. Nilsen then loosened the corpse's limbs and took colour photographs of it with a polaroid camera he had bought specially, after clothing it in underpants, vest and socks.

He wrote:

> I arranged the body in various positions and took several photos (which I destroyed with the last burning). I lay in bed fully clothed, with him lying spreadeagled on top of me as I watched television. I would sometimes speak to him, as though he were still listening. I would compliment him on his looks and anatomy. By crossing his legs I had sex between his bare thighs (although no penetration of the body occurred). I wrapped him well before putting him under the floorboards. I took him up on about four occasions in the next two weeks. It was cold down there and he was still very fresh . . . I would sit him in the other armchair next to me, as I watched an evening's TV, drinking . . . Before he returned to his 'bed' I would sit him on my knee and strip off the underwear and socks, wrap him in curtain material and put him down (actually saying: 'Goodnight, Ken').

Nilsen expected, as with the Irish boy, that someone would remember seeing him with Ockenden, at the Princess Louise, or in the off-licence. But although Ockenden's disappearance was reported in the papers, on posters and on 'Police 5' on TV (Nilsen saw the programme), no one came knocking at his door. Ockenden's parents came to London to look for their son, but no trace of him could be found – not for another three years.

None of Nilsen's 14 other victims was given as much official and public attention as Ockenden, although some were reported as missing. The Salvation Army attempts to trace 5,000 missing persons every year, following up *half* the requests it receives, and succeeds with as many as 70 per cent of its enquiries. Every year, in London alone, about 7,000 people, mainly girls and boys between the ages of 14 and 18, are registered as missing, and as many as 6,000 people can be sleeping outdoors every week. Although most of the missing are found, or return home, some totally disappear. By the end of 1990, the number of persons still missing in the Metropolitan Police District was nearly 2,000, of whom over half were male. Of this 2,000, 1,700 had been missing for more than a year, 151 for more than five years, and 48 for more than ten years.

The sorrow of Nilsen's victims was that society had little interest in them. They were generally unemployed, destitute, homeless, homosexual, friendless, with problem childhoods and mentally and emotionally disturbed. If they had been middle-class, or girls, more official concern would have been shown for them. As it was, few cared about them when they went missing, nor when their fates were known.

Such a one was Nilsen's third victim, Martyn Duffey, aged 16. Nilsen told the police that Duffey was '19 to 20 years old'. Soon after 13 May 1980, Duffey left Merseyside and came to London, carrying a suitcase in which reposed the kitchen knives he had used on a catering course. They were etched with his name. He was about 5′ 6″, had been in care, had been seen by social workers and psychiatrists about his propensities for thieving, drugs, gay clubs, and running away from home. On a Saturday (it is not known precisely where or when) he encountered Nilsen, who had been attending a CPSA conference in Southport. They went back to Melrose Avenue where, after drinking two cans of lager, Duffey went to bed. Nilsen said later, talking to the police: 'I was out on the piss that night drinking heavily. We came back to my flat. I remember the next morning he was dead on the floor. I don't remember any violence at all. He had my tie around his neck . . . I put Duffey straight under the floorboards.'

Later he wrote: 'I remember sitting astride him (his arms must have been trapped by the quilt). I strangled him with great force . . . As I sat on him I could feel my bottom becoming wet. His urine had come through the bedding and my jeans.' Duffey, unconscious, was then drowned head-down in the water-filled kitchen sink. He was stripped and washed in the bath, which Nilsen also entered, lying under Duffey. Then Duffey was dried, parked on a kitchen chair, and Nilsen dried himself. He then took the naked boy to bed. Nilsen wrote: 'I talked to him and mentioned that his body was the youngest-looking I had ever seen. I kissed him all over and held him close to me. I sat on his stomach and masturbated. I kept him temporarily in the cupboard. Two days later I found him bloated in the cupboard. He went straight under the floorboards.'

Nilsen used a luggage ticket he found on Duffey to collect the boy's suitcase from Euston Station. He disposed of all its contents, but kept the suitcase and Duffey's glasses, and remembered to leave Duffey's catering knives in the garden to rust before throwing them away – but not until he had used them himself. 'You can't put a brand new set of knives into the dustbin,' he told the police. 'Someone would have got suspicious.' He also said: 'I knew this would happen again. The killing would happen again. I was resigned to this, and I was also resigned that I would be caught eventually. But I would do as best as I could to dispose of the evidence. I wasn't talking at that stage of turning over a new leaf. If I had been arrested at 65 years of age, there might have been thousands of bodies behind me.'

That summer he disposed of the corpses of Ockenden and Duffey because of the smell. One night he dismembered them both on the kitchen floor, using Duffey's knives. He wrapped the pieces of both young men in plastic bags and packed them into two suitcases. The two heads were put in separate carrier bags. These and the suitcases were stored in a garden shed that Nilsen had built for Bleep and then encased in a makeshift tomb of bricks, which he also filled with newspapers and magazines. The shed was not locked. Periodically he sprayed it with disinfectants and aerosols. As there was no room in the suitcases for Duffey's arms and hands Nilsen buried them by a bush.

Billy Sutherland was the next to die. The third of eight children, he was brought up on a rough council estate in Edinburgh. His father was a merchant seaman. Billy was good fun, but wild. He was often in trouble, and had been in prison, as well as at an approved school. On his knuckles were tattooed LOVE and HATE. An eagle was tattooed on his chest, and swallows on his hands; on his arms were tattoos commemorating his family, and there was a dagger on his leg. Although he had several girlfriends and had sired a child, he also had sex with men, usually for money, on his sprees in London, whither he escaped when evading his responsibilities and the police. He had trained as a chef. It was probably around 12 August, Billy's 26th birthday, that he was killed.

Nilsen was vague about Billy's death. He said they met in a West End pub and that the young Scot invited himself back to Melrose Avenue. He said: 'We started drinking. I remember he had some food. We had a great binge and I killed Billy Sutherland. I remember having a tie around his neck and pulling the tie . . . I did it from the front . . . I always felt I was two or three times as strong when I had drink. I felt I had amazing strength . . . I don't remember when I put Billy under the floor.'

He was also curiously vague about his next seven victims, remembering little about them and what he did to them. Perhaps what he did with their bodies made him want to forget. On the other hand, he was killing now at the rate of about one a month.

The fifth victim, after Billy Sutherland, was a Mexican or Philippino, met in The Salisbury, who accosted Nilsen and followed him outside. He was 'probably' strangled and put under the floorboards. At some stage he was dissected and packed in a suitcase and put in the shed. The sixth to die was Irish, possibly a building worker in his late twenties, who wore an old suit jacket and old shoes; they might have met in the Cricklewood Arms. The seventh was a vagrant, encountered while Nilsen was looking for a taxi at the top of Charing Cross Road, by Oxford Street. Nilsen said:

> His features were pale, hollow, withdrawn. He had a general appearance of looking grossly undernourished. He wore a long ragged

> trench-coat, ridiculously outsize trousers . . . He was carrying an old plastic carrier bag with bits and pieces . . . We got a taxi eventually, and we got back to Melrose Avenue. He said he wanted something to eat – he was starving. I fixed some food and coffee. He said he was tired and ate the food completely. He was not interested in alcohol at all. He was sitting there and dozed off to sleep. I started drinking.

After drinking most of a bottle of Bacardi and listening to Rick Wakeman's *Incantations*, high on drink and the music, Nilsen strangled his guest with a tie. 'There was a weak struggle. There was no sound. His legs were lifting and separating in slow motion, rather like riding a bicycle. I kept on for about a minute and a half before his legs stopped . . . It was as easy as taking candy from a baby . . . I remember thinking to myself: "You've got no more trouble now, squire" . . . I couldn't cut him up. He was so thin.'

By the end of 1980, of the many young men and boys who had entered Nilsen's flat, seven had not departed. The body of one had been burnt, but those of six others still remained, under the floorboards or in the garden shed. On a cold weekday in December, these six were consumed in a large bonfire on wasteland at the rear of the garden. He tended the fire all day, to the sound of *Tubular Bells*. He said:

> I managed to get off work . . . I woke about 6.45 am. I went out into the garden and checked that nobody was about. I pulled up the floorboards and put each bundle into huge pieces of carpeting and tied them up. I dragged these onto the pile by removing palings from the back fence and keeping fairly low . . . I managed to drag the heavy suitcases through the hole in the fence and into the hollow of the bonfire . . . The fabric and structure crumbled, exposing mostly brown-coloured bones and bits of flesh . . . There were thousands of fly chrysalis. Maggots and dead flies were everywhere . . . I put an old car tyre on top of the bonfire to disguise the smell . . . I put bits of wood on from time to time. Kids from a nearby house attracted by the fire gathered around and started throwing things in. I strongly reminded them to keep well out of the way . . . Near the end of the day there was only a pile of ash. I crushed a skull with a rake.

He would write more poetically later, seeing the bonfire as 'a great visual display of living natural forces', and comparing it to 'some Viking ship glowing westwards to Valhalla'. He wrote: 'I thought on those who now magnified my empty life, seeing their sweetness pervading the London air. I stood like an obedient usher . . . They were not in the flames but in me . . . Not for them the insulting monotony of a uniform and anonymous corporation cemetery . . . The sun is setting on the glowing embers and I, weeping, drink the bottle dry.'

Such was the corporeal end of Ockenden, Duffey, Sutherland and three other young men. Douglas Stewart might also have joined them. But he was the second of those (seven, according to Nilsen) who escaped with his life.

Stewart, a sandy-haired Scot, about 5′ 9″, was an unemployed barman, aged 26, from Thurso, who came south to see football matches and his mother – his parents were divorced. He was in the Golden Lion in Dean Street, Soho, when Nilsen, whom he had noticed there before, approached him. It was a Wednesday in mid-November 1980. After closing-time Stewart went in a taxi with Nilsen to Melrose Avenue, where the pair of them watched TV and drank. Nilsen was very attentive, though a tedious talker, and plied his guest with spirits and beer. But Stewart was a slow drinker and seldom drank spirits, and he refused much of what was offered. He also refused to share Nilsen's bed: he said he would sleep in the chair. He dozed off as the older man lay on the bed, listening to the record-player. He awoke to find Nilsen, wearing only jeans, standing astride him and trying to strangle him with a tie. In a choking panic his fingers clawed Nilsen's cheek. For a moment the tie round his neck slackened as Nilsen turned, enabling Stewart to smash his fist into Nilsen's face. Nilsen fell back, and Stewart then fell as he heaved himself out of the chair – to which his feet had been tied. None the less he flung himself on Nilsen, pinning him down. 'What the fuck were you trying to do?' he gasped. Nilsen calmly replied: 'I could kill you now, if I wanted to.' 'Go on!' said Stewart. 'Go ahead!' 'Don't be silly,' said Nilsen. 'I wasn't trying to kill you. I never even touched you.' 'You must think I'm an idiot!' Stewart said. He got to his feet. He said he was leaving and would go to the police. 'They'll never believe you,' Nilsen said. 'Take my money,' he added. 'Go on! Take my money!' 'I don't want your money!' said Stewart, and when he tried to leave Nilsen threatened him with a knife. Stewart succeeded in pacifying Nilsen and fled. He ran to a call-box and telephoned the police. But he was so overwrought by the time a patrol car from Kilburn police station arrived that they believed the older man's cool and positive assurances that there had been a drunken row, a lovers' quarrel. They asked Stewart to make an official complaint when he was sober. He never did. And when the police checked on the London address Stewart gave them, they found it was unoccupied. If Douglas Stewart (as with Andrew Ho) had brought charges and made a statement to the police, eight others might not have died.

The eighth victim, a long-haired hippy, aged about 25 and wearing a bleached denim jacket and jeans, was killed in December 1980. His severed remains were packaged and stuffed under the floorboards. Three others were killed in the first three months of 1981. The ninth victim was a fair-haired, blue-eyed Scot, about 18 years old, who wore a green shirt, a track-suit top, and black and white football socks. Picked up in the Golden Lion, he was strangled on the platform-bed and stored under the floorboards intact. The tenth to die was 'a Billy Sutherland type' but from Belfast – 'slimmish' and 'very ordinary'. Nilsen told the police: 'I don't remember putting anything around his neck. He was just wrapped up in material, tied, and put under the floorboards. At that point there were two intact bodies and one dismembered one down there. That was it. Floorboards back, carpet replaced, and back to work at Denmark Street.'

He felt invincible, as if he were 'a quasi-god'. He told the police: 'I thought

I could do anything I wanted while this was going on. There were people upstairs, people next door. But nobody knew.'

In May 1981 the eleventh of Nilsen's victims, and the last of the eight who were never identified and named, was killed. Aged about 19 and about 5′ 5″, he was a skinhead. He wore a black leather, studded belt and black bovver boots. He was also tattooed with a Union Jack and *England Rules OK*. Around his neck was a row of dots and the legend ***Cut Here***. Later, Nilsen would do just that.

They met in Leicester Square. Of the skinhead, Nilsen said:

> He boasted about his toughness. How hard he was. All the bundles he had been in, and so on. How much he could drink as well. He could drink anyone under the table, he said, and I said, comparatively speaking, I was an old man – under-exercised, clerical pen-pusher – and that I would have no objection matching him drink for drink. We would drink straight whisky . . . Eventually he flaked out in his armchair, where he was sitting. He was dribbling a vomit-like substance down his clothing. I remember thinking he wasn't very hard. I put a tie around his neck and strangled him. After killing him, I went to bed. End of the day, end of a drink, end of a person.

The skinhead was stripped, washed and taken to bed, where Nilsen achieved orgasm between the corpse's thighs. He was later wrapped up in a bundle and rammed under the living-room floor.

Soon after this, his flat was vandalised – as was the flat above. Everything was wrecked and creosote splashed about. Nilsen called in the police, who stood on floorboards concealing four bodies. The wreckers were never caught.

Although Nilsen's remembrance was avowedly uncertain about his fifth to eleventh victims, all unnamed, he was able to write a very exact account, after the trial, of the death of one of them, probably the ninth – the fair-haired, teenage Scot.

> We climbed our drunken way naked up to the wooden platform-bed. Later, I remember being straddled over him, my knees each side of him, with the back of my head pressed against the ceiling. I was squeezing his neck and remember wanting to see more clearly what he looked like . . . I got up shaking and nearly fell down the ladder. I put all the room-lights on and comforted Bleep to go back to sleep. I put a chair beside the ladder and climbed up. I pulled aside the bedding and pulled his ankles until he half hung off the platform. I got onto the chair and pulled his warm, limp, naked body into my arms. I got down from the chair and saw my reflection in a full-length mirror. I just stood there and looked at myself with the lad's naked body in my arms . . . I washed him in the bath and sat him dripping wet on the loo, and bathed myself in the water. It was an act to purify him and apparently (with hindsight) me also . . . I dried his body carefully with a bath towel, and the steam rose

> from him in the cold air. When I moved or carried him a deep sigh would come from his throat . . . Putting him again over my shoulder I carried him up the ladder and laid him on the bed . . . A tape was playing of Copeland's *Fanfare for the Common Man*. I was crying. I got into bed and held him close to me. I was whispering to him: 'Don't worry. Everything's fine. Sleep.' I explored his body . . . I held him so close in my arms that my erect penis was held between his thighs. I stripped off his pants and pulled the bedding back. I took his genitals in my hand and masturbated myself with the other hand . . . I remember first thing in the morning thinking: 'This is absolutely ridiculous.'

Nilsen went to work. On his return he fed the cat and Bleep, turned on the TV and made himself a meal. He took the body from the cupboard where it had been stored, dressed it and sat it in an armchair.

> I took his hand and talked to him – my comments for the day, with cynical remarks about the TV programmes . . . I placed him on the table and slowly stripped him. I would always remove his socks last. I would closely examine (slowly) every part of his anatomy . . . his naked body fascinated me. I remember being thrilled that I had full control and ownership of this beautiful body. I would fondle his buttocks, and it amazed me that there was no reaction from him to this . . . I was fascinated by the mystery of death. I whispered to him, because I believed he was still really in there . . . I would hold him close often, and think that he had never been so appreciated in his life before . . . After a week, I stuck him under the floor . . . I wanted him to lie there underneath in a bed of white roses.

It was far from that. Despite the disinfectant that Nilsen daily sprayed under the floorboards, the 'slight smell problem' from four rotting corpses could not be dispelled. So one Friday evening in August 1981 he reluctantly decided to dismember the three that were intact and repackage them. Before he did so he sent the dog and cat into the garden and removed all his clothes. He said:

> I deliberated this task reluctantly. I fortified myself with about half a bottle of drink before I lifted up the floorboards. The whole task took till after midnight. I removed the intact bundles one at a time, placed them on the kitchen floor . . . I put the wrapping to one side. I removed the clothing from the bodies and set about dissecting them. The smell was grossly unpleasant, and in some cases there existed large colonies of maggots.

He wrote later: 'The flesh looked just like any meat one would see in a butcher's shop, and having been trained in butchery I was not subject to any traumatic shocks.'

He poured salt on the maggots and at one stage was violently sick. More than once he went naked into the garden for some fresh air. Using a kitchen knife, he first cut off the head, then the hands and feet, all of which were washed in the kitchen sink, then dried, wrapped in paper towels, and put in plastic carrier bags, as were the internal organs. Each body was then cut in half; the arms were severed and the legs below the knee. These parts and the others were packed in large black plastic bags, to which deodorants were added, before being wedged under the floor. The internal organs were spilled between the garden's double fencing. Nilsen then took the dog for a walk.

The last of those who were murdered at Melrose Avenue, and the twelfth to die, was Malcolm Barlow, an epileptic, aged 23, from Sheffield. He was without parents, friends, morals or much hope and had been in and out of care and mental institutions for much of his life. On the morning of 17 September 1981, he happened to collapse in Melrose Avenue. Nilsen, on his way to work, came to Barlow's aid. Being the Good Samaritan was, after all, his job, helping the underprivileged, deprived and unemployed. He helped Barlow back to No. 195, gave him a coffee and went out again to phone for an ambulance. The following evening, when Nilsen returned from work, Barlow was outside No. 195. 'You're supposed to be in hospital,' Nilsen said. Barlow replied that he had been discharged. 'Well, you'd better come in,' said Nilsen. He made Barlow a meal. They watched TV and drank, despite the fact that Nilsen had warned his guest about drinking and taking some pills. 'Be it on your own head,' said Nilsen.

He told the police:

> Much later . . . I let the dog out. On returning, I said: 'Are you still awake?' I tried to rouse him, but he was deeply unconscious. I thought: 'Not an ambulance again.' I got halfway to the phone-box and came back . . . I was slapping his face to wake him up. There was no response. I sat there for a full 20 minutes, wondering what to do. I got up and put my hands around his throat and squeezed tightly. I held that position for two or three minutes and released my hold. I didn't check, but I believed him now to be dead. I didn't have to call an ambulance . . . The next morning, not feeling much like prising up the floorboards, I dragged him through into the kitchen, put him under the sink and closed the doors. I went to work.

There Barlow's body remained for two weeks, until it was destroyed with four others in a bonfire in the rear garden, which Nilsen lit on 4 October, the day before he left Melrose Avenue. The landlord, who wished to redecorate the flats in the house and sell them off, had offered Nilsen alternative accommodation in an attic flat near Muswell Hill.

> The day before the move [he said], I made preparations for the burning of the human remains at 195. I made a huge, well-constructed bonfire, using furnishings, and cabinets and things from the house. I left a sizeable hollow in the centre of the structure. This I did the day before. Early in the morning, I lifted the floorboards and started to pack the packages into the centre of the wooden structure, the base of which was two large

> doors on house bricks . . . Going into the kitchen, I opened the doors of the cupboard under the sink. I noticed that the body had become bloated. I removed the body and dragged it through the house and laid it inside the structure . . . The fire burned fiercely, extraordinarily fiercely. There were spurts, bangs, cracks and hisses and a continual hissing and sizzling coming from the fire. This I took to be fat and other parts of the bodies burning . . . The next morning I packed . . . I replaced the floor-boards before I went and checked there was nothing I had left, no evidence . . . I waited out front for the removal van [his belongings were partly contained in two tea-chests] . . . Driving away from 195 Melrose Avenue was a great relief.

Seven weeks later, on 23 November (Nilsen's 36th birthday), a university student, aged 19 and called Paul Nobbs, was strangled in Cranley Gardens, but allowed to live – apparently because Nilsen suddenly remembered, while strangling Nobbs, that the student had earlier phoned his mother about his plans that night.

They met in the Golden Lion. Nobbs later told the police:

> I took off all my clothes and went to bed. Nilsen did the same. We kissed, cuddled and fondled each other, and I attempted to have sex, but was unable because of my state . . . I woke up between two and three in the morning with a splitting headache and felt very ill. I got out of bed, still naked, and went to the kitchen . . . I got a glass of water . . . At about 7.30, I woke again, and I noticed my face was very, very red. I had no whites of the eyes. They were completely red . . . I felt sick and had a sore throat and a pain in the head. I thought it was from the drink. Nilsen told me I looked bloody awful. I said: 'Thank you very much.' We parted on good terms and he offered me his address and telephone number. He seemed no different from the night before.

Nobbs's tutor sent him to a hospital, where doctors concluded that someone had tried to strangle him. But Nobbs was reluctant, because of his homosexuality, to go to the police: he told the doctor he had been mugged. As a result, another three men died.

John Howlett was killed in March 1982; Graham Allen in September; and Stephen Sinclair in January 1983. In between, Martyn Hunter-Craig and others came, and went, and two more potential victims escaped.

One was Carl Stottor, aged 21, whom Nilsen met in the Black Cap in Camden Town on 5 May 1982. Stottor was unhappy because he had recently broken up with a boyfriend in Blackpool. He said he wished he was dead. To which Nilsen replied: 'Don't be so silly. You've got your whole life in front of you.'

Stottor later told the court: 'I remember hearing the bell for last orders and he invited me back to his flat. I think he said how pretty I was.' Nilsen held his hand in the cab taking them to Cranley Gardens. In the attic flat Stottor had two glasses of whisky before they both went to bed. No sexual activity took place. Stottor said later:

> I fell asleep and woke up feeling something around my neck, and I couldn't breathe properly. I put my hands up to this thing around my neck and couldn't release it . . . He was behind me as this was happening. He didn't shout, but in a whispered voice said: 'Keep still' . . . I then became semi-conscious. There was an increasing pressure and I couldn't breathe. I vaguely remember being carried and then I felt very cold. I knew I was in water and he was trying to drown me. He kept pushing me into the water. The third time I came out of the water I said: 'No more! Please – no more!' He pushed me back in again. I felt this man is trying to kill me, and this is what it feels like to die. I felt very relaxed and then passed out . . . The next thing I knew the dog was licking my face. Then I passed out again . . . Next I woke up in bed, and Des was in bed with me and his arm was around me. I couldn't stay awake for very long . . . When I finally came round and could get up, my face was bloated, and my neck was sore with cuts and burns. My tongue was swollen. He said I had had a nightmare . . . He said he had to throw cold water over me because I was in a state of shock . . . He asked me if I would meet him again.

Stottor went to a hospital and was told that he had probably been strangled. But, as with Nobbs, he was reluctant to go to the police. There were no witnesses and he still wondered whether it had all been a dream.

In June 1982, Nilsen was promoted and transferred to the Jobcentre at Kentish Town. He was now earning £7,000 a year.

In September, Graham Allen, from Glasgow and aged 28, was killed. He had been in a fight in Soho and was very drunk. Nilsen took him home, made him a large omelette, which Allen began to eat and then passed out, with a piece of omelette hanging out of his mouth. Nilsen removed the plate from Allen's lap and strangled him. His naked body was kept in the bath, full of cold water, for several days. He was eventually dismembered in the bath, and his head, hands and feet were boiled, and pieces of flesh flushed down the loo. Said Nilsen later: 'What was left of him was put into two black plastic sacks. One was placed in a secret cubby-hole at the end of the bath, the other was put into a tea-chest.' Allen was identified later through dental records.

For seven days, over Christmas, Trevor Simpson, an ex-prisoner, aged 20, from Derbyshire, stayed with Nilsen in the flat despite the sickly smell in the front room and the bathroom. Nothing special happened on Christmas Day: there were no presents; nor were there any decorations or cards. Nilsen scolded Simpson for reading the *Sun* and suggested they visit the tomb of Karl Marx in Highgate Cemetery. They generally ate in, with daily excursions to cinemas and pubs. Simpson was not a heavy drinker, which seemed to annoy Nilsen. One night Simpson awoke to find the room was full of smoke. Nilsen was in the kitchen and behaved very calmly, blaming Simpson for dropping a lit cigarette on to a pair of Nilsen's jeans which smouldered on the floor. Simpson left the following day.

A few days later, after midnight on New Year's Eve, a Japanese student,

Toshimitsu Ozawa, was assailed in the flat by Nilsen, who approached him (while Ozawa was wide awake) with a tie held taut in his hands. He seemed calm and Ozawa thought that his host was joking, even when the tie was put around his neck. Ozawa pushed Nilsen away. But the performance was repeated. Ozawa panicked, kicked out and fled, causing such a commotion – the dog was barking also – that the girls in the ground-floor room emerged to check on Nilsen's safety. He appeared on the stairs, holding a torch; he was very drunk.

Four weeks later Stephen Sinclair, the fifteenth of Nilsen's victims to die, was killed.

It seems clear that Nilsen originally killed to acquire, to own and to keep the bodies of young men and use them as he wished. He killed them all at night, when both he and they had drunk a good deal, and when they were insensible, defenceless and asleep. They were strangled so that their bodies would barely be marked, and probably because he enjoyed the extreme pleasure of holding life or death in his hands. Drowning was another means of suffocation, as was attempted asphyxiation by smoke. Those he killed were deliberately chosen: they were smaller than him, and much younger, generally social misfits and down-and-outs, without homes, with few friends and whose absence would not be missed. It seems that as the killings continued, Nilsen became increasingly indifferent to the physical quality of his victims, and killed because he felt he had been angered, offended or slighted in some way – and because he wanted to kill again.

The most gruesome, cold-blooded and protracted of Nilsen's murders was the thirteenth, that of John Howlett, aged 23, known to Nilsen as John the Guardsman.

He was the first to die in Cranley Gardens, in March 1982. They had met in a pub the previous December. In March they met again in The Salisbury in St Martin's Lane. It seems that Howlett, who came from High Wycombe, was after a bed for the night. They walked to Cranley Gardens from the Highgate Underground station, and once in the attic flat of No. 23, Nilsen made a meal and they watched TV and drank. After midnight Howlett announced he was tired. He said: 'I wouldn't mind getting my head down.' He left Nilsen on his own, watching TV, and went to sleep next door – the bed was then in the front room. At about 1.00 am Nilsen, displeased and drunk, put the lights out and went into the other room.

> He was in the bed [said Nilsen later]. I think I said: 'I thought you were getting your head down. I didn't know you were moving in.' I roused him and he mumbled a reply. He indicated to me that he didn't feel like moving. I went into the back room, got the bottle of Bacardi, and sat on the bed. I noticed he'd taken most of his clothes off . . . I didn't feel like getting into the bed with him in it. I remember it was getting a bit cold. I remember finishing the bottle. I went to the armchair and under the cushion there was a length of loose upholstery strap. I approached to where he was lying in bed under the blankets. I wound this material round his neck. I think I said: 'It's about time you went.' I was astride

> him and I tightened my grip on the material. He fought back furiously and partially raised himself up. I thought I'd be overpowered. He was a very fit person. Summoning up all my strength I forced him back down and his head struck the rim of the head-rest on the bed. He still struggled fiercely, so that now he was half off the bed. In about a minute he had gone limp. There was blood on the bedding, and I assumed it was from his head. I checked if he was still breathing and he was – deep rasping breaths. I tightened my grip on him again around his neck for another minute or so. I let go my grip again, and he appeared to be dead. I stood up. The dog was barking in the next room. I went through to pacify it. I was shaking all over with the stress of the struggle . . . I returned to the front room and was shocked to see that he had started breathing again. I looped the material round his neck again, pulled it as tight as I could, and held on for what must have been two or three minutes. When I released my grip he had stopped breathing. But I noticed as he lay there on his back his heart was still beating quite strongly. I couldn't believe it. I dragged him off the bed and into the bathroom. I pulled him over the rim of the bath, so his head was hanging into the bath, put the plug in, still holding him, and ran the cold water full on. His head was on the bottom of the bath. In a minute or so the water reached his nose. The rasping breath came on again. The water rose higher and I held him under. He was struggling against it. There were bubbles coming from his mouth or nose, and he stopped struggling. I held him in that position for four or five minutes. The water had become bloody, and a substance, as well as particles of food, was coming from his mouth. Because of the blood, I emptied the bath. Having emptied the bath I put him in with his knees bent . . . I left him there all night. I washed my hands, changed the bedding and went to bed. I was smoking and shaking. I called the dog, and it came through looking a bit sheepish. I tapped the bed, saying 'Come up here', and it curled up by my feet . . . Before going to work and before dressing I pulled him out of the bath and put him into the cupboard. I got some blood on my hands and my legs. I bathed and went to work . . . For a week afterwards, I had his finger-marks on my neck.

A few days later, as a friend of Nilsen from Scotland was coming to stay, John Howlett was dissected in the bath. His internal organs, in 'half-pound lots' were flushed down the loo, as were lumps of flesh. His head, hands and feet were boiled, as were his ribs. The severed remnants of his arms, legs and pelvis, were packaged in several plastic bags and sacks and put in a tea-chest in the front room. There they remained for nearly a year.

On 10 and 11 February 1983, the foul relics of Howlett, Allen and Sinclair were retrieved from 23 Cranley Gardens by the police.

Dennis Nilsen was transferred to Brixton Prison in March, where he was confined in a single cell, as a Category A prisoner, for 23 and a half hours a day. Resentful of the way he was treated, he became alternately awkward, angry, frustrated, depressed, rebellious and paranoid. He went on hunger-strike twice, tore up depositions, refused to wear prison uniform, assaulted warders by throwing his chamber-pot contents at them and was banned from attending church services as his presence 'disturbed' the other prisoners. Curiously, he was never given any kind of medical examination, although he was questioned by psychiatrists. In April, Nilsen decided to dispense with his solicitor, Ronald Moss, and with legal aid and defend himself. A few weeks later he reapplied. This happened twice more. In September Moss was finally dismissed, five weeks before the trial, and another solicitor, Ralph Haeems, took his place. Haeems, who had been involved in the trials of the Great Train Robbers and the Krays, had been recommended by David Martin, a young gunman, convicted in September of malicious wounding and other offences, and with whom Nilsen fell in love in prison, although apparently nothing sexual occurred. On Haeems's advice, Nilsen changed his plea from guilty to not guilty, thus prolonging his trial.

While in Brixton Prison Nilsen wrote nearly 200 letters and filled 49 exercise-books with his specious, egocentric and contradictory thoughts, seeking to self-dramatise, elevate and excuse what he had done. None of these writings, which revealed much more than his police statements, was used in evidence at his trial. The author, Brian Masters, who had acquired Nilsen's trust when writing his account of the man and the murders, offered to make the journals available – Nilsen had assigned all 49 to him. But the offer was never taken up by the lawyers or the police.

Nilsen wrote: 'Killing is wrong, and I have reduced my own principles to ashes . . . My murders were for no useful end as murders never are' – 'I look back with shame that the small space on that living-room floor could have witnessed 12 deaths' – 'I have always believed they are, in a sense, living on within me' – 'I sometimes wondered if anyone cared for me or them. That could easily be me lying there. In fact a lot of the time it was. It may be that when I was killing these men, I was killing myself' – 'We are not dealing with murder here, although I have killed.'

The trial of Dennis Nilsen began at the Central Criminal Court on Monday, 24 October 1983 – a month before his 38th birthday. He was defended by Ivan Lawrence, QC, MP. The prosecution was led by Allan Green, and the judge was Mr Justice Croom-Johnson. Allan Green became Director of Public Prosecutions in 1987 and was knighted. He resigned as DPP in 1991, following a police allegation that he had been kerb-crawling and approaching prostitutes near King's Cross.

Nilsen was charged with the murders of Ken Ockenden, Martyn Duffey, Billy Sutherland, Malcolm Barlow, John Howlett and Stephen Sinclair, and with attempting to murder Douglas Stewart and Paul Nobbs. Nilsen wore gold-rimmed glasses, a grey-green jacket, pale blue shirt, and a dark blue tie with white spots. The *Daily Express* reported: 'There is a primness of the fussy clerk about him, a nervy respectability.' The *Daily Mirror* commented on his pale blue eyes and his large hands 'very still in his lap'.

It was not disputed that Nilsen had killed. The question was whether, as the defence alleged, his abnormality of mind was such that it substantially reduced his responsibility for what he had done. The prosecution claimed that the accused was fully aware of his acts, and that they were deliberately done. Oddly, the prosecution conceded in advance that neither the murders nor the victims were homosexual by nature, and the very essence and cause of the murders, the homosexuality of the accused, and of most if not all of his victims, was played down in court. Mr Green, who also wore glasses, said that Nilsen had admitted that he was bisexual and emotionally homosexual, but denied that any homosexual activity had occurred before his victims' deaths.

After Mr Green had paraphrased and quoted at length from Nilsen's detailed statements to the police, three witnesses for the prosecution were called. They were: Douglas Stewart, Paul Nobbs and Carl Stottor. The thickness of Stewart's Scottish accent and his jaunty self-assurance made a poor impression, as did the revelation that his story had been bought by the *Sunday Mirror*. The defence cast doubts on his reliability as a witness. Although Stewart denied being homosexual and said he had married two years before, the sexual proclivities of Nobbs and Stottor were not in doubt. Both were very nervous and spoke so quietly they could hardly be heard. Both testified that Nilsen's behaviour before and after each attempted murder was calm and concerned. 'How odd that was,' said Mr Lawrence.

DCI Peter Jay, after agreeing that Nilsen had been very co-operative and had no previous criminal record, read various self-analytical statements made by Nilsen and a letter to the police. One document, written on 25 February, was entitled 'Unscrambling Behaviour'. In it Nilsen wrote:

> I guess I may be a creative psychopath who, when in a loss of rationality situation, lapses temporarily into a destructive psychopath, a condition induced by rapid and heavy ingestion of alcohol. At the subconscious root lies a sense of total social isolation and a desperate search for a sexual identity . . . God only knows what thoughts go through my mind when it's captive within a destructive binge . . . It may be the perverted overkill of my need to help people . . . There is no disputing the fact that I am a violent killer under certain circumstances . . . It amazes me that I have no tears for these victims. I have no tears for myself or for those bereaved by my actions. Am I a wicked person, constantly under pressure, who just cannot cope with it, who escapes to reap revenge against society through the haze of a bottle of spirits? Maybe it's because I was just born an evil man.

DCS Chambers read out the whole of Nilsen's statements about the murders. The recitation took four hours, during which the jury of eight men and four women gazed at the impassive bespectacled person hunched in the dock with varying degrees of shock, incredulity, horror and disgust, which were heightened when the cooking-pot, wherein three heads had been boiled, was produced along with some other exhibits, in court. As Chambers spoke, Nilsen scanned a transcript of his confession, to make sure that what Chambers said was correct.

Two psychiatrists, Dr MacKeith and Dr Gallwey, were called by the defence. Dr MacKeith contended that the accused suffered from a severe personality disorder and had difficulty expressing any feelings apart from anger.

He was suspicious, paranoid, schizoid and craved attention. His problem was depersonalisation, which meant he regarded people as components of his fantasies. Allan Green, in cross-examination, maintained that Nilsen was cunning, resourceful, articulate, plausible, 'a jolly good actor', and frequently lied. Dr Gallwey said Nilsen had a False Self problem, which was magnified when he was socially and emotionally isolated. The killings were motiveless, but they prevented Nilsen from going insane or committing suicide: his self-loathing and urge for self-destruction were directed elsewhere. Gallwey agreed with Green that Nilsen knew what he was doing intellectually but was not emotionally aware. 'Did he know the nature and quality of his acts?' demanded Mr Green. 'No,' replied Gallwey. 'He knew the nature of the acts only. He did not know the quality of them.'

The prosecution was allowed a rebuttal witness, another psychiatrist, Dr Bowden, who declared that Nilsen, though abnormal, had no mental disorder, that his feelings of guilt about being homosexual had been redirected into doing something really bad, that he was not especially lonely or without friends, that he had shown remorse, was rational, purposeful, manipulative and had simply wanted to kill. Dr Bowden said: 'In my experience, the vast majority of people who kill have to regard their victims as objects – otherwise they cannot kill them.'

Mr Green summarised his and the defence's closing speeches with the words: 'The defence says: "He couldn't help it." The Crown says: "Oh yes, he could."' Mr Lawrence insisted that Nilsen was 'out of his mind', and in cataloguing a list of his horrific acts, repeatedly asked: 'Is there nothing substantially wrong with a mind like that?'

In his summing-up, Mr Justice Croom-Johnson said: 'There are evil people, who do evil things. Committing murder is one of them . . . What is meant by "substantial"? It doesn't mean *total* . . . You may legitimately differ from the doctors and use your common sense. If you found there was some impairment, but not enough, you would be allowed to find him guilty of murder.'

The jury were evidently divided about this, and having retired on Thursday, 3 November, they were unable to return with a unanimous verdict. But at 4.25 on the Friday they concluded, by a majority of ten to two, that Dennis Nilsen was guilty on the six counts of murder and one count of attempted murder (that of Stewart). They were unanimous in their guilty verdict on the attempted murder of Paul Nobbs.

Nilsen was sentenced to life imprisonment, with a recommendation that he should serve no less than 25 years.

He was sent to Wormwood Scrubs, where a prisoner slashed his face with a razor, causing a four-inch cut across his left cheek. In March 1984 he was moved to Parkhurst Prison on the Isle of Wight, and in June he was transferred to Wakefield Prison. In 1992 he was in Albany Prison, back on the Isle of Wight.

He has a cell to himself, but he mixes with others at meal-times. He is cheerful and far from morose, and still resolute about his rights. In his cell he reads a lot, writes and paints, listens to the radio, and has as his cellmate a budgerigar, called Hamish. For over a year in Wakefield he is said to have enjoyed a physical relationship with an armed robber, called Jimmy, aged 32.

Meanwhile, there were other deaths: David Martin committed suicide in Parkhurst Prison in March 1984, before Nilsen's arrival there; Nilsen's brother, Olav, died of a heart attack (like their grandfather) in 1990; David Gallichan committed suicide in December 1991; and DCS Geoff Chambers died in July 1992.

A few days after his trial Nilsen wrote in his prison journal what amounted at last to a true confession, which confirmed the prosecution's case.

> I had always wished to kill, but the opportunity never really presented itself in safe conditions . . . [This was] substituted by fantasies which had *me* killed in the mirrored images. I had been killing this way for years, killing my own image. The kill was only part of the whole. The whole experience, which thrilled me intensely, was the drink, the chase, the social seduction, the getting the 'friend' back, the decision to kill, the body and its disposal. The pressure needed release. I took release through spirits and music. On that high I had a loss of morality and danger feeling . . . If the conditions were right, I would completely follow through to the death . . . I had no other thrill or happiness.

He had also written, months before: 'Am I mad? I don't feel mad. Maybe I am mad.'

The Nilsen murders, in number and kind, were repeated by tall, fair-haired, nice-looking Jeffrey Dahmer in Wisconsin, in the late 1980s. He was charged in August 1991, when he was 31, with killing 15 non-white young men and boys. He claimed to have killed 17 – there may have been more. Like Nilsen, drink played a significant part in the execution of the murders. Dahmer was a heavy drinker (rum and coke) and drugged his victims with a special potion before strangling them with a strap. The bodies were also dismembered, some heads and skulls, painted grey, being kept in a fridge. Necrophilia (oral sex in his case) was a feature of Dahmer's crimes, as was cannibalism. And he took Polaroid photos of his victims, before and after they were killed, and as he cut them up.

A few weeks after Dahmer was arrested, a Texan, Donald Evans, confessed to the killing of a ten-year-old girl in Mississippi. He also claimed to have killed about 60 other people in the past 14 years. Meanwhile, in New York, Julio Gonzales was convicted of the murder of 87 people, who died in 1990 when, after a row with his girlfriend, he set fire to a social club in the Bronx.

In southern Russia, in April 1992, a 56-year-old former teacher, Andrei Chikatilo, was charged with killing and eating at least 52 young women and children over a period of a dozen years. He was sentenced to death in October 1992 and executed by firing squad.

And so it goes on – a reflective echo of the slaughter of people that occurs increasingly around the world in fatal spasms of civil, tribal, racial and religious strife.

Epilogue

Albert Pierrepoint's own account of his first execution, as head executioner, follows. It took place at Pentonville Prison in 1940, the victim being a professional criminal sentenced to death for a gangland killing. Pierrepoint's assistant was Steve Wade.

At five minutes to nine we were given the signal that the Sheriff had gone to the Governor's office. Wade and I walked across the Prison yard with an officer who led us up to the corridor outside the condemned cell. I think the next minutes of waiting were the worst, not only then but on every occasion. It is impossible not to feel apprehension and even fear at the prospect of the responsibility of the moment, but with me the frailty passed as soon as there was action. At half a minute to nine a small group came down the corridor. There was the Sheriff, the Governor, the doctor and some senior prison officers. I suddenly had a strange realisation. I was the youngest man there, and the eyes of everyone were on me. The party paused at the next door to that of the condemned cell, the door of the execution chamber. A finger was raised and they passed in. The chief opened the door of the cell and I went forward with a strap in my hand.

The prisoner was standing, facing me, smiling. In his civilian clothes he looked as smart as I had already registered him. In my civilian clothes, amid all those uniforms, we might have been meeting for a chat in a club in Leicester Square – but who would have foreseen a robed priest in the room? I quickly strapped his wrists and said 'Follow me.'

The door in the side wall of the cell had been opened as I came in, and I walked through it into the execution chamber. He followed me, walking seven paces with the noose straight ahead of him, and the escorting officers mounting the cross-planks gently stopped him as he stood on the T. I had turned in time to face him. Eye to eye, that last look. Wade was stooping behind him, swiftly fastening the ankle strap. I pulled from my breast pocket the white cap, folded as carefully as a parachute, and drew it down over his head. 'Cheerio,' he said. I reached for the noose, pulled it down over the cap, tightened it to my right, pulled a rubber washer along the rope to hold it, and darted to my left, crouching towards the cotter pin at the base of the lever. I was in the position of a sprinter at the start of a race as I went over the cross-plank, pulled the pin with one hand, and pushed the lever with the other, instinctively looking back as I did so. There was a snap as the falling doors were bitten and held by the rubber clips, and the rope stood straight and still. The broken twine spooned down in a falling leaf, passed through a little eddy of dust, and floated into the pit.

I went to the side of the scaffold and walked down into the pit. I undid the prisoner's shirt for the stethoscope, and the doctor followed me. I came up again and waited. The doctor came back to the scaffold. 'Everything is all right,' he said. It was a curious way for a doctor to pronounce death . . . I suppose his intention was to reassure the Governor and possibly me . . .

At ten o'clock Wade and I returned to the execution chamber. He went down into the pit and, kneeling on the scaffold floor, I complied with a strange requirement. By regulation, I had to measure from the heels of the hanging man to the level of the scaffold from which he had dropped. This measurement was longer than the drop I had given him. The extra length was made up by the stretch of the man's body after death . . . He had been hanging for an hour, and the stretch was considerable . . .

I put the tape measure away, and went below. I stared at the flesh I had stilled. I had further duties to perform, but no longer as executioner. I had been nearest to this man in death, and I prepared him for burial. As he hung, I stripped him. Piece by piece I removed his clothes. It was not callous, but the best rough dignity I could give him, as he swung to the touch, still hooded in the noose. He yielded his garments without the resistance of limbs. If it had been in a prison outside London, I should have left him his shirt for a shroud, and put him in his coffin. In London there was always a post-mortem, and he had to be stripped entirely and placed on a mortuary stretcher. But in common courtesy I tied his empty shirt around his hips.

Wade had fixed the tackle above. I passed a rope under the armpits of my charge, and the body was hauled up a few feet. Standing on the scaffold, with the body now drooping, I removed the noose and the cap, and took his head between my hands, inclining it from side to side to assure myself that the break had been clean. Then I went below, and Wade lowered the rope. A dead man, being taken down from execution, is a uniquely broken body whether he is a criminal or Christ, and I received this flesh, leaning helplessly into my arms, with the linen round the loins, gently with the reverence I thought due to the shell of any man who has sinned and suffered.

Afterword

I operated on behalf of the state, what I am convinced was the most humane and the most dignified method of meting out death to a delinquent – however justified or unjustified the allotment of death may be – and on behalf of humanity I trained other nations to adopt the British system of execution . . .

I do not now believe that any one of the hundreds of executions I carried out has in any way acted as a deterrent against future murder. Capital punishment, in my view, achieved nothing except revenge.

Albert Pierrepoint, 1974

Acknowledgements

In the writing of this book I have been greatly assisted by the work of writers and journalists in times long past, particularly those in the nineteenth and early twentieth centuries who wrote with such care and accuracy for *The Times*, the *Morning Advertiser*, the *Illustrated Police News*, and for local newspapers like the *Surrey Advertiser*, the *Tonbridge Free Press*, the *Essex County Chronicle*, the *Western Morning News*, and the *Torquay Times*. Other and more contemporary newspapers were also useful sources of information, in particular *The Times*, the *Sunday Times*, the *Independent*, the *Daily Telegraph*, the *Daily Mail*, the *Daily Express*, the *Daily Mirror*, the *Sun*, the *People*, the *News of the World*, the London *Evening Standard* and the *Evening News*.

I also owe a large debt of gratitude to the librarians, archivists and local historians who provided me with photocopies, advice and information: to those at the Battersea District Library, the Rugeley Central Library, the Leatherhead Central Library, the Central Library, Torquay, the Devon Record Office, the Essex Record Office, and Westminster Libraries.

My thanks to them, and chiefly to the ever-helpful staff of the Marylebone Library in London, and to Mary Clucas, Eva Wade and the staff of the Commissioner's Library in New Scotland Yard.

Thanks also to the Home Office, the Met Office, the Public Record Office at Kew, the Records Office at the Old Bailey, the Court of Appeal, Madame Tussaud's and Tonbridge School; and to Joyce Bailey, Francis Cazalet, Clare Colvin, Lt.-Col. Dennis Daly, Bernie Davis, Louise Douglas, Stewart Goodwin, Henry Hayward, Jane Herbert, Paul Mallender, Brian Masters, John Miller, Brigadier Andrew Parker Bowles, Sheila Reid, Bryan Rostron, Anthony Seldon, David Thorogood, Marjorie Waddell and Andy Wright.

Special thanks to the new Curator of the Black Museum, John Ross, and above all to his predecessor, Bill Waddell, without whose unstinting assistance, advice and co-operation this book could not have been written.

Some of the photographs in the book are reproduced by kind permission of the Metropolitan Police. These photos, of Museum exhibits, were taken by Alan Chandler.

The author and publishers also wish to thank the following: Her Majesty's

Stationery Office for permission to reproduce the 1990 criminal statistics (p. ix); Times Newspapers for permission to quote from trial reports; Harrap Ltd for permission to quote from *Executioner: Pierrepoint* by Albert Pierrepoint (pp. 358–60).

Sources

ASCOLI, David, *The Queen's Peace*, Hamish Hamilton, 1979
BERRY, James, *My Experiences as an Executioner*, reprinted by David & Charles, 1972
BROCK, Alan, *A Casebook of Crime*, Rockcliff, 1948
COBB, Belton, *Murdered on Duty*, W. H. Allen, 1961
DAVIS, Don, *The Milwaukee Murders*, True Crime, 1992
FLETCHER, George, *The Life and Career of Dr. William Palmer of Rugeley*, T. Fisher Unwin Ltd, 1925
GOODMAN, Jonathan and PRINGLE, Patrick, *The Trial of Ruth Ellis*, David & Charles, 1974
GRIBBLE, Leonard, *Triumphs of Scotland Yard*, John Long, 1955
GUTTRIDGE, Roger, *Dorset Murders*, and *Hampshire Murders*, Ensign Publications, 1990
HANCOCK, Robert, *Ruth Ellis, the last woman to be hanged*, Weidenfeld & Nicolson, 1963
HAWKES, Harry, *The Capture of the Black Panther*, George G. Harrap, 1978
KNOTT, George, *The Trial of William Palmer*
LANE, Brian, *The Murder Guide*, and *Murder Update*, Robinson Publishing, 1991
LISNERS, John, *House of Horrors* (Dennis Nilsen), Corgi, 1983
LOCK, Joan, *Dreadful Deeds & Awful Murders*, Barn Owl Books, 1990
LOGAN, Guy B. H., *Masters of Crime*, Stanley Paul, 1928
MARKS, Laurence and VAN DEN BERGH, Tony, *Ruth Ellis*, Macdonald & James, 1977
MASTERS, Brian, *Killing for Company* (Dennis Nilsen), Jonathan Cape, 1985
MORRIS, Terence and BLOM-COOPER, Louis, *A Calendar of Murder*, Michael Joseph, 1964
Notable British Trials (William Palmer, Franz Müller, Charles Peace, George Chapman), William Hodge & Company, 1912
PARKER, Tony, *Life after Life*, Secker & Warburg, 1990
PIERREPOINT, Albert, *Executioner: Pierrepoint*, George G. Harrap, 1974
PROTHERO, Margaret, *The History of the CID and Scotland Yard*, Herbert Jenkins, 1931

SIMPSON, Keith, *Forty Years of Murder*, George G. Harrap, 1978
SPENCER SHAW, E., *A Second Companion to Murder*, Cassells, 1961
STURRY DEANS, R., *Notable Trials*, Chapman & Hall, 1932
TULLETT, Tom, *Murder Squad*, Triad/Granada, 1981 – first published as *Strictly Murder*, Bodley Head, 1979
VALENTINE, Steven, *The Black Panther Story*, New English Library, 1976
WALBROOK, H. M., *Murders and Murder Trials, 1812–1912*, Constable, 1932
WILSON, Colin and SEAMAN, Donald, *Encyclopaedia of Modern Murder*, Arthur Barker, 1983

Issues of the magazine *Murder Casebook*, Marshall & Cavendish, 1990

Index